THE HISTORY AND THEORY OF INTERNATIONAL LAW

Sepúlveda on the Spanish Invasion
of the Americas

THE HISTORY AND THEORY OF INTERNATIONAL LAW

General Editors

NEHAL BHUTA
Chair in International Law, University of Edinburgh

ANTHONY PAGDEN
Distinguished Professor, University of California Los Angeles

BENJAMIN STRAUMANN
ERC Professor of History, University of Zurich

In the past few decades the understanding of the relationship between nations has undergone a radical transformation. The role of the traditional nation-state is diminishing, along with many of the traditional vocabularies which were once used to describe what has been called, ever since Jeremy Bentham coined the phrase in 1780, 'international law'. The older boundaries between states are growing ever more fluid, new conceptions and new languages have emerged which are slowly coming to replace the image of a world of sovereign independent nation states which has dominated the study of international relations since the early nineteenth century. This redefinition of the international arena demands a new understanding of classical and contemporary questions in international and legal theory. It is the editors' conviction that the best way to achieve this is by bridging the traditional divide between international legal theory, intellectual history, and legal and political history. The aim of the series, therefore, is to provide a forum for historical studies, from classical antiquity to the twenty-first century, that are theoretically-informed and for philosophical work that is historically conscious, in the hope that a new vision of the rapidly evolving international world, its past and its possible future, may emerge.

PREVIOUSLY PUBLISHED IN THIS SERIES

The World Bank's Lawyers
The Life of International Law as Institutional Practice
Dimitri Van Den Meerssche

Preparing for War
The Making of the 1949 Geneva Conventions
Boyd van Dijk

Sepúlveda on the Spanish Invasion of the Americas

Defending Empire, Debating Las Casas

Edited and translated by

LUKE GLANVILLE
Associate Professor of International Relations
Australian National University

DAVID LUPHER
Professor of Classics, Emeritus, University of Puget Sound

MAYA FEILE TOMES
Lorna Close Lecturer in Spanish, Murray Edwards College,
University of Cambridge

Great Clarendon Street, Oxford, OX2 6DP,
United Kingdom

Oxford University Press is a department of the University of Oxford.
It furthers the University's objective of excellence in research, scholarship,
and education by publishing worldwide. Oxford is a registered trade mark of
Oxford University Press in the UK and in certain other countries

© Luke Glanville, David Lupher, and Maya Feile Tomes 2023

The moral rights of the authors have been asserted

First Edition published in 2023

All rights reserved. No part of this publication may be reproduced, stored in
a retrieval system, or transmitted, in any form or by any means, without the
prior permission in writing of Oxford University Press, or as expressly permitted
by law, by licence or under terms agreed with the appropriate reprographics
rights organization. Enquiries concerning reproduction outside the scope of the
above should be sent to the Rights Department, Oxford University Press, at the
address above

You must not circulate this work in any other form
and you must impose this same condition on any acquirer

Public sector information reproduced under Open Government Licence v3.0
(http://www.nationalarchives.gov.uk/doc/open-government-licence/open-government-licence.htm)

Published in the United States of America by Oxford University Press
198 Madison Avenue, New York, NY 10016, United States of America

British Library Cataloguing in Publication Data

Data available

Library of Congress Control Number: 2022951828

ISBN 978–0–19–886382–3

DOI: 10.1093/oso/9780198863823.001.0001

Links to third party websites are provided by Oxford in good faith and
for information only. Oxford disclaims any responsibility for the materials
contained in any third party website referenced in this work.

Series Editors' Preface

The famous "debate" between the Dominican, Bartolomé de Las Casas, Bishop of Chiapas, and official, "Defender of the Indians", and the humanist historian, self-styled theologian, honorary royal chaplain, and translator of Aristotle, Juan Ginés de Sepúlveda, held in the Colegio de San Gregorio in Valladolid in 1550-1, has become legendary. It has been described as the "first morality debate about European colonization"—which it most certainly was not. It was seen in the nineteenth century as part of a largely imaginary heroic struggle of the Dominican order against the Castilian crown. "These excellent monks" as Sir Travers Twiss, former Queen's Advocate General, salaried champion of Leopold II's occupation of the Congo and one of the founders of the highly influential *Institut de droit international*, wrote in 1856, had been "impelled to vindicate the right of the oppressed against the authority of the Church, the ambitions of the Crown, the avarice and pride of their countrymen, and the prejudices of their own Order". They were, he concluded, "the early streaks of dawn the earnest of the coming day". In the twentieth century the "debate" acquired a hallowed, if largely spectral, place in what the North-American historian Lewis Hanke famously and misleadingly described as the "Spanish Struggle for Justice the New Word". By 1949, the "debate" itself, all that was claimed to have preceded it, and all that was believed to have emanated from it, had become, as Carl Schmitt observed sourly "transformed into a journalistic myth."

The "real" Valladolid Debate in fact, as Luke Glanville, David A. Lupher, & Maya Feile Tomes demonstrate in their brilliantly painstaking historical reconstruction of the whole affair was quite unlike what it has subsequently become in the modern political imagination. In the first place although routinely described as a "debate"—although such a thing would have been barely conceivable in the universities of sixteenth-century Spain—it was in effect a traditional *Junta* of the kind the Castilian crown convoked on repeated occasions, in order to resolve complex moral issues. It consisted of a group of judges—in this case there were fourteen—selected from among the recognized areas of expertise: theology, and canon and civil law. Their task was to decide whether Sepúlveda's inflammatory tract *Democrates secundus* (which was indeed written as "debate"—or at least as a dialogue), widely considered to be the most extreme attempt to defend the Spanish conquests of the Americas, and already denied a license to be printed after long acrimonious debate by the University of Salamanca, in 1548 should now be given royal approval. Sepúlveda, of course, claimed that it should. Las Casas argued that it should not. The terms of the subsequent conflict between the two men, went, however, far beyond questions of royal and ecclesiastical censorship.

vi SERIES EDITORS' PREFACE

Sepúlveda and Las Casas were called to present their arguments to the judges of the *Junta* on separate days. Each phase of these cumbersome events was presided over, and commentate upon, at some length, by Domingo de Soto—Francisco de Vitoria's successor in the Prime Chair of Theology at Salamanca and possibly the most radical and influential of the so-called "School of Salamanca", who had as early a 1535, as the editors point out, asked in a public lecture (*relectio*) the question : "By what right, then, do we retain the overseas empire that has just been discovered? The fact is, I don't know."

From Soto's wry account of the events, the whole affair was something of a shambles. Sepúlveda, as requested, provided only a summary of his arguments and kept pretty much to the question under consideration. Las Casas, however, went on at very great length in an attempt to respond, as Soto put it, "to everything which the doctor has ever committed to paper and all the objections which one can offer to his opinion." Between them, however, both Las Casas and Sepúlveda in their different ways had, as Soto made clear, hijacked a meeting whose original purpose had been to discover, "by what manner and under what laws our Holy Catholic Faith could be preached and promulgated" and how the Indians might be "subjected to the majesty of the Emperor our lord, without harming the royal conscience in conformity with the Bulls of Alexander". In other words the issue at stake had been intended to be the true meaning of the famous "Bulls of Donation" of 1493 and the various theological, and scriptural problems that they raised. It had also been one which had studiously attempted to avoid any consideration of the still highly contentious issue of the legal status of the Spanish occupation of the Americas. Instead, remarked Soto,

> The fact of the matter ... is that the two gentlemen arguing the case have not approached the task in this way, in general terms and as a formal recommendation; rather, they have addressed themselves to and debated the following specific issue, namely whether it is lawful for His Majesty to wage war on those Indians and render them subject to his empire prior to preaching the faith to them so that, once they have been subjugated, they may more easily and conveniently be instructed in and enlightened by the teachings of the gospel as to the errors of their ways and the Christian truth.

Sepúlveda argued that "war of this sort is not only lawful but expedient". Las Casas, of course, maintained the contrary. Not only was war in these circumstances, not lawful, it was also "wicked and antithetical to our Christian religion". It is important to remember, however, that neither man questioned the legitimacy of the Spanish presence in the Americas as such nor of the lasting validity of the Alexandrine donation. It was on this, Las Casas insisted, and on this alone, that the "juridical and fundamental basis" of the Castilian title to the Indies was based. Las Casas' prime concern was not with the legitimacy of the occupation, about which, as he said again and again, and even reiterated in the preamble to his will, he was never in any doubt, but with the *behaviour* of the occupiers. What was at stake was the legitimacy of the *means* by which the Amerindians had been, as Las Casas expressed it elsewhere, "brought into history", so as to become, as both the pope and God had intended, Christians and subjects of the Spanish crown. On Las Casas' reading of history, sacred and profane, America was unique, a true donation, not only of Pope Alexander VI, to Their Catholic Majesties but of God to humankind. For Las Casas, no less than, over two centuries later, for Edmund Burke, true empire was a "sacred trust"—which, in Las Casas' view, the Castilian crown had repeatedly failed to honour. It is little wonder that Soto, so obviously chaffing at the limits his commission had imposed upon him, not "to express or otherwise insinuate my own opinion here…but rather faithfully to convey the essence of their views and the gist of their arguments", protested vehemently that he might otherwise, "insofar as my meagre intellect permits, have been able to impart a sheen of a different order to this synopsis".

Las Casas, however, had another reason for insisting on the validity of the Bulls. For if Francisco de Vitoria—whom he rarely mentions by name- had been right in his refutations of the pope's claims to universal jurisdiction then the only rights which the Castilian Crown could claim in America would have to have been acquired as the outcome of a just war, or, as Las Casas phrased it, they would have to have been grounded "in arms and in power". And if that were the case, then in his view, the Kingdoms of the Indies could only have been founded, "as that great Alexander and the Romans and all those who were famous tyrants, as today the Turk harries and oppresses Christendom" had founded their empires. And that would have been a blatant denial of Las Casas' image of the Spanish empire as the means of fulfilling God's not-so-hidden plans for mankind.

Las Casas' objective throughout all of his voluminous writings on the subject was to demonstrate that while the Spanish occupation of the Americas was fully justified by the Donation it served only one end: namely the conversion of the Indians. The wars of conquest, which he denounced at every turn, were an aberration brought about by the rapacious, unprincipled and un-Christian behaviour of the Spanish settlers. Since the Indians were, on his account, docile and rational beings, and Christianity was a docile and rational faith, the conquests should never have taken place at all. For this same reason Las Casas replied, to Sepúlveda's use of a version of Vitoria's "defence of the innocent" as grounds for depriving the Indians of their sovereignty and their goods, under the *ius gentium*, by arguing that while the protection of the subjects of a state from the tyranny of its ruler was clearly a moral obligation, and that the papacy was bound to defend the innocent even if they were pagans, "because they belong potentially (*in potentia*) to the Church", this could not be achieved through conquest. If war were the only means available then, "it would be better to relinquish that protection" for when compared with all the evils of warfare, even human sacrifice was the lesser of the

viii SERIES EDITORS' PREFACE

two. (To this Sepúlveda retorted that "our good sir has got his sums quite wrong: for in New Spain ... more than twenty thousand people were sacrificed each year; and if one multiplies this figure across the thirty years that have elapsed since New Spain was annexed and this form of sacrifice abolished, this would amount to six hundred thousand people already, whereas I doubt that in the course of the conquest of the entire region more people were killed than victims formerly sacrificed by them in a single year".)

To the claim which Sepúlveda had made repeatedly that the Indians were incapable of self-government, and the dependence of this—discussed here at length by the editors—on Aristotle's famously contentious and widely misunderstood, theory of natural slavery Las Casas replied that this, and anything which might possibly be deduced from it, could not be applied to the peoples of the Americas. (Notoriously—although he later abandoned his position—he took a verry different view on Africans.) The Amerindians, he argued, were as advanced, as sophisticated and as civil as any of the societies—including the ancestors of the modern Spaniards—to be found the pre or non-Christian world, and he wrote a massive rambling tome, the *Apologética historia sumaria*, in an attempt to demonstrate this point empirically. True the Indians still "suffer from many and great defects in their societies", an inescapable consequence, as he understood it, of their paganism, which would be remedied once they had all been converted to the true faith—and that was something which, in his view, would require a radical reform of the present colonial administration. Vitoria, had taken a similar position. Although the Indians were certainly not "natural slaves" (in any case in his view a false category), they did nevertheless "seem to us insensate and slow-witted". This, however, was something that was due "mainly to their evil and barbarous education". Once exposed to Christianity and the civilizing ways of the Spanish, they would eventually be transformed into true civil beings. For those who, like Las Casas, accepted the validity of the papal bulls, the ultimate objective of this civilizing process could only be full incorporation into the Spanish monarchy. If the Americas had indeed been ceded legitimately to the Spanish crown by the papacy, the fully-civilized Indians would never be in a position to claim anything resembling a right to "self-determination". On the other hand, neither could there be any grounds for treating them any differently from any of the other subjects of the Spanish monarchy.

For Las Casas, and on this point he was fully in agreement with Sepúlveda, the polities which had existed prior to the arrival of the Spanish had been dissolved by papal decree in 1493, and a new entity which this act had created, the "Kingdoms of the Indies" had been incorporated into the Crown of Castile by royal decree in 1519. The "Spanish Monarchy" was a God-ordained, papally-sanctioned state which would continue in its present course until the end of time.

SERIES EDITORS' PREFACE   ix

In the end the *Junta* of Valladolid never arrived at any decision, and *Democrates secundus*, despite Sepúlveda's many subsequent attempts to acquire an *imprimatur* remained unpublished until 1892.

This book offers the best most complete translation of all the major texts which were written in the course, and in the context, of the Valladolid *Junta*. For the first time, scholars of the history of the European colonization of the Americas, of the prolonged struggle to establish a legal, theological and moral justification for warfare, and of the history more broadly, of the evolution of modern international law, have a collection of scrupulously edited texts on which to draw. In addition, Luke Glanville, David A. Lupher, & Maya Feile Tomes, introduction, provides the most exhaustive most detailed account of the complex history of the "debate" itself, together with an analysis of the arguments of the major participants, many of which have still lingering implications for the evolution of modern international law. It is, in itself, a work of outstanding scholarship.

Anthony Pagden
Los Angeles October 2022

Editors' Preface and Acknowledgements

This volume offers annotated translations of four central documents that precipitated, recorded, and reacted to the debate convoked by the Spanish Crown in Valladolid in 1550–51 to assess the merits of the defence of the Spanish invasion of the Americas composed by the prominent Aristotelian scholar and royal chronicler, Juan Ginés de Sepúlveda, *contra* Bartolomé de las Casas. Despite many Anglophone scholars' vivid awareness of this climactic event of the so-called 'controversy of the Indies' and their extensive familiarity with Sepúlveda's ideas, this familiarity is perforce mostly at second hand, for none of these key Sepúlvedan documents has hitherto been made available in English translation.

While all three editors share responsibility for the finished work, the primary division of labour was as follows. In addition to acting as principal editor and taskmaster, Luke Glanville is the author of the general introduction. David Lupher provided the translations of the Latin-language material—Sepúlveda's *Democrates secundus* and *Apologia*—and prepared the reference notes and prefaces thereto. Maya Feile Tomes produced the translations of the Spanish-language pieces—*Aquí se contiene una disputa o controversia* (combining pieces by Domingo de Soto and Las Casas as well as Sepúlveda) and the Sepúlvedan *Proposiciones temerarias* (*PT*), along with their respective shorter companion pieces, the *Postreros apuntamientos* and *Declaración*—and penned the respective prefaces. She also (re)located manuscripts *S* and *C* of the *PT*. David almost single-handedly produced the majority of notes for the aforementioned works too, tackled many of their thornier Latin passages, and generated working collations (not printed in this volume) of the manuscripts of both *Aquí se contiene* and the *PT*. He also authored the epilogue. Throughout this process, each of the three editors continually fed back on the work of the other two, and our near-constant communications, conducted in the period 2018–22 from three continents across three time zones and interrupted three times by our respective brushes with COVID-19 (and, for Maya, three job changes in as many years), were lively, substantive, sometimes intense, but always amicable—in sharp and refreshing contrast to the vituperative debate around which the works in this volume centre.

Luke is grateful to Benjamin Straumann, who suggested David as an ideal companion on this project and who generously provided support and advice as series editor alongside Nehal Bhuta and Anthony Pagden, as well as to all the members of the International Law editorial team at OUP—Merel Alstein, Robert Cavooris, Eleanor Hanger, Jack McNichol, and John Smallman—whose lot it has been to shepherd us along the way. Thanks are also owed to David, for wisely

xii EDITORS' PREFACE AND ACKNOWLEDGEMENTS

recommending Maya as an indispensable addition to the team. Daniel Schwartz and Daniel Brunstetter both provided invaluable advice in the early stages of the project. Liane Hartnett, David Lantigua, Nicolas Lémay-Hebert, Alana Moore, and Cian O'Driscoll each provided thoughtful feedback on the general introduction. David Lantigua and Jörg Tellkamp both graciously provided pre-publication copies of excellent volumes on the intellectual history of Spanish imperialism that are now in print—Lantigua's *Infidels and Empires in a New World Order* and Tellkamp's *Companion to Early Modern Spanish Imperial Political and Social Thought*. An Australian Research Council grant made possible numerous aspects of this project, including a visit to Whitman College in 2016, where Luke and David first mapped it out in the delightful company of Elizabeth Vandiver, Clare Glanville, and baby Arthur.

David is pleased to see this volume appear in a series co-edited by Anthony Pagden, for some three decades ago Pagden's groundbreaking book *The Fall of Natural Man* was not only his first proper introduction to Sepúlveda, but also served as a stimulus to his 2003 *Romans in a New World*. He also wishes to record his gratitude to James J. O'Donnell, especially for assistance with references to Augustine and other church fathers. Anders Winroth of the University of Oslo gave vital help with references to Gratian and canon law. Series editor, former Alberico Gentili collaborator, and friend Benjamin Straumann provided crucial assistance with questions of Roman law and also offered welcome encouragement throughout. Elise Bartosik-Vélez was a frequent source of assistance and encouragement. Thanks are also owed to David Butterfield of Cambridge University for his excellent preliminary version of certain key passages of the *Democrates secundus*. Finally, Elizabeth Vandiver has been a constant source of wise scholarly judgement, encouragement, and companionship throughout his work on this project.

Maya is grateful to Christ's College, Cambridge, for the Junior Research Fellowship, which first afforded her the latitude to countenance embarking upon this project, to Murray Edwards College for welcoming her into her new post in a way that still allowed her to finish it, and to the Spanish & Portuguese Section of the Modern and Medieval Languages Faculty for the funding which enabled her to seek the services of a research assistant for a brief spell in the middle. That R.A. was Rachel Dryden, who painstakingly waded her way through an unwieldy document in pursuit of many scriptural references. Natalia K. Denisova kindly supplied a digital copy of her own edition of the *Proposiciones temerarias* at a time when in the depths of the pandemic it was difficult to come by the hard copy. Pablo Andrés Escapa of the Real Biblioteca in Madrid, and Óscar Lilao Franca, of the Biblioteca General Histórica at the University of Salamanca, were instrumental in helping to relocate the second known manuscript (*C*) of the *Proposiciones temerarias*, and the latter kindly fielded a number of further queries about it. José María Burrieza Mateos and Silvia Soto Fernández of the Archivo General de Simancas were in turn invaluable in tracking down the long-lost third manuscript (*S*). José Antonio Bellido Díaz, Alejandro Coroleu, Juan Carlos Galende Díaz, Miguel Herrero de Jáuregui, Asunción Miralles de Imperial y Pasqual del Pobil, Antonio Sánchez de Mora, Alessio Santoro, Ángel Sanz Tapia, Julián Solana Pujalte, and David Woodman generously corresponded on points of detail. Hannah Skrinar (in Brussels), Rasmus Sevelsted (in Cambridge), and Oliver Francis (in general) all kindly coexisted with this project in various invaluable ways. Above all, she is grateful to her fellow editors for their friendly intellectual fellowship, and especially to David, whose *Romans in a New World* has been a beacon since her own student days and with whom she would never have thought that she would one day be collaborating.

Contents

Introduction	1
• Sepúlveda: Theologian, philosopher, or humanist?	3
• *Democrates secundus*	10
• Seeking a licence to print	22
• *Apologia*	28
• The Valladolid debate	33
• The disputants' arguments	37
• Aftermath	50
• Legacies and reverberations	56
Key for Canon Law References	63
***Democrates Part Two, on the Just Reasons for the War against the Indians* (*Democrates secundus, sive de iustis belli causis apud Indos*)**	65
• Preface to the translation of *Democrates secundus*	65
• *Democrates Part Two, on the Just Reasons for the War against the Indians*	86
• *Preface to the Dialogue 'On the Just Reasons for War' by Ginés de Sepúlveda to His Excellency, Luis Mendoza, Count of Tendilla and Marquis of Mondéjar*	86
• *The Dialogue which is Entitled Democrates Secundus on the Just Reasons for War by Juan Ginés de Sepúlveda, Doctor of Arts and Sacred Theology*	87
• Book I	87
• Book II	150
• Appendix: Passages from early drafts	180
The Defence of the Book*, On the Just Reasons for War** (Apologia pro libro de iustis belli causis***)	191
• Preface to the translation of *Apologia*	191
• *Apologia*	198
***Contained Herein Is a Debate or Disputation* (*Aquí se contiene una disputa o controversia*)**	225
• Preface to the translations of *Aquí se contiene una disputa o controversia* and *Postreros apuntamientos*	225
• *Contained herein is a debate or disputation*	236
• Bartolomé de las Casas's 'The Subject of This Work'	237
• Domingo de Soto's 'Summary'	240
• Juan Ginés de Sepúlveda's 'Twelve Objections'	269
• Bartolomé de las Casas's 'Twelve Replies'	289

xvi CONTENTS

- Appendix: *Final points of argument presented to the congregation by Sepúlveda (Postreros apuntamientos que dio Sepúlveda en la congregación)*   347

Outrageous, Scandalous, Heretical Notions (Proposiciones temerarias, escandalosas, y de mala doctrina)   351
- Preface to the translations of *Proposiciones temerarias* and *Declaración*   351
- *Outrageous, scandalous, heretical notions*   366
- Appendix: *Itemization (Declaración) of the grounds on which the pretexts offered for the falsehoods in the bishop of Chiapa's book neither suffice nor serve to exonerate anything*   385

Postscript: From Valladolid to the 'Black Legend'   389

Bibliography of Post-1492 Works   395
Index of Authors and Works Cited in the Translated Texts   407
Index of Biblical Passages Cited in the Translated Texts   413
General Index   417

Introduction

As Juan Ginés de Sepúlveda himself tells it, it was the backlash from Spanish colonists against Emperor Charles V's New Laws (1542) that generated renewed controversy within the royal court about the justice of Spain's subjugation of the Amerindians. And this in turn prompted the president of the Council of the Indies to ask Sepúlveda to write something about the matter.[1] The book that he produced, *Democrates secundus*, a learned and impassioned defence of Spain's wars that deftly combined the resources of Renaissance humanism, Aristotelian philosophy, and Christian theology, only amplified the controversy. The Dominican friar Bartolomé de las Casas schemed to ensure that Sepúlveda was denied a licence to print his manuscript. Sepúlveda returned the favour, seeking royal condemnation of one of Las Casas's own manuscripts, written against the subjugation and mistreatment of Amerindians. Tensions were so heightened and consciences so unsettled that the emperor called a halt to further wars pending the outcome of a meeting of prominent theologians and jurists to be held at Valladolid. Here, in 1550–51, Sepúlveda and Las Casas debated bitterly, albeit it seems without ever being in the same room as each other. When Las Casas printed without licence a summary of the opening session of the Valladolid deliberations and the protagonists' respective responses, and introduced this text with a narrative of events that denigrated his rival, Sepúlveda retaliated by penning a furious response that accused Las Casas of an array of heresies and strove to have Las Casas's text publicly banned by the Inquisition.

This volume presents translations of four key texts of this bitter dispute: Sepúlveda's *Democrates secundus* (composed around 1544); his *Apologia* (1550), which defended that text; the composite record of the Valladolid Junta that Las Casas published (1552); and Sepúlveda's enraged riposte (around 1553). The Valladolid Junta was the climactic event in the controversy within Spain about its wars in the Americas. It was also a foundational moment in the history of international legal thought as Sepúlveda and Las Casas argued over fundamental matters of empire and colonial rule; natural law and cultural difference; the jurisdiction of the church, the responsibilities of Christian rulers, and the rights of infidel peoples; the just reasons for war and just grounds for resistance; and the right

---

[1] Sepúlveda, *Proposiciones temerarias*, §2.

Sepúlveda on the Spanish Invasion of the Americas. Luke Glanville, David Lupher and Maya Feile Tomes, Oxford University Press. © Luke Glanville, David Lupher, and Maya Feile Tomes 2023.
DOI: 10.1093/oso/9780198863823.003.0001

2 SEPÚLVEDA ON THE SPANISH INVASION OF THE AMERICAS

to punish idolatry, protect innocents from tyranny, and subjugate unbelievers for the purpose of spreading the Christian faith.[2]

We tend to know the arguments of Las Casas quite well in the Anglophone world, not least because we have for several decades enjoyed easy access to English translations of several of his treatises condemning the subjugation and coerced conversion of the Amerindians.[3] Sepúlveda's ideas tend to be less well known. His defences of Spain's activities in the Americas have been available only in Latin, Spanish, and, quite recently, Italian and German.[4] As a result, while not discounting the contributions of scholars such as Lewis Hanke and Anthony Pagden, who have done much to bring Sepúlveda's ideas to an Anglophone audience,[5] received wisdom about Sepúlveda's claims has been shaped to a significant degree by the summaries and allegations offered by his opponent, Las Casas. Some readers of this volume may find that Sepúlveda's arguments turn out to be quite different from what they expect. He does not endorse the enslavement of the Amerindians, for example. Nor does he support their forced conversion to the Christian faith. He does apply Aristotle's doctrine of natural slavery to the Amerindians in order to establish their inferior status and thus justify their subjugation to the rule of natural masters for their own benefit. But he moderates this argument over time and ultimately, it seems, abandons the controversial language of natural slavery altogether. It is at least in part due to the dominance of Las Casas's version of his dispute with Sepúlveda that certain misunderstandings of Sepúlveda's position have crept into the narrative. It is vital, then, that we hear Sepúlveda's side of the story.

It is not our intention, though, to rehabilitate Sepúlveda. Not at all. His arguments are nuanced and carefully made, yet no less problematic for this fact; they are often brilliantly constructed, yet still frequently repulsive, as the brutal subjugation of the Amerindians is justified with terms and claims that dehumanize them, excuse their suffering on the basis of abstracted calculations, and silence their appeals for justice via myopic appeals to church doctrine and papal jurisdiction. But

---

[2] For a valuable recent examination of Valladolid as a founding moment, see David M. Lantigua, *Infidels and Empires in a New World Order: Early Modern Spanish Contributions to International Legal Thought* (Cambridge: Cambridge University Press, 2020).

[3] English translations include Bartolomé de las Casas, *History of the Indies*, translated and abridged by Andrée M. Collard (New York: Harper & Row, 1971); George Sanderlin, *Bartolomé de las Casas: A Selection of His Writings* (New York: Knopf, 1971); Bartolomé de Las Casas, *The Only Way*, edited by Helen Rand Parish and translated by Francis Patrick Sullivan (New York: Paulist Press, 1992); Bartolomé de Las Casas, *A Short Account of the Destruction of the Indies*, edited and translated by Nigel Griffin with an introduction by Anthony Pagden (London: Penguin, 1992); David Thomas Orique, O.P., *To Heaven or To Hell: Bartolomé de las Casas's* Confesionario (University Park, PA: Pennsylvania State University Press, 2018); Bartolomé de Las Casas, *In Defense of the Indians*, edited and translated by Stafford Poole (DeKalb, IL: Northern Illinois University Press, 1992). Note that the title, *In Defense of the Indians*, is the concoction of its editor and translator, Poole. The work in question is Las Casas's Latin *Apologia*, a reworking of part of the text that he delivered at the Valladolid Junta, discussed below.

[4] We detail these non-English editions of Sepúlveda's writings in the translator prefaces.

[5] Lewis Hanke, *Aristotle and the American Indians: A Study in Race Prejudice in the Modern World* (Chicago: Henry Regnery, 1959); Anthony Pagden, *The Fall of Natural Man: The American Indian and the Origins of Comparative Ethnology* (Cambridge: Cambridge University Press, 1982; rev. 1986).

INTRODUCTION 3

it is worth reading and understanding his arguments rightly. If anything, it is more disturbing, rather than less, to discover that Sepúlveda is not so much the cartoonish villain as he is sometimes presented. He is not some absurd figure whose arguments Las Casas and others could quickly and easily dismiss. He was a learned and agile thinker who embraced or at least adopted the theological, moral, and legal frameworks of his critics and made careful use of the same authorities that these critics so cherished—especially biblical examples and exegesis and the writings of the church fathers and medieval theologians and canonists—while putting them to entirely different ends. His finely-grained arguments, moreover, spoke to grand and enduring themes that are recognizable to us today. Accordingly, his ideas not only proved challenging in his day to Las Casas and other critics of Spain's invasion of the Americas, but may also offer challenges to us today since, when we look beyond the contextual specificities and view his arguments in full, we might be disturbed to find that his thinking about the just reasons for war is in important ways not so far different from our own.

This introduction narrates the story of the four translated texts. It is a complex story that takes some telling, not least in order to understand how and why Sepúlveda modified his arguments across the four texts in response to the criticisms and machinations of Las Casas and certain Dominican theologians who worked to ensure that Sepúlveda was not granted a licence to print his *Democrates secundus*. The introduction concludes by reflecting on some of the disturbing reverberations of Sepúlveda's ideas that continue to be felt today in the theories and practices of war.

Sepúlveda: Theologian, philosopher, or humanist?

We begin by examining Sepúlveda's intellectual and vocational development leading up to his engagement with debates about Spain's activities in the Americas. This will help us to understand not only why he was asked to write the text that he would title *Democrates secundus*, but also what kind of thinker he was, how he would have been viewed by others within Spain, and why a manuscript composed by him would have been regarded as weighty enough and potentially persuasive or dangerous enough to have occasioned the extraordinary meeting at Valladolid in 1550–51.

Born in Pozoblanco, near Córdoba, around 1490, Sepúlveda studied philosophy at the University of Alcalá de Henares and theology at the University of Sigüenza before leaving Spain in 1515 to take up a scholarship at the Colegio de San Clemente, the Spanish college in Bologna.[6] Sepúlveda seems not to have completed

---

[6] For an English-language overview of Sepúlveda's life and career, see Aubrey F. G. Bell, *Juan Ginés de Sepúlveda* (Oxford: Oxford University Press, 1925). See also Teodoro Andrés Marcos, *Los imperialismos de Juan Ginés de Sepúlveda en su Democrates Alter* (Madrid: Instituto de Estudios Políticos, 1947); Ángel

the theological studies he began at Bologna, and so he may not have been fully entitled to the title of 'doctor' when he left there and was removed from the register of students in 1523. Nevertheless, from that year onwards, with the printing of his translation of Aristotle's *On Generation and Decay* (*De ortu et interitu*) in Bologna, he developed a habit of styling himself 'doctor of arts and theology' (artium et theologiae doctor) on the title-pages of his publications.[7] Others addressed him the same way. Las Casas identified his opponent as 'el doctor' on the title-page and in subsequent passages in the composite account of the Valladolid debate that he printed in 1552. The Dominican theologian Domingo de Soto used the same title for Sepúlveda in his summary of the disputants' remarks before the judges at Valladolid, which Las Casas included in that printed account. Perhaps there was a tinge of irony in Las Casas's use of the title, perhaps Soto used it out of courtesy, or perhaps neither was aware of Sepúlveda's apparent resumé inflation.[8]

Nevertheless, even if he was not fully credentialed as a doctor of theology, Sepúlveda's theological training at both Sigüenza and Bologna is not in dispute. He displayed this training proudly, most notably in a 1526 treatise against Luther, *On Fate and Free Will* (*De fato et libero aribitrio*), and in his involvement in the question of Henry VIII's attempt to secure papal approval of his divorce from Catherine of Aragon (his treatise *On the Marriage Ceremony and Dispensation* (*De ritu nuptiarum et dispensatione*) in three books was published in London in 1553, early in the reign of Mary I). Nor should we underestimate the mastery of the church fathers and medieval theology and canon law that, as we will see, he subtly demonstrated in his *Democrates secundus* before putting it on somewhat ostentatious display in his *Apologia* as not only a defence of the former text, but also a counterweight to its humanist format and style. Thus, there is much to be said for Katie Benjamin's thesis that, while Sepúlveda's credentials as a theologian may have been

---

Losada, *Juan Ginés de Sepúlveda: a través de su "Epistolario" y nuevos documentos* (Madrid: Consejo Superior de Investigaciones Científicas, 1949; repr. 1973); Francisco Castilla Urbano, *El pensamiento de Juan Ginés de Sepúlveda: Vida activa, humanismo y guerra en el Renacimiento* (Madrid: Centro de Estudios Políticos y Constitucionales, 2013); Marco Geuna (ed.), *Guerra giusta e schiavitù naturale: Juan Ginés de Sepúlveda e il dibattito sulla Conquista* (Milan: Edizioni Biblioteca Francescana, 2014).

[7] Sepúveda's right to the title has been disputed since at least 1780. See the introduction to his works published that year by the Real Academia de Historia, vol. 1, iv. While Losada (*Juan Ginés de Sepúlveda*, 38–39) indignantly rejected these doubts, basing himself largely on the 1523 Bologna title-page, Antonio Pérez Martín's magisterial study of the records of the Spanish College at Bologna has given support to these doubts: *Proles Aegidiana* (Bologna: Publicaciones del Real Colegio de España, 1979), vol. 2, 604–06, cited in Katie Marie Benjamin, *A Semipelagian in King Charles's Court: Juan Ginés de Sepúlveda on Nature, Grace, and the Conquest of the Americas* (Th.D. diss., Duke University Divinity School, 2017), 196.

[8] Incidentally, it is often forgotten or overlooked that Sepúlveda was in fact officially a secular priest. He was ordained back in 1510, when matriculating at Alcalá. But his being in minor orders would have had no necessary impact on his identity as a theologian. See Benjamin, *A Semipelagian in King Charles's Court*, 90.

INTRODUCTION 5

lacking (or at least inflated), his theological pretensions and contentions need to be taken seriously.[9]

Sepúlveda's years of study at Bologna proved decisive for his future career, achievements, and identity. It was at Bologna that he became the pupil and protegé of the great Italian Aristotelian Pietro Pomponazzi, who had come to Bologna after years of teaching at Padua.[10] Pomponazzi was a product of a tradition of Italian Aristotelianism, often referred to as 'Paduan Averroism', but which the great scholar of Renaissance thought Paul Oskar Kristeller preferred to call 'secular Aristotelianism'.[11] While Pomponazzi knew no Greek, he 'eagerly seized upon the new source material made available by his humanist contemporaries', and he showed in his writings 'the impact of the broad humanist movement of his time'.[12]

It was during Sepúlveda's second year at Bologna, 1516, that Pomponazzi published his most celebrated—and excoriated—work: On the Immortality of the Soul (De immortalitate animae), a justification of controversial views that Pomponazzi had been teaching for some time by that point.[13] Indeed, Pomponazzi's teachings on the immortality of the soul had received implicit condemnation at the Fifth Lateran Council and in the resulting papal bull Apostolici regiminis (1513).[14] In his 1516 treatise, Pomponazzi combined a scholastic style with a quasi-humanist determination to understand Aristotle on his own terms, not as filtered through medieval scholastic theology. Equally importantly, he stoutly defended the autonomy of both philosophy and theology, resisting any attempt to confuse their claims, procedures, and domains. On the question of the immortality of the soul, Pomponazzi maintained that philosophy, above all as represented by texts of Aristotle accessed as directly as possible, pointed unambiguously to the soul's mortality, while theology—and Christian revelation—no less unambiguously declared its immortality. Though Pomponazzi concluded by accepting on faith the

---

[9] Benjamin insists upon this even while dubbing Sepúlveda 'semi-Pelagian', which is to say, inter alia, semi-heretical. Benjamin, A Semipelagian in King Charles's Court.

[10] For a lucid account of Pomponazzi's life, ideas, and importance, see the chapter devoted to him in Paul Oskar Kristeller, Eight Philosophers of the Italian Renaissance (Stanford: Stanford University Press, 1964), 72–90.

[11] See the discussion of medieval vs Renaissance Aristoteliansim in Paul Oskar Kristeller, Renaissance Thought: The Classic, Scholastic, and Humanist Strains (New York: Harper Torchbooks, 1961), ch. 2 ('The Aristotelian Tradition'); and for the term 'secular Aristotelianism', see Kristeller, Eight Philosophers, 75. We should add that in our use of the term 'humanist' we are following Italian student slang for a teacher or student of the studia humanitatis, defined by Kristeller as 'a clearly defined cycle of scholarly disciplines, namely grammar, rhetoric, history, poetry, and moral philosophy, and the study of each of these subjects was understood to include the reading and interpretation of its standard ancient writers in Latin and, to a lesser extent, in Greek' (Renaissance Thought, 10). As the sixteenth century advanced, a knowledge of Greek became ever more characteristic of the genuine 'humanist'.

[12] Quoted words are from Kristeller, Renaissance Thought, 42, and Eight Philosophers, 75.

[13] For an English translation, see Pietro Pomponazzi, 'On the Immortality of the Soul', translated by William Henry Hay II, revised by John Herman Randall Jr, with an introduction by John Herman Randall Jr and annotations by Paul Oskar Kristeller, in The Renaissance Philosophy of Man, edited by Ernst Cassirer, Paul Oskar Kristeller, and John Herman Randall Jr, 257–381 (Chicago: University of Chicago Press, 1948).

[14] Benjamin, A Semipelagian in King Charles's Court, 200–211.

6 SEPÚLVEDA ON THE SPANISH INVASION OF THE AMERICAS

theological position, his so-called 'double truth' was bound to make theologians uncomfortable.[15]

Pomponazzi's teaching was inspirational to Sepúlveda. Above all, Pomponazzi was Sepúlveda's introduction to Greek philosophy as a subject of immense value in its own right, and not only as a welcome pre-Christian ancillary to Christian theology (as it had been for Thomas Aquinas and many other medieval theologians). Though Sepúlveda was not the first to apply Aristotle's doctrine of natural slavery to the Amerindians when he did so in his *Democrates secundus*, we can perhaps blame Pomponazzi for inspiring his Spanish pupil with a reverence for the Greek philosopher that made virtually inevitable Sepúlveda's infamous appeal to Aristotle's doctrine. But Sepúlveda surpassed his teacher in a vital respect. Sepúlveda was able to read Aristotle in the original Greek, and he no doubt saw the series of Aristotelian translations that he produced from 1522 to 1548 as a means of offering to the Greekless more accurate Latin translations than those that Pomponazzi had been obliged to use. Also, Pomponazzi was quick to make use of the Aristotelian commentaries by Alexander of Aphrodisias (late second, early third century CE) that began to appear around the turn of the sixteenth century, and he passed this enthusiasm on to Sepúlveda, whose translation of Alexander's commentary on Aristotle's *Metaphysics* was printed in Rome in 1527. Thus, if in his attempt to approach Greek philosophy as directly as possible Pomponazzi revealed himself as a quasi-humanist, his student Sepúlveda was able to enter more fully into the Renaissance humanist project of pushing boldly *ad fontes* and experiencing Aristotle and his great ancient commentator in their own words.

Sepúlveda sought not only to emulate and even to surpass Pomponazzi in the quest for direct access to the texts of Greek philosophy, but also to push the claims of philosophy further than had his teacher.[16] He came to believe that his teacher was mistaken in demarcating philosophy and theology so sharply as autonomous realms, and thus he rejected Pomponazzi's controversial notion of a 'double truth'. But he also rejected the argument of theologians that the value of philosophy (and, above all, Aristotelian philosophy) was ancillary to theology. Instead, it became Sepúlveda's settled belief that natural reason, if properly followed, should suffice to take one deep into the territory that most theologians reserved for divine revelation. Hence his famous contention, which would be repeatedly evident in his engagement with the Amerindian question, that there is fundamentally no sharp distinction between natural law and divine law.

In breaking down the wall within his teacher's 'double truth', Sepúlveda not only implicitly exalted philosophy over theology (or at least seemed in danger of doing

---

[15] The 'double truth' emerges most clearly in ch. 15, the final chapter of Pomponazzi's treatise. See also Kristeller, *Eight Philosophers*, 81–84.

[16] We are indebted in what follows to the analysis in Benjamin, *A Semipelagian in King Charles's Court*, 199–200, 210–11.

so), he also manufactured a handy justification for the coercive subjugation of the Amerindians even before peaceful conversion was attempted. Given the powers he ascribed to natural reason, quite unaccompanied by divine revelation, the Amerindians had no excuse for human sacrifice, cannibalism, and other egregious violations of natural law. Indeed, Sepúlveda's exaltation of the powers of human reason meant that the Amerindians had no excuse for not following natural law all the way to a close approximation of Christian truth. Or, rather, they did have one excuse: they were less advanced humans who were not fully capable of grasping natural (and hence divine) law on their own and thus it was for their benefit that they be made subject to the rule of civilized, Christian Spaniards. Thus, Sepúlveda extended the claims of his teacher's own field of philosophy and at the same time made a case for philosophy's contribution to a practical dispute involving a newly expanded world undreamed of by Aristotle.

We will see that Las Casas and his supporters—most notably the Dominican theologian Melchor Cano—sought to neutralize Sepúlveda's claims to be taken seriously by theologians by framing him as a mere Aristotelian, a proponent of Italian humanism, a lightweight man of letters. In recent years there has been a similar tendency to pigeonhole him as a humanist, even when the categorization is intended as laudatory. For instance, Alejandro Coroleu Lletget, the noted Spanish scholar of classical receptions—and editor of the *Democrates secundus* in the Pozoblanco *Obras completas*—has declared Sepúlveda 'one of the most distinguished representatives of Spanish humanism, alongside Juan Luis Vives and Antonio Agustín'.[17] More productive, perhaps, is the approach of other scholars who have acknowledged the elusive complexity of Sepúlveda's intellectual composition. Thus, Joaquín J. Sánchez Gásquez, while labelling Sepúlveda 'un humanista' in the subtitle of an article, is alert to the inadequacy of that label, even going so far at one point as to call Sepúlveda 'a Scholastic theologian', and concluding that 'Sepúlveda, in addition to being a theologian, never neglected the *studia humanitatis* and to cultivate his humanist side.' He compares him to Luther's associate, Philip Melanchthon, 'also a theologian, but also a humanist'.[18]

Sepúlveda's development was further shaped by another mentor whom he met at Bologna: Alberto Pio, prince of Carpi, who was nephew of the great humanist philosopher Pico della Mirandola and a patron of the Colegio de San Clemente. Pio selected Sepúlveda to be a part of the rich intellectual environment that was his court at Carpi. Pomponazzi had had a stay there himself, prior to his move to

---

[17] Alejandro Coroleu Lletget, 'The *Fortuna* of Juan Ginés de Sepúlveda's Translations of Aristotle and of Alexander of Aphrodisias', *Journal of the Warburg and Courtauld Institutes* 59 (1996): 325–32. See similarly Richard Tuck, *The Rights of War and Peace: Political Thought and the International Order from Grotius to Kant* (Oxford: Oxford University Press, 1999), 43–44; Matthias Vollet, 'Sepúlveda: Traductor y comentarista de Aristóteles, *Política I', Ideas y Valores* 119, 2002: 137–43.

[18] Joaquín J. Sánchez Gásquez, 'La *Pro Alberto Pio Carpensi, Antapologia in Erasmum Roterodamum* de Juan Ginés de Sepúlveda: Testimonio de una singular asímilación cultural y retrato de un humanista', *Humanistica Lovaniensia* 47 (1998): 75–99, quoted words on 98–99.

8 SEPÚLVEDA ON THE SPANISH INVASION OF THE AMERICAS

Bologna. Sepúlveda spent much of the period between 1522 and 1525 there. Pio was at that time engaged in an increasingly bitter dispute with Desiderius Erasmus, accusing him of sharing some of Martin Luther's heretical opinions and paving the way for the Reformation.[19] Pio involved Sepúlveda in this quarrel to the point that Erasmus claimed that much of Pio's final attack against him, published posthumously in 1531, was actually written by Sepúlveda. When Erasmus countered this tract with a lengthy and bitter *Apology*, Sepúlveda took it upon himself to compose a defence of his deceased patron (*Antapologia pro Alberto Pio, Comite Carpensi, in Erasmum Roterodamum*).

Sepúlveda's involvement in this theological dispute may have influenced his antagonism to some of Erasmus's pacifist claims. While at Carpi, Sepúlveda composed a dialogue, *Gonzalo—A Dialogue in Defence of the Pursuit of Glory* (*Dialogus de appetenda gloria, qui inscribitur Gonsalus*), a forthright riposte to the pacifist arguments of Erasmus and his Spanish humanist associate Juan Luis Vives, which was printed in Rome in 1523.[20] In addition to displaying Sepúlveda's early ideas about war, the *Gonzalo* reveals that, in a departure from Pomponazzi's rather scholastic style, Sepúlveda had begun to cultivate the art of presenting his ideas in the form of classical philosophical dialogues. Though he would describe his *Democrates secundus* as a Platonic dialogue, both that dialogue and those that preceded it owed more to the kind of Ciceronian dialogue practised by Renaissance humanists (the *Ciceronianus* of Erasmus springs to mind) than they did to actual Platonic dialogues.[21]

While at Bologna, Sepúlveda had also met Giulio de' Medici, the future Pope Clement VII. In 1526, Sepúlveda accompanied Pio to Rome and joined Clement VII's papal court, where he based himself—with some eventful exceptions—for much of the next decade. While under the pope's patronage, Sepúlveda not only published his anti-Lutheran tract *On Fate and Free Will* and his translation of Alexander of Aphrodisias, he also found himself on familiar terms with the great Dominican theologian and Thomist scholar Tommaso de Vio (Cajetan), who can be said to have sown the seeds of the Valladolid debate.[22] As Master General of the Dominican Order in 1510, Cajetan had sent a contingent of Dominican friars to Española, one of whom, Antonio de Montesinos, delivered in December of 1511 the fiery Advent sermon denouncing Spanish maltreatment of the Amerindians

---

[19] See Desiderius Erasmus, *Collected Works of Erasmus: Volume 84: Controversies with Albert Pio*, edited by Nelson H. Minnich (Toronto: University of Toronto Press, 2005).

[20] For discussion, see Luna Nájera, 'Masculinity, War, and Pursuit of Glory in Sepúlveda's *Gonzalo*', *Hispanic Review* 80/3 (2012): 391–412. On the development of Sepúlveda's ideas in relation to those of Erasmus and Vives, see J. A. Fernández-Santamaría, *The State, War, and Peace: Spanish Political Thought in the Renaissance 1516–1559* (Cambridge: Cambridge University Press, 1977), 163–95.

[21] Sepúlveda claimed in the preface of his *Democrates secundus* that he had written the text 'in the Socratic format'.

[22] See Sepúlveda's note to this effect in the appendix of passages from earlier drafts of *Democrates secundus* (I.14.4). As Losada (*Juan Ginés de Sepúlveda*, 61n7) noted, this draft passage is our only evidence that Sepúlveda associated with Cajetan in Rome in 1526–27, before the Sack of Rome.

that ignited the broader controversy about Spain's activities in the Americas.[23] When Cajetan received reports from the friars he had sent, his shock led him to ask a returned friar, 'Do you doubt that your king is in hell?'—or so, at least, Las Casas claimed.[24] Cajetan's indignation subsequently drove him to incorporate into his commentary on Aquinas's *Summa theologica* a declaration that non-believers who had never been subjected to the dominion of Christian rulers 'are not to be dispossessed of their political jurisdiction on account of their unbelief, since *dominium* is from positive law, and unbelief is from divine law, which does not take away positive law'.[25]

The story of the connection between Cajetan and Sepúlveda further complicates our appreciation of the complex role that the latter played in the intellectual life of his time. When Rome was sacked by imperial forces and Lutheran *Landsknechte* in 1527, Sepúlveda took refuge in the Castel Sant' Angelo along with the pope, Cajetan, and others, but he was soon expelled by Cardinal Orsini as a suspect Spaniard. He fled to Naples, while Cajetan, after ransoming himself and his household, withdrew to his native Gaeta, on the coast between Rome and Naples. Sepúlveda records that he was facing the hardships of the impending siege of Naples when Cajetan 'summoned me so that I might collaborate with him on his labours. He was working on a commentary on the New Testament and wished that I would resolve certain difficulties and help him out with my knowledge of Greek.'[26] (Like Pomponazzi, Cajetan had no Greek.) Two decades later, Sepúlveda would find himself in the uncomfortable position of countering his (by now deceased) rescuer's influential rejection of the idea that unbelief constituted just grounds for subjugation by Christian rulers when advancing his defence of Spain's invasion of the Americas.

In 1529, Sepúlveda was sent by Clement VII to greet Charles V upon his landing at Genoa and to accompany Charles to Bologna, where the pope crowned him emperor. To mark the occasion, Sepúlveda composed an *Exhortation to Charles V to Make War upon the Turks* (*Cohortatio ad Carolum V ut bellum suscipiat in Turcas*), which was printed in Bologna at the end of that year. A few years later he composed another dialogue, *Democrates primus*. According to the prologue addressed to the Duke of Alba, Sepúlveda had found that many young Spanish noblemen serving as knights in the train of Charles V were tormented by their awareness of 'certain views according to which the profession of a noble warrior ... did not fit well with

---

[23] Note that Lewis Hanke's pioneering study, *The Spanish Struggle for Justice in the Conquest of America* (American Historical Association, 1949), began with a chapter, 'The Sermons of Friar Antonio de Montesinos'.

[24] Las Casas, *Historia de las Indias, in Obras completas*, vols. 3–5, edited by Miguel Ángel Medina, with introductory material by Jesús Angel Barreda and Isacio Pérez Fernández (Madrid: Alianza, 1994), Bk. 3, ch. 38.

[25] See Lantigua, *Infidels and Empires in a New World Order*, 85–92; quoted passage on 87.

[26] Sepúlveda, a passage from his *Chronicle of Charles V*, quoted in Losada, *Juan Ginés de Sepúlveda*, 61 (our translation).

10 SEPÚLVEDA ON THE SPANISH INVASION OF THE AMERICAS

the mandates of Christian philosophy'.[27] Alarmed by such claims, particularly given Spain's ongoing wars with the Turks, Sepúlveda made the case in the dialogue that Christians were not prohibited from undertaking wars waged for just reasons. In so doing, he demonstrated an impressive aptitude for bringing together theological, Aristotelian, and Italian humanist reasoning and directing them towards a common end. Sepúlveda published the dialogue in Rome in 1535.[28]

Charles V arrived in Rome that same year and offered him the post of official chronicler, with an additional honorary title of 'chaplain'. Sepúlveda, whose papal patron Clement VII had recently died, gladly accepted. Thus, in 1536, having spent two decades immersed in Italian intellectual culture, Sepúlveda returned to Spain. He was by now a remarkably protean intellectual: theologically-trained opponent of both Luther and Erasmus, distinguished translator of and commentator upon the works of Aristotle, author of dialogues in the elegant Latin of a Renaissance humanist, and newly appointed royal chronicler and chaplain. Given the impressive multiplicity of his identities and areas of plausible competence, we may perhaps have sufficient reason to see why he would be at once a formidable and elusive antagonist for Las Casas and his supporters.

Democrates secundus

Debate within Spain about the justice of royal policies regarding the wars in the Americas and the treatment of indigenous peoples subjugated by the Spaniards had by now been raging for several decades. Soon after Sepúlveda arrived on the scene, questions that had sometimes been raised about the humanity and rationality of the Amerindians were settled by Clement's successor, Pope Paul III, in his 1537 bull *Sublimis Deus*. Prompted by the testimonies of Dominicans who had witnessed the mistreatment of Amerindians, Paul condemned those Spaniards who asserted that the Amerindians should be reduced to slavery and made to serve them like brute animals. His bull proclaimed that the peoples of the Americas were fully human and capable of receiving the Christian faith, that the faith should be preached to them peacefully, and that even those who remain outside the faith should not be deprived of their liberty and possessions or be in any other way enslaved.[29]

---

[27] Numerous scholars have repeated the mistaken claim of Losada (*Juan Ginés de Sepúlveda*, 148) that the young Spanish noblemen were students who Sepúlveda encountered during a visit to the Colegio de San Clemente in Bologna in the entourage of Clement VII. Castilla Urbano (*El pensamiento de Juan Ginés de Sepúlveda*, 95–96) has shown, however, that Sepúlveda made clear that they were knights accompanying Charles V. One of the characters in the dialogue, Democrates, indicated that he consorted with them in the encampment of the emperor in Hungary.

[28] For discussion of *Democrates primus*, see Fernández-Santamaría, *The State, War, and Peace*, 172–88.

[29] On the influence of the Dominicans on *Sublimis Deus*, see Gustavo Gutiérrez, *Las Casas: In Search of the Poor of Jesus Christ* (Maryknoll, NY: Orbis, 1993), 302–08. For the text of the bull, see Lawrence A.

But while the bull *Sublimis Deus* prohibited the enslavement of Amerindians, it did not address the system of the *encomienda*, by which groups of Amerindians were allotted to individual Spanish colonists (*encomenderos*) and compelled to provide their labour and tribute to them while supposedly remaining free as a matter of law. This institution served the colonists as a morally palatable alternative to formal enslavement. However, not only did it impose destructive burdens on many Amerindians, but its feudal nature was increasingly perceived to undercut the authority of the Spanish Crown.

In 1540, Las Casas, a Dominican friar who had been led by his conscience to renounce his own *encomienda* in Cuba in 1514 and had spent most of the intervening years in the Americas, ministering, preaching, and writing for the protection of the Amerindians, returned to Spain. He quickly set about seeking to persuade the emperor to enact legislation to abolish the *encomiendas* and prohibit further conquests.[30] On 20 November 1542, after Las Casas had spent several months tirelessly arguing his case before a special council meeting established by the emperor in Valladolid, Charles V passed the New Laws.[31] These radical reforms aimed to ensure the preservation and good governance of Amerindians via provisions that both drastically limited the power of colonial elites and forcefully asserted the direct authority of the Spanish Crown in the Americas. The laws prohibited the enslavement of any Amerindians, including those who rebelled against Spanish rule, prohibited royal and ecclesiastical officials from holding Amerindians in *encomiendas*, and stipulated that abusive *encomenderos* be deprived of their *encomiendas* and their Amerindians placed under the direct authority of the Crown. Most significantly, the laws ordered that no new *encomiendas* be granted to anyone and that, upon the death of the present holders of *encomiendas*, their Amerindians not pass to their descendants but revert to the Crown.[32]

Not satisfied with the New Laws, Las Casas and another Dominican friar, Rodrigo de Ladrada, petitioned the emperor for additional reforms, urging him in 1543 to explicitly prohibit further conquests on the basis that they were unjust, destructive to the Amerindians, and scandalous to the Christian faith.[33] But the New Laws alone proved more than sufficient to provoke uproar in Spain and fierce resistance from colonists in the Americas. In Peru, widespread rebellion culminated in the revolt of Gonzalo Pizarro and the military defeat and decapitation of

---

Clayton and David M. Lantigua (eds), *Bartolomé de las Casas and the Defense of Amerindian Rights: A Brief History with Documents* (Tuscaloosa: University of Alabama Press, 2020), 86–87.

[30] For English-language overviews of Las Casas's life and career, see Henry Raup Wagner with the collaboration of Helen Rand Parish, *The Life and Writings of Bartolomé de las Casas* (Albuquerque: University of New Mexico Press, 1967); Gutiérrez, *Las Casas*; Lawrence A. Clayton, *Bartolomé de las Casas: A Biography* (Cambridge: Cambridge University Press, 2012).

[31] Clayton, *Bartolomé de las Casas*, 270–84.

[32] Clayton and Lantigua, *Bartolomé de las Casas and the Defense of Amerindian Rights*, 56–59.

[33] Lantigua, *Infidels and Empires in a New World Order*, 150.

12 SEPÚLVEDA ON THE SPANISH INVASION OF THE AMERICAS

the viceroy Blasco Núñez Vela in 1546. In Mexico, passionate opposition to the New Laws prompted provincials of the religious orders and representatives of the council of Mexico City to set off for Spain to lodge their protests.

As Sepúlveda tells it, the delegation's arrival gave rise to a lot of discussion at court regarding the justice of the conquest of the Indies.[34] A Spanish translation of Sepúlveda's dialogue examining the just reasons for war, *Democrates primus*, had been printed in Seville in 1541, and he had been going around claiming that he could provide proof of the justice of Spain's conquest of the Indies. Having heard this claim, Francisco García de Loaysa, the archbishop of Seville and president of the Council of the Indies, asked him to commit his thoughts to paper. And so Sepúlveda composed a book, *Democrates secundus*, 'in a matter of just a few days'.[35]

He addressed the justice of Spain's subjugation of the Amerindians by way of a dialogue between the characters of Leopoldus, a German influenced by the errors of Lutheranism, and Democrates, a Greek who served as the mouthpiece of Sepúlveda. Leopoldus and Democrates had been introduced in the earlier dialogue, *Democrates primus*, in which they had discussed with Alphonsus, an old Spanish soldier, whether war was prohibited to Christians. That dialogue was set at the Vatican. They now met in the gardens at Sepúlveda's place in Valladolid, on the banks of the Pisuerga.[36]

Democrates secundus begins with a recapitulation of the earlier account of the just reasons for waging war, an account grounded in the authority of natural law. The three just reasons for war are said to be self-defence, the recovery of things wrongly seized, and the punishment of injuries received.[37] Sepúlveda then suggested an additional reason for war—a reason less widely acknowledged and arising less often, but no less just: to reduce to subjection those whose natural condition is that they should be ruled by others. This was the first of four justifications that he proceeded to offer for the Spanish wars in the Americas.

Natural slavery

This first justification rested on Aristotle's claim, found in the first book of his *Politics*, that some people are 'slaves by nature' (*natura servi*). Sepúlveda's unabashed

---

[34] Sepúlveda, *Proposiciones temerarias*, §2.

[35] Sepúlveda, *Proposiciones temerarias*, §2. Note that one early manuscript, known as the P (Santander) manuscript, gives the title of Sepúlveda's book as *Democrates alter*. The four other known manuscripts are entitled *Democrates secundus*. Alejandro Coroleu Lletget, 'Introducción filológica', in Juan Ginés de Sepúlveda, *Obras completas, vol. 3: Demócrates Segundo*, edited by Alejandro Coroleu Lletget, and *Apología en favor del libro sobre las justas causas de la guerra*, edited by Antonio Moreno Hernández, xxxi–xxxvi (Pozoblanco: Ayuntamiento de Pozoblanco, 1997), xxxi.

[36] On Sepúlveda's lengthy residency in Valladolid, see Marcos, *Los imperialismos de Juan Ginés de Sepúlveda*, 27–28.

[37] Sepúlveda, *Democrates secundus*, I.1–4.

INTRODUCTION 13

application of this doctrine to justify Spain's wars has since become the primary source of his notoriety. As noted earlier, he was not the first to make use of the doctrine. John Mair, the Scottish theologian at the University of Paris, had applied it to peoples of the Americas in his commentary on the second book of Peter Lombard's *Sentences*, published in 1510.[38] The *licenciado* Gregorio introduced it into Spanish debates about the Americas two years later.[39] Numerous others had repeated it in the years since.[40] But few had invoked it and applied it to the Amerindians with such apparent conviction and enthusiasm as Sepúlveda now did.

Compare the 'intelligence, ingenuity, magnanimity, temperance, humanity, and religion' of the Spaniards with those 'lesser humans' (*homunculi*) in the Americas among whom one scarcely finds any vestiges of humanity, he urged. These barbarians have no learning, no writing, and surely little virtue given that they used to feast upon human flesh. Add to their uncivilized nature and customs their idolatry and their monstrous rite of human sacrifice and it could not be clearer that they are slaves by nature.[41] They are surpassed by the Spaniards in every respect, 'as children are by adults, as women are by men, as savage and fierce people are by the most gentle people', and, as he put it in an early version of the text, 'I might also say: as apes are by human beings'.[42] It is not only just but also beneficial for such people to be subjected to the rule of civilized, Christian Spaniards.

And what benefits the barbarians have gained! In exchange for their gold and silver, which hold little value for them anyway, these people, who were once 'contaminated by heinous sacrifices and impious rites', have received the pious and just rule of the kings and people of Spain, their laws, customs, and alphabetic writing system, and the knowledge of the true God and the Christian religion. Those who have accepted the rule of the magistrates and priests assigned to them differ from their earlier selves 'almost as much as human beings from beasts'.[43]

It is instructive to compare Sepúlveda's argument about the implications of the natural condition of the barbarians with that offered by the Dominican theologian Francisco de Vitoria in his famous relection on the Indies delivered at the University of Salamanca in 1539.[44] Vitoria cautiously affirmed Aristotle's claim that

[38] John Mair, *In secundum Sententiarum* (Paris: Jodocus Badius (Ascensius) and Jean Petit, 1510), dist. 44, q. 3, quoted and discussed in Las Casas, *In Defense of the Indians*, ch. 56, pp. 339–40.

[39] Las Casas, *Historia de las Indias*, 3.12.

[40] See Pagden, *The Fall of Natural Man*, 27–56.

[41] Sepúlveda, *Democrates secundus*, I.10.1, I.11.1.

[42] Sepúlveda, *Democrates secundus*, I.9.1. Note that, just as Sepúlveda removed the mention of apes from the later S (Salamanca) manuscript, which was completed in or after 1547, so too did he moderate his tone by removing all but one of the uses of the word *homunculi* found in earlier versions of the dialogue. Christian Schäfer, 'Einleitung', in Juan Ginés de Sepúlveda, *Democrates secundus / Zweiter Demokrates*, edited, translated, and introduced by Christian Schäfer, xiii–lxxiv (Stuttgart-Bad Cannstatt: Frommann-Holzboog, 2018), lxv.

[43] Sepúlveda, *Democrates secundus*, I.11.1, I.19.3.

[44] Anthony Pagden and Jeremy Lawrance explain that a relection was a 'rereading' of a problem— commonly a problem 'of some immediate political or social significance'—which had been raised during that year's lectures. Relections at Salamanca were typically more formal than a lecture, up to two hours long, and delivered prior to Midsummer's Eve. Anthony Pagden and Jeremy Lawrance,

14   SEPÚLVEDA ON THE SPANISH INVASION OF THE AMERICAS

some people are slaves by nature and that it is better for them to be ruled by natural masters. He insisted, however, that Aristotle should not be read as arguing that those who are in a condition of natural slavery lack true dominion over their own bodies and possessions or that others can rightly arrogate to themselves power over them on the mere ground of their natural condition. Therefore, Vitoria claimed, the barbarians of the Indies possess true dominion regardless of their natural inferiority, and so they cannot rightly be subjugated to Spanish rule without just reason.[45]

Sepúlveda similarly accepted that the barbarians possessed true dominion. However, he claimed that their condition of natural slavery *itself* constituted just reason to subjugate them through war, should they fail to submit themselves willingly to the rule of natural masters.[46] Composing *Democrates secundus* at the same time as he was at work translating Aristotle's *Politics* into Latin (printed in Paris in 1548), Sepúlveda had no trouble finding a suitable passage: 'for the art of hunting is a part of warfare which it is fitting to use sometimes against beasts, and sometimes against those humans who, though they have been born to obey, reject rule'.[47] Wary, perhaps, of being perceived to be embracing a controversial claim of thirteenth-century canonist Hostiensis, or indeed a supposed heresy associated with Lutherans of his own day, Sepúlveda clarified awkwardly that he did not deny that the barbarians rightfully governed themselves prior to the promulgation of Alexander VI's 1493 papal bull, *Inter caetera*, and the arrival of the Spaniards. The regions of the New World had indeed belonged to the Amerindians, he insisted. But it was nevertheless right for them to be subjected to Spanish rule, by force if necessary, for the plain reason that those regions were not ruled by civilized Christians.[48]

'Introduction' and 'Glossary', in Vitoria, *Political Writings*, edited and translated by Anthony Pagden and Jeremy Lawrance xiii–xxviii, 380 (Cambridge: Cambridge University Press, 1991), xvii.

[45] Francisco de Vitoria, 'On the American Indians', in *Political Writings*, q. 1, conclusion.

[46] Vitoria, it should be said, contemplated a similar argument at the end of his relection, though he insisted that he mentioned it 'for the sake of the argument, though certainly not asserted with confidence', and that he did 'not dare to affirm or condemn it out of hand'. Vitoria, 'On the American Indians', q. 3, art. 8.

[47] Aristotle, *Politics*, 1.3.8 (1256b23–27), quoted in Sepúlveda, *Democrates secundus*, I.5.4. Vitoria had cited this same Aristotelian passage in his relection. However, he mentioned only the part about the right to hunt beasts, and he did so in order to contrast these beasts' apparent lack of dominion with the natural condition of rational men such as the barbarians of the Indies. He completely ignored Aristotle's clear statement here that war is also sometimes rightly waged against natural slaves. Vitoria, 'On the American Indians', q. 1, art. 4.

[48] Sepúlveda, *Democrates secundus*, I.20.5–6. Las Casas would accuse Sepúlveda of this Lutheran heresy at Valladolid. Bartolomé de las Casas, 'Replies', in *Aquí se contiene una disputa o controversia . . .* , Twelfth Reply, §11. For discussion of Hostiensis's argument that infidels could not legitimately possess dominion, expressed in his commentary on the decretal of Pope Innocent III, *Quod super his*, and how this opinion became tainted by its association with the supposed heresies of John Wycliffe and Jan Hus in the fourteenth and fifteenth centuries and then Martin Luther in Sepúlveda's time, see James Muldoon, *Popes, Lawyers, and Infidels* (Philadelphia: University of Pennsylvania Press, 1979), 15–18, 107–19; Xavier Tubau, 'Canon Law in Juan Ginés de Sepúlveda's *Democrates secundus*', *Bibliothèque d'Humanisme et Renaissance* 73/2 (2011): 265–77, at 274–75.

INTRODUCTION   15

Sepúlveda does not appear to have hesitated in founding this first justification for war on Aristotle's doctrine of natural slavery. He supplemented the doctrine with conventional humanist appeals to the bravery of the Spaniards, the cowardice of the barbarians, and the glory of conquest (reprising a theme he had developed in his *Gonzalo* and repeated in book two of his *Democrates primus*).[49] We will see, however, that he would abandon his reliance on Aristotle's doctrine as well as his enthusiastic invocations of humanist virtue in subsequent iterations of his argument as he came to understand how they provoked the ire of Dominican theologians who were called to inspect *Democrates secundus*.[50] It is worth noting, moreover, that the centrality of Aristotle for Sepúlveda's argument even in *Democrates secundus* has at times been overstated. This unfortunate feature of Anglophone scholarship can be traced in large part to Lewis Hanke's influential and in many ways excellent mid-twentieth-century study, *Aristotle and the American Indians*.[51] In reality, in Sepúlveda's three remaining justifications for conquest in the Americas, and even at certain points when defending his first justification, he leant more heavily on the authority of Scripture and of Augustine, among other theologians.

Punishing violations of natural law

Sepúlveda's second justification for war to subjugate the barbarians was that it was just punishment for their violations of natural law, specifically those laws prohibiting idol worship and human sacrifices. The impious and wicked crimes of the Amerindians, he claimed, violate not only divine law, but also natural law, which applies to all peoples. It was for such crimes that God meted out the punishment of war not only against the Israelites, at the hands of the Assyrians and Babylonians, but also the pagan peoples inhabiting the Promised Land, at the hands of the Israelites, before the coming of Christ.[52] Christ, in turn, commanded his Apostles not only to preach the Christian faith to all peoples, but also to teach them to observe the laws of nature as contained in the Decalogue and the love of one's neighbour. And since all people are subject to these laws and can be taught and persuaded to obey them, it is most just that violators be punished by Christian princes on the authority of the church.[53]

---

[49] Sepúlveda, *Democrates secundus*, I.8.4, I.10.1–2.

[50] On Sepúlveda's misrepresentation of Augustine's understanding of glory at I.8.4, which may well have exacerbated the disapproval of the Dominican theologians, see David A. Lupher, *Romans in a New World: Classical Models in Sixteenth-Century Spanish America* (Ann Arbor: University of Michigan Press, 2003), 115–17. On Sepúlveda's revised description of the Amerindians as a noble and brave people in later writings, see Rolena Adorno, *The Polemics of Possession in Spanish American Narrative* (New Haven: Yale University Press, 2007), 126–32.

[51] Hanke, *Aristotle and the American Indians*.

[52] Sepúlveda, *Democrates secundus*, I.11.3–4.

[53] Sepúlveda, *Democrates secundus*, I.12.3.

16 SEPÚLVEDA ON THE SPANISH INVASION OF THE AMERICAS

Certainly, Sepúlveda acknowledged, Augustine had defined just wars as 'those which avenge injuries received', and the barbarians had not injured the Spaniards (or at least not prior to resisting the Spaniards' just wars against them). However, the worship of idols injures God, and Christians justly wage holy war (*bellum sacrum*) to avenge wrongs done to God.[54] How kind and merciful the kings of Spain have been to the barbarians, therefore, in refraining from punishing them to the fullest extent. Instead of justly depriving them of their possessions and lives, they have reduced them to Christian rule and pursued their correction and salvation.[55]

Sceptical of this second justification for war, at this point in the discussion Leopoldus introduced Paul's words in 1 Corinthians 5:12: 'What business is it of mine judge those outside the church?' Vitoria had invoked this verse to show that the church had neither spiritual nor temporal jurisdiction over the infidel barbarians.[56] Sepúlveda had Democrates interpret it very differently: Paul meant merely that the church should not spend time passing judgment futilely on the unbelief of pagans, since it is unable to force people to believe against their will. And yet, while the church should not strive in vain to compel belief, the church is authorized, and indeed obliged, to do all it can to bring about the conversion of unbelievers, including, where possible, by punishing and correcting those who violate the law of nature.[57] As Augustine had declared in a letter to the Donatist bishop, Vincentius, 'The church corrects those whom it can and tolerates those whom it does not have the power to correct.'[58] And where violations of natural law are not merely perpetrated by individuals, as in many societies, but a whole people allows these sins to go unpunished and does not even think that they merit punishment, as in the Americas, Christians justly punish and correct such a people through war.[59]

Protecting innocents

Sepúlveda supplemented this argument for punitive war with a third justification for war against the barbarians, claiming that war to avenge injuries done to God is especially warranted if it also serves to ward off injuries to innocent people. This was certainly the case with respect to the wars in the Americas, he claimed. Prior to the arrival of the Spaniards, the inhabitants of New Spain had been in the habit of sacrificing over 20,000 people each year.[60] Far fewer lives were lost in the course of

---

[54] Sepúlveda, *Democrates secundus*, I.15.7.
[55] Sepúlveda, *Democrates secundus*, I.11.6.
[56] Vitoria, 'On the American Indians', q. 2, art. 2 and art. 5.
[57] Sepúlveda, *Democrates secundus*, I.12.2–3, I.15.5.
[58] Augustine, Letter 93.9.34, quoted in Sepúlveda, *Democrates secundus*, I.12.2–3.
[59] Sepúlveda, *Democrates secundus*, I.15.1–5.
[60] This figure of 20,000 had been widely invoked at least since the first bishop of Mexico, Juan de Zumárraga, had asserted it in 1532. Luis N. Rivera, *A Violent Evangelism: The Political and Religious Conquest of the Americas* (Louisville, KY: Westminster/John Knox, 1992), 261.

reducing all of New Spain to Spanish rule, with the exception of the city of Mexico/ Tenochtitlan where obstinate resistance led to more substantial loss of life. He appealed to well-known scriptural and theological proof-texts for support, from the parable of the good Samaritan, to Psalms and Proverbs endorsing the rescue of the poor and the guiltless, to the writings of Ambrose, Augustine, and Jerome.[61] But he then quickly moved on.

When Sepúlveda was defending his previous justification for Spain's wars he repeatedly acknowledged that unbelief alone does not provide just reason for war. Only when unbelief is accompanied by violations of natural law are Christian princes justified in taking up arms. This claim mirrored that which had been offered by the thirteenth-century canonist-pope Innocent IV in his influential commentary on Pope Innocent III's decretal, *Quod super his*. Noting that a 'very learned man' (identified only in a marginal gloss as Cajetan) had argued that unbelief alone is not a just reason for war, Sepúlveda insisted that the notion that the natural law violations of unbelievers provided just cause for war was supported by the opinions of 'very learned men'.[62] But he did not name Innocent IV.[63] This was perhaps because Sepúlveda knew that he himself at times collapsed the distinction between the crimes of unbelievers and their mere unbelief, pushing his argument beyond the limits of what Innocent IV had been willing to permit. In certain passages, the absence of Christian faith alone seemed to provide grounds for war. He suggested that if there was discovered in the Americas a civilized and humane people who, despite not possessing faith in Christ, obeyed the law of nature and worshipped the true God according to nature, Christian princes could not justly wage war against them on account of their infidelity.[64] But this was a rather circumscribed category of hypothetical infidels.[65] And as he further developed the case for punitive war, the possibility of war against even these infidels began to emerge: it is lawful to subject unbelievers to the rule of Christians, he declared, 'especially' if they violate the law of nature, such as by failing to 'acknowledge and worship the one, eternal, highest, greatest God'.[66] Such an argument was closer to the controversial position of Hostiensis, Innocent IV's student, whose claim that unbelievers lack dominion,

---

[61] Sepúlveda, *Democrates secundus*, I.15.8–9.

[62] Sepúlveda, *Democrates secundus*, I.12.1 and 3.

[63] At some point, perhaps in the course of writing his *Apologia*—in which he did explicitly invoke the authority of Innocent IV as well as Hostiensis, Joannes Andreas, and Panormitanus in support of this justification for war—Sepúlveda added a marginal note beside this passage in *Democrates secundus* referring to the commentaries of these four canonists on Innocent III's decretal: 'Super cap. quod super his de voto'.

[64] Sepúlveda, *Democrates secundus*, I.12.2.

[65] For evidence of the possibility of such people, Sepúlveda pointed to Paul's remarks in Romans 2:14, about Gentiles doing by nature that which is required by the law, and also to examples of Greek philosophers who recognized that there is only one god (*Democrates secundus*, I.12–14).

[66] Sepúlveda, *Democrates secundus*, I.12.3.

18 SEPÚLVEDA ON THE SPANISH INVASION OF THE AMERICAS

expressed in his own commentary on *Quod super his*, Sepúlveda had tried to mark his distance from.[67]

Sepúlveda's suggestion that failure to worship the true God itself constitutes a violation of natural law and is justly punished on the authority of the church wherever it occurs, paved the way for his fourth justification for war. He pivoted to this justification, turning from punishment and the protection of bodies to correction and the conversion of souls, thus:

> For not unbelief by itself, but the monstrous sacrifices made with human victims, the extreme wrongs done to innocent peoples, the horrible feasts upon human bodies, the impious worship of idols—these constitute the justifications for war against those most unjust barbarians. Nonetheless, unbelief in itself would offer sufficient justification not for punishing but for correcting and for converting from the false religion to the true one—which is the ultimate goal of this war.[68]

Spreading the Christian faith

This fourth justification, Sepúlveda claimed, is also the most just: war is rightly waged against the barbarians in order to guide them by the shortest and most direct path to the truth of the gospel.[69] Were it not for the fact that the will cannot be forced, he admitted, he would argue that pagans should be compelled to belief. But while it is ineffectual to baptize unwilling pagans, Christians are nevertheless obliged at least to pull them back from the precipice, even against their will, and to lead them towards the true path through gospel preaching, so long as they can do so at no harm to themselves. This was made clear by Christ's command to 'do unto others as you would have them do unto you' (Matthew 7:12). The Spaniards should lead even unwilling barbarians towards the true faith, since the Spaniards would wish this to be done for themselves if they were to go dangerously astray. 'What sane man would not?', he asked. And such efforts to spread the Christian faith in the Americas, he declared, can only be safely done and will only bear fruit if the barbarians are first brought under Spanish rule.[70]

Sepúlveda was not alone in defending the subjugation and pacification of the barbarians by the Spaniards in the interests of getting them to hear and receive the Christian faith. John Mair had argued as much in his commentary on the second book of the *Sentences*, and Alexander VI's bull, *Inter caetera*, was widely interpreted

---

[67] On the contrasting positions of Innocent IV and Hostiensis and the preference of later canonists for Innocent's position, see Muldoon, *Popes, Lawyers, and Infidels*, 3–28; Lantigua, *Infidels and Empires in a New World Order*, 33–45.

[68] Sepúlveda, *Democrates secundus*, I.15.9.

[69] Sepúlveda, *Democrates secundus*, I.15.11.

[70] Sepúlveda, *Democrates secundus*, I.15.13, I.16.

as commending and authorizing the same.[71] However, several theologians, including Vitoria, had recently rejected both the justice of subjugating the barbarians for this purpose as well as the pope's power to authorize it. In this they echoed the revered opinion of Cajetan, who in his commentary on Aquinas's *Summa* had declared that Christ sent his Apostles into the world not to crush, despoil, and subjugate unbelievers, but to preach the gospel to them peacefully; not as armed soldiers, but as sheep among wolves.[72] To support his argument, Sepúlveda turned again to the weighty authority of Augustine, and specifically two of Augustine's letters endorsing measures to lead heretical Donatists back to the true faith by force.

Among the numerous passages from these letters that proved useful to Sepúlveda was a creative interpretation of Christ's parable of the banquet that Augustine had advanced to explain why the fourth- and fifth-century church was right to use compulsion to lead people towards the faith even though the first apostles did not. The fact that the host of the banquet had his slave first invite and then compel people to come to the banquet, Augustine explained, was meant to symbolize the fact that, whereas the early church, lacking the power to do more, merely invited outsiders into the faith, now that the church's power was fortified by the power of Christian rulers, it was right to 'compel them to come in'.[73] It was for this reason, Sepúlveda reported, that Augustine, and Ambrose before him, approved of the Roman imperial law (which was taken by Sepúlveda and others at his time to be an edict of Constantine) that prohibited offensive sacrifices by pagan subjects and provided for the punishment not only of perpetrators, but also of provincial governors who allowed these crimes. Likewise, Pope Gregory I endorsed wars waged by Christians against pagans for the sole purpose of bringing them under Christian rule, so as to enable Christian teaching, and Gregory praised Gennadius, the exarch of Africa, for waging such wars. Add to this that the Israelites were instructed in Deuteronomy 20 as to how to wage war against people of a different religion, should they refuse to serve under tribute, and it is plain that 'there is sufficient justification in the matter of religion why unbelievers may be reduced to rule by believers', so that they may be led by the teachings and examples of pious men to worship God.[74]

And he did not stop there. Departing still further from the opinions of Cajetan and Vitoria, Sepúlveda argued that the barbarians of the Indies should be reduced to Spanish rule not only so that they could be forced to listen to preachers, but also to remove their fears of their own priests and rulers and to inspire in them fear of

---

[71] Mair, *In secundum Sententiarum*, dist. 44, q. 3, quoted and discussed in Las Casas, *Defense of the Indians*, ch. 53, pp. 326–29.

[72] Vitoria, 'On the American Indians', q. 2, art. 2; Cajetan (Tommaso de Vio Gaetano), 'Commentary on Aquinas's *Summa theologica*', in *Sancti Thomae Aquinatis ... Opera Omnia Iussu Impensaque Leonis XIII P.M. Edita*, vols. 8 and 9 (Rome: Typographia Polyglotta, 1895 and 1897), II-II, q. 66, art. 8.

[73] Sepúlveda, *Democrates secundus*, I.17.1–2, citing Augustine, Letter 173.10, and Luke 14:15–24.

[74] Sepúlveda, *Democrates secundus*, I.17.3.

20 SEPÚLVEDA ON THE SPANISH INVASION OF THE AMERICAS

the Christians instead—a fear that would encourage them to accept the true faith. He again found support in Augustine's writings on the Donatists. It is not that a person can become good against their will, Augustine had claimed. But rather, 'in the process of fearing what he does not want to suffer he either gives up a hostility that stood in the way or is forced to acknowledge a truth of which he had been unaware . . . and now willingly embraces that which he had not been willing to embrace'. When Christian teaching is accompanied by 'useful terror', Augustine maintained, not only do rational arguments and divine testimonies persuade listeners, but 'the power of fear would break the bonds of evil custom', leading to the salvation of many. Sepúlveda insisted that this was confirmed both by the experiences of Augustine with the Donatist communities in North Africa and of the Spaniards with barbarians in the Indies.[75]

As for the pope's power to authorize the Spanish wars for these ends, Sepúlveda acknowledged that the power granted by Christ to his vicar is properly exercised in matters of the spirit, such as the salvation of souls. And yet, the pope also necessarily has authority over temporal affairs with a bearing on such spiritual matters, and the subjugation of the barbarians is such an example, directed as it is towards the teaching of natural law and gospel truth.[76] It was therefore with just reasons and right authority, Sepúlveda declared at the end of Book I, that Pope Alexander VI had entrusted to the rulers of Castile the task of reducing the barbarians to their rule and not merely inviting, but compelling them into the Christian faith.[77]

Ruling justly

Having expounded his four just reasons for subjugating the Amerindians, Sepúlveda addressed, in what became in the final version the much shorter second book of *Democrates secundus*, how they ought to be ruled. It was to prove a source of frustration to him that some who read his manuscript took him to be arguing that the barbarians ought to be enslaved by the Spaniards. He had sought to head off such confusion as he appealed to Aristotle's doctrine of natural slavery in Book I, explaining that the philosophical concept of natural slavery is different to the legal or civil condition of enslavement.[78] Now, at the beginning of Book II, he

---

[75] Sepúlveda, *Democrates Secundus* I.18.3–4, quoting Augustine, Letter 93.5.16, 93.1.3. For an illuminating discussion of Augustine's claims, see P. R. L. Brown, 'St. Augustine's Attitude to Religious Coercion', *Journal of Roman Studies* 54/1–2 (1964), 107–16. For a detailed history of the Donatist controversy, see Brent D. Shaw, *Sacred Violence: African Christians and Sectarian Hatred in the Age of Augustine* (Cambridge: Cambridge University Press, 2011). For more on Sepúlveda's use of Augustine, see Lantigua, *Infidels and Empires in a New World Order*, 169–73.

[76] Sepúlveda, *Democrates secundus*, I.16.2.

[77] Sepúlveda, *Democrates secundus*, I.20.

[78] Sepúlveda, *Democrates secundus*, I.5.2. Some commentators in recent decades have pondered whether, in claiming that the barbarians were *natura servi*, Sepúlveda had in mind the serfdom of some medieval Spanish peasants or a form of chattel slavery. As he tried to make clear, however, he was

bluntly rejected the 'childish belief' that barbarians, by virtue of being slaves by nature, possessed no liberty or property of their own.[79] Vitoria had said much the same in 1539.[80] Sepúlveda argued that if the barbarians willingly subject themselves to Spanish rule, they cannot be justly enslaved and deprived of their possessions. Rather, they should be made 'subject to taxation and tribute in accord with their nature and condition'.[81] As for those who stubbornly resist subjugation and therefore need to be defeated through war, they should in most instances be subjected to the same treatment. However, he took a circuitous route towards that conclusion, first justifying and then rejecting the defeated barbarians' enslavement along the way.[82] If some readers mistakenly read him as defending Amerindian slavery, it was not entirely their fault.

In any case, while he declared that the pacified barbarians should retain their liberty and possessions, Sepúlveda insisted that they ought not to enjoy legal equality with the Spanish Christian subjects of the kings of Spain, nor should they be subject to the same methods of rule—or at least not at first. The barbarians, slaves by nature as they are, are properly subjected to 'an almost masterly rule', or perhaps 'a certain mixture of masterly and paternal power', rather than the 'royal or civil rule' administered to Spaniards.[83] He did not consider the nature and condition of the barbarians to be immutable, however. He believed that people who are by nature slaves are capable of being made more civilized (*humanus*) over time.[84] And so, as time passes and the barbarians become more civilized and Christianized, such that they are more like free men in their nature and condition, they ought to be treated as such. The precepts of Aristotle can aid the kings of Spain in seeking the right balance, he suggested: barbarians should not be oppressed nor subjected to forms of servitude that prompt them to rebel, but nor should they be indulged and given such freedom that they are inspired to reembrace their earlier condition and customs.[85]

Thus, Sepúlveda concluded, it is right that wise, just Spaniards exercise rule over barbarians in their cities and regions, instructing them in civilization and initiating them into the Christian religion and, in exchange for their labour and riches, ensuring that their basic needs are met—as was incumbent upon them under the *encomienda* system. But those Spaniards who have not only failed to look after those

---

concerned when making this claim not with the barbarians' legal or civil condition under Spanish rule, but solely with their natural condition, which justified merely their subjugation to Spanish rule. For further discussion, see the Preface to the translation of *Democrates secundus*.

[79] Sepúlveda, *Democrates secundus*, II.1.1.
[80] Vitoria, 'On the American Indians', q. 1, Conclusion.
[81] Sepúlveda, *Democrates secundus*, II.7.5.
[82] Sepúlveda, *Democrates secundus*, II.2–7. For further discussion, see the Preface to the translation of *Democrates secundus* at pp. 83–85..
[83] Sepúlveda, *Democrates secundus*, II.8.1.
[84] Sepúlveda, *Democrates secundus*, I.11.1, I.15.10.
[85] Sepúlveda, *Democrates secundus*, II.8.1–2.

22 SEPÚLVEDA ON THE SPANISH INVASION OF THE AMERICAS

entrusted to them, but also tortured and even killed them by subjecting them to unconscionable servitude and unbearable labours are wicked and detestable. The king of Spain must put an end to such crimes for the sake of his reputation and salvation, for the sake of those Spaniards who treat the barbarians well and deserve their just rewards, and for the sake of the barbarians themselves, who should be ruled with justice, gentleness, and humanity.[86]

Seeking a licence to print

Sepúlveda and Las Casas provide contrasting reports of what happened next. As Las Casas tells it, Sepúlveda first presented his book to the Council of the Indies. The Council's members 'ascertained the evil of the work and its very deadly poison' and refused to permit its printing. Sepúlveda then contrived to have it considered by the Royal Council of Castile, 'where they were not abreast of the goings-on in the Indies' and, thus, where the book stood a better chance of being endorsed.[87] Sepúlveda begins his own account by claiming that, upon writing his book and finding that it was approved by all who read it at the royal court, he presented it to the Council of Castile, requesting a licence to have it printed. The Council soon submitted the book for examination to one of the royal councillors and then to two Dominican monks, one of whom was Vitoria's brother, Diego de Vitoria. Each examiner endorsed the book. It was at this moment, Sepúlveda reports, that 'certain figures of authority staged an intervention, saying that, excellent though the book might be, it was not a suitable moment for it to be printed'.[88] He wrote to Emperor Charles V, asking what was going on. The emperor responded by ordering the Council of Castile to examine the book again and, unless they found a reason to decide otherwise, to grant a licence for it to be printed. And so it was passed again to the *licenciado* Francisco de Montalvo, who declared his approval of the book.[89]

At this point, however, in mid-1547, Las Casas returned from the Americas where he had been serving as bishop of Chiapa. As he himself puts it, upon learning that Sepúlveda's book was being assessed by the Council of Castile, being apprised of its contents, and fearing the 'irreparable damage' to which it could give rise, he quickly set about opposing it 'with all his might'.[90] He engineered to have it undergo examination all over again. The Council of Castile requested that it be inspected

---

[86] Sepúlveda, *Democrates secundus*, II.8.3–4.

[87] Las Casas, *Defense of the Indians*, ch. 57, p. 342; Bartolomé de las Casas, 'The Subject of This Work', in *Aquí se contiene una disputa o controversia* .... Las Casas claims that Sepúlveda also sent the book to the Council of Trent around this time, 'but, after having read it thoroughly and seeing that the material was scarcely Christian, some of the Council fathers refused to discuss the matter'. Las Casas, *Defense of the Indians*, ch. 57, p. 342.

[88] Sepúlveda, *Proposiciones temerarias*, §2.

[89] Sepúlveda, *Proposiciones temerarias*, §2.

[90] Las Casas, 'The Subject of This Work'.

INTRODUCTION   23

by the universities of Alcalá and Salamanca. And rightly so, Las Casas claimed, since the book's subject matter was 'above all theological in nature'.[91] Sepúlveda contends that Las Casas then, 'by means of machinations, fabrications, and favour-mongering', worked to ensure that the universities ruled against the book. Those from Alcalá judged that it ought not to be printed, but gave no reason for their decision. Those from Salamanca reached the same conclusion, giving reasons that Sepúlveda claims the Council of Castile found 'frivolous and insubstantial'.[92]

One of eight members of the tribunal at Salamanca that considered the book and issued the university's judgment in mid-1548 was Melchor Cano, who two years later would be appointed as one of the judges at the Valladolid Junta. Cano had moved from Alcalá to succeed Vitoria as Prima Professor of Theology upon the latter's death in 1546.[93] Towards the end of 1548, Sepúlveda sent Cano a letter complaining both about the tribunal's judgment and also some rumours that had since emerged. Sepúlveda accused Cano of mocking him in the presence of students at Salamanca and boasting of his leading role in ensuring that the tribunal rejected the book. Sepúlveda had also heard that Cano was accusing him of blasphemy for his characterization in *Democrates secundus* of the Apostle Paul's angry response to being struck on the mouth.[94] Maybe, Sepúlveda suggested, Cano was issuing the charge of blasphemy in order to suppress the sound arguments for war contained in the book. He then turned to what he suspected to be a fundamental reason underlying the decision on the part of Cano and the rest of the tribunal to oppose the book: their belief that his arguments relied on displays of humanist eloquence rather than serious theological learning. One can be both eloquent and learned, Sepúlveda insisted. He was an expert on Aristotle and was appreciated by intellectuals in Italy, and also by Erasmus, he claimed.[95] He had devoted himself to serious theological study and had impressed Pope Clement with his debating skills. But you, Cano, have responded to the book not by treating its arguments seriously but by issuing lies and threats.[96]

---

[91] Las Casas, 'The Subject of This Work'.

[92] Sepúlveda, *Proposiciones temerarias*, §3.

[93] Also among the eight committee members at Salamanca was Diego de Covarrubias, professor of canon law, who delivered his own relection on the justice of war against the Amerindians in 1547–48. Diego de Covarrubias, 'De iustitia belli adversus indos', in *Corpus Hispanorum de Pace*, vol. 6, edited and translated by Luciano Pereña et al., 343–63 (Madrid: Consejo Superior de Investigaciones Científicas, 1981). For the full list of committee members, see Francisco Castilla Urbano, 'The Debate of Valladolid (1550–1551): Background, Discussions, and Results of the Debate between Juan Ginés de Sepúlveda and Bartolomé de las Casas', in *A Companion to Early Modern Spanish Imperial Political and Social Thought*, edited by Jörg Alejandro Tellkamp, 222–51 (Leiden: Brill, 2020), 224.

[94] The passage is from Sepúlveda, *Democrates secundus*, I.2.2, referring to Acts 23:3.

[95] In the aftermath of Sepúlveda's involvement in Pio's quarrel with Erasmus, Sepúlveda and Erasmus developed and sustained an amicable correspondence, usually on matters of Greek philology, until the latter's death in 1536. Lupher, *Romans in a New World*, 106.

[96] Letter 74, from Sepúlveda to Melchor Cano, 26 December 1548, in Juan Ginés de Sepúlveda, *Obras completas, vol. 9.1: Epistolario*, edited by Ignacio J. García Pinilla and Julián Solana Pujalte (Pozoblanco: Ayuntamiento de Pozoblanco, 1997), 189–203.

Cano replied some months later, insisting that, while he may have criticized the book, he had never maligned Sepúlveda nor accused him of blasphemy. As for the judgment of the tribunal appointed at Salamanca, Cano insisted that he was not the leader of the tribunal, but he was not sorry that he was a member, nor was he about to change his mind about the book. Nor, for that matter, was he inspired by personal motives to take the position that he had. Sepúlveda had intimated that Cano opposed the book because it went against arguments Cano had presented in a relection on the dominion of the Amerindians (*Relectio de dominio Indorum*), delivered at Alcalá in 1546. Cano had indeed taken quite a firm stance against the justice of Spain's wars in this relection, ruling out wars waged on grounds of the natural condition of the barbarians, or with a view to punishing idolatry or other sins, or on the mere authority of the pope or the emperor, and expressing more caution than Vitoria had about the resort to force to protect innocents.[97] In his letter to Sepúlveda, however, he claimed that he had long since forgotten what he had written for the relection. Instead, the fact that Sepúlveda's arguments were contrary to those presented by Vitoria, 'a learned man neither undistinguished nor worthy of being despised', in his famous 1539 relection was enough to convince everyone that 'your view might not seem so certain and indubitable, but rather could most justly and for the best of reasons be called into question.'[98] Even if Cano had forgotten much of his own relection, he surely remembered that he had come out more plainly against the justice of Spain's wars than Vitoria, and he likely recalled that he had at one point criticized an unnamed Vitoria for offering 'certain frivolous arguments' in favour of using force against the barbarians for their own good.[99] The fact that Sepúlveda's arguments were contradicted even by Vitoria's relatively gentle critique of Spain's wars, then, would have been sufficient for Cano to oppose the book.

Cano then turned the knife. Responding to Sepúlveda's allusions to the praise he received for his ideas and eloquence in Italy, he remarked:

> Those wonderful Italians, to whom you show a kindness similar to their own, will render a decision about your book in accord with your hopes. But I, a Spaniard, from the most distant regions of the earth, who has scarcely had the opportunity to see Italy once, what am I to do? I don't know how to lie. If a book is bad, I cannot praise or express an interest in it. But now it annoys and disgusts you to have been

---

[97] Melchor Cano, 'De dominio Indorum', in *Corpus Hispanorum de Pace,* vol. 9, edited by Luciano Pereña (Madrid: Consejo Superior de Investigaciones Científicas, 1982), 555–81.

[98] Letter 81, from Melchor Cano to Sepúlveda, undated, in Juan Ginés de Sepúlveda, *Obras completas, vol. 9.2: Epistolario,* edited by Ignacio J. García Pinilla and Julián Solana Pujalte (Pozoblanco: Ayuntamiento de Pozoblanco, 1997), 214–25, at §19, p. 222 (our translation).

[99] Cano, 'De dominio Indorum', 561 (our translation). On why it was Vitoria whom Cano had in mind here, as opposed to Sepúlveda as Luciano Pereña suggests, see Lupher, *Romans in a New World,* 86–87.

born in Spain, and you come close to disowning our native country because it is stingy in its praise of your genius.[100]

As for Sepúlveda's objection that his book had been approved by the three theologians tasked by the Royal Council of Castile with examining it (an objection that he would not tire of repeating), Cano noted that, while he admired those theologians, Sepúlveda was presumptuous to cast them as the leading experts and to denigrate as 'lesser ones' the universities' theologians who, when asked for an opinion by the same council, voted against the book.[101] Leaving no doubt that he did not take seriously Sepúlveda's pretensions to contribute meaningfully to a controversy that was essentially a matter of theology, Cano concluded by noting condescendingly that he would refrain from responding to other points that Sepúlveda had raised since he did not wish provoke a reply and spark a quarrel that would 'give extra trouble to a man who is enjoying his leisure in the field of literature.'[102]

Nevertheless, Sepúlveda did soon reply. His letter to Cano, written in mid-1549, provides a clear sense of his interpretation of the reasons for which the theologians at the universities had rejected his book. The first was their refusal to treat his theological arguments seriously, despite the fact that it was his position—not theirs—that was theologically sound.

> Instead of the gospel, you offer us the sophistries of old heretics twisting the gospel and the example of Christ to fit their own meaning; but we are [i.e. I am] adducing for you the gospel, as it has been interpreted by the holy doctors and by the church itself in actions and in pronouncements. You make mention of Cajetan and Francisco Vitoria, whom my book very clearly shows to have been partly on my side and partly in error. Against them I name Augustine, Ambrose, and Gregory, Aquinas, Duns Scotus, Nicholas of Lyra, not to mention other more recent theologians, and everyone who is most important and experienced in pontifical law. You offer Salamancans and those of Alcalá—that is, the opinion of a few men speaking in the name of the university; to these men, we oppose all the rest of Spain.[103]

The second reason for which the universities' theologians had decided against his book, he had come to realize, was their opposition to his use of Aristotle's doctrine of natural slavery. He recalled that when he had invoked the doctrine in a meeting at Salamanca, Cano had responded that Aristotle had offered the doctrine to gratify Alexander the Great, who was at that time waging war against barbarians.

---

[100] Letter 81, from Melchor Cano to Sepúlveda, §22, p. 223 (our translation).
[101] Letter 81, from Melchor Cano to Sepúlveda, §20, p. 222 (our translation).
[102] Letter 81, from Melchor Cano to Sepúlveda, §25, p. 223 (our translation).
[103] Letter 82, from Sepúlveda to Melchor Cano, 15 July 1549, in Sepúlveda, *Obras completas, vol. 9.2: Epistolario*, 226–47, at §29, p. 244 (our translation).

26 SEPÚLVEDA ON THE SPANISH INVASION OF THE AMERICAS

And when Sepúlveda had attempted to impress upon him the importance and authority of Aristotle, Cano had replied, 'Oh no, he was wicked and flawed'.[104]

The third reason for which the theologians judged as they did, Sepúlveda contended, was that they had fallen victim to the machinations of an unnamed individual whose efforts were 'contrary and persistent'. This was clearly a reference to Las Casas. Sepúlveda explained that he did not mean to charge the theologians with 'avarice or corruption'. But they admit that they were pressured by 'entreaties, letters, and clever rhetoric'—so much so that some of them voted contrary to their inclinations.[105] The universities' decisions, he concluded, were tainted.[106]

Sepúlveda countered Las Casas's manoeuvres against his book by seeking the condemnation of the latter's own book, the *Confessionary* (*Confesionario*).[107] This book of twelve rules for confessors sought to utilize the sacrament of confession as a means of motivating Spaniards in the Indies to stop opposing and violating the New Laws. It stipulated that confessors should only grant confession and absolution to conquistadors, *encomenderos*, miners, ranchers, slave-owners, and other Spaniards who had mistreated or exploited Amerindians on the condition that those seeking confession first pledged to restore what they had taken unjustly from Amerindians and to make restitution for the spiritual and physical harms done to them. In the process of explaining the guilt of the Spaniards in Rule Seven, Las Casas condemned unambiguously everything that they had done in the Indies:

> Everything that has been done throughout all the Indies both during the Spaniards' invasion of each of its provinces and in the course of the subjugation and servitude that they have imposed upon these people, together with all the means and ends and everything else they have employed in their dealings with them and in matters pertaining to them, has been against all natural law and the law of nations and also against divine law and is, consequently, all completely unjust, iniquitous, tyrannical, and deserving of all eternal fire and, as such, null, void, and without any value or weight in law.[108]

Las Casas submitted his *Confesionario* for examination to six theologians at Salamanca in February 1548 and he soon received their approval. (Among the six were Cano and Bartolomé de Carranza, both of whom would be appointed judges at the Valladolid Junta.[109]) However, in November that year, the Council of the

---

[104] Letter 82, from Sepúlveda to Melchor Cano, §24, p. 239 (our translation).
[105] Letter 82, from Sepúlveda to Melchor Cano, §23, pp. 238–39 (our translation). See similarly Sepúlveda, *Proposiciones temerarias*, §§3, 16; Letter 72, from Sepúlveda to Martín Oliván, 1 November 1548, in Sepúlveda, *Obras completas, vol. 9.1: Epistolario*, 184–86, at §1, p. 184.
[106] Letter 82, from Sepúlveda to Melchor Cano, §24, p. 239.
[107] For an English translation of this text, see Orique, *To Heaven or To Hell*.
[108] Bartolomé de las Casas, 'Aquí se contienen unos avisos y reglas para los confesores', edited by Lorenzo Galmés, in *Bartolomé de las Casas, Obras completas, vol. 10: Tratados de 1552*, edited by Ramón Hernández O.P. and Lorenzo Galmés O.P., 367–88 (Madrid: Alianza, 1992), 375 (our translation).
[109] Orique, *To Heaven or To Hell*, 42n30, 75.

INTRODUCTION 27

Indies issued a decree (*cédula*) ordering that the book be confiscated from monasteries in the Indies and sent to the council. Sepúlveda would later recall this event with no small amount of satisfaction, noting that, while the council never issued a ruling against his own book, it deemed Las Casas's 'false, scandalous, and outrageous'.[110] Las Casas was subsequently hauled before the council on the charge that Rule Seven implied that the rulers of Castile had no lawful entitlement to the Indies.[111] He quickly prepared a text, *Thirty Most Juridical Propositions* (*Treinta proposiciones muy jurídicas*), affirming the Spanish title to dominion in the Indies on the basis of Alexander VI's donation and injunction to the Spaniards to pursue the peaceful conversion of the people in those lands, but denying the right of Spaniards to wage war against them for that purpose, or to enslave them or distribute them among themselves in *encomiendas*. He promised to present a fuller account of this argument to the council soon.[112]

Despite the Council's order for the confiscation of copies of the *Confesionario* from the Indies, Sepúlveda pushed for still further action to be taken. In a letter penned to Prince Philip in September 1549, he reported that the council had referred the 'scandalous and diabolical *Confesionario*' to the king, whose response he now awaited. Noting that the book went against what he argued in his own book, he reminded the prince of his duty 'to support the cause of justice and not permit brazen men to obscure the truth with their fictions and wiles, especially in a business that so greatly affects the public good and the reputation and conscience of your fathers and grandfathers'. He beseeched him to command Doctors Escudero and Figueroa, who were apparently examining both the *Confesionario* and *Democrates secundus*, to do so carefully and to communicate their findings to the king. And he expressed his hope that, once the king issued a decision against the *Confesionario*, he might be granted a licence to print his *Democrates secundus*.[113]

While he engaged in these machinations against Las Casas, Sepúlveda responded to what he believed to be the university theologians' first and second reasons for opposing *Democrates secundus*—their dismissal of his competence in theology and their unease over his use of Aristotle—by writing and circulating several defences of his book.[114] One such defence, the *Apologia pro libro de justis belli causis* (*Defence on Behalf of the Book* On the Just Reasons for War), was printed in Rome on 1 May 1550. He reported that it was printed after having been approved

---

[110] Sepúlveda, *Proposiciones temerarias*, §16.

[111] Orique, *To Heaven or To Hell*, 42–45; Wagner and Parish, *Life and Writings*, 171–73; Bartolomé de las Casas, 'Aquí se contienen treinta proposiciones muy jurídicas', in *Tratados de Fray Bartolomé de las Casas*, vol. 1, transcribed by Juan Pérez de Tudela Bueso (Buenos Aires, 1965, repr. Mexico City: Fondo de Cultura Económica, 1974 and 1997), prologue; Sepúlveda, *Proposiciones temerarias*, §16.

[112] Las Casas, *Aquí se contienen treinta proposiciones muy jurídicas*, prologue and §§17–18, 30.

[113] Letter 86, from Sepúlveda to Prince Philip, 23 September 1549, in Sepúlveda, *Obras completas*, vol. 9.2: *Epistolario*, 251–53, at §§3–4, pp. 252–53 (our translation).

[114] Sepúlveda indicated in his September 1549 letter to Prince Philip that he had written and distributed copies of three such *apologiae* that year, as well as a 'summary of my Indies book of which I told Your Highness'. Letter 86, from Sepúlveda to Prince Philip, §3, p. 252.

by the deputy of the Pope, the *maestro* of the Holy Palace, and an adjudicator of the Rota, and praised by many other learned men in the Roman Court.[115] Las Casas sneered that Sepúlveda sent his *Apologia* to Rome 'in open contempt for the judgment of the universities and of both Royal Councils' since he knew that 'there was no one there of a contrary mind who would fling back his poisoned darts'.[116]

Apologia

Perceiving that a primary cause of the antagonism towards *Democrates secundus* from the theologians at Salamanca and Alcalá was his use of humanist methods to advance an argument about matters of a theological nature, Sepúlveda pursued a markedly different approach in his *Apologia*. In place of a dialogue, he now defended his claims 'in the scholastic manner', outlining seven objections that had been made against his book, presenting his argument, and then responding to the seven objections in turn.[117] Hoping to leave no grounds for rebuttal, he largely eschewed recourse to humanist literature and references to Greco-Roman authors. Much muted were the rhetorical flourishes, the allusions to the barbarians' lesser-humanity, and the humanist appeals to the glory of conquest. Instead, he built his case almost entirely on the claims of authorities whom the theologians most revered and could not dismiss, foremost among them the Bible, Augustine, and Aquinas. Sepúlveda had already relied heavily upon these authorities in *Democrates secundus*. But they were now more deliberately placed at the centre of discussion, supplemented, where convenient, with the conclusions of medieval canonists. Thus, rather than taking Cano's hints and ceding the theological ground to the theologians, Sepúlveda sought to demonstrate that he was capable of playing on their terms and beating them at their own game.

Before proceeding to his argument, Sepúlveda began the *Apologia* by explaining that the purpose of *Democrates secundus* had been misconstrued. He had not, as some were claiming, set out to justify depriving the barbarians of their dominions and possessions, reducing them to slavery, and killing those that resist. His book clearly condemned such unjust and impious behaviour. Rather, his argument was merely that the barbarians should be subjected to the rule of Christians so that obstacles to their reception of the faith could be removed and so that they might obtain the benefits of true religion and civilization.[118] It seems, though, that Sepúlveda was aware that he had not expressed this as plainly in the book as he might have. In his *Apologia*, therefore, he avoided repeating the suggestion that the barbarians

---

[115] Juan Ginés de Sepúlveda, 'Objections', in *Aquí se contiene una disputa o controversia ...*, Twelfth Objection, §7; Sepúlveda, *Proposiciones temerarias*, §16.
[116] Las Casas, *Defense of the Indians*, ch. 57, p. 343.
[117] Sepúlveda, *Apologia*, I.5.
[118] Sepúlveda, *Apologia*, I.7–9.

were suitable for 'almost masterly rule', in contrast to the 'royal or civil rule' exercised over Spanish Christians. Indeed, in an undated letter to Francisco de Argote, he reversed his position on this matter, stating that the Amerindians 'ought to be ruled not as a master rules but in a kingly and civil way for their own utility'.[119]

The most dramatic revision that Sepúlveda made to his argument was with respect to his first justification for war, which was grounded in the Amerindians' nature. In *Democrates secundus*, Leopoldus had expressed concern that Democrates's argument about natural slavery was 'beyond the received opinion of learned men'. Democrates responded by explaining that it was in accord with the position of pagan philosophers such as Aristotle and defended the value of making use of their ideas.[120] Having since come to realize how troubled the theologians were by this doctrine, and how little they were swayed by appeals to the authority of Aristotle, Sepúlveda now changed tack. The defence of this first justification for war in the *Apologia* was brief. Gone was any mention of the Amerindians being slaves by nature. Instead, Sepúlveda claimed merely that they were all barbarian in their customs and most were barbarian in nature. He invoked Aristotle in explaining that, by the law of nature, such peoples should be ruled by superior peoples, and they should be forced to such rule if they reject it. However, this reference to Aristotle was sandwiched between references to theologians, Aquinas and Augustine, who Sepúlveda claimed said the same thing.[121]

He gave much more weight to the second justification for war, namely that it constitutes just punishment for the barbarians' practices of idol worship and human sacrifice. To the scriptural passages and theological authorities that he had invoked in *Democrates secundus*, he now added the opinions of Pope Innocent IV and, somewhat surprisingly, Hostiensis, as well as two other medieval canonists, each of whom in their respective commentaries on Innocent III's decretal *Quod super his* had defended the pope's power to authorize the punishment of any people who violate the law of nature.[122] In his 1539 relection on the Indies, Vitoria had explicitly rejected both the authoritative opinion of Innocent IV and the more controversial view of Hostiensis.[123] Sepúlveda made no mention of Vitoria here, or indeed anywhere, when setting out his case in the *Apologia*, despite Cano's remarks about how significant it was that Sepúlveda's arguments diverged from Vitoria's. While Vitoria's relection was not printed until 1557, it was in circulation in the 1540s and Sepúlveda presumably would have had access to it if he wished. But he gave little indication that he had read it closely. The only reference he made to the

---

[119] Letter 101 from Sepúlveda to Francisco Argote, undated, in Sepúlveda, *Obras completas, vol. 9.2: Epistolario*, 296, at §2 (our translation).

[120] Sepúlveda, *Democrates secundus*, I.5.1, I.3.2.

[121] Sepúlveda, *Apologia*, III.1. Sepúlveda's efforts to distance himself from Aristotle's doctrine are noted in Pagden, *Fall of Natural Man*, 112; David M. Lantigua, 'The Freedom of the Gospel: Aquinas, Subversive Natural Law, and the Spanish War of Religion', *Modern Theology* 31/2 (2015): 312–37, at 323.

[122] Sepúlveda, *Apologia*, III.2.xii.

[123] Vitoria, 'On the American Indians', q. 2, art. 5.

30 SEPÚLVEDA ON THE SPANISH INVASION OF THE AMERICAS

relection in either *Democrates secundus* or the *Apologia* was a rather ambiguous handwritten citation that he added to the margins of the former manuscript at some point, perhaps in the aftermath of his exchanges with Cano.[124]

In the *Apologia*, instead of addressing Vitoria's clear rejection of the right of war against infidels to punish violations of natural law, Sepúlveda instead chose to address Cajetan's rebuttal of the notion that infidels may be justly defeated in war on account of their unbelief. He did so by echoing the opinion of Innocent IV, as against that of Hostiensis, declaring that while unbelief alone does not provide grounds for punishment, such grounds are provided by unbelievers' idol worship and other violations of natural law.[125] Left unmentioned was that Vitoria had challenged this very move, claiming that the assertion that the sins of infidels against natural law provide grounds for war 'is tantamount to saying that the barbarians may be conquered because of their unbelief, since they are all idolaters'.[126] Sepúlveda's appeal to the authority of the medieval canonists here may have been unlikely to win over the theologians who had previously expressed their opposition to his *Democrates secundus*, but we will see that it would help to convince several of the jurists before whom he would soon present his argument at Valladolid.

As in *Democrates secundus*, Sepúlveda treated his third justification for war—to save the lives of innocents—only briefly in the *Apologia*.[127] It is perhaps surprising that he did not make more of this justification since, of the four that he advanced, this was the one that had been most consistently endorsed by leading theologians and jurists within Spain.[128] It is especially surprising that he did not note Vitoria's well-known endorsement of this justification. While Vitoria denied that the church had the power to authorize the punishment of the barbarians for violations of natural law—specifically their idol worship and human sacrifice (Sepúlveda's second justification)—he had repeatedly asserted that war might

---

[124] Sepúlveda's marginal note at I.15.3 of *Democrates secundus* indicated that Vitoria was one of 'certain recent theologians' who argued that if individuals within a society commit sins against nature, the whole society can on that account be said to fail to observe the law of nature. Sepúlveda presumably had in mind here a passage from Vitoria's relection in which the theologian argued that, since the pope may not wage war against Christian kingdoms for sins against nature committed by individuals, the pope may not do so against the barbarians for that reason either (Vitoria, 'On the American Indians', q. 2, art. 5). Sepúlveda's point was that, while a society should not be said to violate the law of nature on the basis of the crimes of individuals, it could be said to be in violation if such crimes are approved by public customs and institutions, as was the case in the Indies. To be fair to Vitoria, though, he had noted in a relection on dietary laws delivered in 1538 that Christian societies also customarily accepted certain violations of natural laws, and 'surely it would be strange that fornication should be winked at in Christian society, but used as an excuse for conquering the lands of unbelievers!' (Francisco de Vitoria, 'On Dietary Laws, or Self-Restraint', in *Political Writings*, 230).

[125] Cajetan, 'Commentary on Aquinas's *Summa theologica*', II-II, q. 66, art. 8; Sepúlveda, *Apologia*, III.2.ix.

[126] Vitoria, 'On the American Indians', q. 2, art. 5.

[127] Sepúlveda, *Apologia*, III.3.

[128] For an overview, see Daniel Schwartz, 'The Principle of the Defence of the Innocent and the Conquest of America: "Save Those Dragged Towards Death"', *Journal of the History of International Law* 9/2 (2007): 263–91.

INTRODUCTION 31

be justly waged by Christian princes to protect the innocent victims of these nefarious rites (Sepúlveda's third justification).[129] Vitoria drew this distinction between punishment and protection clearly. Sepúlveda, by contrast, presented the obligation to protect innocents as little more than a mere addendum to his defence of wars waged to punish sins against nature. This third justification reads in both *Democrates secundus* and the *Apologia* almost as if it were an afterthought. And yet we will see that Las Casas would need to work hard, and even to flirt with heresy, to rebut this argument at Valladolid.

Sepúlveda then proceeded to devote more space to defending his fourth justification for war than to the first three combined. People can be brought towards salvation either by preaching alone or 'through the application of force and the fear of punishments', which aims not to compel belief—which is impossible—but rather to remove impediments to the teaching and receiving of the faith. And as Augustine taught, in accordance with the parable of the banquet, whereas Christ and the Apostles made use of the first method, the church, having been 'fortified by the power and protection of Christian kings and princes', rightly makes use of the second.[130]

To defend this position, Sepúlveda appealed once again to arguments and examples found in the writings of Augustine, Ambrose, and Gregory. It seems that some readers of *Democrates secundus* had objected that these theologians only advocated compelling heretics who remained under the jurisdiction of the church despite straying from the faith, or pagans who were already subject to Christian rule, but not pagans like the barbarians of the Americas who had never before received the faith and were not already ruled by Christians. Sepúlveda addressed this objection both in passages that he added to early versions of the dialogue and also in his *Apologia*.[131] Not only did Augustine endorse the supposed law of Constantine, which prohibited the idolatrous rites of pagans, Sepúlveda explained, but Augustine's interpretation of the parable of the banquet actually makes more sense applied to pagans than to the heretic Donatists, since those subjected to compulsion in the parable were being compelled not to 'return' to the faith, but to 'come in' for the first time. And when Gregory praised Gennadius for waging wars for the sole reason of spreading the Christian faith, he was referring to wars waged not against heretics, as some claim, nor Muslims, who did not yet exist, but against pagans.[132] Sepúlveda's reference to the implausible idea that Gennadius waged war

---

[129] Vitoria, 'On Dietary Laws, or Self-Restraint', q. 1, art. 5, fifth conclusion; Vitoria, 'On the American Indians', q. 3, art. 5; Francisco de Vitoria 'On the Evangelization of Unbelievers', in *Political Writings*, §3.

[130] Sepúlveda, *Apologia*, III.4.i–iv.

[131] Christian Schäfer notes that Sepúlveda added §§I.18.4–6 as part of the modifications made to early states of *Democrates secundus*. Whereas these sections are included in the S (Salamanca) manuscript, which mentions and thus postdates Charles V's victories in the Schmalkaldic War in 1547, they are not included in earlier states of the dialogue's composition represented by the P (Santander) and VTM manuscripts, which do not refer to this war. Schäfer, 'Einleitung', lxvi.

[132] Sepúlveda, *Democrates secundus*, I.18.6, I.17.3; Sepúlveda, *Apologia*, III.4.xii–xxi.

32 SEPÚLVEDA ON THE SPANISH INVASION OF THE AMERICAS

against Muslims was probably a dig at Cano. In one of his letters to Cano, Sepúlveda had mocked him for making such a suggestion when they had met at Salamanca.[133]

Sepúlveda continued his defence of his fourth justification for war in his *Apologia* by highlighting Aquinas's teaching in the second part of Book II of the *Summa* (q. 10, art. 8 and art. 11) with regard to the right to prevent unbelievers from obstructing the faith and practising pagan rites. In doing so, he provided some clarity that had been lacking in *Democrates secundus* as to the relationship that he envisaged between coercion and preaching. Force may justifiably be used first to subjugate the barbarians to the rule of Christians and then to prevent idol worship and other pagan rituals and to remove impediments to preaching. But once these things have been done, 'no further violence, no terrorization should be inflicted to make them Christians'. Rather, once they have been so prepared, they should be taught and exhorted to accept Christianity of their own free will.[134] And yet, fear still plays a useful role. While the gospel should be preached peacefully, it is expedient that the barbarians be not only subjected to Christian rule but made to fear the Christians, so as to prompt them to embrace the faith of their own free will more quickly.[135] This method was the most expeditious means of converting people to the faith. Augustine had come to realize this in the context of the Donatist controversy, and the same had been shown to be true in the Indies. Once the barbarians are reduced to rule and their impious rites forbidden, they respond to gospel preaching so readily that more are converted in a few days than would be converted by preaching alone in three hundred years. This point alone should settle the entire controversy, Sepúlveda declared.[136]

He concluded his *Apologia* by attacking 'a cunning and hostile man'—clearly an unnamed Las Casas—both for turning people against his book and also for having urged the emperor to adopt the disruptive New Laws.[137] The publication of *Democrates secundus* would produce great benefits, Sepúlveda insisted. It would clear the names of the rulers and people of Spain, whom this 'certain person' has falsely accused of subjugating the Amerindians unjustly and tyrannically. It would also clarify for those Spaniards who have returned from the Americas with riches, and also for their confessors, whether or not they acquired these riches justly— a matter that was shown in the book to depend upon each individual Spaniard's treatment of the barbarians, but which had been brought under a cloud by the suggestion in the scandalous *Confesionario* that *all* riches acquired from the Americas had been obtained unjustly.[138] Not for the last time, Sepúlveda noted that—prior to the intervention of Las Casas—his book had been approved by all who read

---

[133] Letter 82, from Sepúlveda to Melchor Cano, §24, p. 239.
[134] Sepúlveda, *Apologia*, III.4.xvii–xix.
[135] Sepúlveda, *Apologia*, III.4.xlv.
[136] Sepúlveda, *Apologia*, III.4.xxv–xxx.
[137] Sepúlveda, *Apologia*, V.5, V.17.
[138] Sepúlveda, *Apologia*, IV.8.

INTRODUCTION   33

and understood it, including those who had assessed it for the Council of Castile. Among the four assessors was Diego de Vitoria, who, he declared, would never have granted his endorsement had his brother, Francisco, not given his full support.[139] As for the New Laws, Las Casas had not merely erred in recommending them to Charles V, but had done so with an 'eagerness for revolution'. Thankfully, the emperor had subsequently been persuaded by Dominican and other monks from the Indies to modify the laws, so as to limit the 'tumults and seditions' that Las Casas had so recklessly provoked.[140]

The Valladolid debate

The bitter dispute between Sepúlveda and Las Casas, combined with the ongoing resistance of the *encomenderos* and their supporters to even the watered-down New Laws, had prompted the Council of the Indies to write to Charles V in mid-1549, urging him 'to order a meeting of learned men, theologians, and jurists, with others according to your pleasure, to discuss and consider concerning the manner in which these conquests should be carried on in order that they may be made justly and with security of conscience'.[141] The emperor did just that. In April 1550, he sent instructions to the Spanish authorities in Peru and New Spain, ordering that all expeditions of discovery and conquest be suspended pending the outcome of a meeting to be held in mid-1550.[142] As Lewis Hanke famously remarked, 'Probably never before or since has a mighty emperor—and in 1550 Charles V, Holy Roman emperor, was the strongest ruler in Europe with a great overseas empire besides— ordered his conquests to cease until it was decided if they were just.'[143]

On 7 July 1550, royal letters were sent summoning fifteen theologians and jurists to a junta at Valladolid, to begin the following month. The fifteen were comprised of the President of the Council of the Indies and six of his councillors, two councillors of the Council of Castile, one councillor from the Council of Orders, the bishop of Ciudad Rodrigo, and four theologians, among whom were three Dominicans (Cano, Carranza, and Domingo de Soto) and a Franciscan (Bernardino de Arévalo).[144] We learn from Sepúlveda that Arévalo, upon being attacked and wounded by a crazed fellow friar and suffering also from foot pains caused most likely by gout, did not make it to the first session of junta, making the number of judges fourteen.[145]

---

[139] Sepúlveda, *Apologia*, V.5–7.
[140] Sepúlveda, *Apologia*, V.16–17.
[141] Quoted in Hanke, *Aristotle and the American Indians*, 36.
[142] Adorno, *Polemics of Possession*, 82.
[143] Hanke, *Aristotle and the American Indians*, 37.
[144] Castilla Urbano, 'The Debate of Valladolid', 226.
[145] Letter 95, from Sepúlveda to Martín Oliván, 1 October 1551, in Sepúlveda, *Obras completas, vol. 9.2: Epistolario*, 267–71, at §5, p. 269.

34 SEPÚLVEDA ON THE SPANISH INVASION OF THE AMERICAS

Suspecting fresh machinations from Las Casas, Sepúlveda wrote to the bishop of Arras, Antoine Perrenot de Granvelle, that he 'shudder[ed] to think' who advised the emperor to select the three Dominicans 'for you couldn't name any others in Spain more at odds with His Majesty's aim with regard to his honour and conscience when it comes to doing what is fitting for the conversion of those peoples' in the Indies.[146] The inclinations of Cano and Carranza to favour the arguments of Las Casas have been noted above. Soto had been expressing his own concerns about Spain's activities in the Indies for even longer than they had, declaring in a relection, *De dominio*, delivered at Salamanca in 1535, 'By what right, then, do we retain the overseas empire that has just been discovered? The fact is, I don't know.'[147] Sepúlveda reports that the legal counsel (*fiscal*) of the Council of Castile was similarly troubled by the inclusion of the three Dominicans on the list of judges on the grounds that their previously stated positions indicated that they were not impartial. The *fiscal* petitioned to have them replaced or at least to have others, such as Sepúlveda himself and also Álvaro Moscoso, who had previously examined and approved *Democrates secundus* on behalf of the council, added to the list. In the end, it was decided that the list would not be altered, but that Sepúlveda and also Las Casas would be invited to appear before the judges to offer their opinion on the matter on which the emperor had asked the judges to pronounce.[148] Meanwhile, the Council of the Indies requested that Sepúlveda deliver to them all the copies of the *Apologia* that he had in his possession. In October and November, *cédulas* were issued prohibiting its export to or circulation in Peru, New Spain, and Tierra Firme, and ordering the return of all copies that had been sent to those territories.[149]

Our understanding of what occurred at Valladolid is primarily informed by the accounts provided by the two disputants. Las Casas printed a four-part composite record of the proceedings, which he titled *Contained herein is a debate or disputation ... (Aquí se contiene una disputa o controversia ...)*, in Seville in 1552. The first part was an introduction written by Las Casas himself, in which he issued a searing attack on *Democrates secundus*—a book that he said was written 'in most

---

[146] Letter 92, from Sepúlveda to Antoine Perrenot de Granvelle, 8 July 1550, in Sepúlveda, *Obras completas, vol. 9.2: Epistolario*, 260–63, at §1, pp. 260–61 (our translation).

[147] Domingo de Soto, *Relección 'De dominio'*, edited by Jaime Brufau Prats (Granada: Universidad de Granada, 1964), 162 (our translation).

[148] Sepúlveda, *Proposiciones temerarias*, §4. Sepúlveda himself petitioned Granvelle to ask the king to modify the list of judges, or at least to add to their number 'others who are properly versed in the truth', such as Moscoso or the Archdeacon of Mallorca. Letter 92, from Sepúlveda to Antoine Perrenot de Granvelle, §4, p. 263; Letter 94, from Sepúlveda to Antoine Perrenot de Granvelle, 3 August 1550, in Sepúlveda, *Obras completas, vol. 9.2: Epistolario*, 265–66, at §4, p. 266 (our translation).

[149] Letter 94, from Sepúlveda to Antoine Perrenot de Granvelle, §2, p. 265; Marcos, *Los imperialismos de Juan Ginés de Sepúlveda*, 67–69; Diego de Encinas, *Libro Primero de Provisiones, Cédulas, Capítulos, y Cartas ... tocantes al buen govierno de las Indias* (Madrid: Imprenta Real, 1596), 230. Las Casas claimed that, prior to the Valladolid Junta, the emperor commanded the confiscation of *all* copies of the *Apologia* throughout Castile. Sepúlveda insisted, however, that many copies of these texts remained in circulation. Las Casas, 'The Subject of This Work'; Sepúlveda, Twelfth Objection, §7; Sepúlveda, *Proposiciones temerarias*, §16.

elegant Latin', but based on information received from Spaniards guilty of inflicting destruction and devastation on the people of the Indies; a book that purports to justify the sovereignty of the Spanish Crown over the Indies, but which in reality defends the cruelties and inhumanities of Spanish conquests and *encomiendas*.[150] Upon narrating his version of Sepúlveda's struggles to attain a licence to print his book, Las Casas then reported that, realizing the dangers of his antagonist's argument, and perceiving these dangers to be heightened by the fact that Sepúlveda had produced a Spanish summary that could be read by and sway the opinions of ordinary Spaniards, Las Casas had resolved to write his own *Apología*, also in Spanish, to counteract Sepúlveda's arguments and to explain 'the dangers, scandalous elements, and damages which his doctrine comprises'.[151] Las Casas would read this *Apología* to the judges at the first session of the Valladolid Junta.

Held in the chapel of the Colegio de San Gregorio, the first session began on 15 August and lasted until sometime in September.[152] Sepúlveda was summoned to speak first and he did so, giving his opinion for two or three hours. The judges then summoned Las Casas, who read his *Apología* for five or six days. Las Casas reports that he read out the entire manuscript. Sepúlveda claims that the judges, tired of listening to Las Casas, asked him to stop before he had finished.[153] Soto was then asked to prepare a summary of the disputants' opinions for the benefit of the fourteen judges. Soto's *Summary* (*Sumario*) constitutes the second part of the composite account published by Las Casas.

Soto noted when introducing his *Sumario* that, whereas the Valladolid Junta had been called to determine the means by which the peoples of the Americas could be justly subjugated to the rule of the Spanish Crown in accordance with Alexander's bull, and the manner in which the Christian faith ought to be proclaimed among them, Sepúlveda and Las Casas had addressed a narrower and more concrete question: 'whether it is lawful for His Majesty to wage war on those Indians and render them subject to his empire prior to preaching the faith to them so that, once they have been subjugated, they may more easily and conveniently be instructed in and enlightened by the teachings of the gospel as to the errors of their ways and the Christian truth'. Sepúlveda had argued that such war was not only lawful but expedient. Las Casas had argued that it was neither.[154]

Soto observed that it was hard to represent the force of the disputants' arguments equally since Las Casas had spoken for so much longer than Sepúlveda. His summary largely focused on Las Casas's claims and he recommended that those judges who wished to gain a fuller sense of the Sepúlveda's argument should consult the latter's book. Soto noted also that Las Casas was not in the room when

---

[150] Las Casas, 'The Subject of This Work'.
[151] Las Casas, 'The Subject of This Work'.
[152] Castilla Urbano, 'The Debate of Valladolid', 226.
[153] Las Casas, 'The Subject of This Work'; Sepúlveda, *Proposiciones temerarias*, §4.
[154] Domingo de Soto, 'Summary', in *Aquí se contiene una disputa o controversia…*, §2.

36 SEPÚLVEDA ON THE SPANISH INVASION OF THE AMERICAS

Sepúlveda presented his argument and so, instead of addressing the latter's arguments as they had been presented to the junta, Las Casas had 'responded to everything which the doctor has ever committed to paper and all the objections which one can offer to his opinion'. Soto sought, therefore, to summarize the key arguments adduced by Las Casas as they related to Sepúlveda's four principal justifications for Spain's wars.

While Las Casas did not hear Sepúlveda speak, he had read one of the Spanish summaries of *Democrates secundus* that Sepúlveda had produced.[155] Las Casas had not read *Democrates secundus* itself.[156] And yet he invoked some particularly objectionable claims made in that book but not in Sepúlveda's *Apologia*, such as the Aristotelian claim that the barbarians might be justly hunted as beasts.[157] Perhaps such claims were included in the Spanish summary of *Democrates secundus* or perhaps Las Casas had been told of them by one of the theologians who had read and been troubled by that dialogue.

After Soto completed his summary and distributed it to the other judges, Sepúlveda requested a copy and wrote a response to twelve objections that he perceived Las Casas had raised against his position. This is the third part of the composite account. (While this third part is divided into twelve 'objections', the twelve sections actually comprise Sepúlveda's responses to these objections.) A copy of Sepúlveda's rejoinder was given to each of the judges and the participants returned to their monasteries and residences. Only when Sepúlveda returned to Valladolid for further deliberations the following year did he discover that his voluble antagonist had offered extensive written replies to each of his twelve points.[158] These replies make up the fourth and final part of the composite account that Las Casas published.

Sepúlveda took no issue with the accuracy of Las Casas's transcription of either Soto's summary or Sepúlveda's own twelve-point response. He did object, however, to Las Casas's decision to print these materials in 1552 with such a scandalous introduction and with such lengthy replies to Sepúlveda's twelve points, and to do so without a licence—an act that was surely all the more infuriating for Sepúlveda due to his failure to secure permission from the royal councils to print his own book.[159] He set about composing his own side of the story of the Valladolid Junta soon after Las Casas's was printed. He supplemented his narrative with

---

[155] Las Casas, *Defense of the Indians*, 17.

[156] This is evident from the fact that, in his introductory letter to Prince Philip that accompanied a Latin version of his Spanish *Apología*, which he seems to have completed in 1552 or early 1553, Las Casas noted that he had not yet been given a chance to read *Democrates secundus* and requested that the prince instruct Sepúlveda to furnish him with a copy so that he might refute his falsehoods 'more completely'. Las Casas, *Defense of the Indians*, 18, 22.

[157] Las Casas, Twelfth Reply, §16.

[158] That, at least, is Sepúlveda's rendering of what transpired after the first session, in *Proposiciones temerarias*, §4.

[159] We discuss the significance, or otherwise, of the fact that Las Casas published his *Aquí se contiene* without a licence below, on p. 53.

further rebuttals and ferocious condemnations of Las Casas, the precise purpose of which we will say more about later, resulting in an impassioned text, *Outrageous, Scandalous, Heretical Notions ...* (*Proposiciones temerarias, escandalosas, y de mala doctrina ...*), which remained unpublished until the late nineteenth century. With Las Casas's *Aquí se contiene* and Sepúlveda's *Proposiciones temerarias* in hand, we can piece together the details of their dispute.

The disputants' arguments

Natural slavery

Soto's brief summary of Sepúlveda's argument about the Amerindians' barbarism justifying their subjugation by the superior Spaniards included multiple invocations of the Aristotelian notion of natural slavery.[160] Sepúlveda had avoided this language in his *Apologia* and it seems likely that he would have done the same in his address to the Valladolid Junta. Perhaps Soto expressed Sepúlveda's argument in these Aristotelian terms because that was how Las Casas put it when offering his critique, or perhaps he did so because it seemed the most straightforward way of summarizing Sepúlveda's position. Either way, Sepúlveda could hardly claim—and in fact did not claim—that he was being misrepresented, given his ongoing efforts to obtain a licence to print *Democrates secundus*, in which his reliance on Aristotle's doctrine was unmistakable.

Las Casas refuted Sepúlveda's argument by contending that there actually exist multiple categories of barbarians and that the Amerindians do not fall into the category of barbarians that Aristotle described as *natura servi*. One category of barbarian denotes people who, while fully capable of governing themselves, exhibit some odd opinions or customs. A second category comprises those who lack writing. Aristotle dealt with these sorts of barbarians in the third book of his *Politics* and never suggested that such people should be considered natural slaves or that war could be waged against them on account of their barbarity. It was a third kind of barbarian, whose habits, intellect, and disposition render them 'akin to wild beasts', which Aristotle had in mind in the first book of his *Politics* when suggesting that it is lawful to wage war against them and to subject them to humane governance, Las Casas argued.[161] And while the Amerindians exhibit some habits characteristic of less civilized people, they are not so barbaric that they fall into

---

[160] Soto, 'Summary', §§10, 14.

[161] Soto, 'Summary', §14. Las Casas added the distinction between the first and third books of Aristotle's *Politics* in his Eighth Reply, §1. He also indicated there that he had outlined not three but four categories of barbarians in his *Apología*. We learn from the Latin version of this *Apología*, which he produced a couple of years later, that the fourth category was simply people who are not Christian. Las Casas, *Defense of the Indians*, ch. 5, pp. 49–53.

that category.[162] Las Casas listed a number of ancient and contemporary peoples who *did* fit this third category. In a Latin version of his Spanish *Apología*, which he seems to have completed in 1552 or early 1553, however, he claimed that such barbarians were rare 'mistakes of nature' and no race, nation, or region would ever be entirely comprised of such people, and he argued that Aristotle had said the same. God's providential plan for humankind, Las Casas insisted, would not include the existence of large numbers of people in the Indies in such a condition of barbarism and natural slavery, and it was irreverent to suggest otherwise.[163]

Sepúlveda responded in his written reply to objections with a brevity that signifies the diminishing weight that he wished to place on this justification for war by the time of the Valladolid Junta. While the barbarians may indeed live in cities and govern themselves, he explained, everyone who has spent time with them, such as the colonist and historian Gonzalo Fernández de Oviedo y Valdés, recognizes that they are 'people of limited understanding and depraved habits'. And since such characteristics fit the definition of barbarian that Aquinas had provided in his commentary on the *Politics*, it is right that they be forced to submit to the more rational and civilized Spaniards.[164] Sepúlveda made no mention of either Aristotle or the doctrine of natural slavery. But Las Casas replied that Sepúlveda did not understand Aquinas and was instead relaying Aristotle's doctrine.[165] Whereas in his initial remarks to the junta Las Casas had merely questioned the application of Aristotle's doctrine to the Indies, here in his written reply he implied that the doctrine itself might be questionable.[166]

The barbarians of the Indies, he continued, are barbarians merely in the sense that the Spaniards themselves once were, and surely Sepúlveda would not have approved of the Romans dividing Spanish people among themselves, seizing their wealth, and causing them to perish in body and soul, as the tyrannical Spaniards do to the Amerindians today. Las Casas catalogued the civilized qualities of the Amerindians and the progress they had made in matters of Christian religion, good habits, and liberal and mechanical arts thanks to the teaching of missionaries and other moral Spaniards. Sepúlveda was unaware of this, Las Casas charged, because he has no experience in the Indies and has been all too quick to believe 'the ungodly, tyrannical men who prevailed upon him to compose his treatise to justify

---

[162] Soto, 'Summary', §14.

[163] Las Casas, *Defense of the Indians*, ch. 2 and 3, pp. 30–41, citing Aristotle, *Nicomachean Ethics*, VII.1. The quote is at ch. 2, p. 34. On the dating of this Latin manuscript, see Stafford Poole, 'Preface', in Las Casas, *Defense of the Indians*, xx–xxi. But see also our note at *Contained herein is a Debate or Disputation*, n. 30.

[164] Sepúlveda, Eighth Objection, §2.

[165] Las Casas, Eighth Reply, §1.

[166] He had previously been willing to condemn the doctrine and its author more plainly, famously dismissing Aristotle in 1519, in the presence of Charles V, as 'a pagan burning in hell'. Las Casas, *Historia de las Indias*, 3.149. He would again offer a blunt assessment of the doctrine in the Latin version of his *Apología*, which he completed a couple of years after the Valladolid Junta: 'Good-bye, Aristotle!' Las Casas, *Defense of the Indians*, ch. 3, p. 40.

the plundering, robbery, and killings they have perpetrated', such as Oviedo who himself was one of those plundering tyrants and whose *History* is 'utterly false'.[167]

Punishing violations of natural law

The fundamental reason Las Casas provided, in both his remarks and his written replies, for rejecting Sepúlveda's second justification for war—namely to punish sins against natural law—was that neither the church nor Christian princes had jurisdiction over the barbarians. Here he focused on the sins of idolatry and failure to worship the true God (and in the process responded also to elements of Sepúlveda's fourth justification, concerning the spread of the gospel), rather than the specific idolatrous rite of human sacrifice, which he treated separately. He began by dismissing Sepúlveda's appeals to the wars of the Israelites against pagans in the Old Testament. The wars against the inhabitants of the Promised Land were fought not on account of their idolatry, he insisted, but because God had promised the land to Abraham, and the wars waged against peoples beyond the Promised Land were permitted not on account of their paganism, but because of the injuries these peoples did to the Israelites. In any case, such Old Testament examples should be considered merely sources for admiration, not models for imitation.[168]

As for the New Testament and its implications for the church, Las Casas argued, given that all humanity was subject to Christ as a man and yet Christ chose to wield his power over those outside the faith not in actuality (*in actu*), but only in potentiality (*in potentia*) and dormant capability (*in habitu*), and given that Christ's church surely has no more power than Christ claimed for himself, the church is not authorized to punish outsiders. Only once people accept the faith does Christ wish for his church to assume jurisdiction over them, for God reserves to himself the right to punish those outside the faith.[169] Las Casas offered a curt dismissal of Sepúlveda's suggestion that Paul meant in 1 Corinthians 5:12 only that the church should refrain from judging outsiders that it lacks the power to correct. 'Just as the doctor readily offers that interpretation off the top of his head', Las Casas declared, 'so too can it be just as readily dismissed'.[170]

As for Sepúlveda's appeals to Augustine and other theologians asserting the authority of the church and Christian rulers to rid infidels of their idolatry and to remove impediments to their receiving the true faith, Las Casas claimed that, despite Sepúlveda's protestations to the contrary, most of the examples provided did not involve pagans who were not already subject to Christian rule and had not already

---

[167] Las Casas, Eighth Reply, §§4–5.
[168] See Soto, 'Summary', §4; Sepúlveda, First Objection; Las Casas, First Reply.
[169] Soto, 'Summary', §7. This argument continued across Sepúlveda's Sixth Objection, Las Casas's Sixth Reply, and Sepúlveda, *Proposiciones temerarias*, §7.
[170] Las Casas, Fifth Reply, §1.

40   SEPÚLVEDA ON THE SPANISH INVASION OF THE AMERICAS

received the faith, such as were the barbarians of the Indies. Las Casas suggested that the banquet host's instruction to 'compel them to come in' referred to the internal compulsion that God exerts on people to bring them to himself and that Augustine had interpreted it as denoting external compulsion only in the case of heretics, who are under the church's jurisdiction.[171] As for the wars that Sepúlveda had invoked that *were* waged by Christian rulers against pagans, these were waged against enemies who had either blasphemed or obstructed the faith, or seized communities and territories belonging to the church—crimes that, in contrast to the idolatry of pagans, were justly punished by Christians.[172]

In his written response, Sepúlveda countered not only by defending his interpretation of the wars of Christian rulers, but also by appealing again to Aquinas's teachings in the *Summa*. Aquinas, he claimed, made clear that Christians justly prevent blasphemy, evil persuasions, and persecutions aimed at obstructing the faith. Las Casas replied by denying that the Amerindians seek to obstruct the faith in any of these ways. And while he conceded that their idolatry is indeed blasphemous, he insisted that this blasphemy is inadvertent and they mean not to offend God but to worship and serve him in this way. Such blasphemy is not what Aquinas has in mind, and it is not justly punished by the church.[173]

Sepúlveda also noted Aquinas's claim that Christians should only tolerate the idolatrous rites of unbelievers if this was necessary to avoid a scandal or disturbance that would hinder the spread of the faith. Aquinas, moreover, had followed Augustine in declaring that, while the church had therefore necessarily tolerated idolatry in its early years, the number and power of Christians had since grown such that it could rightfully use force to rid infidels of their idolatry without risk.[174] In his written reply, Las Casas did not hold back:

> What could be more grievous than inspiring the heathens with hatred, abhorrence, and loathing for the faith before they have even heard its doctrine? What greater form of destruction than butchering countless people in the course of warfare? What greater barrier to the salvation of the heathens than casting vast numbers of souls down into hell and prompting those who escape with their lives never to convert; or if, out of fear, they do go through the motions of converting, for their faith never to be true, but merely feigned?[175]

---

[171] In this context, Las Casas appealed also to Innocent IV's claim that no one can be compelled to become a Christian. But this did not help his case since Sepúlveda argued not for the forced conversion of pagans, which he agreed was impossible, but for the punishment of their crimes against natural law, which, as he had noted in the *Apologia*, Innocent had endorsed.

[172] See Soto, 'Summary', §5; Sepúlveda, Third Objection; Las Casas, Third Reply.

[173] Sepúlveda's Fourth Objection, §4, and Las Casas's Fourth Reply, §§4–9, discussing the *Summa* II-II, q. 10, arts 8 and 11. Sepúlveda defended his interpretation of Gregory's praise of Gennadius's wars against pagans again in his *Propositiones temerarias*, §15.

[174] Sepúlveda, Fourth Objection, §4, discussing the *Summa* II-II, q. 10, art. 11.

[175] Las Casas, Fourth Reply, §5.

INTRODUCTION   41

Las Casas concluded his treatment of the subject of punishment in his remarks to the junta by addressing the justifications for war against idolatrous infidels offered by Innocent IV and other canonists. The church has the authority to punish such infidels through war only in six types of cases, Las Casas declared, and the canonists were correct only insofar as they had such cases in mind. War is justly waged against infidels who violently occupy lands formerly belonging to Christians, as with the Holy Land; in self-defence, as against the Turks; against infidels who besmirch and pollute the Christian faith, as in the case of the Moors and Saracens; and against those who deliberately blaspheme the name of Christ, the saints, or his church. None of these four conditions for war was met in the case of the Indies. This left only two possible cases of justifiable war. These corresponded to Sepúlveda's third and fourth just reasons for war against the Amerindians: to protect innocents from harm and to prevent the deliberate obstruction of Christian preaching.[176]

Spreading the Christian faith

Las Casas addressed the issue of Christian preaching first. Here he presented arguments he had developed more fully in his first book manuscript, *The Only Way to Draw All People to a Living Faith* (*De unico vocationis modo omnium gentium ad veram religionem*), drafted in 1534 but not printed in full during his lifetime.[177] He began by rejecting Sepúlveda's claim that it was expedient first to subjugate the barbarians to Christian rule and to instil in them a fear of Christians with a view to making them more easily instructed in the faith and more inclined to receive it. Reminding his audience, as he often did, that he had spent many years in the Indies whereas his opponent had not, Las Casas insisted that his experience had shown that the model of spreading the gospel recommended by Sepúlveda led the barbarians either to reject the faith, or to accept it merely out of fear, and so in a manner that was ultimately hollow.[178]

When Sepúlveda responded in writing, insisting that—after the barbarians had been subjugated and fear instilled—the faith should be preached to them with gentleness, Las Casas replied that Sepúlveda was deluded if he believed that such a model was anything but coercive, and that as such it was ineffective. When Sepúlveda appealed to Augustine's argument about the usefulness of fear, Las Casas explained that fear may have been rightfully and usefully used to prompt

---

[176] Soto, 'Summary', §9. When Sepúlveda noted in his response to the objections that the canonists had actually defended the church's right to punish pagans on account of their sins against nature and idolatry alone, Las Casas insisted that they had in mind the Moors and the Turks and would not have endorsed the punishment of the peaceful barbarians of the Indies had they known of them and had they seen how preaching alone could convince them to give up their vices (Sepúlveda's Seventh Objection and Las Casas's Seventh Reply, §2).

[177] For an English translation, see Las Casas, *The Only Way*.

[178] Soto, 'Summary', §10.

the heretic Donatists to recognize how they had gone astray and to lead them back to the truth, but it was neither permissible nor effective to attempt the same in the case of the pagans of the Americas. Christians ought instead to invite them into the faith with gentleness and love, 'approaching them like sheep among wolves—not as wolves and plundering brigands among the most meek and guileless sheep', as Christ instructed his church.[179]

As for the right of war to prevent the obstruction of preaching, Las Casas declared to the junta, it depends on what the barbarians think they are obstructing. Whereas the Moors intentionally obstruct the preaching of Christianity, and are thus rightfully punished, the Amerindians, who know nothing of the Christian religion, obstruct Spanish preachers because they see them in the company of soldiers and understandably think they are in danger of being robbed and killed. Furthermore, if an entire pagan people decide that they do not wish to listen to Christian preaching, war cannot be waged against them to facilitate such preaching.[180]

Soto could not help but insert his own opinion here—the only moment in his summary at which he did so. He interjected that it was essential to consider whether Las Casas was right on this point. After all, Christ commissioned his followers to preach the gospel to all the world. Do we not therefore have a right to preach to all peoples, and to protect preachers with armed force if necessary to ensure that they are not prevented from spreading the faith? Soto reported that Las Casas responded to this query by saying that Christ's commission did not oblige Christians to force unbelievers to listen to preaching, but simply to preach to those who are willing to hear. But Las Casas made a mistake here, Soto declared. While Las Casas was likely correct in claiming that the barbarians cannot be forced to listen to sermons, the question of whether they may be forced to allow sermons to be preached was a different matter, and one that many theologians had answered in the affirmative, Soto claimed. Soto was right. Vitoria had done this in 1539, with the condition that such force be eschewed in instances where it was clearly detrimental to the spread of the gospel.[181] So too had Soto himself in his 1535 relection, *De dominio*.[182] It is worth noting, however, that the other two Dominican theologians sitting in judgment at Valladolid had previously offered arguments quite similar to that of Las Casas—Cano, in his 1546 relection, and Carranza, in his 1540 lecture course at Valladolid on Aquinas's *Summa*.[183]

---

[179] Sepúlveda, Ninth Objection; Las Casas, Ninth Reply, quotation is at §2.

[180] Soto, 'Summary', §12.

[181] Vitoria, 'On the American Indians', q. 3, art. 2.

[182] Soto, *Relección 'De dominio'*, 162.

[183] Cano, *De dominio Indorum*, 579–80; Bartolomé de Carranza, 'Ratione fidei potest Caesar debellare et tenere Indos novi orbis?', in *Misión de España en América: 1540–1560*, edited by Luciano Pereña Vicente, 38–57 (Madrid: Consejo Superior de Investigaciones Científicas, 1956), at 40–42. See also Daniel Allemann, 'Empire and the Right to Preach the Gospel in the School of Salamanca, 1535–1560', *The Historical Journal* 62/1 (2019): 35–55. Soto himself would move closer to the position shared by Las Casas, Cano, and Carranza in his 1558–60 commentary on the fourth book of Lombard's

INTRODUCTION   43

Emboldened, perhaps, by Soto's criticism of Las Casas, Sepúlveda suggested in his written response—quite incorrectly, it should be said—that Las Casas's claim that the barbarians cannot be 'collectively forced' to listen to preaching was 'a new and false doctrine'.[184] Sepúlveda insisted that the right to compel listening necessarily followed from the obligation to preach the good news to all the world, since Christ's commission cannot be fulfilled if no one listens to preachers. Las Casas disagreed. Christ didn't command the Apostles to use force against those who did not wish to listen, but to withdraw peacefully, leaving it to God to punish them on Judgment Day. And in any case, the Amerindians do not refuse to listen to the gospel when it is preached peacefully. It is only when they are evangelized in the violent manner that Sepúlveda advocates that they refuse to listen and instead rightfully take up arms against those who foist their preaching upon them.[185]

Protecting innocents

As for Sepúlveda's remaining justification for Spain's wars, namely the duty to protect innocents from harm, Las Casas accepted that, while the church does not have the authority to punish infidels' sins against natural law, the innocent are entrusted to the church by divine law and so the church is responsible for their protection. Vitoria, it will be recalled, had similarly distinguished between punishment and protection.[186] Crucially, however, having listed protection as one of his six just reasons for war against infidels, Las Casas insisted—in contrast to Vitoria, Sepúlveda, and numerous other Spanish theologians and jurists—that if protection cannot be accomplished by other means than war, it is better to refrain from discharging the duty altogether.

This was so for several reasons. First, it is good to choose the lesser of two evils, and allowing a few innocent barbarians to be killed for the purposes of sacrifice or cannibalism, as heinous as that is, is preferable to the ills that arise from war. Not only do more innocents die in such wars than the handful for whose protection the war is waged, but—worse—such wars inspire infidels to hate the faith. Second, the negative commandment not to kill, and especially not to kill the innocent, is

---

Sentences, Domingo de Soto, *In quartum Sententiarum* (Salamanca: Juan María de Terranova, 1561–62), vol. 1, dist. 5, q. unica, art. 10, pp. 265–76. See also Lantigua, *Infidels and Empires in a New World Order*, 135–39.

[184] Each of the Dominican theologians presiding at Valladolid—Cano, Carranza, and also Soto, at least in his *Sumario* and later writings—maintained that the barbarians could not be compelled to listen to preaching.

[185] Soto, 'Summary', §12; Sepúlveda, Tenth Objection; Las Casas, Tenth Reply.

[186] Vitoria, 'On the American Indians', q. 3, art. 5. However, whereas Vitoria claimed that Christian princes could lawfully protect the innocent 'even without the pope's authority', Las Casas ascribed authority for protection to the church.

more binding than the positive duty to protect the innocent, and so one should act to fulfil the latter only if this can be done without violating the former. And this especially in a situation where it is difficult to distinguish the specific wrongdoers worthy of punishment from the many innocents living among them. It is better to leave their punishment to God.[187]

Sepúlveda responded in writing by declaring that Las Casas 'has got his sums quite wrong'. Building on his claims in *Democrates secundus*, he explained that not only has the conquest of New Spain and the subsequent abolition of human sacrifices there saved the bodies of 600,000 barbarians (20,000 per year over 30 years), at a cost of no more than 20,000 lost during the entire conquest, but it has enabled the conversion of countless souls that would otherwise have been lost to the faith. In his written reply, Las Casas challenged Sepúlveda on his own calculations. Far fewer than 20,000 innocents were sacrificed each year prior to the arrival of the Spaniards. Fewer, even, than fifty. Indeed, he added provocatively, pointing to the cruelties and tyrannies of the Spaniards, 'the Spanish have upon arrival in each province sacrificed more people to that most beloved and adored goddess of theirs, Greed, in any given year of those spent in the Indies than the Indians to their gods in a hundred years across all the Indies put together'. And as for Sepúlveda's tears for the few innocents who were victims of sacrificial rites and who died unbaptized, does his heart not break for the twenty million souls that the Spaniards have condemned to perdition by massacring them and depriving them of the opportunity to receive the faith?[188]

In his remarks to the junta, Las Casas offered a further and more controversial reason for rejecting war as a just response to the Amerindians' rite of human sacrifice. Here he pivoted from the protection of innocents back to the punishment of wrongdoers. The barbarians, he explained, are excused for not recognizing their error in performing human sacrifices for two reasons. First, those who perform this depraved rite are following the teachings of their priests, rulers, and forefathers and carrying out a practice that was also widespread in Greco-Roman antiquity. And they understandably perceive the armed Spaniards who tell them of their error as enemies who have come to plunder and kill rather than friends who have come to teach. They are therefore exonerated before men, albeit not before God, for maintaining what Aristotle termed a 'probable' opinion—that is, an opinion that is approved by the wisest members of a community, misguided though they might be. Second, in performing the rite, they are sacrificing the best thing that people have to offer—human life—to that which they understand to be God. They do so with an excusable ignorance since, while they are guided by natural law, which directs them to worship God, they do not know God's grace.[189]

---

[187] Soto, 'Summary', §13.

[188] Sepúlveda, Eleventh Objection, §1; Las Casas, Eleventh Reply, §§1–3, quoted words from §3.

[189] Soto, 'Summary', §13. On the Spanish application of the notion of 'invincible ignorance' to the debates about the justice of the subjugation of the Amerindians, see David Lantigua, 'Religion within

INTRODUCTION 45

This was the most controversial of all the arguments presented by Las Casas at Valladolid. Soto treated it only briefly in his summary, perhaps because Las Casas outlined it only briefly during the junta's first session, or perhaps because Soto understood how scandalous it was and wished to protect Las Casas's reputation.[190] Even so, Sepúlveda perceived an opportunity to attack. In justifying the barbarians' human sacrifices, he declared, Las Casas had offered an argument 'far removed from Christianity'. Even in Greco-Roman antiquity, pagans considered human sacrifice an abomination, or at least those who were not savage barbarians thought as much. The notion that the Amerindians' ignorance can excuse such a crime—a crime that is against nature—is ludicrous, for theologians and canonists agree that 'ignorance of natural law does not serve to exonerate anyone'. And if the barbarians are justified in defending their idolatry by taking up arms against the Spaniards, as Las Casas declares in his *Confesionario* and implies here at Valladolid, it follows that their idolatry is free from sin. This is an argument that no Christian can accept.[191]

If Soto perhaps tried to avoid drawing too much attention to Las Casas's controversial argument in his summary of the first session, Las Casas did not shy away from it in his reply to Sepúlveda. He did not mean to suggest that the barbarians are excused before God, he explained, 'for I do not know what God makes of them, for his judgment is inscrutable'. Rather, his point was that they are excused before men. And yes, while the barbarians may be in error, they are justified in defending their religion and their idols against the Spaniards. Indeed, they would be in violation of natural law and guilty of mortal sin if they did not risk their lives in defence of their rites, since all people are obliged to love and serve God, or that which they consider to be God, even to the point of death. Having equivocated a moment earlier, Las Casas then firmly rejected the suggestion that, in maintaining that the barbarians rightfully defend their religion, he must also maintain that they practise their religion without sin. The pagan Amerindians bring upon themselves eternal damnation whether they defend their gods and their idols or not, he conceded, since while they do not violate natural law in worshipping false gods that they believe to be true, they nevertheless violate God's divine command.[192]

---

the Limits of Natural Reason: The Case of Human Sacrifice', in *Bartolomé de las Casas, O.P: History, Philosophy, and Theology in the Age of European Expansion*, edited by David Thomas Orique, O.P. and Rady Roldán-Figueroa, 280–309 (Leiden: Brill, 2018); Marco Toste, 'Invincible Ignorance and the Americas: Why and How the Salamancan Theologians Made Use of a Medieval Notion', *Rechtsgeschichte—Legal History* 26 (2018): 284–97.

[190] See on this point Glen Carman, 'Human Sacrifice and Natural Law in Las Casas's Apologia', *Colonial Latin American Review* 25/3 (2016): 278–99.

[191] Sepúlveda, Eleventh Objection, §§3–5, quotations from §§3 and 5. While Las Casas affirmed in his eleventh reply (§8) that the barbarians were indeed justified in taking up arms against the Spaniards, David Lantigua notes that he appears to have removed this argument from the *Confesionario* prior to its printing in 1552. Lantigua, *Infidels and Empires in a New World Order*, 163n83.

[192] Las Casas, Eleventh Reply, §§4–9, quoted words from §4.

Sepúlveda amplified his condemnation of Las Casas's defence of human sacrifice in *Proposiciones temerarias*. Las Casas's suggestion that it does not go against natural law to sacrifice innocents to false gods is impious and heretical, he claimed. After all, theologians are in agreement that the precepts of the Decalogue are natural laws, and human sacrifice violates the precepts prohibiting both idolatry and murder. Furthermore, Las Casas's claim that he does not know what God makes of idolaters who sacrifice innocents (a claim from which Las Casas admittedly retreated) is nonsense, befitting only of someone who is either not Christian or insane, for everyone knows that God condemns murderous idolaters.[193] Sepúlveda charged that while Soto had sought to protect Las Casas by sugarcoating his unsound doctrine in the *Sumario*, Las Casas had undone Soto's efforts by expressing his position so plainly in his written replies, leading Soto to become mired in Las Casas's lost cause, thus following in the footsteps of Cano, Carranza, and those other theologians whom Las Casas had pestered into approving his scandalous *Confesionario*.[194]

Concluding disputes

Las Casas concluded his reading of his *Apología* at Valladolid by declaring that none of Sepúlveda's four reasons sufficed as grounds for war to be waged against barbarians prior to preaching. And neither can the barbarians be compelled to listen to preaching if they do not wish to. What, then, would be a lawful and expedient course of action for the Spaniards? Preachers and others who are capable of brokering peace with the Amerindians and instructing them in good habits should, in those cases where it is safe to do so, enter their lands to teach them. Wherever this proves too dangerous, they should instead establish themselves at a distance and make contact from there, seeking to promote the faith slowly through love, peace, and good examples. This, Las Casas claimed, was all that Pope Alexander VI had intended to authorize in his 1493 bull, *Inter caetera*, as Pope Paul III later clarified in his own 1537 bull *Sublimis Deus*.[195] Only once they become Christians should the people of the Indies be made subject to the Spanish Crown, and even then the Crown should exercise jurisdiction only for the purpose of extracting tribute for the protection of the faith, the teaching of good customs, and the implementation of good governance.[196]

---

[193] Sepúlveda, *Proposiciones temerarias*, §§8–13.

[194] Sepúlveda, *Proposiciones temerarias*, §16.

[195] Whereas Dominican theologians, including Soto, Vitoria, Carranza, and Cano, had each argued that Alexander lacked the authority to donate jurisdiction over the Amerindians to the Spanish Crown, Las Casas did not question the pope's authority but instead asserted that the pope had not in fact made such a donation. See Soto, *Relección 'De dominio'*, 158–64; Vitoria, 'On the American Indians', q. 2, art. 2; Carranza, 'Ratione fidei', 40; Cano, 'De dominio Indorum', 568–79.

[196] Soto, 'Summary', §14.

The eleventh and twelfth responses penned by Sepúlveda upon reading Soto's summary of Las Casas's concluding remarks, and Las Casas's replies to these responses, featured numerous accusations of slander and heresy and ongoing claims and denunciations regarding the licensing and printing of their respective books. It also saw them jostling to position themselves as the voice of authority whose arguments truly vindicated the Spanish Crown. And it saw them taking firm stances on matters of Amerindian sovereignty, Spanish reparations, and the feasibility of conversion without conquest, each of which carried profound implications.

Sepúlveda declared that Alexander VI had clearly intended the barbarians to be subjugated to Spanish rule prior to the gospel being preached to them. The Spaniards have always conducted their affairs in the Indies in this way, and Alexander and all subsequent popes have known and sanctioned this.[197] It is worth highlighting how important Alexander's bull had become for Sepúlveda's argument by this time. In *Democrates secundus*, rather than appealing to the authority of the bull to support his argument, he had done the reverse, asserting that his humanist reasoning demonstrated the justice of the bull.[198] He appears to have come to appreciate the usefulness of the bull for his cause through his confrontations with the royal councils and the universities' theologians, to the point that he appended it to the end of his *Apologia* and made much of Las Casas's refusal to interpret it as authorizing Spanish rule over the Amerindians at Valladolid. In his *Proposiciones temerarias*, he went so far as to accuse Las Casas of heresy for denying that Alexander had authority to make his donation and of seeking to obscure this heresy by pretending to read his bull as not in fact constituting such a donation.[199] As for Paul III's bull, Sepúlveda averred in his twelfth response to Las Casas's objections, it did not weaken his case at all, for it was concerned not with the justice of the wars, but with those Spaniards who had, without royal authorization, enslaved and mistreated the Amerindians.[200]

Moreover, Sepúlveda continued, Las Casas's claim that the barbarians should be made subject to the Spanish Crown only upon conversion makes no sense. If it is lawful to subjugate them to protect the faith and prevent apostasy, why would it not also be lawful to do so in order to rid them of idolatry and wickedness and to stop them obstructing the faith being preached and received in the first place? Indeed, if a choice had to be made, it would make more sense to subjugate the barbarians in their state of sin and then set them free again once they received the faith, rather than allowing their idolatry to go unpunished only then to subjugate them punitively when they renounce it. Las Casas's argument is all the more absurd,

---

[197] Sepúlveda, Twelfth Objection, §1.
[198] Sepúlveda, *Democrates secundus*, I.20. See more generally Domenico Taranto, 'La "Bolla Alessandrina" e la guerra giusta: Note sul rapporto tra l'ecclesiastico, il politico e il religioso in Sepúlveda', in Geuna, *Guerra giusta e schiavitù naturale*, 31–52.
[199] Sepúlveda, *Proposiciones temerarias*, §15.
[200] Sepúlveda, Twelfth Objection, §1.

48 SEPÚLVEDA ON THE SPANISH INVASION OF THE AMERICAS

Sepúlveda claimed, since it implies that war may be waged against barbarians if, once converted, they resist Spanish rule.[201]

As for Las Casas's *Confesionario*, it not only commits 'libellous slander' against Spain and its rulers by declaring all the conquests in the Americas to be unjust, but, in calling on the emperor to refrain from further conquests, it effectively asks him to abandon his duty to spread the faith. After all, the emperor would not be able to find military personnel to travel to protect preachers in the Indies if they were unable to reap the rewards of gold and silver that they presently stood to gain via the labour of subjugated barbarians. And if preachers went to the Indies without protection, they would meet the same fate as those sent recently to Florida—a rather callous allusion to the death of one of Las Casas's friends, Luis Cáncer. And even if they survived, 'a hundred years of preaching would still not be as effective as fifteen days' worth of it with the Indians subjugated beforehand'.[202]

Las Casas replied, accusing Sepúlveda of dressing up his own outrageous arguments under the guise of a 'feigned zeal' for serving the king, and suggesting that he should be indicted 'as a capital enemy of the Christian republic, abettor of cruel tyrants, scourge of the human race, and sower of the most mortal blindness throughout these Spanish realms'. He stood by his claim in the *Confesionario* that all the wars waged by the Spaniards in the Indies were unjust and that no Spaniards involved could be saved unless they made reparation, and he now added that Sepúlveda, in seeking to exonerate these Spaniards, was himself guilty of mortal sin and obliged to offer restitution.[203]

Regarding Sepúlveda's concern that Spaniards would not accept the risks and costs of going to the Americas to protect preachers and facilitate the spread of the gospel if they were not allowed to subjugate the barbarians and extract wealth from their lands, Las Casas offered a twofold reply. Firstly, what clearer acknowledgement could there be of the tyranny of the Spaniards? Sepúlveda here concedes that Spanish soldiers go to the Americas not because of their love of God, neighbour, or king, but their lust for silver, gold, and Amerindian labour—a desire to dispossess the Spanish Crown of the Americas, to keep it for themselves, and to apportion the people among themselves as if they were beasts. And secondly, preachers only need armed protection when barbarians have been given grounds to fear the Spaniards, as was lamentably the case in Florida. God desires that the gospel be preached peacefully, Las Casas insisted, drawing on and appealing to his own experiences in Verapaz in the late 1530s. And if barbarians are not converted by such methods quickly, 'God—who died for them—will convert them next year, or ten years from now.' Sepúlveda ought not to presume to be more zealous for their conversion than

---

[201] Sepúlveda, Twelfth Objection, §§2–3.
[202] Sepúlveda, Twelfth Objection, §§4–5, quotation from §5. Sepúlveda had anticipated this outcome in Florida in *Democrates secundus*, I.18.2.
[203] Las Casas, Twelfth Reply, §§1, 12, quoted words from §1.

INTRODUCTION 49

God is and he should not invent a bloodier way to convert them more quickly than God intends.[204]

Las Casas declared that his desire in promoting his model of peaceful evangelization was not to quash the entitlements of the Spanish Crown in the Americas, but to avert the scourges that God would otherwise visit on Spain for its tyrannies. Always taking care to distinguish the justness of Spain's rulers from the injustices of the Spaniards in the Americas, Las Casas insisted, moreover, that not only was Sepúlveda's interpretation of Alexander's bull incorrect, but his claim that the Crown has always acted in accord with this interpretation was slanderous. Spain's rulers had repeatedly prohibited and embargoed warfare against the barbarians and commanded the Spaniards not to give the barbarians reason to fear or despise them since this impedes the spread of the faith.[205]

Las Casas was clearly eager to have the Crown find his arguments desirable. And yet he made clear that if the Crown *had* authorized wars, violence, and devastation wrought by Spaniards upon the bodies and souls of Amerindians (which he again insisted they had surely not done), Spain's monarchs would be guilty of mortal sin no less than the Spanish tyrants in the Americas.[206] In his final major work, the 1564 treatise *Twelve Doubts* (*Doce dudas*), Las Casas would go further and call upon the Spanish Crown itself to make restitution for the injustices committed by Spaniards in the Americas.[207] Calls for reparations for the injustices of European imperialism, then, have a long history.

What of Sepúlveda's claim that it would make more sense to subjugate the barbarians prior to their conversion rather than afterwards? This fails to account for the fact that the church only acquires jurisdiction over unbelievers once they receive the faith, Las Casas insisted. What, then, of Sepúlveda's claim that Las Casas's argument implicitly justified war against converted Amerindians who refuse to accept the jurisdiction of Spain's Christian rulers? This was a trickier matter and it led Las Casas to adjust his position. He first repeated and then limited what he had declared in the nineteenth of his *Thirty Propositions*. He continued to maintain that it would be sinful for converted Amerindians to refuse to accept the jurisdiction of Spain's rulers. But he now insisted that war cannot be justly waged upon them on this account, so long as they maintain their faith and act in accordance with the law.[208] This clarification, it should be said, was not included in the replies that Las Casas submitted to the Valladolid Junta. He added it to his twelfth reply prior to printing the composite record of the Valladolid proceedings in 1552.[209]

[204] Las Casas, Twelfth Reply, §§17–21, quoted words from §21.
[205] Las Casas, Twelfth Reply, §§2–7, 23.
[206] Las Casas, Twelfth Reply, §13.
[207] Gutiérrez, *Las Casas*, 393–95.
[208] Las Casas, Twelfth Reply, §§8–10.
[209] See our note at the beginning of the Twelfth Reply, §8. See also Vidal Abril-Castelló, 'La bipolarización Sepúlveda-Las Casas y sus consecuencias: La revolución de la duodécima replica', in *La ética en la conquista de América*, edited by Demetrio Ramos et al., 229–88 (Madrid: Consejo Superior de Investigaciones Científicas, 1984), 245–46; Gutiérrez, *Las Casas*, 385–87.

50 SEPÚLVEDA ON THE SPANISH INVASION OF THE AMERICAS

Sepúlveda's insistent probing had led Las Casas to claim that, despite Alexander's bull, even converted Amerindians had the right to reject Spanish rule. He would develop this argument further in a 1563 treatise, *The Treasures of Peru* (*De thesauris*), and again in his *Twelve Doubts* the following year, articulating and defending, as Dominican theologians such as Soto, Vitoria, and Cano had done before him, a principle of the consent of the governed that was said to be applicable to all peoples everywhere.[210] This was a universalized vision of self-determination that European imperial powers would continue to deny to many colonized peoples for another four hundred years.

Aftermath

Our knowledge of what happened in the second and final session of the Valladolid Junta, which took place in April 1551, is by contrast quite conjectural.[211] It relies to a large extent on Sepúlveda's own accounts, contained in a letter penned to his friend Martín Oliván in October of that year and in his *Proposiciones temararias* written a year or so later. Sepúlveda claims that he felt no need to respond to the lengthy replies that Las Casas had sent to the judges since he had already addressed everything in them and few if any of the judges had read Las Casas's replies anyway. Nevertheless, Sepúlveda did present a deposition on 12 April requesting an audience with the assembly at which he would debate with the theologians the power of Alexander VI to authorize the Spanish Crown to carry out the conquest of the Indies for the purpose of converting the Amerindians to the Christian faith. We have included a translation of this 'final deposition' as an appendix to the *Aquí se contiene* translation.[212] Sepúlveda reports that he was granted this audience and discussed with the theologians his interpretation of the bulls of Alexander VI and Paul III.[213] At some point, the Franciscan theologian, Bernardino de Arévalo, who had been unable to take his place on the panel of judges the previous year, came

---

[210] Lantigua, *Infidels and Empires in a New World Order*, 270–89.

[211] A Council of the Indies memo of points to be treated further in the second session, which was perhaps drafted by a counsellor who was one of the fourteen Valladolid judges, Gregorio López, offers a tantalizing sense of how the discussions may have proceeded. The twelve points that the memo says require further consideration by the assembly include some of the just reasons for war asserted by Sepúlveda (to punish idolatry and other sins against natural law and to protect innocents), several further just reasons for war that Vitoria had defended in his 1539 relection and that others had since debated (to protect converts and commerce and to assist Amerindian communities waging just wars against other Amerindians), and several issues pertaining to the implementation of the solutions given to these problems. For the text of the Council of the Indies' memo, see Bartolomé de las Casas, *Tratado de Indias y el doctor Sepúlveda*, edited by Manuel Giménez Fernández (Caracas: Fuentes para la Historia Colonial de Venezuela, 1962, repr. 1988), 145–47, and see the discussion on LXIV–LXV.

[212] See in this volume 'Final points of argument presented to the congregation by Sepúlveda'.

[213] Sepúlveda, *Proposiciones temerarias*, §5. On the possibility that Sepúlveda additionally presented his responses to Las Casas's twelve objections and Las Casas presented his replies during this second session, see n. 202 in our translation of *Aquí se contiene*.

INTRODUCTION 51

to Valladolid and intervened in the deliberations. Sepúlveda tells us that, prior to Arévalo's arrival, the older jurists had been on his own side in the debate, whereas the younger jurists had been led astray by the dubious opinions of the theologians and had come to support the arguments of Las Casas. Arévalo, who had written his own treatise adducing arguments similar to Sepúlveda's, delivered an opinion to the junta that caused those who had been led astray to reconsider their views. The wavering jurists requested that the matter be referred to other theologians, and Sepúlveda asked for permission to present his views to the junta again, but the theologians among the judges rejected both requests.[214]

Sepúlveda claims that, in the end, the jurists disputed some of his arguments but agreed with him that the medieval canonists had been right to justify war against infidels on account of their idolatry and other violations of natural law, and that Spain's wars were lawful for that reason.[215] As for the theologians, he asserts, Soto remained firmly against him, Cano had been summoned to the Council of Trent and so was not present for the second session, and Carranza kept putting off writing up his decision due to a reluctance to offend his friends. Arévalo, however, submitted his book justifying the conquests along with a written opinion supporting all four justifications that Sepúlveda had adduced.[216]

Las Casas, by contrast, offered a rather different account of the junta's outcome. He claimed in the Latin version of his *Apología*, written within a year or two of the second session, that the junta pronounced the conquests unjust but made no decision about the allotment of Amerindians to *encomenderos* due to the ongoing rebellion of the colonists in Peru.[217] In a letter written ten years later to the Dominicans of Chiapa and Guatemala, he asserted that he had proved conclusions before the junta 'that no person before me had dared to touch or write about', including that it is not against natural law to sacrifice humans to a god that one believes to be true, and not only were all of the theologians and jurists 'quite satisfied', but some were even 'struck with admiration'.[218]

---

[214] Letter 95, from Sepúlveda to Martín Oliván, §§4–7, pp. 268–70.

[215] The ninth point in the Council of the Indies' memo of twelve points to be treated in the second session, described in n. 211 above, notes that it had been 'determined by the majority' of the fourteen judges that 'neither war nor subjugation of the Indians ought to precede warnings and preaching' (Las Casas, *Tratado de Indias y el doctor Sepúlveda*, 146, our translation). This appears to indicate that the majority of the judges had already decided against one of the four reasons for war defended by Sepúlveda—war to facilitate the spread of the gospel—prior to the beginning of the second session. This is not contradicted by Sepúlveda's own reports and it may explain why he focused more on the authority of Alexander VI's bull during his appearance at the second session, and on both this bull and the right to punish idolatry and human sacrifice in his *Proposiciones temerarias*.

[216] Letter 95, from Sepúlveda to Martín Oliván, §8, p. 270; Sepúlveda, *Proposiciones temerarias*, §5. Cano was replaced for this second session by Pedro de la Gasca. Castilla Urbano, 'The Debate of Valladolid', 227.

[217] Las Casas, *Defense of the Indians*, 9.

[218] Bartolomé de las Casas, 'Carta a los Dominicos de Chiapa y Guatemala acerca de las ventas de las encomiendas del Perú [1563]', in *Corpus Hispanorum de Pace*, vol. 8, edited and translated by Luciano Pereña et al., 235–50 (Madrid: Consejo Superior de Investigaciones Científicas, 1984), 238, quoted in Gutiérrez, *Las Casas*, 183.

52 SEPÚLVEDA ON THE SPANISH INVASION OF THE AMERICAS

Ultimately, the junta did not deliver a judgment. Each of the judges had been instructed to submit his verdict in writing to the king. In 1557, Cano was sent a note explaining that all the other judges had submitted their verdicts and that he was to submit his at once.[219] But whether or not he provided one, no collective judgment was ever issued. The Council of the Indies appears to have decided that the weight of opinion among the judges lay with Las Casas. In a letter sent to Charles V in 1554, the council asserted that the junta had considered Spain's conquests 'dangerous to Your Majesty's conscience for many reasons … and mainly because of the difficulty of excusing the damages and grave sins that are committed in such conquests'.[220] But amid ongoing struggles for authority over the Indies between the Crown on the one hand and the conquistadors and *encomenderos* on the other, Charles soon discarded his moratorium on future conquests. In December 1555, he authorized new conquests for Peru. Philip II ascended to the throne the next month and issued formal instructions in May 1556 on how to proceed with further conquests.[221]

What of the disputants themselves? In 1552–53, Las Casas printed eight treatises on Spain's subjugation of the Amerindians. Each was printed in Seville without licence.[222] Among them were his record of the Valladolid Junta, entitled *Aquí se contiene …* ; the *Confesionario*; the *Thirty Propositions*; the fuller treatment of the Spanish Crown's authority in the Indies that had been promised in the *Thirty Propositions*, entitled *Treatise in Support of the Sovereign Empire and Universal Principate that the Kings of Castile and León Hold Over the Indies* (*Tratado comprobatorio del imperio soberano y principado universal que los reyes de Castilla y León tienen sobre las Indias*); and the notorious *Very Brief Account of the Destruction of the Indies* (*Brevísima relación de la destruición de las Indias*), which documented the horrors of the wars and encomiendas. Around the same time, he revised the Spanish *Apología* that he had read before the judges at Valladolid, producing two texts: a Latin text, *Apologia*, which elaborated on each of his principal arguments, and a Spanish text, *Apologética historia sumaria*, which refuted claims about the inferiority of the Amerindians. Neither would be printed in his lifetime.[223]

---

[219] Hanke, *Aristotle and the American Indians*, 74.

[220] 'Carta del Consejo de Indias a Su Majestad el Rey sobre la Prohibición de las Conquistas en la Junta de Valladolid [1554]', in *Corpus Hispanorum de Pace,* vol. 8, edited and translated by Luciano Pereña et al., 320–24 (Madrid: Consejo Superior de Investigaciones Científicas, 1984), at 322, quoted in Castilla Urbano, 'The Debate of Valladolid', 245.

[221] Adorno, *Polemics of Possession*, 83.

[222] On how the Sevillian printers Sebastián Trujillo and Jácome Cromberger likely perceived that these controversial treatises would prove to be good money-spinners, see Clive Griffin, *The Crombergers of Seville: The History of a Printing and Merchant Dynasty* (Oxford: Clarendon Press, 1988), 105.

[223] Poole dates the writing of the *Apologia* at 1552 or early 1553 (Stafford Poole, 'Preface', in Las Casas, *Defense of the Indians*, xx–xxi). Edmundo O'Gorman puts the composition of the *Apologética historia sumaria* in the years between 1552 and 1559 (Edmundo O'Gorman, 'Estudio preliminar', in Bartolomé de las Casas, *Apologética historia sumaria*, vol. 1, edited by Edmundo O'Gorman, xxi–xxxvi (Mexico City: Universidad Nacional Autónoma de México, Instituto de Investigaciones Históricas, 1967)).

INTRODUCTION   53

It is worth noting that Las Casas's decision to publish his eight Sevillian treatises without licence in 1552–53, including his record of the Valladolid Junta, the *Aquí se contiene*, was probably not as legally dicey as Sepúlveda would soon imply in his *Proposiciones temerarias*. In 1502, Ferdinand and Isabella had written a letter to the Royal Council requiring printers, binders, and booksellers to submit all books for licensing. This was still an official requirement fifty years later. However, as Clive Griffin explains, prior to 1554, 'the power to license works for printing … [was] in the hands of a motley collection of secular and ecclesiastical authorities depending on the region in question'. Only in that year was licensing centralized in the Royal Council. Two years later 'it was decreed that special licenses were required to print any book concerning the Indies'. And from 1557 onwards, 'authorities made a serious bid to control the trade'.[224] So, while Sepúlveda was clearly aggrieved that he had been prevented from printing his own *Democrates secundus* by the interventions of the royal councils and the machinations of his rival, Las Casas's decision to publish his composite account of the Valladolid debate without a licence was likely not a major issue in 1552. As Ramón Hernández O.P. notes, Las Casas had served as bishop of Chiapa and so presumably did not feel that he needed to first secure the permission of the local authority, the bishop of Seville, to publish his own books—and this especially for his *Aquí se contiene* given that it included the *Sumario* penned by the highly respected Soto.[225] Moreover, the publisher of *Aquí se contiene*, Sebastián Trujillo, was a major and highly respected Sevillian printer. It is doubtful that he would have published this and several other unlicensed tracts by Las Casas that year if there was serious risk of confiscation and condemnation.[226]

Nevertheless, Sepúlveda was infuriated by Las Casas's unlicensed publication of *Aquí se contiene*. He responded by penning his own account of the Valladolid Junta, the *Proposiciones temerarias*, sometime between late 1552 and early 1554.[227] He appears to have written this account primarily in order to denounce his rival to the Council of the Inquisition. Sepúlveda has long been suspected of being behind Las Casas's denunciation to the Inquisition.[228] This can be confirmed by a little remarked letter composed by Sepúlveda in March 1554 and sent to Antoine Perrenot de Granvelle, bishop of Arras. Sepúlveda told Granvelle that he had informed the Inquisition of Las Casas's unlicensed publication and sent them his *Proposiciones temerarias*—a tract in which, in addition to narrating some of the controversies

---

[224] Griffin, *The Crombergers of Seville*, 121.

[225] Ramón Hernández O.P., 'Los tratados impresos por Bartolomé de las Casas', in *Bartolomé de las Casas, Obras completas, vol. 10: Tratados de 1552*, edited by Ramón Hernández O.P. and Lorenzo Galmés O.P., 1–21 (Madrid: Alianza, 1992), 8–11.

[226] For a study that, in contrast to Griffin and Hernández, insists on the importance of licensing in this period, though, see Antonio Sierra Corella, *La censura de libros y papeles en España y los índices y catálogos españoles de los prohibidos y expurgados* (Madrid: Cuerpo Facultativo de Achiveros, Bibliotecarios y Arqueólogos, 1947).

[227] On the dating of this text, see the Preface to the *Proposiciones temerarias* at pp. 354–56.

[228] See, for example, Losada, *Juan Ginés de Sepúlveda*, 352; Clayton, *Bartolomé de las Casas*, 455.

54 SEPÚLVEDA ON THE SPANISH INVASION OF THE AMERICAS

and events discussed above, Sepúlveda described and responded to several heresies that he claimed were contained within Las Casas's treatise.[229] He asked Granvelle to read his *Proposiciones temerarias* and to consider asking the king to command the Inquisition to examine *Aquí se contiene* in light of his accusations and, if appropriate, to ban it publicly.[230]

It appears that the Inquisition did consider and respond to Sepúlveda's denunciation of Las Casas's writings, though the details are murky. Our knowledge of the Inquisition's actions relies on a single source, Juan Antonio Llorente's nineteenth-century study of the Inquisition's archives, which includes an entry on Las Casas that reads as follows:

> He is the author of many excellent works ... [I]n one of them he seeks to prove that the monarchs do not hold the power to dispose of the possessions and liberty of their American subjects by imposing any other ruler upon them, be it by way of fiefdom, *encomienda*, or in any other manner. The work in question was denounced to the Council of the Inquisition on grounds of being contrary to the teachings of St Peter and St Paul about the submission of serfs and vassals to their lords. Its author was mightily dismayed upon learning of the action being taken against him; however, the only thing the Council required of him in a legal sense was the submission of the work and its manuscript; this occurred in 1552. It was subsequently printed many times outside Spain.[231]

These denunciations are identical to those that Sepúlveda presented in his *Proposiciones temerarias.*[232] According to Sepúlveda's letter to Granvelle, he did not send his treatise to the Inquisition until early 1554. Thus, Llorente's 1552 dating is probably incorrect. Insofar as the other details that Llorente provides are accurate, it seems that the Inquisition did not pronounce against Las Casas's *Aquí se contiene*, which was the target of Sepúlveda's treatise, but instead ordered the confiscation of a different work. Henry Raup Wagner and Helen Rand Parish helpfully suggest that the work that the Inquisition seized was Las Casas's *Learned and Elegant Explanation* (*Erudita et elegans explicatio*), another of his treatises refuting the right of kings to claim territory and grant *encomiendas* without the consent of indigenous peoples, which was printed posthumously in 1571 in Frankfurt on the Main.[233] Perhaps this was originally a ninth treatise that Las Casas had printed

---

[229] Letter 113, from Sepúlveda to Antoine Perrenot de Granvelle, 15 March 1554, in Sepúlveda, *Obras completas, vol. 9.2: Epistolario*, 324–27, at §3, p. 325.
[230] Letter 113, from Sepúlveda to Antoine Perrenot de Granvelle, §4, p. 325.
[231] Juan Antonio Llorente, *Histoire critique de l'Inquisition d'Espagne*, vol. 2 (Paris, 1817), 433–34 (our translation).
[232] Wagner and Parish likewise note the similarities between Llorente's summary and Sepúlveda's treatise, a discovery made all the more remarkable by the fact that Wagner and Parish appear not to have known of the evidence from Sepúlveda's letter to Granvelle that he had sent his treatise to the Inquisition. Wagner and Parish, *Life and Writings*, 189.
[233] Wagner and Parish, *Life and Writings*, 188.

in Seville and perhaps Sepúlveda informed the Inquisition of this and other un-licensed works after first informing them of *Aquí se contiene*.[234]

Sepúlveda, meanwhile, found himself confronted with rumours that he had been paid by rebellious *encomenderos* to write in support of their interests. It was cer-tainly true that he had been called upon to write *Democrates secundus* in response to the controversies surrounding the New Laws that regulated the *encomenderos'* activities and in his *Apologia* he had condemned Las Casas for recommending the laws to the emperor and endorsed the emperor's subsequent decision to modify them. Las Casas declared in his own Latin *Apologia* that Sepúlveda 'attacks the New Laws with all his might' in *Democrates secundus*, 'though never making ex-press mention of them in any way', and Las Casas consistently framed Sepúlveda's arguments as serving the ambitions of the *encomenderos* and working against the conscience and interests of the Spanish Crown.[235] Sepúlveda complained to the theologian Pedro Serrano that his enemies were saying that he had been bought for five or six thousand ducats to write his *Democrates secundus* in defence of the interests of the 'leaders of the brigands'. He insisted, however, that he had written the book as an expression of his own views.[236]

And this does seem to be borne out by what he wrote. While he consistently de-fended the subjugation of the Amerindians and the colonists' use of their labour, he also reaffirmed the Spanish Crown's title to the Indies, its right to exact tribute from the Amerindians, and its authority over the *encomenderos*. Charles V was, after all, his patron and protector, and Sepúlveda served as Charles's confessor and official chronicler. His arguments would have certainly been welcome to the Spanish col-onizers. Even while rebuking the crimes of individual *encomenderos*—crimes that had contributed to the demands for the New Laws—he offered clear support for the practice of *encomienda*. But his arguments were weighted more strongly in fa-vour of the Crown's prerogatives and image. And his primary concern and focus, in any case, was always the justice of the conquests rather than the governance of the conquered.

Sepúlveda continued to defend Spain's invasion of the Americas in later writ-ings such as *The New World* (*De orbe novo*, not printed in his day) and *On Kingship and the Duty of a King* (*De regno et regis officio*, his final work, printed in 1571). In *De orbe novo* in particular, he revived some humanist elements of *Democrates secundus* that he had learned to avoid in his discussions with the theologians, such as praising the conquistadors for their pursuit of glory. He also expanded upon

---

[234] Wagner and Parish, *Life and Writings*, 187–89.

[235] Las Casas, *Defense of the Indians*, 8.

[236] Letter 104, from Sepúlveda to Pedro Serrano, undated, in Sepúlveda, *Obras completas, vol. 9.2: Epistolario*, 303–06, at §5, at 305 (our translation). The Town Council of Mexico, which had dis-patched representatives to the Spanish court the previous decade to protest the New Laws, voted in 1554 to buy for Sepúlveda 'some jewels and clothing from this land to the value of two hundred pesos' as rec-ognition of what he had done for them and 'to encourage him in the future'. Whether these gifts reached him is unknown. Hanke, *Aristotle and the American Indians*, 76.

56 SEPÚLVEDA ON THE SPANISH INVASION OF THE AMERICAS

his criticisms of the excesses of certain Spaniards, directing his ire particularly at *encomenderos* who continued to ignore the Crown's command not to enslave the Amerindians.[237] But despite his many efforts, he never succeeded in being granted a licence to print his *Democrates secundus*. It was published and also translated into Spanish for the first time by Marcelino Menéndez Pelayo only in 1892.

Legacies and reverberations

In his 1554 letter to Granvelle, Sepúlveda warned that the books Las Casas had recently printed were liable to be 'spread throughout Europe, which could be the source of a great deal of evil, for, in addition to slandering the Spanish monarchs and nation for tyranny and robbery, they might prompt another Christian prince to use them as a pretext to intervene in the conquest of the Indies'.[238] Sepúlveda thus rightly anticipated the role that Las Casas's writings would play in facilitating the development among Spain's Protestant European rivals of the 'Black Legend' regarding the evils of the Spanish conquests—a narrative that in turn served to justify their own imperial projects in the Americas and elsewhere.[239] And of course a central figure in this 'Black Legend' would be Sepúlveda himself, whose reputation as one of the most brazen defenders of Spain's wars and *encomiendas* carries through to this day.

Seeking to defend his honour and establish that Las Casas's arguments against him were not only 'futile and extremely flimsy' but also marked by 'false allegations and fabrications', Sepúlveda sought in his *Proposiciones temerarias* to summarize what he had been arguing in his writings and in his presentation to the Valladolid Junta:

> The conquest of the Indies performed with a view to subjugating those barbarians, ridding them of their idolatry, and forcing them to observe natural law against their will if necessary—and then, having subjugated them, to preach the gospel to them with all due meekness without recourse to any force whatsoever—is just and holy, and that, once they have been subjugated, they should be neither killed nor enslaved nor stripped of their estates but rather turned into vassals of the king of Castile and made to pay an appropriate amount of tribute as appointed and required by our sovereigns and as stipulated in the instructions issued to the captains-general whom they have dispatched, and that anything done in breach of this is wrongfully done and a grave sin for which it will be arduous indeed to

---

[237] Francisco Castilla Urbano, 'La consideración del indio en los escritos sepulvedianos posteriores a la Junta de Valladolid', *Cuadernos Americanos* 142 (2012/14): 55–81, at 71–80.

[238] Letter 113, from Sepúlveda to Antoine Perrenot de Granvelle, §3, p. 325 (our translation).

[239] See similarly Castilla Urbano, 'The Debate of Valladolid', 242. On the place of Sepúlveda and Las Casas's dispute in the 'Black Legend', see our volume's postscript.

INTRODUCTION 57

account before God, and anything taken by force—above and beyond that which can be lawfully seized in war—is robbery and must be restored.[240]

Sepúlveda complained that Las Casas had falsely accused him of endorsing the cruelties and robberies perpetrated by Spanish soldiers in the Americas. In reality, he insisted, 'these evils strike me as even more awful than they strike him'. He had not said more about those evils, he claimed, only because he took his task as being to explain the lawfulness of the wars themselves—a lawfulness that was not invalidated by the sins of individual soldiers.[241] Sepúlveda was here invoking a distinction between justifiable reasons for waging war and justifiable conduct in war that would later come to be framed as a distinction between considerations of *jus ad bellum* and *jus in bello*.[242]

However, while Las Casas certainly drew attention to the iniquities and cruelties of Spanish soldiers (and would do so in much greater detail in his *Brevísima relación*), he recognized that the fundamental tyranny was not the crimes of particular conquistadors and colonists so much as the plain fact that Spaniards had waged unjust wars against the Amerindians and divided them up among themselves in *encomiendas*. The problem was not that just wars had been waged unjustly, but that the wars themselves were unjust. Cruelty and greed marked not just the conduct of certain Spanish soldiers and *encomenderos* but the decision to forcefully subjugate the Amerindians in the first place. Everything that the Spaniards had done in the Indies, Las Casas had declared in his *Confesionario*, from their arrival to the subjection and servitude that they had imposed upon the people there, was 'completely unjust, iniquitous, tyrannical, and deserving of all eternal fire'.[243] And all who authorized, defended, profited from, and participated in such activities were implicated in these injustices. All were in need of repentance. All owed restitution.

Over the centuries following the Valladolid dispute, a body of law would emerge—first conceived as part of the law of nature and the law of nations and subsequently as part of positive international law agreed to by states in treaties and conventions—to regulate conduct in war.[244] A well-established corpus of

---

[240] Sepúlveda, *Proposiciones temerarias*, §17.

[241] Sepúlveda, *Proposiciones temerarias*, §17.

[242] On the surprisingly recent, twentieth-century origins of this framing, see Robert Kolb, 'Origin of the Twin Terms *jus ad bellum/jus in bello*', *International Review of the Red Cross* 37/320 (1997): 553–62. For discussion of Sepúlveda and Las Casas's divergent approaches to this distinction, see Stefano Pietropaoli, 'Las Casas e Sepúlveda: due modelli del diritto internazionale moderno', in Geuna, *Guerra giusta e schiavitù naturale*, 157–68.

[243] Las Casas, *Aquí se contienen unos avisos y reglas para los confesores*, 375.

[244] This law was prefigured by and indeed influenced in part by Las Casas's painstaking documentation of the injustices of individual Spaniards; injustices that Protestant European powers were eager to condemn. However, this law also was and continues to be marked by enduring and problematic colonialist distinctions between civilized soldiers and barbaric enemies. See Frédéric Mégret, 'From "Savages" to "Unlawful Combatants": A Postcolonial Look at International Humanitarian Law's "Other"', in *International Law and Its Others,* edited by Anne Orford, 265–317 (Cambridge: Cambridge University

international humanitarian law now clearly defines and provides for the enforcement of rules prohibiting the mistreatment of enemy combatants and civilians. And we are often quick today to condemn the cruelties and tyrannies of individual participants in war, just as Sepúlveda did. However, while much attention has been given in recent times to this task of making the conduct of war more 'humane', war itself continues to be a distressingly common feature of international life—a feature that, two decades into the 'war on terror', feels increasingly taken for granted.[245]

And it is not hard to detect certain troubling parallels between some of the justifications offered for today's wars—particularly those fought by Western powers against weaker others—and the justifications that Sepúlveda adduced in defence of Spain's wars in the Americas. The four just reasons for war that Sepúlveda advanced have had long afterlives, surviving both the secularization of the law of nations in the early modern period and, in certain senses, even the codification of positive international law since the eighteenth century.[246]

Consider the right of punishment. Protestant natural law theorists such as Alberico Gentili, Hugo Grotius, and John Locke transposed the universal right to punish violations of the law of nature into a secular key in the sixteenth and seventeenth centuries, attributing this right not to the church but to sovereign rulers and peoples.[247] In the hands of Grotius, such violations included cannibalism, piracy, and the inhumane treatment of parents.[248] Other Protestant natural law theorists, such as Samuel Pufendorf, Christian Wolff, and Emer de Vattel, rejected the right of punishment, denying for the most part that sovereigns have a right to punish those beyond their realm who have done them no injury and worrying that such a right would too frequently be abused.[249] Subsequent theorists would tend to be more reticent about recommending this reason for war. And yet a notion of punishment continues to be commonly insinuated in justifications for the

---

Press, 2006); Helen Kinsella, *The Image before the Weapon: A Critical History of the Distinction between Combatant and Civilian* (Ithaca, NY: Cornell University Press, 2011).

[245] Samuel Moyn, *Humane: How the United States Abandoned Peace and Reinvented War* (New York: Farrar, Straus and Giroux, 2021).

[246] On the echoes of Sepúlveda's ideas in early modern English and Dutch justifications for imperial projects, see Lantigua, *Infidels and Empires in a New World Order*, 189–250. On the enduringly 'purposive' nature of war, whereby wars have long been and continue to be waged by powerful states so as to impose particularistic visions of political order on others, see Jens Bartelson, *War in International Thought* (Cambridge: Cambridge University Press, 2018).

[247] Alberico Gentili, *De jure belli libri tres*, vol. 2, translated by John C. Rolfe (Oxford: Clarendon Press, 1933), I.25; Hugo Grotius, *De jure belli ac pacis libris tres*, vol. 2, edited by Francis W. Kelsey (Oxford: Clarendon Press, 1925), II.20.40; John Locke, *Two Treatises of Government*, edited by Peter Laslett (Cambridge: Cambridge University Press, 1960), Second Treatise, II.7–14.

[248] Somewhat surprisingly, Grotius even appealed to the authority of Innocent IV, which he contrasted with the opinion of Vitoria, in making this argument. Grotius, *De jure belli ac pacis*, II.20.40.

[249] Samuel Pufendorf, *Of the Law of Nature and Nations*, translated by Basil Kennett (London, 1729), VIII.3.7; Christian Wolff, *Jus gentium methodo scientifica pertractatum*, vol. 2, edited by Joseph H. Drake (Oxford: Clarendon Press, 1934), II.637–38; Emer de Vattel, *The Law of Nations*, edited by Béla Kapossy and Richard Whatmore (Indianapolis: Liberty Fund, 2008), II.1.7.

resort to force, especially in instances in which great powers take up arms against 'rogue' and 'outlaw' regimes and rulers, whose behaviours are said to violate universal moral principles. The 2003 invasion of Iraq by the US-led 'Coalition of the Willing' is a clear example. Such wars of punishment are framed as just and necessary for the purposes of disciplining wrongdoing, deterring further injustice, and prompting the defeated other to embrace the true and the good, just as they were in the writings of Sepúlveda.[250]

Consider the obligation to protect the innocent. This was the justification for war presented by Sepúlveda that Las Casas was most willing to endorse in principle, even if not in its application to the Americas. It would be embraced by countless theologians, jurists, philosophers, and rulers over the centuries that followed as, for example, Queen Elizabeth intervened to defend the people of the Low Countries against tyrannical Spaniards in the 1580s, Protestant rulers intervened to protect persecuted co-religionists in the Holy Roman Empire in the decades following the Westphalian settlement of 1648, European powers intervened to rescue Christian minorities from atrocities in the Ottoman Empire in the nineteenth and early twentieth centuries, and numerous 'humanitarian interventions' were waged by both Western and non-Western states in response to genocides and other mass atrocities from the 1970s onwards.[251] Today, such wars of protection are fought in the name of the 'Responsibility to Protect' (R2P), a principle that accords to states a responsibility to intervene in the affairs of other states—peacefully if possible, forcefully if necessary—should the latter fail to protect their own populations from atrocities.[252] Whatever the differences between R2P as it has been constructed by states in our own century and the duty to protect as adduced by Sepúlveda half a millennium earlier—and we will note shortly that the differences are significant—the danger of doing more harm than good when resorting to violence to protect innocents endures as the horrors and tragedies that have followed NATO's 2011 intervention in Libya all too clearly show.

Consider even the right to wage war to facilitate the spread of the gospel. The echoes of Sepúlveda's words are perhaps fainter, but nevertheless worth hearing.

---

[250] Gerry Simpson, *Great Powers and Outlaw States: Unequal Sovereigns in the International Legal Order* (Cambridge: Cambridge University Press, 2004); Cian O'Driscoll, 'Re-negotiating the Just War: The Invasion of Iraq and Punitive War', *Cambridge Review of International Affairs* 19/3 (2006): 405–20.

[251] Brendan Simms and D. J. B. Trim (eds), *Humanitarian Intervention: A History* (Cambridge: Cambridge University Press, 2011); Lauren Benton, Adam Clulow, and Bain Attwood (eds), *Protection and Empire: A Global History* (Cambridge: Cambridge University Press, 2018); Luke Glanville, *Sharing Responsibility: The History and Future of Protection from Atrocities* (Princeton: Princeton University Press, 2021), 17–71.

[252] See Luke Glanville, *Sovereignty and the Responsibility to Protect: A New History* (Chicago: University of Chicago Press, 2014); Glanville, *Sharing Responsibility*. Recognition of the parallels between R2P and Sepúlveda's argument for war to protect the innocent prompted the editor of a recent volume of essays on Sepúlveda to declare, 'Sepúlveda our contemporary, then' ('Sepúlveda nostro contemporaneo, dunque'). Marco Geuna, 'Ripensare Sepúlveda e la tradizione della guerra giusta', v–xviii, in Geuna, *Guerra giusta e schiavitù naturale*, xvi (our translation).

60 SEPÚLVEDA ON THE SPANISH INVASION OF THE AMERICAS

While Gentili and Grotius endorsed the punishment of atheists, they joined with Las Casas and other Dominicans in denying a right of war against those who sincerely profess a false religion. Neither belief in a false god nor a refusal to listen to gospel preaching provided just grounds for war, they declared.[253] For many years to come, certain Protestant apologists for empire did continue to appeal to the duty to spread the Christian faith as a just reason for subjugating indigenous peoples. But others eschewed this justification, often in order to mark their distance from the tyrannical Spaniards.[254] Even so, European colonizers commonly constructed and asserted rights to wage war to facilitate the spread of other beliefs—beliefs that were often inextricably linked to their understanding of Christianity—such as belief in the free flow of trade, the duty to cultivate and improve the land, and the amorphous and evolving collection of values and virtues that would be labelled the 'standard of civilization' in the nineteenth century.[255] In our own time, wars are again fought to facilitate the spread of belief, especially faith in liberal democracy. Reverberations of Sepúlveda's arguments were clearly felt in the twenty-year-long war waged by Western powers in Afghanistan as well as in Iraq and elsewhere. To facilitate the spread of this latest gospel, regimes and institutions are once more forcibly torn down, populations are quelled and made subject to new rulers, outside experts are parachuted in under the protection of armed personnel, people are taught to embrace the true doctrines of good government, and tribute is exacted in the form of favourable trade agreements—and the results tend to range from unsuccessful to calamitous.

Consider finally the distinction between the civilized and the barbarian. After Sepúlveda, most writers shied away from invoking the Aristotelian doctrine of natural slavery to justify war.[256] But hierarchical distinctions between the civilized and the barbarian, the pious and the monstrous, the cultured and the savage, the advanced and the backward, would continue to be put to work to justify wars fought by supposedly superior peoples against and for the benefit of supposedly inferior others. Today, such distinctions are still invoked in support of wars, whether to help

---

[253] Gentili, *De Jure Belli*, I.9; Grotius, *De Jure Belli ac Pacis*, II.20.48.

[254] See Andrew Fitzmaurice, *Humanism and America: An Intellectual History of English Colonization, 1500–1625* (Cambridge: Cambridge University Press, 2003), 138–40. On English ambivalence about the Spanish model and justifications for colonization in the Americas, see Eliga H. Gould, 'Entangled Histories, Entangled Worlds: The English-Speaking Atlantic as a Spanish Periphery', *American Historical Review* 112/3 (2007): 764–86; Edmund Valentine Campos, 'West of Eden: American Gold, Spanish Greed, and the Discourse of English Imperialism', in *Rereading the Black Legend: The Discourses of Religious and Racial Difference in the Renaissance Empires*, edited by Margaret R. Greer, Walter D. Mignolo, and Maureen Quilligan, 247–69 (Chicago: University of Chicago Press, 2017); Jorge Cañizares-Esguerra, 'The "Iberian" Justifications of Territorial Possession by Pilgrims and Puritans in the Colonization of America', in *Entangled Empires: The Anglo-Iberian Atlantic, 1500–1830*, edited by Jorge Cañizares-Esguerra, 161–77 (Philadelphia: University of Pennsylvania Press, 2018).

[255] Fitzmaurice, *Humanism and America*; Anthony Pagden, *The Burdens of Empire: 1539 to the Present* (Cambridge: Cambridge University Press, 2015), 120–52; Gerrit W. Gong, *The Standard of 'Civilization' in International Society* (Oxford: Clarendon Press, 1984).

[256] Pagden, *Burdens of Empire*, 97–119.

justify the punishment of the barbaric, the protection of their innocent victims, or the forceful propagation of civilized virtues and institutions among those who have not yet been taught or have refused to assent to such things themselves.[257] And in some cases, these wars are authorized once again by an institutionalized international authority—not the pope and his church anymore, but the United Nations Security Council.[258]

Indeed, hierarchical views of humanity underpin not only the justifications for particular wars but international law and international order more generally. Antony Anghie shows how international law continues to reproduce the 'dynamic of difference' that characterized the Spanish debates about the colonization of the Americas, a dynamic that entails 'the endless process of creating a gap between two cultures, demarcating one as "universal" and civilized and the other as "particular" and uncivilized, and seeking to bridge the gap by developing techniques to normalize the aberrant society'. Powerful states, Anghie explains, thus continue to present their domination over others across multiple domains, including aid, development, trade, governance, and of course war, in terms of an 'imperial narrative in which "we" are civilized, peace-loving, democratic, humanitarian, virtuous, benevolent, and "they" are uncivilized, violent, irrational, backward, dangerous, oppressed, and must therefore be sanctioned, rescued, and transformed by a violence that is simultaneously defensive, overwhelming, humanitarian, and benevolent'.[259]

The identification of Sepúlvedan antecedents of certain justifications for war may not in itself warrant giving up on all such justifications today. Concerning the obligation to protect the innocent that Sepúlveda adduced, for example, it is surely significant that R2P is not asserted merely by apologists for empire but has been in the present century endorsed unanimously by all states. And it is noteworthy that R2P does not justify the subjugation of peoples to foreign rule, but merely forceful measures aimed at defending and upholding the sovereign will of a people in need of protection.[260] Nevertheless, Sepúlveda's arguments for protection offered in defence of Spain's brutal wars haunt R2P and should give pause to anyone contemplating the resort to force to protect a vulnerable people today. There may be good reasons to cling to the possibility that wars of protection can on certain occasions be justified. But it is vital to wrestle with how the lures of civilizational self-confidence continue to lead powerful states to intervene in the affairs of weaker others in ways that do more harm than good. Whatever we may think of Las Casas's excuses for

---

[257] Mark B. Salter, *Barbarians and Civilization in International Relations* (London: Pluto Press, 2002); Daniel R. Brunstetter and Dana Zartner, 'Just War against Barbarians: Revisiting the Valladolid Debates between Sepúlveda and Las Casas', *Political Studies* 59/3 (2011): 733–52.

[258] Anne Orford, 'Jurisdiction without Territory: From the Holy Roman Empire to the Responsibility to Protect', *Michigan Journal of International Law* 30/3 (2009): 981–1015.

[259] Antony Anghie, *Imperialism, Sovereignty and the Making of International Law* (Cambridge: Cambridge University Press, 2005), 4, 317.

[260] See UN General Assembly, '2005 World Summit Outcome', A/Res/60/1 (24 October 2005), paras. 138–39; Glanville, *Sharing Responsibility*.

the Amerindians' rites of human sacrifice and cannibalism, we can surely learn from his reply to Sepúlveda that the always-horrific consequences of war must be carefully considered, and that arms should never be taken up to save the lives of some innocents at the cost of killing many more. At the very least, the observable parallels between the just reasons for war laid out by Sepúlveda and the reasons frequently offered to justify the resort to arms today point to a need to reckon carefully not only with the horrors of Spain's wars in the Americas, but also with the arguments that were provided to defend them—arguments that in the unabashed voice of Sepúlveda are so plainly dehumanizing, marked by such obvious myopia and hubris, but whose fundamental claims and assumptions may not be so different from those that we continue to use to reason about the justice of war today.

Key for Canon Law References

Reference notes identifying passages in canon law follow current standard practice, taking the forms indicated by the following samples (drawn from canons that are cited with particular frequency in these texts).

1) **Gratian, *Decretum*, D. 45, c. 3.**
   D = *Distinctio* (Distinction). Book 1 of Gratian is composed of *Distinctiones*.
   c. = *caput* (chapter). In the body of the text, one will not find chapter numbers; instead, a chapter will usually be identified by an incipit, i.e. the first two or three Latin words of the canon. In the case of D. 45, c. 3, the chapter would be identified in the text as *Qui sincera* (the beginning of a letter of Gregory I to Paschasius, bishop of Naples).

2) **Gratian, *Decretum*, C. 23, q. 5, c. 32.**
   C = Causa (Case). Book 2 of Gratian is given over to *Causae*.
   q. = quaestio (question)
   c. = caput (chapter), though some take the c. as referring to *canon* (prooftext). This will be an extract from Scripture, a church father, a papal letter or decree, or a canon of a church council, sometimes with an interpretive comment by Gratian.
   As with references in the text to the *Distinctiones* of Bk. 1, these chapters (or canons) will be identified in the text by their incipits: in this case, *Si audieris* (from Cyprian of Alexandria's *Ad Fortunatum de exhortatione martyrii*).
   Incidentally, the frequency of citations of Causa 23 is explained by its subject matter, warfare: the reasons for going to war and the proper conduct of wars.

3) **X.3.42.3**
   X: Somewhat confusingly, this is not the Roman numeral; rather, it is an abbreviation for *Liber Extra* ('Additional Book'), a common way of referring to the *Decretales* of Gregory IX, an extensive supplement to Gratian issued on the pope's command in 1234 and largely the work of Raymond of Peñafort and William of Rennes.
   3: In this sample reference, this refers to Book 3 of the Gregorian *Decretales*.

Sepúlveda on the Spanish Invasion of the Americas. Luke Glanville, David Lupher and Maya Feile Tomes,
Oxford University Press. © Luke Glanville, David Lupher, and Maya Feile Tomes 2023.
DOI: 10.1093/oso/9780198863823.003.0002

42: This is the number of one of the thematic titles into which a book of the *Decretales* is subdivided. In the text, titles are referred to by their Latin names, not by numbers. In this particular instance, the title is *De baptismo et eius effectu* ('On Baptism and its Effects').

3: This is the chapter (or canon) number within the title. In this instance, it is a letter by Innocent III to the Archbishop of Arles; its incipit is *Maiores ecclesiae* ('The leaders of the Church'), which is how it will be referred to in the texts—though this tends to be abbreviated to *Maiores*.

Democrates Part Two, on the Just Reasons for the War against the Indians

(*Democrates secundus, sive de iustis belli causis apud Indos*)

Preface to the translation of *Democrates secundus*

Manuscripts and evolution of the text

There are five surviving manuscripts of the *Democrates secundus,* though at least two others were known to the editors of the collection of Sepúlveda's works published in Madrid in 1780—one of them apparently destroyed in the French siege of Valencia in late 1811 and the beginning of 1812.[1] Of the five extant manuscripts, only one was known to Marcelino Menéndez y Pelayo for his *editio princeps* of 1892.[2] By 1952, Ángel Losada had discovered three more, one of which, bearing corrections and annotations in Sepúlveda's own hand, he used as the basis of the first critical edition of the dialogue. Alejandro Coroleu Lletget's 1997 edition and translation in the Pozoblanco *Obras completas* (fundamentally a revision of Losada's) took account of one further manuscript, bringing the total to five, though Coroleu followed Losada in using as his basis the manuscript with the marks of Sepúlveda's *ultima manus,* as have Domenico Taranto (2009), Christian Schäfer (2018), and the present translator.

There seems little doubt that the most advanced stage in the evolution of *Democrates secundus* is represented by the manuscript currently in the Biblioteca Universitaria in Salamanca—hence Coroleu has dubbed it 'S' (though Losada had called it 'A'). This manuscript is in the hand of one of the two scribes Sepúlveda

---

[1] For these lost manuscripts, see Francisco Cerdá y Rico et al., 'De vita et scriptis Joannis Genesiae Sepulvedae', in *Sepúlveda, Opera, vol. 1,* I–CXLIII (Madrid: Academia de la Historia, 1780), LXIV, n. 1; Marcelino Menéndez y Pelayo, 'Advertencia preliminar', *Boletín de la Real Academia de la Historia* 21/4 (1892): 257–59, at 259; Ángel Losada, 'Introducción', in Juan Ginés de Sepúlveda, *Democrates Segundo, o de las justas causas de la guerra contra los Indios,* edited by Ángel Losada, VII–XXXII (Madrid: CSIC, Instituto Francisco de Vitoria, 1951; repr. 1984), XXIX.

[2] 'Sepúlveda, Democrates Alter, sive de justis belli causis apud Indos, edited by Marcelino Menéndez y Pelayo', *Boletín de la Real Academia de la Historia* 21/4 (October 1892), 257–369.

Sepúlveda on the Spanish Invasion of the Americas. Luke Glanville, David Lupher and Maya Feile Tomes, Oxford University Press. © Luke Glanville, David Lupher, and Maya Feile Tomes 2023.
DOI: 10.1093/oso/9780198863823.003.0003

66 SEPÚLVEDA ON THE SPANISH INVASION OF THE AMERICAS

employed for his official chronicles *De rebus gestis Caroli Quintis historia* and *De orbe novo*. It contains several revisions and marginal annotations in Sepúlveda's own hand.[3] The latest datable reference in the main text occurs in a list of Spanish victories at which Charles V was present: 'most recently (*proxime*) in the war in Germany against the Lutheran heretics' (I.9.2)—that is, the Battle of Mühlberg on 24 April 1547, when Charles presided over the defeat of the Schmalkaldic League. The adverb *proxime* here implies that the main text of this manuscript represents a revision reasonably close to 1547, but we have of course no idea how long Sepúlveda continued to add corrections and notations once the text had been copied.[4] Perhaps he continued to harbour the hope that it might someday be published, at least posthumously in a collected edition of his works. The manuscript seems to have remained in Córdoba after Sepúlveda's death, for it came into the possession of the Córdoban antiquarian and local historian Pedro Díaz de Rivas (1587–1653), who hoped to issue an edition of it.[5] Subsequently, it passed into the possession of the library of the Colegio Mayor de Cuenca at the University of Salamanca, then to the Biblioteca Real del Palacio in Madrid (where Losada found and edited it), and finally, in 1954, to the university library in Salamanca. It is this manuscript that forms the basis of our translation.

Of the other four manuscripts extant, three clearly belong to the same family, derived from a single lost archetype. The earliest of these copies is the last to be collated with the others (by Coroleu in his edition of 1997). First located by the team assembled by the industrious Paul Oskar Kristeller,[6] it is a sixteenth-century manuscript bound in a folio of miscellaneous content in the Biblioteca Vallicelliana in Rome. Coroleu has named this the V manuscript. The other members of the family are later copies of the same archetype. One of them (named T by Coroleu, but B by Losada) is in the Archivo y Biblioteca Capitular in Toledo, but in the late eighteenth century it had been in Rome, in the possession of Cardinal Francisco Saverio de Zelada, a diplomat of the Roman curia. It is in a late seventeenth-century hand. Given its presence in Rome, it seems plausible that the original of T and V was also in Rome—unless, perhaps, T is a copy of V. The other, called M by Coroleu (and C by Losada) is in the Biblioteca Nacional de España in Madrid. Written in lettering of the early eighteenth century, it was acquired by the noted jurist Fernando José

---

[3] For a sample page, with Sepúlveda's corrections and additions, see Losada's edition, Plate VI, opposite p. 57.

[4] Ignacio Javier García Pinilla has argued for a date post-1565 for the draft of S. See Francisco Castilla Urbano, 'La consideración del indio en los escritos sepulvedianos posteriores a la Junta de Valladolid', *Cuadernos Americanos* 142 (2012/14): 55–81, at 55–56 and n. 2; Francisco Castilla Urbano, *El pensamiento de Juan Ginés de Sepúlveda: Vida activa, humanismo y guerra en el Renacimiento* (Madrid: Centro de Estudios Políticos y Constitucionales, 2013), 158n732. Castilla Urbano does not accept García Pinilla's arguments.

[5] Losada, 'Introducción', XXVII.

[6] Paul Oskar Kristeller, *Iter Italicum: A Finding List of Uncatalogued or Incompletely Catalogued Humanistic Manuscripts of the Renaissance in Italian and other Libraries, Vol. 2: Italy: Orvieto to Volterra [and] Vatican City* (Leiden: Brill, 1967), 131.

de Velasco y Ceballos (1707–1788). As of this writing, this manuscript is accessible online through the BNE's Biblioteca Digital Hispánica.

The other surviving manuscript was labelled P by Coroleu (and D by Losada). Dating to the early seventeenth-century, this manuscript is in Santander, in the Biblioteca Marcelino Menéndez Pelayo. Working from a transcription made around 1883 by Julián Pereda, parish priest of Villadiego, Menéndez y Pelayo used this manuscript as the basis of his 1892 *editio princeps* of the dialogue.[7] Through Menéndez y Pelayo's edition and translation, the P manuscript also formed the basis of the German and Italian translations by Dietmar Schmitz (1991) and Giuseppe Patisso (2008). The title this manuscript gives to the dialogue is *Democrates alter sive De iustis belli causis apud Indos*. Thus, in the sixty years between the *editio princeps* and the first critical edition (Losada's 1952 edition of the S manuscript), it was common to refer to the dialogue as the *Democrates alter*. But the title appears as *Democrates secundus* in all the other manuscripts.

Among the scholars who have written about the manuscript tradition of the *Democrates secundus*, there has been a consensus on certain key issues.[8] All are agreed that the Salamanca manuscript (S; Losada's A) represents the final state of Sepúlveda's work on the dialogue and in this respect constitutes 'el texto definitivo'.[9] The corrections and annotations in Sepúlveda's own hand, as well as the two-book structure, make this virtually certain. Similarly, there is a consensus that the V, T, and M manuscripts belong to a single family (named A by Coroleu) and derive from a single lost archetype (designated α2 by Coroleu). Similarly, it seems agreed that P and S form a distinct family (named B by Coroleu). As Coroleu noted, a glance at the *apparatus criticus* of his edition will immediately reveal wording that P and S have in common that differs from that of VTM.[10] It is also agreed that the archetype of P represented an 'intermediate state of the text', antedating S,

---

[7] It does not seem to be entirely clear whether the document in the Biblioteca Menéndez Pelayo is the original P manuscript, Pereda's copy of it, or both.

[8] The scholars in question are: Losada (in the introduction to his edition, XXVI–XXXII, and in his earlier biography of Sepúlveda, *Juan Ginés de Sepúlveda: a través de su 'Epistolario' y nuevos documentos* (Madrid: Consejo Superior de Investigaciones Científicas, 1949; repr. 1973), 189–95); Coroleu (in his 'Introducción filológica', in Juan Ginés de Sepúlveda, *Obras completas, vol. 3: Demócrates Segundo*, edited by Alejandro Coroleu Lletget, and *Apología en favor del libro sobre las justas causas de la guerra*, edited by Antonio Moreno Hernández (Pozoblanco: Ayuntamiento de Pozoblanco, 1997), XXXI–XXXVI, and in a nearly contemporaneous co-authored article, Alejandro Coroleu Lletget and Julián Solana Pujalte, 'Un nuevo manuscrito del *Democrates secundus sive de iustis belli causis* de Juan Ginés de Sepúlveda', *Analecta Malacitana* 20/1 (1997): 127–31), and Christian Schäfer (in his 'Einleitung', in Juan Ginés de Sepúlveda, Democrates secundus / Zweiter Demokrates, edited, translated, and introduced by Christian Schäfer, XIII–LXXIV (Stuttgart-Bad Cannstatt: Frommann-Holzboog, 2018), LXIV–LXVII).

[9] The phrase is Losada's ('Introducción', XXVI; *Juan Ginés de Sepúlveda*, 191). Coroleu calls S 'the final state of the text' ('el estado último del texto'; 'Introducción filológica', XXXII), and Coroleu and Solana Pujalte call it 'the most developed state of the text' ('el estado más evolucionado del texto'; 'Un nuevo manuscrito', 129). Schäfer calls S 'the end-result of the revised and expanded text' ('das Endresultat des verbesserten und erweiterten Textes'; 'Einleitung', LXIV).

[10] Coroleu, 'Introducción filológica', XXIV.

68 SEPÚLVEDA ON THE SPANISH INVASION OF THE AMERICAS

but postdating VTM.[11] This inevitably implies that the A family (VTM and their archetype) represents 'the most primitive state in the elaboration of the work.'[12] This assumption has led Schäfer, the most recent scholar to discuss the dialogue's manuscript tradition, to assert that the A family 'plays no decisive role for the question of the evolution of the content of the text, for P turns out to represent a fuller version of it'.[13]

Schäfer's extreme assertion unwittingly calls attention to a misconception that naturally arises from the three-stage hypothesis of the evolution of the dialogue and of the relationships among its surviving manuscripts: 'primitive' (VTM), 'intermediate' (P), and 'definitive' (S). In itself, the hypothesis is surely correct. Family A does indeed seem to represent the earliest surviving stage of the manuscript; P a later stage; and S the last stage of all. Thus, it would seem to be natural to suppose that Sepúlveda drafted the archetype of P as a revision of the archetype of VTM, and then later composed S as a revision of the archetype of P. But the reality is more interesting—and not so simple.

It is certainly true that the archetype of P was a revision of the archetype of VTM. And it is also plausible to assume, as did Losada (followed by Schäfer), that Sepúlveda intended this revision for publication, for P is the only manuscript prefixed by a dedicatory epistle (to Luis de Mendoza, Count of Tendilla and Marqués of Mondéjar).[14] But it is too often forgotten that P represents not only a revision of the VTM tradition but also a considerable abridgement of it. Thus, Schäfer was quite mistaken in supposing that P represents a much fuller version of the A family. More to the point, the most extensive passages present in the VTM manuscripts but omitted from P were not discarded by Sepúlveda; in fact, they were reused (with revisions, of course) in the final version, S. Thus, in Book I of the S manuscript we are treated to a very extensive digression (chapters 13 and 14 in Coroleu's division) on the monotheism of the great pagan (especially Greek) philosophers and the possibility that their faith, derived from their adherence to natural law, might well make them in some sense beneficiaries of God's grace—but at the very least these philosophers show that the Amerindians had no excuse for not following natural law to reject idolatry and recognize one true God. This remarkable set of reflections is indeed missing in P, and yet it is present in VTM.

---

[11] 'El manuscrito P representa un estado intermedio del texto' (Coroleu, 'Introducción filológica', XXXII = Coroleu and Solana Pujalte, 'Un nuevo manuscrito', 129).
[12] 'El estado más primitivo de elaboración de la obra': This phrasing by Coroleu and Solana Pujalte in the conclusion to their article ('Un nuevo manuscrito', 131) is more explicit than any statement by Losada in his two discussions or Coroleu in the introduction to his edition.
[13] '...für die Frage der inhaltlichen Entwicklung des Textes keine ausschlaggebende Rolle spielen, da sich P als eine Art ausführlicherer Version davon erweist', Schäfer, 'Einleitung', LXVII. In footnote 100 to this passage, Schäfer cites the article by Coroleu and Solana Pujalte, whose conclusion he has taken too far.
[14] Losada, 'Introducción', XXXI; Schäfer, 'Einleitung', LXIV. Both note that P is also followed by two 'approbations', by Alvaro Moscoso and Diego de Vitoria (brother of Francisco). But it should be noted that these endorsements are also appended to VTM.

So, it was part of both the 'primitive' and the 'definitive' state of the dialogue, but not the 'intermediate'. Curiously, among the scholars writing on the manuscripts of the dialogue, only Losada explicitly drew attention to this, though he drew no conclusions from it.[15] But even more curious is the fact that, a few pages earlier, Losada declared that the S manuscript (his A) offers 'very numerous additions to the text known up to now' (i.e. P), and by way of example he offered nearly half of the Salamanca manuscript's Book II.[16] And yet that extensive chunk of Book II (along with some other parts of Book II missing in P) was present in the 'primitive' stage represented by VTM.

The solution to this tangled manuscript tradition seems inevitable, though none of the scholars who have written on this matter has attempted to follow it through. For instance, Coroleu posits two archetypes, α1 for Family A (VTM) and α2 for Family B (PS), but then neglects to explain how the 'most evolved state' could have emerged from them, given that it manifests a significant correspondence to both.[17] An obvious scenario of development suggests itself:

1) In the first phase, apparently from the second half of 1544 to the second half of 1545, Sepúlveda drafted a fairly extensive manuscript, the archetype of VTM, and circulated it among readers who could have been expected to find it appealing—or at least unobjectionable.[18] Hence all three surviving exemplars sport the *approbaciones* (blurbs, if you like, verging on imprimaturs) of Moscoso and Diego de Vitoria (an especially prized 'catch', given that he was not only himself a Dominican but also the brother of the distinguished Francisco).

2) In the second phase (presumably around 1546), Sepúlveda revised the archetype of VTM, streamlining it considerably, and furnishing it with a formal dedicatory preface, clearly in the fond hope that the manuscript would promptly be approved for publication. Thus came into being the archetype of P (which we can call, with Coroleu, α2).

3) A few years later, with Sepúlveda's hopes for immediate publication decisively dashed, the disappointed Córdoban found himself unable to simply let his elegant and (in his view) persuasive dialogue sink under the weight of the criticism of pesky Dominicans. A lifelong controversialist, he was naturally itching to have the last word—though he was probably resigned to the likelihood that it would not be publicly uttered until after his death, perhaps in a suitably elegant 'complete

---

[15] Losada, 'Introducción', XXXI; *Juan Ginés de Sepúlveda*, 195.

[16] '... numerosísimas adiciones sobre el texto ya conocido, algunas tan extensas como la que aparece entre las páginas 98 y 117', Losada, 'Introducción', XXVIII. Pages 98–117 in Losada's edition correspond to II.3.9–II.7.5 (pp. 114–28) in Coroleu's edition.

[17] Coroleu, 'Introducción filológica', XXXIV.

[18] For this dating of the first draft of the dialogue, see Teodoro Andrés Marcos, *Los imperialismos de Juan Ginés de Sepúlveda en su Democrates Alter* (Madrid: Instituto de Estudios Políticos, 1947), 24, followed by Losada, *Juan Ginés de Sepúlveda*, 198–99. Anthony Pagden declares that the dialogue was 'probably composed in 1544': Anthony Pagden, *The Fall of Natural Man: The American Indian and the Origins of Comparative Ethnology* (Cambridge: Cambridge University Press, 1982), 109.

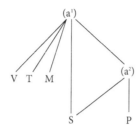

Figure 1.1 The MSS Tradition of *Democrates secundus*

works'. (In this, he would long be disappointed, for it was included neither in the *Opera omnia* published by Arnold Mylius in 1602 nor in the fuller 1780 *Opera*, though the editors of the latter did make a point of praising, summarizing, and quoting from it in the introduction.[19]) In composing this final version (which he would continue to tinker with, making numerous corrections and marginal additions), he naturally set before him *both* the extensive archetype of VTM *and* the revised and abridged version that was the archetype of P. And then he set to work, restoring (and revising) lengthy passages cut from the 'intermediate' version, while also supplying extensive reworkings of passages that the archetypes of VTM and P had in common.

Thus, when Coroleu posited a common archetype ($\alpha 2$) for both P and S, he was correct—but only up to a point. The archetype of the early seventeenth-century manuscript P, after serving as the template for various copies circulated by Sepúlveda in the mid-1540s, later served him as *one* archetype for his 'definitive' revision, S. But S also drew very extensively upon the archetype (Coroleu's $\alpha 1$) of the earlier state represented today by VTM. Though none of the scholars who have written about the manuscripts of the dialogue has offered a stemma, one would surely be useful for visually grasping the likely evolution of the text (see Figure 1.1).

It should be noted that, while traditional stemmata reconstruct the activity of generations of scribes, this one differs in also indicating the activity of the author himself (using scribes under his direct supervision). Thus, VTM and P represent scribal copies of lost archetypes produced by Sepúlveda himself, while S is an autograph (or, rather, an authorially supervised and autographically corrected) revision of two lost autograph (or authorially supervised) manuscripts. Thus, this stemma is meant to illustrate both the process of authorial composition and also the process of textual transmission after the author's death.

---

[19] Francisco Cerdá y Rico, et al., 'De vita et scriptis Joannis Genesii Sepulvedae', XLIX–LXV. From the quoted passages, it is clear that they were using a manuscript of the VTM family—most likely M (Madrid).

A couple of specific examples will not only illustrate the process assumed here, but also can illuminate the development of Sepúlveda's thinking on the Americas.

In Book II of the Salamanca manuscript, at the beginning of what we (following Coroleu) label II.1.3, Leopoldus asks a short but highly pertinent question: 'So, then, by what right, by what law can a certain population or individual of those people be deprived of liberty and goods?' This is how the question appears in all three versions (though with *quisquam* in S vs. *quisque* in VTMP). Thereupon follows a speech by Democrates that is short in VTM, longer in P, and longer still in S. One may compare all three texts by consulting our main translation (which follows the S version) and the other two versions as supplied in the Appendix. In a nutshell, the three versions make these points:

1) VTM: The law of nations (*ius gentium*) justifies the dispossession and enslavement of those defeated in a just war.
2) P: Repeating the single sentence of VTM but crucially adding 'and the law of nature', this expanded version invokes biblical examples of the Israelites punishing idolatrous nations, thus advancing the argument beyond traditional 'just war' theory into the territory of the tension between the positions of Innocent IV and Hostiensis.
3) S: Much the longest of the three versions of Democrates's speech, the S version dispenses with the VTM and P versions altogether and constructs its response around a new gambit: an infidel people's misuse of their natural gifts justifies their forced subordination to those who know how to put those gifts to better uses. And among those natural gifts susceptible to disenfranchising misuse are both communal and personal liberty.

After these three distinct versions of Democrates's answer, VTM, P, and S all present Leopoldus's objection that this argument violates the natural law according to which 'all men are said originally to have been free' (II.2.2). Though all three versions have Leopoldus asking essentially the same question, the specific wording is instructive, for while the phrase *a natura abhorere* is shared by VTM and P and not by S, VTM and S agree in using the verb *feruntur* for P's more common *dicuntur*. This is a striking confirmation of the hypothesis that in composing the S version Sepúlveda had the archetypes of both VTM and P on his desk before him.

A broader and more intense light upon the dialogue's evolution is cast by three substantial passages in what Coroleu (followed by our translation) labels chapters 11 and 12 of Book I:

1) Immediately following the end of chapter 10, VTM, followed by P, offer an extensive passage on the Amerindians' political and social lives (see Appendix). The point is that the manifest willingness of the Amerindians to obey tyrannous overlords not only reveals a naturally servile disposition

72 SEPÚLVEDA ON THE SPANISH INVASION OF THE AMERICAS

but also promises an easy transition to a domination by new masters (the Spaniards) that will in fact benefit them. When composing his final version, Sepúlveda chose to omit this section entirely, but rejoined the earlier versions when they turned to focus on the more appealingly lurid question of the Amerindian's unnatural religious practices—a point the S version embellished by adding an aside on the supposed atheism of certain Amerindian societies, which is offered as an indication of an even more debased nature.

2) At the end of this section (I.11.3–6), VTM, followed by P, offer a passage (see Appendix) that was reworked and considerably expanded in S. The VTMP version offered several passages from the Old Testament to make the point that idolatry and other sins against natural law were justly punished by the Israelites, then cited Cyprian of Alexandria to make the point that such instances provide proper precedent for Christian behaviour as well.[20] The S version at first elaborates these points, offering even more biblical passages and reinforcing Cyprian with citations from Ambrose and Augustine. But then the S version takes a remarkable turn and strikes an entirely new note. After beefing up the Israelite precedent and the Church Fathers' validation of it, Democrates tosses all that aside. While it would indeed be perfectly permissible to imitate the Israelites smiting Canaanites and Amorites, that's not what we're doing over there in the Americas, he now insists. We're not there to smite and exterminate; we're there to bring the temporal advantages of civilization and the spiritual blessings of Christianity to benighted peoples. Thus, the 'definitive' version of the dialogue simultaneously intensifies the validity of the Israelite precedent and rejects its appropriateness to Spanish behaviour in America. Not only is this a deft bit of rhetoric in itself, but it also reads like an implicit response to Sepúlveda's critics, who denounced the genocidal implications of an invocation of the Israelites in Canaan. If so, this is not the only instance where Sepúlveda's final version was evidently designed to respond to criticisms of earlier versions.

3) In all versions, I.12 begins with Leopoldus reminding Democrates that leading modern theologians insist that infidelity does not in itself furnish Christians a just cause for war. That is, Leopoldus is suggesting that his interlocutor shares the quasi-heretical position of Hostiensis, while a marginal note in all the manuscripts makes it clear that the main recent theologian sharing Leopoldus's view was the celebrated Dominican (and onetime patron of Sepúlveda himself), Cajetan. The bulk of the rest of S's chapter 12 (Democrates's response) represents a thorough reworking of the version shared by VTM and P. That earlier version is, on the whole, a rather tired rehash of the biblical precedents trotted forth in the previous chapter, with a verbatim repetition of the citation from Cyprian. But one new feature was

---

[20] Interestingly, this passage in VTMP also contains the dialogue's only citation of 'Berosus'—i.e. the notorious forger Annius of Viterbo. This was omitted in S's expansion of the passage.

an appeal to the supposed anti-pagan legislation of Constantine the Great and Gregory I's praise of the wars conducted by the exarch Gennadius against North African pagan tribes. The version in S trims the Israelite precedent, turning instead to Augustine for help in properly understanding what Paul really meant when he declined to pass judgment on 'those outside' (1 Cor. 5: 12), then focusing on the apostolic duty to evangelize 'all peoples', promoted by the Alexandrine bulls. While Democrates here is made to jettison the invocation of Constantinian legislation and Gregory's praise of Gennadius, that useful portion of the VTMP version would be recycled (largely verbatim) in I.17.3.

At the end of chapter 12, however, VTM and P part ways. VTM here made the point that one could argue that in a very real sense infidelity is in itself a violation of natural law, for the greatest pagan philosophers showed that a belief in a single, beneficent God did not depend upon Christian revelation. This triggered Leopoldus's astonishment, which in turn led to the lengthy digression about the faith of the pagan philosophers and the possibility that they might receive divine grace for that faith. All of this was omitted by P when Sepúlveda decided to abridge the dialogue for publication. But when he came to expand and revise the dialogue for its final version (and possible eventual, probably posthumous publication), he restored this lengthy digression that was clearly so congenial to him as a leading Aristotelian humanist.[21] But halfway through section 4 of chapter 14, there is a remarkable passage present in VTM that Sepúlveda chose to omit (see Appendix), in which Democrates cites none other than Cajetan as asserting that 'the philosophers, under the guidance of God and with nature as their teacher, knew that God was one—and that he had a care for good and pious men'. Indeed, Democrates claims to have heard this from Cajetan's own lips, for 'I was on familiar terms with him sometimes at Gaeta, after the sack of the city [Rome], sometimes in the city itself'. It is easy enough to see why Sepúlveda realized that he had to excise this from the final version, for it is perhaps the only moment in the versions of the dialogue when the mask slips and the Greek Democrates speaks from the personal experience of Sepúlveda himself. Still, it must have cost Sepúlveda a pang, so soon after having Democrates defend his position against the implied objections of Cajetan, to sacrifice an opportunity to irritate his Dominican opponents by reminding them that he had once been on close terms with the great Dominican theologian who had powerfully reasserted and expanded the validity of infidel *dominium*.[22]

---

[21] Confusingly, in his app. crit. for I.13–14 Coroleu labels variants offered by S as SP, which would imply that this digression is in P as well. It is not. Losada's app. crit. correctly notes '*om*. D' [i.e. P] for his lines 1157–419, i.e. what Coroleu called chapters 13–14. This appears to be a case where Coroleu's treating of P and S as a single family (B) had led him into misleading expression.

[22] On the importance of Cajetan's position on infidel *dominium* to the Controversy of the Indies, see esp. David M. Lantigua, *Infidels and Empires in a New World Order: Early Modern Spanish Contributions to International Legal Thought* (Cambridge: Cambridge University Press, 2020), 85–92.

74 SEPÚLVEDA ON THE SPANISH INVASION OF THE AMERICAS

These examples may suffice to give some indication of the evolution of the text of the *Democrates secundus* and the likely relationships among the archetypes of the surviving manuscripts. Focusing finally on the final version, we note that it is not only an expansion and revision of both the archetypes of VTM and of P, but that it is also a more elegant and polished work than its predecessors, its two-book structure allowing for a bit more scene-setting and even a 'cameo' appearance by Sepúlveda himself as host before the resumption of the discussion on 'the same green and shady bank of the Pisuerga', the river that flows through Valladolid, often the seat of the royal court and the location of the palace of Prince Philip, whose tutor Sepúlveda was. But also, as mentioned above, the final version provided Sepúlveda the gratifying opportunity to address several criticisms that had been directed at his dialogue in its earlier incarnations.

Of the scholars who have discussed the stages of the dialogue's composition, Christian Schäfer has been the one to address most fully ways the S manuscript answered criticisms.[23] He thus offered the S version of I.12, discussed above, as a response to the objection that one cannot hold against the Amerindians the fact that they had never heard of Christ or monotheism before the arrival of the Spaniards. That is a plausible assumption, and this eagerness to respond to criticism surely also encouraged Sepúlveda to restore from the archetype of VTM the immediately subsequent long passage (I.13–14) on the monotheism of the pre-Christian pagan philosophers. Also, we have already noted that S's extensive reworking of the VTMP version of I.11.3–6 reads very much like a response to the objection that the behaviour of the Israelites in the conquest of Canaan is no proper model for Spanish behaviour in America.

Schäfer also suggests that I.18.4–6 was an answer to the objection that the citations that Sepúlveda was fond of marshalling from Augustine's letters on the Donatists were irrelevant when one is dealing with peoples who had never accepted Christianity in the first place. This is likely enough, but one should note that the new material in S here extends beyond that passage, all the way to I.20.2. This embraces a key passage (I.19.4) that surely offers a further response to criticisms: the consideration of a hypothetical in which Spaniards might encounter an American society openly eager to accept Christianity. Here a lack of attention to Latin usage (as well as to the logic of the passage itself) had led modern translators (Losada/ Coroleu, Taranto, and Schäfer) to misunderstand Sepúlveda's actual answer. See the passage in our translation and the note supplied to it. Suffice it to say that our reading of this passage is in line with another feature of S noted by Schäfer: its more self-consciously humane tone.

One way in which this kinder, gentler tone manifests itself is in a pruning back of the use of a damning diminutive that is applied three times in VTM and P to

---

[23] Schäfer, 'Einleitung', LXVI.

the Amerindians but only once in S: *homunculi* (rendered 'lesser humans' in our translation). While this slur is found in all the manuscripts in a passage (I.10.1 in S) contrasting the singular moral superiority of the Spaniards to the 'lesser humans' of the Americas, it was excised as part of a similar passage (where the Romans were linked with the Spaniards) in the revision of what became I.15.11 of S (see the Appendix for the discarded passage) and in the omitted passage on Amerindian political and social structures (see the Appendix). Thus, though it is common to read the sweeping assertion that 'Sepúlveda calls them *homunculi*', one should note that this is truer of earlier versions than of the final one.[24]

But the most striking—and controversial—example of mitigating revision in the Salamanca manuscript is its apparent suppression of what Schäfer calls 'the always scandalous and stir-causing quasi-comparison of the Indians with apes'.[25] This refers to a passage early in I.9.1. Asserting the propriety of the rule of more culturally advanced peoples over more primitive peoples, Democrates proceeded to claim that

> it is by the highest right that the Spaniards rule over those barbarians of the New World and the adjacent islands, people who in intelligence, native wit, and every sort of virtue and human feeling [*humanitate*] are as far surpassed by the Spaniards as children are by adults, as women are by men, as savage and fierce people are by the most gentle people, as the wildly intemperate are by those who are self-controlled and temperate—and finally I might almost say: as apes are by human beings (*denique quam simiae prope dixerim ab hominibus*).[26]

Or so the VTM family and P concluded the sentence. Even there, one should probably acknowledge a slight soft-pedalling in the 'I might almost say' (*prope dixerim*): hence Schäfer's qualification 'quasi-comparison' ('Beinahe-Vergleich').

This is a prime instance of the importance of which version of the dialogue one is using. When he published his groundbreaking book *The Spanish Struggle for Justice in the Conquest of America* in 1949, Lewis Hanke focused on this passage and offered a paraphrase of it concluding 'as monkeys from men'.[27] A decade later, after the appearance of Losada's edition, Hanke's widely read and cited *Aristotle and the American Indians* quoted the passage in a very similar discussion, but this

---

[24] The quoted phrase ('Sepúlveda li chiama *homunculi*') is from Luca Baccelli, 'Nihil humanum a me alienum puto: Sepúlveda e l'umanità degli Indios', in *Guerra giusta e schiavitù naturale: Juan Ginés de Sepúlveda e il dibattito sulla Conquista*, edited by Marco Geuna, 89–116 (Milan: Edizioni Biblioteca Francescana, 2014), 106.

[25] Schäfer, 'Einleitung', LXV: 'den seit jeher als skandalös aufsehenerregenden Beinahe-Vergleich der indios mit Menschenaffen'.

[26] I.9.1: Menéndez y Pelayo, ed., p. 304. In the Madrid MS, it appears on the top of p. 25v. For the S version, see Coroleu's edition and app. crit., p. 64 and Losada's, p. 33.

[27] Lewis Hanke, *The Spanish Struggle for Justice in the Conquest of America* (American Historical Association, 1949), 122.

76 SEPÚLVEDA ON THE SPANISH INVASION OF THE AMERICAS

time omitting the scandalous phrase.[28] Curiously, Christian Schäfer himself has
exhibited a similar shift with regard to this passage. In an article published in 2002,
he cited the ape comparison with no comment on the textual history, for in writing
that article his access to the dialogue had been through Menéndez y Pelayo's edition of the P text.[29] Sixteen years later, however, he based his edition and translation on Coroleu's edition of the S text, and he drew proper attention to the ape
passage as from an earlier phase of the dialogue's evolution.[30] But the ape simile
remains a favourite of those who paint with a broader brush. For example, Aldo
Andrea Cassi has multiplied the offending phrase in claiming that 'in certain instances Sepúlveda seems straightforwardly to assimilate the Natives to apes'.[31]

But even further care seems called for here. In his 2018 edition, Schäfer, noting
that this phrase 'has ensured a considerable stir in the secondary literature', simply
notes that it 'is found in the earlier version of the text, which P, V, T and M unanimously offer', implying that the phrase is entirely lacking from the Salamanca
manuscript.[32] This is a plausible assumption if one is primarily relying, as Schäfer
was, on Coroleu's *apparatus criticus*, which simply lists the earlier manuscripts as
including the phrase.[33] But here, as often, Losada's 1951 edition is still worth consulting. There we read in a note *ad loc.* that this passage was expunged (*suprimida*)
from the S manuscript.[34] Anthony Pagden, in his magisterial and influential *The
Fall of Natural Man*, quotes the sentence with the ape simile intact in his text and
in an end-note declares: 'The final phrase ... has been erased from the manuscript ... used by Ángel Losada for his edition. The erasure, however, was certainly
not done by the scribe and I doubt that it represents a modification of the text.
Had Sepúlveda wished to moderate his language, as Losada seems to think, it is
unlikely that he would have left the passages quoted below unaltered.'[35] Among
the passages that Pagden proceeded to cite and to single out for their 'acerbity' is
one where Sepúlveda claims that the Amerindians under Spanish rule differ from
their pre-Conquest selves 'as much as human beings from beasts' (*quantum pene
homines a belluis*, I.11.1). Interestingly, this passage is found only in S. One could
argue that it intentionally restates the earlier offending phrase in a less absolute
manner, for its larger point is not that the Amerindians are inherently bestial, but

---

[28] Lewis Hanke, *Aristotle and the American Indians: A Study in Race Prejudice in the Modern World*
(Chicago: Henry Regnery, 1959), 47. See p. 43, where he declared his allegiance to Losada's edition.
[29] Christian Schäfer, 'La *Política* de Aristóteles y el Aristotelismo político de la conquista', *Ideas y
valores* 119 (2002): 109–35, at 130f.
[30] Schäfer, 'Einleitung', LXV; see also his end-note 99, p. 226.
[31] Aldo Andrea Cassi, *Ultramar: L'invenzione europea del nuovo mondo* (Rome-Bari, 2007), 102 ('In
alcuni casi Sepúlveda sembra addirittura assimilare gli indigeni alle scimmie'), quoted in Baccelli, '*Nihil
humanum a me alienum puto*', 89.
[32] Schäfer, 'Einleitung', 226n99.
[33] Corloleu's edition, p. 64: '*Post* temperatis ad. denique quam Simiae prope dixerim ab
hominibus **VTMP**'.
[34] Losada, 'Introducción', 33n28.
[35] Pagden, *The Fall of Natural Man*, 117, 232n35.

that they appeared so in their former state of backward culture. Francisco Castilla Urbano, however, has argued that 'the greater part of the alterations of the S manuscript relate not so much to an intention to soften the language used in referring to the Indians, which does not seem to have excessively worried the humanist; rather, they have to do with the correction of certain errors, stylistic changes in certain phrases, and an amplification of the content, much of it having nothing to do with the Indians'.[36] Thus, Castilla Urbano, like Pagden, does not regard it as likely that the erasure of the ape phrase represents a modification of Sepúlveda's own views, but at the same time he does not follow Pagden in insisting that the erasure cannot be attributed to Sepúlveda. Rather, he regards it as a stylistic improvement, not a substantive change.

Our intention here has not been to achieve blinding or binding clarity on this infamous and highly problematic passage. Rather, this textual and interpretive conundrum may serve as a glaring example of the importance, too frequently overlooked, of keeping in mind the manuscript tradition and the likely evolution of the text of this dialogue.

Editions and translations

The first edition of the Latin text, accompanied by facing Spanish translation, was published in 1892 in the bulletin of the Royal Academy of History by Marcelino Menéndez y Pelayo. Menéndez y Pelayo's Latin text was that of the P (Santander) manuscript, as transcribed by Julián Pereda (ca. 1883), parish priest of Villadiego. Though Ángel Losada noted that both the edition and the translation show many signs of haste and carelessness, it was reissued a half century later, errors intact, in Mexico, accompanied by an introduction by the distinguished Spanish legal scholar and Civil War emigré Manuel García-Pelayo.[37] Menéndez y Pelayo's edition and translation also formed the basis of a 1991 German translation by Dietmar Schmitz and, more recently, of an Italian translation by Giuseppe Patisso.[38]

The first edition to be based on the later Salamanca manuscript (S) was that of Ángel Losada (1951).[39] This edition, with facing Spanish translation, was supplied with a full *apparatus criticus* with variant readings and entire longer passages from

---

[36] Castilla Urbano, 'La consideración del indio', 56; see also his *El pensamiento de Juan Ginés de Sepúlveda*, 157–58.

[37] Sepúlveda, *Tratado sobre las justas causas de la guerra contra los indios* (México: FCE, 1941, repr. 1979 and 1996). For Losada's complaints about both editions, see *Juan Ginés de Sepúlveda*, 190; 'Introducción', XXXI–XXXII.

[38] Sepúlveda, 'Dialog über die gerechten Kriegsgründe', translated by Dietmar Schmitz, in *Der Griff nach der neuen Welt*, edited by Christoph Strosetzki, 210–69 (Frankfurt: Fischer, 1991); Sepúlveda, *Democrate secondo, o della giusta causa della guerra contro gli Indos*, translated by Giuseppe Patisso (Galatina: Congedo, 2008).

[39] Sepúlveda, *Democrates Segundo, o de las justas causas de la guerra contra los Indios*, edited by Ángel Losada (Madrid: CSIC, Instituto Francisco de Vitoria, 1951; repr. 1984).

the other manuscripts known to Losada (MTP, but not V). In addition to his own historical and editorial introduction, Losada also included an analysis of the dialogue by noted Sepúlvedan scholar Teodoro Andrés Marcos, and his edition was illustrated with several plates of key passages, mainly in the S manuscript.

The title page of the third volume of the Pozoblanco *Obras completas* (1997) attributes the critical edition and translation of the dialogue to Alejandro Coroleu Lletget, but on the internal title page (p. XXIX) it is more accurately identified as Coroleu's revision of Losada's text, translation, *apparatus criticus*, and register of sources, with a philological introduction by Coroleu, as well as an introductory historical study by Jaime Brufau Prats. Coroleu also introduced helpful section and subsection numbers to Losada's text, and these have been retained in our translation.[40] (The titles given to the chapters, however, are our own.) In general, Coroleu follows Losada's text and translation fairly closely, though the Latin text is marred by many typographical errors, usually not present in Losada's edition. Coroleu had the advantage of being able to take account of the V manuscript (Rome: Biblioteca Vallicelliana), not available to Losada. One surprising omission is that Coroleu fails to note marginal references and notations added to the S manuscript.[41]

In 2009, Domenico Taranto presented the Latin text printed by Coroleu, with many (but not all) typos corrected (noted at the bottom of the pages), with facing Italian translation, prefaced by a substantial and illuminating introduction.[42] Taranto's edition offers no *apparatus criticus* and does not supply any of the extensive passages where earlier versions markedly differed from the S manuscript. Taranto's footnotes are largely confined to notations of sources, often supplying useful corrections and improvements to those supplied by Losada and Coroleu.

Christian Schäfer's bilingual Latin–German version (Stuttgart, 2018) is, like Taranto's, based on the Losada–Coroleu Latin text.[43] His end-notes supply sources (often correcting both Losada–Coroleu and Taranto) and also Latin texts and German translations of the more important divergent passages from the earlier manuscripts. On pp. 247–49, he listed the typos he corrected in the Coroleu text. Schäfer also supplied a very useful (sixty-page) introduction.

---

[40] While Losada did not subdivide the text into chapters and subsections, he did supply marginal line numbers. While these were of course only applicable to his edition, they prove extremely helpful when Losada's app. crit. notes extended omissions in certain manuscripts, for his line-number ranges are much easier to follow than Coroleu's habit of referring only to a pair of frame-words embracing the omitted passage, when those words may be pages apart.

[41] For example, when Leopoldus (I.12.1) alludes to 'certain distinguished theologians' as reasserting the principle that infidelity doesn't invalidate *dominium,* and in the S version indicates that he is thinking about one theologian in particular, Coroleu fails to mention the marginal notation citing Cajetan that is present in S (Losada ed., 43n110), P (Menéndez y Pelayo ed., 318n2), and M (33v)—and presumably also in V and T. Similarly, Coroleu fails to mention the marginal reference to Vitoria in S alongside a reference to 'more recent theologians' found only in that manuscript (I.15.3). Losada not only noted that reference, but also included a plate of that page of the manuscript (Pl. VI, 57).

[42] Sepúlveda, *Democrate secondo, ovvero sulle giuste cause di guerra /Democrates secundus sive de iustis belli causis,* edited and translated by Domenico Taranto (Macerata: Quodlibet, 2009).

[43] Sepúlvdeda, *Democrates secundus / Zweiter Demokrates.*

The present translation

Despite the considerable attention that the disputation at Valladolid has received in Anglophone writings, some of it (notably the various writings of Lewis Hanke) aimed at a relatively wide audience, no complete English translation of the *Democrates secundus* has appeared until now. In 1969, John Leddy Phelan translated from Menéndez y Pelayo's edition a few pages in a volume intended for students, and this was reprinted in a widely circulated reference work in 1984.[44] Also, for some years Columbia University has included extracts from the dialogue in its celebrated first-year Core Curriculum, but access to the assigned text seems restricted to Columbia students and faculty.[45]

The present translation resembles those of Taranto and Schäfer in being based on the Latin text established by Losada and Coroleu rather than on a fresh examination of the manuscripts (apart from the M manuscript, which is available online). Unfortunately, it joins Patisso and Schmitz in breaking with the tradition maintained by Menéndez Pelayo, Losada, Coroleu, Taranto, and Schäfer of including a Latin text. This is a source of considerable regret for the translator, who must direct those wishing to consult Sepúlveda's exact words to one or more of those earlier volumes. An appendix supplies translations of the more substantial passages in earlier manuscripts that differ from the text offered by the Salamanca manuscript. (These have been taken from the critical apparatuses of Losada and Coroleu.)

Writing shortly after Losada's edition of the Salamanca manuscript appeared, Lewis Hanke noted that 'Losada believes that the text he has published represents the true thought of Sepúlveda, and the reader who follows the minute and exhaustive collation of the four manuscripts he provides is bound to agree.'[46] This implies, of course, that the earlier versions failed to represent Sepúlveda's 'true thought'—perhaps a highly dubious assumption. Tellingly, Hanke offered as one example of this 'true thought' the fact that the S manuscript 'omits some of the harsher expressions on the nature of the Indians'—as though such expressions had been somehow insincere or insufficiently pondered. Of course, it is just as easy to argue that the S manuscript represents not so much Sepúlveda's 'true thought' as a more polished and elegant version that implicitly responded to negative reactions triggered by earlier versions.

Also, one highly relevant—but, alas, obscure—question is: when did Sepúlveda produce the S version (and its corrections and marginal notations)? We noted

---

[44] John Leddy Phelan, trans., in Frederick B. Pike (ed.), *Latin American History: Select Problems* (New York: Harcourt, Brace, and World, 1969), 47–52; reprinted in J. . Parry and Robert G. Keith (eds), *New Iberian World: A Documentary History of the Discovery and Settlement of Latin America to the Early Seventeenth Century, vol. 1, The Conquerors and the Conquered* (New York: New York Times Books, 1984), 323–27.

[45] A teaser of the Columbia reading is available online at http://www.columbia.edu/acis/ets/CCREAD/sepulved.htm

[46] Hanke, *Aristotle and the American Indians*, 43.

80 SEPÚLVEDA ON THE SPANISH INVASION OF THE AMERICAS

above that its *terminus post quem* is the Battle of Mühlberg in April of 1547, and the comment that this was recent (*proxime*) implies that it was composed not long after. But how long after—and how widely was it circulated, if indeed it was circulated at all?[47] Given that it may well postdate the Valladolid Junta of 1550–51, a strong case could be made that those whose interest is primarily in the Controversy of the Indies in general and in the Valladolid Junta in particular, rather than in the intellectual biography of Sepúlveda himself, would be better served by an edition and/or translation based primarily on an earlier version, either that represented by the VTM family (no such edition or translation currently exists) or that represented by P. Presumably Schmitz and Patisso had this in mind in basing their translations on Menéndez y Pelayo's edition of the P manuscript.

Nonetheless, this translation follows the tradition established by Losada, Coroleu, Taranto, and Schäfer in offering a version of the fuller and more polished S manuscript. But some guidance should be given to a reader who, perfectly plausibly, wants some sense of the earlier versions which caused such a stir from around 1544 or so. Given that the dedicatory preface to the P manuscript implies that this was the version for which Sepúlveda sought official approval and licence to publish, one should be offered a chance to sketch out a rough reconstruction of that version from the translation and alternate passages offered here. Here, then, are some key steps to take to restore this version to an approximation of the P version:

- P's dedication to Luis de Mendoza is in fact prefaced to our translation of the S text.
- I.4.5: For a substantial passage in P omitted from S, see Appendix.
- I.11.1: At the beginning of this section, S has cut an account of the tyrannical nature of Amerindian societies found in P (as well as in VTM). See Appendix.
- I.11.3 (beginning): In an apparent response to criticisms, S has expanded and sharply modified an appeal in P (and VTM) to the precedent of the ancient Israelites in punishing pagan idolatry. See Appendix.
- I.12.2–3: For the substantially different version in S (largely following VTM) of this section, see Appendix.
- I.13–14: These chapters, on the monotheism of the pagan philosophers, though present in VTM, were cut in P.
- I.1.4.4: Here S cuts an interesting personal reminiscence of Cardinal Cajetan: see Appendix.
- I.15.11: This section replaces a lengthier passage in P (as well as VTM): see Appendix.
- I.18.5—I.20.2: This is an addition in S not found in either P or the earlier VTM.

---

[47] See above (n. 4) for García Pinilla's claim that the S version is post-1565, as well as Castilla Urbano's rejection of this suggestion.

- I.21.6–7 through the second sentence of II.1.1: This narrative transition between Books I and II is, of course, missing from P (as well as VTM).
- II.1.3—II.2.1: A much shorter version of this appears in P: see Appendix.
- II.2.4 (*ad fin.*)—II.3.8 (halfway through): A much shorter version was in P: see Appendix.
- II.3.9—II.7.4: This very extensive section is missing in P (but present, from II.4.1, in VTM).

* * *

A reader or translator familiar with classical Latin will generally feel at home with the Latin text of Sepúlveda's *Democrates secundus*. As the introduction to this volume has noted, Sepúlveda's range of genres as a writer was extensive, and he knew how to suit his style to the genre. Like its predecessors, the *Gonsalus* and the *Democrates primus*, this dialogue is composed in a supple and reasonably elegant Latin style. Though the genre into which these dialogues fit is the Ciceronian adaptation of the style of Plato's middle and late dialogues (where the elenchus of the earlier Socratic dialogues gives way to the authoritative pronouncements of a confidently wise figure—whether Socrates or the Athenian stranger in the *Laws*), Sepúlveda avoided the distinctive Ciceronian periodic style. It seems fair to say that in these dialogues, and perhaps especially in the *Democrates secundus*, he was determined to keep the reader's focus on the substance of his arguments, while at the same time avoiding the more austere style of the jurists and theologians. This creates a striking contrast with his more succinct and businesslike defence of the *Democrates secundus*, the *Apologia* he published in Rome in 1550, which bristles with citations from canon law and eschews literary pretensions (though the later defence does nonetheless appropriate certain passages from the dialogue).

Though the *Democrates secundus* is a relatively lucid work, it does at times present challenges for the translator. These primarily involve the difficulty of finding adequate English equivalents for particular words that play a major role in Sepúlveda's argument. These problems begin with the work's very title (in the S manuscript): *Democrates secundus, de iustis causis belli.* One obvious problem here is the inappropriate generality of the title, for Sepúlveda is not discussing justifications for wars in general, but for the specific wars that had been and were still being carried on against the Amerindians. Thus, in rendering the title, we have taken the liberty of adding the specificity that was present in the title of the P manuscript (*Democrates alter sive De iustis belli causis apud Indos*) and rendering the title: *Democrates Part Two, on the Just Reasons for the War against the Indians.* But the lexical problem here is the word *causa.* In the title, and often in text, one will find the word *causa* rendered 'reason', as in a reason offered for going to war. The Latin word *causa* was most at home in a legal context, where it referred in the first instance to 'judicial proceedings, a legal case, trial' (*Oxford Latin Dictionary*), but more often referred to the case presented by one party in such a trial: as the *OLD* put it (*s.v. causa* 2): 'the case (including the interests) of one side in a legal or other dispute, plea, cause, side'. Thus, in addition to 'reason', we have also often used words like 'motive' (e.g. 'A second motive for a just war', I.4.7) or 'justification' (e.g. I.15.11). As always, it would have been useful to have the facing Latin text in order to see when such words as 'reason', 'motive', and 'justification' render the same word *causa*. At least the reader can rest assured that the translator has carefully avoided any temptation to render *causa* by its deceptive English derivative 'cause'.

One family of words often found in this dialogue generated frequent discussion among the collaborators. This comprised the cognates *humanus* and *humanitas* and the negative *inhumanus*. The general concept *humanitas* can have the sense of 'human nature or character' (*OLD*), with a strong suggestion of 'status as a human being', and the adjective *humanus* can designate a person or group as genuinely human. But it can also refer to the display of proper human feeling, especially in the sense of kindness or mercifulness, and the adjective *humanus* in the context of human relations would naturally be rendered 'humane'. This sense is often relevant in Sepúlveda's dialogue in the context of behaviour in warfare. But *humanitas*, both in classical and Renaissance Latin, also had the sense of 'civilization' ('the quality distinguishing civilized man from savages or beasts', *OLD*)—or, to use a term common in early modern English colonial discourse, 'civility'. This usage, it should be noted, implies a potentially temporary, improvable nature, and accordingly we find Sepúlveda applying this adjective to the Amerindians in the comparative degree: when the Amerindians 'shall become more civilized (*humaniores*) ... , they will need to be treated more freely and generously' (*liberius ... liberaliusque*, II.8.1). Thus, depending on the context, *humanus* could be rendered 'human', 'humane', or 'civilized', while *inhumanus* could be 'inhuman', 'inhumane', or 'uncivilized'. Not only are the boundaries among these senses often uncertain, there is also the fact that the single Latin words *humanus* and *inhumanus* carry along with them the suggestion of the other senses in ways that no English rendering can imitate. In the process of this translation, in particular its revision, there has been an increasing tendency to choose 'civilization/civilized/uncivilized' for *humanitas/humanus/inhumanus*. But the other renderings have been used or retained when the context seems to require it. And the root senses of 'human status' and 'human' may always be lurking in a way that an Anglophone reader of the dialogue may not fully suspect. Thus, in his starkest contrast between the nature of the Spaniards and that of the Amerindians (I.9.1), he twice singles out the superior *humanitas* of the Spaniards shortly before the notorious comparison of Amerindians to apes that was (controversially, as we have seen) erased in the S manuscript. Also, even the comparative adjective *humaniores,* noted above, is susceptible to harsher translation than we have chosen, as when Anthony Pagden singled out that passage and put this phrase in italics: 'when they have become more human'.[48]

---

[48] Pagden, *Fall of Natural Man,* 116. Interestingly, in his note *ad loc.* (233n40), he noted: 'The word *humanus* is also used merely to mean "polite" or "civilized" and as a synonym for "urbanus". ... But it is

A related and even more complex and controversial challenge is posed by the nouns *servitus* and *servus,* commonly rendered 'slavery' and 'slave'. When dealing with Aristotle's concept of the 'slave by nature', Sepúlveda, whose translation of the *Politics* was published in Paris in 1548, was rendering the Greek δοῦλος, a word with the clear sense of a slave as the disposable property of a legal owner. The classical Latin word *servus* also carried this meaning of chattel slave (as did the term *mancipium*). But after the Roman Empire in the West gave way to the Germanic kingdoms of the Dark Ages, followed by the Middle Ages and the early modern period, the Latin words *servus* and *servitus,* while still used of chattel slavery, became extended to more varied forms of subordination and servitude, most notably serfdom.

Thus, while Sepúlveda is notorious as a supposedly frank advocate of the enslavement of the Amerindians, one could argue that the use of the Latin words *servitus* and *servus* in his day allowed for a more nuanced—or, if you prefer, evasive—intended meaning. In his pioneering study of Sepúlveda's views on the question of the enslavement of the Amerindians, Robert E. Quirk maintained that the bad reputation under which Sepúlveda suffers is largely due to the fact that 'two Latin words used by both disputants at Valladolid have been misinterpreted and mistranslated, to the disadvantage of Sepúlveda. The Latin words are *natura servus,* the mistranslation, "slaves by nature".[49] Quirk attributes part of the blame for the misunderstanding and mistranslation to the stylistic register of Sepúlveda's humanist Latin. While in his day the post-classical Latin coinage *esclavus* was used for a chattel slave, freeing the classical word *servus* to be applied to a serf, Sepúlveda's humanist vocabulary could not admit a barbarous word like *esclavus* into his elegant dialogue, thereby exposing his intentions to frequent misunderstanding.[50]

---

evident from the context that Sepúlveda wishes to suggest that the Indians are also something less than real men.' Rolena Adorno is too sweeping in asserting simply that Sepúlveda used 'humano' to mean 'civilized': Rolena Adorno, *The Polemics of Possession in Spanish American Narrative* (New Haven: Yale University Press, 2007), 115f. (Note that she is referring to the word that Losada tended to use in his Spanish translation; on p. 116 she even dutifully consults Covarrubias's 1611 dictionary, apparently forgetting that Sepúlveda was writing in Latin.)

[49] Robert E. Quirk, 'Some Notes on a Controversial Controversy: Juan Ginés de Sepúlveda and Natural Servitude', *Hispanic American Historical Review* 34/3 (1954): 357–64; quoted passage on p. 358.
[50] Quirk was fully aware that Sepúlveda believed that Amerindians captured in a just war could justly be *made* slaves (359). Thus, Francisco Castillo Urbano is too sweeping when he claims, citing Quirk as his authority, that Sepúlveda used *servus* only to refer to a serf-like subordinate 'who needed to pay tribute to his lord' ('a un siervo que debía pagar un tributo a su señor'): *El pensamiento de Juan Ginés de Sepúlveda,* 175, followed by Christian Schäfer, 'Conquista and the Just War', in *A Companion to Early Modern Spanish Imperial Political and Social Thought,* edited by Jörg Alejandro Tellkamp, 199–221 (Leiden: Brill, 2020), 203. Cf. also Horst Pietschmann, 'Aristotelischer Humanismus und Inhumanität? Sepúlveda und die amerikanische Ureinwohner', in *Humanismus und Neue Welt,* edited by Wolfgang Reinhard, 143–66 (Weinheim: VCH, 1987), 160. Luca Baccelli noted that earlier than Sepúlveda, Palacios Rubios had used *servus* to refer to various kinds of obligatory labour that could nonetheless be consistent with free status: '*Nihil humanum a me alienum puto*', 94.

84 SEPÚLVEDA ON THE SPANISH INVASION OF THE AMERICAS

Our practice is to render *servus* and *servitus* as 'slave' and 'slavery'. But we ask the reader to stay alert to the specific way in which Sepúlveda was using those terms in any given context.[51] Significantly, as we emphasized in the introduction to this volume, when introducing the concept of the Amerindians as *natura servi* in Book I, chapter 5, Sepúlveda was at pains to distinguish this concept of the 'philosophers' (interestingly, he doesn't mention Aristotle by name) from the formal status established by the jurists (referring here above all to Roman law).[52] Rather, the concept of 'the philosophers' is one of a general subordination of natural inferiors to natural superiors—or so he claimed here, in a passage that occurs in all states of composition. Thus, while the concept would certainly include slaves, it could also include various forms of free servitude—including serfdom or its American analogue in the institution of the *encomienda*.

Of course, while the Amerindians may be abstractly considered 'slaves by nature' solely in this extended, 'philosophical' sense, and while it is conceivable that an Amerindian society could avoid loss of *dominium* by a sincere and thorough acceptance of Christian preaching (the hypothetical case envisioned in I.19.4), the facts on the bloody ground of the Americas reveal a harsher reality. Given that Sepúlveda regarded most of the military actions of the Spaniards in America as just wars (the practice of idolatry alone constituting a breach of natural law sufficient to guarantee such wars' justice), the defeated Amerindians were liable to the fate that the law of nations (*ius gentium*) allowed for those captured on the wrong side of a just war: enslavement (as well as dispossession of goods, including territory). In chapters 2 and 3 of Book II, Sepúlveda took pains to justify this provision of the *ius gentium*, urging the tender-hearted Leopoldus to consider that enslavement is preferable to death and that it is also useful as a deterrent, hence presumably averting the enslavement of other Amerindian groups. But Sepúlveda proceeded to note that in practice the Israelites, the Greeks, and the Romans—even Julius Caesar in his conquest of Gaul—often chose not to exercise their right to enslave defeated populations. Indeed, mercy and moderation will often serve the cause of peace and security.

It is in this context and in accord with this line of thought that we should take note of an important passage (II.8.1) that appears late in the dialogue in all of its stages of evolution.[53] Here Sepúlveda drew upon the analogy of a substantial household

---

[51] We are following here the practice and warning of Christian Schäfer ('Einleitung', LXX–LXXI), who notes that he renders the words as *Sklave* and *Sklaverei*, but admits that what Sepúlveda actually meant by his Latin words varies with the context. See also Schäfer, 'Conquest and the Just War', 203.

[52] Though Sepúlveda does not cite Aristotle in the text here, there is a reference to Book 1 of the *Politics* in the margin of the S and P text here (Losada ed., p. 120; Menéndez y Pelayo ed., p. 288) and also in the Madrid manuscript (M, p. 14r)—and presumably in V and T as well.

[53] In the P version, the passage is on p. 364 of the Menéndez y Pelayo edition; in the M manuscript, it is on 89r. It also occurs in V and T.

in Spain, where a master would exercise authority over three categories of subordinates: 1) sons; 2) 'slaves or bondsmen (*servi seu mancipia*)'; 3) 'servants of free-born status (*ministri conditionis liberae*)'. Thus, not only did Sepúlveda's classical Latin allow him (*pace* Quirk) to express the status of free servants without using *servi* in its extended, post-classical sense, but his words here also serve as a useful reminder that in a substantial household in the Spain of his day there would likely have been actual slaves.[54] Using this analogy of a household, Sepúlveda asserted that the American 'barbarians ought to be governed like servants (*ministros*)— albeit free ones—through a power that is a certain mixture of masterly and paternal power', with the promise of being 'treated more freely and generously' as they become more civilized (*humaniores*, see above). True, even then they would not be granted the rights and privileges of freeborn Spaniards, but they would have travelled a marked distance from the slaves that the *ius gentium* would have allowed them to become (provided, of course, one accepted Sepúlveda's claim that the Spaniards were engaged in just wars in the Americas).

Given this complexity of Sepúlveda's views on the status of Amerindians as, variously, 'slaves by nature' (in a sense more metaphorical than Aristotle intended), losers in just wars whose enslavement the *ius gentium* fully allowed, and yet also people whom it was merciful and expedient to treat as free servants, the reader needs to exercise due caution when encountering the terms 'slave' and 'servitude' here for *servus* and *servitus*.[55] And yet one is seldom entirely free of the suspicion that Sepúlveda's views on the status of the Amerindians were not so much complex as they were strategically evasive. While clearly eager to counter those who accused him of advocating outright slavery for the Amerindians, he was no doubt content to allow a considerable measure of hermeneutic leeway to readers who were sympathetic to the *encomenderos*.

Finally, we should note that when quoting biblical passages Sepúlveda often supplied his own Latin versions rather than following the Vulgate readings. Our practice in translating has been to keep close to Sepúlveda's own version, while at the same time approximating as far as possible the wording of the New Revised Standard Version.

---

[54] See Tamar Herzog, 'How Did Early-Modern Slaves in Spain Disappear? The Antecedents', *Republic of Letters* 3/1 (2012): 1–7, a useful reminder of how common slaves were in the households and streets of early modern Spain.

[55] For an influential recent study that scrupulously avoids the common assumption that Sepúlveda was an advocate for enslaving the Amerindians, see Adorno, *The Polemics of Possession*, 117–19. See also David A. Lupher, *Romans in a New World: Classical Models in Sixteenth-Century Spanish America* (Ann Arbor: University of Michigan Press, 2003), 113–14.

Democrates Part Two, on the Just Reasons for the War against the Indians

Preface to the Dialogue 'On the Just Reasons for War' by Ginés de Sepúlveda to His Excellency, Luis Mendoza, Count of Tendilla and Marquis of Mondéjar

Whether it is by means of a just war or instead through injustice that the kings of Spain and our countrymen have reduced to rule and continue to see to the subjugation of those barbarian peoples inhabiting the western and southern region whom Spanish custom calls Indians, and what would be a justification for ruling over those people—this, as you are well aware, distinguished marquis, is a subject of major dispute, and serious consequences are involved in its resolution.[56] For it affects the fame and justice of great and religious princes, and it has a bearing on the governance of very many peoples. And so it stands to reason that there has been a dispute with serious wrangling about these matters, sometimes among learned men in private, but also publicly debated in the highly authoritative royal council established for the governing of those peoples and regions—a council which Emperor Charles, our king and also the Roman emperor, has willed that you preside over and guide, in view of your deep intellect and wisdom.

Therefore, in the midst of so great a disagreement involving the most learned and serious men over extremely important matters, given that I have had some thoughts on these matters that seemed able to settle the dispute, I have decided that I should not hold back in a matter of public concern when so many people have become caught up in it, nor should I keep silent when they are speaking, especially since I have been advised by many men of great authority to lay out my thoughts in writing and make clear my opinion, which they seem to have approved when I earlier presented it to them in a few words. Therefore I have willingly taken the trouble to pursue the question in a dialogue in the Socratic format which our Jerome and Augustine had adopted on several occasions, and I have brought together the just reasons for undertaking a war in general and the proper method of conducting it, and have along the way laid out various other subordinate questions germane to the subject which are very useful for understanding it. This is the book I am sending to you, as a token and testimony of my most ready goodwill and respect for you, whom I have for a long time devotedly venerated and respected on account of your exceptional virtues of every sort and your singular humanity.

---

[56] While the rest of this translation is based on the Salamanca manuscript (S), this preface is found only in the earlier Santander manuscript (P). Luis Mendoza was president of the Council of the Indies (1535–50) and the older brother of Antonio Mendoza, first viceroy of New Spain (1535–50), afterwards viceroy of Peru (1550–52).

Therefore, please accept this little gift, a trifle, indeed, but one nonetheless arising from great affection and extraordinary goodwill, and a work concerning a matter especially suited to your interests, official duty, and established practice. For since you have for a long time now carried out with great personal distinction in both peace and war the will and command of Emperor Charles, who has fully noted your loyalty and virtues in both spheres of activity, it follows that nothing tends to be more important to you, as common opinion consistently testifies, than justice and religion, in which the essence of all virtues is comprehended. Given that no one could cultivate these virtues who exercises an unjust power over any people or who is in any capacity a prefect or minister of a prince who does so, I have no doubt that you will find most welcome a little book in which you will find confirmed and demonstrated by the securest and plainest arguments the justice, until now mired in ambiguity and obscurity, of the rule and administration which has been entrusted to you. In addition, I have set forth many things here relating to the just and proper method of ruling that have been handed down by great philosophers and theologians as being fully consistent with the laws of nature, the common laws, and Christian teachings.

In a work entitled *Democrates primus*, which I published earlier with the aim of refuting heretics who condemn any war as though it is prohibited by divine law, I had introduced two men conducting a dispute in Rome who uttered certain things relevant to the present question. Accordingly, I have thought it not improper to have the same men holding a discussion about these matters in the gardens at my place on the shore of the Pisuerga, so that they could bring to completion the disputation already begun on the respectability of warfare, with a few of their earlier views inevitably repeated. Of these men, the German Leopoldus, repeating through a kind of hereditary contagion a good deal of the errors of the Lutherans, begins the discussion in this way:

The Dialogue which is Entitled Democrates Secundus on the Just Reasons for War by Juan Ginés de Sepúlveda, Doctor of Arts and Sacred Theology

Book I

1 [*Whether war may ever be justly undertaken*]
(1) **Leopoldus:** Democrates, I shall say once again and indeed many times over that there is no line of reasoning by which the waging of war, especially by Christians, is acceptable to me. I recall that we have already had a long dispute of three days about this matter in Rome, at the Vatican.

Democrates: So, then, it seems that what you want is that human life be free of great nuisances and disadvantages, and, in short, of great calamities. If only the

88   SEPÚLVEDA ON THE SPANISH INVASION OF THE AMERICAS

greatest and best God would grant to all kings and princes of whatever state the sort of attitude that would make each one content with his own possessions and not make an armed invasion of the territories of others through avarice, nor seek glory or fame at others' cost through savage and impious ambition—both of which evils have driven many princes at cross-purposes and have armed them for the mutual destruction of peoples and for remarkable losses for the human race, with tranquillity spurned and peace held in contempt. Peoples who lack peace seem to me to lack the greatest portion of happiness that can fall the lot of states. We say that those states are happy and blessed only when they guide their lives with virtue in the enjoyment of tranquillity. For I judge that it is not a trivial or minor thing but the greatest good we seek when we pray with the angelical utterance in our services: 'Glory to God in the highest, and peace on earth to men.'[57]

(2) **Leopoldus:** Sacred Scripture is full of such testimonials. For what else did Christ order his Apostles to pray upon entering houses than happiness, in those words that he prescribed: 'Peace to this house'; or those other words: 'I shall give peace in your territories; seek peace and follow it'?[58] What else do those words declare than that in peace lies the greatest good? Though this is how matters stand, nonetheless I see—and am indeed astonished—that certain Christian kings never withdraw from arms and wage war so constantly that they seem actually to take delight in wars and discords.

Democrates: It makes a major difference whether, on the one hand, someone conducts wars undertaken for just and even necessary reasons, not in a sluggish and retiring frame of mind but resolutely and intently, not unwilling to undergo dangers when duty requires; or, on the other hand, whether he takes delight in wars for their own sakes, wars sought out on any random excuse. The former is the mark of a great man and one pre-eminent for virtue, whose innate and mature excellence, the philosophers teach, is indicated by his delight in its exercise; while the latter is the characteristic of a disorderly man who stands far apart, not only from Christian piety but even from humanity and who (as Homer says and Aristotle repeats) 'lacks law and tribe and home'.[59]

For a war should never be sought out for its own sake any more than hunger, poverty, pain, or other evils of that sort. But just as those calamities that bring discomfort but not disgrace are sometimes endured properly and piously by most excellent and pious men for the sake of some great good, so the greatest princes are on occasion forced through necessity to undertake a war for the sake of great benefits. For wise men judge that good men ought to wage a war in such a way that by means of the war 'nothing other than peace might seem to have been sought'.[60] In

---

[57] Luke 2:14.
[58] Luke 10:5; Leviticus 26:6 and Psalm 34:14 (33:15).
[59] Homer, *Iliad* 9.63; Aristotle, *Politics* 1.1.9 (1253a5).
[60] Aristotle, *Nicomachean Ethics* 10.7.6 (1177b6); *Politics* 7.13.16 (1334a15–16).

sum, a war ought not to be undertaken unless hesitantly and soberly and on the basis of the most just and even necessary reasons. 'A war', says Augustine, 'ought to be a matter of necessity in order that God might free us from that necessity and preserve us in peace. For peace is not sought in order that war may be waged, but rather war is waged in order that peace may be obtained.'[61]

Leopoldus: It is as you say, Democrates. I, however, believe that either there are no justifications for undertaking a war or that they are extremely rare.

Democrates: I, on the contrary, believe them to be many and frequent. For it is neither human goodness nor religious piety that offers or creates just reasons for undertaking a war, but men's crimes and wicked desires, of which the life of men is full and by which it is constantly troubled. For it is the nature of a most excellent prince to do nothing rashly, nothing passionately, to explore all the avenues of peace, to abandon nothing untried if he might be able in any way apart from warfare to repel the outrages of unjust and troublesome men and to look out for the safety and benefit of peoples entrusted to his care, and to live up to his duty. For this is what virtue, this is what religion, this is what humanity demands. But if after having tried everything he will have had no success and he will have seen his fairness and moderation defeated by the pride and baseness of unjust men, he has no reason to fear that, upon taking up arms, he will appear to be waging war rashly or unjustly.

(3) Leopoldus: But would he not be acting more properly and more in the spirit of Christian piety if he yielded to the wickedness of bad men, endured injuries with a calm spirit, and regarded men's customs and all human laws as less important than divine and gospel law? It was in accord with that law that Christ ordered us to love even our enemies and to endure insults and losses with patience.[62]

Democrates: You're resorting to nonsense again, Leopoldus, and I see that we expended a lot of effort to no purpose in that Vatican discussion of ours on the propriety of warfare which you mentioned just a bit earlier. For I have not been able to persuade you that wars are sometimes waged without the law of the gospel standing in opposition to them.

Leopoldus: On the contrary, we occupied ourselves well there; for during those three days you discussed in a varied and full way many matters concerning religion and every kind of virtue, especially those that touch upon warfare, and after the recent error of some of my fellow Germans had led me astray, you led me to think that not all wars have been forbidden to Christians—at least not those which are undertaken for the purpose of repelling injuries. For you persuaded me that this is permissible for all men through the law of nature, and you discussed many noteworthy things about the laws of nature that have by now largely slipped my mind.

---

[61] Augustine, Letter 189.57.6.
[62] Luke 6:27–29.

Therefore, now that a piece of luck has brought it about that we could meet in this royal and very famous town of Spain and we have found some free time in these beautiful gardens by the banks of the Pisuerga, it would be most pleasing to me to hear from you some things that are germane to that earlier discussion, and if certain matters which you dealt with more fully in that Roman discussion shall strike you as worth repeating in summary fashion, it would do no harm to hear those same things twice.

(4) **Democrates**: So what new point touching on that question of the respectability of warfare would you wish to hear from me?

Leopoldus: Just a few things, indeed, but not inconsequential—for they pertain to the justice of war, without which an upright man will never induce his spirit to take up arms. Moreover, they are matters that have occurred to me when I have been thinking about the New World—that is, about those very remote islands and that other continent that not so long ago have been discovered by the voyages of the Spaniards and have been reduced to rule by their arms. For when I recently happened to be strolling about with friends at the court of Prince Philip, Hernán Cortés, the Marqués del Valle, walked by. Inspired by the sight of him, we embarked upon an extended discussion concerning the deeds performed by him and other captains of Charles in that western and southern region that was utterly unknown to the ancient men of our world.

These doings were, I confess, occasion of much wonder to me on account of their varied and unexpected novelty. But as I subsequently reflected upon those same things, it occurred to me again and again to doubt and to fear that it may not have been sufficiently on the basis of justice and Christian piety that the Spaniards inflicted war upon those innocent human beings who have done nothing to deserve bad treatment at their hands. Therefore, I would like to know what you think about that war and others like it that have come about through no binding necessity but from a certain settled intention—not to say through inordinate desire and greed. At the same time, I wish you would set forth concisely for me all the reasons for which a war would seem to you to be justly undertaken, and that you would pursue the question in a few words with your customary skill by virtue of your remarkable talent and deep mind.

2 [*The authority of natural law*]

(1) **Democrates**: I shall indeed do what you demand, not indeed relying upon talent or any special ability, since I am only too aware of how little I have, but because, as you say, we find ourselves at leisure, and you come upon me at a time when I am not entirely unprepared for discussing those matters. For you are neither the only nor the first of those who have conferred with me when these same scruples have troubled them. But as you were saying just a bit earlier, some things from that earlier discussion of ours will need to be brought up again in summary fashion, and foremost among them the following principle, which is the foundation stone of this

DEMOCRATES PART TWO 91

question and of many others: that whatever comes about through the right or law of nature happens also in accord with divine and gospel law.

(2) For if Christ (according to the Gospel) orders us not to resist evil, and when someone strikes us on one cheek he urges us to offer him the other to be struck, and when someone wishes to take our tunic he bids us to yield him our robe as well, it shouldn't seem as though he was immediately abolishing the law of nature in accord with which everyone is allowed to repel violence with violence when acting under the direction of innocent self-defence.[63] For we ought to fulfil those commands not always in actual fact, but (as Augustine puts it) 'in the training of the heart, so that, if a particular situation and reasons of piety should ever demand that we do that, we would not refuse.'[64]

As an authority for this interpretation we have not only Paul, but also Christ himself. For when a blow had been delivered to him at the order of the high priest, Paul was so far from offering his other cheek to be struck that, indignant at the injury, he made sure that the one who ordered the blow was squelched with a reproach: 'God will strike you, you whited wall', he said—that is, as Augustine puts it, 'You hypocrite; you sit there and judge me in accord with the law, but it's against the law that you order me to be struck.'[65] Moreover, as Augustine points out, when Christ was struck in the same way, he himself did not offer his other cheek, but reproached the man who struck him in order that he not increase the injury: 'If I have spoken badly, furnish testimony about the wrong; if I have spoken well, why do you beat me?'[66]

So these are not laws that are mandatory in some way different from what we have said; rather, they are advice and exhortations that pertain not so much to daily life as to apostolic perfection. As Gregory the Great says: 'It is by a special commandment for the few who are more perfect and not in a general way for everyone that the words that the rich young man heard were uttered: "Go and sell all that you have, and give it to the poor, and you will have treasure in heaven, and come and follow me".'[67] For Christ wished that our common and civil life be comprehended and maintained simply by the laws of the Decalogue and other natural laws, and he taught that there is sufficient assistance in those same laws for gaining eternal life. When someone asked him, 'Master, what good thing should I do in order that I might have eternal life?', he replied, 'If you wish to enter upon Life, observe the commandments.' 'Which ones?', he asked, and Christ said, 'You will not commit murder, you will not commit adultery', and he goes on through the other laws of the Decalogue. 'But if you wish to be perfect', he said, 'go and sell all you have, and give

---

[63] Luke 6:29.

[64] Augustine, Letter 138.2.13 and *Contra Faustum* (*Against Faustum*) 22.79.

[65] Acts 23:3; Augustine, *De sermone Domini in monte* (*On the Sermon on the Mount*) I.19.58.

[66] John 18:23; Augustine, *De consensu Evangelistarum* (*On the Harmony of the Evangelists*) 3.6 and *In Evangelium Ioannis tractatus* (*Tractates on the Gospel of John*) 113.4.

[67] Gregory I, *Moralia in Iob* (*Commentary on Job*) 26.27.

92 SEPÚLVEDA ON THE SPANISH INVASION OF THE AMERICAS

it to the poor, and follow me.'[68] That is similar to the admonitions and exhortations about the enduring of injuries that we just mentioned. Therefore, Christ said in another place with the same intent, 'Do unto others as you would have them do unto you. For this is the law and the prophets.'[69] The most sagacious men pre-eminent for learning and Christian piety interpret these words in such a way as to show that by means of them Christ affirmed all natural laws.

(3) To this also pertains what Paul wrote to the Romans: 'He who loves his neighbour has fulfilled the law; for "You shall not commit adultery; you shall not kill; you shall not steal; you shall not give false testimony; you shall not covet", and whatever else is ordered is contained in this utterance: "You shall love your neighbour as yourself" '[70]—no doubt because all natural and divine laws about things that ought to be done pertain to keeping men to their duty and preserving human society in this life, in order that in this way one may take a step to that other, eternal life. This society is most especially held together by mutual love and goodwill; indeed, in the mutual love of men we also understand piety and love for God. For the love of God is most especially to be perceived in this: whether one observes the laws of God. 'If anyone loves me', Christ said, 'he will keep my word.'[71] For, though there may occur among Christians no fewer controversies than formerly occurred among the Romans, and there might seem to be need of no fewer laws for properly curtailing and settling them than those contained in the Twelve Tables and the fifty books of the Digest, nonetheless Christ, after repeating a few laws of the Decalogue, rolled up those and all other laws touching upon customs and proper actions into one law which supports that law of nature by which human society is held together.

For by natural law, as the most eminent author Gratian propounds, 'nothing else is ordered than that which God wants to happen; nothing else is forbidden but that which God forbids to happen.'[72] For indeed the truth is that, since there are, all told, three fit and proper kinds of government (kingship, the public order of the best men, and that which in common parlance is termed a republic), no law can be passed conformably to any of them that would not also be in accord with nature— or at least none that would deviate from the natural order. For the aim of all of them is safety and the public good—that is, felicity, which is to be understood in two senses. One is perfect and final and the end-goal of all good things, which the clear vision and contemplation of God brings about; and, as such, it is called eternal life. The other is imperfect and incomplete, the sort that can fall to the lot of human beings in this life—this moreover consists in the practice of virtue, as the philosophers make clear, and it is the road and as it were the stairway to perfect felicity.[73]

---

[68] Matthew 19:16–21.
[69] Matthew 7:12.
[70] Romans 13:8–9.
[71] John 14:23.
[72] Gratian, *Decretum*, D. 9, c. 11.
[73] Aristotle, *Nicomachean Ethics* 10.7.1–10.8.3 (1177a12–1177b24).

It is through this felicity that 'blessed are the peacemakers, blessed are the pure of heart', and others of whom Christ makes mention in that passage in the Gospel.[74]

(4) Since, then, according even to the pagan philosophers, not to mention religious and Christian men, in every good state all laws ought to be oriented to the practice of virtue, and virtue by its very nature is, second to God, the thing most to be sought out and cultivated, it turns out that all the best laws are most especially fitted to nature, in accord with the view not only of the best and wisest men but also of God. Therefore this is all the more the case in that state of which God is himself the founder and the legislator.

3 [*Natural laws are known to all men*]
(1) **Leopoldus:** You seem to me to have established and confirmed the power and authority of natural laws abundantly, copiously, and by laying deep foundations. Still, you have not yet established and declared to us here just what the law of nature is.

Democrates: The philosophers define the law of nature as 'that which everywhere has the same power, not because there is an agreement on this or that'.[75] For their part, the theologians define it in different words, but ones that tend to the same end, along these lines: 'The natural law is the participation in the eternal law in a created being capable of reason'.[76] Moreover, the eternal law, as Augustine defines it, is the will of God, 'which orders that the natural order be preserved and forbids that it be disturbed'.[77]

Furthermore, man has a share in this eternal law through right reason and a propensity to duty and virtue. For while a man may be prone to evil through some eager desire, he has nonetheless a tendency towards the good through reason. Therefore, proper reason and a proclivity to performing duties and approving the tasks of virtue both are and are called natural law. This is that law of which Paul spoke when he referred to the good men among the pagans who were in the habit of doing what is right through a natural instinct. 'They are', he said, 'a law unto themselves, who manifest the work of the law written in their own hearts'.[78] Therefore, to those asking in the psalm, 'Who will show us good things?', this answer is given: 'The light of your countenance, Lord, has been signed upon us',[79] for this is the light of right reason, which is understood to be natural law.

For that which is good and just and, contrariwise, that which is wicked and unjust, this law makes clear in good men, not only Christians, but in all men who have not ruined upright nature through twisted practices—and all the more so

---

[74] Matthew 5:8–9.
[75] Aristotle, *Nicomachean Ethics* 5.7.1 (1134b19–20).
[76] Aquinas, *Summa theologica* (*ST*) II-II, q. 91, art. 2.
[77] Augustine, *Contra Faustum* 22.30.
[78] Romans 2:14–15.
[79] Psalm 4:6.

94 SEPÚLVEDA ON THE SPANISH INVASION OF THE AMERICAS

to the extent that any given individual is better and more intelligent. It was concerning this law that a very important author, Cyprian, at once bishop and martyr, spoke: 'Nor does the written sacred law contradict natural law in anything; but the condemnation of evil and the choosing of the good are divinely implanted in the rational soul in such a way that no one could rightly make excuses, given that no one is lacking the knowledge for the pursuit of these things, and given that we both know what ought to be done and are able to perform what we know.'[80]

(2) **Leopoldus**: Why so much about natural laws and pagan philosophers?

Democrates: Simply to make it clear that the discernment of natural laws is not to be sought only from Christians and through gospel writings, but also from those philosophers who are considered to have discoursed best and most wisely about the nature of things and about human behaviour and about every sort of system of government. It was about this that Augustine wrote in the second book of *On Christian Teaching*: 'The works of the philosophers contain some very useful moral precepts, and even some things about the worship of the one true God himself are to be found among them, much like gold and silver that they didn't create themselves but dug up, as it were, from certain mines of the divine providence that has been poured forth everywhere. Just as the Jews (took gold and silver) from the Egyptians, so a Christian ought to take from those men for the purpose of spreading the gospel.'[81]

It is agreed that the foremost of the philosophers are Plato, whom Augustine preferred to all others, and Aristotle, whose teachings—except on a very few subjects, which lie beyond human capacity and cannot be explored by a human without the help of divine revelation—have been received by subsequent ages with such great agreement and approval that nowadays they seem not the words of some philosopher but the shared ideas and decisions of wise men generally. For it was not without reason that our Jerome wrote that Aristotle was the prince of philosophers and without any doubt was a marvel and a great miracle in the whole of nature, into whom seems to have been poured virtually whatever the human race could receive in accord with nature.[82]

4 [*The just reasons for war*]

(1) **Leopoldus**: Then let's return to the point at issue, and if you think there are any reasons that offer a basis for undertaking and waging a war justly and piously, set them forth now.

---

[80] Not, in fact, Cyprian, but Arnaldus Bonaevallis (Arnaud de Bonneval), *De cardinalibus operibus Christi* (*On the Principal Doings of Christ*), §4, *De baptismo Christi* (see *Patrologia Latina,* vol. 189, col. 1632B).

[81] Augustine, *De doctrina christiana* 2.40.60 (largely paraphrased at end).

[82] Pseudo-Jerome, *Regula monachorum* (*The Monks' Rule*) 11 (see *Patrologia Latina,* vol. 30, col. 415A, not 402B–C, as Taranto, followed by Schäfer, claimed).

Democrates: A just war needs not only just reasons for its undertaking, but also a legitimate initiator, the good intention of the one waging it, and a proper method of conducting it. For it is not allowed to any random person to undertake a war, except for the purpose of warding off an injury, for to repel an injury within the limits of innocent self-defence is allowed to anyone by the law of nature—or, better, as Pope Innocent [IV] affirmed in the Council of Lyon: 'All laws and all rights allow everyone to repel violence with violence and defend oneself. Therefore, the initiation of a war, either conducted personally or through a deputy, is permitted to no one except a prince or those who have the supreme authority in a state.'[83] For, as Augustine says in his dispute with Faustus, 'The natural order, in accordance with the tranquillity of the human race, requires that the power and the decision to make war lie within the hands of the prince.'[84]

(2) Also, Isidore of Seville denied that a war waged without a formal declaration is just.[85] Furthermore, to declare a war—that is, to publicly summon citizens to arms—belongs to the supreme power of the state, for it arises from those matters in which the leadership of a state is most involved. Thus princes are to be understood as those who are in charge of a proper state, who govern with the highest authority and without recourse to some more powerful leader. For others, who are not in charge of the whole but only of part of a kingdom or state or who exercise rule on the orders of a superior, are not called princes but more accurately prefects.

I have said that for the justice of a war there is need of an upright intention on the part of the one who is undertaking and waging it—that is, a good aim and a proper plan—since, according to Dionysius, 'this is the nature of virtue and duty, that unless it has all of its parts, it loses the name of virtue and duty.'[86] For sinning in any given case occurs in many ways; but to act rightly occurs only in one way (provided, to be sure, that other incidental things, which the crowd of philosophers call 'circumstantial matters', are taken into account), just as the mathematicians declare that there is only one straight line that can be drawn from one point to another, but that curved or oblique lines are infinite; and just as there is only one way for archers to hit the target, while there are as many ways as you could imagine of bending aside from it. Therefore sinning happens in many ways in one and the same affair, as the philosophers teach, but proper action occurs in only one way.[87]

In the case of circumstantial things, however, the consideration of the end holds the principal place. For in things that need to be done the end is, according to those same philosophers, the same thing as propositions among the mathematicians,

---

[83] Acts of the First Council of Lyon (1245); see Gian Domenico Mansi, *Sacrorum conciliorum nova et amplissima collectio*, vol. 23 (Venice: Antonio Zatta, 1779), 673. This was based on *Digest* 9.2.45.4: 'vim enim vi defendere omnes leges omniaque iura permittunt' ('for all laws and rights allow warding off violence by means of violence').

[84] Augustine, *Contra Faustum* 22.75.

[85] Isidore of Seville, *Etymologiae* (*Etymologies*) 18.1.2.

[86] Pseudo-Dionysius the Areopagite, *Divine Names*, Bk. 4.31.

[87] Aristotle, *Nicomachean Ethics* 2.6.14 (1106b29–31).

and it is just that all things be given their designation on the basis of their end.[88] This holds true to such an extent that someone who commits adultery for the sake of gain ought to be called unjust and greedy rather than an adulterer.[89] Therefore it makes a major difference with regard to the justice of a war in what spirit each person undertakes the war—that is, what aim he sets forth for himself for waging the war. It was with this in mind that our Augustine said, 'To go to war is not a sin, but to go to war for the sake of booty *is* a sin.'[90] Nor is it a criminal act to govern a state, but to govern a state for the sake of augmenting one's wealth appears worthy of condemnation.

(3) I also pointed out that, just as in other things, so also in the waging of wars moderation needs to be observed, so that, if possible, no injury would happen to the innocent, nor harm come to emissaries, foreigners, priests, or sacred things, nor enemies be harmed more than is just, for word must be kept even with enemies once it has been given to them, and anger against them must not be indulged in more than as accords with the degree of their guilt. Therefore the same Augustine says in another passage: 'A lust for doing harm, cruelty in taking vengeance, a militant and implacable spirit, a savageness in rebellion, a passion for dominating, and things of this sort—these are the things which are held blameworthy in wars.'[91] With these words he makes it clear that moderation, too—in addition to good intention, which is most especially said to be the end aimed at—is called for in undertaking and waging a war. Moreover, the aim of a just war is living in peace and tranquillity justly and with virtue, with the elimination of bad men's ability to do harm and to sin—in sum, in order that measures may be taken for the public good of men. For this is the aim of all laws that have been passed in a way befitting a state that has been established properly and in accord with nature.

(4) **Leopoldus**: So, then, the authority for initiating a war undertaken not from the necessity of repelling an immediate injury (which necessity grants everyone that power through the law of nature) but from other motives—this authority you determine rests with princes (that is, those properly understood to be such) or the magistrates of some free republic, by whose deliberations and supreme power the commonwealth is governed—and you deny that they can justly decide upon war if they resort to arms when induced by any other motive than the public good, or when it is in their power to look out for the public good in some other way.

Democrates: That is exactly what I believe.

Leopoldus: Therefore will we be able to doubt that *any* war that has been initiated in accord with the conditions that you have set forth was waged justly? What if some prince, induced not by avarice or lust for rule but in order to look after his

---

[88] Aristotle, *Nicomachean Ethics* 7.8.4 (1151a17–18).
[89] Aristotle, *Nicomachean Ethics* 5.2.4 (1130a24–28).
[90] Pseudo-Augustine, *Sermon* 82, *De verbis Evangelii Lucae* ('On the Words of the Evangelist Luke') 3.12–14 (see *Patrologia Latina*, vol. 39, col. 1904).
[91] Augustine, *Contra Faustum* 22.74.

own state suffering from insufficiencies of fields and territories, should inflict on his neighbours a war by which he might take possession of their fields and virtually essential booty?

(5) **Democrates**: By no means. For that would be brigandage, not warfare. But in order for a just war to be undertaken there ought to be underlying just motives,[92] of which the most weighty and the one most especially congruent with nature is that force inflicted may be repelled with force, when no other way is allowed. For as we said before, on the authority of Pope Innocent, 'all laws and all rights allow one to repel force with force and grant to all the right to defend themselves and their possessions'—not only at that moment in time when the violence is inflicted, but also if the resistance happens at the first moment possible, for example as soon as the matter comes to be known, and when the resources have been assembled for somehow warding off the injury and recovering things that have been carried off. Still, unless this happens under the direction of a prince or on a prince's authority, this will not properly be called a war but a defensive action, which will be just only so long as it happens within the guidelines of blameless self-defence. For if it exceeds the limit of self-defence, punishment will be levied concerning the violence or damage incurred, as the rescript of the same Innocent makes clear. Therefore in that sort of dispute the things seized will not remain in the possession of those who seized them, and wrongs inflicted will have to be punished by laws or by the authority of the prince.

(6) Another line of reasoning is this: if a prince or state is provoked by war or by a wrong which ought to be warded off by war through open hostilities, it is precisely for this sort of war that nature has armed even the other living beings with claws, horns, hooves, or in other ways, but to man she has given in place of all these arms manual dexterity through which his hand is able to make use of spear, sword, and any other sort of weapons.[93] Moreover, as the same Philosopher says in another passage, man is able to make use of cleverness and the natural power of his mind, which the Philosopher himself calls prudence and virtue—but since he says that man is able to make use of these faculties for both good and bad purposes, he reveals that he has misused these terms, for in another place he affirms that no one can misuse virtue.[94]

(7) A second motive for a just war is in order to recover things that have been carried off. We see that Abraham followed this motive in the war in which he proceeded against Chedorlaomer, king of the Elamites, and his allied princes, who

---

[92] The rest of I.4.5 replaces a substantially different passage in the P (Santander) manuscript. See Appendix.

[93] Aristotle, *De partibus animalium* (*On the Parts of Animals*) 687a7. In this passage I have followed the text offered by the Rome, Toledo, and Madrid manuscripts. Also, Losada seems wrong in taking *alia ratio est* to mean *caso distinto es*. This section clearly offers a further justification for war based on nature. Given that nature has equipped animals for self-defence, it stands to reason that nature intended man's hands and their artificial extensions for self-defensive warfare.

[94] Aristotle, *Politics* 1.1.12 (1253a34–36); *Magna Moralia* 1206b17.

after the pillaging of Sodom led off his nephew Lot as a captive, along with a huge amount of booty.[95] By this it is made clear that it is lawful to undertake a war in order to recover not only one's own things but also one's friends' things that have been wrongly seized—and to seek requital for wrongs done to friends.

(8) A third motive is to punish people who have inflicted an injury when they haven't been punished by their own state, which is in the habit of overlooking wicked deeds. Not only is this done in order that both the malefactors and those who, by their consent to the deed, became partners in wrongdoing may, as a result of their just punishment, become slower to commit wicked acts in the future, but also so that others may be deterred by their example. Here I could mention many wars that were waged by the Greeks and Romans on this motive with the great approval of men, whose consensus is considered a law of nature. Such was the war that the Spartans waged against the Messenians on account of Spartan maidens raped in the course of a solemn sacrifice conducted by the Messenians—a war that the Spartans extended for a ten-year period. Likewise the war in which the Romans punished the Corinthians on account of ambassadors who were treated outrageously contrary to the law of nations. But examples will be more properly sought from Sacred Scripture. There it is recorded that, on account of rape and murder inflicted upon the wife of a Levite in the town of Gibeah of the tribe of Benjamin, war was inflicted by the other sons of Israel upon this city and upon the consenting tribe, a war in which almost the entire tribe was destroyed in a massacre, and cities with their villages were burned to the ground.[96] Similarly, the Maccabees Jonathan and Simon, having taken up arms in order to avenge the death of their brother John, attacking the sons of Jambri, made a great slaughter of them.[97]

(9) **Leopoldus**: Are you saying that the avenging of injuries is permissible for good and religious men? What force, then, have those divine words in Deuteronomy: 'Vengeance is mine, and I myself shall render retribution?'[98] Don't they make it clear that the right of taking vengeance rests solely in the power of God?

Democrates: I don't deny that, but God does not always carry out vengeance himself directly, but often through his deputies—that is, through princes and magistrates. For the prince 'is God's minister', according to Paul, 'an avenger for God's wrath against the person who does evil'.[99] Accordingly, a private person is not allowed to proceed with arms against injuries done to him, though he *is* allowed to ward off immediate injuries and to oppose those who are pressing upon him, nor is he forbidden to seek punishments through laws and magistrates, provided that he

---

[95] Genesis 14:8–16.
[96] Judges 20.
[97] 1 Maccabees 9:36–40.
[98] Deuteronomy 32:35.
[99] Romans 13:4.

does so without giving way to hatred—but this is so that a limit may be placed upon injury, and so that wicked men may be deterred by the example of the punishment.

Those who represent the state, however, are permitted to proceed against injuries done both to themselves (insofar as the injuries spill over into the state itself) and to individual citizens, for the good order and dignity of the state demand it— indeed, it is not only permitted; it is even necessary. If indeed they are willing—as they most certainly ought to be willing—to undertake the duty entrusted to them by God, they then bear the sword not without proper justification.

These, then, are the three motives for a just war that Isidore brought together in the few words that I have mentioned and that have been gathered into the Decreta of the church. Isidore includes the punishment of injuries in the discussion of the recovery of things seized, for while punishments may now and then be demanded in and of themselves, they are more commonly demanded along with the return of things that have been seized.

(10) There are also other motives for a just war that are indeed less broadly recognized and occur less frequently. They are nonetheless considered very just, and they are supported by both natural and divine law. There is one of these that most especially applies to those barbarians, popularly called Indians, whose advocacy you seem to me to have taken upon yourself. It states that when those people whose natural condition is such that they ought to obey others nonetheless resist their rule, they may be reduced to subjection by force of arms if no other path lies open. For the greatest of the philosophers affirm that this is a just war according to the law of nature.[100]

5 [*The barbarians are slaves by nature*]

(1) **Leopoldus:** These are astonishing things you are saying, Democrates, and beyond the received opinion of learned men.

Democrates: Astonishing, perhaps, but only to those who greet philosophy from the threshold. Therefore, I am all the more astonished that you, a learned man, suppose that an old teaching of the philosophers and one judged especially in accord with nature is new.

Leopoldus: Has anyone been born with such bad luck that he would have been condemned to slavery by nature? For what else is it to be subjected by nature to the rule of another than to be a slave by nature? Or do you think those jurists who often pursue the rationale of nature are joking when they affirm that all men were in the beginning born free and that slavery was brought in by the law of nations contrary to nature?

(2) **Democrates:** I certainly do say that jurists both are quite serious and lay down rules most prudently, and yet by the word 'servitude' the jurists mean something

---

[100] Aristotle, *Politics* 1.3.8 (1256b23–27).

far different from what the philosophers express. For the jurists call by the name of 'servitude' a condition that is unusual and results from the violence of men and the law of nations and sometimes also civil law, while the philosophers use the word 'servitude' to mean a native slowness of wit and inhumane and barbaric customs. Moreover, you ought to bear in mind that not all kinds of rule are embraced within a single category, but within many. For in one manner and with one sort of right a father rules over his children; in another way a husband rules over a wife; in yet another way a master rules over a slave; in another way a magistrate rules over citizens; in yet another way a king rules over the peoples and individuals who have been subjected to his rule. Though these forms of rule may be diverse, given that they exist in accord with right reason they all rest upon the law of nature—a varied law, to be sure, but one derived, as wise men teach, from a single natural principle and ordinance: that things that are perfect rule over and dominate things imperfect, strong things over weak things, things outstanding in virtue over things unlike themselves.

(3) This is in accord with nature to such an extent that in all things which consist of many or connecting or divided elements we see that one thing—that is, that which is greater—holds power, while another thing is subject, as the philosophers make clear.[101] Since even among inanimate things, things composed of matter and form, form (because it is more perfect) is superior and, as it were, acts as master, while matter is subordinate and, as it were, acts as a slave. For though the matter of all things which come into being and pass away is the same, nonetheless we see each thing moved about in just such a way as matter is moved in whatever direction form will have led, just as a maidservant follows her mistress. Thus, when fire has been made from earth, as the so-called elements tend to be generated one from another, matter that at one moment was being carried downward now strives upward in accord with the ruling power of form.

They say that this occurs even much more manifestly among living beings—that is, that the soul holds the ruling power and is, as it were, the mistress, while the body is subject and is, as it were, the slave. Then, in the same manner, in the soul itself the part that is capable of reason is superior and exercises power (albeit a kind of civil power), while the part devoid of reason is subordinate and submits to rule—and they all do this in accord with that decree and law of God and nature that the more perfect and powerful things are to hold the power over things unlike and unequal to themselves. The philosophers bid us to contemplate this in things that retain an uncorrupted nature and in men who are best endowed with mind and body. Indeed, this situation is manifest in them because their nature is unimpaired; for in faulty and depraved beings the body often rules over the mind and emotion

---

[101] This subsection and most of the following paraphrase Aristotle, *Politics* 1.2.9–15 (1254a28–1255a3). Though Sepúlveda often cites 'the philosophers' and refers to them in the plural ('they say', etc.), he usually means Aristotle.

over reason, specifically because the being is in bad shape and beyond the bounds of nature. Therefore, in a single man one may behold the rule of a master, which the soul exercises over the body, and also a civil and regal rule, which the mind or the faculty of reason exercises over the emotional element.

(4) In these things it is clearly evident that it is natural and advantageous that the soul have lordship over the body, that reason govern the emotions, and that an equality or an opposite method of governing is harmful—and they [the philosophers] teach that through the same law this is the case in both man and in the other animals. For though the tame animals are superior to the wild ones, nonetheless it is better and more advantageous for the domesticated ones to be subjected to the rule of man. For in this way and no other are they kept safe. By the same reasoning males have power over females, adults over children, just as the father over his children—in short, the better and more perfect over the worse and the more imperfect. In the same manner, they teach that this reasoning holds good in the case of different men among themselves, and that there is a certain category among them within which some are by nature masters, while others are by nature slaves. For those who are powerful through intelligence and wit, but not through strength of body, are by nature masters. On the other hand, those who are slower-witted and more sluggish, but powerful in body for undertaking vital tasks are by nature slaves, for whom it is not only just (they declare) but even profitable that they serve those who are by nature masters. We see that this has also been ordained by divine law; for it is written in the book of Proverbs: 'He who is stupid shall serve the wise'[102]—and such, they teach, are barbarous and uncivilized peoples who stand apart from civility and gentler customs and virtues, for whom it is advantageous and just by nature that they be subject to the power of princes or peoples who are more civilized and superior in virtue, so that when their savagery has been set aside they may be brought back to a more civilized way of life, gentler customs, and the cultivation of virtues through the virtue, laws, and wisdom of those others.

That those peoples may be forced by arms if they reject that rule, and that this war is just by the law of nature, they teach in these words: 'Whence it happens', he [Aristotle] says, 'that even the method of acquiring wealth by means of war originates in a certain manner from nature, for the art of hunting is a part of warfare which it is fitting to use sometimes against beasts, and sometimes against those humans who, though they have been born to obey, reject rule. For a war of this sort is just by nature.'[103]

(5) These words were written by Aristotle, whom Augustine supports. Augustine writes in this way to Vincentius: 'Or do you suppose that no one can be compelled to justice, when you read that the father of a family said to his slaves, "Whomever you might find, compel them to come in."[104] And in another passage he says,

---

[102] Proverbs 12:29.
[103] Aristotle, *Politics* 1.3.8 (1256b24–27).
[104] Augustine, Letter 93.2.5 (citing Luke 14:21).

102 SEPÚLVEDA ON THE SPANISH INVASION OF THE AMERICAS

'Many things must be done even with unwilling people who need to be beaten with a certain benevolent harshness, for one needs to take more thought of what is good for them than for what they want. For in the reprimanding of a son, no matter how harshly, a father's love is never really lost; instead, something happens which he doesn't wish for, and the other suffers pain who appears in need of healing through pain, even against his will.'[105]

In sum, they determine that for upright men, outstanding in virtue, intelligence, and humanity, to rule over those unlike themselves is advantageous for both and is just by nature. This very point is made clear by both the shared opinion of mankind and by the tested custom of nations—which are both, philosophers teach, the law of nature. For all states which use a correct political system and also upright kings, in assigning magistracies to those by whose judgment the greatest matters are managed, tend to look solely or most especially at virtue and prudence, for they judge that the state will be safe and rule will be just only if upright and wise men put restraints on the common people. For it is not easy for such men to be driven to wrongdoing through greed and vice, nor do they tend to slip into error through lack of prudence the way people unlike them do. And if you look into it, it is upon this foundation that the whole political teaching of the philosophers rests—that is, their account of the state.

6 [*The justice of war against barbarians contrasted with the injustice of civil war against an unintelligent or wicked prince*]

(1) **Leopoldus:** If supreme commands belong by right of nature to the more intelligent and those outstanding for virtue, then assume, for the sake of argument, that the kingdom of Tunis (for I prefer to refer to unbelievers in an example of a disaster than to our own people) has fallen through the law of paternity and seniority to a certain prince who has younger brothers and other relatives who are much more intelligent and more virtuous. On your view, wouldn't one of those men contend that the rule is owed to himself, as the best man, rather than to that inappropriate prince?

Democrates: If it's the truth we're seeking, Leopoldus, and what the procedure of the natural order requires, rule ought always to be in the hands of the best and most intelligent men. For, as the philosophers make clear, kingdoms that are truly kingdoms are always governed by the best man and most intelligent man, one who looks to the public good.[106] But if it happens in a different manner, the name of kingdom is lost. For that reason, the government of the optimates [*respublica optimatum*] is the most just and the most in accord with nature, for in it the most

---

[105] Augustine, Letter 138.2.14.
[106] Losada/Coroleu and Taranto cite Aristotle, *Politics* 3.5.1 (1279a27), but as Taranto notes, that passage does not in fact specify the rule of a single man.

intelligent and the best men [*optimi*] (hence it gets its name) hold the power.[107] But human felicity is not such that the best and most advantageous things are always able to be chosen by men or to happen or be secured without great disadvantages.

Doctors believe that it is very important for the natural and proper state and health of the human body that good humours dominate in it, and when the opposite occurs, with inferior and corrupted humours becoming powerful, if there is any safe way of healing this disorder by diminishing the bad humours, they don't overlook it. But if there is a danger that while they are striving to weaken these humours they might undermine the whole body, wise doctors omit the dangerous cures—not because they are unaware that such a disorder of humours is bad and contrary to nature, but because they judge it better that the man experience an unfavourable state of health than to utterly pass away.

Cautious men imitate this wisdom of the doctors and, when kingdoms are sick and, as it were, suffering in their heads, sometimes unsuitable princes are tolerated, on the authority of the Apostle Peter[108]—not because it would not be far more just and more natural to be governed by whatever best man there be, but lest internal wars and seditions arise, which are much worse evils in comparison to which those others would seem good. For the lesser evil, as the philosophers affirm, fills the place of a good.[109] Thus, Augustine says, 'Bad men are to be endured for the sake of peace, nor should we withdraw from them physically but spiritually. This we ought to do for the correction of the wicked in so far as it is allowed in accord with each person's station, with peace preserved.'[110]

This is how Thomas discusses this matter: 'A prince's sin needs to be endured, if it is not possible for it to be punished without harm to the multitude—unless perchance the prince's sin would be such that it would do greater harm to the multitude, either spiritually or temporally, than the harm which would arise from hence [i.e. from punishing it].'[111] From these considerations it is to be understood that the advice to tolerate wicked, unsuitable, and unjust princes, as also other aspects of the administration of a state, is guided by the public good.

(2) **Leopoldus:** If for the sake of avoiding disasters we ought to be content with the current condition of a state, however unsuitable it may be, why should we not in the same manner abstain from rule over the barbarians, lest wars and the greatest evils come about? And if that other war [civil war] is impious, why should *this* war not be considered base?

---

[107] In classical Latin, the *optimates* are the nobility; in the late Republic, the term was used to refer to the Senatorial party.

[108] 1 Peter 2:18.

[109] Aristotle, *Nicomachean Ethics* 5.3.15 (1131b31–32).

[110] Attributed to Augustine by Gratian, *Decretum,* C. 23, q. 4, c. 1. The text offered by Gratian (followed here by Sepúlveda) is paraphrased from *Sermons* 88.20.23 (see *Patrologia Latina,* vol. 38, 551).

[111] Aquinas, *ST* II-II, q. 108, art. 1.

Democrates: Because the rationale is far different in the two cases. For when a king, however wicked and unqualified, succeeds to power in accord with the laws and ancestral custom, the reason he ought to be endured is not so much in order to avoid disasters if we should attempt to drive him out and replace him by force of arms; rather, it is in order that we don't violate the laws, by which the safety of the state is maintained, by undertaking a war against a legitimate monarch. This is impious and wicked, in the first place because it happens without the authority of the prince, without which a war cannot be just, unless perhaps it should come about through the public deliberation and will of the entire state. Next, because it is against the laws and customs of our ancestors to whom this most prudently seemed the right course in order to do away with the disputes of rivals and the discords which often pull fellow-countrymen apart in a spirit of faction and produce civil wars and, often, tyrants.

Also, it has been with great consensus among most peoples sanctioned by law that someone always succeeds to power from a certain family which they most especially approve of, and in accord with the law of heredity and seniority, someone who would govern peoples and communities partly through his own wisdom and that of his ministers, partly through ancestral and just laws. To be perfectly honest, this is in fact what generally happens, and wise and just kings—or at least acceptable ones—succeed to the throne, as we read that it happened among the Spartans from the single family of the Heraklids, and even more among the Spaniards from the family of the Pelagids, if you will allow me to designate in the manner of my people the descendants of Pelayo, to whom rule was first given by his countrymen after the slaughter inflicted by the Saracens and Moors. From that time right up to this age which Charles, king of Spain and also Roman emperor, makes glorious, over the course of more than eight hundred years, in the unbroken succession of this family, hardly one or two—very few, at any rate—could be discovered who wouldn't be fit to be justly counted in the list of excellent kings.

Therefore if it ever happens that such a disease falls upon some kingdom—a situation that God on occasion allows on account of the sins of peoples and for the sake of punishment—the unfit king will have to be endured, and God will need to be petitioned to give him a good mind and take away his recklessness, so that those things that he is unable to perform through his own intelligence he may arrange through the advice of the best and most prudent men and also govern in accord with ancestral customs and principles.

(3) In sum, just as the philosophers say that laws that are not downright savage and barbarous ought not be changed without a great and manifest good for the state, even if better laws might be found, so nothing should be done or decided contrary to the laws, nor without a decree of the king or the state, except in the case of the most certain and major advantage.[112] Rather, a tolerable inconvenience

---

[112] Aristotle, *Politics* 2.5.10–14 (1268b25–1269a28).

ought to be endured for the same reason—that is, in order to avoid a situation where people grow accustomed to altering or abrogating or transgressing laws for any reason that falls short of the very most serious, thereby diminishing the full force of the laws, which is the salvation of the state and which is sustained by the habit of obedience.

Take notice, then, what a difference there is between this war against the barbarians and the war that would occur if an insufficiently suitable prince were rashly exposed to armed attack by factions. The latter war would be undertaken without public authority and against a legitimate ruler; the former, when properly administered, is being waged in accord with the order and will of the prince. The latter would occur in defiance of a sworn oath and against laws, ordinances, and ancestral customs and would be accompanied by the greatest disturbance of the state; while the former is happening in accord with the law of nature for the great benefit of those who are defeated, so that they may learn civilized behaviour from the Christians, may grow accustomed to the practice of virtues, and with the help of sound teaching and pious advice may make their minds ready for gladly accepting the Christian religion.

7 [*The reputed massacres of barbarians*]

(1) **Leopoldus:** But in that war against the barbarians there have occurred (as tends to happen) great slaughters and massacres. These should constitute as powerful arguments in their favour for ruling out warfare as would the dangers of civil dissensions among ourselves.

Democrates: No, much less, given how great a difference there is between a just and pious war and wicked civil struggles. For in the latter the innocent are often harassed by an unjust war, while in the former those who are conquered and fall are visited with just punishments, a fact that should by no means deter firm, brave, and just princes—according to Augustine, who, as I was saying earlier, addresses Faustus in this way: 'What is held blameworthy in war? Is it the fact that people who are going to die someday anyway give their lives so that those who are going to live may be ruled in peace? To find fault with this is the mark of cowards, not religious people.'[113] And yet, in case you are unaware, the nature of these barbarians is such that by means of the death of very few on both sides the greatest possible number may be battled into subjection.

(2) **Leopoldus:** In a just war, Democrates, at least according to you, not only is a just motive required, but so also are a good intention and a proper method of waging war. But this war against the barbarians, as I hear, is not being carried out with a good intention, since there is no other aim for those waging it than to reap the benefit of as much gold and silver as possible by fair means or foul—quite

---

[113] Augustine, *Contra Faustum* 22.74.

against that precept of Augustine which you have mentioned: 'To wage war is not a crime, but to go to war for the sake of booty is a sin.'[114] The view of Ambrose is similar: 'Those who are stirred up by some hidden inspiration of God to proceed against wicked men are themselves liable to reproach when they seek with wicked intention not to punish the sins of the wrongdoers but to run off with their goods or subject them to their own rule.'[115] Thus, the war is being carried on by the Spaniards neither justly nor with proper rationale, but to the great detriment of the barbarians and with cruelty and in the manner of brigandage, so that the Spaniards are no less obligated to restore to the barbarians the things taken than are brigands to the wayfarers whom they have plundered.

(3) **Democrates**: One who approves of the rule of a prince or state over client states and subjects, Leopoldus, is not to be imagined as automatically approving of the sins of prefects and administrators. Thus, if something is done avariciously, cruelly, or basely by unjust and very wicked men, as I hear many things have been done, this does not make the cause of the prince and good men worse, except insofar as crimes are perpetrated through their negligence or with their permission—for in that case the consenting princes are involved in the same guilt as the ministers and ought to be punished with the same penalty by the judgment of God. For there is that well-known and pious decree of Innocent III: 'An error which is not resisted is approved, and truth, when it is too weakly defended, is suppressed. Indeed, to overlook wicked people when it is in your power to trouble them is nothing other than to encourage them. And he who forbears to oppose an open crime is not free from the uneasy suspicion of secret involvement.'[116]

Therefore, if the war is being waged as you say it is, Leopoldus, it is being waged impiously and criminally, and it is my view that one ought to punish those who are waging it thus as though they are brigands and kidnappers. For to perform just actions is little or nothing unless we perform those actions justly. 'That which is just', says God, 'you must pursue justly.'[117] But the war has not been conducted in this way by everyone—if those things are true which are recorded in certain reports I have recently read about the things done during the conquest of New Spain. Besides, we are not disputing about the moderation or the criminal behaviour of soldiers and prefects, but about the nature of this war as it relates to the lawful ruler of the Spaniards and his duly appointed ministers, and I declare the nature of the war to be of such a sort that it can be conducted correctly, justly, and piously, and with some advantage to the conquering people, but much more to the defeated barbarians. For, as I said before, their nature is such that they can be conquered

---

[114] Pseudo-Augustine, *Sermon* 82, 3.12–14 (*PL* 39, col. 1904). Cf. above, I.4.2 and n. 90.

[115] The words are not, in fact, those of Ambrose, but of Gratian commenting on Ambrose's *On Cain and Abel* (2.4.15): *Decretum*, C. 23, q. 5, c. 49.

[116] Innocent III, as quoted in Gratian, D. 83, c. 3. Coroleu, Taranto, and Schäfer all incorrectly limit the quoted passage to just the first sentence.

[117] Deuteronomy 16:20.

and forced to surrender with little trouble and the loss of few lives. If men who are not only brave but also just and even moderate and humane are put in charge of this duty, the matter may be settled easily without any wickedness or crime, and while the advantages of the Spanish would get some consideration, as I have said, to a much greater degree and in many more ways would those of the barbarians be provided for.

8 [*The proper method of waging war*]

(1) This, then, is the unavoidable procedure for making war: that first war be declared—that is, that the barbarians first be urged to accept the rule of the king of Spain so that, for their own great advantages, they may be governed by the best laws and customs and may be initiated into the true religion—lest, if they do otherwise and reject the rule, they justly undergo hostilities at the hands of the Spaniards who have been sent by their king for this purpose. If the barbarians request some time for deliberation, they should be granted as much as would be sufficient for gathering a public council and conferring on courses of action; a longer space of time should by no means be granted. For if there were to be a long wait while those people make a prior investigation concerning the nature, customs, and intelligence of the Spaniards and of themselves, about the differences between the two peoples, about the justice of ruling and obeying, about the differences in customs and religion, about honour and truth—it would be a long, endless, and fruitless delay, for they cannot come to know all this except in the course of daily association with our men and through the lessons of teachers of morality and religion once our rule has been accepted.

(2) If therefore after having been exhorted in this way they do what they are ordered to do, they ought to be taken under our protection, and they should be granted the terms of a peace that is not unjust when one takes their own nature into account—so that, in accord with Deuteronomy, 'they may serve under tribute'.[118] But if, after having rejected the exhortation or after having foolishly refused to receive ambassadors and having stubbornly rejected a conference, they will have assembled to resist by fighting and then will have become defeated in war, both they themselves and their goods will be in the power of the victorious prince so that he will be able to make a decision about them in accord with his own judgment, though with prudence and the consideration of peace and the public good guiding the will along with the standard of treatment that should always be applied in punishing enemies after a victory.

But especially to be avoided is craftiness, lest through deception and cunning they may be led into serious error and the hope or necessity of resistance. For unless everything happens in good faith and in such a way that they manifestly

---

[118] Deuteronomy 20:11.

understand the exhortation and what demands are being made of them, deception and ill will confer nothing valid, do no good, and actually stand in the way of justice.

But if, the exhortation being omitted and the time for consideration that I mentioned being refused, war is rashly inflicted, since this would happen contrary to the law of nature and the will and command of a just prince, it will be utterly unjust and ought not so much to be called a war as an act of brigandage. For 'enemies', as the jurist Ulpian defined them, 'are those against whom the Roman people have publicly declared war, or who have themselves declared it against the Roman people';[119] others, however, are called brigands and pirates—for in the term 'the Roman people' we understand a prince or state. For all the goods that have been seized should be restored to those who have been wrongfully pillaged in the manner of brigandage—just as if a praetor [judge] were to deprive of his goods someone accused of treason when the case had not in fact been publicly declared. For if they had been warned, perhaps they would have submitted themselves and their goods to authority without recourse to arms, and peace, for the sake of which a war ought to be waged, could have come about.

(3) There are other matters which pertain to the proper method of waging war—that nothing happen overzealously, cruelly, avariciously, immoderately. For if all these and similar factors are overlooked, the resulting actions are, on the authority of Augustine, rightly censured as though they are basely done and sins.[120] But if a war is undertaken from just motives and under the authority of a prince and is publicly declared against the enemy, although it may be waged in a spirit which is base and not focused on justice but on booty—a situation which, as I have said, is not without wickedness and sin—nonetheless, on the authority of major theologians that defective intention does not bring it about that a soldier or lieutenant should be forced to restore booty which was in other respects justly wrested from the enemy—any more than a greedy judge who has punished with loss of all his possessions a man accused of treason whom he had found guilty in a process that was strictly legal, albeit carried out in a highly self-interested and twisted frame of mind.[121] For it was not the twisted mind of either the judge or the soldiers that was the reason for punishing the one or the other with loss of goods; rather, it was the crime which those who were punished perpetrated—the one in subverting sovereign authority, the other in harming and disturbing human society by an unjust war—for, in accord with common laws, this latter crime is also punished with capital punishment and loss of goods.

(4) Therefore, let it remain and be established, on the authority of the very wisest men, that it is just and in accord with nature that intelligent, upright, and humane

---

[119] Ulpian, in *Digest* 49.15.24.
[120] Augustine, *Contra Faustum* 22.74.
[121] Aquinas, *ST* II-II, q. 66, art. 8.

men rule over those who are unlike themselves. For this is the justification that the Romans had for ruling most peoples with a legitimate and just rule, as St Thomas mentions in his book *On the Government of Rulers,* following Augustine, who discussed the rule of the Romans in this way in Book 5 of *The City of God*: 'For the purpose of overcoming the weighty evils of many peoples, God granted the greatest and most illustrious rule to the Romans, who for glory's sake curbed their own greed and many other vices'—that is, so that they might destroy and correct the barbarous customs and vices of many peoples by means of the good laws which they used and the virtue in which they were pre-eminent.[122]

For if Romans who were considered upright and wise—such as Curius, Fabricius, the Scipios, Fabius Maximus, Metellus, and the Catos—were in the habit of seeking glory, they should not automatically be supposed to have rejected virtue. For as the philosophers teach, the person who most especially cultivates and pursues virtue is the person who seeks glory—not, of course, an empty glory in an absurd manner and through the performance of bogus duties, but a solid glory pursued in a correct manner, with reason, and with upright methods. For solid glory is, as the most learned men define it, 'the approving praise of good men, the uncorrupted voice of those who judge well concerning superior virtue'.[123] For though one should despise the common chatter of stupid and base men in whose eyes the servants of Christ find no favour, one mustn't despise the judgment and discourse of good and intelligent men, in which (according to the Philosopher) the proper measurement of good things and bad inheres.[124] For to hold the latter in contempt is 'the characteristic of an arrogant or dissolute man', as Ambrose affirms.[125]

Thus, no law forbids us to seek glory—that is, good reputation—since it is a respectable and very fine thing and is often a great assistance to virtue. For, as the Philosopher says, the longing for honourable things is praiseworthy; but it needs to be sought with reason, not as the proper end of things rightly performed but as a means of generating virtue.[126] This will happen in the best way if, ultimately, virtue itself, arising from the precepts of Christian philosophy, is oriented to God as the supreme good. Thus Augustine more openly testifies in another passage that it was through the virtues of the ancient Romans that, through God's providence, their rule grew. He wrote back to Marcellinus in this way: 'Let us tolerate, if we can't correct, those who wish the state, which the first Romans established and expanded through their virtues, to stand with its vices unpunished.' And a bit later: 'God thus

---

[122] Pseudo-Aquinas (Ptolemy of Lucca), *De regimine principum* (Sepúlveda often cites this with the singular *principis* for the plural *principum*) 3.5; Augustine, *De civitate Dei* 5.13.

[123] Cicero, *Tusculan Disputations* 3.2.3.

[124] According to marginal notes in the manuscripts, Sepúlveda was thinking of *Nicomachean Ethics*, Bk 10. That would appear to be 10.5.10 (1176a17-20). But also relevant are *Topics* 1.1 (100b22-24) and *Rhetoric* 1.2 (1356a6-7).

[125] Ambrose, *De officiis ministrorum* (*On the Duties of Clergy*) I.47, 226.

[126] Aristotle, *Nicomachean Ethics* 10.5.6 (1175b28).

showed in the case of the very wealthy and famous empire of the Romans just how much power civil virtues may possess even without true religion.'[127]

9 [*The superior intelligence, virtue, and religion of the Spaniards*]

(1) To return to the matter at hand: if it is lawful and permitted for those who are superior and more advanced in nature, customs, and laws to rule over those who are their inferiors, you certainly do understand, Leopoldus, provided you are familiar with the customs and natures of the two peoples, that it is by the highest right that the Spaniards rule over those barbarians of the New World and the adjacent islands, people who in intelligence, native wit, and every sort of virtue and human feeling are as far surpassed by the Spaniards as children are by adults, as women are by men, as savage and fierce people are by the most gentle people, as the wildly intemperate are by those who are self-controlled and temperate.[128]

(2) Nor do I suppose that you are actually waiting for me to discuss the intelligence and genius of the Spaniards, for you have, I imagine, read Lucan, Silius Italicus, and the Senecas, as well as Spaniards later than these: Isidore of Seville, second to none in theology, Averroes and Avempace, those men pre-eminent in philosophy, and King Alfonso, pre-eminent in astrology—to say nothing of others, whom it would take too long to list.[129] Moreover, who is unaware of their other virtues: bravery, humanity, justice, and religion?—I'm speaking here of princes and of those men whose assistance and industry princes make use of for the administration of the state. In short, I am speaking about those who are liberally educated. For even if certain individuals among the Spaniards are wicked and unjust, their baseness should not stand in the way of a whole people's fame, which ought to be judged in civic-minded and noble men and in public customs and institutions, not in slave-like and depraved men, whom this very nation especially loathes and detests.

And yet there are certain virtues that are to be seen in almost every social rank, such as bravery, of which in almost every period of history Spanish troops have given testimonies which surpass men's belief—such as the things done in the Numantine War and in those in which Viriathus and Sertorius were the leaders, when great armies of the Romans were routed and sent under the yoke by a small band of Spaniards—and in our fathers' time when Gonzalo the Great Captain was leader, and in our time under the auspices of the Emperor Charles at Milan and

---

[127] Augustine, Letter 138.3.17.

[128] Here all the earlier manuscripts (VTMP) added: 'and finally I might almost say: as apes are by human beings (*denique quam simiae prope dixerim ab hominibus*)'. This phrase was erased in the S manuscript (see preface). Also, S offered the following marginal note here: 'On the nature and customs of these barbarians, read the general history published about them: Bk. 3, ch. 6'. As Losada noted, the reference is to the first part of Gonzalo Fernández de Oviedo's *Historia general de las Indias,* published in Seville in 1535. In the chapter indicated, see esp. fol. xxvii r, on 'the great, ugly, and enormous sins and abominations of these savage and bestial peoples (*gentes salvajes y bestiales*)'.

[129] Like others of his time, Sepúlveda assumed that the late-first-century-CE epic poet Silius Italicus was born in the Ibero-Roman city of Italica, near modern Seville. In fact, his place of origin is uncertain.

Naples, and with Charles himself as leader at Tunis in Africa, and recently in the Flemish and French wars, and most recently in the war in Germany against the Lutheran heretics, who were utterly defeated to his greatest glory. In these places Spanish troops have furnished a model of excellence duly accompanied by the great admiration of men.

Why should I mention temperance in matters of food, drink, and sex, when there is no other nation in Europe—or at least very few indeed—which can compare with Spain in self-control and sobriety? And yet these days I do see that through association with foreigners luxurious feasting has crept into the tables of the aristocracy, though, since this is commonly excoriated by good men, there is hope that soon the old-time native frugality will be summoned back to our ancestral customs. As for what pertains to the other part of temperance: although the philosophers teach that military men are inclined to lust, nonetheless there is a certain semblance of virtue in not forgetting nature even when committing vices and sins.[130]

(3) How deeply the Christian religion is implanted in the minds of the Spaniards, I have seen many clear instances among those who live in arms. But what seems to me by far the most important is the fact that during the great plague that followed the sack of Rome in the pontificate of Clement VII there was not found a single one of the Spaniards taken off by the plague who did not stipulate in his will that all the things he had carried off be restored to the plundered citizens. There was no one of another nation—at least insofar as I am aware—who discharged this duty that was in accord with Christian piety—and there were far more Italians and Germans there. And I personally took note of this, for I was present with the army and in the city and made a thorough investigation of everything. I recall that we made mention of this fact in that meeting we had in the Vatican. For what can I say of the Spaniards' gentleness and humanity? In battles, when victory has been gained, they have no greater concern and care than how they may save as many of the defeated as possible and protect them from the savagery of their allies.

10 [*The inferior nature and customs of the barbarians*]
(1) Now compare with these Spaniards' intelligence, ingenuity, magnanimity, temperance, humanity, and religion those lesser humans (*homunculi*) among whom you will scarcely find any vestiges of humanity, who not only have no learning but do not even use or know writing, who retain no records of the things they have done apart from a certain skimpy and obscure record of a few things marked out with certain pictures, who have no written laws but only certain barbaric institutions and customs. For, as for virtues, if you are looking for temperance and

---

[130] For the teachings of 'the philosophers', see Aristotle, *Politics* 2.6.6 (1269b 28–32). The point about the 'semblance of virtue' seems more than simply an acknowledgement that sexual desires are natural. It seems likely that Sepúlveda is suggesting that, unlike the Amerindians, the Spaniards refrained from 'unnatural' sex ('sodomy').

gentleness, what would it be possible to hope for from those who have rushed into every sort of intemperance and wicked desires, and many of whom used to feast upon human flesh?

And as for the wars among themselves by which they were almost constantly troubled (for you shouldn't imagine that before the arrival of the Christians they lived in leisure and in that peace under the reign of Saturn feigned by the poets)—these they were in the habit of waging with such frenzy that they didn't consider a victory complete unless they could glut their prodigious hunger upon the flesh of their enemies. This cruelty is all the more remarkable in them given how far they are from the unconquerable ferocity of the Scythians, who likewise feasted on the very bodies of men, since these people are so cowardly and timid that they are scarcely able to endure the hostile sight of our men and often many thousands of them have been scattered in womanish flight by very few Spaniards, not even amounting to a hundred in number.

(2) But lest I hold you up too long here, just grasp the nature and worthiness of those people from a single characteristic act of the Mexicans who used to be regarded as the most intelligent and bravest. Their king was Montezuma, whose empire extended far and wide in those regions and who lived in the city of Mexico, which was located in a vast swamp, very well protected both by the nature of the place and by fortifications, rather like Venice (so they say), but roughly three times as large in number of people and the size of the place. When he learned of the arrival of Hernán Cortés and of certain victories he'd won, and Cortés wished to come to him in Mexico on the pretext of having a conference with him, Montezuma strove to turn him away from this plan by making many excuses. But when he had made no headway in alleging these pretexts, in sheer terror he received him into his city accompanied by a band of about three hundred men. Cortés, having gotten control of the city in this manner, conceived such contempt for the cowardice, inertia, and backwardness of these men that, having struck terror into them, he not only forced the king and his subject princes to accept the yoke and rule of the king of Spain, but also threw the king himself into chains on suspicion of collusion in the murder of some Spaniards perpetrated in one of his provinces—while his townspeople kept quiet through astonishment and cowardice and had no thought of conspiring to take up arms to liberate their king. Thus Cortés, right at the start, with such a small body of Spaniards and with the assistance of a few natives, held in subjection and terror so huge a multitude which seemed to lack not only energy and cleverness but even downright common sense.

Could it be made clear by any greater or more manifest piece of evidence how some men surpass others in ingenuity, energy, strength of mind, and virtue—or more clearly demonstrated how those people are slaves by nature? For as to the fact that some of them seem to be clever at certain arts, that is no indication of a more human intelligence, since we see certain insignificant beasts—bees and spiders, for example—fashion such works as no human industriousness is sufficiently able to imitate.

(3) But to turn to what some people blather about the civil way of life of those people who inhabit New Spain and the province of Mexico (for these people, as I have said, are considered the most civilized of them all) and about those same people's public practices—as though peoples display a perfectly adequate degree of industry and civilization if they possess cities constructed on a plan, have kings to whom rule is granted not by the claim of family or seniority but by the vote of the common people, and conduct commerce in the manner of civilized peoples. See how far those pundits have gone astray and how much I disagree with their opinion, since I have no more decisive evidence for the backwardness, barbarity, and native servility of those peoples than precisely the public practices of those very same people. For almost all of those practices are servile and barbarous. For the fact that they possess houses and some manner of living together and commerce, which natural necessity brings in—what does this prove, apart from the fact that they are not bears or apes utterly deprived of reason?

11 [*The idolatry and abominable sacrifices of the barbarians and the justness of their subjection to Spanish rule*]

(1) I have spoken about the nature and customs of the barbarians; but what am I to say about their religion and their abominable sacrifices?[131] Since they worship demons instead of God, they suppose he can be appeased by no sacrifices but human hearts. Although this is in fact very true, if by 'hearts' you understand healthy and pious minds, those people, by referring the statement not to the Spirit that gives life but to the letter that kills (to use Paul's words[132]) and by interpreting it most foolishly and barbarously, think that he must be worshipped by means of human victims. Thus they used to pluck out hearts from breasts rent asunder, and with these offerings made at abominable altars they would think that they had properly propitiated and placated the gods, and they themselves used to feast upon the flesh of the men they had slaughtered. These crimes, since they exceed every sort of human depravity, are classified by philosophers among savage and monstrous acts of wickedness.[133]

As for the fact that some of their nations are said to have no religion at all and no conception of God—what else is this than to deny that God exists and to lead lives in the manner of beasts?[134] I see nothing more grievous, more base, more foreign to human nature than this. For the basest kind of idolatry is that of those

---

[131] In place of this sentence in the S manuscript, the earlier manuscripts offered a lengthy passage about the nature of American (esp. Aztec) societies. See Appendix.

[132] 2 Corinthians 3:6.

[133] Aristotle, *Nicomachean Ethics* 7.5.2 (1248b 20–23).

[134] The passage on Amerindian atheism we have printed here as a paragraph is found only in the S (Salamanca) manuscript, the final state of the text of the dialogue.

who worship the stomach and the most shameful parts of the body in place of God and those who follow bodily pleasures instead of religion and virtues, always prone upon the ground in the manner of pigs as though they have never looked up at heaven. For these words of Paul most aptly suit them: 'Those whose end is extinction, whose God is the belly, their minds are set on earthly things.'[135]

Therefore, are we going to doubt that these peoples so uncivilized, so barbaric, so contaminated by heinous sacrifices and impious rites have been reduced to submission by a most excellent, pious, and most just king, such as Ferdinand was and as Emperor Charles is now, and by a nation that is pious, most humane, and pre-eminent in every sort of virtue in accord with the best possible justification and with the greatest benefit for the barbarians themselves? Although prior to the arrival of the Christians these people were such as we have declared with regard to their nature, customs, religion, and unspeakable sacrifices, now that they have received, along with our rule, our letters, laws, and customs—at least those who have entrusted themselves docilely to the magistrates and priests who have been assigned to them, as many have indeed entrusted themselves—they differ from themselves and that earlier condition of theirs just as much as the civilized differ from the barbarians, the sighted from the blind, the gentle from the fierce, and the pious from the impious—and, to be perfectly blunt, almost as much as human beings from beasts.

(2) Thus it is understood that it is all the more fitting that those men obey the rule of more prudent, more humane, and pious men, given that most of them are of such a nature that does not resist teaching if they are given instruction, although it be agreed that all of them are—or were, before the rule of the Spaniards and daily interaction with them—barbarians and people brought up in a servile manner without letters, shrinking from a civilized and more humane way of life and customs, and contaminated with those crimes that in themselves constitute another justification for a thoroughly just war.

(3)[136] For those crimes are so impious and wicked that it was mainly through his anger at them that God destroyed the Canaanites, Perizzites, and other sinful peoples through warfare with the sons of Israel, and then afflicted those very Israelites in their turn by means of the Assyrians and Babylonians with many disasters in war, slaughters, and enslavements—on account, that is to say, of two most grievous sins: the worship of idols and sacrifices offered with human victims. Such sacrifices have never been promulgated in a law that is to be made lasting—for that is divine and natural law, laying down the same punishments for the pious along with those pagans who have contaminated themselves with these crimes, as is declared in many places and testimonies of the Divine Scriptures.

[135] Philippians 3:19.
[136] Sections I.11.3–6 in the S (Salamanca) manuscript expand on a considerably shorter passage in the earlier manuscripts. For the earlier version, see Appendix.

DEMOCRATES PART TWO   115

Some of these, which I retain in my memory, I will not hesitate to set forth. As is found in Deuteronomy, Moses, the divine intermediary, urged the sons of Israel not to imitate the peoples whom God was going to destroy at their hands: 'They have performed all the abominations which God turns away from, offering their sons and daughters to their gods and burning them up with fire.'[137] And in Leviticus: 'If a people of the land, neglecting my rule and holding it in contempt, shall have acquitted a man who has given one of his own seed to Molech' (that is, who has immolated his own children to idols), 'and will not have chosen to kill him, I shall set my face against that man and his kindred, and I shall kill the man himself and all those who approve of him after impunity has supposedly been granted to him.'[138]

(4) Although these things were enjoined upon the sons of Israel, God himself has declared that that same law is not only divine, but is also natural and pertains to all peoples, for he has affirmed that he destroyed those sinners because of precisely those sins. For since the pagans before the coming of Christ were subject to no divine law apart from natural law, as the theologians agree, nothing could be objected to as a sin but that in which the law of nature is violated.

Sacred Scripture says, 'When God will have destroyed them, do not say, "It is because of my righteousness that God has led me in so that I might possess this land", for it is because of their own iniquities that those peoples have been destroyed.'[139] And again in Deuteronomy: 'When you shall enter the land which the Lord God will give you, take care lest you choose to imitate the abominations of those peoples; nor let there be found among you anyone who would make an offering involving his son or daughter passing through fire or who consults soothsayers or pays attention to dreams and auguries or who is a sorcerer or spell-caster or someone who consults prophetic spirits or diviners or who seeks the truth from the dead, for God detests all these things, and it is because of crimes of this sort that he will destroy them when you make your entrance.'[140]

Similar to this is that which is found in Leviticus: 'For the inhabitants of the land, who had been there before you, had perpetrated all those abominations and had polluted it. Take care therefore lest the land vomit you out in similar fashion when you have done similar things, just as it vomited out the people who were there before you.'[141] Having said these things, he added a universal law and one applicable to all men: 'Every soul', he says, 'which shall have done any of those abominations shall pass away from the midst of its own people'[142]—which is to say that whoever commits the aforementioned crimes which pertain to the worship of idols and the sacrifices of human victims is to be punished by death, as Moses, the greatest

[137] Deuteronomy 12:31.
[138] Leviticus 20:4–5.
[139] Deuteronomy 9:4.
[140] Deuteronomy 18:9–12.
[141] Leviticus 18:27-28.
[142] Leviticus 18:29.

interpreter of the divine will, declared by means of the most extreme example. For it was he who ordered the Levites, on account of the worship of idols by which the other sons of Israel had defiled themselves, to kill their brothers and friends and nearest of kin; and once this was done, he addressed the Levites thus: 'Today you have consecrated your hands to the Lord, each one in his own son and brother, so that a blessing may be given to you'.[143]

Also, in the book of Wisdom it stands written: 'Those inhabitants of the Holy Land, whom You loathed because they used to do horrible things against You through poisons and unjust sacrifices, slaughterers of their own children and feasters upon human innards and devourers of blood—You have chosen to destroy them through the hands of our fathers.'[144] And in a Psalm: 'They have become mingled among the peoples and have learned their works and have worshipped their statues and have sacrificed their own sons and daughters to demons, and the Lord was angered with fury and abhorred his own heirs and gave them into the hands of the nations.'[145] Likewise in the Fourth Book of Kings [2 Kings], Ahaz, king of Judah, is recorded as having consecrated his own son by having him pass through fire in accord with the idols of the nations, idols that the Lord overthrew in front of the sons of Israel, and because of these crimes the sons of Israel were given into the hands of those who plundered them.[146] And in the time of Hoshea, king of Israel, the Israelites were deported to the land of the Assyrians—'because', it says, 'they worshipped the gods of others and walked in accord with the manner of the nations—gods whom the Lord had destroyed in the sight of the sons of Israel.'[147]

(5) So many and such great testimonies and judgments of God allow no pious man to doubt that these two sins—the worship of idols and human sacrifices, of which it is agreed that those barbarians are guilty—are most justly punished by the killing of the perpetrators and the confiscation of their goods—whether they are believers, as the Hebrews were at that time, or pagans both before and after the coming of Christ, since that law, as we have made clear, rests upon natural law, and such sins, which are committed contrary to the judgment of reason, are condemned with proper punishments not by a temporal law but by the eternal law of God, as the theologians agree.

(6) But in order that the testimonies of the church fathers may also contribute to the most secure line of reasoning, Cyprian, the most learned and also most holy bishop and martyr, in the work entitled *Exhortation to Martyrdom*, upon mentioning those crimes, says, 'But if those precepts concerning the worship of God and the rejection of idols were observed before the coming of Christ, how much more are they to be observed after the coming of Christ, now that he has

[143] Exodus 32:29.
[144] Wisdom 12:3–6.
[145] Psalm 106 (105):35–41.
[146] 2 Kings 16:3 and seq.
[147] 2 Kings 17:1–8.

urged us not only by words but also by deeds?'[148] And St Ambrose: 'When peoples are stirred up by divine commandment to punish sins, just as that Jewish people was stirred up to take possession of the Promised Land and to destroy the sinful peoples, guilty blood is shed without blame, and those things which are wrongly possessed by them properly pass over into the legal right and dominion of good people.'[149] The words of Augustine are also apposite here: 'If we put off attacking or punishing those things by which God is powerfully offended, we most certainly provoke the patience of divinity to wrath.'[150]

Therefore, with the help of God's greatest and clearest judgments we can see that important precedents have been established with regard to the laying waste and pillaging of those barbarians. Therefore if those barbarians had been dealt with according to justice and punished on the basis of their manifest crimes, and we had not chosen to prefer kindness and mercy to severity, not only could they have been deprived of their possessions but also of their lives, given that they imitate the sins of those who were punished in accordance with divine fore-judgments and the curse of the Psalm: 'Pour out your wrath upon the nations who know you not, and upon the kingdoms that have not called [upon] your name.'[151] But I see that the most humane kings of Spain arrived at a different decision and continue to abide by it; for in pursuit of this task that they have been assigned—to subjugate those barbarians to their rule and that of their fellow Christians—they have set forth not the punishment of sins but their correction, as well as the salvation and the public good of those peoples. This is what the pursuit of Christian piety demands, which—unlike the old law, which was of slavery and fear—is the law of Grace and gentleness.

12 [*The authority of the church to bring unbelievers under its rule, especially those who violate the law of nature*]

(1) **Leopoldus**: Why, then, has it occurred to certain theologians of great reputation to deny that it is permitted for Christian princes to bring pagans under their rule if they are discovered inhabiting regions where neither the rule of the Romans nor the name of Christ has ever penetrated?[152] For lack of faith, according to them, does not provide sufficient justification, barring some specific act of wrongdoing,

---

[148] Cyprian, *Ad Fortunatum de exhortatione martyrii* (*To Fortunatus, Exhortation to Martyrdom*) 5.23.

[149] Not in fact Ambrose, but Gratian's comment on Ambrose's *De Cain et Abel* 2.24: *Decretum*, C. 23, q. 5, c. 49.

[150] Not in fact Augustine, but Gregory I, Letter 3.27 (to Manianus and Benenatus), cited in Gratian, *Decretum,* C. 23, q. 4, c. 50, where it is attributed to Augustine.

[151] Psalm 79 (78):6.

[152] A marginal gloss in all the manuscripts cites Cajetan on Aquinas: 'Caiet. 2.a 2.ae. q. 66. ar.8' (though VTM mistakenly have 'q. 67'). See Xavier Tubau, 'Canon Law in Juan Ginés de Sepúlveda's *Democrates secundus*', *Bibliothèque d'Humanisme et Renaissance* 73/2 (2011): 265–77, at 273–74. In a parallel passage in the *Apologia* (III.2.ix in our numbering), Cajetan is explicitly mentioned in the text. For Cajetan's views on infidel *dominium*, see Lantigua, *Infidels and Empires in a New World Order*, 85–88.

for waging war against them and for depriving unbelievers of their possessions. And yet it is not so much the authority of one particular very learned man that advises me here as it is the testimony of the Apostle Paul, who denied that it belonged to the apostolic office and power to pass judgment upon the pagans, in these words: 'For what business is it of mine to make judgments about those who are outside?'[153]

(2) **Democrates:** Pagans, Leopoldus, who are nothing worse than simply being pagans, and against whom no charge can be brought apart from their not being Christians (a condition we call 'infidelity')—there is no legal case for their being justly harassed and punished by the weapons of Christians. For instance, if some polished, law-abiding, and civilized population were discovered in the New World, one which did not worship idols but instead worshipped the true God under the guidance of nature, and one that, to employ the words of St Paul, 'without the law performed the things of the law in a natural way', but did not however follow the gospel law and did not possess faith in Christ, it would be proper by this reasoning to call this people 'infidel'.[154] It is peoples of this sort that that decision of the modern theologians whom you have cited seems to support in the matter of justifying war, arguing that Christian princes may not attack them with offensive arms for the sake of punishing them on any charge of infidelity.

But while we read in the Sacred Scriptures (as the theologians themselves affirm) that no people was slaughtered or crushed by war at God's command solely because of infidelity, nonetheless we know that many utterly collapsed under the weapons of the Hebrews under God's authority on account of crimes associated with infidelity[155]—but mainly on account of two crimes by which those barbarians of yours are especially plagued, the worship of idols and the sacrifices of human entrails, as we have pointed out above through many testimonies drawn from the Holy Scriptures. For this is what Paul meant when he said that it was not his task to pass judgment on those who are outside: 'Why must I pass futile judgment concerning the customs of the unbelievers whom I am unable to correct either in accord with their own will, as I could correct Christians, or against their will, given that the powers of the church do not come to my aid here—though nonetheless these people do not escape God's judgment?'

For this is the custom of the church, as Augustine testifies in a letter to Vincentius: 'that it corrects those whom it can and tolerates those whom it hasn't the power to correct, awaiting the separation at the end of the age'—that is, the Judgment of God.[156] In another passage (in a letter to Marcellinus), discussing

---

[153] 1 Corinthians 5:12. The 'very learned man' (*vir doctissimus*) is, again, Cajetan. This sentence is found only in the Salamanca manuscript, the latest state of the dialogue.

[154] Romans 2:14. 'Polished, law-abiding, and civilized' is our attempt to render *culta, civilis, et humana*.

[155] From here to the end of §12 the S manuscript offers a substantial revision of the version of the earlier manuscripts. For the earlier version, see Appendix.

[156] Augustine, Letter 93.9.34.

the unbelievers who criticized the Christian religion, he said, 'Let us tolerate, if we can't correct, those who wish the state, which the first Romans established and expanded through their virtues, to stand with its vices unpunished.'[157] Therefore it is not a mark of prudence to strive in vain, nor is it the task of an apostle to ask for a rational mode of life from those who live outside, as one would ask it of Christians, and to demand that they live in a Christian manner.

(3) On the other hand, that it *is* the task of an apostle to make an effort to bring it about that those same people be converted to belief in Christ, to preach the gospel to them, and to attempt all things within one's power that serve to produce this result in the right way—to *this* not only Paul but all the apostles bear witness by their lives and by the deaths they met in this cause. Therefore, it is not rashly but highly reasonably that it has been handed down by very learned men that there is sufficient justification for Christians lawfully, on the authority of the Supreme Pontiff, waging war for the purpose of punishing and correcting pagans who do not observe the law of nature.[158]

For lest anyone doubt the power of the church, which we understand was granted among the apostles over every land and over all peoples, Christ himself thus gave the Apostles the right and the commandment of teaching men and of giving laws derived from his teaching, by first declaring that every power in heaven and earth had been given to him, then by speaking not only of peoples but of *all* peoples—in these words: 'Every power has been given to me in heaven and on earth. Go forth, therefore, and teach all peoples, baptizing them in the name of the Father and the Son and the Holy Spirit, teaching them to observe all the things that I have taught you.'[159] For Christ had first and foremost taught his Apostles that along with the Christian faith the laws of nature should be observed, all of which are contained in the Ten Commandments and in the love of one's neighbour.

Since all mortal men are subject to those laws and are able to be taught and persuaded by natural reason, it is by the greatest justice that violators of those laws may be punished by the church and by the vicar of Christ and, through his authority and decree, by Christian princes and may be compelled to natural justice, provided the power to carry it out be at hand, for as I have said, on the authority of Augustine, 'The church corrects those whom it can and tolerates those whom it does not have the power to correct.'[160]

For that reason, St Thomas testifies that the church, administering the authority of God, is able with its own right to pass laws upon the unbelievers, even upon

---

[157] Augustine, Letter 138.3.17.

[158] The identity of these 'very learned men' (*viri eruditissimi*) is indicated in a marginal note in the manuscripts: 'Super cap. quod super his de voto' (Losada edition, p. 45, n. 113), i.e. commentators on Innocent III's decretal *Quod super his*. In the parallel passage in the *Apologia* (III.2.xii.), Sepúlveda mentions by name the commentators he has in mind: Innocent IV and Hostiensis, supported by Joannes Andreas and Panormitanus.

[159] Matthew 28:18–20.

[160] Augustine, Letter 93.9.34.

those who do not belong to the church or are subjected to its members in temporality (as he himself phrases it).[161] Since this is so, the church will by the same reasoning and the same right be able to establish among those same people other things which will have seemed necessary and accordingly to apply the necessary force, provided the means are at hand, to insure that the laws be observed, lest it shall have laid down the law in vain. And a little bit later the same Thomas denies that the rites of unbelievers, which bring Christians nothing of truth or usefulness, should for any reason be tolerated unless perhaps to avoid some evil—as at first, when there was a great number of unbelievers, the rites were tolerated.[162]

It is therefore lawful and permitted on the authority of the church that unbelievers be brought under rule, especially those who do not observe the law of nature, which law,[163] it is agreed, is especially violated by idol-worshippers and those who do not acknowledge and worship the one, eternal, highest, greatest God. For, under the guidance of God and the teaching of nature, Socrates, Plato, Aristotle and the majority of philosophers recognized that God is a single being and is most greatly to be worshipped, according to the testimony of our Paul, who writes thus to the Romans: 'That which is to be known of God is clear to them; for God made it plain to them. For the invisible things of God from the creation of the world are clearly seen, having been understood through the things that were made; among them, his eternal power and divinity.'[164]

13 [*The philosophers recognized that there is only one god*]

(1) **Leopoldus**: Do you, then, think that Plato and Aristotle recognized a single god?[165] For they mention throughout their works many gods, some of whom they even call by name as Jupiter, Saturn, Mars, Mercury, and many others.

Democrates: It is not impious to mention gods through a kind of metaphorical usage, nor is it even contrary to the custom of Scripture. For even in Exodus we read: 'Do not disparage the gods, and do not curse the leader of your people.'[166] And in the Psalm: 'God stood in the gathering of the gods, in their midst he judges the gods.' And in the same Psalm: 'I have said: You are gods and sons of the Highest.'[167] Therefore he calls the sons of God gods, though, granted, the Son of God is by

---

[161] Aquinas, *ST* II-II, q. 10, art. 11.

[162] Aquinas, *ST* II-II, q. 10, art. 11.

[163] The passage from here to the end of this section and chapter, serving as a transition to the discussion of pagan philosophers, was present in VTM, but omitted in P.

[164] Romans 1:19–20.

[165] The long section on the pagan philosophers designated chapters 13 and 14 by Coroleu was entirely omitted in the intermediate P manuscript, but was present, with variations, in the earlier tradition represented by VTM. Coroleu's *app. crit.*, by designating S readings in this passage as SP, misleadingly gives the impression that this section was present in P, even though he correctly noted on p. 75 'textum integrum om. P' (see also the *app. crit.* of Losada's edition, 47). See p. 322 of Menéndez y Pelayo's edition, where the omission is evident.

[166] Exodus 22:28.

[167] Psalm 82 (81):1 and 6.

nature properly only one, the second person of the Trinity. Nonetheless, whoever have faith in Christ are called sons of God by adoption, as it were. 'All men', says Paul, 'are sons of God through faith.'[168] And John in his Gospel says: 'To those who believe in his name, he has given the power to become sons of God.'[169] Therefore the wise philosophers refer to many gods and mention them by name, but only when they speak in a way that appeals to the common people and metaphorically.

(2) Therefore the incorporeal beings that we call angels those men sometimes called intelligences and at other times called gods. But just as we, while admitting that there are many thousands of angels who imitate the single nature of God, believe that God is one single being, so those men, while believing that there were many beings of this sort in heaven, nonetheless held for certain that God was one single being, highest and eternal, whom they called best and greatest, even though he himself was called by many names, as Aristotle himself testifies, who writes thus to Alexander in his book *On the Cosmos*: 'Though God is one, nonetheless he is called by many names, which we have bestowed upon him from his own works. For we call him Jupiter [Zeus] as the author of life [*zō*], and Saturn [Kronos] from time [*chronos*], for he passes through from one age to another without end, and Nemesis because he distributes [*nemō*] to individuals in accord with their deserts.'[170]

And the fact that not just Aristotle but almost all the learned men of the pagans were of this opinion is attested by Augustine in the fourth book of *The City of God*: 'God in the sky is named Jupiter, the same in the air is Juno, in the sea Neptune, in the earth Pluto, in time Saturn, in wars Mars, in the vineyards Liber, in the grains Ceres, and in other things in the same manner.'[171] Likewise Varro, as the same Augustine reports, recounts that Jupiter is worshipped even by those who worship one single God without an effigy, but he is called by another name.[172] The pagan Maximus of Madaura wrote thus to Augustine about this: 'Who is so mad, so beside himself as to deny that it is most certain that there is one single highest God, without beginning, without offspring, the great and splendid prince, as it were, of nature, whose powers, spread throughout the fabric of the world, we call upon by many names, since it is evident that we do not all of us know his true name?'[173]

(3) These same philosophers understood that, compared to this true God, all other beings called gods and goddesses and all other things that were contained in the world were meagre, feeble, and trivial, and ought to be considered as of no value, as that famous 'Homeric chain' makes clear, which Aristotle mentions in his book *On the Movement of Animals*.[174] Aristotle explains the gradation of causes in

---

[168] Galatians 3:26.
[169] John 1:12.
[170] Pseudo-Aristotle, *De mundo* 401a14.
[171] Augustine, *De civitate Dei* 4.11.
[172] Augustine, *De civitate Dei* 4.9.
[173] Maximus to Augustine: Augustine, Letter 16.1.
[174] Aristotle, *De motu animalium* 699b32.

accord with this same principle: that the first cause, which is God, presides over all other things at once, is alone unmoving, but moves and guides all other things. And in Book 3 of the *Politics* he says, 'If there were someone in a state who surpassed all other citizens jointly in intelligence and in every sort of virtue, to wish to subject this man to rule by turns would be as if it were decided that rule among the gods be shared out in such a way that Jupiter would sometimes rule and sometimes obey the rule of another god.'[175]

This same Aristotle, in his work *The First Philosophy* [*Metaphysics*], though he often mentioned many gods, nonetheless in Book 12 affirms and makes clear that there is only one god.[176] That this god has a care for human affairs and justice, he teaches in these words of the last book of the aforementioned *On the Cosmos*: 'As it is handed down in an old saying, since God possesses the beginning, middle, and end of all things, he always rightly proceeds in accord with nature, and justice always attends upon him, punishing those who violate divine law.'[177] Moreover, he says that God rightly proceeds in accord with nature because God orders that the natural order always be preserved and forbids it to be disturbed—'which is the essence of eternal law', as Augustine teaches in his book *Against Faustus*.[178]

As to the fact that Ambrose propounds in his book *On the Duties of Clergy* that Aristotle was of the opinion that the providence of God did not descend below the sphere of the moon, he seems to have been led astray by one of those people who through a passion for faultfinding are in the habit of giving insufficiently candid testimony about great men, as though they were on intimate terms with people whom, as the saying goes, they didn't even know by sight.[179] For nothing is further from Aristotle's teaching than that claim, for in Books 1 and 12 of *The First Philosophy* he teaches that God is the first cause and declares that he is the beginning and cause of all things;[180] and in Book 1 of the *Meteorology* he teaches that the world with the lands that surround us is governed by celestial causes, of which the first cause is God;[181] and in Book 10 of the *Nicomachean Ethics* he affirms that God has charge of human affairs and especially looks out for the best and wisest men.[182] Also, in Book 2 of the *Magna Moralia*, in reference to good luck, he says, 'We judge that God, in whose will things of this sort reside, grants good things and bad to mortals in accord with the merit of each person.'[183] I shall pass over many other passages that very manifestly refute that falsehood.

---

[175] Aristotle, *Politics* 3.8.7 (1284b28–32).
[176] Aristotle, *Metaphysics* (1074a40).
[177] Pseudo-Aristotle, *De mundo* 401b24.
[178] Augustine, *Contra Faustum* 22.30.
[179] Ambrose, *De officiis ministrorum* 1.13.
[180] Aristotle, *Metaphysics* 983a8.
[181] Aristotle, *Meteorologica* 339a22.
[182] Aristotle, *Nicomachean Ethics* 10.8.13 (1179a25–29).
[183] Aristotle, *Magna Moralia* 2.8 (1207a6–7).

I declare that this same Ambrose was led astray in the same manner when he wrote in the second book of the same work that Aristotle placed the happy life in virtue and the pleasures of the body, since Aristotle himself in many passages plainly and clearly left his view about happiness fully declared: that is, that the highest good consists in the use of untrammelled virtue.[184] Nor does he add any other pleasure than that which, arising from the very works of virtue and from worthy deeds, is felt by those who have put on the habit of virtue. This, the truest and most honourable form of delight, is a far cry from bodily pleasures, whose pursuers he tends to affirm are not happy but similar sometimes to beasts, sometimes to bondsmen. Moreover, he calls virtue untrammelled when it is not impeded by poverty or ill health by which it is less able to perform worthy and glorious deeds. So virtue alone is not sufficient for the perfect performance of duty, but the actual doing is also required, as both Ambrose and the Philosopher affirm.

14 [*The possibility of salvation through the law of nature without the knowledge of Christ*]

(1) **Leopoldus:** Now that we've fallen into this subject, I beg you, Democrates, not to be reluctant to disentangle this minor question in a few words: if those philosophers believed that there was one god and that he was of the sort you have said, what did those equipped with this faith lack for acquiring the salvation of their souls?

Democrates: 'Faith without works is dead', says James in his epistle.[185] 'You believe', he says, 'that God is one; good for you! The demons believe it as well—and tremble.'[186] Therefore many of those men, as Paul testifies, 'though they recognized God, did not glorify him or give thanks to him; but they became empty in their cogitations'.[187]

(2) **Leopoldus:** It's not surprising that many of the pagans lived wicked lives even though they had the correct conception of God, for the same thing happens in the case of many Christians. But supposing there were some among those famous ancient philosophers and other men whom the philosophers educated in civil life who at one and the same time had the correct conception of God and lived upright lives on the basis of the law of nature—perhaps such men as Socrates, Plato, Aristotle, Aristides the Athenian, Aratus of Sicyon among the Greeks, and likewise among the Romans the Catos, Curius, Fabricius, the Scipios, Cicero, and others who were regarded as most excellent and just—and supposing also that they committed some sin or other, they would be thought to have made up for it through their great services and the remorse of their hearts. Therefore if men such as these,

---

[184] Ambrose, *De officiis ministrorum* 2.2.4 (*PL* 16, col. 104B); cf. Aristotle, *Nicomachean Ethics* 10.6.1–10.7.3 (1177a1–28).

[185] James 2:26.

[186] James 2:19.

[187] Romans 1:21.

124   SEPÚLVEDA ON THE SPANISH INVASION OF THE AMERICAS

with God and nature as their guides, believed that God is one and that he has a care for human affairs, how much hope do you think we should have concerning their salvation?

(3) **Democrates:** What should I think other than what Thomas Aquinas, the wisest and holiest man, thought, who affirmed that before the coming of Christ the pagans were subject only to the law of nature, not yet to Mosaic law, 'although they would have attained salvation more perfectly and more securely under reverence for that law than by the natural law alone'[188] Here he followed Paul as his authority, who wrote thus in his Epistle to the Romans: 'It isn't those who hear the law who are righteous in the eyes of God, but those who perform the law will be justified. For when the pagans, who do not have the law, perform naturally the things that belong to the law, these people, while not in possession of the law, are a law unto themselves; they show the work of the law written in their own hearts.'[189] Although Thomas had earlier twisted these words about into various meanings in his commentary on the epistles of Paul, nonetheless in the *Summa theologica,* which he composed as an old man, he took them in this plain and very clear sense, an opinion shared also by Augustine in a certain letter.[190] Also, at much greater length, Alfonso el Tostado, a very important author, followed and expounded upon this same view, in his *Fifth Paradox.*[191]

(4) **Leopoldus:** But without faith in Christ no one has ever achieved salvation, 'for there is no other name given to men under heaven by which they must be saved.'[192] For 'both the crowds that came before him and those that followed used to shout: "Hosanna to the son of David; blessed is he who comes in the name of God"'[193] Hence Augustine says, 'That faith which saves us healed the just men of old—that is, faith in Jesus Christ, the mediator between God and men.'[194] In what way, then, could those ancient philosophers and upright pagan men be saved through the law of nature alone?

Democrates: Someone who uses the words 'the law of nature alone' here, Leopoldus, is to be thought of as setting aside the rituals of Moses, but not the grace of God that the theologians call 'sanctifying grace' [*gratia gratum faciens*], without which no one has ever been worthy of salvation—that is, of eternal life. 'For the sufferings of this time are not worthy to be compared with the future glory that shall be revealed in us', as Paul affirms.[195] But faith in Christ is not included in that exception [of Mosaic rituals]—and as you were saying, it is a common teaching of the theologians that there is no salvation without that faith.

---

[188] Aquinas, *ST* I-II, q. 98, art. 5.
[189] Romans 2:12–15.
[190] Augustine, *Contra Faustum* 19.2; *De spiritu et lettera* (*On the Spirit and the Letter*) 28.4.
[191] El Tostado (Alonso de Madrigal), *Paradoxa* (1521), II, V, pp. 124–25.
[192] Acts 4:12.
[193] Matthew 21:9.
[194] Augustine *De natura et gratia contra Pelagium* (*On Nature and Grace against Pelagius*) 44.51.
[195] Romans 8:18.

Still, you know how indulgently and liberally those same theologians interpret this principle, for when it is a question of the salvation of the holy patriarchs who dated back to before the coming of Christ, they do not declare or demand that a manifest and explicit faith in Christ have been in all of them, but they have been content with a still obscure and hidden mystery of some sort.[196] In accord with this line of thought, one is not improperly permitted to conclude that those philosophers and whoever else believed that God is one and has a care for human affairs had some sort of faith in Christ.[197]

For in the following words Thomas, following Paul, affirms that the entire faith in Christ is contained in this formulation: 'All the articles are implicitly contained in certain primary matters of faith: namely, that it is believed that God exists and that he has forethought concerning the salvation of human beings, in accord with this passage in the Epistle to the Hebrews: "He who approaches God ought to believe that he exists, and that he grants rewards to those who seek him"; for in God's existence are included all things that we believe exist eternally in God, and in these things our blessedness consists; but belief in the providence of God embraces all things that are temporally distributed by God for the salvation of human beings, which things are the path to blessedness, and it is in this manner that some of the subsequent articles are contained in other articles, just as in the faith in the redemption of mankind the incarnation and his passion and all things of this sort are implicitly contained.'[198] Those are the words of St Thomas in the second part of Book 2, first question. Just a bit further on the discourses on the same subject in this way: 'If there were those who, although pagans, were saved, people to whom revelation had not been made, they were not saved apart from faith in the Mediator, for even if they did not possess explicit faith, they nonetheless had implicit faith in divine providence, believing as they did that God was the liberator of human beings in accord with means pleasing to himself.'[199] According to this line of reasoning, then, one may suppose—with Thomas or, rather, Paul as one's authority—that the ancient philosophers, as champions of justice, and other upright men who were taught by the philosophers had faith in Christ and were saved through the law of nature before the coming of Christ.

(5) But whether the same reasoning is valid in the case of heathens after the coming of Christ—those who live or have lived uprightly on the basis of the law of nature, people whom the name of Christ has never reached, who have been just as unable as those earlier people to believe in him of whom they had not heard or to hear of him without someone there to preach him—and whether, in the general case of all those who simply observe the law of nature, a certain common way

---

[196] 'Mystery' renders *enigmate*, clearly based on 1 Corinthians 13:12.

[197] Here the manuscripts VTM, representing the earliest state of the dialogue, offered an extensive passage with a personal anecdote concerning Cardinal Cajetan. See Appendix.

[198] Aquinas, *ST* II-II, q. 1, art. 7, quoting Hebrews 11:6.

[199] Aquinas, *ST* II-II, q. 2, art. 7.

of believing of the sort we have laid out would suffice; or whether there would be required a special provision for sending forth those who might more clearly teach righteous men faith in Christ on an individual basis (as was done by means of Peter with the centurion Cornelius and by means of angels with certain other men about whom Dionysius testifies in his *Celestial Hierarchy* in what constitutes his third and most secure argument)—as to what we are allowed to decide concerning all these things, I say, let those who investigate those matters with greater subtlety look into this.[200]

In the meantime, we do not hesitate to affirm that point on which the theologians are of one mind: divine aid has failed no one either after or before the coming of Christ who cultivates justice and does what in him lies. 'For God is no respecter of persons', as the Apostle Peter says, 'but in every people the one who fears him and performs justice has been accepted by him.'[201] And as Paul says: 'The same one is God of all, richly blessing all who call on him.'[202] He backs this up with the testimony of the prophet Joel, in these words: 'Everyone who calls upon the name of the Lord shall be saved.'[203] For we have learned that right up to the time that our fathers could remember there were very many peoples to whom the gospel had not been announced, and that there are even now many in what they call the New World who have never heard the name of Christ—this despite the fact that those of earlier times supposed that there were already no such peoples or very few, such as Augustine, who wrote in his *On Nature and Grace*: 'For there are at this point still the most remote peoples—though, as reported, very few—to whom the gospel has not yet been preached.'[204]

Also Ambrose, in his work *On the Calling of All Nations,* has left this written: 'But if perchance even now in the remotest parts of the world there are certain peoples whom the grace of the Saviour has not yet illuminated, we do not doubt about them that through the hidden judgment of God the time for their summoning has been arranged, when they are to hear and accept the gospel, which they have not yet heard. And yet they have not been denied that measure of general help, which has been offered all men from above, even though human nature has been wounded by so bitter a wound that their own unaided reflection does not have the power to fully instruct any man in the knowledge of God, unless the true light could scatter the heart's shadowy state, the light which, in his inscrutable wisdom, the just and good God did not pour forth upon earlier ages in the way he has done in our days.'[205] This same Ambrose earlier, in Book 1, named this 'general help' as 'the assistance of

---

[200] Pseudo-Dionysius the Areopagite, *Celestial Hierarchy* 9.2 (*PG* 3, col. 257D).
[201] Acts 10:34–35.
[202] Romans 10:12.
[203] Joel 2:32.
[204] Augustine, *De natura et gratia* 2.2.
[205] Pseudo-Ambrose (probably Prosper of Aquitaine), *De vocatu gentium* 2.6.

grace', in these words: 'Although we believe that there are no men from whom the assistance of grace has entirely been taken away'.[206]

This very weighty testimony of Ambrose very fully accords with that view of Thomas, which we have mentioned: 'Pagans could have been saved by the law of nature'—though not without sanctifying grace (as Scotus says), and with more difficulty than if they had been enlightened by the law of Moses.[207] For original sin was wiped out for them [the Jews] through their sacrifices, through their faith in Christ (obscure and enigmatic though it was, as we have mentioned above), and through circumcision, which was given to them earlier.

Relevant to this is what Gregory teaches in the fourth book of his *Moralia:* 'Whoever is not absolved through the water of regeneration is held bound by the chains of the original accusation'.[208] Indeed, the water of baptism has among us the same effect that among men of ancient times faith alone had for children or the efficacy of sacrifice had for adults or the mystery of circumcision had for those descended from the stock of Abraham. For it is not congruent with divine generosity to have given to those who are not of the seed of Abraham (that is, to the gentiles who have been called to the faith)[209] a means of defence for doing away with original sin while having left them no means of obtaining forgiveness for their other sins and for returning into a state of Grace with God.

15 [*The justice of war against peoples who violate the law of nature, do wrong to God, and harm innocents*]

(1) To return to the point from which we digressed: if the law of nature was salutary for those who lived by it and invoked the name of God, while the worship of idols was always harmful (for as Paul said, 'An idolater will not receive an inheritance in the kingdom of Christ and God'), it is sufficiently clear that idol-worshippers do not follow the law of nature, the violation of which in other ways as well is assuredly a very great sin.[210]

Leopoldus: If the violation of the law of nature is a just motive for inflicting war, then either I am wrong or there has been no people who could not be justly attacked in that way on account of the violation of the law of nature and because of sins. For which peoples and how many of them will be found who observe the law of nature?

---

[206] Pseudo-Ambrose, *De vocatu gentium* 1.7.

[207] The passage in Duns Scotus to which Sepúlveda refers has not been identified. Taranto cites an irrelevant passage in Scotus (*Super primum Sententiarum*, dist. 1, q. 4) where *gratificatio* is used, but not (as here) *gratia gratificans*.

[208] Gregory I, *Moralia in Iob* 4.3.

[209] This parenthetical clarification is ambiguous in the Latin: 'id est, gentibus vocatis'. This could be rendered 'that is, those who are called pagans'. This is how the Losada/Coroleu translation renders it: 'es decir, los gentiles'. Similarly, Taranto renders it 'a quelli cioè chiamati genti'. But *vocati* could also have the sense of 'called; invited; summoned [to the faith]'. So Schäfer: 'dass heisst, den zum Glauben berufenen Völkern'. I lean, without strong conviction, to the latter interpretation.

[210] Ephesians 5:5.

Democrates: Many such nations will be found—or, rather, there is no nation among those that are and are called civilized, which would not observe the law of nature.

(2) **Leopoldus:** I don't sufficiently understand what you are calling the law of nature in this context, unless perhaps you are saying that the law of nature is observed by those who at least abstain from criminal lust and similar sins, though they may be involved in other serious misdeeds—although even on this line of reasoning there are very few peoples who observe the law of nature. But I maintain that robberies, adulteries, murders, and other great crimes with which we see Christians contaminated all over the place are against the law of nature, nor could you, if you would care to be consistent with yourself, deny this, since not long ago you defined the law of nature as participation in the eternal law by a creature capable of reason. In accord with this eternal law, all more serious sins are condemned capitally—that is, by eternal death.

(3) **Democrates:** Don't worry, Leopoldus; all sins, insofar as they are more serious, are against the laws of nature. For as Augustine says, 'They wouldn't be sins unless they were contrary to nature.'[211] And St Ambrose, in the first book of *On the Duties of Clergy*, defines that which is fitting—that is, that which is worthy—as living in accord with nature; and the base as that which comes about contrary to nature.[212]

But you, however, must see to it again and again that you do not rashly take any one thing as established for all the peoples of the world. For if there is a sin against nature committed in a given nation by certain people—or even by everyone acting as individuals—one should not say that the whole nation on that account does not observe the law of nature, as certain recent theologians have falsely thought.[213] For the case of a whole society should not be tried on the basis of the doings of certain individual people, but on that of public customs and institutions. For the acts of a state, as the Philosopher teaches in Book 3, chapter 1 of the *Politics*, 'are understood to be those that have been conducted publicly by those by whose supreme authority the state is administered.'[214] It is also the shared opinion of jurists that those things that are done by private individuals, even if they are done by all of them, nonetheless should not be attributed to the society as a whole.

(4) Therefore in those peoples among whom robbery, adultery, usury—add even criminal lust and other sins—are regarded as being among the basest things and are punished in accord with customs and laws, although certain individuals, or even a majority of them, are caught up in those sins, not even for this reason is it to be maintained that those peoples do not observe the law of nature. A state should

---

[211] Augustine, *Contra Faustum* 22.78.

[212] Ambrose, *De officiis ministrorum* 1.221.

[213] A marginal annotation in Sepúlveda's hand to the Salamanca manuscript makes the reference explicit: 'F[ra]n[cisc]us Victoria in relectione'. See Losada's edition, p. 57 (and Pl. 6).

[214] Aristotle, *Politics* 3.1.1 (1274b34ff).

not be punished on account of individuals' crimes which are publicly condemned and punished, any more than if certain individuals rashly, without public authorization, harass with attacks the fields of another country, provided that they are duly punished by their own state, with restoration of the stolen property.

(5) But if some population were so barbarous and uncivilized that it failed to regard all or some of the crimes I've enumerated as belonging to the category of base acts and failed to punish them through laws and customs—or that it visited the lightest punishments upon the most serious crimes—especially those which nature most especially loathes—and did not even think some of them merited punishment at all—this people would justly and properly be said to fail to observe the law of nature. For in this situation we have an augmentation of that famous shouting of the inhabitants of Sodom and Gomorrah, since, as St Augustine testifies, 'Not only were those crimes not punished among them, but they were even repeatedly practised as though in accord with a public law.'[215] He also in another passage says of them, 'It was fitting that those who offended God through a joint endeavour should perish by the same common attack of retribution.' Also, a little later he says that they were people 'who made their sin manifest not only by performing it but by openly proclaiming it.'[216]

Therefore such a people may with the highest justification be utterly defeated in war by Christians, if they reject their rule, on account of their wicked crimes and barbarity and inhumanity—but for their own greatest good, to be sure, in order that very wicked men, barbarians, unbelievers may submit to men who are good, civilized, and worshippers of the True Religion, and may be led by the warnings, laws, and customs of those men to right reason, civilization, and piety—which would be the greatest duty of Christian loving-kindness.

It does not belong to the power or the jurisdiction of the Supreme Pontiff to subject the pagans to the Christians and to the laws of the gospel or to demand that they be punished as violators of the Christian religion which they do not accept— this, as I have said above, is what the Apostle meant when he said, 'For what business is it of mine to pass judgment on those who are outside?'[217] It *is*, however, his duty to offer help, if some not especially difficult way of proceeding may be embarked upon, in order that the pagans may be hindered, as far as possible, from crimes and inhuman acts of wickedness and the worship of idols and in general from impiety and may be summoned back to worthy and civilized customs and true religion. And this he will do on the authority of God, 'who wishes all men to become saved and to come to the knowledge of the truth.'[218]

---

[215] Augustine, *Enchiridion de Fide, Spe, et Caritate* (*Handbook on Faith, Hope, and Charity*), Bk. 1, ch. 80.

[216] These passages are not in fact from St Augustine, but an anonymous Irish writer of the sixth century who goes by the title of 'Augustinus Hibernus' ('the Irish Augustine'), *De mirabilibus sacrae scripturae* (*On the Miracles of Sacred Scripture*), Bk. 1, ch. 10 (see *Patrologia Latina*, vol. 35, col. 2161).

[217] 1 Corinthians 5:12.

[218] 1 Timothy 2:4.

(6) For that utterance of Terence's Chremes—'I am a man; I consider nothing human to be alien to me'[219] (meaning that it belongs to the duty and humanity of every man to look after his fellow man and to be of service to him in whatever circumstances he can, short of doing harm to himself)—this is divine and natural law, which has come forth from that light of the countenance of God, which has been sealed over us[220]—that is, from eternal law—and which has been handed down in the book of Ecclesiasticus: 'God has given a commandment to every single man concerning his neighbour.'[221] For all mortals, as Augustine teaches in Book 1 of *On Christian Teaching*, are neighbours and fellows among each other on account of that fellowship which is most broadly manifest among all men.[222]

But if each private individual is ordered to render this duty in accord with the law of nature, how much more is this true of the highest priest of God and vicar of Christ and also the Christian princes, who themselves also, though in a different manner, represent God on earth, since both pope and princes not only are called but actually are shepherds of the Christian flock! Moreover, it is the duty of a shepherd not only to feed the flock that has been entrusted to him, but if he comes upon some other sheep from another flock or sheepfold of the same lord wandering in the wilderness, it is his duty not to neglect their care, but, if he is able to do so conveniently, drive them into the same pens as his own sheep and thus to a safer place, so that in this way there may gradually come into being a single sheepfold and a single shepherd.

(7) Pagans may not solely on account of unbelief be punished or forced to accept faith in Christ against their will, for as Augustine says, 'Belief belongs to the will, and the will cannot be forced.'[223] They can, however, be restrained from wicked deeds. He says, 'No one can be compelled to faith, but treachery is often punished by the scourges of tribulations through the severity or, rather, through the mercy of God.' The same man addresses heretics thus: 'Those men are considered the most conscientious guides and the most pious counsellors who decree that, in return for so great a sin, you must be so mildly deterred and constrained by warnings of fines or by the confiscation of lands or goods or money, so that, by reflecting on why you are suffering these things, you may shun your sacrilege once you have become aware of it and you may be freed from eternal damnation.'[224] That which has been said against heretics holds true also against pagans; for both are our neighbours and we are ordered by divine and natural law to care for both so that they may be turned away from wicked deeds, especially from those by which nature and

---

[219] Terence, *Heautontimoroumenos* (*The Self-Tormentor*), 77.

[220] An allusion to the Vulgate of Psalm 4:6: 'Signatum est super nos lumen vultus tui, Domine'.

[221] Ecclesiasticus 17:12 (Sirach 17:14).

[222] Sepúlveda is thinking of Augustine, *De doctrina christiana* 1.30.31, but he is not directly quoting Augustine, as Losada, Coroleu, Taranto, and Schäfer all assumed.

[223] Augustine, *Contra litteras Petiliani* (*Against the Letter of the Donatist Petilian*) 2.83.184.

[224] Augustine, *Epistola ad Catholicos contra Donatistas* (*Letter to Catholics of the Donatist Sect*) 20.55.

the author of nature, God, are most violated and offended—in particular from the worship of idols, the very worst of all sins.

Therefore, as to the objection you offered at first, Leopoldus, that this war in which the Spaniards attack barbarians who have not deserved any ill treatment at their hands seems to be unjust—since you are, I believe, applying to this war the standard definition of just wars as being, on the authority of Augustine, 'those which avenge injuries received'[225]—one must understand that in a holy war which is waged by pious men against the worshippers of idols it is not so much the wrongs done to men that are punished as those done to God, these being much more serious.

Moreover, the person who ought to obey another man and yet does not carry out his just demands is committing an injury to the person making the demand. If that person rejects rule after having been given warning, he is a wrongdoer. Accordingly, it is obvious that in this war not only wrongs done to God but also those done to men are punished; but above all it is the wrongs done to God, for they are largely defined by those crimes in particular, and they are wrongs that (as St John Chrysostom observed) we ought not to endure even to hear of, following the example of Christ. Chrysostom went on to say: 'In the case of our private injuries a certain amount of patience is a laudable thing; but to disregard injuries to God is an act of serious impiety.'[226]

(8) For if it is permitted and even praiseworthy for princes to avenge by war injuries done to friends and family members even among foreign peoples, on the model of Abraham who sought from the four kings retribution for the injuries done to Lot and his friends, how much more so in the case of injuries done to God, no matter by whom they may have been perpetrated.[227] This is especially the case if, assuming that a prince has a sufficiently serious reason for the justice of the war, by that same action many injuries may be warded off from many innocent people, as is indeed occurring in a major way in the case of those barbarians reduced to our rule, for it is agreed that in any given year in one region named New Spain they sacrificed over 20,000 people who deserved no such fate. Thus, with the exception of a single city, Mexico, whose inhabitants at the end fought back most obstinately, that entire province, which is much larger than all of Spain, was reduced to the rule of the Christians through the slaughter of far fewer men than they themselves were in the habit of sacrificing in any given single year. For the theologians agree that all men are the neighbours of all men, on account of that fellowship which (as we have mentioned a bit earlier) is very extensively evident among all men—also on the principle derived from the Samaritan in the Evangelist, who is said to have acted as

---

[225] Augustine, *Quaestiones in Heptateuchum* (*Questions on the Heptateuch*), VI ('Questions on Joshua Son of Nun'), 10.

[226] Pseudo-John Chrysostom, *Opus imperfectum in Matthaeum* (*Unfinished Work on Matthew*) V (see *Patrologia* Graeca, vol. 51, col. 668); cf. Aquinas, *ST* II-II, q. 188, art. 3.

[227] Genesis 14:8–16.

132 SEPÚLVEDA ON THE SPANISH INVASION OF THE AMERICAS

the neighbour to the Israelite who was robbed and wounded by brigands, to whom he had brought aid at great danger and damage to himself.[228]

(9) Moreover, it is by that divine law that I have cited from Ecclesiasticus ('God has given a commandment to each man concerning his neighbour') that all men are commanded, if they are able to do so without serious detriment, to bring aid to a neighbour and a fellow, on the model of the upright and humane Samaritan— and all the more if someone is unjustly being taken off to death.[229] There is a precept about this with regard to individual behaviour in the sacred Proverbs: 'Rescue those who are being led off to death'[230]—led off, that is, unjustly and without guilt, as in the case of those wretched men who used to be sacrificed by those barbarians at their impious altars. Among those people this prophecy is fulfilled in our age by the Spaniards: 'For he will free the poor man from the man of power, the poor man who has no one to help him. He will spare that poor and weak man and will save the souls of the needy.'[231]

Therefore, who would deny that it is the duty of a most excellent and pious prince to repel when he can these most serious injustices from so many innocent people? Since, as Ambrose testifies, 'it is not in inflicting but in deflecting injury that the law of virtue consists; for he who does not repel an injury from a fellow man when he able to do so is as much at fault as he who commits the injury.'[232] 'Indeed such crimes and other monstrous sins', as Augustine says, 'are better punished by the judges of the world—that is, by the secular princes—than by the bishops and ecclesiastical guides.'[233] For, as Paul says, 'they are avengers of God's wrath against those who do evil'.[234] Therefore Jerome writes: 'He who smites the wicked for the very reason that they are wicked and possesses the instruments of killing in order that he might kill the worst people—he is God's assistant.'[235]

For not unbelief by itself, but the monstrous sacrifices made with human victims, the extreme wrongs done to innocent peoples, the horrible feasts upon human bodies, the impious worship of idols—these constitute the justifications for war against those most unjust barbarians. Nonetheless, unbelief in itself would offer sufficient justification not for punishing but for correcting and for converting from the false religion to the true one—which is the ultimate goal of this war.

(10) Therefore since the new, gospel law is more perfect and gentler than the old, Mosaic law, for that was a law of fear, while this is a law of grace, gentleness, and charity, even wars ought to be waged in a gentle and merciful manner, and

---

[228] Luke 10:30–37.

[229] Ecclesiasticus 17:12 (Sirach 17:14).

[230] Proverbs 24:11.

[231] Psalm 72 (71):12–13.

[232] Ambrose, *De officiis ministrorum* (*On the Duties of* Clergy) I.36.

[233] In fact, Haymo of Halberstadt (ninth cent.), *In epistolam ad Romanos*, ch. 13 (see *Patrologia Latina*, vol. 117, col. 481). Sepúlveda presumably found the passage in Gratian, C. 23, q. 5, c. 39.

[234] Romans 13:4.

[235] Jerome, *Commentarii in Ezechielem* (*Commentary on Ezekiel*) 3.9.

they ought to be undertaken not so much for the purpose of punishment as for the correction of the wicked. 'For we have not received the spirit of slavery in fear once again', as Paul says, 'but the spirit of the adoption of children, in which we call out, "Abba, Father", nor are we ascribed to Ishmael as the sons of the slave woman, but as belonging to Isaac in freedom.'[236]

Therefore, if Augustine's words are true (as they most certainly are)—'The person whose freedom to sin is taken away is defeated to his own advantage, since there is nothing more unhappy than the happiness of sinners'[237]—what could happen more profitably or in a more salutary way for those barbarians than that they be subjected to the rule of those through whose prudence, virtue, and religion they may be made humane and, to the extent of their ability, civilized beings instead of barbarians and scarcely even human beings, worthy men instead of sinful men, and Christians and worshippers of the true God and the true religion instead of impious men and worshippers of the devils, as they have already become now that the Christian religion has been received through the foresight and the order of Emperor Charles, that most excellent and religious prince, and now that at public expense there have been granted them instructors in writing and learning as well as teachers of morals and true religion?

(11) From this religion arises separately the fourth and most just justification for making war against the barbarians. For this refers to the accomplishing of the gospel teaching of Christ and the guiding of an infinite multitude of men wandering in the most destructive shadows back by the nearest short-cut into the light of truth.[238]

(12) God says, 'If you encounter the ox or ass of your enemy going astray, lead it back to him.'[239] If God orders us to lead wandering brute animals back to the path and to a safer place and to fulfil this duty even for enemies, shall we hesitate to lead back to the path of truth, if we can, human beings, our neighbours and fellows, who are most dangerously astray? And will we regard it as a nuisance to undertake this task whose aim is not that we tend to the advantages of our enemies, but that we obey the will of the most loving God and the Lord of all, who wishes that all men become saved and come to the knowledge of the truth?[240]

(13) Thus it is by the law of nature and of Christian charity that we are ordered not only to show the right path to any people at all who are going astray, but even much more to guide pagans back to the true religion, if it may be done opportunely and without great harm to ourselves. For what sane man would not wish

---

[236] Galatians 4 (paraphrase of general sense).

[237] Augustine, Letter 138.2.14. ('Since there is nothing' translates 'quoniam nihil est', for which Sepúlveda read, more awkwardly, 'nec est quidquam', 'nor is there anything'.)

[238] This short section in the Salamanca manuscript replaced a lengthier passage in the earlier versions. See Appendix.

[239] Exodus 23:4.

[240] 1 Timothy 2:4.

that somebody, no matter who, might call him back, even against his will, and lead him back to the true path when he is dangerously astray and foolishly hastening through the darkness to a precipice? Therefore, since we do not doubt that all who are wandering outside the Christian religion are going astray and are being brought to an inevitable precipice unless we shall have pulled them back in whatever way permitted, even against their will, will we not obey the law of nature and Christ who orders us that those things that we wish to be done for us by other men we ourselves should do for them in turn?[241] Christ teaches that this is the highest of all divine laws.

16 [*The right and duty to subject the barbarians to Spanish rule so that they may be more easily forced to hear the gospel*]

(1) **Leopoldus**: Do you, then, believe that pagans are to be compelled to belief, against the opinion of Augustine, whose testimony you have cited just a little while ago?

Democrates: If I in fact thought that way, I could defend the opinion with the help of great authorities—and indeed, if it could actually happen, I would be of this view and even argue that it is the greatest duty of charity. For what greater benefit can be conferred upon a man who is an unbeliever than faith in Christ? But since, as I said before, the will, without which there is no room for faith, cannot be forced, it is not right, according to Augustine and other great theologians, to take on the vain and sometimes dangerous task of baptizing those who are unwilling and the infant children of the unwilling, who tend, on the whole, to follow the will of their parents. Therefore, I say that the unwilling are not to be baptized, but insofar as it lies within our power they are to be pulled back from the precipice, even against their will, and when they are going astray the path of truth is to be shown to them by means of pious warnings and the preaching of the gospel. Given that this happens most conveniently, as we have already seen, when those same people have been reduced to obedience, and because we understand that in these times of ours it cannot happen otherwise, due to the shortage of preachers of the faith and the lack of miracles, I maintain that the same law by which the barbarians may be forced to hear the gospel serves also to ensure that they may be brought under our rule.

For he who in accord with justice seeks an aim by the same right brings to bear all things that pertain to that aim. For this is what Thomas Aquinas said: 'Every power or art or ability to which an end pertains is permitted to make use of those things that serve that end.'[242] Explaining this natural law Pope Alexander III said: 'The person to whom a cause is committed receives the full power concerning all things that belong to that cause.'[243] And Celestine III: 'It is a principle of settled law that,

---

[241] Matthew 7:12.
[242] Aquinas, *ST* II-II, q. 40, art. 2.
[243] Alexander III, in X.1.29.5.

just as the principal matter is entrusted to delegated judges, so the appurtenance is to be entrusted to them as well.'[244] For in every business the end holds the principal place, and in the matter at hand the end is the propagation of Christian piety and the preaching of the gospel entrusted to Peter and his successors, which cannot easily come about without the subjection of the barbarians. Moreover, the person to whom a business is entrusted is understood to be entrusted also with the other things without which the business cannot be properly carried out, as we are more unambiguously taught by the rescript of Gregory IX in the same title.[245]

(2) Thus, while we admit that the power granted in heaven and earth to Christ in accord with his human nature (according to the last chapter of Matthew) and communicated and passed on by Christ to his vicar and his successors is a power properly to be exercised in those matters which pertain to the salvation of souls and in matters of the spirit, nevertheless the popes are not shut out from temporal affairs insofar as they have a bearing on spiritual matters—here I am gladly making use of the words of Thomas Aquinas, in the third book of *On the Government of Rulers*.[246] Moreover, the subjugation of the barbarians is directed towards opportunely passing on to non-believers the teaching of gospel truth and natural law, both of these being a spiritual duty. For, as the same Thomas teaches, flesh-and-blood wars occurring in a believing people ought to be referred to a divine spiritual good as their end, and that is the proper sphere of priests; and for that reason it is the business of priests to regulate just wars and influence other men to fight them—just as Pope Hadrian, of blessed memory, urged Charlemagne to wage war against the Lombards, concerning which it is written in the ecclesiastical decisions [i.e. Gratian's *Decretum*].[247]

Following Hadrian's example, Pope Alexander urged the Spaniards to utterly defeat the barbarians and reduce them to rule and construct a path for gospel preaching, which preaching was commanded by Christ to Peter and the other apostles not only to those who lived with Christ, but even those of this or any other age, if any path for the spreading of the gospel should manifest itself. For there are apostles even today, and there will be until the fullness of the age, as Paul teaches: 'He himself has indeed given some as apostles, some as prophets, others indeed as evangelists, others as pastors and teachers; for the perfecting of the saints, for the work of the ministry, for the building up of the body of Christ, until we shall all come together into the unity of faith and the knowledge of the Son of God.'[248] Therefore there are apostles who are the successors of the Apostles— that is, bishops and presiding priests of the churches and preachers engaged in that

---

[244] Celestine III, in X.1.29.21.

[245] X.1.29.39. The title in question (29) is called *De officio et potestate iudicis delegati* ('On the duty and power of an appointed judge').

[246] Pseudo-Aquinas (Ptolemy of Lucca), *De regimine principum*, 3.12.

[247] Gratian, *Decretum*, C. 23, q. 8, c. 10.

[248] Ephesians 4:11–13.

which pertains to the duty of preaching. As Paul says: 'How will they preach to those barbarians unless they are sent?'[249] How will they be sent unless the barbarians are first brought to obedience?

(3) **Leopoldus:** They are to be sent in the same way as those first ones were sent, who without weapons, with the sole aid of faith, wandered through the greatest part of the world preaching the gospel.

Democrates: And even without a staff and a bag?[250] Just offer the apostles of our age that perfection of faith, that power of miracles, and the gift of tongues by which those men used to reduce impious men to the yoke of faith and to utterly break down their defences, and, believe me, there will be no lack of preachers to wander all over the New World preaching the gospel. Still, I am utterly convinced that, if such men as those were to show up in this era through the gift of God, they would all proceed to make full use of any advantage and opportunity for doing the job well and would express great gratitude to Christian princes who have constructed the road for the preaching of the gospel by pacifying the barbarians.

Therefore now when, either through our merit or sin or because there is less need, we see no or very few miracles, it is necessary to rely upon discernment, and the business should be guided by forethought, lest, if we have acted otherwise, 'we might seem to tempt God—which is against the law of God'.[251] For the theologians contend that God is tempted by the person who in the face of dangers does not make what preparations he can, but entrusts everything to divine aid, just as though he would like to make trial of his justice or his power. 'No one', says Augustine, 'ought to tempt his own God, when he has something he is able to do with rational deliberation.'[252] And Pope Nicholas said: 'A man seems to tempt God if he has something he can do and does not take measures in advance to look after his own safety and that of others.'[253] Moreover, to send apostles and evangelists to peoples who are barbaric and not yet pacified is a difficult and perilous business, which, being met with obstacles on all sides, seems likely to produce very little fruit or none at all.

(4) **Leopoldus:** God has granted man free will, and according to Ecclesiasticus, 'he has left him in the hand of his own judgment'.[254] Why should we be domineering and meddlesome in the business of others and not allow each person to live as he wishes, provided he does no harm to someone else?

---

[249] Romans 10:15, paraphrased, for Paul does not mention 'barbarians'. Losada and Coroleu misidentify the paraphrased passage as 1 Cor. 10:24.

[250] An allusion to Matthew 10:10.

[251] Deuteronomy 6:16.

[252] Gratian, *Decretum,* C. 22, q. 2, c. 22. Though inspired by Augustine's *Contra Faustum* 22.36, the words are actually those of Alcuin (*PL* 100, col. 535), filtered through Hrabanus Maurus (*PL* 107, col. 534) and the Glossa Ordinaria on Genesis 12:13.

[253] Nicholas I, in Gratian, *Decretum,* C. 23, q. 8, c. 15.

[254] Ecclesiasticus (Sirach) 15:14.

Democrates: I detect here the accusation of the heretic Donatus. But hear not what I but what Augustine replies to this: 'Who does not know that a man is not condemned except through the fault of his wicked will, nor acquitted unless he has a good will? Nonetheless, those whom we love are not for that reason to be handed over, cruelly and without consequences, to their evil will; rather, where at all possible, they are to be prevented from evil and forced to the good.'[255] 'For the point that needs to be kept in mind', the same authority states in his letter to Vincentius, 'is not that someone is forced, but what sort of thing it is he is being forced to, and whether it is good or bad.'[256] For, as the same author says in his *Handbook*, 'Many good things are offered to people against their will, when what is being considered is their advantage, not their will; since they are found to be enemies to themselves.'[257]

17 [*The right and duty to compel the barbarians to justice and religion*]

(1) **Leopoldus:** But we read of none who were compelled by Christ or the Apostles either to accept the faith or to hear the gospel; rather, they were only invited to do so.

Democrates: When Paul was harassing the church, Christ restrained him with his voice, threw him to the ground with might, and forced him to faith.[258] That same Christ debarred the buyers and sellers and cast them out of the temple, beaten with whips. But since our discussion is about war inflicted upon wicked idol-worshippers, do you suppose that, since this never happened in the beginnings of the church's birth, there is no time that it can properly be done by the church, not even when she has been augmented by the might and fortified by the power of kings and princes?

Leopoldus: Indeed, I see no reason why I shouldn't think that.

(2) **Democrates:** But Augustine saw why, for when a certain heretic made a similar objection to him, he said, 'You do not notice that at that time the church was just beginning to sprout with new shoots, and that as yet this prophecy had not been fulfilled: "And all the kings of the earth shall pray to him, and all the peoples shall serve him." This certainly comes closer to fulfilment the more the church makes use of its power not only to invite, but also to compel to the good. This is what the Lord wished to indicate by the fact that, although he possessed great power, he nonetheless chose to recommend humility first.'[259]

---

[255] Augustine, Letter 173.2.

[256] Augustine, Letter 93.5.16.

[257] Augustine, *Enchiridion de fide, spe, et caritate* 19.72. Losada, Coroleu, and Schäfer assign the first part of the passage from the *Enchiridion* to Letter 193, but Taranto divided the Augustine passage correctly.

[258] Acts 9:3–8.

[259] Augustine, Letter 173.10, quoting Psalm 72 (71):11. Losada and Coroleu attributed the second half of this passage from Augustine to Sepúlveda, but Taranto and Schäfer correctly extended the quotation.

138 SEPÚLVEDA ON THE SPANISH INVASION OF THE AMERICAS

In order to support this opinion with a teaching from the Gospel, Augustine added this: 'This he taught clearly enough also in the famous parable of the feast: after the host sent word to those who had been invited, and they proved unwilling, he said to his slave, "Go forth quickly into the cities and the streets and the neighbourhoods of the city, and bring here the poor and the weak, the blind and the lame": and the slave said to his master, "It has been done as you have ordered, but there is still room"; and the master said to the slave, "Go into the highways and the hedges and force them to come in, so that my house may be made full". See how it is said at one point concerning those who had come first, "Bring them in"; and then it is said, "Compel". That symbolized the beginnings of the church as it was still growing to the point where afterwards there would be the power of compelling.'[260]

(3) Thus it follows that Augustine declares that there was a famous law of the best and most just prince [Constantine] against the pagans and their sacrifices, with capital punishment and seizure of possessions established as the punishment—not only for those who actually performed the sacrifices, but also for the governors of provinces, if they neglected to punish the crime.[261] Augustine mentions that this law was approved and praised by all Christians, and Ambrose most obstinately defended it in the presence of later emperors.[262]

And lest you think that this course of action, which has been given such a sanction both by law and by nature itself, is allowed only against those pagans who have already been subjected to the rule of Christians (which would be the claim of a man hallucinating in the light of midday), Gregory, an exceptionally wise man and at the same time a most pious pope, most emphatically approves of wars that are inflicted upon unbelievers by the pious, and he claims that these wars are holy and most pleasing to God—even if there is no other underlying reason than that the name of Christ and faith in him may be preached to those people when they have been brought under the rule of the Christians. In a letter he roundly praises Gennadius, the exarch of Africa, because he harried the pagans in war solely for the sake of spreading the faith, 'so that Christ's name may run in every direction through the subdued peoples by means of the preaching of the faith'.[263] For we should not suppose that the prefects and generals of the Romans were in the habit of waging war against people who had already been pacified and subjected to the Roman people.

---

[260] Augustine, Letter 173.10, citing Luke 14:21–23. (*In civitates*, 'into the cities', is not in Augustine's text.)

[261] Sepúlveda is thinking of Augustine, Letter 93.3.10. Though Augustine was referring to emperors in the plural, Sepúlveda took the reference to be to Constantine. See his reference to a supposed edict of Constantine in I.21.4. Usually, the emperor in question is taken to be Constantius II (in 341), though even some modern scholars make a case for an edict of Constantine (now lost). The word 'famous' renders *notam*, Schäfer's palmary emendation for *non tam* (read by the other editors, though Losada did note that the 'n' at the end of *non* was missing).

[262] Ambrose, Letter 6.30.

[263] Gregory I, Letter 1.73.

Relevant here also is this passage from Deuteronomy: 'When you approach a city to attack it, first offer it peace. If it accepts and opens its gates to you, all the people who are in it shall be saved, and it shall serve you under tribute. But if, on the other hand, etc.'[264] Further on it says: 'This is what you shall do to all the cities which are at a considerable distance from you'[265]—that is, which are of a different religion, as an interlinear gloss makes clear, making it clear that there is sufficient justification in the matter of religion why unbelievers may be reduced to rule by believers, so that the impious, by obeying better, pious men, may be led to the true worship of God through their teaching or example. Therefore, I say that those barbarians are not only to be invited, but even compelled to the good—that is, to justice and religion—especially since the business can be carried out and the barbarians reduced to rule with so little trouble and through the killing of so few people on either side, while at the same time one may, with but small loss, attend to the salvation and the great advantages of both present and future members of an almost limitless multitude.

18 [*Preaching is usefully supplemented by threats of force*]
(1) **Leopoldus:** Do you not think that some other safe plan may be formed for the opening of an avenue to preach the gospel than that those nations be compelled to accept rule by force of arms?

Democrates: Indeed, I see that not even this plan has been sufficiently safe for some.

Leopoldus: How is that? Do you think that anyone has experienced danger among the barbarians on account of preaching the gospel?

(2) **Democrates:** Has it, then, not yet reached your ears that in many places preaching friars have been killed by incompletely pacified barbarians when a garrison of Spaniards has withdrawn? And have you not heard that two Dominicans have been cut to pieces by barbarians who rejected the Christian religion in the province of Pirito? Moreover, I have ascertained that a few years later in Chiribiche and Cubagua, provinces of the same continent, two convents of Dominicans and Franciscans were destroyed by the barbarians. In Chiribiche the monk Dionisio was cruelly killed, while the others fled to a boat which was moored nearby; but in Cubagua all the monks, whom the barbarians attacked while they were offering up their sacrifice, were cut down. In that place the barbarians desecrated even the sacred vestments in mockery of the ceremonies and sacrifice that we call the mass.

If that happens to our apostles even after our rule has been accepted by those people, and such a crime has been committed after our troops have taken possession of provinces but had been removed a short distance away, what do we think

---

[264] Deuteronomy 20:10–12.
[265] Deuteronomy 20:15.

is going to happen when preachers have been sent to instruct barbarians whom no fear of our forces could restrain from wickedness and impiety?

So I hope I am a false prophet! But I fear for those men concerning whom, I hear, plans are currently in progress to send to Florida to preach the gospel without the protection of armed men. The originators of these plans are the kind of men who, upon worming their way into public deliberations, are in the habit of bravely making decisions about such things at the cost of others' danger and labour. Indeed, the worthy ones are those who achieve the glory not only of being first to form a bold plan but also of being leaders in a pious undertaking.

(3) And yet I maintain that it is not only in order that they might listen to the preachers that the barbarians should be reduced to rule; but also in order that threats may be added to teaching and admonitions and that terror may be struck into them—if we follow Augustine, who replied thus to Vincentius the Donatist: 'If they are made afraid but not taught, it would seem in effect a wicked domination. But if, on the other hand, they are taught but not made afraid, they would be hardened by the hoary antiquity of custom, and they would more sluggishly be moved to strive to reach the path of salvation. For there are indeed many of whom we are well aware who, when they have been given rational arguments and the truth manifest from divine testimonies, used to answer us that they wished to cross over into communion with the Catholic Church, but they feared the violent hatreds of wicked men.... When, therefore, salvific teaching is joined to useful terror so that not only would the light of truth drive away the shadows of error, but also the power of fear would break the bonds of evil custom, then, as I have said, we rejoice over the salvation of many.'[266]

(4) What Augustine said about heretics we may also truly affirm about the barbarians, very many of whom have accepted the Christian religion through the terror which was applied along with the teaching, who would have rejected it through teaching alone, frightened as they were by the fear of their own priests and rulers. It is highly probable that those priests and rulers, for the sake of their own interests and because they are suspicious of anything new, were going to resist the new religion as inexpedient for their plans. Therefore, it was necessary to remove from the common folk the fear of those people and to inspire in them fear of the Christians instead. For as it is stated in the holy Proverbs: 'An obstinate slave will not be improved by words. For even if he will have understood, he will not obey.'[267]

On that point the Philosopher argues thus: 'It is impossible—or at least very difficult—that when people have adhered to customs for a long time those customs may be completely transformed by words and reasoning.'[268] And a little bit further on: 'The majority of people comply with force more than with words and reasoning

---

[266] Augustine, Letter 93.1.3.
[267] Proverbs 29:19 (in the Vetus Latina version cited by Augustine, Letter 93.5.17).
[268] Aristotle, *Nicomachean Ethics* 10.9.5 (1179b17–18).

and are more compelled by punishments than are guided by a sense of decency.'[269] Therefore he assures us that there is need of laws and force in order to constrain wicked men through the fear of punishment and to engender virtue in them. 'For law', he says, 'which is reason emanating from a certain wisdom and intelligence, has a coercive power.'[270]

This does not mean, as Augustine points out, that 'someone could become good against his will, but rather it is because in the process of fearing what he doesn't want to suffer he either gives up a hostility that stood in the way or is forced to acknowledge a truth of which he had been unaware, so that because of his fear he either rejects the falsehood about which he had been disputing or seeks out the truth of which he was ignorant, and now willingly embraces that which he had not been willing to embrace'.[271] He supports this idea not only by the example of many individuals, but also by that of whole communities. Although these communities had been Donatist, they were then Catholic through the opportunity offered by this kind of terror. As the same Augustine says, 'The church, therefore, corrects those whom it can and tolerates those whom it does not have the power to correct.'[272]

(5) **Leopoldus:** Augustine's remarks were directed against heretics, not pagans, concerning whom there is a different method.[273] For heretics, since they had been initiated into Christian sacraments, and they come to oppose the teachings of the Christian religion to which they had pledged themselves, are, as troublemakers and deserters, to be compelled to their duty and to justice by force of arms, if no other way is granted. But as for pagans, who have nothing in common with us, and who govern their state without any injury to Christians—what charge of this sort, finally, can be lodged against them, on the grounds of which they ought to be punished by the arms of the Christians?

Democrates: If it is about sins and the right of punishing you are inquiring, Leopoldus, just as in the case of heretics the transgression of the law of the gospel may be punished, so in the case of the pagans may the violation of the law of nature, as we have declared above. But Augustine in that passage was not indeed referring so much to the punishment of wrongdoings, as the subject matter itself makes clear, as to how one might look out for the salvation and well-being of men in accord with Christian charity. For just as doctors sometimes heal men who are unwilling and even tied up by cutting and cauterizing in order to provide for the safety of those who are sick, just so Augustine believes that Christian piety should attend to those whose minds have gone astray in religious matters, even when they are unwilling and actively resisting—not heretics only, but also pagans, so that both

---

[269] Aristotle, *Nicomachean Ethics* 10.9.9 (1180a4–5).
[270] Aristotle, *Nicomachean Ethics* 10.9.12 (1180a22–23).
[271] Augustine, Letter 93.5.16.
[272] Augustine, Letter 93.9.34.
[273] It should be noted that the passage that begins here and extends through I.20.2 is an addition to the Salamanca manuscript, the last state of the text. It is missing in VTMP.

may be compelled against their will to come into the Gospel banquet, in accord with the precept of Christ, if upon being invited they showed themselves unwilling.

(6) For although Augustine is addressing a heretic, nonetheless you could not doubt that he was giving precepts not only to them but also to pagans, if you carefully examine the passage and reread the letter to the Donatist Vincentius that we have often mentioned, where he mentions the law of Constantine against the pagans. There, on the basis of the greater force most justly brought to bear upon the pagans so that they might enter the Gospel banquet, he strives to prove to the heretics that they, too, are justly compelled to return to the Catholic faith. For here is what Augustine writes to Vincentius: 'In truth, the pagans may blaspheme more against us concerning the laws which Christian emperors have brought against idol-worshippers; and yet many among them have been corrected and converted to the living and true God, and they are still daily being converted.'[274]

And, really, Leopoldus, if we're seeking the truth, this passage of the Gospel is much better suited to the pagans than to the heretics, for the banquet was being prepared not so much for the heretics, of whom there were none at the time, but for the Jews and the pagans. Therefore, the Jews, who were invited first, were not willing to come; then very many of the gentiles who were, as it were, lame and blind, not supported by the crutches of the holy written law or enlightened by their intellects, were guided in through the preaching of the gospel. Finally, in these times of ours pagans, who have been sought out from the streets and hedges beyond the city walls—that is, from the most remote places—are being compelled by divine commandment to enter the banquet of Christ, for heretics should be said to 'return' rather than 'enter' when they are summoned back to the Catholic faith.

Nonetheless, Augustine's precepts suit both groups, arising as they do from the same font—that is, from Christian charity towards our neighbours. For we do not, as you claim, have nothing in common with the pagans, but many things; for they are our fellows and our neighbours and are called sheep of the same Lord, albeit not of the same sheepfold. For, 'there is one Lord of all, richly blessing all who call upon him, and who desires that all men be saved and come to the knowledge of the truth.'[275]

19 [*Whatever evils may be done in subjugating the Indians will be more than outweighed by the material and spiritual benefits they will receive*]

(1) **Leopoldus:** You, then, Democrates, are teaching that bad things ought to be done so that good things may result—in flat contradiction to what Paul says in his Epistle to the Romans.[276] For it is impossible—or at least extremely difficult—that

---

[274] Augustine, Letter 93.8.26.
[275] A conflation of Romans 10:12 and 1 Timothy 2:4.
[276] Romans 3:8.

this war can be waged without sins and many evils, as the simple facts make clear. For it never has been waged without injustice and wrongdoing and great injuries and losses for the barbarians.

Democrates: This line of reasoning, Leopoldus, if it has any validity at all, poses no more of a problem for this war than for others that have been waged for whatever reason. For there has scarcely ever been a war waged without great misfortunes and losses, without some sort of injustice and wrongdoing. Furthermore, while it may be difficult for someone waging war even from a just motive to avoid injustices and wrongdoings, it is not utterly impossible, nor should crimes committed by soldiers against his will be ascribed to a prince whose just or unjust motive makes a war just or unjust, nor do those crimes make the motive unjust instead of just or mean that it should be condemned.

But if we are ordered by Christian laws to avoid the risks and even the occasions for sinning, nonetheless that does not apply in cases where necessity urges us at the same time to avoid some greater evil, or where a great advantage for the state beckons. For, granted that no one may be forced into straits where it would become necessary for him to commit a sin, if nonetheless two maxims which cannot both be fulfilled press upon one at the same time, the person who obeys the more serious of the two and lets the other fall aside does not sin, as we are taught by the decision of the Council of Toledo in Gratian, by the testimony of Gregory and Bede, by the moral rule of Gerson, and by the teaching of Aristotle.[277]

This is the method that ought especially to be pursued in wars, as the same Jean Gerson, a very important writer, teaches, for in the same work he makes this point: 'In the waging of wars, which are full of innumerable evils sometimes to one group of innocent people, at other times to another, only the good of the state excuses people from mortal sin—or, at times, the avoidance of a public harm that is markedly worse than a private harm proceeding from the war would be.'[278]

Therefore, since a lesser evil happens or is taken on when some less serious law is passed over, in order that obedience be given to a more serious law that bids one to attend to or perform some great good, a law that it would be a greater evil to transgress, in a case where it is not possible to obey both laws at the same time, in such a case, given that the lesser evil, as the philosophers teach, is considered to take the place of the good,[279] it isn't that evil is done in order that good may come about; rather, through a prudent plan, one derived from eternal law, a lesser evil is preferred to a more serious one, so that what happens in this way by reason of the immediate

---

[277] Gratian, *Decretum,* D.13, c. 1–2 (where the 7th Council of Toledo and Gregory's *Moralia in Iob* are cited); Bede, *Homiliae* 23 (on birthday of John the Baptist), cited as Homily 44 in Gratian, C. 22, q. 4, c. 6; Jean Gerson, *Regulae morales (Ethical Guidelines)* 26; Aristotle, *Nicomachean Ethics* 5.3.15 (1131b21–22).

[278] Jean Gerson, *Regulae morales,* 73. (In the translation, 'excuses people' renders 'excusat eos', 'eos' being present in Gerson, but not in Sepúlveda.)

[279] Aristotle, *Nicomachean Ethics* 5.3.15 (1131b21–22).

circumstances may be understood not to be an evil but a good—which is something that Paul himself would most emphatically commend.

(2) Moreover, for a worthy prince no law ought to carry more weight than one that orders him to take thought for the state and to regard the public good as his paramount consideration. But since in this case the public good is two-fold—both that of the Spaniards and that of the barbarians—I say that both need to be taken into account, so that those Spaniards who have done their duty should not be defrauded of their due reward, and so also that proper regard be paid to the safety of the barbarians—in particular the safety of their souls—and to their advantages. It is agreed that it should come about that, if any loss should be inflicted, it should be balanced out by much greater advantages. For if we were to calculate the bad and the good things that this war brings about, there is no doubt that the bad things would be overwhelmed by the number and importance of the good things.

(3) For the sum total of their misfortunes is that they are being forced to change their rulers—not all of them, but those whom it has seemed necessary to change—and that they are deprived of their portable goods—in particular gold and silver, which metals were held of little value by them, for indeed they made use of neither gold or silver coins—and in their place they receive from the Spaniards the metal iron, which is far more suitable for the widest uses of life. For, setting luxuries aside, human life can easily dispense with gold and silver, and if coins do come into being from those metals, it is not nature that gives them value but the law and voluntary agreement of men—in accord with which line of reasoning, iron and bronze could be preferred to gold and silver. But if you were to take iron away from human usages, you would have taken away very many necessary tools, for with iron, as Pliny says, 'we cleave the earth, we sow plants, we set out fruit trees, we yearly force vines to regain youthful vigour when the crud has been cut away—with iron we construct houses, we cut rocks, and we employ iron for very many other uses'.[280] Thus, all the metals which the Spaniards seize from the barbarians are compensated for by iron alone, and thus a benefaction is most lavishly rendered back to them.

Then how much more lavish a benefaction if you add wheat, barley, and other kinds of grains and legumes? Add in addition horses, mules, donkeys, cattle, sheep, goats, pigs, vines, and very many kinds of trees, all of which now grow abundantly in those parts of the world, but which were never seen or heard of by the barbarians before this time, but have been brought in by the Spaniards. The usefulness that the barbarians used to get from gold and silver is far surpassed by the benefit they get from any single one of these things.

By how much more is it surpassed if you consider letters, with which the barbarians were utterly unfamiliar, having been ignorant of reading and writing, or if you

---

[280] Pliny the Elder, *Naturalis historia* (*Natural History*) 34.39.138.

consider civilized behaviour, the best laws and customs, and that which by itself surpasses all the advantages of all other things: knowledge of the true God and the Christian religion, by which care is taken for the salvation of many thousands of souls, which were surely going to perish without that religion—a benefit that ought to be sought out even through great losses of other things and through slaughters, according to Augustine, who, writing to Bishop Auxilius, affirms that it is a greater loss for one soul to perish without baptism than for countless men, even innocent ones, to be slaughtered.[281]

The men of old, as Aristotle relates, conferred upon certain worthy men the rule of their nation or state precisely because they had been graced with some great benefaction by them, and we even read of certain men who have been translated into gods by earlier ages because they were the inventors of useful things for men.[282] Therefore, since the kings of Spain are, as it were, the inventors of so many very useful and necessary things unheard of in those regions, with what acts of reverence, what duties, and what honours could the barbarians render thanks equal to so many and such great benefactions?

When one recognizes and reflects on these matters, those who strive to hinder this expedition in order to prevent the barbarians from coming under the rule of the Christians are not, I argue, humanely favouring the barbarians, as they themselves would like to seem to be doing; rather, they are doing their best to cruelly begrudge those very people the greatest and most numerous good things—which good things these peoples' cowardly and churlish opinion either utterly destroys or very seriously retards.

(4) Still, I would not deny that an occasion might occur when, even though one had the power of exerting compulsion, it would be the right thing to refrain from the subjugation of the barbarians.[283] This might happen if some prince with his state or people were to request teachers of the Christian religion from us—not out of fear or simulation, but of his own accord, in good faith, inspired by the spirit of God—or if through some other chance, in the great variety of human affairs, right reason, which we cannot measure by a single rule, might urge us to attend to the salvation of the barbarians in some other way. For while it is by laws and precepts that what ought to be done on any given occasion is usually established, other things, occurring outside the normal course of affairs, are left to the sagacity of just princes and upright men who are in charge of things that need to be done,

---

[281] Augustine, Letter 250.2 (*PL* 33, col. 1067).

[282] The first part of this sentence seem to refer to (without directly quoting) Aristotle, *Politics* 3.9.7 (1285b6–9), but apotheosis is not mentioned there, though there is a brief mention of it at *Nicomachean Ethics* 7.1.2 (1145a23–24).

[283] Losada/Coroleu, Taranto, and Schäfer all take *a subiectione ... temperandum* to mean exercising moderation in subjection ('mitigar', 'temperarsi', 'die Herrschaft ... gelockert werden kann'). But *temperare* used with *a/ab* means 'to restrain oneself, hold back, refrain (from)' (*OLD*).

146 SEPÚLVEDA ON THE SPANISH INVASION OF THE AMERICAS

according as the consideration of the good of the whole people will require that those things be managed—as the Philosopher declares.[284]

20 [*The pope's prudential grant to the Spaniards of lands hitherto unclaimed by Christian rulers*]

(1) To return, then, to the general question: since all men are connected among themselves by a certain kinship and affinity, and at some times are called partners or neighbours and at other times brothers, it follows that there are many duties that men are ordered by divine and natural law to render to fellow men by virtue of the very fact that they are men, and this law, as learned men teach, is embraced above all in a single precept: whatever good can be bestowed without harm is to be granted even to one who is unaware of it, and this indeed includes not only pointing out the right path to one who is astray and wishes guidance, but also calling a wayfarer back from a precipice even against his will, if the opportunity is given us to do so with no harm to ourselves. This is the point of the precepts of Augustine and Gregory—derived, as we have said, not only from divine law but also from natural law.

It was in following these authorities and the arguments we have mentioned that Pope Alexander VI in 1493 entrusted to the kings of Castile, willing as they were and in fact requesting this task for themselves on the basis of their own right, the task of reducing these barbarians to rule and not only inviting them to the Gospel banquet—that is, to faith in Christ—but even compelling in the way we have mentioned those who persisted in resisting.

Given that the justice of this war has been made clear by this impartial judgment and rescript of the Highest Priest, I am utterly amazed if there is anyone from the ranks of the pious—anyone, at least, who has been made aware of this—who could harbour doubts about the propriety of this cause and would dare to oppose his own judgment or the opinion of any private person to the sacrosanct authority of the church. For just as wars waged under the authority of God cannot be unjust, as Augustine says, so it is ordained that we regard as just those wars that are waged with the approval and encouragement of the Highest Priest of God, the Vicar of Christ. For if through the special providence of God the hearts of kings are guided by God himself in the administration of public affairs—as we are taught in that verse of Proverbs: 'The heart of a king is in the hand of God'[285]—how much more is the heart of the Highest Priest, the Vicar of Christ, guided by God?

It is concerning this matter that St Bernard treats in the book *On the Precept and the Dispensation*: 'From whom is divine counsel more to be sought than from that

---

[284] Apparently a reference to Aristotle's distinction between 'equity' and 'legal justice' in *Nicomachean Ethics* 5.10.3–7 (1137b12–35). Coroleu, followed by Schäfer, glosses *Politics* 3.11.13 (1288a30), but this is not very close.

[285] Proverbs 21:1.

man to whom the divination of the mysteries of God has been entrusted? In the same way, we ought to listen to that man whom we regard in the place of God as though it is God himself we hear in those matters that are not manifestly contrary to God.'[286] Also, Thomas Aquinas affirms that greater faith should be shown to the pontiff alone when he is deciding or passing judgment on anything in the church than to many wise men in concert.[287] In sum, in the same way that in a kingdom that which pleases the king has the force of law in disputed matters, as the jurists teach, so in the church does that which pleases the supreme pontiff.

(2) For the so-called decretals [*epistolae decretales*], in which a large portion of pontifical law is brought together—what are they other than rescripts of the pontiffs similar to this one of Alexander VI, which we have mentioned? And lest you suppose that the matter is supported by the view of only one pope, this same view has been confirmed by the judgment and authority of all the other Roman pontiffs who have subsequently followed him. When they fully ascertained and very gladly learned, with great wonder at things that challenged credulity, that new peoples in the most remote regions of the world were being reduced to Christian rule far and wide by the threatened or even inflicted arms of the Spaniards, and that through this opportunity the name of Christ and belief in him were being spread throughout a world unknown to the men of old, each of the popes, rejoicing for the church and for his own future memory, did not cease to support the intention and pious efforts of the Spanish kings with letters, charters, and indulgences, and to offer help in many places. Indeed, through their authority and favour bishoprics, priesthoods, cathedrals, monasteries, and other pious places have been established and erected in many regions, and many things have been generously granted that are most especially conducive to the accomplishment of this task.

(3) **Leopoldus:** Let it be as you propound, Democrates, and let Christians be allowed to force barbarous and impious peoples under their rule and to forbid them atrocity and abominable religions, for I have nothing to say against that. But if excellence in intelligence and virtues and the motive of religion have assigned this right to the Spaniards against the barbarians, could not the French or the Italians or, in short, any Christian nation that is more intelligent, better, or more humane than those same barbarians lay claim to the same power in the same way and by the same right?

(4) **Democrates:** At first it seems that the matter could indeed have met with doubt or dispute, and yet in this contention each nation has a greater right to this to the extent that it is more intelligent, better, more just, and more religious, and in all these things there are very few nations which, if we are looking for the truth, could

---

[286] Bernard of Clairvaux, *De praecepto et dispensatione* (*On the Precept and the Dispensation*) 9.21.

[287] Taranto notes that this claim is not found in Aquinas, 'whose views on the position of the pope in the church are clear, as emerges from *ST* II-II, q. 39, art. 1, but are not accompanied by the comparison with the many wise men' (123n232).

be compared with the Spaniards. But now, through the law of nations, according to which things that belong to no one become the property of those who seize them, it has been brought about that the rule over these barbarians properly devolves upon the Spaniards—not on the ground that those regions lacked just princes and lords, but because those peoples belonged to the rule of no Christian prince.

(5) For those people are mistaken who deny that pagans are true and just princes and lords of their own things solely on the ground that they are unbelievers, though their rule may in other respects be just. For Nebuchadnezzar was a pagan and an unbeliever, but the prophet Daniel affirmed that he was a valid and just king and lord of the things he possessed, for he addressed him thus: 'You are king of kings, and the God of heaven has given you a kingdom and fortitude and rule and glory, and all areas in which the sons of men and the beasts of the field live; also the birds of heaven he has given into your hands and established under your sway.'[288] Nor was this only before the coming of Christ, but even in Christian times the Apostle Paul declared that the kingdoms and empires of pagans were valid and just in a very important testimony in the Epistle to the Romans, framed in these words: 'There is no power but that from God, and the powers that be have been established by God.'[289] For Paul was not giving a command concerning Christian rulers, for there were none at that time, but concerning pagans, by whose rule the globe was being governed.

(6) Therefore, those regions had true lords and just princes by a right that suited their own society, one in which those who were slaves by nature were subordinate to slaves who were a bit more intelligent than they, and the latter were able by their own right to shut out foreigners and to prevent them from digging up gold and silver and fishing for pearls in each one's kingdom. For, just as fields and farms have their own lords, thus a whole region and whatever is in it, both seas and rivers, belong to a state or to rulers, as the jurists teach, although for certain uses those things are to be shared by all. Therefore, it was not because those regions belonged to no one, but because those very mortals who held those regions were free from the rule of Christians and civilized peoples that they passed by the law of nations over to the rule of the Spaniards who occupied them—and also because of the aforementioned decree of the Supreme Priest and Vicar of Christ, to whose power and duty it belongs to look out for opportunities for removing disputes among Christian rulers and to put the appropriate person in charge of the duty of extending the Christian religion through reason and justice should any way of doing so reveal itself. Thus, for many reasons, and through the most excellent divine law and natural law, those barbarians may be reduced to obedience by the arms of the Spaniards if they reject their rule.

[288] Daniel 2:37–38.
[289] Romans 13:1.

DEMOCRATES PART TWO 149

21 [*The enlightened Leopoldus summarizes Democrates's arguments so far*]

(1) **Leopoldus:** There is no further dispute we can have, Democrates, concerning the justice of this war and rule, a justice which you have made clear and fully supported by weighty arguments derived from the most profound theology and philosophy and from deep delving into the very nature of things and the eternal law of God. For I confess that, after I have heard you discourse, I have cast aside every doubt and scruple by which I used to be troubled.

(2) For if I correctly grasp in my mind the sum of the above disputation, you have laid out four reasons on the basis of which, considered each in itself, it seems that war can justly be waged by the Spaniards against those barbarians. First, [it may be waged] if, since they are by nature slaves, barbarians, uncultivated, and uncivilized, they were to reject the rule of the more intelligent, more powerful, and more perfect, a rule which they ought to accept for their own great benefits and by the same law of nature by which matter ought to obey form, the body the soul, appetite reason, brute animals human beings, in short the imperfect the perfect and the worse the better, so that it may be well for both. For this is the natural order, which divine and eternal law everywhere orders to be observed, as St Augustine says—and in support of his view you have cited not only Aristotle, whom the most distinguished philosophers and theologians have employed as a teacher of justice as also of other moral virtues and as the most sagacious interpreter of nature and of natural law, but also St Thomas, easily the prince of scholastic theologians, Aristotle's expounder and emulator in interpreting the laws of nature, all which laws you have declared to be divine and to derive from the eternal law of God.

(3) You have brought forward another reason: so that the unnatural crimes of feasting on human flesh could be abolished, by which the nature of things is most extremely violated, and so that demons not be worshipped in place of God (something that most especially provokes God's wrath)—and worshipped in the monstrous rite of sacrificing human victims. Next—a point that in my opinion has very great force and weight for affirming the justice of this war—in order that grave harms be warded off from the innocent mortals whom the barbarians sacrifice every year. You have taught that natural law bids all men repel such injuries from any men at all if they can do so.

(4) In the fourth place you have laid it down that the Christian religion be spread far and wide through preaching the gospel through any convenient means, wherever an opening shows itself, once a pathway for preachers and teachers of morality and religion has been built—and built in such a way that not only will the preachers have the power to pass along gospel teaching safely, but also so that the fear of their own rulers and priests may be removed from the ordinary barbarians, so that being persuaded freely and without fear of punishment they will receive the Christian religion. In short, this will happen when all the impediments and the worship of idols have been removed to the furthest possible extent, and once the pious and most just law of the Emperor Constantine against the pagans and the worship of idols

150 SEPÚLVEDA ON THE SPANISH INVASION OF THE AMERICAS

has been renewed—all of which, you have taught (citing the authority of Augustine and Cyprian), will have to be done. But it cannot be done unless the barbarians have been pacified by war or by some other means.

(5) In order to make these reasonings clear, you came to use the example of the Romans, whose rule over other nations you affirmed to have been just and lawful, following the authority of Augustine and Thomas, and you made it clear that their rule came about on the basis of justifications that carried less weight than ours. Also, you believed that one should not pass over in silence the authoritative decree of the Highest Priest and Vicar of Christ that was invoked and issued on behalf of this war and rule. You maintained the justice of this war and rule in such a way that you nonetheless most emphatically condemned any kind of recklessness in waging and managing the war, any cruelty or greed, and you taught that the blame for these crimes, when they are perpetrated by soldiers or commanders, redounds upon the princes, who are to be condemned by a judgment of God equal to the crime, unless they see to it with all their might and in every possible way that such crimes by unjust men not be allowed. Have I properly brought together in a few words the things that you have discussed in far more words while explaining the justice of this war?

(6) **Democrates:** Indeed you have, most accurately. But this is enough about these matters for now, since our host is now present and invites us to lunch. If there are any matters pertaining to this question that seem to you in need of further discussion, it will be possible to pursue them in the afternoon.

(7) When they had said these things, they adjourned to the lunch that their hidalgo host had prepared in the garden with the lavishness to be expected for close friends.[290]

Book II

1 [*Do those who are slaves by nature lose their right to liberty and property?*]
(1) After they had been greeted with friendly, merry, and yet not unlearned conversation and had then passed a few quiet hours, as the afternoon advanced they returned to the same green and shady bank of the Pisuerga. Leopoldus said, 'If it's alright with you, Democrates, let us return to the discussion we had begun about the war against the barbarians, and let us consider that question which, no less than the earlier one, manages to involve the minds of good and pious men in an

---

[290] Losada (*ad loc.*) was surely right in rendering *hospite generis Italici* as 'el huésped de hidalga prosapia'. He refers to the end of a letter Sepúlveda wrote earlier to Prince Philip (27 October 1543, *Epistolarum libri* III.6) in which he derived *hidalgo* from the adjective *italicus*, as in the *ius italicum*, by which Roman law conferred on certain provincial communities the rights of those born in Italy. Taranto attempted to attach *generis italici* to the feast itself: 'alla maniera italica', and he has been followed by Schäfer ('nach italienischer Weise'). But this strains the word order. The host is, of course, Sepúlveda himself, who thus makes a 'cameo' appearance at the end of the first book of the dialogue.

indecisive judgment. Is it because those men are barbarians and slaves by nature—and add in their crimes and worship of idols—is it for these reasons, I say, that they ought to be robbed of their fields and cities and, in short, all their goods and their civil liberty by men who are more intelligent, just, and upright—actions that I hear have often been perpetrated by certain men through the most extreme greed and cruelty? And is it because those unfortunate men have been born more for subjection than for rule that they ought to be judged devoid of civil liberty and in possession of things that rightly belong to others?'

(2) **Democrates:** Those things that are the worst or that happen in the worst manner no one but the worst man will commend. But you are wrong, Leopoldus, if you suppose that there has been no just reason why some of those people were deprived of their liberty and their goods—*not* on the grounds that they are (as in fact they are) slaves by nature and for that reason possess no liberty nor any possession of their own. That is a childish belief, for one may see certain people, even among the more civilized nations, who are slaves according to the standard of nature, but according to the standard of society are not only free, but are even considered very noble people and lords of great patrimonies and possess veritable herds of servants, some of whom, by the highest law of nature, should be able to rule over *them*. This is what the verse in *Ecclesiasticus* means: 'Free men will serve a wise servant.'[291] Nor is it because they live in a criminal manner nor because they are idol-worshippers, for no vices, no error brings it about that someone is not master of those things that he has otherwise justly acquired and possesses. Even if one had committed a crime that would be punished in due legal process by confiscation of goods, one should not be condemned as soon as the case had been brought nor deprived of goods while not yet formally convicted, for the use of those goods is not forbidden by any law at all before formal condemnation and execution take place.

(3) **Leopoldus:** So, then, by what right, by what law can a certain population or individual of those people be deprived of liberty and goods?

Democrates:[292] There are many things that bring it about that someone could legally be deprived of his own goods, but this in particular: if someone is making ill use of those goods, especially as an affront to God or an evil for the state, according to Augustine, who in supplying the explanation and unfolding the law by which the goods of heretics are to be confiscated and justly passed into the possession of the Catholics, addressed the heretic Petilianus in this way: 'The things that you used to possess have become ours through the power of the one who owns everything (that is, through divine law). For you were making use of them for division, whereas we shall use them for unity.'[293] The same authority,

---

[291] Ecclesiasticus 10:28 (10:25).

[292] This long speech by Democrates in the Salamanca manuscript expands on shorter versions attested by the VTM and P manuscripts. For these earlier versions, see Appendix.

[293] Augustine, *Contra litteras Petiliani* (*Against the Letter of Petilianus*) 2.59.134.

explaining why the previous inhabitants were removed from the Holy Land by the order of God and gave way before the children of Israel, declared: 'They were driven out because they were making ill use of that land.'[294] Likewise, in Book 22 of *Against Faustus*, explaining why the Hebrews seem rightly to have taken the goods of the Egyptians, he says: 'Because the Egyptians were sacrilegious and unjust, and they were serving their idols by making use of that gold—that is, God's creation—in order to do wrong to the Creator.'[295] Gregory, too, supported this view in that very well-known decree: 'The person who abuses a power entrusted to him deserves to lose that privilege.'[296] And the same person in another place: 'A person deprives himself of the power to bind and untie if he exercises that power on behalf of his own pleasures and not in order to insure the good behaviour of his subjects.'[297]

(4) Moreover, those people most especially abuse their faculties for the contempt of God who worship demons in place of God or who live a life that is at variance to divine and natural laws; for goods and resources, as the philosophers teach, are tools for life, whose use cannot avoid being most vile when it is adapted to such a life as that.[298] Therefore Augustine concludes that all heretics and all impious people and idol-worshippers possess their resources unjustly—that is, they may be justly deprived of them by the Catholics and the pious. He writes thus to Vincentius: 'Moreover, if we consider what was written in the Book of Wisdom: "Therefore the righteous plundered the ungodly", and likewise what one can read in Proverbs: "The riches of the impious are stored up for the righteous"— then we shall see that what needs to be asked is not who possesses the goods of the heretics, but who are members of the society of the just?' [299] And again: 'No earthly thing can be possessed by anyone unless it is either by divine law, according to which all things belong to the just, or by human law, which is in the power of the kings of the earth. Therefore, you falsely call yours things which you do not possess justly and which you have been ordered to give up in accord with the law of earthly kings. In vain you say, 'We have toiled in amassing these things', when you read it written that 'the just shall consume the labours of the impious'.[300]

And, again, writing against Petilianus: 'If you complain about ecclesiastical objects or places that you used to possess and now possess no longer, the Jews, too, could call themselves just and cast our unfairness in our teeth because the Christians now possess the place in which the impious once held sway. So what

---

[294] Augustine, *Contra litteras Petiliani* 2.59.134.
[295] Augustine, *Contra Faustum* 22.71.
[296] Gratian, *Decretum*, D.74, c. 7.
[297] Gratian, *Decretum*, C. 11, q. 3, c. 60.
[298] Aristotle, *Politics* 1.2.4 (1253b31–32).
[299] Augustine, Letter 185.9.37, citing Wisdom 10:19 and Proverbs 13:22. In fact, this letter was to Boniface, not Vincentius. The quotation from Augustine immediately following is from the letter to Vincentius.
[300] Augustine, Letter 93.12.50.

is unfitting if the Catholics, through a similar will of the Lord, now possess those things that the impious used to hang onto? Against all the unrighteous and the impious that famous word of the Lord holds valid: "Let rule be taken from them and given to a people that performs justice". Or was it written in vain: "The pious shall eat the labours of the unrighteous"? Hence you ought to be more amazed that you still possess anything rather than that you have lost something.'[301]

The words of Ambrose also have a bearing on this: 'When the people are stirred up to punish sins by the command of God (that is, by divine law), guilty blood is shed without sin, and the things which were wrongly possessed by them rightly pass into the right and power of the good.'[302] St Thomas supports this view in the second part of the second book [of the *Summa*] in these words: 'The unbelievers possess their things unjustly to the extent that they have been ordered to forfeit them in accord with the laws of earthly princes. Thus they may be deprived of those things through violence—not by private but by public authority.'[303]

(5) Such testimonies make it clear that not only heretics but also pagans and idol-worshippers are rightly deprived by Christians of their goods and resources through public authority, in some cases because they make ill use of them for a way of life condemned by divine law, at other times on account of the worship of idols and sins that incur capital punishment and confiscation of goods through divine and natural law—with the exception of those unbelievers who are under the rule of Christians and are tolerated by them. The most learned men approve of this exception, since those people seem to hang onto their own goods through the will and generosity of the Christians.

(6) Nor am I pressing this point in order to teach that pagans are not true masters of their own things that they have acquired justly and through good arts, for as I said earlier, I don't judge that to be true. Rather, I'm trying to establish that it is on account of misuse and idol-worship, a violation of divine and natural law, that people are rightly deprived of their goods by Christians through an act of public authority. And I argue that those people are in a case similar to those who have committed a crime punishable by confiscation of goods, though the decision of the judge has not yet been formally issued. Those people are legally able to make use of their goods until they have been convicted and deprived. For in the case of the sorts of crimes that are to be punished by war, the declaration of war itself corresponds to a judicial decision.

---

[301] Augustine, *Contra litteras Petiliani* (*Against the Letter of Petilianus*) 2.43.102. The printed texts (Losada, Coroleu, Taranto, and Schäfer) all omit 'tenebatis et' ('you used to possess and') through haplography, and they translate accordingly. I have translated the missing words from Augustine's text, which add necessary precision. But the haplography may go back to Sepúlveda.

[302] Gratian, *Decretum*, C. 23, q. 5, c. 49.

[303] Aquinas, *ST* II-II, q. 66, art. 8.

2. [*Slavery and confiscation of goods are the just fate of those justly defeated in war*]

(1) There is another argument, and that with the most justice of all, one which extends more widely and which is embraced by the law of nations—that is, by the law of nature. When people have been defeated in a just war undertaken for whatever reason, both they themselves and their goods become the property of the victors and those who seize them. For this is the origin from which slavery as a social institution was born.

(2) **Leopoldus:** Do you actually think that this law derives from nature when it is flat-out contrary to natural law, in accordance with which all men are said originally to have been free? Unless perhaps we suppose that two just and natural laws can fight between themselves. But what could be said or happen that would be more absurd than that?

Democrates: No laws that are just—I don't mean only laws of nature, but civil laws as well—can be thoroughly at variance with each other, since nothing fights with the just except that which is unjust, nothing fights with the good except that which is bad. For just as in truth all things that are true are in agreement, as the philosophers teach, just so all just things accord with just things and all good things with good things.

(3) Still, an occasion can occur when, of two very just and natural laws, one would have to be neglected, on the guidance of nature itself, and the other observed. For example, it is a law of nature to conceal the hidden crime of a friend; but it is also just by the law of nature to attend to the advantage and safety of one's country. If a good and religious man is the only person who realizes that his friend is plotting against his country, if he were unable to deter his planned evil in any more suitable way, he will place the safety of his country ahead of the advantages and desires of his friend and report his impious attempts to the prince or a magistrate.

And he will do this with God and nature as his guide; for in this sort of disagreement of laws he prefers that the law that should be overlooked will be the one that will involve the lesser amount of harm, as the holy and most serious fathers declared in the Eighth Council of Toledo: 'Granted that two evils should be most scrupulously avoided; if, however, the exigencies of danger compel one to commit one of them, we ought to settle on the one that is recognized as binding with a looser knot. But which would be of lesser weight or which would be more serious needs to be searched out with the keenness of piety—that is, the judgment of right reason.'[304] And Gregory added: 'When the mind is constrained between lesser and greater sins, if absolutely no opening without sin is evident, the lesser sins are always to be chosen.'[305]

---

[304] Gratian, *Decretum,* D. 13, c. 1.
[305] Gregory I, *Moralia in Iob* 32.30.29.

DEMOCRATES PART TWO 155

(4) It is unnecessary, after so many and such important authorities, to use as witnesses scholastic theologians who tend to this view with what is indeed an impressive unanimity. Therefore, though it is by nature just that each person should enjoy his natural liberty and his justly acquired goods, nonetheless reason and the natural necessity of men have through a tacit consensus of nations established or approved that, when there will have been a recourse to arms,[306] the things that will have been captured in war—to use the words of Aristotle—'become the property of the victors';[307] that is, as the jurists make clear, people who have been captured are to become slaves and their goods are to pass into the power of those who seize them—indeed, for the most profound of reasons, which is something agreed upon by universal law, though it goes against the nature of a private person or single individual, as Thomas teaches in the second part of Book 2, question 65.[308] This law, then, is natural and is secured with much stronger bonds of justice than that aforementioned law of natural liberty.

3 [*Slavery and confiscation deter injustice, but should be imposed with moderation*]

(1) **Leopoldus:** I see clearly enough that this law rests on and is supported by a superiority of arms. But I don't understand how it is made secure by the bonds of justice. To me, it seems instead unjust and in violation of any sort of fairness, for often just wars come about from grievances that are not all that serious. But slavery and the confiscation of goods are, after death, the most serious of all punishments. Since, then, moderate grievances ought to be punished by moderate punishments, I have trouble imaging how it would not be contrary to justice in such wars, even granted that they are just, to reduce the defeated to slavery and despoil them of their goods, especially when I see eminent theologians advising that, when we have fallen into a war of this sort, our best men are to be established as calculators of the injuries, losses, and expenses incurred, lest we demand penalties greater than what is in accord with the calculation of the wrongs and inconveniences received. For, as it is stated in Deuteronomy, 'The manner of the blows ought to be in proportion to the measure of the wrongdoing.'[309]

(2) **Democrates:** Indeed, nothing can be more just or more holy than that precept of the theologians. But do be alert to make sure that some of those same men may not be accurately enough assessing injuries received, an assessment that peoples have conducted with extreme accuracy when enacting this law. For those who, for example, unjustly ravage the fields of other peoples and drive off booty are not just

---

[306] From here to the quotation from Colossians in II.3.8, the Salamanca manuscript restored a passage present in the VTM manuscripts that was considerably reduced in the P (Santander) manuscript. For the P version, see Appendix.

[307] Aristotle, *Politics* 1.2.16 (1255a7–8).

[308] Aquinas, *ST* II-II, q. 65, art. 8.

[309] Deuteronomy 25:2.

inflicting damage and loss upon that state or people, but also wrong and indignity, and at the same time they are doing harm to the universal political order of men and to human fellowship, which, just as it is most especially supported and preserved by peace and tranquillity, so it is most shaken up and caused to totter by war. Since people everywhere in the world think this way, establishing that it is impious to disturb the public peace and tranquillity, they have publicly ordained through a tacit yet substantial consensus that all those who have brought it about that their accomplices have through wrongdoing provided just cause for a war should have their crime punished both by death and the confiscation of goods—that is, that their enemies, by waging war with their own justification, may kill them and reduce them to slavery and appropriate for themselves whatever they have seized from them—in order to deter unjust and wicked men from such crimes.

Therefore, wars, enslavements, the sackings of cities, and the seizing of kingdoms are not sanctioned by the law of nations for any other reason than as punishments of an inflicted injury and the crime of a violation of human fellowship. For just laws never decree the infliction of disasters and losses except when it is for the purpose of imposing just punishments on wicked men and violators of the law—as for instance if one infringes national sovereignty or drives away ambassadors, an office that ought to be inviolate among all nations. 'Indeed, it is for this reason', as Augustine says, 'that great and holy men have punished some sins with death, in order that a useful fear be struck in those who are alive, not so that the death itself might do harm to those who were being punished by death, but so that the sin that could have been augmented if they had lived would be diminished.'[310]

(3) On this basis it is clear that when the victor in a just war saves an enemy for slavery although he could kill him with full justification (whence 'slaves' [*servi*, preserved] get their name), this person is not acting unjustly, but humanely; and this law rests to the greatest degree upon natural law. For it is directed in the highest degree to the preservation of human fellowship, which comes about through nature. For that which is suited to the preservation of natural fellowship or, as the jurists say, is in general instituted for the sake of human necessities is, according to the philosophers, just by nature.[311]

(4) This, then, is the source, this the most just and natural origin from which proceeded the law that deprives those defeated in a just war of life or liberty or goods. 'For laws have been made', as Isidore says, 'so that human recklessness may be restrained by fear of them, and so that innocence may be safe amidst the wicked, and so that among the wicked themselves insolence and the power to do harm may be bridled by the threat of punishment.'[312] Thus you may now understand that those calculators of injuries and losses of whom you have made mention either do

---

[310] Augustine, *De sermone Domini in monte* (*On the Sermon on the Mount*) 1.20.64.
[311] Cf. Aristotle, *Politics* 1.1.8–9 (1252b28–1253a3).
[312] Isidore of Seville, *Etymologiae* (*Etymologies*) 2.10.5.

not properly make their calculation or else they follow a species of fairness and humanity rather than the laws of war, which have been adapted to nature and to the shared requirements of human fellowship. Therefore it is permitted to a victor in a just war, if he relies upon the full extent of the law, to kill his enemy, reduce him to slavery, and deprive him of his goods, unless some other custom stands in the way, as happens among Christians, for one ought to abide by custom even more than on written laws, as the philosophers teach.[313]

(5) But because extreme justice is sometimes extreme injury, and 'although all things are permitted, nonetheless not all things are expedient' (as St Paul says),[314] accordingly it is the characteristic of a just and humane ruler to prefer due proportion to the full extent of the law and to give the case of the enemy a balanced hearing, and to take into account their customs, cruelty, gentleness, reasons for fighting, willingness to oblige, and in turn their stubbornness; to resist giving way to hatred or avarice; and to refer everything to the public good and to the deterrence of wicked men. In sum, one should strive or rage no further than is called for by calculation of the crime committed or the injury inflicted and by public tranquillity and secure peace, a peace that would be utterly free of treasonous plots. Thus, the law concerning the punishment of enemies ought to be tempered by this restriction: it is granted by the law of nations and by natural law to kill enemies defeated in a just war and to reduce them to slavery and to confiscate their goods, but only to the extent that considerations of peace and public benefit would demand.

(6) For this is the aim of a just war—so declares the common consensus of men (which is to say, it is a decree of nature)—and many great men have mentioned this. And we see that the most civilized peoples have maintained this custom—the Macedonians, the Athenians, the Spartans, and the other Greeks, upright and wise men, and above all the ancient Romans, 'who have been regarded as very moderate in the waging of war', as Augustine testifies.[315] For certain states defeated by them they reduced to provinces, burdened only by light discomforts and subject to taxes with conditions that were not unfair; certain states they left free and allowed them to use their own laws. But when the guilt or the nature of their enemies demanded it, they deprived them of towns and fields; and some they even destroyed from their foundations, such as Carthage, following principally the authority of Cato, as Cicero said, for 'his authority had power even when he was dead'.[316]

And Julius Caesar, the very prudent commander-in-chief in the Gallic War, treated the other Gauls very humanely when he had thoroughly defeated them, but as for the Aduatici, on account of their treachery and rebellion he reduced them to slavery and made a general auction of the booty from their town, as is recorded

---

[313] Aristotle, *Politics* 3.9.6 (1287b5–8).
[314] 1 Corinthians 6:12.
[315] Augustine, *De civitate Dei*, Bk. 5 (but the exact phrase does not seem to appear).
[316] Cicero, *De officiis* 1.79.

in his *On the Gallic War*; and as for the Veneti, who had cast into chains his ambassadors (whose office had always been holy and inviolate among all nations), he determined that there needed to be a more serious punishment—'in order', he wrote, 'that in the future the law concerning ambassadors would be more diligently observed by those barbarians'.[317] Thus, when all their senate had been killed, he sold all the others at auction.

(7) In the same manner—to confirm secular history with sacred examples—King David inflicted a lighter punishment on the Philistines, Moabites, and Syrians whom he had defeated, for they had done less serious harm to the Israelite people, and he thought it sufficient that they render taxes to him; but he very severely punished the Ammonites, because they had treated his ambassadors with contempt, contrary to the law of nations, and insultingly dismissed them. For when their royal city of Rabbah had been taken by siege, as recorded in Second Book of Kings [2 Samuel], he carried off the greatest amount of plunder, and he kept the people alive, leading them forth with their king, and drove iron carriages over them and cut them to pieces with knives.[318] Therefore Ambrose said in Book 1 of his *On the Duties of Clergy*, 'A more violent punishment is applied to more violent enemies and unbelievers and those who have more done more violent harm.'[319]

Therefore, the most prudent and just mortals used to moderate their right against defeated enemies in accord with the reasoning we have mentioned and having looked into the aforesaid considerations, and it is proper for Christians to imitate their prudence and moderation—but in such a manner that they may surpass the most moderate pagans not only in religion but also in clemency and humanity—once they have secured victory, that is, for before victory has been achieved, even just wars are waged according to the custom of the gentiles, with little difference, by killing the enemy, reducing them to slavery, depriving them of goods and arms, plundering camps that have been taken—in sum, by inflicting misfortune upon the enemy in every manner that contributes to the securing of victory.

(8) But to operate now with the testimonies of Sacred Scripture and of holy and pious men: that the things captured in a just war belong to those who seize them, just as it is confirmed by the law of nations, so too is it made clear in that passage that we have cited above from Deuteronomy: 'You shall divide all booty among your army, and you shall feast upon the spoils of your enemies';[320] and what is mentioned in Genesis about the booty that Abraham took from the defeated kings, where there was also mention made of slaves, for this is how the king of the Sodomites, to whose aid Abraham had come, addressed him: 'Give me the living souls; you take the rest for yourself.'[321]

---

[317] Caesar, *De bello gallico* 2.33; 3.9 and 11.
[318] 2 Samuel 12:26–31. (The biblical passage is obscure and subject to less horrific interpretations.)
[319] Ambrose, *De officiis ministrorum* 1.29.
[320] Deuteronomy 20:14.
[321] Genesis 14:21.

DEMOCRATES PART TWO 159

Ambrose discusses this passage in the work entitled *Abraham*: 'Someone will object: "Since he himself was the victor in battle, why did he say to the king, 'I will take nothing from you'?" It's because he is giving a lesson in military discipline: that all things are to be reserved to the king. It is true, however, that he adds that a certain financial advantage ought to be granted to those who may have been associated with the king to offer aid—a wage for labour, as it were.'[322] The same Ambrose, in the book on Tobit, teaches that, just as it is lawful to kill enemies in a just war, so is it to deprive them of their goods—in these words: 'Exact interest from the person to whom you rightly wish to harm. The person against whom arms are justly inflicted is legitimately subjected to interest.'[323] For his teaching means that to exact interest is nothing other than to despoil someone. St Thomas confirms the same point in the second part of Book 2.[324] Those who are most important and most skilled in pontifical law agree,[325] for they say that things that have been seized in a just war are not to be reckoned as compensation for things that have been stolen; rather, the defeated are deprived of their goods and reduced to slavery as punishment for the crime of having violated human fellowship.

This slavery even Paul affirms is just and legal when contracted in a just war: in his Epistle to the Colossians he not only does not regard as unjust slavery contracted in a just war through the law of nations, but even gives precepts and lays out the duties of slaves to masters and masters to slaves: 'Slaves', he says, 'obey your earthly masters in all things, not only obeying them in plain view as those who please men, but fear God in the honesty of your heart.'[326] With these words he makes it clear that that person does not fear God—that is, he gravely sins—who, though a slave, does not serve and act submissively to his master—and he says, 'You masters, offer to your slaves that which is just and fair, for you realize that you too have a master in heaven.'[327] He does not say, 'Manumit your slaves, free your slaves'—which is what he should have said if divine law condemned human servitude—but 'treat your slaves justly and humanely'. And he writes to the same effect in another place: 'Slaves, obey your fleshly masters in fear and trembling… and you masters do the same to them, leaving threats aside.'[328] Also, in an epistle, Peter, the prince of the Apostles, orders slaves to obey not only good and modest masters, but also difficult ones.[329]

---

[322] Ambrose, *De Abraham* 1.3.

[323] Ambrose, *De Tobia* 15.51.

[324] Aquinas, *ST* II-II, q. 66, art. 8. (But Taranto notes: 'The position of Thomas is in reality more complex, as is shown by *ST* II-II, q. 78.')

[325] A marginal note in S here cites Hostiensis on Innocent III's decretal *Quod super his*. Manuscripts T and M (and probably also V) also cite Hostiensis ('hosti'). See Losada's edition, p. 97, n. 270.

[326] Colossians 3:22.

[327] Colossians 4:1.

[328] Ephesians 6:5 and 9.

[329] 1 Peter 2:18.

160 SEPÚLVEDA ON THE SPANISH INVASION OF THE AMERICAS

And lest you be able to be in any doubt concerning the shared opinion of those in earlier days on this matter, even the very pontiffs of the church, and not just the laypeople, made use of slaves and bondsmen, with good and religious men and the pontifical law itself approving of that. But although by the law of nations those captured in a just war become the property of the ones who capture them, nonetheless according to the custom of Christians, when they wage war among themselves, those captured in war are at least deprived of their arms and horses and whatever of value they were wearing, but are not reduced to slavery, unless it happens that rich men are forced to ransom themselves for a price, on account of their wealth.

(9)[330] But we are speaking here of external wars which are waged with a legitimately declared enemy, not civil disputes, which are also called wars—civil wars. For the procedure of these is far different, and it makes no difference if the citizens of a single city or state are fighting among themselves or the cities of a single kingdom are fighting among themselves. For in a kingdom, cities and peoples that are accustomed to be summoned by kings to public deliberations and to convene through ambassadors and representatives possess through laws and customs the power of deliberating, as happens in Castile. All these compose, as it were, a single city, whose citizens are all citizens of the individual cities.

Therefore, if, as sometimes happens, a civil war rages among these cities and citizens when some great internal strife concerning the state arises, once those who support the wrong cause have been defeated by their adversaries, it is in accord with the law of nations and the shared custom of men (which has the force of natural law) that they neither *should* nor generally *do* undergo the terms applied to those who have been soundly defeated by foreign enemies in a just and legally declared war—i.e. that they be deprived of their towns or their private or public liberty or suffer some other rather serious consequence. Rather, they are punished in accord with civil custom and ancestral laws, and in such a way that, once punishment has been meted out to seditious and disorderly citizens and those who were the leaders of the rebellion and the stirring up of disturbances, the common people should be spared. We know that this has been the practice in all recorded history and among all human societies, and it is a fact so well known that we do not need to support it by examples—and it is declared also by Roman law which agrees with natural law.

(10) **Leopoldus:** Only those who have committed a crime that is punishable by law are subject to the penalty of the law. When, however, a war has broken out between two cities or nations, though one side may have a base cause while the other supports a worthy cause, we nonetheless see whichever side is defeated afflicted indiscriminately by the same penalty that it itself would have visited upon the enemy had it been victorious—and slaves come into being on both sides.

---

[330] This section is found only in the Salamanca manuscript, i.e. the final version.

DEMOCRATES PART TWO 161

Democrates: We are not investigating what happens in human life, which is full of wrongdoing and wickedness, since everyone advocates for himself in the arguments for war, as in other matters—whence it comes about that the civil law of the Romans holds both kinds of defeated as slaves. Rather, we are concerned with what happens rightly and with the approval of good men. So just as he who supports a just cause in war has the power as victor to seek the legal penalties from unjust men who are enemies in a legitimately declared war, so the person who either inflicts a war through wrongdoing or wrongly repels a war that has been inflicted upon him is not allowed to kill an enemy or reduce him to slavery or afflict him with any loss without himself incurring guilt. For the greatest of philosophers affirm that slavery contracted in an unjust war is itself unjust.[331]

4 [*Are those princes (and their soldiers) who repel a just enemy acting unjustly?*]

(1) **Leopoldus:** But what if both sides have a worthy motivation and the war is just on either side, as some have thought was the case once upon a time in the war in which the Jews attacked the Amorites and Perizzites and those other peoples?[332] For just as the Jews justly fought against those impious and wicked nations because of their crimes, so long as the Jews followed the law and will of God, so those peoples, in their ignorance of justice, justly protected themselves and their goods against the violence of the Jews. It cannot be doubted that whoever relies upon this excuse is defending a just cause.

Democrates: I know that there are some men of great authority in other respects who have discoursed in this way about the justice of that war, having been defeated by the same reasoning that you have just used—not because they actually assented to it, but because they weren't able to disentangle it. Indeed, I am amazed that they have not noticed that it seems contrary both to common sense and to what has been established by the common judgment of men to reach a conclusion utterly absurd in the eyes of wise and serious men only because they have been overcome by specious arguments.[333] For what is more established among sane men than the fact that two thoroughly opposite reasons for war cannot at the same time be just, exactly as two contradictory propositions cannot both be true? For if a war were to be just on both sides by any line of reasoning, it would have to follow that both sides would be performing the same actions both justly and unjustly.

(2) For the man who supports a just cause in a war justly kills his enemy, and in the same way the man who kills someone who supports a just cause in a war acts

---

[331] Aristotle, *Politics* 1.2.18 (1255a24–26).
[332] From this sentence through the first sentence of II.7.5 the S manuscript restores a very extensive passage omitted from the P version.
[333] These first two sentences of Democrates's speech in the S version replaced the earliest version (represented by VTM), which offered an anecdote about Diogenes' refutation of Zeno's paradox. See Appendix.

162 SEPÚLVEDA ON THE SPANISH INVASION OF THE AMERICAS

unjustly. But both men are performing both actions if the war is held to be just on both sides. Therefore, both are acting both justly and unjustly at the very same time, which is an impossibility. It must follow, then, that the cause of one side is just and that of the other side unjust. Therefore, since in that war currently under discussion divine law and the revealed will of God, which willed those peoples to be destroyed because of their sins and idol-worship, forbid us to harbour doubts about the justice of the Jews, it is utterly necessary that we determine that those sinful peoples waged an unjust war.

Therefore, in the same way that in a court trial it cannot happen that plaintiff and defendant are simultaneously maintaining a just case, but one has a just case, in accord with what is ultimately adjudged, while the other may have a reasonably credible case and should be dealt with rather mildly after he has been defeated; so in that war, when the Jews inflicted a just war, the pagans had a plausible case for repelling the war, but not, however, a just case; for they had openly committed, in defiance of divine and natural law, sins that needed to be punished by the forfeit of life and property—and if they did not know that these were sins or were unaware of the law on which the Jews relied, ignorance of divine and natural law lets no one off the hook. Therefore, it is allowable that such ignorance may mitigate the penalty, but it does not take away the guilt or the calculation of the sin and the disgrace. For when Paul was harassing the church in a hostile manner he was unaware that he was acting basely and against the law of God, but he did not evade the sin for that reason.

(3) Nonetheless he rather easily obtained forgiveness, as he himself testifies: 'Earlier I was a blasphemer and a persecutor and a man of violence, but I secured the mercy of God because I acted in ignorance.'[334] For if ignorance of temporal and civil law does one harm and does not free an individual from guilt, even less does ignorance of the perpetual and eternal divine and natural law excuse an entire city or people—the law that ought to be known to all good and prudent men and even to all grown-ups. Hence Gregory wrote: 'Those who understand those things that are of God are themselves known by God; and those who do not know the things that are of God are themselves not known by God.'[335] Paul agrees, saying: 'If someone does not know, he shall not be known';[336] and also: 'Whoever is stupid in sin shall be wise in punishment'[337]—and we have as authorities for this declaration not only the men most wise in both kinds of law but also the philosophers.

(4) For if ignorance of the law or of that which one ought to do were to do one any good and remove one's sin, no one would ever sin; for every wicked man, as those

---

[334] 1 Timothy 1:13.
[335] Gregory I, *Regula pastoralis* (*Pastoral Rule*) 1.1.
[336] 1 Corinthians 14:38.
[337] Gratian, *Decretum*, D. 38, c. 10.

same philosophers teach, does not know what he ought to do and what he ought to avoid.[338] But that doesn't mean that every kind of ignorance frees the ignorant man of guilt, but only that kind which removes the element of volition—as in the case in war when somebody roaming around among the enemy for the sake of spying kills an ally under the impression that it's an enemy. He wouldn't be at fault, for he acts against his will. Nor would someone who in the darkness slept with a substituted woman (as is recorded of Leah) under the impression that it was his own wife, because he acts not of his own free will, but unwillingly, through ignorance—a situation that is most clearly revealed through his subsequent grief after the matter becomes known. But if he had known it was someone else's wife, but nonetheless judged that he was allowed to do it, he committed adultery, because he performed willingly and knowingly an act that was truly base. For if someone wishes to act justly, but nonetheless goes astray in his deliberations and does something against the law, he incurs sin, since ignorance in choosing, as those same philosophers teach, is not a cause of the involuntary but of a perversity of judgment. Nor does an ignorance of the whole do one any good, but only of the details—that is, as the theologians put it, of the individual circumstances.

In his interpretation of this passage [in Aristotle], St Thomas says, 'Although it is possible in a deliberation to be in ignorance in two ways—in a particular instance (as when someone on account of sexual desire decided that on that particular occasion he had to commit fornication) or in general (as in the case where somebody supposes that all fornication is permissible)—neither sort of ignorance creates the element of involuntariness, but rather each is a cause of wickedness—that is, of sin.'[339] Therefore unawareness of the law or of a particular statute does not remove the sin in the way that ignorance of particular details does. For the person who approaches another man's wife who has been substituted for his without his knowledge (as we have said) seems not to be acting voluntarily, for he is unaware of the matter or object that he is dealing with (which is where a moral action derives its outward form (*speciem*)), and he is unaware of that which no law orders him to know. On the other hand, the person to whom everything is known except for justice or the law acts willingly, and ignorance of the law does not remove the volition, since he is unaware of that which he both ought to know and is able to know.

For just as everyone both ought to know and is accustomed to know which foods are healthy and deadly and to avoid the ones he doesn't recognize, thus each person ought to possess full awareness of the precepts of common law—that is, the law which all men use in common—and to keep away from precepts that are dubious. For just as in the choice of the former the health of the body is involved, so in the latter is the health of the soul. Moreover, the natural laws, which (as we have made clear) are considered the same as the divine laws, are common laws, and

---

[338] Aristotle, *Nicomachean Ethics* 3.1.14 (1110b27–28).
[339] Aquinas, *Sententia libri ethicorum* (*Commentary on Aristotle's Ethics*) 3.3.7 (adapted).

all mortals make use of them—in the same way that those for whom a particular or civil law has been passed make use of it after it has been published and can be known by them.

A different line of reasoning obtains if someone is constrained by a just or invincible ignorance—that is, one that cannot be overcome by effort; for just as this removes the will, so it completely removes the sin. According to Augustine, the person who has found no one from whom to learn is also involved in this ignorance.[340]

Since, therefore, those sinful nations made a mistake in deliberating whether they ought to ward off the war or to receive the Jews, their error did not free them from guilt. Furthermore, natural law does not permit every sort of defence, but only that which has as its object the repelling of harm. Otherwise, a thief could legally protect himself by using weapons against the judge. Since, then, ignorance of the law did those peoples no good, one ought to harbour no doubts that they unjustly warded off a war waged by those who were punishing crimes and great injuries inflicted against God on account of idol-worship and human sacrifices.

(5) For there is nothing gained by those theologians' use of the example of the inhabitants of Seir, the Moabites, and the Ammonites, whom God forbade the sons of Israel to crush in war, in their attempt to maintain that idol-worship offers insufficient justification for making war against pagans.[341] For perhaps the iniquities of those three peoples were not yet at their fullest extent, as were those of the Amorites. Moreover, while the common people of those nations may have worshipped idols, it is likely that there were nonetheless many who observed the law of nature and worshipped the one true God and persisted up to then in the religion and the laws of their ancestors, for all of them (as is recorded in the same place) derived their descent from Esau or from Lot, and God handed over those regions to be inhabited by them after the other peoples had been destroyed, and he called them brothers of the sons of Israel, while he prohibited them from being harassed in war.

Therefore, in the same way that God said to Abraham when he was interceding on behalf of the Sodomites that it would come to pass that he would spare the entire city on behalf of the just men in it, if even ten could be found, so one may believe that, because of the larger number of just men from the seed and family of Abraham, God would spare those cities that had not yet reached the extreme of impiety reached by the Amorites, and he wouldn't let them be destroyed at that time by the sons of Israel. But why are we dealing with conjectures when we may read in many passages of Sacred Scripture that it was on account of idol-worship

---

[340] Pseudo-Augustine, *Quaestiones veteris et novi testamenti* (*Questions on the Old and New Testament*), q. 67 (Souter ed., p. 117). Souter identified the author as the so-called 'Ambrosiaster', an anonymous commentator on the Pauline epistles in the papacy of Damasus I (361–84). Sepúlveda's source was Gratian's *Decretum*, D.37, c. 15.

[341] Deuteronomy 2:4–5, 9, and 18–19.

that the Jews were utterly defeated and overwhelmed and led off into slavery in very just wars—that is to say, wars issuing forth from the will and the concealed command of God—as was done by Shalmaneser the king of the Assyrians and by Nebuchadnezzar the Babylonian king, as is recorded in the Fourth Book of Kings [2 Kings],[342] and also by Antiochus and his deputy Philip, about whom we read in the Second Book of Maccabees?[343] Therefore the Amorites unjustly pushed back against the war brought upon them by the Jews who were justly attacking their great crimes and wrongs in accord with divine law.

(6) However that may be, this ignorance does far more harm to princes or the highest magistrates—in a word, those by whose advice the state is administered and who deliberate concerning war and peace—than to soldiers, whose duty it is to perform the decrees and orders of the prince, not to debate about the justice of a war, and they seem to be exempt from blame if, while they keep ranks instead of accepting peace (as we have said, following Augustine), it is either certain that the order given them is not contrary to God's command, or it is at least not absolutely certain that it *is*. 'Just as', he says, 'perhaps injustice in giving an order makes a king guilty, so the rank that involves obeying orders makes the soldier innocent.'[344]

Therefore, soldiers, who are merely executors of a decision passed by a prince or magistrates, are not involved in the same guilt as the princes and magistrates, whose error in a doubtful case does them no good at all. If this were perhaps the case on both sides, it could be granted that the soldiers on either side waged war without sin and were innocent in the eyes of God. Nonetheless, those on either side could be regarded as guilty by the other side, on the ground that they had been condemned through the prince or council whose decision and order they followed while not knowing if the order was decided upon against the will of God—for if this could be determined, it would be better to obey God than men. For, in determining the justification for a war, a prince turns into the judge even of the enemy, in accord with the law of nations. The case of a soldier, then, seems similar to that of an executioner who kills a man condemned by the judge on the judge's order and through public authority, even when it may be doubtful whether that man had been convicted justly or unjustly.

5 [*Soldiers may without sin obey orders to wage a war of dubious justification*]

(1) **Leopoldus:** So you suppose that ignorance in a doubtful rationale for war aids the soldiers. But the consensus of philosophers is that ignorance of what one ought to do is of no help to anyone. Moreover, I cannot conceive how soldiers can be without guilt when by supplying military help they appear to be agreeing with a

---

[342] 2 Kings 17:1–23 and 24:1–25:21.
[343] 2 Maccabees 6:11.
[344] Augustine, *Contra Faustum* 22.75.

prince who is clearly sinning because he is inflicting war in a doubtful cause, and they are thus exposing themselves to the danger of sinning in many ways.

Democrates: In pontifical law care has been taken to insure that, even if a subordinate judge knows that the decision that he has been ordered by a commissioner to carry out is unjust, he should nonetheless carry it out. Therefore, all the more ought a soldier in a doubtful case obey the authority of his prince, the necessity of obedience being added to the factor of his ignorance.

(2) **Leopoldus:** Certainly—if the reasoning were the same or similar, which in fact it is not. For it is completely different. For a judge ought to execute a sentence although he knows it to be unjust only when by executing it he does nothing that by its nature is base and against the law of God—as, for example, when he confers upon someone a priesthood or a piece of land about which there is some dispute—or things of that nature. For, while it may be that the piece of land had been unjustly awarded to this man through the injustice or sin of the superior judge, nevertheless to put him into possession of it does not seem by its nature base or against the law of God, especially due to the authority of the law which in itself forbids one to hesitate—since if that which he is ordered to carry out were manifestly against divine law (such as the execution of an innocent man), he ought to bring it to the attention of the superior judge or prince and obey God rather than men.

And very learned men interpret this same law in this sense by means of other ecclesiastical decrees and the testimonies of Augustine and Jerome. Likewise, Isidore says, 'If someone prohibits you from doing what has been ordered by God, or orders something to be done that God prohibits, let him be detestable to all who love God'—by which it is understood that one is not to obey.[345] 'When a master', says Augustine, 'orders those things that are contrary to God, then he is not to be obeyed.'[346] Moreover, to wage an unjust war—that is, to kill innocent men or reduce them to slavery and plunder them—is automatically profoundly base and has been condemned both by natural and divine law. In light of these things, if the case of a judge were equivalent to that of a soldier, the soldier would obey without guilt even if he knew that the war that he is being ordered to wage is unjust—something Augustine denies in the very same passage that people draw upon for justifying themselves in a doubtful case: for he says that a soldier needs to consider whether what he is being ordered to do might be contrary to the law of God.

Therefore, that pontifical law you mention seems to me to be just and consonant with Christian piety only when it is taken in the sense that I have mentioned, so that it be understood to have been passed concerning those things that you Greek

---

[345] Isidore of Seville, in Gratian, *Decretum*, C. 11, q. 3, c. 101. (Gratian does not indicate which work. Taranto and Schäfer simply refer to Gratian.)

[346] Cited as Augustine in Gratian, *Decretum*, C. 11, q. 3, c. 92, but it doesn't appear in any of Augustine's surviving writings. Anders Winroth believes that it might be Gratian's comment on the sentence from Ambrose's *De Paradiso* immediately preceding (personal communication, 28 October 2020).

scholars call ἀδιάφορα and the Latin philosophers, as I see, call *indifferentia,* and not about those people who are condemned by divine or even natural law.

(3) **Democrates:** But, to take your example, knowingly to transfer a piece of land from a just to an unjust owner—and indeed whatever is decided upon or happens contrary to justice—if you will look into the matter more closely you will scarcely be able to doubt that it *is* contrary to divine law, since divine law, which we call everlasting, is law itself and the everlasting yardstick of justice. Therefore, I do not see any other way this particular law can be defended than by a contest of two evils, under the pressure of which the natural order, whose preservation eternal law ordains, demands that, if it is necessary to endure one or the other of them, the lesser evil is the one to be preferred, as we are instructed by the authority of the Council of Toledo and Gregory the Great, as we have mentioned above.

For it is a bad thing to be the minister or executor of depriving a just owner of a piece of land, but it is much worse to seriously harm the state by rejecting the authority of a superior judge. For a public injury is considered far more serious than a private injury. This line of reasoning holds true in the same way for a judge who is the only person to know the truth of a matter; for he ought to render his verdict not on the basis of his own knowledge, but on the basis of things alleged and proven. And in the same way soldiers do serious harm to the state if they diminish the authority of a prince in a doubtful case.

(4) **Leopoldus:** You ought to say the same thing even if the war were clearly unjust, since the reasoning would be the same in both cases.

Democrates: No, the reasoning is completely different. For unless a subordinate judge carries out a decision handed down by a superior judge—no matter what that decision might be—a great disruption in the state would necessarily result, nor would the state be in a position to be administered without great harm to many, nor would a dispute reach any conclusion—all which inconveniences would happen in the same way if the judge, by invoking his own private knowledge (which could be alleged falsely), were permitted to neglect legitimate proofs and regard them as less important—and I make the same judgment about the executioner.

But if soldiers obey when ordered to wage a war that is almost certainly unjust, they are preferring human orders to divine precepts, and that is impious and criminal. But it is quite another matter if there is doubt about the justice of a war; for in that case, if they were to diminish the prince's power to command, they would be doing very great harm to the state, whose good, because it is the most important thing, we are ordered to attend to by the law of nature, which is derived from eternal law.

(5) **Leopoldus:** No, they would be benefitting rather than harming the state, for by reminding the prince of his duty they would be deterring him not only from wars that are manifestly unjust but also from those of doubtful justice, so that he might realize that he should flee not only evil but even the appearance of evil, if he wishes his soldiers to be obedient to his word. This would be a great benefit for the

168 SEPÚLVEDA ON THE SPANISH INVASION OF THE AMERICAS

state. For a solider in a dubious cause cannot offer his ignorance as an excuse, since the person who has doubts about a war is not unaware that the war, the object of another person's sinful action, is of dubious justice. Therefore, if he supposes that to wage a war of uncertain justice under the command of a prince is not against divine law, he is involved in an ignorance of law and of the entire question, not just of some single factor or action.

Democrates: In a proper state, Leopold, which can take three forms, it is not the duty of the soldiers—or of the common people as a whole—to deliberate about matters pertaining to the state, among which matters war is one of the most important; rather it is their duty to obey the commands and decrees of the prince and the highest magistrates, as the most important philosophers teach.[347] For where the common people make a claim to deliberation about the most important matters, that is not properly a state at all, but the aberration of a state, and this form of government is called 'popular', unjust, and harmful to the state. Just as it is the duty of any good Christian man of whatever station in life never knowingly or willingly to prefer human orders to divine laws, so it is the duty of soldiers and other private citizens not to debate about doubtful matters pertaining to the state, most of the reasons and causes of which are unknown to them, but to obey the decrees of the prince or the senate and have a proper respect for their intelligence and prudence—indeed, this is what is just in accordance with natural law.

For it has a bearing on the safety of a state that is established in accord with nature, the sort of state that often gets into a crisis and is troubled by great disturbances, if religion should provide the common people that sneaky means of diminishing military authority—and this is contrary to eternal law and the fixed will of God, to whom it is especially pleasing that all those things that are managed in accord with the natural order be held valid, as we have made clear in following the authority of Augustine.

Therefore, if soldiers who in good faith follow the authority and orders of a prince or state should be thrust into error and wrongdoing, they would be without fault; and if there will be any guilt, it will be assigned to those in authority; for the necessity of obedience comes to the aid of the soldiers, as does their ignorance—for that kind of ignorance, which is termed 'invincible', does not demand tireless and unsuitable diligence, but it is quite enough if each person displays the diligence that is proportionate to his duty and his station.

(6) **Leopoldus:** To wage an unjust war is base by its very nature. When something is of this sort, even though it may be thought to be honourable, it cannot come about without some guilt. 'For the good', as the philosophers and theologians teach, 'exists on the basis of the full cause, but evil derives from individual

---

[347] Coroleu, followed by Schäfer, offers *Nicomachean Ethics* 1134a19, which does not seem relevant. Losada and Taranto offer no citation.

defects'.[348] Therefore, in order that it be rightly done, 'it is insufficient', Aquinas says, 'that what is done be embraced as a good thing, unless it is by its very own nature a good thing'.[349]

Democrates: The person who is profoundly ignorant that a war is unjust does not wage an unjust war unjustly, except contingently, nor is he committing a sin. For the person who acts out of ignorance when he would definitely not be about to act if he were in possession of knowledge—that person is judged to act unwillingly, as the philosophers declare.[350] Moreover, the person who acts unwillingly acts neither justly nor unjustly, except contingently, according to those same philosophers. For it so happens that the things he does may be just or unjust, but a deed is determined to have been done justly or unjustly on the basis of volition or its opposite.[351] Whence it happens that (to use the words of St Thomas) 'exterior actions may be disordered; nonetheless, if they are done without any disordering of the will they are not sins'—as in the case where a man commits murder either out of ignorance or through an excessive zeal for justice.[352] Aristotle says, 'To sleep with another man's wife is not to commit adultery or to do an injury, but it *is* when one is in the following condition: knowing and willing and making a choice.'[353]

(7) Soldiers who wage a war that they do not know is unjust do so neither knowingly nor willingly. For not to know that the war is unjust is an ignorance of a particular thing or act—which is an ignorance that helps one—not of the law, which is an ignorance that doesn't do one any good. It would be ignorance of the law if they either didn't know that it was base and against God's law to wage an unjust war and thought that that was instead a good thing, or if the person who didn't know the war was unjust also didn't consider the waging of an unjust war either a good thing or a bad thing.

Similarly, Jacob in no way realized that he was sleeping with the wrong woman—and the wrong woman is the object of adultery for a man who knows what he is doing. And in the same way an unjust war is not the object of that sin we are asking about, because it is not understood as such by the soldier we are imagining, who does not perceive this war as unjust or either as a good thing or a bad thing, since he is unaware that it is unjust—just as the act of Jacob was not adultery because of his ignorance of the matter or object; for though it be granted that he knew that Leah was a woman, he didn't know that she was not his own, and accordingly his will was not inflicted upon a woman who was not his own.

---

[348] Pseudo-Dionysius the Areopagite, *Divine Names* 4.30 (*PG* 3.729C). Coroleu, followed by Taranto, suggests Aristotle, *EN* 1103b24, but Losada and Schäfer correctly identify the source.

[349] Aquinas, *ST* I-II, q. 19, art. 6.

[350] Aristotle, *Nicomachean Ethics* 3.1.13 (1110b18–19).

[351] Aristotle, *Nicomachean Ethics* 5.8.4 (1135b4).

[352] Aquinas, *ST* II-II, q. 24, art. 4.

[353] Aristotle, *Nicomachean Ethics* 5.6.1 (1134a19–21).

Thus the person who through plausible and invincible ignorance does not know that a war is unjust does not commit this sin, any more than the man who out of ignorance kills a friend who is mixed in with enemies commits murder—through which ignorance he failed to know the object, which is to say that the man is innocent and not to be condemned. Therefore, on account of the opinion that some recent theologians of no little reputation have vainly introduced contrary to the widely shared and received view, it has not seemed irrelevant to have discoursed in a rather detailed manner about the case of soldiers who, though harbouring doubts about the justice of a war, nevertheless are obedient to the command of the prince when they are summoned to arms.

6 [*A prince who wages a war of dubious justification sins*]

(1) **Leopoldus:** What is to prevent the same thing from happening in the case of the princes on both sides, and thus the war would be waged without guilt on either side, with neither prince harbouring any doubts about the justice of the war?

Democrates: The most important factor stands in the way: namely, that it is impossible.

Leopoldus: How so?

Democrates: Because princes and their counsellors cannot be unaware of the reason that the war is being undertaken—for it is precisely that that enters into the deliberation: whether the rationale for undertaking a war is sufficiently important and just. And that cannot happen in such a way that it would abolish every bit of doubt on both sides—unless some ignorance of the law entered in on one of the two sides, as, to take the case of the Amorites, when they didn't think that worshipping gods and idols and offering up human sacrifices or the doing of other things that are most base constituted actions that were foul and contrary to any law—which is manifestly ignorance of the law.

Leopoldus: But princes are capable of being mistaken and each one can suppose his own cause is just.

Democrates: They may, but not without a certain element of doubt. For in questions of what is to be done there is no truth so obliterated by obscurity that it doesn't possess some plausibility that would force a dissident to entertain some doubts—unless blindness or sluggishness of mind got in the way, evils that do not remove guilt. For it is good men, intelligent men, men learned in usage and law who tend to be and ought to be called in to public deliberations and the weighing of motives. Once matters have been thought through and the motive has been criticized from every angle, these men will indeed be able to make a mistake in their opinion, but not in such a way that they would fail to see the plausibility of the other side of the argument which is truly just and so decide that what is unjust is in fact just and free from any sort of uncertainty.

(2) The prince ought to be involved in the disputation of these men discussing the justice of the war, and he ought to assess most diligently the weight of the

arguments on both sides of the question, although when the facts have been made known there can be no ignorance apart from that of the law, and that does no one any good, as we have made clear above.

There is often, however, a double dispute concerning the law: one involving, for example, the legal right to fields occupied by one's neighbours; the other, about the justice of undertaking a war aimed at recovering the fields that are under dispute. While the former of these disputes may fail to reach certainty, the latter ought to admit of no doubt at all. For it is certain that one ought not make war for a dubious reason. Therefore a war cannot be unambiguously just on both sides, nor can it be decided upon by the princes and counsellors of both sides without sin when the motive is dubious. It can, however, be waged without sin by soldiers in a cause which is dubious (either because of its natural obscurity or because it is doubtful even to the princes), provided that the soldiers themselves do not harbour doubts, given that the facts and the motives are unknown to them due to an ignorance that, while it does involve them in injustice, is justifiable for themselves.

If, however, they wage an unjust war either knowingly or through ignorance, they will nonetheless lawfully endure every sort of hostile action at the hands of those others who are waging a just war that involves them in no guilt, and they will endure all this on account of the error and sin of those upon whom the power of deliberating on behalf of the state was bestowed by all the citizens. But the evils that these soldiers themselves inflicted on their own unjustly suffering enemies will be attributed by divine judgment to their prince and to those who instigated the undertaking of the war.

Therefore, since (according to Paul) one should in all things avoid even the appearance of evil,[354] a war ought not to be undertaken except for the most righteous and necessary causes (according to Augustine), on account of the slaughters, conflagrations, plundering, and other disasters that tend to be inflicted in war. Thus, while a prince who wages a war with a dubious cause is in a state of great sin, the soldier in a doubtful cause needs not be in doubt himself, but he ought to respect the judgment of his prince and to follow his orders. For such an ignorance, in conjunction with the necessity of obedience, will free the soldier from guilt.

7 [*Though ignorance of their unjust cause exempts soldiers from sin, they may still justly suffer the evils of war*]

(1) Leopoldus: What, then, will a prince do in a doubtful case—if, for example, there is a dispute over the right to fields or boundaries, and it is a point of dispute in law whether their seizure by neighbours was just or unjust? Is he to undertake a war in a dubious cause, or should he abandon the advantages of his state and a rationale that could well be just and honourable?

---

[354] 1 Thessalonians 5:22.

Democrates: I do not judge that to be something that falls within the duty of a prince. But since there are two species of fighting an issue out (as Cicero very wisely teaches in Book 1 of *On Duties*)—one through arbitration, the other through violence—since the former is proper to human beings, the latter to beasts, we ought to take refuge in the latter only when it is not allowed to make use of the other.[355] Thus, in a case where there is a doubtful controversy, the prince ought to demand of his adversaries that arbitration about the question of justice be effected by judges who are worthy men and skilled in the law selected from both sides. If that can be achieved, there will be no need of arms. If, however, the adversaries obstinately reject a fair and just agreement they will be doing a wrong, which turns the case for going to war from doubtful to certain and just.

(2) As to the case of the one who is in possession of the fields concerning which there is a dispute, if the fields are rashly recovered from him by force of arms, he will justly repel the war—not only because in a dubious case the legal position of the possessor is stronger, but also because the other party is committing a wrong in that he is attempting to achieve by arms what in a dubious case he ought to have done by legal means. Therefore, if he were defeated by the one who was repelling a wrong, by the law of war and the law of nations he will lose his right to those fields and also to such other things as the victor seized. By both Roman and pontifical law, which agrees with natural law, this has been established as the penalty for the man who acts violently.

(3) Moreover, here is the reason why, even though it is granted that soldiers may ignorantly wage an unjust war without sin (likewise the common people who were not admitted to the councils), they justly suffer acts of war at the hands of those with whom the war is waged. It is because the prince and the highest magistrates represent the entire state, and by common consent the power of deliberating on behalf of everyone has been entrusted to them by the whole state and by all the common people. Whatever will have been determined by them will appear to have been determined by everyone, and everyone will appear to have consented to that.

For as reality itself teaches and as the philosophers who have written about the state make clear, in every state that is not a downright tyranny—that is, in a state in which power is exercised upon willing subjects—the supreme power of deliberating on behalf of the entire population is entrusted by consensus to a single man, such as a prince, or to several men, such as a senate, or to an assembly of the entire people—and whatever is openly resolved upon by this man or these men is judged to have been resolved upon by everyone.

Therefore, just as by the sin of a single man, Adam, in whom the whole human race was contained, all men have sinned, so the action of a prince, who acts the part of the whole people, reaches to and is binding upon all the common people. Hence

---

[355] Cicero, *De officiis* 1.34.

DEMOCRATES PART TWO   173

the jurist says, 'The prince's pleasure has the force of law, since by the Royal Law that was passed concerning his rule the people have yielded all their own authority and power to him.'[356] The consensus of the people is corresponding to this Royal Law when they initially appoint an individual prince or king on the basis of his personal qualities or birth, or when they salute and affirm as prince and king, either directly or through representatives, someone chosen by their ancestors. And the same rationale belongs to a public council in a state.

(4) Moreover, soldiers are a portion of the people, which is the reason that, while soldiers who do not know that a war is unjust may not sin in waging the war, they nonetheless justly suffer hostile acts, as we have said above. That is, although they are not harassed by spiritual punishments, they may be so by bodily ones—as sons are sometimes punished for the sin of their father—which line of reasoning holds good even for the rest of the state.

Therefore, this is what differentiates the parties in regard to the reason for a war: in that party that upholds the just cause in a war, everyone is exempt from sin; in the other party, if the soldiers have not learned for certain about the justice of the war, the deaths and the losses incurred by them are principally imputed to the initiators of the war and those by whose advice and command it was undertaken. If you are looking for a judge of both sides: the truth itself, which is God, and upright and wise men using the light of right reason, which derives from eternal law, settle the motives and justice of those who wage war.

(5) To return to the point from which we have digressed: slavery contracted through a just war is just, and booty legally acquired passes into the possession and full ownership of the victor. Therefore, in the matter of these barbarians, the case of those who have been overcome by Spanish arms and by a properly declared war is far different from that of those who, influenced by advice or fear, have handed themselves into the power and good faith of the Christians. For just as the victorious prince may by his own right and pleasure make whatever determination seems conducive to the public good concerning the liberty and goods of the former, so by the common laws and the law of nations it is unjust to reduce the others to slavery and to deprive them of their goods. Still, it is permitted to hold them subject to taxation and tribute in accord with their nature and condition.

How great a difference exists between those who have surrendered and those who have been defeated by force God himself made clear when he gave the sons of Israel rules for waging war: 'When you approach a city to fight against it, first offer it peace; if it accepts it and opens its gates to you, all the people who are in it shall be saved, and it shall serve you under tribute; but if it does not wish to enter upon a treaty and makes war against you, you shall besiege it, and when your God will

---

[356] The jurist Sepúlveda refers to here is the celebrated Roman jurist Ulpian (c. 170—c. 228), and his famous dictum *quod principi placuit legis habet vigorem* is in the *Digest,* 1.4.1. But Sepúlveda is quoting the paraphrase in the sixth-century *Institutes* 1.2.6. The 'Royal Law' is the so-called *Lex regia de imperio*.

have given it over into your hands you will smite with the edge of the sword everything in it which is male, leaving aside the women and infants and cattle that are in the city. You may divide all the booty among the army, and you may eat of the spoils of your enemies.'[357]

Lest someone suppose that God had given an order not about peoples far distant, but only about those cities that he was offering to the sons of Israel to inhabit, he immediately added: 'Thus you shall do to all the cities that are at a considerable distance from you and are not among those cities that you are going to receive into your possession. But concerning those cities that will be given to you, you are to allow nothing at all to live, but you shall kill them with the edge of the sword.'[358]

(6) It is, however, the task of a good and religious prince to maintain the principle of justice towards those who have yielded themselves up, but the principle of due proportion and humanity towards the others, and not to will or permit a rule of cruelty against either—and this all the more so because, just as the Spaniards, if they were led by a good intention, had a just and pious motive for making war, so those peoples had a plausible motive for repelling and resisting force, given that they did not yet know justice and the truth, which they were not able to come to know simply through a declaration by the Christians or in just a few days, nor could they be revealed to them in any other way than by actual deeds over a long period of time. Nor should it be held against the Spaniards that in the pursuit of their very noble cause they granted them only a short space of time for deliberation rather than a long time that would have been in vain; nor should one blame the Indians because they did not think that they should rashly make a decision about the most important of their affairs on the authority of unknown and foreign men.

Therefore, unless we are to observe the procedure of punishing the public sins of which we have spoken above (the worship of idols and human sacrifices) in accord with God's ancient condemnation—a procedure which does not please the kings of Spain in light of their own humanity and Christian mercy—if we turn to the other consideration of the law of war it would seem to me to be beyond any sense of due proportion to reduce the barbarians to slavery or to deprive them of their goods solely on the charge of resisting war (apart from some who through cruelty or obstinacy or treachery and rebellion rendered themselves unworthy)—for they would judge that against these people one should use the method of moderation rather than the law of war. This is especially the case given that the whole rationale for undertaking and waging the war is to be referred to its purpose—which in every question ought to carry the greatest weight—namely, that the pacified barbarians become prepared for more civilized customs and for receiving the sacrosanct religion, a goal that the Christians will more easily and honourably pursue the more they show themselves to be more humane and more kindly than the barbarians.

[357] Deuteronomy 20:10–14.
[358] Deuteronomy 20:15–17.

DEMOCRATES PART TWO   175

8 [*The Indians ought not to enjoy legal equality with the Spaniards, but they should be ruled with moderation*]

(1) **Leopoldus:** Would you actually go so far as to commend this highly humane and generous method of ruling: namely, to bring it about that those mortals who, once they had accepted the Christian religion, did not reject the rule of the Spanish monarch should enjoy an equal legal status with the other Christians and the Spaniards themselves, who are subjects to the rule of the same king?

Democrates: No indeed, I strongly disapprove of it. For nothing is more contrary to the kind of justice called distributive than to apportion equal shares to unequal people and to make those who are superior in dignity or virtue or merits equal to their inferiors in advantages or honour or legal parity. For that is the very objection that Achilles in Homer made to king Agamemnon in the presence of his ambassadors as the most extreme wrongdoing (as Aristotle confirms): that Agamemnon assigned equal advantages and honours to good and bad, brave and cowardly alike. 'The base', Achilles said, 'and the worthy are honoured alike.'[359] This is something to be avoided not only in the case of individual men, but even much more in the case of entire peoples, for indeed the different status of men creates different methods of ruling justly and different types of just regimes.

Over upright, humane, and intelligent men a civil form of government is suitable, one befitting free men, or a royal rule, which imitates paternal rule; but over barbarians and those who have too little cleverness and humanity, the rule of a master is suitable. Therefore not only the philosophers but also the most eminent theologians do not hesitate to affirm that there are certain peoples over whom masterly rule is more suitable than royal or civil rule.[360] They teach that this occurs in two ways: either because they are slaves by nature, which they say come into being in certain regions and certain climes of the world, or because as a result of moral depravity or some other cause they cannot in any other way be restrained to do their duty—and both of these factors coincide among these not yet pacified barbarians. Therefore, to the extent that there is a difference between those who are by nature free and those who are by nature slaves, there ought to be just as much difference in the methods of ruling over the Spaniards and those barbarians—namely, that for the one group royal rule is suitable, for the other an almost masterly rule.

Royal rule, as the philosophers teach, is very similar to the running of a household. For they teach that the running of a household is a kind of kingdom of the house, and in turn a kingdom is the household management of a state or of a single people or of several peoples.[361] Since, therefore, in a great house there are sons, slaves,[362] and, rubbing shoulders with both, servants of freeborn status, and the just

---

[359] Homer, *Iliad* 9.319; Aristotle, *Politics* 2.4.7 (1267a2).
[360] Pseudo-Aquinas (Ptolemy of Lucca), *De regimine principum* (*On the Government of Rulers*) 2.9.
[361] Aristotle, *Politics* 3.10.2 (1285b31–33).
[362] 'Slaves' here translates *servi seu mancipia*. Both are classical Latin terms for chattel slaves. Though *servus* could refer in later Latin to a free bondservant (esp. a serf), Sepúlveda's humanist Latin followed

176　SEPÚLVEDA ON THE SPANISH INVASION OF THE AMERICAS

and kindly (*humanus*) father of the family rules over all of them—not, however, in one single manner, but in accord with the rank and condition of each—I say that the Spaniards ought to be governed by the paternal power of a most excellent and just king who wishes, as he should, to imitate a most excellent and just father.

But those barbarians ought to be governed like servants—albeit free ones—through a power that is a certain mixture of masterly and paternal power, and they ought to be treated in accord with their own condition and that of the current time. For when, with the passage of time, those same men shall become more civilized and their moral probity and Christian religion shall have been firmed up along with our rule, they will need to be treated more freely and generously.

(2) For I greatly approve and have always approved of this precept of the great philosophers who have written about the state: that even in the best founded state, when it comes to the distribution of public advantages and honours, there should be consideration not only of wise and respectable men but even of the masses. For while it may be admitted that the highest powers and those that are administered by single prefects or among just a few men ought to be entrusted to the best and the most prudent men, as the natural order of things demands, still, because the best and wise are everywhere few while the multitude of the people is great, and because when the common people are disaffected it is very hard for the power of the few good men to last securely, those philosophers teach that it is advantageous that offices of lesser importance and also those that are entered upon by many people at the same time may be shared with the common people and men from among the common people, lest, if a different course should be taken, the alienated spirits of the majority might throw the condition of the state into confusion or even cause it to totter.

Aristotle treats of this matter very wisely in many passages, but listen to what he says in Book 3 of the *Politics*, and I'm not reluctant to quote you his exact words (for I know them by heart) from the translation by our friend Ginés: 'So this is how we might settle that controversy over what things ought to be entrusted to the will and the power of the multitude of free men and citizens who do not possess riches or are marked out by virtue—for it is not safe to hand over to them the highest magistracies, since through injustice and lack of self-control they would easily fall sometimes into wrongdoing, at other times into error—but to grant them nothing, to share nothing with them is a course full of danger. For if the many and needy are deprived of honour, it must be that the city will be full of enemies.'[363]

---

classical usage. Here, where he is contrasting chattel slaves (often present in prosperous Spanish households of his day) with free servants (*ministri conditionis liberae*), he was careful to remind the reader of what he meant by *servi* by adding as an alternative term (*seu* = 'or') the unambiguous word *mancipia* (pl. of *mancipium*). Since English does not offer a clear synonym for 'slave', I have reduced the alternative Latin terms to the single English term. For this passage, see the preface to this translation, pp. 83-85.

[363] Aristotle, *Politics* 3.6.6 (1281b22–31).

These things that Aristotle said about the state can properly be applied to kingdoms and entire provinces. Therefore, the king of Spain and his advisers may be advised by these precepts of the philosophers to establish their rule over these pacified barbarians in such a way that, on the one hand, they do not get uppity through indulgence and a greater freedom than befits their condition, and through this inducement and licence conspire to recover their earlier condition and their ingrained way of life, nor, on the other hand, are they to be oppressed by such harsh rule nor treated in such a servile manner and so without honour that out of disgust over their servitude and demeaning treatment they might be bent upon disasters for the Spaniards and be on the watch for all opportunities to shake off their yoke. For it has been mentioned by these same philosophers that for this same reason the Helots so acted against the Spartans and the Penestae against the Thessalians, often conspiring to take up arms against their masters while they bore a resented servitude with a discontented attitude.[364] For the Thessalians and the Spartans used the Penestae and Helots who lived round about their cities almost as slaves to cultivate their fields.

Thus, then, rule should be moderated so that the barbarians may be held to their duty, partly through fear and force but partly though benevolence and an even temper, so that they will be neither able nor willing to contrive a rebellion against the rule or the security of the Spaniards. For this moderation seems to have enough power and security even for securing a perpetuity of rule.

And it is agreed that once upon a time the Romans, those most prudent of men, used these same means for firming up their rule over peoples not yet well pacified, which makes it plain to grasp that it is not only unjust, but also is not conducive to long-term stability and downright dangerous to treat those barbarians as slaves, except in cases where some may show themselves worthy of that punishment and misfortune though crime, perfidy, cruelty in waging war, and obstinacy.

(3) Thus it does not contradict either justice or Christian religion to put upright, just, and wise Spaniards in charge of some of them throughout their cities and regions—especially those men by whose aid they were reduced to rule—men who would take care to instruct them in civilized and upright customs and initiate them into the Christian religion (which is to be handed on not by violence, which is contrary to what we have laid out, but by examples and persuasion), and at the same time by means of their labours and their riches support and help them for the requirements of life, not only the essential ones, but also those befitting free men. 'For the labourer is worthy of his hire', as Christ says in the Gospel, and Paul says: 'For if the Gentiles have become partakers of their [the Christians'] spiritual things, they ought also to be of service to them in material things.'[365]

---

[364] Aristotle, *Politics* 2.5.6 (1269a37–38).
[365] Luke 10:7; Romans 15:27.

178 SEPÚLVEDA ON THE SPANISH INVASION OF THE AMERICAS

But cruelty in ruling and avarice are especially to be avoided by everyone. For as Augustine proclaims, kingdoms without justice are not kingdoms at all, but public acts of brigandage. Hence, when Alexander of Macedon reproached that famous pirate and asked him, 'Why do you harass the sea?', he answered, 'Why do you harass the earth? But because I do what I do in a little boat, I am called a pirate; but because you do it with a large fleet, you are called an emperor.'[366] That which is said of kingdoms extends very broadly and is relevant to all kinds of rule and prefectures that are unjustly and cruelly managed. Paul teaches and advises that these evils are especially to be avoided by saying, 'Masters, offer your slaves what is just and fair.'[367]

Neither motives of humanity or justice nor Christian philosophy forbid ruling over subject mortals or exacting tribute, which is a just pay for labours and is essential for supporting princes and magistrates and soldiers; nor do they forbid one to own slaves or to make use of the toil of slaves in a moderate way; rather, they forbid one to rule avariciously and cruelly, to oppress slaves with an unbearable servitude, slaves whose temporal and spiritual welfare[368] and necessary advantages must be attended to, as though they are parts of oneself—for, as the philosophers make clear, the slave is, as it were, a part of the master—with a soul, although separate.[369] All these and similar crimes not only religious people, but also all good and humane people detest.

For if, on the authority of Paul, 'the person who takes no care for his own people has denied the faith and is worse than an unbeliever',[370] how much more wicked and detestable ought that man to be considered who not only takes no care to look after those who have been entrusted to his good faith, but even tortures and kills them with intolerable exactions and unconscionable servitude and constant and unendurable labours, as certain men have been recorded to have done in some of the islands through the most extreme cruelty and avarice?

As I have often said, a just and religious prince must see to it by every possible means that such crimes be perpetrated no longer, lest through his negligence the crimes of others might procure for him a bad reputation in this age and eternal damnation in the next. For as that pope [John VIII] said, it does no one any good if, though he is not punished for his own sin, he needs to be punished for the sin of another. He says, 'That person has doubtless the guilt of the perpetrator who neglects to emend that which it is in his power to correct.'[371] And Pope Damasus said,

---

[366] Augustine, *De civitate Dei* 4.4.
[367] Colossians 4:1.
[368] Here (as in the last sentence of the work) I am assuming that Sepúlveda intended the word *salus* to cover both protection in this life and eternal salvation in the next. See Democrates's comments at I.19.2.
[369] Aristotle, *Politics* 1.2.6 (1254a12–13).
[370] 1 Timothy 5:8.
[371] John VIII, quoted in Gratian, *Decretum,* D. 86, c. 3.

'When someone is able to obstruct and trouble the wicked and does not do so, it is nothing other than to show favour to impiety.'[372]

(4) So, then, in order to conclude and draw together what I think into a few words: I believe that all these evils need to be counteracted and looked into, in order both that those men who have deserved well of the state not be defrauded of their just rewards, and so that a rule may be exercised upon pacified peoples that is, in proportion to their nature, just and also gentle and humane—in a word, the kind of rule that suits Christian princes—a rule accommodated not only to the utility of the ones in power, but also to the subject peoples' welfare, both temporal and spiritual, and a liberty appropriate to their own nature and condition.

---

[372] Damasus to Stephen, bishop of Mauretania (probably spurious), quoted in Gratian, *Decretum*, C. 23, q. 3, c. 8.

180 SEPÚLVEDA ON THE SPANISH INVASION OF THE AMERICAS

Appendix to Democrates secundus: Passages from early drafts

I.4.5

The Santander MS (P), published by Menéndez Pelayo in 1892, offered a substantial passage not present in the earlier (VTM) manuscripts and later omitted in the Salamanca MS (S), for it dealt with matters that Sepúlveda would handle more extensively in the second book (which is largely lacking in the earlier P version). The initial words in brackets are in common between P and the other manuscripts (including S).

[By no means. For that would be brigandage, not warfare. But in order for a just war to be undertaken there ought to be underlying just motives,] which are much more to be looked into by princes than by soldiers. 'For the just man', says Augustine, 'even if he is perchance fighting under a king who is actually a sacrilegious man, is able to wage war righteously under his orders, thereby observing the proper order of civic peace [i.e. as an obedient soldier]—provided that the order he was given was either definitely not contrary to the commandment of God or at least that it was not certain that it was contrary—in such a way that the wickedness of the command would perhaps make the king guilty, while the proper duty of obedience would show the soldier to be innocent.'[373] For this to be so, however, it must be understood that the soldier is under the direct power of a state or a prince. For those whom no necessity of obedience excuses may not without sin fight and offer service to a state or prince waging an unjust war, or even if there is some doubt about its justice, and they ought to return things carried off, as the most learned men declare. Supporting this opinion is Ambrose, who wrote in his book *On the Duties of Clergy*: 'If it is not possible to come to the aid of one party unless another is harmed, it is more fitting that neither be helped than that one of the two be harmed.'[374]

Textual notes on the Latin text of Coroleu's edition
(*apparatus criticus*, p. 51):

- *rege et homine sacrilego*—The *et* does not occur in Augustine (even as cited by Gratian), but occurs in Menéndez Pelayo's transcription of P, followed by Losada and Coroleu. I have translated the Augustinian text, in which *homine sacrilego* is in apposition to *rege*.
- *potest*—This is the reading in Gratian, followed by Sepúlveda in P, and it is what I have translated. But the *PL* text of this passage (vol. 40, col. 448) offers

---

[373] Augustine, *Contra Faustum* (*Against Faustus*) 22.75 (via Gratian, *Decretum*, C. 23, q. 1, c. 4).
[374] Ambrose, *De officiis ministrorum* 3.9 (via Gratian, *Decretum*, C. 14, q. 5, c. 10).

poscit, which makes little sense and seems to be a slip for *possit,* which would work ('he would be able').

- *si vice*—This follows Gratian, but makes no sense. Augustine wrote *civicae* (it would have been spelled *civice* in the Middle Ages), and I have followed this.
- *servans quod*—This should be *servans—cui quod.* The *cui* was omitted by Gratian, who was followed by Sepúlveda. I have followed the Augustinian text.
- *praeceptum*—Coroleu has introduced the erroneous *praeceptorem.*
- *sensu*—This is Menéndez Pelayo's reading of the P text, followed by Losada and Coroleu. It makes no sense. Augustine (also as quoted in Gratian) wrote *reum,* which is what I have translated.
- *quam alterum*—Coroleu mistakenly omitted *gravari* between these words.

I.11.1 (first sentence)

In place of the first sentence of this section in the Salamanca manuscript (S), the earlier manuscripts (VTMP) offered the following extensive passage on the nature of the society of the Amerindians (especially the Aztecs).

The fact that they have a state arranged in such a way that nobody possesses anything of his own, not a house, not a field that one could sell piecemeal or leave to whomever one wished in one's will—for all things are in the power of the lords who are inappropriately referred to as kings—and the fact that they live not according to their own choice but according to that of the kings, and that they devote themselves to those men's will and pleasure and not to their own liberty, and that they do all these things not after having been overwhelmed by force of arms but willingly and of their own accord—these are the most indisputable indications of a barbarous, abject, and servile mentality. For fields and estates have been distributed in such a way that one part was awarded to the king, another part to public shows and sacrifices, and a third for the uses of individuals, but in such a way that the same men would cultivate royal and public lands and also live off of lands individually granted and, as it were, rented at the will of the king, and they would also pay tribute. Moreover, when a father died the eldest son would receive the patrimony of all the children, unless the king saw fit otherwise. Thus it came about that very many suffered under poverty, and also for this reason some were forced to undergo a harsher mode of servitude. Overwhelmed by want, they used to approach petty kings and ask for little bits of land and obtain terms under which they not only paid a yearly rent but were even personally obliged, when works projects were required, to assume the legal status of slaves (*iure mancipiorum*). If this servile and barbarous system of government had not been in accord with their intelligence and nature, it would have been easy for them to alter it, upon the death of a king who had no successor, to a freer, better, and nobler form of

182 SEPÚLVEDA ON THE SPANISH INVASION OF THE AMERICAS

government. Given that they failed to do this, they declared that they were born for servitude and not for the life of citizens and freeborn men. Therefore, if you wished to reduce these peoples not only to rule but also to a rather more gentle servitude, what you would be determining for them would be nothing worse than forcing them to change masters—and to receive in place of barbarous, impious, and inhuman masters Christian ones, men who cultivate the more civilized virtues and the true religion. Therefore we know that they are—and certainly were before the arrival of the Spaniards—such lesser humans [*homunculi*] in mind and manners, so barbarous, so uncultivated, so uncivilized [*inhumani*]. And yet we haven't even mentioned their impious religion and wicked sacrifices. Since they worship a demon …. [then as in the S manuscript]

I.11.3 (beginning)

From the beginning of I.11.3 through the end of I.11.6, the Salamanca manuscript (S) expands on a shorter passage in the earlier manuscripts. What is offered here is a translation of the version in the Santander manuscript (P), but similar versions are found, with variants, in V (Rome), T (Toledo), and M (Madrid).

These sins, crimes, and impious behaviour of the barbarians are so unspeakable and so odious to God that it is principally because he is offended by these things that he is recorded to have destroyed all mortals—Noah and a very few innocents excepted—in a universal flood. For in explicating the words in Sacred Scripture 'the earth was corrupted in the face of God and filled with iniquity', a very ancient writer by the name of Berosus (for that is the title of the book) says: 'They used to devour human beings and bring about still-births and prepare them as food, and they mated with their mothers, daughters, sisters, men, and beasts.'[375] Subsequently, for those crimes, he records that that very great flood followed. For Sacred Scripture itself bears manifest witness that it was because of that unspeakable crime of lust that Sodom and Gomorrah and all the surrounding region and all its inhabitants, apart from Lot with a very few righteous people of his household, were destroyed to utter extermination by sulfur and fire divinely sent down from heaven.[376] Later on, would there have been just cause for the Jews to attack in a very harsh war, at God's instigation, the Canaanites, Amorites, and Perizzites

---

[375] Genesis 6:12; Pseudo-Berosus (Giovanni Nanni = Annius of Viterbo), *Berosi sacerdotis Chaldaici Antiquitatum … libri quinque* (Antwerp: Jan Steels, 1545), 6. This forgery was first published in Rome by Eucherius Silber in 1498 as *Commentaria super opera diversorum auctorum de antiquitatibus loquentium.* But Sepúlveda's wording implies that he was using one of the more recent Antwerp editions by Steels, for their title-pages place *Berosi* first. Most modern scholars tend to cite Steels's edition of 1552, in which the bogus fragment appears on p. 44. In both those editions, *abortus* appears as *aborsus.* Also, in my translation I have supplied *in* before *edulium,* present in Nanni's text but missing from Sepúlveda's.

[376] Genesis 18–19.

and even to exterminate their herds and flocks if their justification did not derive from these crimes and, most important of all, from the worship of idols? Scripture says, 'God loathes all sins of this sort, and I will destroy them when you enter the land.'[377] And it says, 'If the people of the land negligently and as though holding my power in contempt let off the man who has given of his seed to Moloch—that is, who has become an idol-worshipper—and they don't wish to kill him, I shall set my face against that man and against his family, and I shall cut off that man from the midst of his people along with all who agree with him to fornicate with Moloch.'[378] Similar to these words is what is found in Deuteronomy as an expression of abhorrence at the worship of idols: 'If you hear in one of your cities certain people saying, "The sons of Belial have gone out from among you", and they have led astray the inhabitants of your city, and they have said, "Let us go and worship foreign gods whom you do not know", investigate carefully and diligently. When the truth of the matter has been thoroughly perceived, if you find what has been said to be confirmed and that this abomination has actually been perpetrated, you shall without delay utterly smite the inhabitants of that city with the edge of the sword. Destroy it and all the things in it, right down to the cattle.'[379] Bearing this command and this sternness in mind, Mattathias killed the man who had approached the altar with the intention of sacrificing, as is recorded in the book of Maccabees.[380] Therefore by means of God's greatest and clearest signs great precedents concerning the slaughter of those barbarians seem to have been brought to pass.[381] And there is no shortage of very learned theologians, deeply versed in Sacred Theology, who maintain that that decision and law passed sometimes against Jewish transgressors, and sometimes against Canaanites and Amorites and other pagan idol-worshippers, was not only divine but also determined to be natural. Moreover, they contend that it pertains not just to Jews but also to Christians, and that it has been permitted to Christians not only to subject to their rule those barbarians who have been contaminated with wicked crimes and impious worship of divinities and thus to compel them to sanity and to the true religion by means of suitable arguments and through preaching of the gospel, but even to harass them with rather more severe warfare. Cyprian agrees with this view. Having cited that passage in Deuteronomy and other passages, he added: 'But if these commands concerning the worship of God and the rejection of idols have been observed before the coming of Christ, how much more ought they to be observed after the coming of Christ, when in coming he urged us not only with words but even with deeds.'[382]

---

[377] Deuteronomy 18:12 (where, however, God's action is presented in the third person).
[378] Leviticus 20:4–5.
[379] Deuteronomy 13:12–15.
[380] 1 Maccabees 2:23.
[381] I have read *praeiudicia* ('precedents') for *praeindicia* here. A few words earlier *indicia* (which I have rendered 'signs') may well be *iudicia* ('judgments'). Either makes sense in this context.
[382] Cyprian, *Ad Fortunatum de exhortatione martyrii* (*To Fortunatus, Exhortation to Martyrdom*) 5.23.

184 SEPÚLVEDA ON THE SPANISH INVASION OF THE AMERICAS

I.12.2–3

The earlier versions (VTMP) all offer a substantially different version of section 12 of the S version, starting with what we have printed as the second paragraph of Democrates's speech in section 2 and proceeding to the end. The bracketed words at the beginning of this passage were retained in the S revision.

[But while we read in the Sacred Scriptures (as the theologians themselves affirm) that no people was slaughtered or crushed by war at God's command solely because of infidelity, nonetheless we know that many utterly collapsed under the weapons of the Hebrews under God's authority on account of crimes associated with infidelity—], such as, on account of unspeakable lust, Sodom and Gomorrah—and, both on account of these and other crimes and also on account of idol-worshipping, the Canaanites, Amorites, and Perizzites, as we have pointed out above and as can be confirmed by many other proof-texts. Ambrose says that sins are punished by means of witting agents, just as God wanted the sons of Israel to punish the sins of the Amorites and other peoples whose land he gave the Israelites to possess,[383] and God himself said: 'Do not defile yourselves in any of these ways, for by all these practices the nations I shall cast out before you have defiled themselves. Thus the land has become defiled, and I will punish it for its iniquity, so that it will vomit out its inhabitants.' And a little further on, he says, 'All those abominations were done by the inhabitants of the land who were there before you, and they polluted it. See to it that it does not similarly belch you forth when you shall have done like things, just as it belched forth those who were before you.'[384] By which words God teaches that those crimes, of which the greatest is idol-worship, are to be punished in the same way in a believer as in a pagan. He declares this even more clearly in the verses that follow. That these crimes and impiety are to be punished by the same penalties even in Christian times is a point made by Cyprian, a very important author, whose words we cited above: 'But if these commands concerning the worship of God and the spurning of idols were to be observed before the coming of Christ, how much more ought they to be observed after his coming, when by his coming he urged us not only by words but also by deeds?'[385] And Augustine: 'If we put off attacking or punishing those things by which God is powerfully offended, we most certainly provoke the patience of divinity to wrath.'[386] For it is established that God is offended by nothing

---

[383] The reference to Ambrose is not a direct quotation, but a paraphrase of Gratian's comment on a passage from Bk. 2.4 of *De Cain et Abel*. (*Decretum*, C. 23, q. 5, c. 49, §5). The passage discusses both witting and unwitting agents of God's punitive will.

[384] Leviticus 18:27–28.

[385] Cyprian, *Ad Fortunatum de exhortatione martyrii* 5.23.

[386] Not Augustine, but Gregory I, Letter 3.27 (to Manianus and Benenatus), cited in Gratian, *Decretum*, C. 23, q. 4, c. 50 (cf. I.11.6).

more than by idol-worship, as God himself made clear; for it was on account of this crime, as recorded in Exodus, that God ordered that every single man kill a brother and friend and neighbour, and when this had been done by the Levites, Moses said, 'Today you have consecrated your hands to the Lord, everyone in his son and his brother, so that a blessing may be given to you.'[387] Hence he also says, 'Every soul that will have done any one of these abominations will perish from the midst of his own people.'[388] This is also the source from which flowed the law of the pious and utterly just Constantine against the sacrifices of the pagans—that is, against the worship of idols—a law that established the penalty of death and confiscation of goods not only for those perpetrating impious sacrifices but even for provincial prefects if they should neglect to punish the crime. Augustine mentions that this law was approved and praised not only by all pious Christians, but also by heretics.[389] And lest you think that these actions, which have been given such a sanction by both law and by nature itself, are allowed only against those pagans who have justly been subjected to the rule of Christians (which would be the claim of a man hallucinating in the light of midday), Gregory, an exceptionally wise man and pious man, in a letter praises Gennadius, the exarch of Africa, because he was harrying the pagans in war specifically so that, when their idol-worship had been taken away, Christian piety might be spread, for he was not waging war against people who had already been pacified and subjected to the Roman people.[390] For it was not for nothing, but for an important reason that it has been handed down by very learned men that there is sufficient justification why Christians lawfully may punish and persecute pagans—on the authority of a pope—if perchance there happen to be any who do not observe the law of nature, as is the case with idol-worshippers.[391]

- The section on Constantine's law, etc. is virtually identical to the passage in I.17.3 in the S. manuscript.

Textual notes on the Latin text of Coroleu's edition (p. 73)

- In the passage cited from Ambrose, Coroleu has incorrectly written *similem* for *similiter*.
- Two sentences later, Coroleu prints *apertis etiam suiectis verbis*. This should read *apertius etiam subiectis verbis*. While *suiectis* is just a typo. Coroleu

---

[387] Exodus 32:29.
[388] Leviticus 18:29.
[389] Augustine, Letter 93.3.10 (to Vincentius).
[390] Gregory I, Letter 1.73 (quoted in Gratian, *Decretum*, C. 23, q. 4, c. 49).
[391] The pope in question was Innocent IV, in his commentary on Innocent III's decretal *Quod super his*.

186   SEPÚLVEDA ON THE SPANISH INVASION OF THE AMERICAS

follows Losada and Menédez Pelayo in reading *apertis*, but note not only the word order but also the *aperte* in the previous sentence—i.e. God makes it clear there, but he made it even clearer further on. Accordingly, I would emend the text with the comparative adverb *apertius*.

- In the passage from Gregory I misattributed to Augustine, for *quibus Deus vehementer ostenditur*, read *quibus Deus vehementer offenditur*. The same error is found in Losada and Menéndez Pelayo. But Coroleu and Losada got it right in I.11.6. (There is also a misplaced comma after *irascendum*.)

I.14.4 (halfway through section 4)

Here the Rome (V), Toledo (T), and Madrid (M) manuscripts offer a passage omitted in the Salamanca (S) version (as well as the P manuscript, of course, which omitted the entire chapter). The bracketed words are shared with the Salamanca manuscript.

[In accord with this line of thought, one is not improperly permitted to conclude that those philosophers and whoever else believed that God is one and has a care for human affairs had some sort of faith in Christ]—on the basis of that passage of Paul touching upon the philosophers' knowledge of God.[392] This passage the Gloss interprets in this way: 'By "the invisible things", it says, is meant the Person of God the Father, according to that passage of 1 Timothy 5: "whom no man has seen". By "eternal power" is meant the Person of Christ, according to the passage in 1 Corinthians 1: "Christ is the power of God". By "divinity" is meant the Person of the Holy Spirit, to whom goodness is appropriated.'[393] Clarifying [*declarans*] these words, Thomas [Aquinas] says, 'Not that philosophers, under the guidance of reason, could arrive by means of created things at a knowledge of the Persons so as to know what their properties are, which do not signify the condition of a cause towards created beings, but only by way of appropriation.'[394] This, then, is one manner in which the philosophers and those taught by the philosophers may seem to have had some kind of faith, however obscure, in Christ, who is the son of God. Another manner is the one Thomas Cardinal Vio [Cajetan], a man famous for learning and religion, used in my hearing (I was on familiar terms with him sometimes at Gaeta, after the sack of the city [Rome], sometimes in the city itself) when he advocated for the philosophers in this matter. This is how I sometimes heard him discoursing: 'The philosophers,' he said, 'under the guidance of God and with nature as their teacher, knew that God was one—and that

---

[392] Romans 1:20.
[393] Sepúlveda was not quoting the interlinear gloss directly, but accessing it through Aquinas. See next note. (The Timothy passage is actually 6:16; the passage in 1 Corinthians is 1:24).
[394] Aquinas, *In Epistolam ad Romanos, Caput Primum*, Lectio VI, 122.

he had a care for good and pious men.' For this is what Paul said in his Epistle to the Hebrews: 'Whoever would approach him must believe that he exists, and that he rewards those who seek him.'[395] Moreover, the person who believes that there is a reward must logically be believed to have faith in the author of the rewarding. In truth, the author of the rewarding is Christ, who revealed the path and opened the hitherto closed gates to the celestial prizes which are set forth for all good and pious men.

Textual notes on the Latin text of Coroleu's edition (p. 80)

- The passage from the Gloss and Aquinas is garbled. The first *per bonitatem* should be omitted; for the second, *divinitatem* should be substituted for *bonitatem*.
- For *a philosophi* read *a philosophis*. (The same error is in Losada's edition.)

I.15.11

The short section I.15.11 in the Salamanca (S) manuscript replaced a lengthier passage in the Santander (P) manuscript and present also, with minor variants, in the earlier VTM manuscripts):

Come, then: it is on the basis of numerous and very important reasons that those barbarians are ordered by the law of nature to accept the rule of the Spaniards—rule which is more advantageous to themselves than to the Spaniards, just as virtue, humanity, and the true religion are considered more precious than any gold or silver. Therefore, if they should reject rule, they may be forced by arms, and that war will be, as we have declared above on the authority of the greatest philosophers and theologians, just by the law of nature—even much more just than the war the Romans waged against other nations in order to subjugate them to their rule, to the extent that the Christian religion is better and more certain than the Roman religion, and the Spanish are superior to those lesser humans [*homunculi*] through a greater excess of intelligence, prudence, humanity, and strength of mind and body than the ancient Romans were to the other peoples—particularly when you add the authority of the supreme pontiff, who takes the place of Christ, and his declaration of the justice of this war. For just as wars that were waged under the authority of God, as were many of those in Sacred Scripture, cannot be unjust, as Augustine says,[396] one is allowed to consider equally just those waged

[395] Hebrews 11:6.
[396] Augustine, *Contra Faustum* 22.75.

188 SEPÚLVEDA ON THE SPANISH INVASION OF THE AMERICAS

with the consensus and approbation of the Apostolic Council of the highest priest of God, the vicar of Christ. This is particularly the case with those wars waged to carry out Christ's evangelical command, which is another reason, and indeed the most just reason of all, why war seems justly waged against those barbarians.

Textual notes on the Latin text of Coroleu's edition (p. 87)

- For *virtuti,* read *virtus.*
- For *praestantque,* read *praestant quam.*
- For *si iusta,* read *sic iusta.* (Losada noted the error, as has Schäfer, but Coroleu overlooks it.)

II.1.3–II.2.1

The long speech of Democrates in the S. manuscript was represented by this short passage in VTM:

> **Democrates:** Indeed, by that (law) which is ready to hand, which even good men commonly make use of, which is contained in the law of nations (*ius gentium*): that those who have been defeated in a just war become, along with their goods, the possession of the victors and those who seize them. For from this was born civil slavery.

Manuscript P began with the VTM sentence (though adding 'and the law of nature') but then offered more, though still far short of the S version:

> **Democrates:** Indeed, by that (law) which is ready to hand, which even good men commonly make use of, which is contained in the law of nations (*ius gentium*) and the law of nature: that those who have been defeated in a just war become, along with their goods, the possession of the victors and those who seize them. For from this was born civil slavery. Although this is common to all just wars, nonetheless when things that have been carried off are sought back, wise and religious men judge that damages ought to be imposed on the enemy proportional to the injuries and inconveniences received. But when by the command or law of God sins and idol-worship among impious men are being punished, if they recalcitrantly fight back, the Sacred Scriptures teach by example that more is permitted against the bodies and goods of the enemy. And the very important writer Ambrose declares in these words: 'When peoples are stirred up thus by divine command to punish sins, as that Jewish people was stirred up to occupy the Promised Land, guilty blood is shed without incurring blame for the sake of destroying sinful peoples; and the things that were wrongly possessed by them properly pass over into

the power of the good men.'[397] On this rationale also it would appear that the war waged by our people against those barbarians does not depart from divine law, and agrees with the *ius gentium*—which is congruent with nature, and by which enslavements and the seizures of hostile goods are introduced.

Textual note on the Latin text of Coroleu's edition (p. 105)

- Before *quamquam*, add *quod*.

II.2.4–II.3.8

From the beginning of II.2.4 to the quotation from Colossians in II.3.8, the Salamanca manuscript (S) restored a passage present in the VTM manuscripts that was considerably reduced in the P (Santander) version, which latter is offered here. The portion in brackets is in all the manuscripts.

[Therefore, though it is by nature just that each person should enjoy his natural liberty and his justly acquired goods, nonetheless reason and the natural necessity of men have through a tacit consensus of nations established or approved that, when there will have been a recourse to arms,] those who have been captured in a just war become the slaves of those who capture them—not only because that which conquers is greater through some excellence [or power, *virtute*], as the philosophers teach, and that it is just by the law of nature that the worse be subordinate and obedient to the better, but also so that through this inducement they prefer to save [*servare*] men whom they have conquered (hence they were called 'slaves' [*servi*]) than to kill them, which contributes to the protection of human society. For there is a certain natural fellowship, as I have said and as the philosophers teach, of all human beings among themselves. Wise men affirm that what is necessary for the protection of natural fellowship is just by the law of nature. In sum, the philosophers declare that what has been introduced through human necessity is founded upon the law of nature. Moreover, once they have lost their liberty, how are they able to keep their possessions? When these things become the property of the ones who seize them, it comes about that they would be more apt to refrain from burning down buildings or laying waste to fields. When people, buildings, and trees have been spared, things are not so very bad for the defeated, nor is the hope absent that through the clemency of the victors liberty or even their possessions may be restored to the defeated, if not on the fairest terms, at least on tolerable terms—as often happens at the hands even of men who

---

[397] Not Ambrose, but Gratian commenting on a passage in Ambrose's *De Cain et Abel* (2.4): C. 23, q. 5, c. 49.6.

190 SEPÚLVEDA ON THE SPANISH INVASION OF THE AMERICAS

are not remarkably humane, unless a prior cruelty and obstinacy in fighting back doesn't stand in the way. And through these justifications and through human necessities I judge this law of war to have been sanctioned or approved by the law of nations, since there ought not to be any doubt of the justice of a law which has been approved by the behaviour and consensus of peoples, since wise men judge the common consensus of men about any matter to be the voice or verdict of nature. But why are we bothering with human reasonings when we may use the testimonies of the Apostles or, rather, of Christ speaking through the Apostles. For Paul [not only does not regard as unjust slavery contracted in a just war through the law of nations, but even gives precepts and lays out the duties of slaves to masters and masters to slaves: 'Slaves', he says, 'obey your earthly masters in all things, not only obeying them in plain view as those who please men, but fear God in the honesty of your heart.']

Textual note on the Latin text of Coroleu's edition (p. 108)

- For *Quae cum efficitur*, read *Quam cum fiant capientium, efficitur*.

II.4.1

Manuscripts VTM presented a fuller version of the first two sentences of Democrates's speech, offering an anecdote about Diogenes's kinetic refutation of Zero's paradox. The bracketed words are found also in the S manuscript.

[I know that there are some men of great authority in other respects who have discoursed in this way about the justice of that war, having been defeated by the same reasoning that you have just used—not because they actually assented to it, but because they weren't able to disentangle it,] as Aristotle testifies happened to certain men who were unable to solve the arguments by which Zeno affirmed that, contrary to our senses, nothing was in motion; they admitted that nothing is moved. In order to refute their stupidity and Zeno's boldness, Diogenes began to walk around in the presence of all of them. When Zeno was astonished and asked what all that inappropriate walking about signified, he replied, 'Don't you see that by walking around I am refuting your sophistries'?' This very intelligent action of Diogenes shows that it is stupid to affirm anything contrary to the senses that has been established by the common approval of men simply because you are unable to solve sophistries.

The Defence of the Book, *On the Just Reasons for War*

(*Apologia pro libro de iustis belli causis*)

Preface to the translation of *Apologia*

History of the text: Overview

The textual history of Sepúlveda's *Apologia* is far less problematic than that of the *Democrates secundus,* and it has accordingly received far less scholarly discussion. Indeed, the only full account of the surviving manuscripts and their relation to the early printed editions is the painstaking and exhaustive survey offered by Antonio Moreno Hernández in the introduction to his 1997 edition of the *Apologia* in the Pozoblanco *Obras completas.*[1] We adopt his conclusions here and direct the reader to his introduction for detailed accounts of variant readings.

Manuscripts

There are four manuscripts of the *Apologia,* and they divide evenly into two groups, to which Moreno Hernández gave the names *B* and *C* (his group *A* refers to the first three printed editions). Group *C* can be dealt with expeditiously. Its earlier member is a sixteenth-century manuscript (dubbed *J* by Moreno) currently in the John Carter Brown Library of Brown University. It is manifestly a copy taken of the edition published in Rome in May of 1550. The fact that a copy was made of the printed book might seem to give some force to the claim made by Las Casas that a royal *cédula* ordered the confiscation of Sepúlveda's *Apologia* 'por toda Castilla'.[2] Sepúlveda himself, however, implicitly denied that such a confiscation had taken

---

[1] Antonio Moreno Hernández, 'Introducción' to the edition of the *Apologia*, in Juan Ginés de Sepúlveda, *Obras completas*, vol. 3, cxxviii–clxxxvi (Pozoblanco: Ayuntamiento de Pozoblanco, 1997), '5. El texto: tradición manuscrita y ediciones', clviii–clxxx.

[2] Bartolomé de las Casas, 'The Subject of This Work', in *Aquí se contiene una disputa o controversia*.

Sepúlveda on the Spanish Invasion of the Americas. Luke Glanville, David Lupher and Maya Feile Tomes, Oxford University Press. © Luke Glanville, David Lupher, and Maya Feile Tomes 2023.
DOI: 10.1093/oso/9780198863823.003.0004

192 SEPÚLVEDA ON THE SPANISH INVASION OF THE AMERICAS

place and asserted that the summary of his dialogue was 'available in printed form' (*anda impressa*).[3] No copy of a *cédula* prohibiting the book in Spain seems to have survived though there do exist three *cédulas* prohibiting its export to or circulation in Peru, New Spain, and Tierra Firme, and ordering its confiscation in those territories.[4] Another possible explanation for a need to copy a scarce printed text is Arnold Mylius's claim, prefacing his 1602 edition, that the original print run was very limited.[5]

Whatever may have been its own reason for existence, manuscript *J* formed the basis of another copy (Moreno's manuscript *G*), made a century later by the Sevillan scholar Nicolás Antonio (1617–1684), presumably while working on his *Biblioteca Hispana Nova*, published in Rome in 1672. Though Antonio was working from *J*, he felt free to make a number of emendations and stylistic 'improvements' and variations. Obviously, though, neither *J* nor Antonio's copy *G* have anything to contribute to the essential history of the text of the *Apologia*.

Much more intriguing are the two manuscripts forming Moreno's Group *B*, both of which derived from Sepúlveda himself, for not only are they the work of scribes he often used, but both bear corrections and notations in the author's own hand. And yet, only one of these manuscripts (*M*, currently in the Biblioteca Nacional in Madrid) antedates the publication of the work in Rome. Included in a codex of various content, *M* corresponds to the bulk of the *Apologia* (our sections II–IV.8 = sections 3–27 in the numbering of the 1780 edition, adopted by Moreno). It is headed not by the title *Apologia*, but by a prolix title beginning *Summa quaestionis ad bellum barbaricum* …. This caused its first editor, A. M. Fabié, to

---

[3] Juan Ginés de Sepúlveda, 'Objections', in *Aquí se contiene una disputa o controversia*, edited by Bartolomé de las Casas, Twelfth Objection; Sepúlveda, *Proposiciones temerarias*, §7. In the *Proposiciones temerarias*, §16, he claimed that the Royal Council had no problem with the book, and that objections spearheaded by Las Casas did not 'prevent numerous copies of it from continuing to do the rounds publicly at court without anybody else raising objections'. But in a letter to Antoine Perrenot de Granvelle, Sepúlveda did note that the Council of the Indies requested him to deliver to them all the copies of the book in his possession, though it did not issue a ruling against it (Letter 94, from Sepúlveda to Antoine Perrenot de Granvelle, 3 August 1550, in Sepúlveda, *Obras completas, vol. 9.2: Epistolario*, §2, p. 265). Santiago Muñoz Machado, in the fullest biography of Sepúlveda, simply asserts without evidence that Las Casas managed 'to get the book blocked from entry into Spain, and the existing copies were confiscated' (*Sepúlveda, Cronista del Emperador* (Barcelona: Edhasa, 2012), 413). Francisco Castilla Urbano likewise takes Las Casas's claim at face value (*El pensamiento de Juan Ginés de Sepúlveda* (Madrid: Centro de Estudios Políticos y Constitucionales, 2013), 198).

[4] The *cédula* sent to the Audiencia of Peru on 19 October 1550 is transcribed and discussed by Teodoro Andrés Marcos in *Los imperialismos de Juan Ginés de Sepúlveda en su Democrates Alter* (Madrid: Instituto de Estudios Políticos, 1947), 67–69 (and a facsimile photo is included in an appendix). The identically worded *cédulas* to the governor of Tierra Firme (3 November) and the Audiencia of New Spain (28 November) are in Diego de Encinas, *Libro Primero de Provisiones, Cédulas, Capítulos, y Cartas … tocantes al buen govierno de las Indias* (Madrid: Imprenta Real, 1596), 230.

[5] Arnold Mylius, prefatory note to his edition of the *Apologia* in *Ioannis Genesii Sepulvedae Cordubensis … Opera quae reperiri potuerunt omnia* (Köln: Arnold Mylius in Officina Birckmannica, 1602), 422: 'Editus igitur Romae … sed cum … pauca admodum exemplaria excusa essent, ad exteros non pervenit … '.

THE DEFENCE OF THE BOOK, *ON THE JUST REASONS FOR WAR*   193

fail to recognize that it was identical to the greater part of the *Apologia*.[6] Moreno Hernández plausibly conjectures:

> We are faced here, surely, with an earlier version of the central section of the *Apologia*, probably composed for his stay in Alcalá and Salamanca around 1548–49 to defend the printing of his *Democrates secundus*. This version was reworked for the text established in the Roman edition, which incorporated the corrections that M had undergone, though it also omitted certain passages, altered the order of others, added or omitted variants, and emended certain readings.[7]

Manuscript *S*, the other member of the *B* group, resides in a miscellaneous codex in the library of the University of Salamanca, having formerly been housed in the Colegio Viejo de Salamanca. The bulk of it is the work of one scribe; the last two pages are by another. But both scribes were ones that Sepúlveda himself often used, and there are marginal notations in Sepúlveda's own hand on the portion transcribed by the first amanuensis. The presence of the preliminary letter by Antonio Agustín to Sepúlveda and the colophon at the end indicate clearly that this manuscript was made from a copy of the edition published in Rome, and Moreno's painstaking analysis of the variants makes this even clearer.[8] Addressing the natural question of why Sepúlveda assigned his scribes to take a copy of a printed copy of his book, Moreno Hernández opined: 'The most likely reason derives from Sepúlveda's interest in promoting the circulation of his work through all means at his disposal, bearing in mind the scarcity of copies brought about by the recall of the edition on royal orders'.[9] But see above for the problems with this 'recall'.

For all Moreno's diligence in examining and collating the manuscripts, it cannot be said that the manuscript tradition of the *Apologia* presents problems comparable to that of the dialogue that it summarized and defended. Nor do the manuscripts offer significant divergences from the text of the Roman edition of 1550—setting aside, of course, the irrelevant 'improvements' introduced by Nicolás Antonio in the mid-seventeenth century (apparently for an edition of the work that he never carried out).

---

[6] A. M. Fabié, *Vida y escritos de Fray Bartolomé de las Casas, Obispo de Chiapas* (Madrid: 1879), vol. 2, Appendix XXIII ('Objectiones y respuestas relativas al *Democrates Alter*'), 519–37. Similarly, Ángel Losada regarded the manuscript as a summary of the dialogue with no apparent relation to the Apologia: *Juan Ginés de Sepúlveda: a través de su 'Epistolario' y nuevos documentos* (Madrid: Consejo Superior de Investigaciones Científicas, 1949; repr. 1973), 331, 652–53.

[7] Moreno Hernández, 'Introducción', clxix.

[8] Moreno Hernández, 'Introducción', clxix–clxxi.

[9] Moreno Hernández, 'Introducción', clxxi–clxxii.

194 SEPÚLVEDA ON THE SPANISH INVASION OF THE AMERICAS

Editions

The circumstances surrounding the first printed edition of Sepúlveda's *Apologia* have been presented in the introduction [pp. 27–28]. It was dated 1 May 1550 and published in Rome by the brothers Valerio and Luigi Dorico.[10] Natives of Brescia, upon moving to Rome in 1539 the fratelli Dorico worked primarily for the Roman Academy, producing books of considerable beauty until 1555. Specializing in the printing of musical texts, they launched the career of the great Palestrina (1525–94), whose first book of Masses they printed in 1554. The musical notation software Dorico is named in their honour. Their edition of the *Apologia* is prefaced by a letter to Sepúlveda by the humanist historian and jurist Antonio Agustín y Albanell, then an auditor of the Roman Rota, and it is followed by the text of Alexander VI's bull *Inter caetera* (1493).

Unlike the *Democrates secundus*, the *Apologia* was included in both of the first two editions of Sepúlveda's collected works. The first of these was published in 1602 in Köln by Arnold Mylius (1540–1604), who had married into and inherited the famous bookselling and printing firm of Arnold Birckmann and his heirs.[11] The *Apology* appears on pp. 423–45, and it includes the Alexandrine bull, but not the letter by Agustín. As Mylius noted in the introduction to his volume, his text of the *Apologia* was based on a printed copy of the 1550 edition that he acquired in Italy.[12]

The third edition of the *Apologia* appeared in 1780, in the fourth and last volume of the impressive *Opera, cum edita, tum inedita* (*Works, Both Published and Unpublished*), edited under the auspices of the Real Academia de la Historia in Madrid, under the direction of a group of scholars led by Francisco Cerdá y Rico.[13] As Moreno Hernández has shown, the editors made use of both the 1550 Rome edition and the 1602 Köln edition.[14] They also introduced 33 section numbers, which were subsequently adopted by Losada in his 1975 translation and by Moreno in 1997.

The only other edition of the *Apologia* is that published in volume 3 (the same volume that contains the *Democrates secundus*) of the *Obras completas* published by the Ayuntamiento de Pozoblanco in 1997, with introduction and text by Moreno Hernández and translation and notes by Ángel Losada (revised by Moreno). This is the only critical edition of the *Apologia*—that is, the only one with a full *apparatus*

---

[10] Ángel Losada printed a full facsimile of this edition in his 1975 translation of the *Apologiae* of both Las Casas and Sepúlveda. (This edition also included a facsimile of the manuscript of Las Casas's *Apologia*.) *Juan Ginés de Sepúlveda and Bartolomé de las Casas, Apologia* (Madrid: Editora Nacional, 1975).

[11] Sepúlveda, ed. Mylius, *Opera quae reperiri pouterunt omnia.*

[12] Arnold Mylius, *De vita scriptisque ... Sepulvedae*, p. 3 (unnumbered), in the front matter of *Opera quae reperiri potuerunt omnia.*

[13] *Ioannis Genesii Sepulvedae Cordubensis Opera, cum edita, tum inedita, accurante Regia Historiae Academia* (Madrid: Imprenta Real de la Gaceta, 1780), vol. 4, 329–51.

[14] Moreno Hernández, 'Introducción', clxv.

THE DEFENCE OF THE BOOK, *ON THE JUST REASONS FOR WAR* 195

criticus, as well as a lucid and full account of the manuscripts and editions and the relationships among them. Also, Moreno's Latin text has very few misprints, unlike the Latin text of the *Democrates secundus* in the same volume. It is in every way a commendable edition.

Translations

As far as we have been able to ascertain, only two translations of Sepúlveda's *Apologia* exist: one into Spanish, the other into English.

The Spanish translation was the work of the esteemed scholar Ángel Losada García.[15] It appeared in 1975 in a volume containing translations of both Sepúlveda's *Apologia* and Las Casas's *Apologia* (often referred to in English as *In Defense of the Indians*, the title Stafford Poole gave to the English translation the year before Losada's volume appeared). Losada accompanied his translations with a useful introduction and also included facsimiles of both the 1550 edition of Sepúlveda's *Apologia* and the manuscript of Las Casas's *Apologia*. It should be noted, however, that Losada was not attempting to produce a critical edition of Sepúlveda's *Apologia*. Indeed, while he included a facsimile of the 1550 edition, he based his translation on the text of the 1780 edition. Losada's translation was adopted, with revisions, by Moreno Hernández in his 1997 Pozoblanco edition.

The only other translation of the work, that into English, is an unpublished 1973 undergraduate Honours Thesis by Lewis D. Epstein, then in his Senior year majoring in Classics at Bowdoin College in Brunswick, Maine.[16] Epstein's often admirable translation profited from the supervision of Nathan Dane, a legendary teacher of Greek and Latin, and also from the advice of Lewis Hanke, who was then nearing the end of his rich academic career at the nearby University of Massachusetts, Amherst.[17] It should be noted that Epstein took the trouble to consult all three Latin editions of the *Apologia* then available—not something as easy to do in 1973 as it is today. Following a distinguished undergraduate career as a Classics major at Bowdoin, Epstein earned a law degree from the University of Virginia Law School and embarked on a successful law practice in Maine and Upstate New York. He died in November of 2020.

---

[15] Sepúlveda and Las Casas, *Apologia*. For an account of Losada's career, with an emphasis on his work on Sepúlveda, see Antonio Truyol y Serra, 'In Memoriam Ángel Losada García', in Sepúlveda, *Obras completas*, vol. 3, VII–X.

[16] As noted by Luna Nájera in her extremely useful *Oxford Bibliography of Sepúlveda*, Epstein's translation 'is not easily accessible'. Nájera was incorrect, however, in identifying this translation as an 'MA diss'. Bowdoin is a distinguished undergraduate liberal arts college; it offers no graduate programmes.

[17] It is highly likely that the 1970 paperback reissue of Hanke's 1959 *Aristotle and the American Indians* inspired Epstein to undertake this project (as, in fact, it first sparked the present translator's interest in this subject). Epstein's preface also records gratitude to Ángel Losada, but it would seem that his communication with him was *via* Hanke.

The present translation

The present translation is based on the Latin text established by Antonio Moreno Hernández in the third volume of the Pozoblanco *Obras completas* of Sepúlveda. We have also profited from consultation of the translations by Losada and Epstein. For certain challenges offered by Sepúlveda's Latin vocabulary, see the translator's preface to the *Democrates secundus*.

As noted above, the 1780 edition introduced 33 section numbers that were subsequently adopted both by Losada in his 1975 translation and by Moreno is his 1997 edition and revision of Losada's translation. We have, however, introduced section and subsection numbers of our own, more closely corresponding to the structure of the treatise. Below is a key correlating our sections with those of Moreno's edition:

Our edition	Moreno Hernández's edition
I (Introduction)	1–2
II (Objections to Sepúlveda's argument)	3
III (Sepúlveda's argument)	4–18
III.1	4
III.2	5–7
III.3	8
III.4.i–viii	9
III.4.ix–xiv	10
III.4.xv–xxi	11
III.4.xxii–xxvii	12
III.4.xxviii–xxxi	13
III.4.xxxii–xxxvi	14
III.4.xxxvii–xxxviii	15
III.4.xxxix	16
III.4.xl–xlv	17
III.4.xlvi–l	18
IV (Sepúlveda's response to the objections)	19–27
IV.1	19
IV.2	20
IV.3	21

Our edition	Moreno Hernández's edition
IV.4	22
IV.5	23
IV.6	24–25
IV.7	26
IV.8	27
V (Conclusion and testimonials)	28–33

198 SEPÚLVEDA ON THE SPANISH INVASION OF THE AMERICAS

Apologia

Antonio Agustín greets Juan Ginés de Sepúlveda

I have shared the summary of that question concerning the war against the Indians, which you discussed at greater length very learnedly and eloquently in the book *On the Just Reasons for War*, with the most excellent priest Felipe Archinto, papal vicar, with that deeply pious man Gil Foscarario, theologian of the pontifical household, and with other very important and learned theologians and jurists—for this was the task you had enjoined upon me in a letter.[18] (2) We have all ever admired and esteemed your unparalleled learning and sharp intelligence in every literary genre. Moreover, this question has seemed to us worthy of being dealt with under the gaze of all men, for the subject matter is extremely important and affects very many men of our nation and people—nor is it a matter foreign to Christendom as a whole. (3) Therefore we have allowed the little book to be transcribed and sent out in several copies—perhaps not contrary to your own wishes. True, you did not write this with the intention that it be diffused among the general public, but if you had supposed that it was something unworthy of you that was going to be circulating, you really should have kept it suppressed and hidden. Bear us in your affections, and farewell. Rome. 1 April.

The Defence by Juan Ginés de Sepúlveda of his Book On the Just Reasons for War, *to the most illustrious and learned prelate Don Antonio Ramírez, bishop of Segovia*

I. [Introduction]

(1) It was not without some surprise over the position you have taken, most illustrious prelate, that I have read through the treatise *On War against the Barbarians*, which you painstakingly composed against my book *On the Just Reasons for War*

---

[18] In 1550, the humanist lawyer Antonio Agustín y Albanell (1517–1586) was at an early stage of a distinguished career as a historian of canon law and member of the church hierarchy (culminating as Archbishop of Tarragona for the last ten years of this life). Educated in Alcalá, Salamanca, Bologna, and Padua (where he studied Greek), he was made Auditor of the Sancta Rota Romana (the highest appellate tribunal of the Catholic Church) at the request of Charles V in 1544. Though his first major work (1544) was on the textual history of the Digest (civil law), he devoted much of his life to the critical study of the text of Gratian (canon law). Sepúlveda no doubt found him of invaluable assistance in the composition of the *Apologia*, given its heavy dependence on canon law.

and which you sent to me at Córdoba. (2) I wondered what motive could have driven you to resolve to wield a carefully composed book to attack an opinion of mine of this nature, given that it is, in the first place, the opinion of one who is a supporter and admirer of you and your excellences and honour, and also of one who makes use of the most obvious and weighty testimonies of the Divine Scriptures and the doctors of the church, the most reliable assistance of rational arguments, and the authority of the church in order to defend against the insolence of certain persons the communal and most honourable cause of our nation and of the prince to whom you owe so much. (3) For nothing could make me believe that you, a prudent man and a highly important bishop, were slave to an ambition to display your talent and learning in so inappropriate an area, especially since you are bringing forward little or nothing of your own. Almost everything was other people's material and not sufficiently worthy of your remarkable learning, for you had borrowed from those who, in my opinion, imprudently and intemperately (to put it mildly) make use of misrepresentations and deceptions to attack imprudently and immodestly the very honourable cause of our state and our rulers.

(4) But now that I have examined everything with troubled mind and wavering judgment, I have been principally led to the view that, since you are a most excellent and very humane man, you have followed no other aim than what I would consider your duty. By composing a little book in which you have gathered together the key arguments on which my adversaries have chiefly relied and in sending it to me, your aim has been either to make me yield to the arguments and thus to lead me back to the true path after my wandering astray or, were I to persist in my view, to more clearly understand from my response how I would refute the objections.

(5) I shall do, then, what you implicitly bid me—and indeed more than you bid me: for I shall lay out not only your arguments, but also all those that have been lodged against me either at Alcalá or Salamanca; and, with the bases and supports of my arguments interspersed in the scholastic manner, I shall respond to the individual points and confute the misrepresentations—not made by you (for I have come to know the integrity and honesty of your mind), but by certain men suffering from an eagerness to curry favour or even more serious diseases of the mind—men who I am convinced have managed with every means at their disposal to delude both you and many others by displaying the same tricks.

(6) But before we go on to anything else you must set aside a false belief—if, that is, you really do perhaps believe that the Universities of Salamanca and Alcalá have passed judgment against my little book. For that was not the judgment of a university but the artifice of a few corrupt men, not a unanimous determination

but the deceptions of two or three people in either place, men whose authority on account of their superior learning other men have preferred over their own better judgment.

(7) This, then, is how you set up the disputation. 'The question', you say, 'is whether it is permissible to harass the Indians with warfare by depriving them of their dominions, possessions, and goods, and by killing them if they offer resistance, in order that, once they are despoiled and subjected, the faith may be more easily urged upon them through preachers'. (8) But to lay out the question in this manner in order that there may be a discussion of my views—what is it other than to stumble on the threshold, as they say, and to reveal right at the beginning of the disputation the wiles of those men from whom you have adopted those points? Those men, lacking confidence in the weakness of the other contrivances with which they attack my book, seek out the assistance of false charges and feign that I have undertaken to serve as advocate for those outrages and impious acts of brigandage that my book most bitterly attacks, in order to create ill will against me and to curry popular favour for themselves—unless, perhaps, they simply have not read my book or, having read it, have failed to understand it on account of their unfamiliarity with a style of writing a bit on the sophisticated side.

(9) I have noticed that this has been the case of many of those to whose vote the matter has been entrusted—to wit, that the book has been condemned by many as soon as the case has been announced, even though both divine and natural law clash with them. Therefore, in order that my position, about which there is complaint, may not be concealed from you, I declare that those barbarians should not be plundered of their possessions and powers, nor should they be reduced to slavery, but they should be subjected to the rule of Christians so that they may not impede the faith and its propagation by resisting preachers and committing blasphemy against God through idolatry—and also for the sake of other advantages for those barbarians themselves. Therefore, the question needs to be posed differently, in the following way:

II. [Objections to Sepúlveda's argument]

(1) 'The question is whether the barbarians whom we call Indians are to be justly subjected to the rule of the Christian Spaniards so that when their barbaric customs and idol-worship and impious rituals have been taken away, their souls may be prepared for accepting the Christian religion'. Those who deny this are guided by these arguments:

First they put it as follows: 'The war by which those barbarians are reduced to the Christians' power is not just; therefore, they are not justly subdued by warfare. This point is proved thus: as Augustine says in [Gratian] Case 23, question 2, canon

THE DEFENCE OF THE BOOK, *ON THE JUST REASONS FOR WAR*   201

'Dominus', "It is customary that just wars be defined as those that punish injuries".[19] But those barbarians have inflicted no injuries upon the Christians. Therefore, it follows that war is not justly inflicted upon them.'

(2) Secondly: 'A war which has as its aim the spreading of religion cannot be just: therefore war cannot be justly waged against the barbarians on the pretext of religion. For Augustine testifies in his letter to Petilianus that no one is to be forced into faith (and this is included in [Gratian] Case 23, question 5, canon "Ad fidem").[20] Also a decretum of the Fourth Council of Toledo holds that violence is to be done to no one in order to enforce belief, from which there is an extract in the canon "De Iudaeis" of [Gratian] Distinctio 45 and in the chapter "Maiores" of title "De Baptismo et eius effectu"' [Gregorian Decretals].[21] Gregory the Great bears witness to the same point in his letter to Pascasius from which there is an extract in the same Distinction [in Gratian], canon "Qui sincera".[22]

(3) Thirdly: 'This war is contrary to the example of Christ and the Apostles, who taught religion by persuasion alone, with no violence used at all; therefore, the war is not justly inflicted. Moreover, the whole behaviour of Christ ought to be a source of instruction to us, on the authority of Paul in Romans 15.'[23]

(4) Fourthly: 'The aim set forth for this war, the conversion of the barbarians to the faith, could more readily be obtained by another method, and without weapons—through the preaching of the gospel, with apostles or preachers having been sent out, as was done in the early church. Therefore, war is not to be inflicted. For as Augustine affirms (quoted in [Gratian] Case 23, question 1, canon "Noli"), "War ought to be a matter of necessity"—that is, when it is not possible to pursue the end of war and peace by any other method.'[24]

(5) Fifthly: 'War is not to be inflicted on any people unless with advance notification, followed by unmistakable obstinacy, for it is highly unjust to offer violence to those who comply. Therefore, although war may be justly inflicted on those who are unwilling to set aside idol-worship and to admit preachers, nonetheless they must first be warned to do these things, so that war may be inflicted in no other circumstances than against obstinate people when the warning has been spurned. This, however, has never been done by the Spaniards in this war; thus, they have never inflicted this war justly.'

---

[19] Augustine, *Quaestiones in Heptateuchum* (*Questions on the Heptateuch*) 6.10 (quoted in Gratian, *Decretum*, C. 23, q. 2, c. 2).

[20] Augustine, *Contra litteras Petiliani* (*Against the Letter of Petilian*) 2.83 (quoted in Gratian, *Decretum*, C. 23, q. 5, c. 33).

[21] Fourth Council of Toledo, canon 56 (quoted in Gratian, *Decretum*, D. 45, c. 5, and by Innocent III to Imbert d'Aiguières, Archbishop of Arles, in X.3.42.3).

[22] Gregory I, Letter 11.15 (quoted and discussed in Gratian, *Decretum*, D. 45, c. 3).

[23] Moreno Hernández assumes that Sepúlveda was referring to Romans 15:18, but it is more likely that the reference is to 15:3 and 7, where Christ is proposed as a model for specific behaviour (pleasing others rather than oneself; welcoming one another).

[24] Augustine, Letter 189.4, to Boniface (quoted in Gratian, *Decretum*, C. 23, q. 1, c. 3).

202 SEPÚLVEDA ON THE SPANISH INVASION OF THE AMERICAS

(6) Sixthly: 'It is impossible—or at least very difficult—for this war to be waged without sins and many evils, as the course of events has shown, for it has never been waged without wrongdoing and wickedness and barbarian casualties. Therefore, it should not be waged, not even on the hope of a good, no matter how great, that might eventuate. For evils are not to be done that good things may result, on the authority of Paul in Romans 3.'[25]

(7) Seventh: 'It is not part of the right or power of the church or of the pope to judge unbelievers; therefore the pope cannot either by himself or through another person compel unbelievers to observe any law. For such power was not granted to the Apostles, as Paul testifies in 1 Corinthians 5, saying: "For what business of mine is it to judge those who are outside?" Therefore, neither is it the job of the church.'[26]

(8) Against these points operate the most manifest testimonies of the holy fathers and the church's duly made decree and declaration.

III. [Sepúlveda's argument]

(1.i) The response is: It is with the fullest justice that those barbarians are being reduced to the rule of Christians.

First: Because they are—or certainly were before coming under the rule of the Christians—all barbarians in their customs and most also in their nature—without letters, without knowledge, and defiled by many barbaric vices, as is attested by the *General History* (Bk. 3, Ch. 6) which was written about them and approved by the authority of the Council of the Indies.[27] As Aquinas says in the first passage of the first book of his commentary on the *Politics*, 'For those are called barbarians in the basic sense who are deficient in reason, either on account of a climatic region in which for the most part dull-witted people are found, or on account of evil habituation, by which men become virtually beastlike.'[28]

(1.ii) Moreover, peoples of this sort ought by the law of nature to obey more civilized (*humanioribus*), wiser, and superior peoples, so that they may be governed by better customs and laws; and if after having been warned they reject rule, they may be constrained by arms, and that war will be just according to the law of nature, on the authority of Aristotle in the first book of the *Politics* (chapters 3 and 5) and Aquinas on the same passage.[29] Thus it was brought about that the imperial rule of the Romans over other peoples was just and was willed by God, as Augustine declares in *The City of God* (Bk. 5, Ch. 12); and he subsequently adds,

---

[25] Romans 3:8.

[26] 1 Corinthians 5:12.

[27] Gonzalo Fernández de Oviedo, *La historia general de las Indias* (Seville, 1535; repr. Salamanca, 1547), Bk. 3, ch. 6 (esp. fol. xxvi *v* – fol. xxvii *r*).

[28] Aquinas, *Sententia libri politicorum* (*Commentary on Aristotle's Politics*), Bk. 1, lect. 1, c. 23.

[29] Aristotle, *Politics*, Bk. 1. Sepúlveda appears to be thinking of passages in chapters 1 (1252a 30–35) and 2 (1254b 15–21), on the advantages of subordination for the slave, and in ch. 2 (1255b 38–41) on warfare as a means of acquiring slaves. Aquinas, *Sententia libri politicorum*, Bk. 1, Lect. 1, c. 19.

THE DEFENCE OF THE BOOK, *ON THE JUST REASONS FOR WAR*   203

'God granted to the Romans the greatest and most illustrious empire for the sake of taming the serious evils of many peoples.'[30] These Romans for the sake of glory suppressed many vices—that is, they practised virtues. (1.iii) Therefore, for the same reason—and with even better justification—the Spaniards may reduce the Indians to their own rule. Saint Thomas Aquinas makes the same point in *On the Government of Rulers* (Bk. 3, Ch. 4) and proceeds to cite Augustine.[31]

(2.i) Secondly: Those barbarians were involved in the most serious sins against the law of nature, ignorance of which gives no one an excuse—on account of which sins God destroyed the sinful peoples who inhabited the Promised Land. For all of them were worshippers of idols and almost all offered up human sacrifices. (2.ii) For Holy Scripture declares not obscurely but in the most straightforward language that God destroyed those peoples not through some hidden judgment but because of this sort of idolatry. (2.iii) For thus it is written in Chapter 9 of Deuteronomy: 'When God has destroyed them in your sight, do not say, "It was because of my righteousness that God brought me here so that I might possess this land", since those peoples were destroyed on account of their own acts of impiety.'[32] And in Chapter 12: 'All the abominations that God recoils from they have performed for their gods, even offering up their sons and daughters and burning them up in the fire.'[33] And in Chapter 18, laying out the abominations on account of which those peoples were destroyed, Scripture says: 'When you enter the land that your Lord God shall give to you, make sure that you do not wish to imitate the abominations of those peoples; and let no one be found among you who would make his son or daughter pass through fire, or who consults soothsayers or who pays attention to dreams and auguries, or who is a sorcerer or a singer of incantations, or consults oracle-mongers or diviners, or seeks the truth from the dead. For all these things God abominates, and it is because of sins of that sort that he will destroy those people upon your entry.'[34]

(2.iv) By these testimonies it is manifestly declared that these peoples were destroyed on account of the worship of idols; for all the sins that are mentioned here relate, according to the general agreement of the theologians, to the worship of idols or impious superstition. Virtually the same thing is handed down in Leviticus 18 and 20 and in Psalm 105.[35] Likewise, in the same psalm it is declared that the Israelite people were in large part destroyed and led off into captivity and slavery on account of the same sins: 'They mingled among the peoples and adopted their customs. They sacrificed their sons and their daughters, and God was roused to furious anger against his own people and handed them over into the hands of the

---

[30] Augustine, *De civitate Dei* 5.12.
[31] Pseudo-Aquinas (Ptolemy of Lucca), *De regimine principum* 3.4.
[32] Deuteronomy 9:4.
[33] Deuteronomy 12:31.
[34] Deuteronomy 18:9–12.
[35] Leviticus 18:1–5; 20:2–5; Psalm 106 (105):49.

204 SEPÚLVEDA ON THE SPANISH INVASION OF THE AMERICAS

peoples.'[36] (2.v) Wisdom 12 and Exodus 32 support this, where it is declared that the law of nature is violated by these sins, given that for the same things both believers and unbelievers alike have been punished.[37] Therefore, referring to these same things, Cyprian in his *Exhortation to Martyrdom* adds: 'But if before the coming of Christ these precepts concerning the worship of God and the spurning of idols were observed, how much more ought they to be observed after the coming of Christ?'—words that are found in [Gratian] Case 23, question 5, canon 'Si audieris.'[38] Ambrose manifestly supports him: see [Gratian], Case 23, question 5, canon 'Remittuntur.'[39]

(2.vi) Since, according to these testimonies, the worship of idols, sometimes for itself and sometimes for the sacrifices of human victims that happen in it, is mentioned as a reason for a just war and extermination, idolatry per se is manifestly declared to offer believers sufficiently great and just reason for waging war against unbelievers, as was the opinion of Nicholas of Lyra on Numbers 31, citing especially that passage from Deuteronomy 12: 'Overturn all the places in which the peoples whom you are dispossessing worshipped their gods.'[40] (2.vii) This is also supported by the teaching and testimony of St Thomas Aquinas, who wrote in his *Secunda secundae* (quaest. 10, art. 8): 'Unbelievers may be compelled in war by believers—not so that they may believe, but so that they may not hinder the faith with blasphemies or evil persuasions or persecutions.'[41] Later, in quaest. 94, art. 3, he maintains that great blasphemy is contained in idolatry and that faith is assaulted by its action.[42]

(2.viii) This teaching Lyra follows, in the passage we have mentioned. He says: 'One reason for a just war is that it be against a land in which God is blasphemed through idolatry.'[43] Likewise Augustine in Letter 50, which is addressed to Boniface, teaching pious kings to serve God by opposing the worship of idols, said this: 'Thus Hezekiah served God by destroying the groves and temples of the idols and the high places that had been constructed against God's order (2 Kings 18), and Josiah by doing the same thing (2 Kings 23), just as the king of the Ninevites served him in forcing his city to placate the universal God (Jonah 3), and just as Darius

---

[36] Psalm 106 (105):35–41.

[37] Wisdom 12 (entire chapter); Exodus 32 (entire chapter).

[38] Cyprian, *Ad Fortunatum de exhortatione martyrii*, §5 (quoted in Gratian, *Decretum*, C. 23, q. 5, c. 32).

[39] Ambrose, *On Cain and Abel*, Bk. 2, ch. 4 (quoted in Gratian, *Decretum*, C. 23, q. 5, c. 49).

[40] Nicholas of Lyra, commentary on Numbers 31 in *Postillae perpetuae in universam S. Scripturam* (*Running Commentary on the Whole of Sacred Scripture*), a massive biblical commentary composed 1322–31 and first published in Basel in 1498. But Sepúlveda is more likely to have consulted it as a marginal commentary in *Biblia Sacra cum glossis, interlineari et ordinaria* (Lyon, 1545), where the commentary on Numbers 31 is on pp. 318–20. The Deuteronomy passage is 12:2.

[41] Aquinas, *Summa theologica* (*ST*) II-II, q. 10, art. 8, co.

[42] Aquinas, *ST* II-II, q. 94, art. 3, ad 2.

[43] Nicholas of Lyra, Commentary on Numbers 31 (see n. 40).

THE DEFENCE OF THE BOOK, *ON THE JUST REASONS FOR WAR*   205

served him by putting the idol in the power of Daniel to be shattered (Daniel 14), and just as Nebuchadnezzar served God', etc.[44]

(2.ix) As to the fact that Cajetan denied that unbelievers may justly be defeated in war by Christians on account of lack of belief, his words need to be understood as referring to punishing them solely for the sake of unbelief; but that doesn't hold true if they are at the same time worshippers of idols or are in some other way failing to observe the law of nature.[45] [If he meant something other than this, he should not be listened to—all the more so because in his support for his position he slipped up twice in the same place, for he made use of the trick of the heretics concerning the model of Christ who compelled no one, a claim refuted by Augustine in many passages, and concerning the reason for destroying the sinful peoples he offers arguments contrary to Sacred Scripture, as we have taught.][46]

(2.x) In addition, it is proved by another argument that it has been allowed to Christians to harass idol-worshippers with war—through public and papal authority. For to Christ, in accord with his human nature, 'has been given all power in heaven and on earth', as it is written in the last chapter of Matthew,[47] and Christ shared this power with Peter, his vicar, and with Peter's successors, as Thomas teaches in *On the Government of Rulers* (Bk. 3, Chs. 10 and 12).[48] (2.xi) Though this power is properly exercised in those things that pertain to the salvation of the soul and in spiritual goods, it is nonetheless not excluded from temporal things to the extent that they are directed towards spiritual things, as is found in chapter 13 of the same book.[49] (2.xii) Therefore the pope has power over peoples everywhere, not only for the purpose of preaching the gospel, but even in order to force peoples, if the opportunity arises, to observe the law of nature to which all men have been subjected—as Innocent [IV] and Hostiensis, very serious authorities, have taught, commenting on the chapter 'Quod super his' of 'De voto' [in the *Decretals* of Gregory IX]—and Joannes Andreas and Panormitanus support them.[50]

---

[44] Augustine, Letter 185.5.19 (to Boniface); 2 Kings 18:3–4 (Hezekiah); 2 Kings 23:4–20 (Josiah); Jonah 3:6–10; Daniel 14:22 (i.e. the 14th book of Daniel in the Greek version, part of the Apocrypha under the title Bel and the Dragon—the reference is in fact to Cyrus, not Darius); Daniel 3:29–30; 4:34–37 (Nebuchadnezzar).

[45] Tommaso de Vio (Gaetano), Commentary on Aquinas, *ST* II-II, q. 10, art. 8, in *Sancti Thomae Aquinatis Opera Omnia Iussu Impensaque Leonis XIII P.M. Edita*, vol. 8 (Rome: Typographia Polyglotta, 1895), 89–90. Sepúlveda would have used the 1540 edition of Cajetan's commentary.

[46] The bracketed words are preserved only in a manuscript (*J*) in the John Carter Brown Library, Brown University.

[47] Matthew 28:18.

[48] Pseudo-Aquinas (Ptolemy of Lucca), *De regimine principum* 3.10: 1–75; 3.12: 100

[49] Pseudo-Aquinas (Ptolemy of Lucca), *De regimine principum* 3.13: 25.

[50] The reference is to four canonists commenting on the papal decretal *Quod super his* of Innocent III (sent in 1200 to Hubert Walter, Archbishop of Canterbury) = X.3.34.8. The first was Innocent's successor, Innocent IV (Sinibaldo dei Fieschi), writing around 1245. He declared that, while God allowed infidels *dominium* over their territories, the pope had the God-given right to order that such infidels be punished for violations of natural law, including idolatry. Hostiensis (ca. 1200–1271) went further and denied infidels dominion. The later canonists commenting on the decretal were Joannes Andreas (ca. 1275–1348) and Nicolò de' Tudeschi, *alias* Panormitanus (1386–1445).

206 SEPÚLVEDA ON THE SPANISH INVASION OF THE AMERICAS

(2.xiii) For Christ, who thus commanded the Apostles in the last chapter of Matthew: 'Teach all the peoples everything I have entrusted to you',[51] likewise ordered that the laws of nature, which are contained in the Decalogue and 'love thy neighbour', be especially observed.[52] (2.xiv) But in order for unbelievers to be constrained to hear gospel preaching and observe the law of nature, it is necessary that they be subjected to the rule of Christians—therefore 'collaterally' (to use a pontifical term) this also pertains to the power of the pope, which is especially directed at the spiritual things that belong to that same power (see chapter 'Per venerabilem' in the title 'Qui filii sint legitimi' [Bk. 4, *Decretals* of Gregory IX]).[53]

(2.xv) Furthermore, those who worship idols are the ones who most especially violate the law of nature. Therefore, idolaters may justly be coerced by Christians in war so that after being subjected to their rule they may be forced to live in accord with the law of nature, and also so that God may not be blasphemed and offended by them through their worship of idols. (2.xvi) If one grasps what it means for any people at all to fail to observe the law of nature, one will find it impossible to doubt that idolaters utterly fail to do so. For although all mortal sins are contrary to the law of nature (as Augustine teaches in Book 22 of *Against Fasutus*),[54] nonetheless if mortal sins are committed within a certain people one should not immediately declare that those men as a whole do not observe the law of nature, as certain fairly recent theologians incorrectly believe. (2.xvii) For if one were to take that particular line, no people anywhere would be observing the law of nature. For the case of a whole people needs to be judged in line with the whole people's customs and institutions, as Aristotle teaches in Book 3 of *Politics,* not in accord with the deeds, whether performed rightly or wrongly, of particular individuals.[55] Rather, a people should only be understood to fail to observe the laws of nature when among them some mortal sin is not classed among base deeds but is publically approved—as, for example, among those barbarians, the murder of innocents, who in many regions are offered in sacrifice, and idolatry, which is the most serious sin of all, which is found among all of them. (2.xviii) In accord with these considerations it is plainly to be understood that those peoples have been destroyed not through some special act of will or hidden judgment of God but through the common law of nature, on account of the sins already mentioned, which all belong to idolatry.

(2.xix) Thus, through these testimonies of Sacred Scripture and holy men of learning, one grasps that if we were acting in accord with the strictest justice, those barbarians could have been justly punished with loss of life and lands and all their

---

[51] Matthew 28:18–20 (the 'Great Commission').

[52] Matthew 19:17–19; 22:38.

[53] Innocent III in X.4.17.13. The 'pontifical term' is the rare adverb *causaliter*. Albert Blaise offers 'par accident' as a translation for the word (*Lexicon Latinitatis Medii Aevi*, 162). In his discussion of the term in this passage, Andrés Marcos notes that it refers to 'the indirect power of the Roman Pontiff': that is, the temporal power of the pope may use incidentally in the course of exercising his direct power over spiritual matters (*Los imperialismos de Juan Ginés de Sepúlveda*, 114).

[54] Augustine, *Contra Faustum*, Bk. 22, c. 78.

[55] Aristotle, *Politics* 3.1 (1274b34ff); cf. *Democrates secundus* I.15.3.

THE DEFENCE OF THE BOOK, *ON THE JUST REASONS FOR WAR* 207

goods. Therefore, by how much more right may they be subjected to the rule of the Christians—not so that they might suffer those things (for it is forbidden by a law of the kings of Spain to deprive them of their possessions or liberty), but in order that, once having been subjected to the rule of the Christians, they may be forced to abstain from such crimes, by which God is most greatly offended, and through becoming accustomed to better things and acquainted with pious men they may be prepared for receiving the worship and religion of the true God.

(2.xx) Also pertinent to this point is the passage in Deuteronomy 20: 'Whenever you approach a city in order to besiege it, offer it peace-terms first. If it accepts and opens its gates to you, the whole people who are in it shall be allowed to live and shall serve you under payment of tribute. If, however, ... etc.'[56] Further on: 'Thus you shall act with regard to all the cities which are a considerable distance from you'[57]—that is, which are of a different religion, as the interlinear gloss explains— which especially fits the case of idolaters and thus is a way of referring to worshippers of idols, even though their iniquities may not be full-scale, as were those of the Amorites[58]—so that by obeying better men, pious men, they may be directed by those men's teaching or example to the worship of the true God.

(3.i) Thirdly: all men are ordered by divine and natural law to save the lives of innocent men, lest they be slaughtered in an undeserved death—if they are able to do this without some great disadvantage to themselves. (3.ii) Since, therefore, those barbarians sacrifice on the impious altars of demons many thousands of innocent people a year (for it is established that in New Spain alone more than 20,000 used to be sacrificed each year), and this could be forbidden by only one means—that they be subjected to the rule of worthy men, men who abhor such savage crimes, men of the sort the Spanish are—who would doubt that even for this reason alone the barbarians could have been and could still be reduced by the Christians to their rule with the greatest justice?

(4.i) Fourthly: when men are most perilously wandering astray and hastening to their certain destruction, whether they do this ignorantly or knowingly, calling them back and pulling them back to safety even against their will is part of both divine and natural law—and a duty that all sane men would want offered to themselves even if they were unwilling at the time. (4.ii) Moreover, no one who is a real Christian doubts that all men who wander outside the Christian religion die an eternal death. Rightly, then, are the barbarians compelled to justice for the sake of their own salvation.

(4.iii) But this duty can be offered in two ways: in one way through teaching alone and through exhortation, the other way through the application of force and the fear of punishments—not in order that they may be forced to believe, but so

---

[56] Deuteronomy 20:10–12.
[57] Deuteronomy 20:15.
[58] Cf. Genesis 15:16.

that the impediments may be removed that could stand in the way of the preaching and spreading of the faith. (4.iv) Christ and the Apostles made use of the first method; the church, after it was fortified by the power and protection of Christian kings and princes, made use of the second. And as Augustine teaches, both things have been done in accord with the divine and evangelical command contained in the parable of Luke 14.[59] For when the first ones invited proved unwilling to come, the second ones were led into the divine feast through admonition and teaching; but it was ordered that the last ones be compelled to enter.

(4.v) In his last letter (it is included in [Gratian] canon 'Displicet', Case 23, question 4), when the example of the first periods [of the church] was thrown in his teeth by the heretic Donatus, Augustine wrote, 'You're not noticing that at that time the church was sprouting from the recently planted seed, and that the following prophecy had not yet been fulfilled: "And all the kings of the earth shall worship him, all the people shall serve him". (4.vi) Assuredly, the more that prophecy is fulfilled, the more power the church makes use of, so that it not only invites, but also uses constraint for the good'—in confirmation of which he brings forward the Gospel parable of which I have spoken.[60]

(4.vii) For that which is in the [Fourth] Council of Toledo and in chapter 'Maiores', title 'De baptismo et eius effectu' [in Bk. 3 of the *Decretals* of Gregory IX]—that no one should be forced into believing—has a plain and obvious sense: that no one is to be compelled by violence or war or threats in order that he become a Christian and undergo baptism against his will.[61] (4.viii) The reasoning for this is that such violence would be useless, for no one can be made a believer when his will, which cannot be forced, resists. And so one must make use of teaching and persuasions.

(4.ix) Moreover, it is upon the authority of Augustine, Ambrose, and Gregory that it is utterly just that someone is forced by threats and the fear of punishment to lay aside all impediments that might hinder the teaching of the faith—such as pride and the unrestrained desire for sinning. (4.x) For as to what was stated in the Council of Toledo, Augustine, who approved of force, said the same thing much earlier: 'No one', he said, 'is to be forced to believe, as you [Donatists] all say.' But he thus addresses the heretic Petilianus (included in [Gratian] Case 23, question 5, canon 'Ad fidem'): 'But you people are not being forced by imperial law to do good; rather, you are being prohibited from doing evil. For no one is able to do good unless he chooses that which is in his free will. Therefore, when the laws lay down something against you, you must believe that you are being admonished to consider why you are suffering these things.'[62]

---

[59] Luke 14:15–24.

[60] Augustine, Letter 173.10 (quoted in Gratian, *Decretum,* C. 23, q. 4, c. 38). The biblical citation is Psalm 72 (71):11, and the Gospel parable is Luke 14:15–24. Sepúlveda made two errors in quoting Augustine here: *quod* for *quia* and *novo* for *novella*.

[61] Innocent III in X.3.42.3, citing the Fourth Council of Toledo, can. 56.

[62] Augustine, *Contra litteras Petiliani* 2.83 (quoted in Gratian, *Decretum,* C. 23, q. 5, c. 33).

THE DEFENCE OF THE BOOK, *ON THE JUST REASONS FOR WAR*   209

(4.xi) The same man writes thus in his letter to Vincentius (included in [Gratian] Case 23, question 6, canon 'Vides'): 'You see that what needs to be considered is not the simple fact that someone is being subjected to force, but rather what sort of thing it is he is being forced to, whether it is a good thing or a bad thing. The aim is not that someone would be able to be good against his own will; rather, it is that, in fearing what he does not wish to endure, he either gives up his obstructive hostility or is compelled to acknowledge a truth of which he had been ignorant, so that in fear he might reject the false notion about which he had been contending or might seek the truth which he did not know, so that he might now willingly hold that which he used to be unwilling to hold.'[63]

(4.xii) While it is true that it was against heretics that Augustine made these points, the fact that his arguments are equally valid against pagans is something that Augustine himself teaches in that same letter to Vincentius, in the passage where he mentions laws passed against both groups. He declares that neither Christ nor the Apostles offered violence against either, but later on violence was inflicted on them by the church when it had been armed with the power and the laws of Christian emperors (as is included in [Gratian] Case 23, question 4, canon 'Non invenitur').[64] In that letter, he makes use of the same reasoning to show that the law passed against the pagans' sacrifices was just and praised by all Christians[65]—a law included in the chapter 'On the pagans and their sacrifices' in Book 1.[66] (4.xiii) For there capital punishment and confiscation of goods are laid down should anyone make further use of pagan rites and rituals. This law, first passed by Constantine (as Eusebius testifies in his *Ecclesiastical History* and Jerome in his *Chronicle*) and afterwards confirmed by his son Constantius and other emperors, Ambrose very aggressively defended as pious and very just in the presence of the Emperor Valentinian (Letters 30 and 31).[67] (4.xiv) Gregory, moreover, in his letter to Aldibert [Ethelbert] king of the Britons (in number 60 of Book 9) says this about these same matters: 'For thus once upon a time the very devout Emperor Constantine, calling back the Roman state from the perverse worshippers of idols, subjected it to all-powerful God and

[63] Augustine, Letter 93.5.16 (quoted in Gratian, *Decretum*, C. 23, q. 6, c. 3).

[64] Augustine, Letter 93.3.9–10 (quoted in Gratian, *Decretum*, C. 23, q. 4, c. 41).

[65] Augustine, Letter 93.3.10 ('Quis enim nostrum, quis vestrum non laudat leges ab imperatoribus datas adversus sacrifica paganorum?').

[66] *Codex Justinianus*, Bk. 1, title 11.1. This refers to an edict of Constantius II of 354. See next note.

[67] The Eusebius reference seem to be instead to his *Life of Constantine* 2.45 and 4.25. The reference to Jerome's *Chronicon* (largely translated from Eusebius) seems to be to the entry for 331: 'Edicto Constantini gentilium templa subversa sunt' ('By an edict of Constantine the temples of the pagans were overthrown'). The letters of Ambrose (now numbered 17 and 18; Sepúlveda was following the numbering in the third volume of Amerbach's 1492 Basel edition of Ambrose's works), directed at the thirteen-year-old emperor Valentinian II in 384, were designed to counteract the attempts of the pagan Prefect of Rome, Quintus Aurelius Symmachus, to restore the Altar of Victory to the Senate House in Rome and to secure support for other pagan institutions (such as the Vestal Virgins). But the reference there is not to Constantine, but to Constantius II's edict of 354. For the vexed question of Constantinian anti-pagan legislation, see Scott Bradbury, 'Constantine and the Problem of Anti-Pagan Legislation in the Fourth Century', *Classical Philology* 89/2 (1994): 120–39.

210 SEPÚLVEDA ON THE SPANISH INVASION OF THE AMERICAS

our Lord Jesus Christ', etc.[68] Nor does it matter whether the pagans to whom salvific force is to be applied are subjected to the rule of the Christians or otherwise.

(4.xv) Sisebut, king of Spain, who compelled Jews to become Christians, applied force to people who were already his subjects, but his action is not similarly approved, because such force simply or directly exerting compulsion to Christian belief is regarded as useless, because it is unable to force the will, and it makes people more stubborn. (4.xvi) A prohibition from wrongdoing, on the other hand, which is what happens with the law of Constantine (which is the same as that of Constantius), is a great benefit—and to bestow this upon all men as upon our neighbours, provided we can do so without harm to ourselves, is something we are commanded to do by divine and human law: 'God gave a commandment to each one concerning his neighbour.'[69]

(4.xvii) This, then, is the justification derived from the Gospel parable and the teaching of Augustine, Ambrose, and Gregory, for compelling pagans to come in to the banquet of Christ: first to bring it about that those who have not been subjugated may now be subjected to the rule of the Christians, provided it can happen without major inconvenience to us; then to see to it that by the law of Constantine they may be suitably forbidden the worship of idols and all pagan rituals, and that all the impediments that might stand in the way of preaching the gospel might be removed.

(4.xviii) Taught by these arguments and testimonies, St Thomas (*Secunda secundae*, quaest. 10, art. 11) says that the rites of unbelievers (except for Jews) ought not in any way be tolerated, if means are available, 'although they had been tolerated at one time', he says, 'that is, when there was a great multitude of unbelievers'[70]—i.e. before there were Christian princes who could compel.

(4.xix) But when these measures have been taken, no further violence, no terrorization should be inflicted to make them Christians. Rather, once they have been prepared in this way, they should be taught and introduced to the preaching of the faith so that they would accept Christianity of their own free will, as is declared in the decree or testimony of the most wise and holy Pope Gregory (included in [Gratian] Case 23, question 4, canon 'Si non'), where he praises the most excellent and most Christian Gennadius and declares that he is praised by everyone, because he took pains that pagan peoples who had manifestly not been subjugated might be reduced by war to the sway of the Christians—not for any other reason than that when they had been thoroughly defeated, they might more easily be led to the Christian religion through the free preaching of the faith.[71] (4.xx) For he writes that Gennadius is praised everywhere, 'because he often sought wars, not from a

---

[68] Gregory I, Letter 11.37.18–21 (to Ethelbert).
[69] Ecclesiasticus 17:12.
[70] Aquinas, *ST* II-II, q. 10, art. 11 (paraphrased).
[71] Gregory I, Letter 1.75 (Norberg 1.73), to Gennadius, exarch of Africa (quoted in Gratian, *Decretum*, C. 23, q. 4, c. 49).

THE DEFENCE OF THE BOOK, *ON THE JUST REASONS FOR WAR*   211

desire to shed blood, but solely in order to extend the state in which we see God worshipped, so that the name of Christ might spread in every direction among subjugated peoples through the preaching of the faith'.

(4.xxi) Moreover, he is speaking not, as some fancy, about Saracens or Mohammedans, none of whom yet existed, nor (as others suppose) about the Vandals, who had already been destroyed by Belisarius, nor (as still others imagine) about heretics, who needed to be punished, not defeated in war, and who shouldn't be referred to by the inappropriate name of 'peoples'; rather, he is speaking about peoples in the interior of Africa, the peoples nearest to the Roman empire, as is made clear at the end of the same letter (which is the 73rd of Book 1)—and not, as certain people falsely allege, because they were harassing the Christians, for this is ruled out by Gregory through the word 'solely', but so that after having been thoroughly defeated by the Christians they would not impede the preaching and spreading of the faith.

(4.xxii) For this is what St Thomas says in *Secunda secundae,* quaest. 10, art. 8: 'Frequently Christ's faithful wage war against unbelievers—not, indeed, in order to force them to believe, but in order to compel them not to obstruct the faith'[72]—evidently unfolding the reason why Gennadius frequently waged a pious war against unbelievers. (4.xxiii) For in many places, peoples who have not been subjected to the rule of the Christians impede the faith and its propagation if someone wishes to bring it in. In the first place, this is because they do not allow its public preaching. Thus, on the authority of St Thomas in *On the Government of Rulers* (Bk. 3, Ch. 16), it is established that before the time of Constantine it was never permitted to preach the faith publicly without running the risk of death.[73] Then, it is because they kill even the preachers who act secretly, and they take measures against any of their people being converted, and they attempt to turn back converts with persuasions or even persecutions, as was done often and by many before the rule of Constantine, and as happened everywhere at the beginning of the church.

(4.xxiv) There is also the fact that unbelievers who have been subjected to Christians are more easily drawn to follow our customs and religion; therefore, one is not to use solely preaching and disputation either against pagans or heretics, as in the early church when none of the princes had become a believer, but, when the opportunity is at hand, useful and permissible force should be applied, in the manner we have laid out. (4.xxv) This is the most expeditious method of converting peoples to the faith of Christ, as in every age the actual facts and specific examples have taught us—which examples have the power of a proof, on the same authority of Augustine in the same letter to Vincentius (words which were put into [Gratian] Case 23, question 6, canon 'Vides'). 'Originally', he says, 'it was

---

[72] Aquinas, *ST* II-II, q. 10, art. 8.
[73] Pseudo-Aquinas (Ptolemy of Lucca), *De regimine principum* 3.16: 25–100.

my view that no one should be forced to unity with Christ and the church, but that one should act by means of words, contend by means of disputation, triumph by means of reason. (4.xxvi) But this opinion of mine was overcome not by the words of people who disagreed with me, but by the examples of those who showed me the truth. For the first refutation of me was my own city, which though it had been utterly in the party of Donatus was converted to Catholic unity through the fear offered by imperial laws. Today we see that that city so detests the plague of your hostility that it is believed never to have shared it. (4.xxvii) And this is true of many other cities as well.'[74] St Thomas also, in *On the Government of Rulers* (Bk. 3, Ch. 16), wrote: 'In the year when Constantine was converted to the faith, more than 100,000 people were baptized in the various Roman regions.'[75]

(4.xxviii) It is an established fact that this is happening in the same manner in the conversion of the Indians: when they have been reduced to rule and forbidden their impious religious rites, no sooner has gospel preaching been heard than they flow together in hordes demanding baptism. For it is something almost determined by the custom and nature of mankind that the defeated easily pass over into the way of life of the victors and those giving orders, and that they gladly imitate their deeds and words. (4.xxix) Thus, in this way, over the course of a few days more people are being converted to belief in Christ—and more safely as well—than perhaps would be converted in 300 years by preaching alone. For, as the Philosopher says in Book 10 of the *Nicomachean Ethics*, 'It cannot happen—or at least cannot easily happen—that those things that have been imprinted by custom and retained for a long period of time can be changed and rooted out by words.'[76] Therefore, he says, there is need of force, which is the origin of laws, which have a coercive force.

(4.xxx) The teachings of Augustine and Ambrose thoroughly cohere with this dogma of nature, as does the decree of the church and the very wise Pope Gregory in the aforementioned canon 'Si non'.[77] This alone by itself can settle the entire controversy in this case by means of common law and reason. (4.xxxi) Also in agreement is the teaching of John Duns Scotus, who believes that even greater force is to be offered in the passing on of religion to unbelievers and the children of unbelievers (4 *Sententiarum*, dist. 4, quaest. ultima) and of John Mair (4 *Sententiarum*, dist. 44, quaest. 3), who specifically approves of this expedition against the barbarians.[78]

(4.xxxii) In 1493, when our monarchs Ferdinand and Isabella, called 'Catholic' for their exceptional piety, requested a response and decision of the Holy See in

---

[74] Augustine, Letter 93.5.17 (quoted in Gratian, *Decretum*, C. 23, q. 6, c. 3).

[75] Pseudo-Aquinas (Ptolemy of Lucca), *De regimine principum* 3.16.

[76] Aristotle, *Nicomachean Ethics*, 10.9.5 (1179b16–18).

[77] Gratian, *Decretum*, C. 23, q. 4, c. 49, where Gregory I's letter to Gennadius is quoted (1.75; Norberg 1.73).

[78] John Duns Scotus, *Quaestiones in quattuor libros Sententiarum*, dist. 4; John Mair, *In primum et secundum Sententiarum* (*On the First and Second Books of Peter Lombard's* Sententiae), dist. 44, q. 3.

THE DEFENCE OF THE BOOK, *ON THE JUST REASONS FOR WAR*   213

connection with what is handed down in Deuteronomy 17 and in Bk. 4 [of the *Decretals* of Gregory IX], title 17, 'Qui filii sint legitimi', canon 'Per venerabilem',[79] Pope Alexander VI, following the above arguments and decrees, exhorted them and gave them the task, willing as they were and seeking it with their due right, to subjugate those barbarians to their rule and to take pains that they be reduced to faith in Christ, using these words that were written down in the papal bull: (4.xxxiii) 'Wherefore, after all considerations have been carefully weighed—and especially the exalting and spreading of the Catholic Faith, as befits Catholic monarchs and princes—following the custom of your ancestors, monarchs of blessed memory, you have proposed to subjugate the aforesaid mainlands and islands and to lead their inhabitants to the Catholic faith, with Divine mercy favouring you. (4.xxxiv) Therefore, fully approving in the Lord's name this holy and laudable intention of yours and eagerly wishing that it may be brought to the conclusion it deserves, we urge you as strongly as possible in the Lord's name and by your reception of holy baptism, whereby you are bound to our apostolic commands, and by the bowels of the mercy of our Lord Jesus Christ we strictly demand that when you set about pursuing and taking on this expedition as a whole with eager mind and a zeal for the true faith, it will also be your desire and your duty to lead the peoples living in such islands and territories to accept the Christian religion. And may no dangers or toils ever at any time deter you, once you have conceived the firm hope and trust that God Omnipotent will favourably attend your undertakings.'[80]

(4.xxxv) These are the words of Pope Alexander. Not only are Christians ordered by that decree to stand by it and by similar decrees, but also if someone does not obey or contradicts it, by the same law (in accord with the aforementioned Bk. 4 [of the *Decretals* of Gregory IX], title 17 'Qui filii sint legitimi', canon 'Per venerabilem'[81]) he is excommunicated—and as a general rule we must listen to the vicar of Christ 'as to Christ himself, in those matters that are not manifestly contrary to God', as Bernard says in his book *De dispensatione*.[82] (4.xxxvi) Major theologians have taught that it is heretical to hold in contempt his decrees and rescripts in those matters that touch upon faith or morality (see Sylvius under the word 'canonization').[83] Therefore, by this right, the Vicar of Christ may prohibit all peoples from the worship of idols, if the means of preventing this is to hand, and to compel them to listen to preaching of the gospel. By the same right he has the power to subjugate those same peoples to the rule of Christians either by himself or through Christian princes, since this method is most expeditious and best suited for accomplishing these ends and securing the salvation of souls. [For while it is true

---

[79] Deuteronomy 17:2–3, cited by Innocent III in X.4.17.13.
[80] Alexander VI, *Inter caetera*.
[81] Innocent III in X.4.17.13.
[82] Bernard of Clairvaux, *De praecepto et dispensatione* (*On the precept and dispensation*) 9.21.
[83] 'Sylvius' was Silvestro Mazzolini (1456/7–1527), *Summa summarum quae Sylvestrina dicitur* (Bologna, 1515, but frequently reprinted), a kind of theological dictionary or encyclopedia.

that the power Christ shared with his vicar operated primarily in spiritual matters and those belonging to the salvation of souls, that power was nonetheless not cut off from temporal affairs to the extent that these are directed to spiritual ends, as St Thomas affirms in *On the Government of Rulers,* Bk. 3, Ch. 3, along with Ch. 10,[84] as we have said above.][85]

(4.xxxvii) In addition, certain men who are indeed learned but not equally experienced in practical matters have taught that, before preparing for war, ambassadors should be sent to warn the barbarians to desist from the worship of idols and openly allow in preachers of the Christian religion, so that if they acquiesce in these demands, they may take thought for the salvation of their own souls without warfare. If, however, these results cannot be obtained from them, they may be compelled to behave as ordered after having been thoroughly defeated by righteous arms. (4.xxxviii) I grant that this issuing of a warning is not to be rejected or omitted, if it can prove useful and can be done without great difficulties. For it is similar to that admonition that Christ orders to occur in fraternal correction, before one proceeds to condemnation.[86]

(4.xxxix) Still, just as in the case of fraternal correction, it is the consensus of theologians that a useless admonition is to be omitted and it is necessary to proceed to condemnation, especially if the public interest demands it. This is the way it should be determined concerning this sort of admonition in this war against the barbarians—that it should be completely omitted, if it should seem useless in the eyes of those who prudently weigh the matter.

(4.xl) For 'he who ploughs ought to plough, in the hope of receiving the crop', according to Paul in 1 Corinthians;[87] and that which is useless is regarded as nothing, as is stated in Bk. 1 [of the *Decretales* of Gregory IX], title 'De translatione Episcopi', chapter 'Inter corporalia'.[88] (4.xli) Moreover, it is declared on many sides that admonition is useless in such a case as this, and for this reason it has never been carried out. In the first place, that is because it is something difficult to do—and at the beginning of the war it was especially difficult. For to approach and advise peoples so barbaric, separated from us by an immense distance of ocean and lands and with no commonality of language, and to then await not only what they might answer but what they might do—all this would be a thing so difficult, involving such expense, and requiring such a long time that it would easily deter all Christian princes from such an endeavour. (4.xlii) Thus, to bring this admonition in as a necessary step would have been simply to thoroughly impede an expedition that was pious and salvific for the barbarians and accordingly impede the conversion

---

[84] Pseudo-Aquinas (Ptolemy of Lucca), *De regimine principum* 3.3 and 10.

[85] The bracketed words are found only in the manuscript in the Biblioteca Nacional de Madrid. They do not occur in the text printed in Rome.

[86] Cf. Matthew 18:15–17.

[87] 1 Corinthians 9:10.

[88] Innocent III in X.1.7.2.

THE DEFENCE OF THE BOOK, *ON THE JUST REASONS FOR WAR*   215

of those same people, which was the aim of the war. It is, then, useless and hence something to be eschewed.

(4.xliii) 'Whatever is directed to an end, becomes good through being directed to the end; therefore, those things that impede the end do not have the character of the good', as St Thomas puts it in *Secunda secundae*, quaest. 33, art. 6.[89] (4.xliv) Hence this admonition, even if it could happen after the difficulties had been overcome, would nonetheless do too little good or none at all, and would therefore be useless and best omitted; for it is not probable or likely that any people could be brought by admonition alone and by the exhortation of a foreign people to forsake an ingrained religion and one received from their ancestors. (4.xlv) For, in the words of Augustine in his letter to Vincentius: 'If unbelievers are taught and not made to feel fear, they would be moved too sluggishly to head for the path of salvation, due to the antiquity of hardened custom.'[90]

(4.xlvi) But if someone should say that the barbarians should not be admonished by words alone but should also be intimidated by the fear of an army advanced against them so that by fear, at least, they might do what they are ordered, this would simply mean increasing the difficulty of the admonition to the greatest degree and would cause the very violence that those same people propose admonition to avoid. If violence ought to be done at all, we must not omit the most useful kind of violence, that which forces them to accept the rule of Christians. (4.xlvii) Moreover, although the barbarians upon being driven by fear might admit preachers and set aside for the time being the worship of idols—or rather pretend to do so—nonetheless, there is no doubt that once the fear had been removed, they would return to their original customs and drive out the preachers or kill them and those who had been converted by them (unless they were to return to their original impiety), as used to happen at the beginning of the growth of the church.

(4.xlviii) All these inconveniences and difficulties are easily removed once the barbarians have been thoroughly defeated in war, and thus more progress is made in their conversion in one month than would be made in a hundred years through preaching alone without prior pacification of the barbarians. The preachers of our time, I imagine, would not accomplish more without miracles than the Apostles once did, 'with the Lord working with them and confirming the message with accompanying signs'.[91] These signs are not now to be demanded of God, when it is allowed for us to follow his command with prudent judgment and force the barbarians into the Gospel banquet in the way we have discussed. (4.xlix) In addition, the subjugation of the barbarians is an occasion for a great coming together

[89] Aquinas, *ST* II-II, q. 33, art. 6, ad 3 (paraphrased).
[90] Augustine, Letter 93.1.3.
[91] Mark 16:20.

of Christians, and by having dealings with them and getting accustomed to them those people are more easily converted, and upon being converted they are more readily taught, they persist more steadfastly in the faith they have received, they are not allowed to slip into heresies, and they more easily shed barbarism and put on more civilized and Christian customs.

(4.l) Therefore, since there are two paths by which it seems one can advance towards the conversion of the barbarians—one, operating through admonition alone and teaching and preaching, which is difficult, long, and hampered by many dangers and toils; and the other, operating through the subjugation of the barbarians, which is easy and quick and useful, with many advantages for the barbarians—it is not for a prudent man to hesitate as to which path to follow, especially since we have Augustine as an authority, who makes clear that one should proceed by the more expeditious path, unambiguously using those words that we cited a little earlier: 'If they are taught and not made to feel fear, they would be too sluggishly moved to head for the path of salvation, due to the antiquity of hardened custom'[92]—by which words Augustine plainly teaches that we must not act by teaching alone, but salvific force, which builds the path of teaching, needs to be applied. Now that we have laid these points out, it remains for us to reply to the objections.

IV. [Sepúlveda's response to the objections]

(1.i) To the first point, then, I answer: the war that is inflicted upon idol-worshippers punishes not so much the injuries done to men as those done to God, which are much more serious. Besides, the person who does not perform just requests inflicts an injury upon the one making the request, and the person who ought to obey another but upon being warned rejects that rule is committing an injury. So it appears that by means of this war not only divine but also human injuries are being punished. (1.ii) For it is not allowed either to inflict an unjust war or to resist the infliction of a war that has been properly declared without committing thereby an injury; for not only is it an injury to inflict rough treatment, but also to act unjustly against someone, no matter what the circumstances.

(2.i) To the second point: I grant that no one is to be forced to the faith so that he may believe against his own will, so that he may be baptized against his own will, so that he may be compelled to become a Christian through punishments and fear—all of which is the gist of the decretals and testimonies offered in objection. For it would be useless force and ineffective activity, for belief is a matter of free will, which cannot be forced. (2.ii) But to subject idol-worshippers to the rule of

---

[92] Augustine, Letter 93.1.3.

THE DEFENCE OF THE BOOK, *ON THE JUST REASONS FOR WAR*   217

Christians in order that they may abstain from impious rites, observe the law of nature, and, once impediments have been removed, be forced to listen to preachers of the gospel—this is just and pious and approved and carried out by the church, in accord with the testimony of those same holy doctors Augustine (in [Gratian] Case 23, question 4, canon 'Non invenitur') and Gregory in his letter to Aldibert [Ethelbert].[93]

(3.i) To the third objection: To imitate the deeds and actions of Christ if we can is divinely permitted and pious, but only if Christ does not command otherwise. Therefore, although Christ did not compel anyone, either pagan or heretic, to the Gospel feast, i.e. to the faith—neither he himself nor the Apostles—nonetheless, the same Christ in the Gospel parable ordered us to compel both pagans and heretics in the manner we have mentioned once the ability of Christian kings and princes to do so existed, as Augustine, Ambrose, and Gregory explain, and so it was done by the church in the time of Constantine, and also in that of Gennadius, whose wars Gregory most greatly praises, as we mentioned above.[94] (3.ii) This third objection Augustine confutes most accurately in Letter 50, addressed to Count Boniface: 'They do not keep in mind', he says, 'that that was then another period in history, and all things are done in accord with their times. For which of the emperors at that time believed in Christ?' etc.[95] Therefore, the fact that some people quibble that that evangelical compulsion [in the parable] should be referred back to the power of examples and miracles is simply the fabrication and trickery of heretics, refuted by Augustine in that same letter to Boniface.[96]

(4.i) To the fourth objection: I deny that the barbarians are more conveniently drawn to the faith solely by preaching than if they have first been thoroughly defeated in war. In fact, unless they have been thoroughly defeated, many great difficulties stand in the way of preaching and conversion—about which we have written above. All these impediments are removed if peoples have first been reduced to the rule of the Christians. (4.ii) Therefore war is necessary for preaching and conversion, not directly, but because the business cannot come about properly—that is, without great difficulties—unless the peoples have been thoroughly defeated. (4.iii) For though something is called 'necessary' in five ways, according to Aristotle in the fifth book of the *Metaphysics,* one way in which something is understood to be necessary is that, in its absence, something cannot come about at all or at least not properly.[97] Therefore, war is necessary, unless perchance the barbarians are reduced to rule voluntarily and without force of arms. For the method of preaching without any force is lengthy and impeded by many difficulties.

---

[93] Augustine, Letter 93.3.9 (quoted in Gratian, *Decretum,* C. 23, q. 4, c. 41); Gregory I, Letter to Ethelbert of Kent, 11.66 (Norberg 11.37), also found in Bede's *Ecclesiastical History of the English People,* 1.32.
[94] Gregory I, Letter 1.73 (Norberg; 75 in PL 77).
[95] Augustine, Letter 185.5.19.
[96] Augustine, Letter 185.6.24.
[97] Aristotle, *Metaphysics* 5, 1015a–b.

218 SEPÚLVEDA ON THE SPANISH INVASION OF THE AMERICAS

(5.i) In answer to the fifth objection: In this war, 'admonition' can be understood in two senses. One is when peace is offered if they will do what they are ordered, as is advised in Deuteronomy 20 in these words: 'Whenever you shall approach a city in order to besiege it, offer it peace-terms first. If it accepts and opens its gates to you, the whole people who are in it shall be allowed to live and shall serve you under payment of tribute.'[98] (5.ii) This admonition is necessary not only in this war, but in every war properly waged, if we are able, by means of reasoning and notification of the danger, to force our enemies to surrender, and to gain our ends without shedding blood. The other kind of admonition is the kind we have mentioned above—and which we have demonstrated will be useless and hence omitted—and rightly omitted.

(6.i) To the sixth objection, I respond that that argument has no greater weight against this war than against any other wars, waged on whatever rationale. For there has scarcely ever been any war waged without great misfortunes and losses, without some sort of wrongdoing and crime. (6.ii) Still, even though it is difficult even for someone waging a just war to avoid injurious and wicked actions, it is not absolutely impossible; nor should a prince whose just or unjust cause makes a war just or unjust be made to bear responsibility for the crimes committed by soldiers contrary to his will, nor do those crimes turn a just cause into one that is unjust and to be condemned.

(6.iii) Although we are ordered by Christian laws to avoid risks and occasions of sinning, that does not hold true when necessity urges us at the same time to avoid some still greater evil, or if some great public benefit were to summon us in another direction. While, granted, no one may be forced into such straits that it would be necessary for him to sin, nonetheless if two commands that cannot both be fulfilled are simultaneously pressing, the person who obeys the more serious one, the other having been omitted, does not sin, as we are taught by the decree of the Council of Toledo and the testimony of Gregory (in [Gratian] Distinction 13, canons 'Duo mala' and 'Nervi') as well as the teaching of Gerson in his *Moral Guidelines* and of Aristotle in the third book of his *Nicomachean Ethics*.[99] (6.iv) This is the method that ought especially to be pursued in wars, as the same Jean Gerson, a very important writer, teaches, for in the same work he makes this point in the chapter 'On Avarice': 'In the waging of wars, which are full of innumerable evils, sometimes to one group of innocent people, at other times to another, only the good of the state excuses people from mortal sin—or, at times, the avoidance of a public harm that is markedly worse than a private harm proceeding from the war would be.'[100]

---

[98] Deuteronomy 20:10–11.
[99] Eighth Council of Toledo, c. 2 (quoted in Gratian, *Decretum,* D. 13, c. 1); Gregory I, *Moralia in Iob,* Pt. 6, Bk. 34, ch. 14 (quoted in Gratian, *Decretum,* D. 13, c. 2); Jean Gerson, *Regulae morales (Ethical Guidelines)* 26 (Moreno Hernández has '32.20'); Aristotle, *Nicomachean Ethics,* Bk. 2.9 (not Bk. 3), 1109a35–36.
[100] Gerson, *Regulae morales* 73 (in the section *De avaritia*).

THE DEFENCE OF THE BOOK, *ON THE JUST REASONS FOR WAR*   219

(6.v) On the basis of this precept, if we make a calculation about the bad things and the good things that this war brings upon the barbarians, there is no doubt that the bad things are utterly overwhelmed by the number and seriousness of the good things. (6.vi) For the essence of these evils is as follows: 1) they are forced to change their rulers, but not all of them—only those it has seemed necessary to change; 2) they are deprived to a large extent of their movable goods: that is, gold and silver, which were metals of small value among them, given that they used to make no use of gold or silver coinage; and in exchange for these they are receiving from the Spaniards the metal of iron, which is much more suitable for the most extensive uses of life; and in addition, wheat, barley, legumes, and many species of fruit trees and oils, horses, mules, donkeys, sheep, cows, goats, and many other things never seen by barbarians, which upon being brought in from here flourish very fruitfully in those regions. (6.vii) The usefulness that the barbarians used to receive from gold and silver is far and away surpassed by the advantage of each one of these things. Now add letters, which the barbarians utterly lacked, being utterly ignorant of reading and writing; add civilized behaviour, most excellent laws and customs, and that which all by itself surpasses all the advantages of all the other arts: knowledge of the true God and the Christian religion. When these matters have been recognized and taken into consideration, I contend that those who are trying to impede this expedition to keep the barbarians from coming under the rule of the Christians are not humanely favouring the barbarians, as they themselves wish to appear to be doing, but rather to be cruelly begrudging those same people the greatest and most abundant good things. These good things are either utterly abolished or at least greatly hindered by those same men's indolent and misguided opinion.

(6.viii) Still, I would not deny that an occasion might occur when, even though one had the power of exerting compulsion, it would be the right thing to refrain from the subjection of the barbarians. This might happen if some prince with his state or people were to request teachers of the Christian religion from us—not out of fear or simulation, but of his own accord, in good faith, inspired by the Spirit of God—or if through some other chance, in the great variety of human affairs, right reason, which we cannot measure by a single rule, might urge us to attend to the salvation of the barbarians in some other way. For while it is by laws and precepts that what ought to be done on any given occasion is usually established, other things, occurring outside the normal course of affairs, are left to the sagacity of just princes and upright men who are in charge of things that need to be done, according as the consideration of the good of the whole people will require that those things be managed—as the Philosopher declares in Book 3 of the *Politics* and in Book 5 of the *Nicomachean Ethics*.[101]

---

[101] The references to Aristotle are not clear. See n. 284 to the end of *Democrates secundus* I.19, from which this passage was lifted verbatim (though there only with a vague reference 'as the Philosopher declares'). Moreno Hernández takes the *Politics* reference to be Bk. 3.4, 1278b, but it is not clear why.

220 SEPÚLVEDA ON THE SPANISH INVASION OF THE AMERICAS

(7.i) To the seventh point: Paul's saying that it was not his business 'to pass judgment on those who are outside'[102] has this meaning: it is not the task of an apostle to demand an account of one's way of life from those who are outside the faith, as it is to demand it of Christians, or to demand that they live like Christians. (7.ii) On the other hand, that it *is* the task of an apostle to make an effort to bring it about that those same people be converted to belief in Christ, to preach the gospel to them, and to attempt all things within one's power that serve to produce this result in the right way—to *this* not only Paul but all the apostles bear witness by their lives and by the deaths they met in this cause.

(8.i) As regards the publication of the book in which is set forth the justice and rationale for waging the war, and what is happening justly and what wrongfully, and in which the things that are done with cruelty or through avarice are censured—if some soldier or official will have said that he has sinned through the opportune excuse of the book, he will easily be convicted of having acted wickedly through manifest ignorance or malice or through Pharisaic scandal.[103] (8.ii) On the contrary, in fact, these very great benefits will follow from the publication of the book: a great stumbling-block and slander will be removed from our kings and our people, who, due to the false or misunderstood teaching of certain theologians, are popularly supposed to have unjustly and tyrannically reduced these barbarians to their rule—as recently a certain person has most impudently set forth. (8.iii) Finally, as to those who have brought back gold or silver from this expedition, it will be easily understood by them and by the priests to whom they confess their sins what they have justly acquired and what unjustly, what they may rightly keep and what they ought to give back. For as it is now, both sides are caught in a massive ignorance of the law.

V. [Conclusion]

(1) Finally, you [Antonio Ramírez] concluded with the question: 'If the king persists in his judgment and his confessor holds a different view, could the king be justly and piously absolved by the confessor?' And your answer and decision is that he can, because either opinion has the appearance of truth and is defended by an equal number of learned men. But if that is so, please tell me, most respected prelate, how it occurred to you and those high judges of mine to condemn with your decision in a doubtful case your king and your people and to mark them with infamy and, scandalizing the entire world, to reject the judgment and decree of the pope and the church so groundlessly as to appear to be showing contempt for

---

[102] 1 Corinthians 5:12.
[103] 'Pharisaic scandal' occurs when someone maliciously misinterprets and professes to be scandalized by another person's innocent action. See Aquinas, *ST* II-II, q. 33, art. 7.

THE DEFENCE OF THE BOOK, *ON THE JUST REASONS FOR WAR* 221

them. (2) This, then, is what I would be saying if the case were in fact doubtful, as it appears to you to be. But now that my arguments have been set forth, there really is no ambiguity at all, provided we are actually seeking the truth. For the opinion of those men is neither true nor probable. As to what you say about the number of learned men and judges, just make sure that you aren't being careless in your calculation of the votes. For among those who have written on the subject, only Thomas Cajetan advocates for their view—and that not positively[104]—while none of the others who have clearly grasped my principles either from me or from my writings do so, apart from just a few who, corrupted by ambition, fight knowingly and persistently against the truth, lest they appear to depart, with some loss of reputation, from that which they or their sworn allies have proclaimed orally or in little treatises.

(3) But our view has as authorities: among the philosophers, the prince of them: Aristotle, *Politics*, Book 1, chapters 3 and 5;[105] among those learned in pontifical law, all the most learned men are on our side (those who commented on Book 3 [of the *Decretals* of Gregory IX], title 34 'De voto', canon 'Quod super his');[106] of the theologians, Augustine, Ambrose, Gregory, and Thomas, men of sanctity and famous for their teaching, who all very openly approve of force—against pagans every bit as much as against heretics—as I have made clear. (4) Likewise John Duns Scotus, who judged that even more force ought to be applied to unbelievers and their sons (4 *Sententiarum*, dist. 44, quaest. ultima).[107] Also Nicholas of Lyra (*Numerorum* 31),[108] Master Roa explicating Book 1 of Aristotle's *Politics*,[109] and John Mair, who explicitly approves of this expedition against the barbarians

---

[104] Cajetan (Tommaso de Vio Gaetano), Commentary on Aquinas, *ST* II-II, q. 66, art. 8, in *Sancti Thomae Aquinatis Opera Omnia Iussu Impensaque Leonis XIII P.M. Edita*, vol. 9, 94–95 (Rome: Typographia Polyglotta, 1897). Cajetan had died in Rome in 1534, so he was not directly involved in the controversy over Sepúlveda's *Democrates secundus*. But this passage in his commentary on Aquinas, published in 1517 (seven years after he had sent Dominican preachers to Hispaniola), was often cited by Las Casas and his allies. See David M. Lantigua, *Infidels and Empires in a New World Order: Early Modern Spanish Contributions to International Legal Thought* (Cambridge: Cambridge University Press, 2020), 85–92.

[105] Following Sepúlveda's translation of and commentary on Aristotle's *Politics* (Paris, 1548), what he calls 'ch. 3' is what we would now call ch. 2.1–15 (1253b1–1255a3), and his 'ch. 5' = ch. 3.1–9 (1256a1–1256b39).

[106] The reference given here is to Innocent III in the *Decretales* of Gregory IX (X.3.34.8). But by 'all the most learned men' (*consultissimi quique*), he means the four canonists cited earlier (see n. 50) who commented on this passage.

[107] John Duns Scotus, *Quaestiones in quattuor libros Sententiarum*, dist. 4.

[108] Nicholas of Lyra, commentary on Numbers 31 in *Postillae perpetuae*. See above, n. 40.

[109] Moreno Hernández (218n59) supposes that this is a reference to Juan Roa Dávila, author of *De regnorum iustitia*. Given that Roa Dávila (1552–1630) wasn't yet born when Sepúlveda published his *Apologia*, this seems unlikely. Clearly, Sepúlveda meant the fifteenth-century Salamantine master Fernando de Roa. See now Pedro de Osma and Fernando de Roa, *Comentario a la Política de Aristóteles, vol. 1*, edited by José Labajos Alonso (Salamanca: Universidad Pontífica de Salamanca, 2007). Also, Moreno Hernández's Latin text (p. 218) offers 'cap. 10'. There is no ch. 10 of Bk. 1 of the *Politics*. What Moreno Hernández misread as '10' was in fact 'Io', the abbreviation for 'Ioannis' (sc. Maioris; John Mair).

222 SEPÚLVEDA ON THE SPANISH INVASION OF THE AMERICAS

(4 *Sententiarum,* dist. 44, quaest. 3).[110] Also Alfonso Castro (*De iusta haereticorum punitione,* Book 2), who after having recently thoroughly read and pondered at Salamanca the summary of the question that I had diligently composed (as is stated openly in a handwritten document in my possession), approved of my little book and my view without any exception.[111] (5) In short, before a cunning and hostile man scattered about fantastical tares, no one read and understood my book without greatly approving of it—in particular, four very learned and important men: Royal counsellors, Fernando Guevara and Francisco Montalvo, and Dominican monks, Àlvaro Moscoso and Diego de Vitoria, to whom individually the assessment of my book was entrusted by the Royal Council. The judgment of these theologians, which each wrote under the work in his own hand, I have recorded below:

(6) 'I have read through this work, and I have found in it nothing foreign to the truth, but rather many things worthy of being read—and for this reason I not only commend, but also admire both the work and its author.' Friar Diego de Vitoria. (7) He would never have uttered this opinion in opposition to the shared view of his fellow Dominicans so freely and without hesitation had he not been fully supported by the authority of his brother Francisco, a most learned man and one of noble and open spirit, who was two days distant from him. I have complete confidence that he discussed my book (which he held onto for a long time once the charges had been filed) and my advice with him.

(8) Moreover, Moscoso subscribed as follows: 'I, too, have read this work, which is learnedly composed, and I have found nothing that in my opinion lacks probability. Indeed, the things adduced here from Sacred Scriptures and holy learned men are such a clear indication of this learned man's aim that no one, however shameless, would dare to affirm the opposite.' Moscoso. (9) Nor should we pass over in silence the very weighty testimony of that most distinguished and learned man Fernando de Valdés, Archbishop of Sevilla and Inquisitor General. Once he had repeatedly read my book and the summary of the question I have mentioned, recently, after that notorious judgment passed in an assembly of very learned and important men, when he discussed these matters that were then in everybody's mouth (for to whom was so unexpected a matter not a stumbling-block?), he said, (10) 'I will say what I think: those who were at the start the people responsible for impeding this book would have done their duty much better had they diligently seen to it that it be printed in larger letters and preached from pulpits throughout Spain.' Pedro Ortiz often declared the same thing—a theologian of outstanding teaching in whose premature death theological studies have experienced a serious loss.

---

[110] John Mair, *In primum et secundum Sententiarum,* dist. 44, q. 3.
[111] Alfonso de Castro, *De iusta haereticorum punitione* (*On the Just Punishment of Heretics*), Bk. 2, ch. 14 (p. 204 of the 1568 Antwerp edition).

THE DEFENCE OF THE BOOK, *ON THE JUST REASONS FOR WAR*

(11) Pedro de Soto, Dominican friar and confessor to the Emperor Charles, in a letter that he sent to me, says that he has no doubts at all about the justice of this war, and yet in the same letter earnestly and repeatedly urges me, led by reasoning obscure to me, not to hasten the publication of the book. (12) The same thing [sc. the justice of the war] is openly maintained by two eminent theologians: Juan Gil, who teaches theology at Salamanca as professor, and Honcala, canon of Ávila. (13) Also Alfonso de Herrera, Dominican friar and royal preacher, a very learned man, a man of frank and noble mind, who upon reading my writings and listening to my discourse said, 'I'm drawing my own conclusion, Ginés, and I do not think that anyone would disagree with you unless he hasn't listened to you and your writings or hasn't understood.' (14) Also voting in support of me in massive consensus are the theologians of Sevilla who not long ago diligently read the summary of the question—and in particular two very learned men, Luis Carvajal, the Franciscan provincial, and the Dominican friar Agustín de Esbarroya, who teaches theology from the cathedra in their college.

(15) In addition, there is Miguel de Arcos, a man outstanding not only for influence but also for learning, the provincial of the Dominican order in Andalusía, who recently in the convent at Córdoba, after the matter had been thoroughly examined on the basis of my writings and of discussions with me and in consultation with several learned monks, not only openly approved of my views—with the agreement of others whom I have mentioned and especially Martín Mendoza, the superior of that convent, a very important man of excellent learning—but even professed that he wondered what reason there could be for delaying the publication of this book that would be highly conducive to doing away with the mistaken view of many and to disentangle minds from scruples and pangs of conscience which might have been wrongly instilled. This is a view shared by a man of similar authority and learning, a Dominican by the name of Santa Cruz, the provincial of that same order for Castilla.

(16) This was recently reported to me by a Dominican named De la Cruz, also a provincial, for New Spain, who along with other monks of noted honesty and religion had been sent from that other world so that in the presence of Emperor Charles they might offer a lesson on what consideration of the public good and justice might require, and so that they might request (a request in which they were successful) that, in accord with his wisdom and sense of fairness, he might take measures against the tumults and seditions of the Spanish inhabitants by modifying the laws, and that, in accord with his wisdom, he might limit such great evils. (17) These evils—if we want to know the truth—had their origin from one man's error maintained contrary to this viewpoint of mine—or even from his recklessness and eagerness for revolution. It is contrary to my nature and custom to wish or pray evil for this man in return for these evils and for his restless mind, which harasses me even over here. Rather, I pray that God might furnish him with better thinking so that he may learn at long last to prefer peaceful thoughts to disruptive plans.

(18) In sum, to return from where we digressed, on our side are all learned men to whom I have set forth my view and reasoning, apart from a few whom I have mentioned, men who have a quarrelsome mind corrupted by ambition or some other more serious disease. But I have debated these people and reduced them to take refuge, evading and flailing, in the most trivial and manifestly ignorant fabrications (for I don't wish to call them puerilities) in the manner of men engaged in faction-fighting, who open the prisons in civil disturbances and in great crises. (19) For there's a great distance between our case and that of our adversaries. If in other matters we are as thoroughly defeated by them as we are superior to them, nonetheless the single sacrosanct authority of the pope and the church, on which we are relying in this case that publicly affects morality and religion, would far overcome all the decisions of all other judges—and not only overcome them but even convict those who stubbornly resist it of being heretics.

(20) Therefore, to declare what I think, and to finally make a conclusion, I simply do not see how those men's opinion could be defended, when it rests upon the foundation and the tricks of heretics, is opposed to the gospel and the unanimous declarations and testimonies of the holy doctors of the church, dissents from the ancient judgment of the church, and shows contempt for the new and very weighty decree of that same church and the apostolic response sent to our rulers when they asked for the pope's response on the basis of Deuteronomy and Bk. 4 [of the *Decretals* of Gregory IX], title 17 'Qui filii sint legitimi', chapter 'Per venerabilem'.[112] Nor do I see how their view would not be heretical if it is defended with stubbornness after true reasons have come to be recognized.

This work was published in Rome by the brothers Valerio and Ludovico Dorico of Brescia on 1 May 1550, having been examined and approved by Felipe Archinto, vicar of our most holy lord the pope, Egidio Foscarario, master of the Sacred Apostolic Palace, and Antonio Agustín, auditor of the Roman Rota, and having been commended by the consensus of many other highly learned men.

---

[112] Deuteronomy 17:2–3, cited by Innocent III in X.4.17.13.

Contained Herein Is a Debate
or Disputation

(Aquí se contiene una disputa o controversia)

Preface to the translations of *Aquí se contiene una disputa o controversia* and *Postreros apuntamientos*

The texts

This is the first complete translation into English of the collection of materials which, in the wake of the Valladolid sessions of 1550–51, Bartolomé de las Casas arranged to have published in September 1552 in Seville, at the print shop of Sebastián Trujillo, under the heading: *Aquí se contiene una disputa o controversia* ... (*Contained herein is a debate or disputation* ...). This volume comprised four documents:

1) A brief prefatory statement introducing the context and subject of the material to follow—*Argumento de la presente obra*—which is anonymous but which, in light of the tenor of the piece, is clearly the work of Las Casas himself. This statement of subject must have been composed already sometime in 1551, for he refers in it to the first session at Valladolid as 'last year'. Clearly, then, Las Casas was making ready to publish these works from 1551 onwards.

2) Fray Domingo de Soto's *Sumario* (*Summary*) of the arguments presented by both parties at the first session of the Valladolid Junta in 1550, at which Sepúlveda had spoken first and Las Casas (whose over-long contribution to proceedings Soto was primarily charged with abridging) second. Soto prepared this summary in Autumn 1550 before the first session of the junta was formally adjourned.

3) Sepúlveda's subsequent written responses to twelve objections which had been raised by Las Casas in the course of his lengthy anti-Sepúlvedan deposition before the junta. Sepúlveda prepared these rejoinders upon reading Soto's précis of Las Casas's arguments as schematized in the *Sumario*: the

---

Sepúlveda on the Spanish Invasion of the Americas. Luke Glanville, David Lupher and Maya Feile Tomes,
Oxford University Press. © Luke Glanville, David Lupher, and Maya Feile Tomes 2023.
DOI: 10.1093/oso/9780198863823.003.0005

226   SEPÚLVEDA ON THE SPANISH INVASION OF THE AMERICAS

Muñoz manuscript, on which more below, attests to the feverish annotations which he penned in so doing. (Sepúlveda had, of course, not heard Las Casas deliver his disquisition in person.) Counterintuitively, these Sepúlvedan rebuttals of Las Casas's objections are themselves known as the *Objections*. Whenever this designation is used, then, it must be borne in mind that these are not in fact Sepúlveda's own objections but rather his effort to defend his viewpoint against those which had been levelled against it by Las Casas himself.

4) The twelve *Replies* in turn composed by Las Casas to refute Sepúlveda's responses to the objections he had himself put to the latter.[1] These replies, which were composed after the junta had adjourned for 1550 and before it reconvened in April 1551, are generally much lengthier than the Sepúlvedan answers to which Las Casas was notionally merely 'responding'.

The main documents in Las Casas's *Aquí se contiene* volume thus orbit around the junta's first session of August–September 1550 and span the lead-up to the second session of April–May 1551. Soto himself produced his summary around September 1550, and Sepúlveda likewise prepared his (answers to Las Casas's) *Objections* at that time and had them distributed to the members of the assembly before the first session was adjourned.[2] He may even have dared to imagine that that was the end of that. But when Sepúlveda returned to Valladolid in April 1551, it was only to discover—as he himself recalls in section 4 of his subsequent account, the *Proposiciones temerarias* (*PT*)—that Las Casas had gone on to produce twelve *Replies* to Sepúlveda's so-called *Objections* and submitted them in readiness for the meeting of the second session. Sepúlveda was later in turn to deliver his own resounding 'riposte' to these subsequent Lascasian *Replies* when, upon learning that Las Casas had had the aforementioned materials sent to press in his Seville volume of 1552, he prepared an emphatic rejoinder in the form of his *PT* (1553–54), which he submitted to the Inquisition by way of formal denunciation: see the general introduction, above, and our preface to the *PT*, below, for further discussion of this point.

But while still in Valladolid during the second meeting of the junta in April 1551, Sepúlveda sought permission to address the assembly in person once more. The petition he submitted, which offers an outline of the points he proposed to deliver more fully in oral form, is dated 12 April 1551 and has come to be known as

---

[1] Further indications of the arguments presented by Las Casas at Valladolid can be derived from two other documents which he produced after the 'debate': his Latin *Apologia* (familiar to Anglophone readers under the title of Stafford Poole's 1974 translation, *In Defense of the Indians*) and, to a lesser extent, the massive Spanish *Apologética historia sumaria* (a proto-ethnological work never translated into English). The *Apologia* in particular often casts instructive light on the more abbreviated account of his views presented in Soto's *Summary* and even on occasion serves to flesh out the picture painted by the *Replies*, prolix though they already are.

[2] As recounted by Sepúlveda himself in *PT* §4.

the '*Postreros apuntamientos que dio Sepúlveda en la congregación*' ('Final points of argument presented to the congregation by Sepúlveda').[3] The arguments offered in this short document are primarily devoted to the subject of the bull of Alexander VI—or rather to taking issue with Las Casas's (ab)use of it in the course of his own argumentation. Traditionally there has been some uncertainty as to whether or not Sepúlveda was indeed afforded the opportunity to air these points at the second session or whether this document is our only record of his final set of intended remarks. However, by Sepúlveda's own account in the *Proposiciones temerarias* (§5), he was indeed granted an audience at the second session and seems to have used it as an opportunity to discuss his interpretation of the bull of Alexander VI—as well as that of Paul III—with the junta's theologians.[4] His final oral intervention in the Valladolid Debate in April 1551 will thus presumably have borne some kind of resemblance to the content of the *Postreros apuntamientos*, of which we are offering a translation here by way of appendix.

The editions

In preparing our translations of these documents, the following materials have been used. For the text of *Aquí se contiene* we have largely followed the Lascasian *editio princeps*, published at the print shop of Sebastián Trujillo in Seville in 1552.[5] (From time to time, however, we do depart from this version of the text—and therefore also from most modern transcriptions of *Aquí se contiene*—in instances where the 1552 *editio princeps* exhibits certain questionable features: on those occasions we have sought to arrive at—and, in turn, offer translation of—an emended version of the text on the basis of consultation of two *Aquí se contiene* manuscripts, on which more in the next section.) Various copies of the 1552 *editio princeps* survive and are held today in libraries and private collections around the world.[6] For ease of access, however, we have in practice worked primarily from the facsimilar copy of it reproduced in *Bartolomé de las Casas—Tratados I*,

---

[3] On the date of 12 April, see n. 469 in our translation of the *Postreros apuntamientos*. The Spanish term '*apuntamientos*' can simply mean 'notes' or 'written observations'—though it can also have a more technical sense, pertaining to official accounts of, or indeed formal objections lodged at, legal proceedings. (See Covarrubias on '*apuntamiento*', under '*apuntar*'; and, for the technical sense in the modern context, see RAE entry 2 on '*apuntamiento*'.)

[4] For the best study of the second session of the junta, see Vidal Abril-Castelló, 'La bipolarización Sepúlveda-Las Casas y sus consecuencias: La revolución de la duodécima replica', in *La ética en la conquista de América*, edited by Demetrio Ramos et al., 229–88 (Madrid: Consejo Superior de Investigaciones Científicas, 1984).

[5] On the reception of the *Aquí se contiene*, including how a 'pirated' edition appears to have already been in circulation by the end of 1552, see our postscript to this volume.

[6] For an earlier catalogue of extant editions, see Isacio Pérez Fernández O.P., *Inventario documentado de los escritos de Fray Bartolomé de las Casas*, revised by Helen Rand Parish (Bayamón, PR: Centro de Estudios de los Dominicos del Caribe, 1981), 596–601.

228   SEPÚLVEDA ON THE SPANISH INVASION OF THE AMERICAS

edited by Lewis Hanke et al. (Mexico City: Fondo de Cultura Económica, 1965, repr. 1974 & 1997), 216–459 (*verso* sides), which the reader can also readily access. The particular copy of the 1552 *editio princeps* from which the Fondo de Cultura Económica facsimile is reproduced is that which at the time belonged to a prominent businessperson and bibliophile named Bruno Pagliai.[7] Moreover, this 'Pagliai' copy contains a number of marginal annotations, all in the same anonymous—but certainly early modern—hand, which are consequently all duly reproduced (mostly, if not always, legibly) throughout the Fondo de Cultura Económica facsimile as well: we have therefore always also had sight of these often useful annotations—generally devoted to signalling various *errata*, be they typographical or citational—and have from time to time had occasion to mention them in our footnotes where relevant.

In addition to the Fondo de Cultura Económica facsimilar edition, we have also been aided by a number of partial and complete modern transcriptions (though we have not relied on any one in particular or to the exclusion of any other). The complete transcriptions from which we have primarily worked are: (**1**) that prepared by Juan Pérez de Tudela Bueso, first published in 1958 and again offered *en face* with the facsimilar reproduction of the 1552 edition in the aforementioned 1965 Fondo de Cultura Económica volume (217–459, *recto* sides);[8] (**2**) that in volume 10 of the *Obras completas* of Las Casas (Madrid: Alianza, 1992), 101–93, edited and transcribed by Lorenzo Galmés O.P. We have most recently also had access to the transcription in (**3**) Natalia K. Denisova, *Proposiciones temerarias: Recopilación de textos de Juan Ginés de Sepúlveda, Bartolomé de Las Casas y Domingo de Soto que tratan del debate del Nuevo Mundo* (Madrid: Fundación Universitaria Española, 2019), 75–192.

Of partial transcriptions, we have further consulted the stand-alone editions of Soto's *Sumario* in: (**1**) Jaime Brufau Prats, *Domingo de Soto, O.P.—Relecciones y Opúsculos*, I (Salamanca: Editorial San Esteban, 1995), 199–233; and (**2**) Saverio di Liso, *Bartolomé de Las Casas, Juan Ginés de Sepúlveda: La controversia sugli indios* (Bari: Edizioni di Pagina, 2016), 168–99 (with translation into Italian at 70–137), following the text of Brufau Prats.[9] Like Di Liso, in our translation we have adopted the schema of fourteen sections first introduced by Brufau Prats in his edition of the *Sumario*; and we have gone on to supply section numbers of our own to divide up Sepúlveda's often substantial *Objections* and Las Casas's even lengthier *Replies*. Note, however, that the text of the *Sumario* as printed by Brufau Prats—and followed by Di Liso—is not identical to that in the 1552 edition from which we are

---

[7] See *Bartolomé de las Casas—Tratados I*, vii. Bruno Pagliai was an Italian-born industrialist who resided in Mexico, where the 1965 Fondo de Cultura Económica edition was published.

[8] Tudela Bueso's transcription of Las Casas's *Aquí se contiene* was first published in vol. 5 of his *Obras escogidas de Fray Bartolomé de las Casas: Opúsculos, cartas, memoriales* (Madrid: Ediciones Atlas, 1958), 293–347, as part of the Biblioteca de Autores Españoles series (vol. 110).

[9] See Di Liso, *Bartolomé de Las Casas, Juan Ginés de Sepúlveda*, 70.

CONTAINED HEREIN IS A DEBATE OR DISPUTATION   229

working: in addition to the *editio princeps*, Brufau Prats had also consulted another major manuscript witness—the so-called Muñoz manuscript, on which more below[10]—and thereby arrived at a somewhat different text of Soto's *Sumario*, subtended by a useful *apparatus criticus*.

Further information about the many earlier editions and other formats in which the texts of *Aquí se contiene* are available can be found in Isacio Pérez Fernández O.P., *Inventario documentado de los escritos de Fray Bartolomé de las Casas*, revised by Helen Rand Parish (Bayamón, PR: Centro de Estudios de los Dominicos del Caribe, 1981), esp. 589–601; also 570–73.

By contrast, we have had access to the text of the brief *Postreros apuntamientos* through but a single source: pp. 29–31 of *Fr. Bartolomé de las Casas: Tratado de Indias y el Doctor Sepúlveda*, ed. Manuel Giménez Fernández (Caracas: Academia Nacional de la Historia, 1962; repr. 1988),[11] produced as part of the 'Fuentes para la Historia Colonial de Venezuela' series (Biblioteca de la Academia Nacional de la Historia, 56). The text of the *Postreros apuntamientos* printed there is a transcription of a manuscript belonging to a bundle of several almost certainly original sixteenth-century Sepúlvedan–Lascasian documents (including manuscript copies of the major constituent elements of *Aquí se contiene*) that were later bound together into an unusual codex on which more below. The manuscript of the *Postreros apuntamientos*, which runs to just three small folios, dates from the mid-sixteenth century and appears to have been produced by the same Sepúlvedan scribe involved in the production of other key Sepúlvedan works, notably a major manuscript of the *Democrates secundus*.[12] The Caracas edition transcription of the *Postreros apuntamientos*, from which we have worked, was prepared in 1959 by Dolores Bonet de Sotillo under the direction of María Teresa Bermejo de Capdevila, erstwhile Professor of Palaeography at the University of Madrid.

[10] See Brufau Prats, *Domingo de Soto*, 198. He refers to this 'Muñoz' manuscript as '*Códice M*'—not to be confused with the *PT* manuscript which we have termed *M* (for 'Madrid'), which also features extensively throughout our volume and on which see the *PT* preface. Further confusion could arise from the fact that the *M(uñoz)* MS. of *Aquí se contiene* and the *M(adrid)* MS. of the *PT* are in fact both held in Madrid.

[11] Manuel Giménez Fernández's name is curiously absent from the title-page of the 1962 edition, though it does then appear on that of the 1988 reprint (where 'Giménez' is spelled 'Jiménez'). He is the author of the extensive preliminary study with which the volume opens, albeit unsigned in the 1962 printing.

[12] A description of the *Postreros apuntamientos* manuscript is offered at *Tratado de Indias*, LXVIII–LXIX. The matter of the distinctive scribal hand is discussed on p. LXVIII: it is said to be identical to that used to produce the *Democrates secundus* manuscript of which a facsimilar sample is reproduced on the second plate ('Lámina IV') inserted at pp. 192–93 of Ángel Losada, *Juan Ginés de Sepúlveda a través de du 'epistolario' y nuevos documentos* (Madrid: Consejo Superior de Investigaciones Científicas, 1949/73). Note that this manuscript of the *Democrates secundus* is listed there as MSS. 518 from the Biblioteca de Palacio in Madrid but in fact, as with the *C* manuscript of the *PT* (on which see further the *PT* preface), is now back in Salamanca, as MS. 2634 at the Biblioteca Universitaria.

230 SEPÚLVEDA ON THE SPANISH INVASION OF THE AMERICAS

Aquí se contiene manuscripts

Our translation of *Aquí se contiene* remains first and foremost based on the text as printed in, and best known from, the *editio princeps* of September 1552. However, the texts of the pieces as published in that volume—one of no fewer than ten which Las Casas sent to press at around that same time, nine of them at the print shop of Trujillo—inevitably also contain a number of *errata*: some no doubt the result of slips in the version of the text supplied by Las Casas himself, others clearly introduced by the typesetters at the press working in haste or without due heed. Indeed, the grand term *editio princeps* should not distract us from the fact that the original printing of these materials was more of a glorified pamphlet, presumably produced with relative alacrity. The most common *errata* are those which occur in the referencing information for the proof-texts and other authorities cited in such abundance throughout all the texts of *Aquí se contiene*. There are also regular problems with certain other elements: for instance, Latin words are more commonly misrendered than Spanish. At times, where the sense or syntax of a phrase is truly obscure, comparison with the available manuscript witnesses reveals that Trujillo's typesetters had not infrequently omitted whole words or even, on more than one occasion, several lines of text at once. These and other errors have in turn widely made their way unaltered into the aforementioned modern transcriptions and editions of *Aquí se contiene*.

In preparing our translation, therefore, we have supplemented our understanding of the text as printed in the *editio princeps* through consideration of the evidence from two manuscript witnesses containing part or all of the texts of *Aquí se contiene*. These are:

(1) MS. 9/4811 (formerly MS. A-75) from the Colección de Juan Bautista Muñoz in the library of Spain's Real Academia de la Historia in Madrid, which we have consulted in digitized form.[13] This manuscript, also known simply as the 'Muñoz' manuscript, contains two of the elements in question: Soto's *Sumario* (fols. 210*v*–227*v*) and Las Casas's *Réplicas* (fols. 228*r*–269*v*). Moreover, it bears extensive marginal annotations in Sepúlveda's own hand. Vidal Abril-Castelló has suggested that the marginal annotations to this copy of Soto's *Summary* will most likely have been made in the process of drafting his *Objections* (in Autumn 1551), while his notes on the

---

[13] A description of the complete contents of MS. 9/4811 is available in Real Academia de la Historia, *Catálogo de la colección de D. Juan Bautista Muñoz, vol. 1* (Madrid: Real Academia de la Historia, 1954), 172–74. See further Vidal Abril-Castelló, 'La bipolarización Sepúlveda–Las Casas', esp. 229–31; also 238n16. He refers to the Muñoz manuscript by its now obsolete former catalogue number, A-75, as does Isacio Pérez Fernández, *Inventario documentado*, 573.

CONTAINED HEREIN IS A DEBATE OR DISPUTATION   231

Lascasian *Replies* appear to constitute a preliminary stage in his composition of the later *Proposiciones temerarias* (in 1553).[14] In the footnotes to our translation, we refer to the copies of the *Summary* and *Replies* contained in this 'Muñoz' manuscript as 'MS' (not to be confused with 'MS', the abbreviation for manuscript) and 'MR'.

(2) The Caracas codex, which contains all three major constituent elements of *Aquí se contiene*: Soto's *Summary*, Sepúlveda's *Objections*, and Las Casas's *Replies*. These, too, bear a close connection to Las Casas's own archive: its copy of the *Objections* appears to have been the one of which Las Casas made use in the composition of his *Replies*, while its version of the latter is a scribal copy bearing the autograph signature of Las Casas himself.[15] In fact this remarkable codex is a collection of no fewer than sixteen documents apparently deriving from Las Casas's personal papers. The pieces were assembled under dubious circumstances in the first years of the nineteenth century by the Benedictine monk Benito María Moxó y Francolí (1763–1816)—reputed to be the illegitimate son of Carlos IV—who, having seemingly purloined them from the Spanish state repository,[16] emigrated to the Americas, where he was appointed bishop of Charcas (in modern-day Bolivia) in 1804. The papers, which he had had bound together into a single codex in around 1800,[17] accompanied him. Items 1, 13, and 16 of the codex correspond to the *Summary*, *Objections*, and *Replies* of *Aquí se contiene*; item 3 is the *Postreros apuntamientos*. Upon Moxó's death, the codex passed, along with many of his books, to the Oratory of San Felipe de Neri in Sucre (also in modern-day Bolivia). Many years later, the cash-strapped Oratorians sold the lot to bookdealers in Buenos Aires, from whom the Fundación Creole in turn purchased the codex and in 1958 presented it to the Biblioteca Nacional de la Historia in Caracas, where it remains. We have not had the opportunity to consult it at first hand; however, we have had indirect access to it in the transcription of the complete codex prepared by Dolores Bonet de Sotillo in 1959 and first printed in the above-mentioned 1962 Venezuelan volume, *Fr. Bartolomé de las Casas: Tratado de Indias y el Doctor Sepúlveda*. In our footnotes, we refer to the *Summary*, *Objections*, and *Replies* of the Caracas codex as 'CS', 'CO', and 'CR'.

Consultation of this pair of manuscripts has frequently allowed us to form an enhanced understanding of what was intended in areas of difficulty in the 1552 *editio princeps*, enabling us to identify and correct many textual problems and so to arrive

---

[14] Abril-Castelló, 'La bipolarización Sepúlveda–Las Casas', 238n16.
[15] *Tratado de Indias*, LXV, LXVII.
[16] *Tratado de Indias*, LXX.
[17] *Tratado de Indias*, LXX–LXXI.

at an improved overall version of the text. As a result, anyone tracking our translation against the original Spanish-language text as contained in the *editio princeps* (or against a faithful modern transcription thereof) will, at times, find that the text we appear to be translating diverges from that represented in the Spanish of the *editio princeps*. Unfortunately, as constraints of space mean that we are here offering only our translation into English as opposed to a fuller edition with the original text *en face*, it has not been possible for us to represent such instances in proper context by printing a fully amended version of the text. The corrected version of the text from which we have worked in producing our version must therefore remain a spectral presence for now, glimpsed only through the lines of the translation. However, though we do not provide the original text *en face* (or otherwise), we have always made sure to signal points at which the version of the text we are translating differs from that available in the 1552 edition and to explain the nature of the divergence. We hope that some of these indications will represent a helpful first step in any future attempt to produce a proper critical edition of the whole.

We have also, wherever possible, taken the opportunity to offer corrections to many of the errors inadvertently introduced, or inaccurate citational information provided, by various more modern transcribers and editors. These, too, we signal in our footnotes (although, again, our commentary on these problems should not be taken as any kind of comprehensive effort to compare and contrast the readings and reference notes of all available modern editions). Where we are commenting on difficulties in the transcription practices or the reference information of modern editions, we simply do so in the form of this sort of footnoted observation. When it comes to citational errors and other key *errata* present in the original 1552 edition, by contrast, it seemed important to retain the traces of these in order to allow the reader to appreciate the nature of the *editio princeps* and the types of intervention required. After all, evidence of original *errata* can be useful in helping to understand the working practices not only of the typesetters but also—at least to a certain degree—of the authors themselves; they can even on occasion provide clues as to the sources or reference works from which they were working. Rather than supply these sorts of corrections 'silently', therefore, we have adopted a system of strikethroughs: in other words, we retain the problem in the main body of the text and then employ ~~this form~~ this kind of formatting both to signal the original problem and simultaneously to offer the solution. A typical corrected reference of this sort will therefore read, e.g. 'Jeremiah in Chapter ~~24~~ 23'. Thus, even without providing a proper critical edition complete with full *apparatus criticus*, we hope that what we are offering here will nonetheless constitute a substantial advance on all existing editions of *Aquí se contiene* in terms both of the overall completeness of the text from which we have been working (as offered in translation here) and of the accuracy of the citations and other reference material provided. A full critical edition of *Aquí se contiene*, collating the text of the 1552 *editio princeps* with that of

CONTAINED HEREIN IS A DEBATE OR DISPUTATION   233

the available manuscripts and other sources and working to reconcile the views of its various editors, remains a scholarly desideratum for the future.[18]

* * *

In addition to supporting us in our interpretation of the 1552 *editio princeps* by helping to iron out textual difficulties of a (generally) more minor nature, our consultation of the Muñoz and Caracas manuscripts has inevitably also involved consideration of the more meaningful variant readings to which they attest. As we are not offering a full critical edition, we do not systematically signal these in what follows. However, a brief word about the major patterns of difference in this regard is still in order here.

For the Soto *Summary*, the differences are broadly inconsequential: both the Caracas manuscript and the Muñoz version differ from the 1552 printed version of the *Summary* only in discrepancies in spelling and minor copying errors.[19] When it comes the Lascasian *Replies*, by contrast, both the Muñoz manuscript and the Caracas copy differ from the text as offered in the printed 1552 *editio princeps* in several key regards. Both these manuscripts represent the version of the replies which Las Casas sent to the junta for the second session of April 1551. However, the version he then sent to press in 1552 exhibited certain significant differences— at least one of them amounting to a complete revision of ideological position—as compared with that of the 1551 draft. While ten of the twelve 1552 *Replies* exhibit only very minor changes vis-à-vis the 1551 versions, in two cases the revisions are more noteworthy. The first entailed the addition of a substantial new segment at the start of the Fourth Reply.[20] For our purposes, meanwhile, by far the more significant is the degree to which Las Casas took the opportunity to expand and revise a key portion of the Twelfth Reply.[21] This revision attests to a striking new interpretation of the power of the pope as formulated in the key bulls directed to the Spanish monarchs, arguing for the freedom of the Amerindians to resist Spanish rule. In the earlier version, Las Casas had acknowledged that the pope had the authority to expropriate and reassign Amerindian dominions where there were just grounds to do so; however, in the printed 1552 version his position had changed such that he now held that, while the Amerindians were indeed obliged upon baptism to obey the pope in spiritual matters and ecclesiastical discipline, they were under no

---

[18] Previous modern editors have individually signalled some percentage of problems identified in the *editio princeps*; to date, however, no one edition has reliably identified, collated, and dealt with these problems all together. The otherwise generally excellent quality of the work in Alianza's *Obras completas* series of Las Casas's *oeuvre* sadly does not extend to its edition of *Aquí se contiene*, which leaves much to be desired. A definitive edition thus remains a desideratum.

[19] *Tratado de Indias*, LX.

[20] In his discussion of divergences of the printed version from the Caracas manuscript, Giménez Fernández neglected to mention this expansion (*Tratado de Indias*, LXVII). Compare Abril-Castelló, 'La bipolarización Sepúlveda–Las Casas', where it is properly noted (244 with 244n35).

[21] The previous redaction of this section as known from the Caracas and Muñoz manuscripts can be consulted in n. 439 below.

234 SEPÚLVEDA ON THE SPANISH INVASION OF THE AMERICAS

obligation to recognize the pope's authority to curtail or transfer their sovereignty to the advantage of the Spanish Crown unless they freely elected to accept Spanish rule.[22] This is a highly noteworthy revision of his earlier stance and forms the basis of Vidal Abril-Castelló's seminal article, 'La bipolarización Sepúlveda–Las Casas y sus consecuenicas: La revolución de la Duodécima Réplica' ('The Sepúlveda–Las Casas Dichotomization and Its Consequences: The Revolution of the Twelfth Reply'). This still unsurpassed 1984 study illuminates the nature of this strategic shift in Las Casas's position as evidenced by the divergences between these printed and manuscript versions of the Twelfth Reply.

The approach

Lastly, a word on various points of practice. All the texts translated in this section were originally produced in the language in which Sepúlveda and Las Casas had themselves addressed the Valladolid Junta: Castilian Spanish.[23] However, both Sepúlveda and Las Casas (and, consequently, Soto) also make fairly substantial use of Latin, for which accompanying translation into Spanish is—as per early modern convention and in accord with the nature of the target audience envisaged— never offered. Recourse to Latin normally occurs in the context of direct citation (from Scripture, the church fathers, and so forth) or else in well-known formulaic phrases—though by no means only. When Latin is used in contexts above and beyond these standard modes, it is generally to offer some kind of lapidary pronouncement at the end of a point or else to elaborate on an idea which may have commenced in cited Latin form but on which our authors then go on to expand in an extended Latinate excursus of their own confection. In these cases, Latin is maintained as the language of expression well beyond the confines of the citation, be it for reasons of consistency, as the language of logical disputation, or for rhetorical flair.

Whereas translation of Latin into Spanish was not thought to be necessary for the original readers of *Aquí se contiene*, it naturally raises a dilemma for us. In what follows, its Spanish and Latin passages alike have been rendered into English for reasons of complete Anglophone accessibility: the aim of our volume, after all. However, this has a 'flattening' effect on what was originally a more textured

---

[22] See Abril-Castelló, 'La bipolarización Sepúlveda–Las Casas', esp. 264–65.

[23] Las Casas's address at the first session of the junta was an oral delivery of his *Apología*, a tract written in Spanish (not to be confused with the Latin-language *Apologia* which he then produced after Valladolid, on which see n. 1 above): on the fact that this work was certainly in Spanish, see further the description of events in what is surely the Lascasian preface ('The subject of this work') to *Aquí se contiene*. This Spanish-language *Apología* does not survive: we can piece together its contents only from Soto's *Sumario*, as well as from Las Casas's own later writings (on which see, again, n. 1 above).

multilingual work;[24] thus, in an effort to retain and recreate at least something of the original dynamic of the patterning of alternation between the two, we have opted to reconstitute this linguistic variation at the level of formatting, with those passages or phrases which were originally in Latin now printed here *in italics*. If it is a citation, the originally Latin-language text will also come *'in inverted commas'*; if it is a spontaneous sentiment vouchsafed in Latin by one of our sixteenth-century authors, it appears *without inverted commas*. Although we have in general tried to avoid it, we do occasionally also employ italics to convey emphasis, and we trust that in those cases the context will be such that it will be clear enough when *that* kind of italics is being used. All titles of works, whether originally given in Latin or Spanish, are also formatted in italics and it is likewise hoped that this will not be cause for undue confusion.

There were various terminological dilemmas, too. In the end we have generally adopted a policy of retaining original terms: thus, for instance, Las Casas is referred to as the bishop of 'Chiapa' (rather than modern 'Chiapas'); Aristotle is frequently referred to as 'the Philosopher', as was common at the time; and the term 'Indians', used in these texts to denote the indigenous inhabitants of the Americas, is retained in accordance with the patterns of usage of a time in Europe when the world was perceived—geographically and otherwise—in a manner very different from the way it is generally understood today. Indeed, all the texts in this volume attest, at all levels, to this.

---

[24] For interesting recent discussion of similar considerations in an emphatically modern context—albeit by no means ungermane to the questions which rear their heads for the translation of our texts here—see Ellen Jones, *Literature in Motion: Translating Multilingualism across the Americas* (New York: Columbia University Press, 2022), especially the introduction at 1–35.

Contained herein is a debate or disputation conducted between
the Bishop Fr. Bartolomé de las Casas or Casaus, former bishop of
the Royal City of Chiapa—which is a place in the Indies, situated
within New Spain—and Dr Ginés de Sepúlveda, chronicler of our
lord the emperor, in which the doctor contended that the conquests
undertaken in the Indies against the Indians were lawful, whereas
the bishop opposed this position and argued that they were—and
could never be anything but—tyrannical, unjust, and wicked. The
matter was aired and argued before a large audience of many learned
men, comprising both theologians and jurists, in an assembly which
His Majesty ordered to be convened in the year 1550 in the town of
Valladolid.

1552

The Subject of This Work

Dr Sepúlveda,[25] chronicler of our lord the emperor, composed a book in the form of a dialogue in most elegant Latin,[26] observing all its laws or rules and rhetorical refinement (as befits someone so distinguished and well versed in the Latin language), in which, convinced by the information with which he had been furnished by certain Spaniards who numbered among those most guilty and blameworthy in the destruction and ravages which have been wrought upon the inhabitants of the Indies, he arrived at two principal conclusions. The first is that the wars which have been waged by the Spanish against the Indians were just from the point of view both of the grounds and of the authority for undertaking them, and that, in general terms, this is a course of action which can and should be pursued against them. The second conclusion is that the Indians are obliged to submit to Spanish rule as people of lesser understanding to those of superior intellect, and, should they prove unwilling, he asserts that war may be waged against them. These are the two reasons behind the devastation and death of such an infinitude of people and the desolation of more than two thousand leagues of land at the hands of the Spanish, who have perpetrated killings and depredation by means of the manifold new-fangled forms of cruelty and inhumanity which they practise in the Indies in the course of their so-called 'conquests' and the *encomiendas* to which they came to refer as '*repartimientos*'.[27] The aforementioned Dr Sepúlveda further trussed up his treatise by alleging, so as better to mask the creed which he sought to spread throughout these realms and throughout those of the Indies themselves, that its purpose was to substantiate the title of the monarchs of Castile and León to sovereignty and to supreme, universal dominion over that sphere of the Indies.

The doctor submitted the book in question to the Royal Council of the Indies, pleading and pestering most insistently to be granted a licence and permission to have it printed. Time and again they refused to grant any such thing, all too aware of the renewed calamity and disaster which would inevitably come of publishing it. Seeing the impossibility of having it printed under the auspices of the Council of the Indies, he endeavoured with the help of certain friends of his resident at the imperial court to obtain a *cédula* from His Majesty granting him permission to submit it to the Royal Council of Castile, which news of matters pertaining to

---

[25] This 'Argumento de la presente obra' was composed by Las Casas by way of introduction to the three pieces he was sending for publication at the print shop of Sebastián Trujillo in Seville in 1552.

[26] The *Democrates secundus*.

[27] Both terms refer to grants of the Amerindians' labour, not land, to Spaniards in America, in exchange for ensuring instruction in the Christian faith. Those who received *encomiendas* ('entrustments') were called *encomenderos*. Later, starting with the New Laws of 1542, a more centrally controlled system of *repartimientos* ('distributions') gradually replaced the *encomiendas*, but these remained grants of labour, not land.

238 SEPÚLVEDA ON THE SPANISH INVASION OF THE AMERICAS

the Indies did not tend to reach. Just as this edict was on the point of being issued, while the court and councils were at Aranda de Duero, Fr. Bartolomé de las Casas or Casaus, bishop of the Royal City of Chiapa, returned from the Indies in the year 1547. Upon becoming aware of Dr Sepúlveda's treatise, he grasped the nature of its contents and its thoroughly injurious blindness, as well as the irreparable damage to which it would give rise if printed. So he opposed it with all his might, exposing and revealing the poison with which it brimmed and the objective on which it was bent.

Since the subject matter with which it dealt was above all theological in nature, the esteemed members of the Royal Council of Castile resolved in their wisdom and justice to send it to the universities of Salamanca and Alcalá, enjoining them to inspect and examine it and put their names to it if they deemed it printable. After much painstaking deliberation, the universities concluded that it should not be printed, as its doctrine was unsound.

Not content with this—on the contrary, almightily aggrieved at the universities—the doctor, undeterred by the numerous rebuffs he received from both Royal Councils, decided to send his treatise to his friends in Rome to arrange for it to be published there, albeit under the guise of a certain *Apologia* which he had written to the bishop of Segovia:[28] for, having had occasion to peruse the book in question, the latter had penned a letter in which he offered a series of corrections volunteered in a brotherly spirit, as is common practice among friends and acquaintances. Upon learning that the aforementioned book—the *Apologia*—had been printed, the emperor lost no time in issuing an edict decreeing that all the books or copies thereof be rounded up and kept from appearing. And so the order went out for them to be confiscated throughout all of Castile.

And since the doctor also authored a Spanish-language summary[29] of his book in order to boost its dissemination throughout the realm and enable ordinary people and anyone else unable to read Latin to derive enjoyment from it—for its subject matter is appetizing and appealing to all those who seek and strive to become rich and rise to statuses never before enjoyed by them or by their forebears and, moreover, at no expense to themselves but rather by dint of the sweat, despair, and even deaths of others—the bishop of Chiapa resolved to compose an *Apología* of his own,[30] also in Spanish, in defence of the Indians and in opposition

---

[28] Antonio Ramírez de Haro. The *Apologia* printed in Rome in 1550 is the second work translated in this volume.

[29] Sepúlveda produced at least three summaries (in both Latin and Spanish) defending the *Democrates secundus*. See his letter of 23 September 1549 to Prince Philip (Letter 86 in the Pozoblanco *Obras completas*, IX.2, 252) and Losada (*JGS a través de su 'Epistolario'*, 206).

[30] Las Casas's Spanish *Apología* was never published, nor was it shown to Sepúlveda, who had to rely on Soto's summary of it. Our own reliance on Soto's summary can be supplemented by the Latin *Apologia* that Las Casas subsequently produced. This survived in manuscript and was first published by Losada in 1975, the year after Stafford Poole issued an English translation under the title *In Defense of the Indians*. Some material in the Spanish *Apología* contributed to Las Casas's later massive ethnographic survey, the Spanish-language *Apologética historia sumaria*. Las Casas frequently mentions his

CONTAINED HEREIN IS A DEBATE OR DISPUTATION   239

to the doctor's summary, countering and quashing its premises and rebutting its arguments and every single thing which the doctor believed worked in his favour, thereby alerting people to the dangers, scandalous elements, and damages which his doctrine comprises.

After many other ensuing events in the intervening period, last year—in the year 1550—His Majesty commanded an assembly to be held in the town of Valladolid at which many learned men, both theologians and jurists, would join forces with the Royal Council of the Indies to discuss and pronounce on whether the kinds of wars termed 'conquests' could be waged lawfully and justly against the inhabitants of those realms when they had perpetrated no wrongs besides those committed in their heathenism.

They summoned Dr Sepúlveda to come and give his opinion by making a statement of whatever he wanted to say on the subject. He came and spoke in the first session and said all that he wished to say. They then proceeded to summon the bishop, who read out his *Apología* in its entirety over a period of five consecutive days. And in view of its great length, all the esteemed theologians and jurists of the assembly bade one of their own number, the distinguished priest *Maestro* Fr. Domingo de Soto,[31] confessor to His Majesty and a member of the Dominican Order, to produce a summary of it and for as many copies thereof to be made as there were members of the assembly—which is to say fourteen—so that they could avail themselves of it in considering the matter and then vote on what, by the will of God, they deemed best. In his summary the aforementioned priest, *Maestro* Soto, set out the arguments advanced by the doctor and the counterarguments composed by the bishop. The doctor subsequently requested a copy of the summary so that he could offer his response, formulating a list of twelve objections levelled against him, to which he proceeded to supply twelve answers. The bishop in turn then offered twelve replies to these. And that is the reason and rationale behind this whole treatise which follows.

End of statement of subject.

Apología/Apologia in his 'Replies' in this 1552 pamphlet. We translate it as his Spanish *Apología* on the assumption that he was likely referring to the completed treatise that he read out to the Valladolid Junta and which Soto summarized. However, we cannot be entirely confident about this, since Las Casas appears to have used his Latin *Apologia* as his source at at least one point (see n. 413). Thus, while Poole (*Defense of the Indians*, xx–xxi) dates the Latin *Apologia* to sometime in 1552 or early 1553, Las Casas appears to have already been at work on it while penning his 'Replies' in late 1550 or early 1551.

[31] *Maestro* ('Teacher') refers to Soto's position as Professor of Theology at the University of Salamanca, a position he had held since 1532, as a protegé of his celebrated teacher and fellow-Dominican, Francisco de Vitoria.

240 SEPÚLVEDA ON THE SPANISH INVASION OF THE AMERICAS

Domingo de Soto's 'Summary'

This is a copy of a summary which, at the behest of the assembly which His Majesty ordered to be convened in Valladolid in the year '50, the most reverend and learned priest, *Maestro* Fr. Domingo de Soto, produced of the *Apología* which the bishop of Chiapa composed and read out before the aforementioned assembly in opposition to Dr Sepúlveda.

Prologue by *Maestro* Soto

(1) Most illustrious, magnificent, and reverend sirs and fathers: what your lordships, mercies, and worships have commanded of me is to produce a systematic summary of the arguments which these two gentlemen—the distinguished Dr Sepúlveda and the most reverend bishop of Chiapa—have advanced against one another in this most sage council, so that the thrust and basis of their dispute, all distilled into this digest, might serve as a source of greater illumination to your lordships and mercies in your capacity as the adjudicators thereof. And you commanded me not to express or otherwise indicate my own opinion here, nor am I to expand on the case advanced by either party with any additional line of reasoning, but rather faithfully to convey the essence of their views and the gist of their arguments. This, then, has been my procedure, although with freer rein I might conceivably, insofar as my meagre intellect permits, have been able to impart a sheen of a different order to this synopsis; however, I shall refrain from doing so until such time as your lordships and mercies might see fit to call on me to offer my own opinion.

(2) The matter over which your lordships, mercies, and worships seek to deliberate here is that of probing and determining the proper manner and laws by which our holy Catholic faith may, in a manner best serving God, be preached and propagated in that New World which he has unveiled to us, and to determine the means by which the people there may be rendered subject to the majesty of our lord the emperor without pricking his royal conscience, in accordance with the bull of Alexander.[32] The fact of the matter, however, is that the two gentlemen arguing the case have not approached the task in this way, in general terms and as a point of deliberation; rather, they have addressed themselves to and debated the following specific issue, namely whether it is lawful for His Majesty to wage war on those Indians and render them subject to his empire prior to preaching the faith to them so that, once they have been subjugated, they may more easily and conveniently be instructed in the teachings of the gospel and so enlightened as to the errors of their ways and the Christian truth. Dr Sepúlveda is the proponent

---

[32] Alexander VI, *Inter caetera* (1493).

CONTAINED HEREIN IS A DEBATE OR DISPUTATION   241

of the affirmative view, asserting that war of this sort is not only lawful but expedient. The esteemed bishop holds the opposite position, maintaining not only that it is not expedient but that it is not lawful either; rather, it is wicked and antithetical to our Christian religion.

Two considerations, however, must be borne in mind. The first is that it is difficult to do as much justice to the doctor as to the bishop, for the doctor did not read his book aloud but rather rehearsed the salient points of his case in an oral paraphrase, whereas the bishop read out his writings at enormous length, meaning that the force of each side cannot be represented equally in this account; and therefore whosoever of your lordships or mercies wishes to get more fully to grips with this dispute can consult the doctor's book directly.[33] The second proviso is that, since the esteemed bishop did not hear the doctor speak, in his answer he did not follow the order in which the doctor stated his case (nor did he restrict himself in his response solely to its content), but rather sought to counter everything the doctor has ever committed to paper and to raise all possible objections which can be levelled at his position, as a result of which it will not be necessary to do more than summarize the key points of his response, with the principal arguments made and proof-texts adduced.

(3) Dr Sepúlveda, then, established his position briefly, by means of four arguments: firstly, on account of the severity of the misdeeds of that people, notably their idolatry and their other sins against nature; secondly, the coarse cast of their minds, rendering them by their nature a servile, barbarous people who are accordingly obliged to serve those of more refined intellect, such as the Spanish; thirdly, in the interests of the faith, for this manner of subjection is far more convenient and expedient for preaching and persuading; and, lastly, in view of the abuses which they inflict on one another, killing human beings in order to sacrifice them and in some cases to eat them.

He adduced three arguments in support of the first point: firstly, through proof-texts and examples taken from the Holy Scripture; secondly, on the authority of the esteemed doctors of the church; thirdly, by painting in its ugliest colours the sheer enormity of their wrongdoing. With regard to the proof-texts drawn from the Holy Scripture, he did not rehearse all the ones adduced in his book, but merely two or three of them. The first was Deuteronomy 20, adduced not so much to prove that such warfare was lawful but rather to explain how to conduct it; for it reads as follows: '*When you approach a city to fight against it, you shall first offer it terms of peace*',[34] etc. It goes on to say that if the latter acquiesce to the offer of peace and open their doors to them, they should do them no harm but rather take them on as tribute-payers;[35] however, if the latter defend themselves by armed means, they

---

[33] This is most likely a reference to Sepúlveda's *Democrates secundus*. The members of the junta would each have had access to a manuscript copy of this unpublished book.

[34] Deuteronomy 20:10.

[35] Deuteronomy 20:11.

242   SEPÚLVEDA ON THE SPANISH INVASION OF THE AMERICAS

should kill all the men, leaving only the women and children[36]—although he noted that this particular extreme was not to be countenanced in the case of the Indians. And he used the fact that it also says there, '*So you shall do to all the cities that are very far away from you*'[37]—on which the gloss reads, '*far away*', which is to say, of a different religion'[38]—to argue that the fact of a particular group of people being of a different religion to our own is reason enough for us to be within our rights to wage war on them. In his book, however, he further seeks to substantiate his argument that war can be waged on them on account of idolatry by adducing that passage from Deuteronomy 9: '*Do not say in your heart when the Lord your God has driven them away from you, "Because of my righteousness the Lord has brought me in, ... when it is because of the wickedness of these nations that he is driving them out from before you*';[39] and in Chapter 12 the Jews were commanded to destroy the temples of the gentiles and to smash their statues and idols to pieces.[40] He further adduced the punishment meted out by God against Sodom and Gomorrah by way of example of the sort of thing which it is lawful to inflict upon the Indians.[41] And, conversely, in the course of his oral delivery he also at this point adduced that passage from Leviticus 26, in which God threatened the Jews themselves with the same punishment that obtained for the gentiles if they adopted any of the latter's abominable practices: ' "*I then will", he said, "destroy your high places, and cut down your incense altars, and you will fall amidst the ruins of your idols ... so I will turn your cities into ruins*",[42] etc.

(4) In response to this point, the esteemed bishop advanced many arguments which can be broadly summarized along the following four lines. The first was that God did not order the wars in question to be waged against the idolatrous gentiles on account of their idolatry but rather specifically against the Canaanites and Jebusites and the seven nations mentioned in Deuteronomy 7,[43] who were in possession of the Promised Land, which had been promised to Abraham and his descendants—although God did also wish to punish them for their idolatry at the same time. His first argument in support of this interpretation was that if God had set out to punish the gentiles on account of idolatry alone, he would have had to punish not just those particular peoples but practically everyone in the whole world, for it was all positively brimming with idolatry; and so the fact that

---

[36] Deuteronomy 20:12–14.
[37] Deuteronomy 20:15.
[38] The reference here is to French theologian Anselm of Laon's interlinear gloss of '*procul valde*' ('very far away') as '*religione diversa*' ('of a different religion'). The *Glossa interlinearis* ('Interlinear Gloss') of Anselm of Laon (d. 1117) and his students was commonly included in the annotated Bibles to which Soto (and Sepúlveda and Las Casas) would have had ready access. For an example, see *Biblia sacra cum Glossis, Interlineari & Ordinaria, Nicolai Lyrani Postilla & Moralitatibus, Burgensis Additionibus, & Thoringi Replicis* (Lyon: Trechsel, 1545), where Anselm of Laon's interlinear gloss on '*procul valde*' is at vol. 1, 353v.
[39] Deuteronomy 9:4.
[40] Deuteronomy 12:2–3.
[41] Genesis 19:24–25.
[42] Leviticus 26:30–31 (where the quoted Vulgate has *cadetis inter ruinas idolorum vestrorum*).
[43] Deuteronomy 7:1–2.

CONTAINED HEREIN IS A DEBATE OR DISPUTATION   243

he ordered war to be waged only against those Canaanites and the other six nations goes to show that these wars were not waged on grounds of idolatry alone
but rather on account of the promise he had made to Abraham. There is explicit
support for this idea in Deuteronomy Chapter 9—which the doctor cited in truncated form—where both motives are given together: '*it is because of the wickedness
of these nations [sc. the peoples of the Promised Land] that they have been destroyed
at your coming in, and in order to confirm the oath which the Lord swore to your fathers*'.[44] He also adduced in this connection that passage from Genesis 15, in which
God made the promise in question to Abraham, and in response to the latter's protestations over the length of time it would take for the promise to be fulfilled, God
himself replies: '*the wrongdoing of the Amorites is not yet complete*',[45] which serves
to prove that God granted those lands to the Jews on account of that promise,[46]
while at the same time biding his time to punish them for their sins. In support of
this, he [the bishop] adduced what God stipulated with regard to the other idolatrous gentiles in Deuteronomy 23: '*You shall not abhor an Edomite ... nor an
Egyptian, for you were a stranger in his land*'.[47]

He then proceeded to respond to the proof-text which the doctor adduced from
Deuteronomy 20,[48] pointing out that since the warfare at issue in that passage was
not waged against the inhabitants of the Promised Land but rather against those
who were '*far away*', as the text states, it could not be waged on grounds of idolatry alone if enmity did not exist between them for some other reason also. The
chapter in question opens as follows: '*When you go out to do battle against your
enemies*';[49] the idea being: either for obstructing the Jews' right of passage or else
for inflicting some other damage or harm upon them or their law. In support of
this, he adduces Nicholas [of Gorran][50] and seeks to make the point more plainly
still by means of appeal to El Tostado, in q. 1 of his discussion of that chapter [i.e.
of Deuteronomy 20][51] and in his discussion of Chapter 8 of the second book of

---

[44] Deuteronomy 9:5 (where the quoted Vulgate has *deletae* [mistranscribed as *delecte* in the 1552 edi-
tion] *sunt introeunte te*, for which phrase we have adapted the Douay–Rheims translation).

[45] Genesis 15:16.

[46] Tudela Bueso and Galmés expand the 1552 edition's 'pmissiõ' as 'permisión', but the manuscripts
(CS, 7r; MS, 212r) offer the surely correct *promissión* (as in the common phrase 'Tierra de Promisión',
'Promised Land').

[47] Deuteronomy 23:7.

[48] Deuteronomy 20:15.

[49] Deuteronomy 20:1.

[50] Nicholas of Gorran was a thirteenth-century French Dominican best known for his commentaries
on the Pauline Epistles and the Gospels. In countering Sepúlveda's claim that idolatrous societies were
proper objects of just war, Las Casas probably cited Gorran to the same effect that he did in his later
Latin *Apologia* (ch. 7: 38r = Poole trans., 63; ch. 8: 43v–44; Poole, 71), where he referred to Gorran's
commentary on 1 Corinthians 5:12–13 (in which Gorran also adduced Luke 12:13–14). Several versions of Gorran's Pauline commentary were in print: see, for example, *Postilla elucidativa et magistralis
super Epistolas Pauli* (Haguenau: Heinrich Gran, 1502), where his discussion of the Pauline passage in
question can be found on pp. m3–m3v.

[51] El Tostado (Alonso de Madrigal), *Commentaria in Deuteronomium*, ch. 20, q. 2 ('Offerre pacem, et
offerre pactum pacis, differunt, & quomodo').

Chronicles.[52] Accordingly, even though the gloss there takes those who were '*very far away*' as betokening those of a different religion,[53] it does not mean that war could be waged upon them for that reason alone, but rather it said '*far away*' in order to distinguish them from the seven nations of the Promised Land who were close at hand, for in the case of the latter there were to be no offerings of peace nor brokering of any pact; rather, all were to be slaughtered with no mercy whatsoever extended to any of them, and their temples were to be demolished, their idols smashed, and their farmsteads burnt down. And the explanation for this can be found in Chapters 7, 9, and 12 of Deuteronomy,[54] namely that, since the Jews were the holy temple of God and those lands were to be their dwelling place, no contaminating remnant of idolatry that might corrupt them was to be allowed to remain there. The same reason is also, as he pointed out, given by St Thomas in Book 4 of his [commentary on Peter Lombard's] *Sentences*, dist. 39.[55] When it came to the other gentiles, however, they were free to make peace with them and were not bound to extinguish their idolatry. Thus, he [Las Casas] is bent on demonstrating that the war against those of the Promised Land—in which none escaped with their lives—is not to be adduced as a parallel in this connection, and, by the same token, that warfare against other gentiles could not be waged on grounds of idolatry alone.

He next proceeded to address himself to the proof-texts which the doctor adduced at this point from Leviticus, in which God punished the Jews themselves for idolatry.[56] His answer here is that the only thing which follows from this is that those who have previously received the law of God but then subsequently become apostates or idolaters may rightly be punished. This, he said, is how one should take Nicholas of Lyra's exposition of Numbers 31, in which the latter says that the Holy Scripture offers precedent for waging just warfare upon lands in which God's name is blasphemed.[57] Furthermore, so as to demolish all the aforementioned proof-texts and examples adduced [by Sepúlveda] on this count, he [Las Casas] went on to point out that the examples of the Old Law are for us to admire but not to imitate in its cruel punishments, as originally asserted by St Gregory[58] and attested in the *Decretum*: 2, q. 7, Chap. *nos si*,[59] and in 22, q. 2, Chap. *si quis*,[60] as well as in 14, q. 5,

---

[52] El Tostado, *Commentaria in librum secundum Paralipomenon*, ch. 8, q. 5 ('On whether Solomon sinned in building within the land of Syria').

[53] See n. 38 above on this reference from the *Glossa interlinearis*.

[54] Deuteronomy 7:1–6; 9:1–5; 12:2–3.

[55] Aquinas, *Scriptum super libros Sententiarum Magistri Petri Lombardi*, Bk. 4, dist. 39, q. 1, art. 1. See Las Casas's fuller citation of this in ch. 13 of his Latin *Apologia* (69–69v; Poole, 108), where the text cited is rather different from later editions of Aquinas on the *Sentences*, but shows close similarities to the edition published by Nicholas Jenson in Venice in 1481 (*Super quarto libro Sententiarum Petri Lombardi*, fol. x5v–x6).

[56] Leviticus 26:27–33.

[57] Nicholas of Lyra on Numbers 31. The remarks in question can be found on pp. 318–20 of the 1545 Lyon glossed Bible (see n. 38 above).

[58] Gregory I ('the Great'), *Moralia in Iob*, Bk. 18. c. 3.

[59] Gratian, *Decretum*, C. 2, q. 7, c. 41 (citing a passage from a letter of Gregory IV).

[60] Gratian, *Decretum*, C. 22, q. 2, c. 19 (citing the passage from Gregory I, see n. 58.

CONTAINED HEREIN IS A DEBATE OR DISPUTATION 245

Chap. *Quid dominus*,[61] where it derives from St Augustine.[62] Anyone who wishes to follow this up there can do so. And so, in view of the above, he responded to the point about Sodom by saying that just because God in his inscrutable wisdom meted out that dire punishment does not mean it is lawful to wage war on account of that sin, for otherwise, by that logic, it would also be lawful to burn all cities containing innocent children, as was done in that instance.

(5) Secondly, still in the context of this same point, he addressed himself to that passage from St Luke 14 which gets used against him—'*Compel them to come in*'[63]—by expounding it in accordance with the interpretations of the saints, asserting that it is not to be taken as referring to external coercion by means of warfare but rather taking it in two senses. On the one hand, if taken with reference to every clan of people who are in sin and most especially to those gentiles who have never encountered the faith, it must refer to the form of internal compulsion which God himself inspires or else enacts by means of angelic intervention.

In support of this, he appealed to the authority of St Chrysostom in the *Incomplete Commentary*, Homily 41,[64] and also to St Thomas in the disputations *On Truth*, q. 22, art. 9, where he says that that parable '*is referring to the type of compulsion which is not duress but rather effective persuasion, be it by means harsh or gentle*'.[65] St Paul says the same thing in 2 Timothy 4: '*Preach the word; be ready in season and out of season; correct, rebuke, and exhort*';[66] and in the Epistle to Titus Chapter 2: '*rebuke with all authority*'.[67] And God says the same thing to the angels and prelates who are there to minister to us, as reported by Dionysius in the ninth chapter of the *Celestial Hierarchy*,[68] and by Jeremiah in Chapter ~~24~~ 23: '*Are my words not like fire and a hammer pulverizing rocks?*'.[69] And so at times through calamity, at others through miracles or by means of inspiration and at others again by words, God compels the stony-hearted by turns. It is for this reason that St Augustine says: '*It is a lucky necessity that compels to better things*';[70] and St Thomas in Part III, q. 44, art. 3, deals with this subject at length, noting that God '*through his divine power changes the minds of men not only by bestowing righteousness and by infusing wisdom, which pertains to miracles, but also by outwardly enticing men—or by terrifying and astonishing them*',[71] as can be quintessentially observed in the case

---

[61] Gratian, *Decretum*, C. 14, q. 5, c. 12.

[62] Augustine, *Quaestiones in Exodum*, q. 39 (in *Quaestionum in Heptateuchum libri septem*, Bk. 2).

[63] Luke 14:23.

[64] Pseudo-Chrysostom, *Opus imperfectum in Matthaeum*, Homily 41, c. 22.

[65] Aquinas, *Quaestiones disputatae. De veritate*, q. 22, art. 9, *ad* 7.

[66] 2 Timothy 4:2.

[67] Titus 2:15.

[68] Pseudo-Dionysius the Areopagite, *De caelesti hierarchia* (*On the Celestial Hierarchy*), c. 9.4.

[69] Jeremiah 23:29.

[70] Augustine, Letter 127.8.

[71] Aquinas, *ST* III, q. 44, art. 3, *ad* 1. The 1552 printer misread the *immutat* ('changes') of the manuscripts (CS, 9r; MS, 213v) as *invitat* ('invites'); the text of Aquinas has the perfect tense *immutavit*. Through haplography, the printer also elided the words rendered here as 'which pertains ... by terrifying' (*quod pertinet ad miracula, sed etiam alliciendo vel terrendo*), words present in both manuscripts.

246 SEPÚLVEDA ON THE SPANISH INVASION OF THE AMERICAS

of the conversion of St Paul and in that of Mary Magdalene and of St Matthew,[72] on account of which St Augustine in his discussion of John 14, remarks that it is a far greater feat to reform a sinner than to create heaven and earth.[73]

It follows, then, that '*compel them to come in*' is not a reference to warfare but to the boundless virtue of God in moving the stony hearts of men. And in this same regard Theophylact[74] and several other doctors in elucidating that parable say that the Jews were called softly, as befits people who were already inside the city—which is to say, people already initiated into knowledge of the law—whereas the gentiles were compelled, for they were on the outside, out on the wide roads of their own sins and in the hedges which serve to imprison them, for they were within them as if corralled and walled in.

The second exegesis of this passage which he subsequently adduced at a later point was drawn from St Augustine. In his writings against the Donatists St Augustine frequently stresses the difference between infidels who have never encountered the faith, and heretics, who did receive it but then abandoned it again:[75] the former must be summoned softly, for they cannot be compelled, since they never undertook to embrace the faith of their own free will (which is a necessary precondition to receiving it), whereas the latter did and thus can be—just as someone who never pledged to do something is consequently under no obligation, but, having made such a pledge, he is bound by it, in accordance with those words from Psalm 75 [76]: '*Make vows to the Lord your God*'.[76]

According to the theologians, the first term there is advisory and the latter a mandate. St Thomas draws this distinction in the *Secunda secundae*, q. 10, art. 8,[77] and it was also one of the resolutions of the Fourth Council of Toledo, as can be seen in the chapter *De Judeis*, dist. 45.[78] It is for this reason that St Augustine in his writings against the Donatists[79]—as can be seen in q. 23, Chap. 4, '*Displicet*' and several subsequent ones[80]—drew a distinction between two different phases of the church: one when the church was in its infancy and did not yet boast kings or populations powerful enough to compel the disobedient to the faith, and then a subsequent one in the wake of the fulfilment of the prophecy that '*all kings shall bow down before him*',[81] at whose hands this coercion can be accomplished.

---

[72] Acts 9:1–19; Luke 8:2 and Mark 16:9; Matthew 9:9–13.

[73] Augustine, *In Evangelium Ioannis Tractatus CXXIV, Tract.* 72, on John 14[:12].

[74] Theophylact, *Enarratio in evangelium S. Lucae*, ch. 14: 21–24.

[75] Augustine, Letter 173.10 (to Donatus); Letter 185.6–7 (to Boniface). See also Letter 76.4 (to the Donatists) and Letter 105.2–3 (to the Donatists).

[76] Psalm 76:11. NB. The 1552 printed text has Psalm 75, as do some modern editions (= 75:12), not in error but rather betokening an earlier psalmic numbering system.

[77] Aquinas, *ST* II-II, q. 10, art. 8.

[78] Fourth Council of Toledo, Canon 57, '*de iudaeis autem hoc praecepit*'. See also Gratian, *Decretum*, D. 45, c. 5.

[79] Augustine, Letter 173.10.

[80] Gratian, *Decretum*, C. 23, q. 4, c. 38.

[81] Psalm 72 (71):11.

CONTAINED HEREIN IS A DEBATE OR DISPUTATION   247

However, that the use of such coercion is to be taken as applying only to heretics can be expressly seen from his [sc. Augustine's] fiftieth letter, *To Boniface the Donatist*.[82] Boniface, together with all his fellow heretics, complained that they ought not to be compelled by the force of the law but by means of arguments and reasoning, and it is in this connection that he [sc. Augustine] is prompted to expound the difference as expressed in that parable from the Gospel, commenting as follows: '*Does it not pertain to a shepherd's care to call back to the Lord's fold, once they have been found, even those sheep that were not snatched away with violence but were led astray by seduction and gentleness, that wandered off from the flock and began to belong to others? Does he not have to call them back, even by the fear and pain of beatings, if they want to resist? He ought especially to do so if the sheep have multiplied through fertility among runaway slaves and thieves, because it is more just that the Lord's brand should be recognized on them ... For in that way the error of the sheep is to be corrected without destroying on it the mark of the redeemer.*'[83] The reference is plainly to heretics who '*have strayed from the flock, having been lured away*', and in this connection St Augustine further adduces that passage from St Paul, 2 Corinthians 10,[84] in which he [Paul] says that first of all, '*taking every thought captive to the obedience of Christ*',[85] men must pledge obedience to the church, and then goes on to add: '*And may you be ready to punish all disobedience, whenever your obedience is complete.*'[86] St Augustine takes this to mean that men cannot be punished for disobedience prior to having pledged any such obedience to the church, and so by way of conclusion he offers his interpretation of that parable from the Gospel, reasoning that those who were first called and gently brought in are the gentiles, while those who were compelled to come in from the roads and thickets are to be understood as referring to heretics.[87]

In this connection he [Las Casas] invoked not only the theologians but also Innocent [IV], that pre-eminent doctor among the canonists, who commenting on the chapter opening with the words '*Maiores*' (from the title '*De baptismo et eius effectu*') offers the following with regard to the phrase in question: '*Let them not compel*', he says, '*so that nobody ever finds themselves forced to become a Christian under duress. The fact that the servant is told to compel the guests to come in to the wedding is no bar to this, for what is meant there is compulsion in the form of persistent use of reasoning, not by the severity of any physical sword or by means of temporal violence, for the use of the physical sword is forbidden to that servant, which is*

---

[82] Augustine, Letter 185 [formerly Letter 50]. Contrary to Soto's formulation here, this Boniface was not, in fact, a Donatist but a general (and orthodox Catholic) charged with dealing with recalcitrant Donatists in Africa.

[83] Augustine, Letter 185.6.23. We have adopted here the translation of Roland Teske, S. J., in *The Works of Saint Augustine: A Translation for the 21st Century: Part II: Letters, Vol. 3* (Hyde Park: New City Press, 1997), 193.

[84] Augustine, Letter 185.6.24.

[85] 2 Corinthians 10:5.

[86] 2 Corinthians 10:6.

[87] Luke 14:15–24.

248   SEPÚLVEDA ON THE SPANISH INVASION OF THE AMERICAS

to say, the Order of Preachers [i.e. the Dominican Order], *or to the Apostles in the person of St Peter and the Lord*.[88] And adding a further consideration, he [Innocent IV] says that it can also be taken to mean that '*Jews and others like them who lack the faith are not to be forced to the faith by means of the physical sword but rather be brought in through the efficacy of reasoning; but those who have turned away from the bosom of the church, such as heretics and schismatics, are to be forced to return to it by secular powers if need be, since they belong to the forum of the church.*'

(6) The third point he derived from this[89] was a demonstration of the falsity of his opponents' contention that, in the days of some of the saints, the emperors waged war upon the gentiles on the recommendation of the saints so as to rid them of their idolatry and bring them to the faith.

He began by showing this to be untrue of the time of Constantine and of St Sylvester, as can be seen in Book 10, Chapter 6 8, of the *Ecclesiastical History*: '*Trusting in his piety, he subdued by means of his own weapons alone the Goths, Sarmatians, and other barbarian nations, unless they had been pacified either through friendly dealings or else spontaneous capitulation. The more religiously he surrendered himself to God, the more God brought all things under his power*.'[90] This is not to be taken to mean that those wars were waged against them for that reason but rather on account of the fact that the Goths were marauding around the world harassing people, and whenever they made peace with Christians—as is noted at an earlier point in the *History*[91]—war was not waged upon them, even

---

[88] This italicized passage and the next translated passage are from the comments of Innocent IV on a letter by Innocent III to the Archbishop of Arles included in Gregory IX's *Decretals* at X.3.42.3. Las Casas cited these same passages in his *Apologia*, in chapters 48 (208; Poole, 300) and 50 (214v–215; Poole, 310). Las Casas probably found the comments of Innocent IV in a glossed edition of the *Decretals*, but there were also several editions offering his commentary separately. For example, in the 1548 Lyon edition of Hugues de la Porte (*Sanctissimi in Christo patris D. Innocentii Papae IIII Apparatus toto orbe celebrandus super V. Libris Decretalium*), these passages are on pp. 173–173v. Note that the text of the citations from Innocent IV offered in the *Apologia* differs in a few points of (minor) detail from the one cited by Soto here; in all cases, the one in the *Apologia* corresponds more precisely to the original wording of Innocent IV.

[89] The 1552 edition offers: '*El tercero punto que derribó de aquí fue ...*' ('The third point he demolished from here was ...'). But both manuscripts (CS, 11r; MS, 215r) give the correct *derivó* ('derived', 'deduced').

[90] This passage is not (as usually assumed) from Eusebius's *Ecclesiastical History*, but from the Latin continuation appended by Rufinus of Aquileia to his free translation of Eusebius in the first years of the fifth century. Rufinus eliminated or otherwise redistributed most of Eusebius's tenth and final book and numbered his continuation as Bks. 10 and 11; this passage, then, is in ch. 8 of Bk. 10 of Rufinus's continuation. See also the beginning of Bk. 44 of Las Casas's *Apologia* for his use of this passage (193v–194; Poole, 279). Las Casas was most likely using the frequently reprinted *Autores Historiae Ecclesiasticae* edited by Beatus Rhenanus and first printed by Johann Froben in Basel in 1523 (where it appears on p. 224). This volume also included the *Tripartite History*; see next note.

[91] Partly due to his radical abridgement of Las Casas's points, Soto failed to make it clear that the 'history' to which Las Casas was referring here was not Rufinus's continuation of Eusebius's *Ecclesiastical History*, but the so-called *Historia Tripartita*: Bk. 1, ch. 9 (p. 274 in the 1523 edition of the *Autores Historiae Ecclesiasticae*)—cf. Las Casas, *Apologia*, ch. 44 (194; Poole, 280). The *Tripartite History* was a sixth-century Latin translation, supervised by Cassiodorus and mainly composed by Ephiphanius Scholasticus, of the work of three early Byzantine church historians: Theodoret of Cyrus, Socrates Scholasticus, and Sozomen (the author of the passage in question).

CONTAINED HEREIN IS A DEBATE OR DISPUTATION   249

if they persisted in their idolatry. Orosius in Book 7 [sc. of his own *History*] attests to the fact that the Goths would sometimes wage war upon the Romans,[92] as does St Augustine in his letter to Heliodorus.[93] The same goes for the Sarmatians, who like the Goths were also Scythians and at one time were even more Arian than the Goths themselves—as recounted in the aforementioned *Tripartite History*[94]—from which it followed that war could be waged against them. And thus he concluded that St Sylvester never endorsed this kind of warfare on religious grounds,[95] for war entails so many evils at variance with the object of the faith; his method, rather, was to grant temporal rewards to the infidels so as to induce them to convert (as can be seen in his history and in the chapter *Quam pio*, ~~10~~ 1, q. 2),[96] recognizing that warfare would inspire the gentiles with hatred for Christians and their faith and their law, prompting them sooner to curse and spit at them than to embrace their faith.

At this juncture he [sc. Las Casas] included other proof-texts from the Gospel and from St Chrysostom which were more germane to Dr Sepúlveda's third point.[97] Let us move on, then, to the other material which Las Casas draws from St Gregory, whom both the adversaries also cite for their own purposes.[98]

What our esteemed bishop said here was that, although powerful Christian emperors did indeed exist in St Gregory's day, the latter never advised them to engage

[92] Orosius, *Historiae adversus paganos*, Bk. 7, ch. 37–39, as cited in Las Casas, *Apologia*, ch. 44 (194v; Poole, 281), with particular reference to Alaric's sack of Rome in 410 (ch. 39). An edition likely available to Las Casas would have been that of Gottfried Hittorp of Köln, first published in 1526 and several times reprinted thereafter.

[93] Jerome (not Augustine), Letter 60, written to Heliodorus in 397 (not, as Brufau Prats claimed, Letter 14, written to Heliodorus in 373 or 374). Soto's confusion of Augustine for Jerome probably derives from the fact that Las Casas's manuscript had paired this reference with one from Augustine (*CD* 5.23).

[94] Cassiodorus and Epiphanius Scholasticus, *Tripartite History*, Bk. 8, ch. 13 (from Theodoret and Socrates: see n. 91 above). This passage does not, in fact, offer support for the notion that the Sarmatians were worse Arians than the Goths, nor did Las Casas claim that it did (see *Apologia*, Bk. 44, 195; Poole, 281). He simply offered it in support of the Arianism of the Goths. In the 1523 first edition of the *Autores Historiae Ecclesiasticae*, this chapter is pp. 537–39.

[95] For a fuller version of Las Casas's claim that Pope Sylvester I (who was pontiff when Constantine converted to Christianity) favoured peaceful means of spreading the faith, see Las Casas, *Apologia*, ch. 44 (195v–196v; Poole, 282–83). The reference to Sylvester's 'history' seems to be to the *Actus Silvestri*, a fanciful account of this rather obscure pope, parts of which may date back to the fourth century. Las Casas and Soto would have known it through the *Sanctuarium sive Vitae Sanctorum* of Bonino Mombrizio (Mombritius), first published in 1477 and frequently reprinted. Towards the end of this work, Sylvester's triumph over a pestilential dragon infesting the city of Rome ensured the baptism of scores of thousands.

[96] Gratian, *Decretum*, C. 1, q. 2, c. 2. Both manuscripts (*CS*, 11v; *MS*, 215v) correctly give the number of the causa as 1.

[97] As is clear from ch. 44 of Las Casas's *Apologia* (196v–197v; Poole, 283–84), Las Casas referred to Matthew 5:16 and a passage from the commentary on it by Pseudo-Chrysostom in *Opus imperfectum in Matthaeum*, Homily 10 (available in Froben's 1530 Basel edition of Chrysostom, vol. 2, p. 536–37). Las Casas also quoted from another passage that he identified as from the fifteenth of the genuine Chrysostom's *Opus perfectum* homilies on Matthew; but most of the passage in question is in fact from (genuine?) Chrysostom's Homily 72 on the Gospel of John in the translation of Burgundio of Pisa (1173), which has remained unpublished to this day; but Las Casas must somehow have had sight of the latter's translation. Nowadays the text may be viewed thanks to the *Chrysostomus Latinus in Iohannem Online* (CLIO) website, where the passage in question is at 72.3.12–15.

[98] That is, Gregory I, pope from 590 to 604.

250 SEPÚLVEDA ON THE SPANISH INVASION OF THE AMERICAS

in warfare of this kind, for, had he done so, there would be some record of it. And in the case of England he did not send armed forces but rather Augustine in the company of forty fellow monks,[99] like sheep among wolves, as the Gospel prescribes.[100] This is reported in the *History of England*, Book 1, chapter 25, composed by Bede as well as in other histories, and in the chapter '*Si gene gens*', dist. 56.[101] And the prayer they offered up whenever they made their way in among the heathens was: 'Lord, we beg you in all your mercy to see fit to lift your wrath and ire from this city and from your holy house, for we have sinned against you. Hallelujah.'[102] This is what Bede reports,[103] as does ~~James~~ Paul the Deacon in his own *History*;[104] and so too does Augustine himself in Book 9, Epistle ~~54~~ 58, in St Gregory's Register [sc. of Letters].[105]

And at this juncture he [Las Casas] offered his rejoinder to those who press the selfsame St Gregory into the service of the opposite position on the basis of the chapter '*Si non*', 23, q. 4,[106] in which St Gregory praises the wars waged by Gennadius the Patrician in order to spread the faith, for Las Casas says that those wars were waged upon subjects of the Roman empire or else against enemies of Rome who obstructed and reviled the faith. The passage in question reads: '*Is there*

[99] This Augustine was not of course the Augustine of Hippo so often cited in this debate, but the monk sent by Pope Gregory I to evangelize England, a peaceful process seized on by Las Casas as a model. He went on to become the first Archbishop of Canterbury.

[100] Matthew 10:16.

[101] Bede, *Historia ecclesiastica gentis Anglorum* 1.25; Gratian, *Decretum*, D. 56, c. 10—though in fact this reference to Gratian is quite irrelevant for, though it does open 'Si gens Anglorum ...', there is no discussion in it of Augustine's activities in England (see n. 99 above). The 1552 edition prints the incipit as '*si gene*', which Galmés altered to '*si genes*'. The manuscripts offer the correct '*Si gens*' (CS, 11v; MS, 214r).

[102] The 1552 edition offers a Spanish version close to the prayer Bede placed at the end of 1.25 of his history. The manuscripts (CS, 11v–12r; MS, 216r) offer a somewhat different version: 'Lord, you who created and redeemed these souls, may it please you to lift your wrath from them, so that piety and mercy may enter in along with us.'

[103] Bede, *Historia ecclesiastica gentis Anglorum* 1.23–25.

[104] Paul the Deacon [Paulus Diaconus] indeed mentions Gregory's sending of Augustine to England in his *History of the Lombards* (*Historia Langobardorum*) 3.25, a passage to which Las Casas also refers again in ch. 48 of his *Apologia* (207v; Poole, 300n1); though Paul's fuller account of the Gregorian mission is in fact that in §22 of his *Life of Gregory* (see *PL*, vol. 75, cols. 51–52) The erroneous reference in Soto's text to 'James' ('Juannes') rather than 'Paul' may have arisen from the fact that a Roman missionary later to be known as James the Deacon did also participate in the Gregorian mission to England, overlapping in lifetime with Bede, who indeed refers to him in his *Historia ecclesiastica* (most substantially at 2.20). However, this James the Deacon is not known to have left any writings, or at least none now extant, whereas Paul the Deacon did produce a *History* containing the promised reference; and the error is not in Las Casas's corresponding discussion of this in the *Apologia*.

[105] Gregory I, Letter 11.28 (in *PL* 77, cols. 1138–41) = Norberg 11.36. This corresponds to what used to be known as Letter 58 of Bk. 9, cited as such by Las Casas in the *Apologia* (ch. 48, 207v; Poole, 300), here miscopied by the 1552 typesetter as Letter 54 (the manuscripts give the correct number: CS, 12r; MS, 216r). For this letter in this earlier numeration system (Bk. 9, letter 58), see, for example, the 1550 Basel edition of Froben (*Gregorii Papae Operum Secundus Tomus*, cols. 1082–84). In it, Gregory congratulates Augustine on his missionary success, but warns him not to take undue credit for miracles he is reputed to have wrought.

[106] Gratian, *Decretum*, C. 23, q. 4, c. 49, citing a substantial portion of Gregory I's letter to Gennadius: see next note.

CONTAINED HEREIN IS A DEBATE OR DISPUTATION 251

anywhere to which the voluble reputation of your merits does not extend, conveying how you keep seeking to undertake wars not in the interests of shedding blood but purely for the sake of amplifying the republic in which we see God worshipped with a view to having Christ's name spread in all possible directions among subject peoples by means of preaching.[107]

(7) The fourth point by means of which he [Las Casas] demonstrates that such peoples cannot be punished on the basis of their idolatry is because they do not fall within the forum of the church, in which connection he expounded that passage from St Paul, 1 Corinthians 5, which runs: '*For what business of mine is it to judge those who are outside? Is it not those inside the church whom you are to judge? But those who are outside, God shall judge.*'[108] He took these words as indicative of the stance that all of humanity is subject to Christ *qua* man *in potentia*, but not *in actu*. This means that Jesus Christ *qua* man did not wish to assume complete temporal power over all humans *in actu* (a power which he most certainly does wield in his capacity as God) for the purposes of anything other than preaching and instructing them in the faith; however, this did not extend to exercising jurisdiction over them until they were within the church, whose door and entryway is through the faith. He thus holds power both *in habitu* and *in potentia* over as many potential Christians as there are in the world, but he does not possess it *in actu* until such time as they actually become Christians. For God has reserved to himself alone the right to punish those who are not Christians, as St Paul notes in that very passage: '*those who are outside, God shall judge.*'[109] And since the church does not possess any more power than Jesus Christ himself wielded as a man, any attempt on the part of the church to become involved in meting out punishments for the sins of gentiles would be an affront to God, usurping the judgment which he has reserved for himself on Judgment Day, whereupon Jesus Christ will exercise his universal power over the good and the bad, faithful and unfaithful alike, as St Paul teaches in his Epistle to the Hebrews, Chapter 2: '*For in subjecting all things to him, he left nothing that is not subject to him,*'[110] denoting power *in habitu*; and it continues as follows: '*But now we do not yet see all things subjected to him,*'[111] which is a reference to power *in actu*. Clearer still is 1 Corinthians 15: '*All things are subject to him, manifestly excluding the one who made all things subject to him,*'[112] by which power *in habitu* is meant; and then with regard to power *in actu* it goes on: '*When all things are subject to him, then the Son himself will also be subjected to*

---

[107] The letter in question is Gregory to Gennadius, Letter 1.73 Norberg (1.75 in *PL* 77), the bulk of which is cited in Gratian's *Decretum*, as per the previous note.

[108] 1 Corinthians 5:12–13.

[109] 1 Corinthians 5:13.

[110] Hebrews 2:8. The 1552 edition omitted the words *non subjectum ei*, which are present in the manuscripts (*CS*, 12v; *MS*, 216v).

[111] Hebrews 2:8.

[112] 1 Corinthians 15:27.

252 SEPÚLVEDA ON THE SPANISH INVASION OF THE AMERICAS

him'[113]—i.e. *to the Father*, meaning on Judgment Day. St Thomas explains the distinction in Part III, q. 8, art. 3, and in q. 59, art. 4,[114] where he says that infidels '*do not belong to the church* in actu [*actually*] *but* in potentia [*potentially*]',[115] and this is true both of Christ—whose virtue extends to the salvation of all men—and also of humans, who are able to come to the church of their own volition.

He cited many saints commenting on those words, including Athanasius, who, ventriloquizing the stance of St Paul at that moment, says: '*I am now most certainly not addressing those who are outsiders, for that would go beyond my rights. Therefore it would be futile for me to enjoin Christ's teachings on those who wander outside Christ's court. For whatever the law pronounces, it pronounces only for those who are under the law*.'[116] He also adduced one of Christ's own statements in Luke 12: '*Man, who appointed me a judge or arbitrator over you?*',[117] whereby our Redeemer was clearly signalling that the people in question were not under his jurisdiction. And, commenting on the same passage, Richard of Middleton observes in Book 4, dist. ~~1~~ 7 that: '*The vicar of Christ was not granted direct power over those who had **not** received the sacrament of baptism, which is the door through which the church militant is entered*.'[118] And St Thomas in the *Secunda secundae*, q. ~~10~~ 12, appeals to the same passage as his proof-text for the idea that the church is not in a position to punish the infidelity of those who have never received the faith.[119]

He [Las Casas] drew this item to a close with a notable proof-text from St Augustine's sixth sermon, '*On the centurion's slave-boy*'[120] (from his sermon

[113] 1 Corinthians 15:28.

[114] Aquinas, *ST* III, q. 8, art. 3, ad 1, and q. 59, art. 4, ad 1.

[115] Aquinas, *ST* III, q. 8, art. 3, ad 2.

[116] Pseudo-Athanasius of Alexandria, *On 1 Corinthians*. This is from a Latin commentary on the Pauline Epistles that turned up in Rome in 1477, purporting to have been translated from Athanasius, fourth-century Patriarch of Alexandria. Erasmus, however, correctly identified it as a translation of the Byzantine–Bulgarian theologian and archbishop Theophylact of Ochrid, and it subsequently began to be printed correctly as such. However, it also sometimes continued to be printed as the work of Athanasius, which appears to be the form in which Las Casas (and Soto?) knew it, as for instance in the edition of his *Opera omnia* published in Lyon by Mechior and Gaspar Trechsel in 1532, where the passage appears on fol. 40v. The 1552 typesetter twice mistranscribed *disserit* as *deserit*; the manuscripts offer the correct reading (CS, 13r; MS, 217r). Las Casas cited this passage in ch. 7 of his Latin *Apologia* (38; Poole, 63).

[117] Luke 12:14.

[118] Richard of Middleto(w)n [Ricardus de Mediavilla], *Super quattuor libros sententiarum Petri Lombardi quaestiones subtilissimae* ... , vol. 4, book 4, dist. 7 (on baptism), art. 2, q. 2. Las Casas cited Richard of Middleton's commentary on the fourth book of Peter Lombard's *Sentences* at *Apologia*, ch. 7 (38; Poole, 64), giving the citation as 'distinctione 7, a. 2, q. 2'. The text as printed in 1552 misidentifies the number of the *distinctio* (as do both manuscripts: CS, 13r; MS, 217r) and omits the crucial *non* before *susceperunt*, which is present in both manuscripts.

[119] Aquinas, *ST* II-II, q. 12, art. 2. The 1552 edition has 'questión décima' here, as do both manuscripts (CS, 13r; MS, 217r), where 'duodécima' was intended, as noted by marginal corrections in several copies. Las Casas referred to this Aquinian passage in ch. 7 of the *Apologia* (39; Poole, 64).

[120] Augustine, *Sermones ad populum*, Sermon 62—though in the sixteenth century this would have been known as one of Augstine's *Sermones de Verbis Domini*, of which it was Sermon 6, as per Soto's reference here; and Las Casas refers to it at length in the *Apologia* in ch. 7 (39–40; Poole, 65–66), likewise citing it as 'Liber de Verbis Domini, Sermone 6'. The tale of the centurion's slave-boy [*De puero centurionis*] discussed here can be found in Matthew 8:5–13 and Luke 7:1–10.

series '*On the words of the Lord*'), featuring remarks germane to this very subject: '*Brothers, it is for us to speak to you, and for you to speak to Christians. For what business is it of mine to judge those who are outside, as the Apostle himself says with reference to those people, meaning pagans. To the latter we address ourselves somewhat differently, as if they were ill; they must be dealt with gently in order to get them to hear the truth. In your case, on the other hand, the rot must be cut out.*'[121] The difference is clearly delineated: gentiles are to be enticed with blandishments, whereas in Christians the rot must be excised by force.[122] And it goes on: '*Do you seek to know how the pagans may be defeated, how they may achieve illumination, how they may be summoned to salvation? Forsake all their rites, turn your backs on their nonsense, and if they do not subscribe to our truth, let them be ashamed of their own falsehood.*'[123] St Augustine thus sets out the means of winning over the pagans, namely not by force but by shunning their company so that they feel ashamed.

And since there were those who dared to go and destroy the idols of the gentiles, he adds: '*Do not engage in these practices when it is not in your power to do so. To go into a frenzy and seek to die in situations where they are powerless is characteristic of wicked men, fanatics, and Circumcellions.*'[124] The reference to 'Circumcellions' is an allusion to those who needlessly offered themselves up to be killed by the pagans so as to be hailed as martyrs. And he appeals to that passage from Deuteronomy 7, where it says: '*When that land comes into your possession ... then you shall tear down their altars.*'[125] And St Augustine says the following: '*Where power has not been granted to us, we do not act*' (as in the case of the gentiles); '*where it is granted, we forbid*' (as with wicked Christian idolaters).[126]

And lest anyone imagine that he is alluding to circumstances in which *de facto* power is lacking, he clarifies that he is speaking purely in terms of the situation *de jure*: '*There are many pagans who harbour these abominations on their own estates. Does it follow, then, that we are to go there and smash them up? We should first, rather, see to it that we smash up the idols in their hearts. Upon becoming Christians, they themselves will either invite us to come and perform so fine a task or else they will beat us to it. For now we should simply pray for them, not lose our tempers with them.*'[127] And further along: '*Are there not places containing idols right under our noses? Or do we really not know where such places are?*'[128] The implication being: we know full well where the idols are, '*and yet we refrain from taking action, for God*

---

[121] Augustine, *Sermones ad populum*, Sermon 62, 7.11.

[122] Reading *cortar* with the manuscripts for the 1552 edition's *quitar*.

[123] Augustine, *Sermones ad populum*, Sermon 62, 7.11.

[124] Augustine, *Sermones ad populum*, Sermon 62, 11.17.

[125] Deuteronomy 7:1, 5. (The Latin corresponding to Deuteronomy 7:1 is quite paraphrased in Soto's text here and so, therefore, is my translation.)

[126] Augustine, *Sermones ad populum*, Sermon 62, 11.17.

[127] Augustine, *Sermones ad populum*, Sermon 62, 11.17.

[128] Augustine, *Sermones ad populum*, Sermon 62, 12.18.

254 SEPÚLVEDA ON THE SPANISH INVASION OF THE AMERICAS

has not given us the power to do so. When will God give us the power to take action? When the owner of the object in question becomes Christian.[129]

St Augustine expands on this point of the argument at length in order to underscore the idea that Christians do not have the authority to quash or punish the idolatry of the unfaithful, in accordance with the words of St Paul—'*those who are outside are none of my business*'[130]—unless it has first been wrenched from their hearts through gospel teaching,[131] thereby bringing them under our jurisdiction by means of the faith. And the esteemed bishop corroborates this view with reference to the selfsame St Paul, who first enumerates all the monstrosities and vices of the gentiles, among which he includes idolatry,[132] and, working his way through all the other sins, he notes: '*For what business of mine is it to judge those who are outside?*'[133] To round things off, he [Las Casas] also appealed to the example of the Apostles and martyrs, for there is no record of any of them ever having destroyed idols by any means other than teaching—as in Acts ~~15~~ 17 when St Paul convinced Dionysius of the falsity of his idol by reasoning alone[134]—or miracles, as when St Bartholomew made the Devil himself emerge from his own statue and destroy it.[135]

And just as we cannot rid them of their idolatry, so too by the same token does he [Las Casas] say that we cannot punish them for it either, for it falls outside our sphere of jurisdiction. And the overarching reason he offered for all this was that, since human beings cannot live without a deity of some kind or other, we cannot forbid them to worship their gods without first instructing them in the falsity thereof and of the truth of our own true God.

So it was by means of these four points that he countered Dr Sepúlveda's first line of reasoning whereby the latter set out to demonstrate by the authority and precedent of the Holy Scripture that war may be waged against gentiles by reason of their idolatry. He added up to twelve further arguments: their main substance is all encapsulated in the points already made against Sepúlveda's other assertion, which centred on the severity of those sins in that they go against nature.

(8) Sepúlveda himself formulated the terms of the problem as follows: All sins go against nature, for they are contrary to reason, which is tantamount to being against human nature. From this it follows that, if war could be waged against

---

[129] Augustine, *Sermones ad populum*, Sermon 62, 12.18.

[130] Paraphrasing 1 Corinthians 5:12.

[131] The 1552 edition reads 'para la doctrina evangélica' here, but the manuscripts correctly offer 'por' (*CS*, 14r; *MS*, 218r).

[132] For the 1552 text ('entre los quales pone la idolatría'), the manuscripts offer words based on 1 Corinthians 5:11: 'Si quis fuerit scortator aut avarus aut simulacrorum cultor' (*CS*, 14r; *MS*, 218r).

[133] 1 Corinthians 5:12.

[134] Acts 17:34, referring to Dionysius the Areopagite. In the corresponding passage in ch. 7 of the *Apologia* (41v; Poole, 68), Las Casas claims that the converted Dionysius began to destroy pagan statues. His source for this is not clear.

[135] This reference to Bartholomew inducing a devil to step out of his statue and destroy it can be traced to a story about Bartholomew in India, told by Jacopo de Voragine in ch. 123 of the *Golden Legend*. It is not mentioned by Las Casas in the *Apologia*.

CONTAINED HEREIN IS A DEBATE OR DISPUTATION   255

them on grounds of idolatry, it could also be waged on account of other sins such as theft and adultery. He then answered by saying that, even if war could not in fact be waged on them on account of the latter, it nevertheless could still be waged against them for those sins which they do not hold to be sins and which no law of theirs prohibits. The esteemed bishop countered that lack of faith, which they do not deem a sin but rather something lawful and good, is a greater sin than idolatry and all the same they cannot be punished for their faithlessness, a point which Dr Sepúlveda himself concedes and which is expressly stipulated in the teachings of St Thomas in the *Secunda secundae*, q. 10, art. 8, and q. 12, art. 2,[136] and in those of all other theologians.

And in support of the idea that faithlessness is the greater sin he pointed out that idolatry stems from the misapprehension of believing those gods to be gods, as noted by St Paul in Acts 17: '*Therefore, what you worship in ignorance, this I proclaim to you.*'[137] By contrast, active faithlessness, which is the sort of faithlessness at issue here, is born of arrogance—of not wishing to yield to the teachings of the preachers of the truth, '*taking every thought captive*' (as St Paul says) '*to the obedience of Christ*'[138]—and is done wilfully and out of sheer obstinacy, all of which renders the sin of faithlessness substantially worse. It is for this reason that St Thomas in the *Secunda secundae*, q. 10, says that when Judgment Day comes the sin of faithlessness shall be most severely punished above all others.[139]

(9) In response to the third line of reasoning—which came second in the scheme of Sepúlveda's discussion—based on the authority of the canonists who seem to suggest that war against idolatrous infidels is lawful, the esteemed bishop proceeded to list six sets of circumstances under which the church has the authority to wage war against such people. He said that the views of the canonists held true only insofar as they pertained to those scenarios.

The first is in instances where infidels have violently usurped lands formerly belonging to Christians, as is the case with the Berber region and especially the Holy Land. Conquest of this sort is discussed in the chapter *Quod super his* of the title *De voto*.[140] It is therefore of such lands that we must understand those learned men to be speaking when they say that their idolatry can be punished.

The second is in cases where their sin takes the form of besmirching and polluting our faith, sacraments, temples, or icons by means of gross acts of idolatry; it was for this reason that Constantine forbade the gentiles to have idols in

---

[136] Aquinas, *ST* II-II, q. 10, art. 8, co., and q. 12, art. 2, co. In the manuscripts, only the first passage from Aquinas is cited. The words 'lo qual concede el mismo doctor Sepúlveda' are found in both manuscripts (*CS*, 15r; *MS*, 218r), but omitted by the 1552 printer.

[137] Acts 17:23.

[138] 2 Corinthians 10:5.

[139] Aquinas, *ST* II-II, q. 10, art. 3, ad 3.

[140] '*Quod super his*' is a letter by Innocent III, of which the text is included in X.3.34.8; but in fact, as also in the scenario in n. 50 in our translation of Sepúlveda's *Apologia*, the reference here is not to the letter itself but to commentary on it by Innocent IV.

places where they might constitute a source of outrage to Christians.[141] And in the chapter '*in nonnullis*' of the title '*De Judeis*',[142] we are admonished: '*We should not turn a blind eye to ignominy done to him who destroyed ignominies for our sake.*' And Innocent [IV], commenting on the chapter *Maiores* in the title *De baptismo*[143] likewise says that the church may not wage war against either the Moors or the Saracens except in either of the two aforementioned circumstances, although the esteemed bishop does not concur with Innocent [IV] that God's punishment of the Sodomites serves as a precedent for punishing infidels for all their vices against nature, for he says that the will of God (as mentioned above) should constitute a source of wonder, not emulation.

The third case is when the name of Christ or of the saints or of the church is deliberately taken in vain.

The fourth is if, again on purpose, they obstruct the preaching of the faith, knowing full well what it is that they are impeding. The same does not, however, go for cases in which they kill preachers in the belief that they are coming to do them harm and deceive them, which is the impression the preachers give when they keep company with military men.

The fifth case is if they wage war against us, as the Turks do.

The sixth is in order to save the innocent, albeit not *because* '*everyone has been given a commandment concerning their neighbour*'[144] nor on account of their sins against natural law, but rather because the innocent have been entrusted to the church by divine law and it is for the church to see to their protection. He added, however, that if this defence cannot be accomplished by any means other than war then it is better to turn a blind eye to this obligation to protect, for, of two evils, the lesser one must be chosen; and the harm which befalls large numbers of innocents as a consequence of warfare far outweighs the evil of having a few innocents die. The views of the canonists, he said, were to be taken with reference to the aforementioned sets of circumstances.

This marked the end of his complete response to Dr Sepúlveda's first line of argument about war being wageable against them on account of their idolatry and

---

[141] Eusebius of Caesarea, *Life of Constantine* (*De vita beatissimi imperatoris Constantini*) 2.45 and 4.23–25. The evidence for actual Constantinian legislation of this sort is ambiguous and contested. See further n. 67 in our translation of Sepúlveda's *Apologia*. Interestingly, this second point in Soto's summary of Las Casas's refutation of Sepúlveda's claim is the only one that doesn't match up with the account Las Casas gave in his *Apologia*, where the second point concerns the practice of idolatry in territories taken by heathens from Christians, and is, moreover, given by far the largest amount of space in the *Apologia*: chs. 15–24.

[142] The reference is to a letter of Innocent III's (not, this time, to Innocent IV's commentary on it), included in X.5.6.15.

[143] As in n. 88 above, this is again a reference to Innocent IV's commentary on Innocent III's letter ('*Maiores*') to the Archbishop of Arles. It can be found on fols. 174–174v of Jean Moylin de Cambrai's 1535 Lyon edition of Innocent IV's commentary, with the reference to not attempting to convert the Saracens by means of war at 174v, §5.

[144] Ecclesiasticus [Sirach] 17:12 (mildly paraphrased: the original reads 'et **mandavit** illis unicuique', i.e. '**He** [God] **gave** them each . . .', i.e. active rather than passive construction).

CONTAINED HEREIN IS A DEBATE OR DISPUTATION   257

crimes against nature, which he had founded on three grounds, namely on the authority of the canonists and by virtue of the gravity of the sins in question.[145]

(10) The doctor's second line of reasoning was that the Indians are barbarians *and slaves by nature*, to which the esteemed bishop addressed himself at the end of his writings, and so we shall follow his sequence and first deal with his response to the doctor's third line of argument, namely that it is lawful to subjugate them by means of war in the interests of the faith, in which they can be more easily instructed after having been quelled. The bishop did not respond to this point merely in one discrete section nor in those exact terms: instead, all his writings are littered with arguments pertaining to this. These all boil down to two or three main points.

The first is that, given that the faith cannot be made evident by means of natural reasoning but rather through the surrender of the intellect (as St Paul says: '*in his service*'),[146] those who are to receive the faith must be piously well-disposed (as St Thomas says)[147] towards those who come to bring and preach it, so that the example of the lives of the latter may serve to attest to the true God, whom they serve, and of the truth of the faith they preach, which will make the former more readily inclined to believe it. Wars undertaken with a view to subjugating them prior to preaching are at odds with all this and mean that they will not only fail to grow fond of the Christians but, on the contrary, that they will despise them, spit upon the God who abides such people and abhor the law which permits such behaviour, leading them to deem the faith that they preach false (as the esteemed bishop says that first-hand experience of the Indies has shown to be the case).

In support of this point—albeit not at this juncture but rather in the section in which he dealt with St Sylvester[148]—he first adduced that testimony of Our Saviour Jesus Christ from Matthew 5: '*Let your light shine before people in such a way that they may see your good works and glorify your Father who is in heaven.*'[149] In the ~~1st~~ 10th homily of his *Incomplete Commentary*, St Chrysostom comments with regard to that passage: '*God is glorified by those who both teach and act, but he is blasphemed by those who do not practise what they preach; for if they teach good things and live even more admirably, the gentiles will see this and say, "Blessed is the God who has such servants: for truly theirs is the true God, since, if he himself were not just, he would never keep his followers so close to justice". For the discipline of a master is evident from the behaviour of his household. If, however, they teach good*

---

[145] In fact, Soto mentions only two of Sepúlveda's *tres maneras* of supporting his contention that idolatry justifies wars of conquest; he omits the supposed scriptural authorization. Neither manuscript supplies this element (CS, 16r; MS, 219v), so it is not a slip by the 1552 typesetter. Brufau Prats's edition (p. 220) does offer an additional phrase after *tres maneras: y por la protecion de los inocentes.* Not only does this fail to supply the missing *manera*, it also seems intrusive in this sentence. Presumably Brufau Prats imported it into his text from a marginal notation—and at least one copy does in fact have those words in the margin in an early hand.

[146] 2 Corinthians 10:5.

[147] Aquinas, *ST* II-II, q. 10, art. 11.

[148] See n. 95 above on St Sylvester.

[149] Matthew 5:16.

things but conduct themselves badly, upon seeing this the gentiles will say: "What manner of God is this if his people behave in this manner? Surely he would not tolerate the nature of their behaviour if he were not in favour of their actions?" So you see how God is profaned by bad Christians, just as a master cannot have a good reputation if his household is found wanting.[150] St Chrysostom concludes his discussion of this with a proof-text from St Paul in his Epistle to the Romans, Chapter 2, where the people of God are addressed: *'For the name of God is blasphemed among the gentiles because of you.'*[151]

St Augustine expresses the same view in his book 'On the Christian [way of] life', noting: *'God wanted his people to be holy and free of all pollution of injustice and iniquity so that there would be nothing with which the nations could find fault but rather only cause for admiration, prompting them to say: 'Blessed are the people who have such a God as their Lord—a people whom he chose as his inheritance.'*[152] St Augustine extends himself at considerable length on this point, all cited by the esteemed bishop in his effort to prove that there is no more suitable way of converting the gentiles than through meekness and exemplary behaviour on the part of Christians, nor any means more ineffectual than through the greed, ferocity, and tyranny which the latter exhibit in the course of warfare, as a result of which the gentiles, in their horror, revile the faith and the God of the Christians. After all, as St Chrysostom says in his fourth homily on Titus 2: *'For the gentiles have traditionally always judged the truth of a teaching not from* [the teachers'] *words but from their actual deeds and way of life.'*[153]

He [Las Casas] also made reference to Jesus when he said: *'learn from me, for I am gentle and humble in heart.'*[154] And that verse of Philippians 2, is also germane: *'so*

---

[150] Pseudo-Chrysostom, *Opus imperfectum in Matthaeum*, Homily 10, on Matthew 5. Both manuscripts give the correct number of the homily. The 1552 edition omitted the beginning of the passage present in both manuscripts (CS, 16v; MS, 220r): '*Per illos quidem qui docent et faciunt magnificatur Deus*.' In the following phrase, the misplaced *quidem* for *autem* shows that the omission was an unintentional haplography. For 'the discipline of the master' ('*disciplina domini*'), correct in both manuscripts, the 1552 printing has '*scientia domini*'. For the passage, see pp. 536–37 of vol. 3 of Froben's 1530 Basel edition of Chrysostom. Las Casas quotes it again in ch. 44 of his *Apologia*, minus the errors of the 1552 text.

[151] Romans 2:24, quoted in Homily 10 of the *Opus imperfectum* (see previous note). The 1552 printing misreads '*unde dictum est ad populum Dei*' (correct in the manuscripts: CS, 17r; MS, 220v) as '*Unum dictum est ad populum Dei*'.

[152] Pseudo-Augustine, *De vita christiana*, ch. 9. Although Soto follows Las Casas (see his *Apologia*, ch. 45, 197v; Poole, 285) in attributing this work to Augustine, that attribution has been questioned since the Middle Ages. For a meticulous attempt to claim the text for the British heretic Pelagius (and to debunk the other most commonly ventured attribution, namely to Fastidius), see Robert F. Evans, *Four Letters of Pelagius* (London: Black, 1968).

[153] John Chrysostom, *Homilies on [the Epistle to] Titus* [*In epistolam ad Titum commentarius*], Homily 4 (on Titus 2:2–5): *PG* 66, col. 685. Chrysostom is here commenting on verse 2:7, where Paul urges Titus not only to preach virtue but also to be exemplary in his behaviour. The passage in question can be seen for instance at fol. 371v, col. 2, in Guillaume Roland, *Quartus tomus operum Divi Ioannis Chrysotomi*... (Paris, 1546). Las Casas cites it again in ch. 45 of the *Apologia* (198v; Poole, 286). Galmés mistakenly prints *rita* for *vita*.

[154] Matthew 11:29.

that you may be blameless ... in the midst of a crooked and perverse nation',[155] which is an allusion to the gentiles; and *'Let your gentle spirit be known to all people.'*[156] Also 1 Peter 2: *'Keep your behaviour impeccable among the gentiles, so that with regard to that very thing for which they slander you as evildoers, they may, thanks to the opportunity to observe your good deeds, instead glorify God on the day of visitation.'*[157] He also invoked the example of Jesus Christ, who did not dispatch armed people to preach the faith by first subjugating the world, but rather said: *'Go forth and preach, saying, "The kingdom of heaven is at hand." Heal the sick, raise the dead, cleanse the lepers, [cast out demons]. Freely did you receive, freely give.'*[158] It is not consonant with this that, prior to preaching the faith, we should make our presence known not by healing the sick but by killing the healthy, nor by casting the devils out from their bodies but rather casting their souls down into hell.

He added Jesus Christ's own instruction to the Apostles themselves to go forth not as wolves to devour sheep but *'as sheep in the midst of wolves',*[159] so that they might attest to the faith not by killing but by dying. On this St Chrysostom in the thirty-fourth homily of the *Opus perfectum* notes: *'He orders them to exhibit every form of gentleness, and not only that but also the simplicity of the dove.'*[160] And further along: *'It is indeed a greater and more marvellous thing to change the minds and hearts of our adversaries than to overcome them with the sword.'*[161] And later on St Chrysostom went on to add: *'Let those who adopt the opposite approach, pursuing their adversaries in the manner of wolves, feel ashamed upon seeing the innumerable wolves (which is to say, gentiles) defeated by such a very small number of sheep: in other words, by the disciples. Indeed insofar as we are sheep we easily overpower our enemies, whereas when we pass over into the guise of wolves we are ourselves overcome; for the shepherd then affords us no protection, since he can have no wolves but only sheep.'* Those are the words of Chrysostom.

---

[155] Philippians 2:15.

[156] Philippians 4:5.

[157] 1 Peter 2:12.

[158] Matthew 10:7–8. The original version (quoted by Las Casas in ch. 45 of the *Apologia*: 200; Poole, 288) also includes the instruction to 'cast out demons' (*daemones eiicite*). Soto probably omitted the phrase (missing also in the manuscripts: CS, 17v; MS, 221r) by accident: note his reference to casting out demons in the next sentence.

[159] Matthew 10:16.

[160] John Chrysostom, *Opus perfectum*, Homily 34 on the Gospel of Matthew (10:16). 'Every form of gentleness' (*omnem mansuetudinem*) which appears here rather than the expected 'gentleness of sheep' (i.e. *ovium mansuetudinem*, corresponding to the Greek 'προβάτων ἡμερότητα', PG 57, col. 389) is not Soto's or Las Casas's error but something already present in the Greek-to-Latin translation of Chrysostom by Francesco Griffolini (1462), revised by Philippe Montanus (1536), which Las Casas was clearly using. That translation can be consulted for instance in the third volume of Froben's 1530 Basel edition of Chrysostom, p. 211.

[161] This passage, and the next one, are both likewise from John Chrysostom, *Opus perfectum*, Homily 34 on the Gospel of Matthew, closely following the text of the Griffolini–Montanus Latin translation. Soto has abridged Las Casas's fuller quotation of this passage, thus breaking it into two. He has also added the parenthetical gloss on 'wolves': 'hoc est Gentiles' [which is to say, the gentiles].

260 SEPÚLVEDA ON THE SPANISH INVASION OF THE AMERICAS

He [Las Casas] also invoked Our Redeemer's other instruction according to St Luke: *'And he said to them, "Take nothing for your journey, neither a staff, nor a pouch, nor money."'*[162] He quoted St Jerome commenting on St Matthew, where he says that if those spreading Christ's tidings carried or set store by gold, the infidels would think that they were only preaching the gospel to them in the interest of personal gain:[163] all the more reason, then, not to steal it from them, so as to avoid falling foul of the situation St Paul describes: *'You who preach that one is not to steal, do you steal? You who say that one is not to commit adultery, do you commit adultery? You who abhor idols, do you commit sacrilege? You who take pride in the law, do you dishonour God in breaking the law?'*[164]

He [Las Casas] really stressed this point, going so far as to say that it would be like going forth to preach the faith in the manner of Mohammed, who ordered his sect to be extended by armed means. And he quoted St Ambrose commenting on St Luke in Book 2 7, Chapter 54 59, where he says: *'Let them carry out the mission of their humble teacher. For he [Jesus] sent them to sow the faith not under duress but through teaching. They were also not to exercise the force of power but to exalt the doctrine of humility. In that passage he averred that patience too should go alongside humility. For (according to the testimony of St Peter) he himself would never curse when he was cursed nor strike back when he was struck.'*[165] And further along St Ambrose says: *'When the Apostles wished to request fire from heaven to consume the Samaritans who refused to welcome Jesus into their city, he turned to rebuke them, saying, "Do you not know of whose spirit you are? The Son of man has not come to destroy souls but to save them."'*[166] So if the faith is to be preached with such great meekness, it is villainous to send in armed forces to subjugate the people first. St Gregory, who witnessed such wars in his own lifetime, speaks out against them in the second book of his letters, in Epistle 52: *'To seek to impose faith by means of the lash is a new and unheard-of mode of preaching indeed.'*[167]

Jesus Christ also opposed this practice, instructing his preachers that, wherever they entered, the first thing they should say was to be, *'Peace to this house.'* And he added that, if there were no sons of peace there, *'Your peace shall return to you.'*[168] It is for this reason that in his first book Vincent [of Beauvais], discussing

---

[162] Luke 9:3.

[163] Jerome, *Commentaria in Evangelium Matthaei*, Bk. 1, ch. 10.

[164] Romans 2:21–23.

[165] Ambrose, *Expositio Evangelii secundum Lucam*, Bk. 7 (not 2, *pace* Galmés), ch. 59 (available at *PL* 15, col. 1714). This passage, and the one that follows, are both again quoted by Las Casas in ch. 46 of his *Apologia* (202v; Poole, 292).

[166] Ambrose on Luke (as in previous note), Bk. 7, ch. 60 (as at *PL* 15, col. 1715).

[167] Gregory I, Letter 3.53 (*PL* 77, cols. 647–49) = Norberg 3.52, 'To John, the bishop' ['Ad Joannem Episcopum'] (formerly Bk. 2, Letter 52—which Las Casas inadvertently inverts and cites as '25' in the *Apologia*, ch. 46: 203v; Poole, 293). In Froben's 1550 Basel edition, *Gregorii Papae Operum secundus tomus*, it is letter 2.52 on cols. 736–37 (this passage on 737).

[168] Matthew 10:13; Luke 10:6. Our translation follows the manuscript readings (CS, 18v; MS, 222r): 'Contra lo qual Iesu christo mandó a los predicadores, que dondequiera entrasen lo primero que

CONTAINED HEREIN IS A DEBATE OR DISPUTATION   261

Mohammed's avowal '*to have been sent in the terror of the sword and the violence of arms*', says: '*Consider whether this manner of preaching ought to befit a prophet of God. These means entail nothing but treachery, violence, and human bloodshed: whatever bandits and highwaymen do, that is precisely what was done*.'[169]

He drew this item to a close, then, by saying that his adversaries are mistaken in claiming that these wars are not waged with a view to spreading the faith by force but rather in order to subjugate the people and then preach it to them. For, truth be told, to do so is not just indirect force but rather sheer, direct force, since they say that these wars are waged with a view to preaching the faith to them afterwards. For to proceed in this manner is to overwhelm them from the outset with fright and a sense of duress which will cause them to embrace the faith in a hollow fashion solely out of fear. For if some of their number see the devastation, plunder, and deaths sustained by their neighbours, they will superficially embrace the faith without sparing a thought for what it is that they are receiving so as to escape the same fate themselves.

(11) The second prong of the esteemed bishop's refutation of this line of Dr Sepúlveda's argument was that the preaching of the faith involves preaching penitence. The last chapter of the Gospel of Luke reads as follows: '*So it is written, that Christ would suffer and rise from the dead on the third day, and that repentance and remission of sins would be preached in his name among all nations*.'[170] That was what John [the Baptist] first preached,[171] as did Jesus Christ in his turn. For since he came to redeem our sins, this was his intention—to forgive all past sins by means of baptism, with no punishment whatsoever—which is why baptism does not involve repentance for bygone sins. And this principle must be observed universally among all peoples, for, as St Paul says in Romans 10, and in Galatians 3: '*There is neither Jew nor Greek, there is neither enslaved nor free, there is neither male nor female; for all are one in Christ*.'[172] And St Paul says that he owes the same thing to all men, '*to Greeks and barbarians alike, to the wise and to the foolish*.'[173] From this, then, the following point can be gleaned: to preach the faith is to preach remission of all past sins. Therefore, even though they might deserve to suffer for their sins, they are not to be punished nor have war waged upon them, but rather be taught

---

dixesen fuesse, *pax huic domui*. Y anadió que si no [h]ubiesse allí hijos de paz, *Pax vestra revertetur ad vos*.' Galmés (124) printed the faulty text of the 1552 edition, where the two instances of *pax* led to the omission of several words, due to haplography (specifically *saut du même au même*).

[169] This pair of remarks is drawn from Vincent of Beauvais [Vincentius Bellovacensis], *Speculum historiale*, Bk. 23, chs. 49 and 42 (in that order). Las Casas cites the passage again in ch. 47 of his *Apologia* (206; Poole, 297).

[170] Luke 24:46–47.

[171] On John the Baptist's preaching of repentance, see Matthew 3:2; Mark 1:4; Luke 3:3.

[172] This blends Romans 10:12 (for the first clause) with Galatians 3:28 (for the rest of the sentence). The 1552 edition mistakenly read '*Non est distinctio iudei et servi*', where '*greci*' correctly appears in both manuscripts (CS, 19r; MS, 222v).

[173] Romans 1:14.

through preaching that all shall be forgiven in the moment of baptism. For '*Christ did not come to judge the world, but so that the world might be saved through him*',[174] just as the prophet foretold: '*Behold your King is coming to you, meek, and mounted on a donkey.*'[175]

This, then, is the esteemed bishop's answer to Dr Sepúlveda's third line of reasoning, which centred on the objective of the preaching of the faith.

(12) Truth be told, when it came to the fourth scenario in which it is lawful for Christians to wage war against infidels—namely when they obstruct the preaching and propagation of our faith—it is fair to say that Las Casas went on at much greater length than the purposes of his response to the doctor strictly merited. For, in his bid to circumscribe the scenarios to which this applies, he said it was first and foremost necessary to identify those cases in which they put up resistance to the faith knowing full well what it was that they were obstructing, as is the case with the Moors who are already aware of our religion, as opposed to those who knew nothing of our faith and obstructed us because they thought we were coming to rob and kill them as enemies are wont to do to one another, in which case they were within their rights to defend themselves against us while we, conversely, could not rightly wage war upon them.

His second qualification was that it was necessary to establish in which instances an infidel population was obstructing the faith solely because their princes and nobles had put them up to it. For if the whole republic by common accord of all individuals were to opt not to listen to us but to persist in their own rites in lands where there has never been any Christian presence (as is the case with the Indians), then in those circumstances we cannot wage war against them. And it is imperative here to reflect carefully on whether or not this holds true for the question we are being asked to consider. For our greatest and most inalienable right is the power and dispensation which Jesus Christ granted to all Christians to preach the gospel throughout the whole world as conveyed by his words in the last chapter of the Gospel of Mark: '*Go into all the world and preach the gospel to every creature.*'[176]

These words would appear to indicate that we have the right to go and preach to all peoples and to protect and defend our preachers, by armed means if necessary, to ensure that they are not prevented from preaching. Las Casas's response to this was that, even though that mandate exists, nonetheless it does not oblige us to force the gentiles to listen to us but, rather, only to preach when they are minded to listen. And I would draw your lordships and mercies' attention to the fact that it seems (if I am not much mistaken) that the esteemed bishop was himself mistaken in taking issue with this as he does. For it is one thing for us to be able to force them to let us preach, as many doctors hold that we indeed can; it is quite another for us to be able

---

[174] Cf. John 3:17.
[175] Matthew 21:5, citing the prophet Zechariah (9:9).
[176] Mark 16:15.

CONTAINED HEREIN IS A DEBATE OR DISPUTATION 263

to compel them actually to attend our sermons, which is not quite so plausible. It was to the latter—the idea that we cannot force them to listen to us—that Las Casas was in fact addressing himself at that point in his argument.

He offered four arguments in support of this view. Firstly: because infidels cannot be forced to embrace the faith—which is the objective of preaching—and so, by the same token, they cannot be made to listen to such preaching either; for if one cannot be forced to adopt any particular religion or doctrine, one cannot be forced to listen to it either, not least because that sort of coercion would sooner inspire listeners with hatred for the very faith being preached than with eagerness to receive it.

His second argument is that we do not even oblige those infidels who live in our own midst to listen to us. In support of this he adduced proof-texts from the Gospels of Matthew and Luke (Chapter 10 in both cases), which in turn constituted the third reason: '*Whatever house you enter, first say, "Peace be to this house"*';[177] and, further along: '*And whoever does not receive you nor listen to your words, as you leave that house or city, shake the dust off your feet. Verily I say to you, it will be more tolerable for the land of Sodom and Gomorrah on the Day of Judgment than for that city*'.[178] We are not instructed here to resort to coercion of any sort, but rather to leave it to God to do the judging. And in support of this Las Casas invoked the example of Jesus Christ, who chose to refrain from encroaching forcibly upon the Samaritans who did not wish to receive him, and forbade fire to be rained down on them from heaven; and in time they received the faith thanks to a Samaritan woman. Commenting on this passage, St Ambrose and Bede remark: '*Ultimately the Samaritans, from whom the fire was kept away, came to believe more swiftly*'.[179]

He then supplied the fourth reason, namely that, seeing as they never pledged to listen to the faith, they cannot be obliged to keep a promise they never made. More, however, will be said on this point in due course as part of this most learned disputation.

(13) Dr Sepúlveda's fourth argument hinges on the atrocity which the Indians inflict upon the innocent, killing them for the purposes of sacrifice or in order to eat them. Despite having conceded in his sixth point that it was incumbent upon the church to protect those innocents, the bishop nonetheless subsequently went on to say that it was neither opportune nor appropriate to do so by means of warfare. He offered three or four reasons for this.

The first has already been touched upon, namely that it is necessary to choose the lesser of two evils, and for the Indians to kill a few innocent people in order to eat them—which is even more heinous than doing so for the purposes of sacrifice—is

---

[177] Luke 10:5; cf. Matthew 10:12: '*As you enter the house, give it your greeting.*'
[178] Matthew 10:14–15; cf. Luke 10:10–12.
[179] Ambrose, *Expositio in Evangelium secundum Lucam*, Bk. 7, n. 27. Bede, *In Lucae evangelium expositio*, Bk. 3, ch. 9.

264   SEPÚLVEDA ON THE SPANISH INVASION OF THE AMERICAS

still unquestionably less terrible than the ills which arise from warfare. For, quite aside from all the pillaging, such wars entail the deaths of many more innocents than that handful who were thereby supposed to be set free. Furthermore, these wars besmirch the name of the faith and inspire hatred in the unbelievers, which is a greater evil still.

The second argument was that we have a negative commandment—'thou shalt not kill'—and, most especially, '*do not kill the innocent and the blameless*', Exodus 23[180] and that this is more binding than the affirmative mandate to protect the innocent. Accordingly, when it is not possible to fulfil the latter without violating the former, the latter should be broken sooner than the former. And since in the course of combat between peoples engaged in just warfare it is possible, when in enemy cities, for a few innocents to be inadvertently killed without the assailants realizing as much or meaning to do so, this makes it all the more advisable in the context of warfare waged in order to punish a handful of wrongdoers—proceeding on the assumption that they will be outnumbered by innocents and that it is impossible to tell the difference between the two—to refrain from meting out that punishment, in accordance with Jesus Christ's command in the Gospel, when he did not permit the tares to be weeded out from the wheat lest the wheat itself be ripped up in turn, preferring instead to leave it all for August, which is to say Judgment Day, when the good can be safely sorted from the bad and the latter punished without posing a risk to the former.[181]

The third means of demonstrating the unlawfulness of the wars waged against those who perform human sacrifice was to say that they have an excuse of sorts which exempts them from having to recognize the error of their ways when first their attention is drawn to it, chiefly in view of the fact that those who attempt to foist it upon them are armed soldiers who show every sign of coming more as foes to kill and plunder than as friends to teach. And insofar as their ignorance continues to exonerate them until such time as they are committed to the faith, they are not guilty of blame and, consequently, do not deserve to be punished. And the fact that they have something of an excuse in the eyes of their fellow man (albeit not before God) is due to the fact that, as Aristotle says in the first book of the *Topics*, the opinion held by the wisest men constitutes the so-called 'probable' opinion.[182] And in the first book of his *Rhetoric*, Chapter 2, Aristotle reiterates that whatever is endorsed by the most prudent in turn becomes the view to espouse.[183] And seeing

---

[180]   Exodus 23:7. Note that the Vulgate usually has '*insontem et **iustum** non occides*', whereas the Latin text as given here by Soto offers a common variant form: '*insontem et **innocentem** non occides*'.

[181]   Matthew 13:28–30.

[182]   Aristotle, *Topics* 1.1 (100b22–24). This passage is also cited by Las Casas in ch. 34 of the *Apologia* (152; Poole, 222).

[183]   Aristotle, *Rhetoric* 1.2 (1356a6–7). The passage is also cited (albeit misnumbered there as 1 *Rhetorices* c. 20) in conjunction with the preceding one from the *Topics* in ch. 34 of Las Casas's *Apologia* (see previous note).

CONTAINED HEREIN IS A DEBATE OR DISPUTATION   265

as among those populations in which this degeneracy holds sway it is their own wisemen, priests, kings, and forefathers who have schooled them in this, it follows that they do have some sort of excuse until such time as they are taught the truth.

He substantiated this point by observing that the practice of human sacrifice is something that was very widespread in antiquity, as reported by Eusebius in the fourth book of his *Preparation for the Gospel*, where he says that even princes used to sacrifice their own children so as better to pay reverence to their gods.[184] St Clement in Book 9 says the same of the inhabitants of the islands of the Orient, who may well be the very same Indians under discussion here.[185] Lactantius reports the same of the Tartars and even of the Latins themselves, who were in the habit of sacrificing children, and the same goes for the Carthaginians.[186] And Plutarch reports that on those occasions when they came across barbarians who practised human sacrifice, the Romans did not punish them for it but simply forbade them from continuing the practice.[187] Las Casas adduced many accounts of this sort to illustrate his point.

The second grounds on which they are not obliged to recognize their blindness forthwith is that anyone who, by virtue of natural enlightenment, conceives of some being as god understands that it is a most excellent entity to which reverence is owed by all and to whom, by way of thanks for favours received from this god and to atone for any affronts perpetrated, it is imperative to sacrifice the best thing which humans have to offer; and as that very best thing is human life itself, they have a kind of shroud for their ignorance and an excuse for offering up human lives to him. ~~I say~~ He said that theirs is an excusable form of ignorance in instances where they are not versed in the law of divine Grace but merely in natural law, and even then only hazily, as is the case among [the] gentiles.[188] For in offering up life

---

[184] Eusebius, *De praeparatione evangelica* 4.16.

[185] The reference is to Chapter 20 of Book 9 of the *Recognitiones* of Pseudo-Clement. Las Casas, citing this passage in ch. 34 of his *Apologia* (152v–153; Poole, 223), refers more clearly to this work, though under its common alternative title of *Recognitiones ad Iacobum, Fratrem Domini*, for the work purported to be addressed to James, brother of Jesus. This pseudo-Clementine work, of which the Greek original is lost, is a long and elaborate work of fiction which survives only in Rufinus of Aquileia's Latin translation. Chapter 20 deals with the Brahmins of India, contrasting their ascetic way of life with the barbarity of others in that region, who were said to be in the habit of sacrificing strangers. The relevant passage is on p. 144 of the edition published by Johann Bebel in Basel in 1526.

[186] Lactantius, *Divinarum institutionum libri septem*, Bk. 1, ch. 21. Las Casas cites this again in ch. 34 of his *Apologia*.

[187] Plutarch, *Quaestiones Romanae*, 83. Las Casas, however, gives this reference in ch. 34 of his *Apologia* (153v; Poole, 223) as being from Plutarch's '*Problemata*, p. 465', revealing that he was using the 1542 Lyon edition of Sebastian Gryphius, *Plutarchi Chaeronei, philosophi, historicique clarissimi Opuscula moralia*, where the text corresponding to QR 83 is indeed to be found on pp. 465–66.

[188] In the 1552 edition and also in the manuscripts (CS, 22r; MS, 225v), the first word of this sentence is '*Digo*' ['I say']; however, unless one wishes to imagine that Soto really is inserting his first-person opinion at this point (which, given the opinion being vouchsafed at this point, seems less than plausible), then it is likely that this is simply a slip for '*Dijo*' ['He said', referring to Las Casas]. Di Liso likewise translates (and glosses) it '[Il Vescovo] *disse*' (134) ['[The bishop] *said*'], i.e. as if reading '*dijo*', as we also do—though he does not correspondingly emend his Spanish text (196), which follows that of Brufau Prats (with 'digo').

266   SEPÚLVEDA ON THE SPANISH INVASION OF THE AMERICAS

to God, they perform the greatest homage and reverence of which they are capable, which is why they offer him innocent, blameless children, for they believe that they are the most pleasing to him and of most use to him in the next life.

There is even precedent for this in the Holy Scripture, for God sought to put Abraham's love and faith to the test by commanding him to sacrifice his beloved son to him. And in so doing he was not making undue demands of him, for '*he is Lord of all things and even over human life and death*',[189] although in his benevolence he did not then allow the sacrifice to come to pass. By the same token he likewise in Leviticus ordered that all first-born sons be spared and redeemed by having an animal sacrificed in their stead.[190] He [sc. Las Casas] further notes that '*no one has greater love than the person who lays down his life for his friends*'.[191] And so it followed that they did have some kind of excuse for offering up life to God, to whom so much love was owed, by those sacrificial means. It is for this same reason that wives who were extremely beloved of their husbands used to be buried alive along with them. And even in our own religion it would seem that there are those who would readily still do so were it not for the fact that the faith keeps the blindness of love in check.

Lastly, Las Casas volunteered a further argument against waging war on them: that it is far easier to persuade them by means of reason than through warfare to give up their idolatry and tear it out of their hearts. For although warfare forces them to stop offering sacrifices in public, they continue to perpetrate the same evils in secret, for their hearts remain corrupted. It is in this way, then, that he answered the fourth argument of Dr Sepúlveda.

(14) It now only remains to answer Sepúlveda's second argument which revolved around the barbarism of those people, on account of which they are said to be slaves by their very nature and, as such, obliged to become our subjects. The esteemed bishop's answer to this was that in texts secular and sacred alike there are three categories or classes of barbarian. The first, taken in the broadest acceptation of the term, refers to any people who exhibit some form of oddity in their views or customs, but are not without the social organization and sense to govern themselves. The second type denotes those who do not have languages that lend themselves to being rendered in characters and letters, as was once true of the English, according to the Venerable Bede, which is why he was moved to translate the liberal

---

[189] In Latin the phrase given here reads '*est Dominus universorum, et etiam vitae et mortis humanae*'. This corresponds to a passage early in ch. 37 of Las Casas's *Apologia* (165; Poole, 240), where Las Casas notes 2 Maccabees 14:35 as the source for '*Dominus universorum*'. However, ultimately the whole formulation appears to be derived from a phrase in a lecture by Vitoria on Aquinas (see Vitoria, *De legibus* (Salamanca: Ediciones Universidad Salamanca, 2010), 128), where Vitoria quotes Aquinas as saying '*Deus est dominus vitae et mortis et dominus universorum*', citing *ST* I-II, q. 94, art. 5, ad 2, where the last two words indeed appear, but probably also recalling I-II, q. 100, art. 8, ad 3, where a version of the first part of the phrase can be found. Both these passages in Aquinas deal with God's temporary suspension of natural law, and the second explicitly concerns the command to Abraham to sacrifice Isaac.

[190] Leviticus 12:6. Cf. Exodus 13:13. The 1552 printed text mistakenly repeats *que todos* ('that all').

[191] John 15:13.

CONTAINED HEREIN IS A DEBATE OR DISPUTATION   267

arts into that tongue.[192] And St Gregory says: '*Behold the language of Britain, which once had only been able to grind out barbaric sounds, has for some time now begun to resound with Hebrew words in praise of God*.'[193] And the Philosopher [sc. Aristotle] never took either of these characteristics to denote those who '*are slaves by nature*' against whom war could be waged on that account; on the contrary, he states in the third book of the *Politics* that certain types of barbarians boast true kingdoms, natural kings, nobles, and governance.[194]

Barbarians of the third category are those whose depraved habits, coarseness of intellect, and brutish disposition render them akin to wild beasts dwelling in the fields, with neither cities nor houses, governance nor laws, rites nor modes of interaction that accord with the *ius gentium*; rather, they roam around '*palantes*', to use a Latin term, which is to say marauding and committing acts of violence, as the Goths and the Alans once did, and as the Arabs in Asia and the people in Africa whom we ourselves have dubbed *Alárabes* are now said to do. It is to these people that Aristotle can be taken as referring when he says that, just as it is lawful to hunt wild animals, so too is it lawful to wage wars of self-defence against those who harm us, striving to drag them into the fold of humane society;[195] and it seems likely that he volunteered this view in connection with some of the people on the receiving end of Alexander's conquests.

At this juncture the bishop proceeded to recount the history of the Indians at great length,[196] showing that even though they do exhibit some traits characteristic of less civilized people, they are nonetheless not barbarians of that degree; rather, they are social, civilized people who boast large settlements, houses, laws, arts, nobles, and governance and who impose the death penalty not only for sins against nature but even for some of the other natural crimes. Their level of civilization is certainly such that war cannot be waged against them on this count of barbarism.

And so he concluded, *contra* Dr Sepúlveda, that none of the latter's four arguments constituted grounds for waging war against them prior to preaching the faith; on the contrary, such warfare would be wicked, tyrannical, and detrimental to the gospel and to the preaching thereof. And he also goes further and—as already mentioned—denies the lawfulness of warfare even against those who stand

---

[192] Soto assumed that Las Casas was quoting Bede here, but in fact he was relating an anecdote that he derived from Aquinas's *Lectio 1* on Bk. 1 of Aristotle's *Politics*: 'Unde et Beda dicitur in linguam Anglicam liberales artes transtulisse ne Anglici barbari reputarentur.' See his citation of this at the beginning of Bk. 2 of his *Apologia*, where he proceeds to cite the exclamation of Gregory that follows here.

[193] Gregory I, *Moralia in Iob*, Bk. 27, ch. 11; quoted in Bede, *Historia ecclesiastica gentis Anglorum* 2.1. The 1552 printing offered *fundere* for the correct *frendere* ('gnash', 'grind out') present in the manuscripts (CS, 22v; MS, 226r).

[194] Aristotle, *Politics* 3.9.3 (1285a18–23).

[195] Aristotle, *Politics* 1.2.13 (1254b16–21).

[196] Although, as noted in p. 235 above, 'Indians' in this text is always—as is also the case in this instance—deployed to mean 'Amerindians', it is worth reclarifying this here as the mention of Alexander the Great in the line immediately preceding might suggest that the inhabitants of the Indian subcontinent were now meant.

268   SEPÚLVEDA ON THE SPANISH INVASION OF THE AMERICAS

in the way of preaching in instances where this is done by the common agreement of the whole republic and all members thereof, nor can they be forced to listen to our preaching.

In response to the question that was, lastly, put to him about what the lawful and expedient course of action would be in his view,[197] he says that, in areas which pose no danger, the course of action prescribed by the Gospel would be for preachers to make their way in on their own, along with those capable of teaching good patterns of behaviour that accord with the faith and those in a position to broker peace with them. And in cases where danger is suspected, the best course of action would be to build some strongholds in adjoining areas so as to begin making initial overtures to them from there and thereby gradually enabling our religion to swell in size, gaining ground by dint of peace, love, and setting a good example.

This, he asserts, was the sole intention of Alexander's bull,[198] as clarified by the subsequent bull of Paul,[199] namely that they should be made subjects of His Majesty upon conversion to Christianity—not *as regards ownership of particular things*,[200] nor so as to enslave the people there or deprive them of their realms, but rather purely as far as supreme jurisdiction is concerned, along with some reasonable level of tribute for the protection of the faith and instruction in good customs and proper governance.

This, then, is the summary and orderly sequence into which, as commanded by your lordships and mercies, I have been able to condense the views of these two gentlemen—notably that of the esteemed bishop, whose verbosity and volubility are an index of the years he has spent engaged in this business and of the passion and devotion with which he has pursued the matter. For this, then, thanks are owed first and foremost to God and secondly to him, as well as to the esteemed doctor for his own commendable zeal, diligence, and industry.

This is the end of the summary which the illustrious Father, *maestro* Fr. Domingo de Soto, prepared of the *Apología* of the bishop of Chiapa and of the arguments of Dr Sepúlveda.

---

[197] Our translation follows the text of the Caracas manuscript (22r), which has the passive participle *preguntado*, rather than the Muñoz manuscript (227r) and the 1552 printing, which offer the active participle *preguntando*.

[198] Alexander VI, *Inter caetera* (1493). For a readily accessible edition with the text of this bull in both Latin and in English translation, see for instance Frances Gardiner Davenport, *European Treaties Bearing on the History of the United States and Its Dependencies to 1648* (Washington, D.C: Carnegie Institute of Washington, 1917), 72–78.

[199] Paul III, *Sublimis Deus* (1537). On the vexed matter of the possible forerunner documents of this bull, see Gustavo Gutiérrez, *Las Casas: In Search of the Poor of Jesus Christ* (Maryknoll, NY: Orbis, 1993), 562n11.

[200] This was not a direct quotation from either of the aforementioned bulls. It was a common legal phrase for power exercised over particular things, usually granted by a contract of some sort. Las Casas's point was that neither Alexander VI nor Paul III was granting anything like this sort of *dominium* in the Indies to the kings of Spain.

Juan Ginés de Sepúlveda's 'Twelve Objections'

Having seen the summary which the aforementioned most reverend Father, *maestro* Fr. Domingo de Soto, produced (as mentioned above) at the behest of the assembly, Dr Sepúlveda drew up a list of twelve objections levelled at his position, to each of which he then proceeded to respond in turn. They are as follows:

Dr Sepúlveda's prologue to the esteemed members of the assembly

Illustrious and most eminent sirs: your lordships and mercies have, in your capacity as judges, spent five or six days listening to the esteemed bishop of Chiapa reading out the book to which he has devoted many years, marshalling all the arguments devised both by himself and by others with a view to proving that the conquest of the Indies conducted in the manner in which our monarchs and people have undertaken it to date in accordance with the bull and donation of Pope Alexander VI[201]—namely subjugating the barbarians first and preaching the gospel to them only afterwards—is unjust. It stands to reason, then—and I do entreat this of you— that you should give me your undivided attention for a spell while I, champion of the righteousness and authority of the Holy See and of the justice and honour of our monarchs and nation, offer a brief and matter-of-fact rebuttal to his objections and specious arguments, seeking—aided by God and by the truth I defend—to expose in no uncertain terms the frivolous and flimsy nature of all the counterarguments he brings before all of you, most solemn and learned judges whom no one could ever suspect of putting any other concern above the justice and truth on which so much rests. I shall proceed to do so, then, in as succinct a manner as possible, for, in the presence of individuals so consumed by momentous matters and the govern- ance of the republic, to go on at undue length would be impolitic indeed.[202]

---

[201] Alexander VI, *Inter caetera* (1493).

[202] The wording of this prologue suggests that Sepúlveda may have presented his responses to Las Casas's twelve objections orally to the assembly in Valladolid. Sepúlveda likewise indicates in §1 of his *Proposiciones temerarias* that he presented his responses to Las Casas's objections to the assembly. He also reports (§4) that his responses to Las Casas's objections were distributed to the members of the assembly while they were still in Valladolid, during or after the first session in 1550. Perhaps he dis- tributed his responses in 1550 before delivering them orally at the beginning of the second session in 1551. Abril-Castelló ('La bipolarización Sepúlveda–Las Casas', 238) claims that in the second session Sepúlveda presented his responses to Las Casas's twelve objections and Las Casas presented his twelve replies.

First objection

(1) His first point is that many other nations outside the Promised Land were idolaters, yet they were not destroyed by the people of Israel; and, further, that those nations of the Promised Land were not destroyed on account of their idolatry, and, consequently, that idolatry is not lawful grounds for war.

My response to this is that by the same logic one would be led to conclude that being a highwayman is not a crime punishable by death because there are many highwaymen who have not been put to death. I aver, then, the inhabitants of the Promised Land were destroyed both on account of their idolatries as well as for engaging in human sacrifice, as stated in the Holy Scripture in Deuteronomy 9 and 12, and Leviticus 18 and 20.[203] And other peoples (whose impieties were not quite as thoroughgoing) could be rendered subject to the faithful Jewish people by means of warfare on account of their heathenism and idolatry, as attested by that passage in Deuteronomy 20: '*So you shall do to all the cities that are very far away from you*',[204] '*which is to say, which are of a different religion*', as specified in the interlinear gloss.[205] This statement comes in the wake of an explanation of how they should proceed in the course of waging such warfare.

(2) And with regard to the esteemed bishop's claim that the peoples of the Promised Land were destroyed simply in fulfilment of God's promise to Abraham, I can only say that when God made this promise, he gave the reason for it.[206] For at that point he did not grant it to him [Abraham] by ousting those then in possession of it [the Promised Land], for at that time, he said, the wickedness of the Amorites was not yet full. And as for his [Las Casas's] contention that the aforementioned passage from Deuteronomy 20 is to be taken as referring to cases in which the Jews waged war on other just grounds but not on account of heathenism or idolatry,[207] I would say that this interpretation goes against the interlinear gloss, since, provided that there were just grounds for warfare, war could be waged justly even against people of the same religion.

(3) And to his point about the examples of the Old Testament not being for us to imitate, I would say that this is true of some of them, but not as regards natural law and its dictates, which are to be observed at all times and in all places by all peoples faithful and unfaithful alike, as for instance in the case of idolatry, which was most severely punished in both groups. On the subject of these commandments and harsh punishments, St Cyprian writes the following: '*If these precepts regarding the worship of God and the repudiation of idols were observed prior to the coming of Christ, how much more should they be upheld since his advent*.'[208] This is quoted in

---

[203] Deuteronomy, 9:1–5; 12:2–3, 29–31. Leviticus 18:3, 21, 24–30; 20:2–6, 23.
[204] Deuteronomy 20:15.
[205] This 'interlinear gloss' is the *Glossa Interlinearis* of Anselm of Laon (d. 1117). See n. 38 above.
[206] Genesis 15:13–20.
[207] Deuteronomy 20:15.
[208] Cyprian, *Ad Fortunatum de exhortatione martyrii*, §5 (*PL* 4, 685).

CONTAINED HEREIN IS A DEBATE OR DISPUTATION   271

23, question 5, [chapter] '*Si audieris*'.[209] This serves as further support, then, for our conviction that war is to be waged against these Indian idolaters not with a view to killing and destroying them, as was the case with those of the Promised Land, but so as to subjugate them, rid them of their idolatry and profane rites, and remove the obstacles to the preaching of the gospel.

Second objection

(1) With regard to his contention that those words from the Gospel of Luke, Chapter 14 ('*compel them to come in*')[210] are not to be taken as denoting physical, armed violence but rather spiritual coercion by means of entreaties and miracles— for that is what some have taken it to mean—I would respond that, as attested by the holy doctors, the Holy Scripture can admit two different acceptations of the same phrase, both apt and true in equal measure.[211]

But in any case, the interpretation of this particular passage as referring to physical force is not mine but comes from St Augustine in his forty-eighth, fiftieth, and final letters—*To Vincentius*, *To Boniface*, and *To Donatus*[212]—which are cited in 23, q. 4,[213] and from St Gregory, Book 1, Epistle 23 73 and Book 9, Epistle 60,[214] and indeed from the whole church which likewise took this to be the meaning, as emerges not only from such words but also in deeds, as asserted by St Augustine in the aforementioned letters, where he says that the church was the agent of the force employed by emperors against heretics and pagans, and, citing the following words from the Psalm—'*all kings shall bow down before him*'[215]—in his last letter, he adds: '*For the more this is accomplished, the greater the power the church will wield, with the result that it will not only be able to encourage but also to enforce the enactment of good.*'[216] He justifies this use of force by means of the aforementioned

---

[209] Gratian, *Decretum*, C. 23, q. 5, c. 32. Sepúlveda cites both Cyprian and Gratian in his *Apologia* at §III.2.vi (in our numbering).

[210] Luke 14:23.

[211] The Spanish text here reads 'como[]dos y verdaderos', with slightly ambiguous spacing in the original typesetting, leading Galmés (133) to print: 'como dos y verdaderos'. But Bonet de Sotillo's transcription of the Caracas manuscript (172v) offers: 'cómodos y verdaderos'. Our translation allows for both possibilities.

[212] These correspond, respectively, to Letter 93 (to Vincentius), Letter 185 (to Boniface), and Letter 173 (to Donatus) in the current numbering system of Augustine's letters. The Donatus of Letter 173 (composed in 416) is a Donatist priest, not to be confused with the other Donatus (no relation) to whom Augustine addressed himself elsewhere.

[213] Gratian, *Decretum*, C. 23, q. 4, c. 41 (the letter to Vincentius), c. 42 (the letter to Boniface), and c. 38 (the letter to Donatus).

[214] These letters of Gregory—to Gennadius, exarch of Africa, and to Ethelbert, king of Kent—are now numbered 1.75 in *PL* 77 (1.73 Norberg) and 11.66 in *PL* (11.37 Norberg). In Sepúlveda's day they were numbered 1.73 and 9.60, as in vol. 2 of Froben's Basel edition of Gregory's works, cols. 683 and 1085–87 respectively; he also refers to them as such in section IV.3.1 of his *Apologia*. Both the Caracas manuscript (172v) and the 1552 edition offer '23' for '73' for the first reference.

[215] Psalm 72 (71):11.

[216] The 'last letter' in question is, as per n. 212 above, Letter 173 (to Donatus the Donatist), where the passage from Psalm 72 (71):11 is discussed in 173.10.

272 SEPÚLVEDA ON THE SPANISH INVASION OF THE AMERICAS

words in the Gospel: *'compel them to come in'*. And in Epistle 50 he decries the school of thought that would have these words denote force exerted spiritually and by means of miracles as opposed to physically.[217]

Third objection

(1) With regard to his contention that physical coercion is not to be used against pagans but only against heretics who had previously embraced the faith, and that in the aforementioned passages St Augustine is referring exclusively to the latter, I would say that—while it is true that in those three letters he is making a case against heretics—he also weaves in the matter of the pagans at various points in the course of his argumentation there, especially in Letter 48, page 110.[218] In fact, he even goes so far as to use the fact of the just deployment of overwhelming force which the church employed against the gentiles in ridding them of their idolatry and pagan rites—the justice of which no Christian would doubt, as he himself states—to prove that war waged against heretics is also just (*as noted in* [C.] 23, q. 4, canon *'Non invenitur'*), in which connection he says: *'Which of us'* (*meaning Catholics*), *'which of you'* (*meaning heretics*) *'does not praise the laws passed by the emperors against the rites of the pagans?'*, etc.[219]

(2) And should those who are of the same opinion as Las Casas point out that this kind of force was used only against those gentiles already subject to the emperor, the fact nonetheless remains that it was physical force, which, if it really is unjust, ought to be even less acceptable to employ against one's own subjects than against outsiders. And as if that were not enough, such force was indeed employed against non-subjects in St Gregory's day in the course of the wars waged by Gennadius against the gentiles, all with a view to making it easier to preach the gospel to them once they had been subjugated, as can be found in the chapter *'si non'*, [C.] 23, q. 4, on which more anon.[220]

(3) And just as it is necessary to resort to this kind of physical force in order to preach to the infidels and rid them of their idolatry albeit against their will, so too when it comes to conversion is it necessary to use every possible tenderness and kindly form of coaxing to induce them to convert of their own accord, for in the matter of conversion force has no place whatsoever. This is what it says in the chapter *'De Judeis'* and in the chapter *'qui sincera'* of *Dist.* 45, and in the formulation

---

[217] Augustine, Letter 185 [formerly Letter 50] (to Boniface), at 185.6.24.

[218] i.e. Augustine, Letter 93 [formerly Letter 48] (to Vincentius). We have been unable to discover an edition with pagination corresponding to Sepúlveda's reference here to the letter in question as being on 'p. 110'. In any case it is not that of Amerbach (Basel, 1493); Petit and Bade (Paris, 1515); Froben (Basel, 1528, judging by the 1556 reprint); Cheavallon (Paris, 1531); or Bonhomme (Paris, 1541).

[219] A passage from Augustine, Letter 93.3.9–10 (to Vincentius), quoted in Gratian, *Decretum*, C. 23, q. 4, c. 41.

[220] Gregory I, 1.75 *PL*; 1.73 Norberg; and Gratian, *Decretum*, C.23, q.4, c.49.

of that tenet of St Thomas and of St Augustine: *'for no one is to be forced to the faith or forced to believe'.*[221]

Fourth objection

(1) With regard to his assertion that the saints never incited Christian kings to wage war on the gentiles to rid them of their idolatry and that there is no record of St Sylvester ever having prompted Constantine to wage war against the pagans on that account, I would respond that I never did say that St Sylvester encouraged Constantine to wage war on the gentiles but, rather, to stamp out idolatry through rule of law, imposing the death penalty and confiscation of property upon the worst culprits, which is precisely what he did.[222] For it stands to reason that Constantine only passed that law at the instigation of the Christians—and first and foremost of Pope St Sylvester, who had converted and baptized him—for St Augustine, to whom we have already referred above, reports that the law in question met with the approval of all Christians.

(2) But what I do assert is that the task of prevailing on kings to undertake just wars falls to prelates and above all to the pope, as for instance when Pope Adrian prompted Charlemagne to wage war on the Lombards, for which St Thomas (*Summa theologica, Secunda secundae*, q. 40, articles 1–3) gives the rationale as follows: '*Every power or art or virtue to which a given end pertains should dictate the means to that end. Among the faithful people, wars or physical actions should have as their end the divine spiritual good to which clerics are beholden, and so it is for clerics to determine and induce others to undertake to wage just wars.*'[223]

(3) It is for this same reason that St Gregory, as is clear to see in Letter 23 73 of his first book of letters, used praise as the means of prevailing upon Gennadius, exarch of Africa, to wage war upon the gentiles so that the gospel might be more conveniently preached to them after their subjugation.[224] To this end it was first necessary to rid them of their idolatry, an action which he praised in lavish fashion; *for he who lavishes utmost praise on a person undertaking an action thereby offers sufficient encouragement for the undertaking of that action.*[225]

---

[221] Gratian, *Decretum,* D. 45, c. 5 (canon 56 of the 4th Council of Toledo) and c. 3 (a letter from Gregory I to Paschasius, bishop of Naples, on the treatment of Jews, *PL* 13.12; Norberg 13.13); Aquinas, *ST* II-II, q. 10, art. 8, co; and Augustine, *Tractatus* 26.2 in *In Evangelium Ioannis Tractatus centum viginti quattuor*. Note that the Augustinian passage is cited by Aquinas in his discussion shortly before, at *ST* II-II, q. 10, art. 8, arg. 3, whence Sepúlveda appears to have taken it.

[222] On this supposed Constantinian anti-pagan legislation, see, for instance, Scott Bradbury, 'Constantine and the Problem of Anti-Pagan Legislation in the Fourth Century', *Classical Philology* 89/2 (1994): 120–39, together with n. 67 of the *Apologia* and n. 261 of the *Democrates secundus* in this volume. Augustine discusses it at Letter 93.3.10.

[223] Aquinas, *ST* II-II, q. 40, art. 2, ad 3.

[224] On this letter from Gregory I to Gennadius (1.75, *PL*; 1.73, Norberg) and the correction to the numeration, see n. 214 above.

[225] In the original, this Latin sentence seems to be offered as a quotation from Gregory's letter to Gennadius, but it is not. Rather, it appears to be Sepúlveda's elegant way of commenting on the tone

274 SEPÚLVEDA ON THE SPANISH INVASION OF THE AMERICAS

(4) And in the same vein St Thomas (Secunda secundae, q. 10, article 11), discussing the case of Constantine, remarked the following: 'The rites of the infidels are not to be tolerated in any way. Although once upon a time they were tolerated by the church, that was back when the population of infidels was extremely large',[226] which is to say before there were Christian princes who could exercise coercion. And in article 8, in the course of expounding the rationale behind the wars waged on the gentiles by Gennadius and the imposition of the gospel under duress, he says the following: 'Infidels who have never received the faith are on no account to be compelled to the faith so that they too become believers; they are, however, to be forced by the faithful (provided the means exist) not to obstruct the faith by means of blasphemy, wicked persuasion, or even out-and-out persecution.'[227]

(5) For those infidels who are not Christian subjects obstruct the faith in all manner of ways, for they do not grant access to the preachers—on the contrary, they are more likely to kill them—and they attempt to lure those who do convert back into sin by means of wicked enticements or outright persecution, as well as by profane means, which is to say, through idolatry.

For, as St Thomas himself says in q. 94, art. 3, ad 2: *'Idolatry entails immense blasphemy and the practice thereof is an assault on the faith.'*[228] Following this point of doctrine, Nicholas of Lyra comments on Numbers 31:[229] *'One rationale for just war is against a land in which God is blasphemed through idolatry.'* It is for this reason that St Thomas, after his opening remarks, goes on to say: *'Believers in Christ regularly* [i.e. *'frequenter']* *wage war against infidels not, in fact, in order to force them to believe but rather to compel them to stop obstructing the faith.'*[230] He borrows the word 'regularly' [*frequenter*] from the aforementioned letter of St Gregory,[231] while *'in order to compel'* comes from the Gospel.[232]

(6) As for the esteemed bishop's discussion of Gennadius waging wars upon his subjects or upon his enemies, everything he says there is false: for those against whom war was waged in this instance were not Roman subjects but rather peoples dwelling adjacent to the Roman empire in inland Africa (as St Gregory himself states at the end of the letter in question, when he makes reference to *'neighbouring*

and aim of Gregory's lavish praise of the exarch. The phrase *ad rem generandam* seems faulty. Antonio Lacavalleria's 1646 Barcelona edition has *ad rem gerendam*, which makes much more sense—and is how we have rendered the phrase.

[226] Aquinas, *ST* II-II, q. 10, art. 11, co., with some minor modifications. The words following the quoted text are Sepúlveda's own gloss, probably based on Augustine. In the Fourth Reply, §4, Las Casas comments on the 'sheer irrelevance' of this gloss.
[227] The reference is to Aquinas, *ST* II-II, q. 10, art. 8. There is no reference to Gregory's letter to Gennadius in this article.
[228] Aquinas, *ST* II-II, q. 94, art. 3 ad 2.
[229] Nicholas of Lyra's commentary is included as a marginal commentary in the *Biblia Sacra cum glossis, interlineari et ordinaria* (Lyon, 1545), which may well be where Sepúlveda consulted it, and in which the commentary on Numbers 31 is on pp. 318–20.
[230] Aquinas, *ST* II-II, q. 10, art. 8, co.
[231] Gregory I, Letter 1.75 *PL*; 1.73 Norberg. *'Frequenter'* appears in the fourth sentence.
[232] i.e. Luke 14:23.

peoples).[233] That he did not wage war on them because they were his enemies nor on any other grounds is confirmed by St Gregory himself, who explains that Gennadius waged war on them purely with a view to enlarging Christendom so that, once they had been subjugated, the name of Christ could in turn be preached to them.

(7) Accordingly, both Gennadius's wars and Constantine's law were designed above all for the improvement and salvation of the infidels. For to claim that Constantine's law was devised chiefly to prevent idolaters from aggrieving the Christians in their midst is patently false: for the heretics were the ones responsible for aggrieving the Catholics far more and did them the most harm by their actions and words, quarrelling with them every day and yet still going by the name of Christians; but in the law passed against them the primary concern was to make provision for their correction and salvation, as attested by numerous passages in St Augustine's forty-eighth, fiftieth, and final letters, namely those *To Vincentius*, *To Boniface*, and *To Donatus*, which are cited in *Decretum* 23, q. 4.[234] The same rationale was at work in the law passed against the pagans, as St Augustine likewise attests in the aforementioned letters, especially Letter 48, p. 116, which contains the following words: '*All the more reason for the pagans to rail against us for the laws passed by Christian emperors against idolaters; and yet as a result of these laws many have been reformed and converted to the true living God and continue to be converted on a daily basis.*'[235]

Fifth objection

(1) As to his claim that the pope does not have jurisdiction over infidels, predicating his argument on that passage from St Paul in 1 Corinthians 5 ('*What business of mine is it to judge those who are outside? For those who are outside, God shall judge*'),[236] I would contend that that passage is to be understood as follows: what good is it for me to pass judgment in vain on the behaviour of infidels who do not comply of their own free will, as Christians do, when I am hardly in a position to reform them against their will? For neither I nor the church have the temporal power to do so—but even though I am not to judge them, God shall judge them.

For, as St Augustine says on page 116 of his letter *To Vincentius*, it is the custom of the church to reform those it can and tolerate those it cannot, leaving the latter

---

[233] Gregory I, Letter 1.75 *PL*; 1.73 Norberg; towards the end.

[234] These correspond, respectively, to Letter 93 (to Vincentius), Letter 185 (to Boniface), and Letter 173 (to Donatus) in the current numbering system of Augustine's letters. The references to Gratian's *Decretum* C. 23, q. 4 are to chapters 41, 42, and 38, respectively.

[235] Augustine, Letter 93.8.26. Our search of several early editions of Augustine's letters has failed to locate one with the pagination cited here and in the next Objection. The Caracas MS. apparently reads 'párrafo' for 'página' (174r).

[236] 1 Corinthians 5:12, 13.

for the judgment of God.[237] He expresses the same view in his letter *To Marcellinus*, page 116:[238] '*If we cannot correct them, let us tolerate*', he says, '*those who wish to allow vices to go unpunished in the interests of enabling that republic first established and enlarged by the Romans with their virtues to continue to enjoy stability.*'[239] And he is referring here to the Roman gentiles who claimed that Christianity was the cause of the ruin of the Roman empire and state. No right-thinking person, then, should become involved in matters in which they stand no chance of prevailing, nor is it for apostles to require infidels to account for the nature of their lives and instruct them to lead a Christian existence, as they can with Christians.

(2) It *is*, however, for apostles to endeavour to get them to them to convert and preach the gospel to them and essay all possible means to this end with all their might, as the life of St Paul himself and that of all the other Apostles attests, as do the deaths which they suffered on that same account. For this much is certain: the pope has the power to preach the gospel and the natural laws enshrined in the Decalogue—either in person or through the mission of others—to all the infidels of the world, for he has instructions to that effect (Matthew, final chapter; Mark 16).[240]

(3) Though this power principally pertains to spiritual matters, its use in temporal affairs is by no means precluded where spiritual ends are at stake, as St Thomas teaches in *On the Government of Rulers*, Book 3, Chapter 13.[241] For he says the same thing in *Secunda secundae*, q. 40, art. 2, ad 3: '*The power to which a given end pertains should dictate the means to that end.*'[242] The church explains this natural decree in the chapters '*Preterea*', '*Prudentiam*', and '*Suspicionis*' of the title *De officio delegati*,[243] where it says that whosoever is entrusted with a primary responsibility is understood to be likewise entrusted with all the ancillary actions which serve to arrive at the objective in question and without which the matter cannot be accomplished. And not being able to do something refers here to that which cannot be done without great difficulty—which is one order of impossibility, according to Aristotle in Book 5 of his *Metaphysics*.[244] And in any matter the primary thing is the ultimate objective, and the things which serve further to accomplish it are known as the ancillary elements.

---

[237] This is Augustine, Letter 93. Sepúlveda's Spanish paraphrase is from §9.34: 'corrigens quos potest, tolerans quos corrigere non potest'.

[238] It is unclear which edition Sepúlveda was using here (see nn. 218 and 235 above), and it is in any case odd that both letters should be listed as appearing on the same page ('p. 116'), suggesting that one or other page reference here is likely a slip. (The same number appears in the Caracas manuscript, 174r.)

[239] Augustine, Letter 138.3.17.

[240] Matthew 28:19–20; Mark 16:15.

[241] This is in fact Pseudo-Aquinas (Ptolemy of Lucca), *De regimine principum* 3.13: 25.

[242] Aquinas, *ST* II-II, q. 40, art. 2, ad 3.

[243] X.1.29.5, 21, 39. This title 29 of Bk. 1 of Gregory IX's *Decretals* is entitled '*De officio et potestate iudicis delegati*', reduced (with intrusive full-stop and upper-case 'D') in the printed text to 'el titulo de officio. De lega'.

[244] Aristotle, *Metaphysics* 5; more specifically, perhaps 5.5.3 (1015a34). See also Sepúlveda in his *Apologia*, IV.4.iii.

CONTAINED HEREIN IS A DEBATE OR DISPUTATION 277

Sixth objection

(1) With regard to his assertion that Christ did not grant St Peter power over all the world, for he himself did not possess it *in actu* but only *in potentia*, I would respond that the power granted to Christ, as described in the final chapter of Matthew, was the right to graze, guide, and govern his flock the world over,[245] which is why he called himself a shepherd (John 10),[246] just as the Holy Scripture routinely refers to princes and kings as shepherds. He bestowed this same authority on his vicar (John 21) by means of the words: *'Peter, graze my sheep.'*[247] That the sheep of the Lord comprise Christians and infidels alike is specified by Christ himself (John 10), saying, *'I am the good shepherd, and I know my own sheep, and my own know me',*[248] which is clearly a reference to the faithful; and he then goes on to say, *'And I also have other sheep that are not of this fold, and I must bring them in too',*[249] which is a reference to heathens, as the doctors affirm. And in order to bring these sheep into the fold he sent forth the Apostles throughout the whole world, saying: *'Go into all the world and preach the gospel to every creature'* (Mark 16).[250]

So Christ and his vicar held this jurisdiction over all the world, as is also evident from that passage in Psalm 2: *'Ask it of me, and I will give you the nations as your inheritance, and the ends of the earth as your possession.'*[251] And to claim that Christ possessed this power and right *in potentia* but not *in actu* runs counter to the gospel, for the following syllogism holds true: *if they do not have it* in actu, *then they do not have it; if it is not the case* in actu *then it is simply not the case*, as Aristotle teaches in Book 9 of his *Metaphysics*.[252] And when it comes to power *pro habitu*, Aristotle says: *'Those who have something* in habitu *truly do have it* in actu *as well, for* habitus *is a certain form of* actus' (Aristotle, *De anima*, Book 2, [as quoted in Aquinas, *Summa theologica*, *Prima secundae*], 12, q. 49, [a. 3, ad] 1);[253] for instance,

---

[245] Matthew 28:18.
[246] John 10:11, 14.
[247] John 21:17.
[248] John 10:14.
[249] John 10:16.
[250] Mark 16:15.
[251] Psalm 2:8.
[252] Sepúlveda is indeed broadly drawing on Aristotle, *Metaphysics* 9 here, though he is neither translating directly nor even paraphrasing closely. In fact, in (standard Latin translations of) *Metaphysics* 9, the word *habitus* does not appear at all. The Latin text Sepúlveda offers here would appear, then, to be his own syllogistic extrapolation from Book 9's discussion of actuality and potentiality.
[253] Again, most of the Latin translated in italics here is not actually drawn directly from Aristotle. The concluding words (*habitus est actus quidam*) are, as Sepúlveda indicates, to be found in Aquinas (albeit not in *ST* I-II, 'q. 49, [art.] 1', as the original reference would have it, but in I-II, q. 49, art. 3, ad 1); however, while Aquinas does cite Book 2 of Aristotle's *De anima* in that section, he was not attributing those precise words to Aristotle, though Sepúlveda appears to have taken (or misremembered) him as doing so; hence his reference here to a specific Aristotelian source for the idea (i.e. *De anima* 2).

when the king of Spain is asleep or at play, he possesses the right to rule over Spain *in habitu*, and indeed he truly and *in actu* is the king, even though he is not exercising his rule at that very moment. And with reference to the words of St Paul in Hebrews 2, '*But now we do not yet see all things subjected to him*',[254] he is talking about subjugation '*by faith*', which is the case with all the faithful, but this is not mutually exclusive with universal subjugation of the whole world so as to be able to enforce natural law, preach the gospel, and undertake all the other actions which serve this end.

(2) With regard to the precedent he adduces from St Augustine's sermon On the centurion's slave-boy—'It is for me to speak to Christians, for what business of mine is it to judge those who are outside?'[255]—I would reiterate that this passage is to be interpreted along the lines set out above, in my answer to the fifth objection. And with regard to what St Augustine says there in that sixth sermon of his on the centurion's slave-boy, in connection with the destruction of idols, the whole point of those remarks is designed to combat the mania of a particular group of heretics known as Circumcellions, who used to frequent the pagans' most renowned rites, to which huge crowds flocked, in order to smash up their idols with the express aim of getting themselves killed, convinced that in so doing they were martyrs acting in the service of God.

St Augustine himself reports this in his fiftieth letter (*To Boniface*),[256] denouncing such madness and stating that it is not the suffering that makes the martyr, but the cause. And at this point he [Augustine] remarks that God does not command us to destroy idols under all circumstances but rather only when they are in our possession, as Daniel did when he destroyed the idol which King Darius had entrusted to him (Daniel 14).[257] And he ordered the Israelites to destroy the statues in the Promised Land only after they had taken possession of it and not under any circumstances where doing so would be detrimental to and dangerous for the faithful, as was the case in St Augustine's own day, when there were many extremely powerful idolaters in the Christians' midst who would fight back if any attempt were made to destroy their idols, prompting great strife between Christians and gentiles.

(3) For even though the emperor was Christian, he did not wish to be as draconian in his dealings with the gentiles as Constantine had been. After Constantine came Julian the Apostate, who persecuted the Christians. And as a result of the enormous resistance with which Constantine's law was met on the part of the gentiles, other emperors turned a blind eye to their observance of their rites in the interests of averting unrest in the empire.

---

[254] Hebrews 2:8.
[255] Augustine, *Sermones ad populum*, Sermon 62, 7.11.
[256] Augustine, Letter 185.2.9
[257] Daniel 14:21, discussed in Augustine, Letter 185.5.19.

CONTAINED HEREIN IS A DEBATE OR DISPUTATION   279

This can be seen from what St Ambrose wrote in Letters 30 and 31,[258] both of which attest to the power enjoyed by the gentiles in his own day, for not only were they strongly represented in the Roman Senate, but even the prefect of the city [Rome]—a man named [Quintus Aurelius] Symmachus—was a gentile. And here is what St Thomas has to say (*Summa theologica, Secunda secundae*, [q. 10], article 11): '*The rites of infidels are not to be tolerated in any way, except perhaps for the purposes of averting some evil, in other words, to avoid a scandal or the devastation which might ensue from it, or an impediment to the salvation of those who, while thus tolerated, are gradually being converted to the faith. For this reason the church once upon a time tolerated the rites of heretics and pagans, back when the population of infidels was extremely large.*'[259]

(4) So St Augustine—who was a contemporary of St Ambrose, albeit somewhat his junior—says that Christians were not in the habit of going around destroying the gentiles' idols because they did not have the power or means to do so without provoking strife and imperilling themselves, nor did divine law oblige them to attempt it unless it were possible to do so without encountering these obstacles, as would come to be the case once the Christians were so numerous and powerful that they could do so with impunity and at no danger to themselves, or else once the gentiles came to the Christians of their own accord, at which point they would set to work smashing them up themselves.[260]

This, then, is how that celebrated passage from St Augustine is to be taken: for in 23, question 4, canon '*Non invenitur*',[261] St Augustine himself confirms that the use of force to rid the gentiles of their idolatry against their volition and on pain of death and of the confiscation of goods is lawful and sacrosanct and meets with the approval of all Christians; this is likewise attested by St Thomas, in the passage just cited [*Summa theologica* II-II, q. 10, art. 11], and St Gregory in Book 9, Letter 6 60, heaping praise upon Constantine on this account.[262]

---

[258] Ambrose, Letters 17 and 18; formerly Letters 30 and 31, as in *Operum Sancti Ambrosii pars tertius* (Basel: Johann Amerbach, 1492), fols. 34r–35r and 36r–38r; Sepúlveda also cites them again at *Apologia* III.4.xiii. These letters from Ambrose to Emperor Valentinian II in 384 were designed to counteract the attempts of the pagan Prefect of Rome, Quintus Aurelius Symmachus, to restore the Altar of Victory to the Senate House in Rome and to secure support for other pagan institutions, such as the Vestal Virgins. In the Amerbach edition of these letters, the account of Symmachus is placed between the two.

[259] Aquinas, *ST* II-II, q. 10, art. 11, co. The 1552 printing inadvertently omitted *salutis* ('salvation') between *impedimentum* and *eorum*, though it was present in the Caracas manuscript (175r).

[260] Sepúlveda is here drawing generally on Augustine in his three famous anti-Donatist letters (see n. 234 above), especially perhaps Letter 173 (particularly 173.10); also Letter 138 (formerly 5).

[261] Gratian, *Decretum*, C. 23, q. 4, c. 41, offering section 3.9–10 of Augustine's Letter 93 (to Vincentius).

[262] Gregory I, *Ad Edilbertum anglorum regem*, Bk. 9, Ep. 60 (misprinted as '6' in Soto's text here); now Letter 11.66 (*PL* 77) or 11.37 (Norberg), and at 1.32 in Bede's *Ecclesiastical History*. See further n. 214 above on this letter from Gregory to Ethelbert, king of Kent.

Seventh objection

(1) As for his assertion that when the esteemed canonists speak in their discussion of the chapter *Quod super his* [from the title] *De voto* of the church's right to wage war and punish idolaters and those who fail to observe natural law,[263] they are referring to cases in which the people in question have commandeered Christian territories or profane the Creator and obstruct the faith or under circumstances where other just grounds obtain, I would say that this is patently fraudulent. For the aforementioned doctors say that people can be vanquished and punished for no other reason than that they flout natural law or are idolaters. Thus, it would be preposterous to say that they can be vanquished on account of blasphemy alone yet not on account of idolatry, which is the most reprehensible of all sins and encompasses both heathenism and blasphemy and is tantamount to an assault on the faith, as I have already argued on the authority of St Thomas (*Secunda secundae*, q. 94, article 3, ad 2).[264]

Eighth objection

(1) As for his argument that, on grounds of the fact that those who have both cities and governance cannot be deemed barbarian, these Indians are not to be considered barbarians to the degree that would warrant their forced submission to the right-thinking and civilized, I would respond that the term 'barbarian' (as defined by St Thomas in *Politics* I, First Lesson)[265] denotes anyone who does not live in accordance with natural reason and engages in wicked patterns of behaviour that are openly endorsed by the community, be this as a result of the absence of religion—a context in which humans are raised in a beast-like state—or be it on account of their wicked behaviour and lack of sound doctrine and system of punishment.

(2) That these are people of limited understanding and depraved habits is confirmed in the testimony of practically everyone to return from the Indies, perhaps most notably in the account of them offered in Book 3, Chapter 6 of the *Historia general*, penned by an earnest chronicler and industrious investigator who has spent many years in the islands and on the mainland of Tierra Firme.[266]

---

[263] The canonists to whose comments on Innocent III's decretal *Quod super his* (X.3.34.8 in the *Decretals* of Gregory IX) is alluding here are principally Innocent IV and Hostiensis, supported by Joannes Andreas and Panormitanus. Compare his discussion of this same point in the *Apologia* III.2.xii.

[264] Aquinas, *ST* II-II, q. 94, art. 3, ad 2.

[265] Aquinas, *Sententia libri politicorum* (*Commentary on Aristotle's* Politics), Bk. 1, lect. 1, c. 23.

[266] Gonzalo Fernández de Oviedo y Valdés, *Historia general de las Indias*, [Part I,] Bk. 3, ch. 6. Sepúlveda would have known Oviedo's work through the editions of Juan Cromberger (Seville, 1535) or Juan de Junta (Salamanca, 1547).

Ninth objection

(1) As to his assertion that war is sooner a hindrance than an aid to the Indians' conversion in view of the harm it does in instilling such hatred for the Christians in them, not to mention the fact that the behaviour and lifestyle of the soldiers is such that their manifold wickednesses preclude any possibility of the religion they profess being deemed a good one, I would answer that the delirious patient also takes against the physician who cures him, and the mischievous boy against the teacher who punishes him, yet in both cases the approaches adopted are no less salutary for it, nor should they cease to be performed, as averred by St Augustine in his fiftieth letter.[267]

(2) Moreover, warfare and soldiers are not supposed to serve to convert or to preach, but rather to subjugate the barbarians, thereby paving and securing the way for preaching, which should in turn be performed by friars and clergymen of sound lifestyle and doctrine who can lead by example. The preaching itself must be carried out with the utmost meekness, as modelled by the Apostles. This is what St Augustine has to say in Letter 48: 'For if the infidels had fear instilled in them but were not offered any teaching, this might look all too akin to dreadful tyranny; but if, on the other hand, they were to be given instruction but not inspired with fear, they would be less swift to embark upon the path of salvation, having become hardened by the ingrained nature of their customary ways.'[268]

Tenth objection

(1) As to his claim that the infidels cannot be collectively forced to harken to preaching, this is a new-fangled piece of false doctrine which is not shared even by those who are of the same opinion as him in all other regards. For the pope has the power and indeed the mandate to preach the gospel both himself and through the ministry of others across the whole world, and this cannot be accomplished if nobody listens to the preachers; it follows, then, that he has the power to force them to listen to them by order of Christ himself. 'For when a task is entrusted to someone, it is taken as read that those things without which it cannot be accomplished are also entrusted, provided that natural law is upheld' (in the chapter 'Suspicionis of De officio delegati').[269] And to cite St Thomas (Secunda secundae, q. 40, art. 2, ad 3): 'The power to which a given end pertains should dictate the means to that end.'[270]

---

[267] Augustine, Letter 185.2.7 [formerly Letter 50] (to Boniface).
[268] Augustine, Letter 93.1.3 (to Vincentius).
[269] Gregory IX in X.1.29.39. Sepúlveda has abridged and adapted the text of this chapter somewhat. On the nomenclature of tit. 29 itself, see n. 243 above.
[270] Aquinas, ST II-II, q. 40, art. 2, ad 3 (paraphrased).

282 SEPÚLVEDA ON THE SPANISH INVASION OF THE AMERICAS

Eleventh objection

(1) As to his contention that, although waging war was justified as a means of saving the lives of the innocents whom they were in the habit of sacrificing, this course of action should nonetheless not be pursued since one must always choose the lesser of two evils, and the evils arising from such warfare are far worse than the deaths of those innocent victims, our good sir has got his sums quite wrong: for in New Spain—as reported by all those who return from those parts and have made it their business to look into the matter—more than twenty thousand people were sacrificed each year; and if one multiplies this figure across the thirty years that have elapsed since New Spain was annexed and this form of sacrifice abolished, this would amount to six hundred thousand people already, whereas I doubt that in the course of the conquest of the entire region more people were killed than victims formerly sacrificed by them in a single year.

(2) Furthermore, this war averts the perdition of the countless souls of those who, upon conversion to the faith, will now be saved, both those alive today and those to be born hereafter. And as St Augustine says in Letter 75, it is far worse to lose a single soul of a person who dies unbaptized than to kill scores of men, innocent though they may be.[271]

(3) For contriving to come up with excuses to justify human sacrifice is so far removed from Christianity that it was even considered an abomination by those gentiles who were not themselves uncivilized barbarians, as noted by Pliny in Book 30, Chapter ± 3 as follows: in the year 656 657 '*a decree forbidding human sacrifices was passed by the Senate and at that time the public celebration of this monstrous rite sank into silence*',[272] and not far from there he also says: '*It is hard to convey how much is owed to the Romans for having abolished those monstrous rites in which killing a man was a most devout act*'.[273] Quintus Curtius, in his fourth book, notes the following: '*Those responsible for seeking to reinstate a rite which has been discontinued in many eras and which I should imagine does not please the gods in the least—namely sacrificing a free-born boy to Saturn, which is more a sacrilege than a holy rite—are mistaken in so doing*',[274] etc. Plutarch in his *Apophthegmata* also reports that, upon defeating the Carthaginians, Gelon (tyrant of Sicily) did not wish to make peace with them except on condition that they stop sacrificing their sons

---

[271] Augustine, Letter 250.2 [formerly Letter 75] (to Auxilius).

[272] Pliny the Elder, *Naturalis historia* 30.3.12. The concluding phrase in the 1552 edition (as in the Caracas manuscript, 176r) reads: '*palamque in tempus siluit sacri prodigiosi celebratio*'. This is the version found on p. 539 of the Froben–Erasmus edition of 1525. We have translated this version. Galmés changed '*in tempus*' to the meaningless '*in templos*' (perhaps intending '*in templis*'). Modern texts of Pliny read: '*palamque in tempus illud sacra prodigiosa celebrata*', translated by W. H. S. Jones (Loeb editon, vol. 8, 287): 'so that down to that date it is manifest that such abominable rites were practised'.

[273] Pliny the Elder, *Naturalis historia* 30.4.13.

[274] Quintus Curtius, *Historiae Alexandri Magni* 4.23. The 1552 printing offers '*nostris seculis*' ('in our own times') where the Caracas manuscript (176r) has the clearly correct '*multis s[a]eculis*' ('in many ages').

CONTAINED HEREIN IS A DEBATE OR DISPUTATION   283

to Saturn.[275] And Justin writes that a king of Persia sent to warn the Carthaginians to desist from human sacrifice on pain of having war waged against them and facing annihilation—and they promised to comply.[276] St Augustine also has relevant remarks in his *Quaestiones super judicum*, q. 49.[277] Accordingly, maintaining that ignorance is a valid excuse in the case of so abominable a crime against nature is unconscionable.

(4) And the point he makes about being obliged to refrain from waging a war aimed at punishing a few guilty parties if it cannot be accomplished without a much larger number of innocent people coming to grief is irrelevant. For in a city or community where human sacrifice was performed by public authority, all are guilty, since all approve of the practice.

I would point out that visiting evils and harm upon innocent and guilty parties alike is a feature of practically all wars. But this is inadvertent and contrary to the wishes of the monarch; and thus, so long as the cause is just, the objective holy, and the intention of the monarch sound, the sins of the soldiers—which are committed against the monarch's will and which he does his best to avert—inflict harm upon themselves and their own souls, which offends God, but does not damage the monarch or the cause itself.

Gerson, that redoubtable authority, says the following in the chapter 'On avarice' of his moral precepts: '*In the waging of wars, which are full of innumerable evils, sometimes to one group of innocent people, at other times to another, only the good of the state excuses people from mortal sin—or, at times, the avoidance of a public harm that is markedly worse than a private harm proceeding from the war would be.*'[278] For when it comes to this sort of war—be it waged on account of idolatry alone, or both on that account and also[279] so as to prevent the deaths of the innocents who were sacrificial victims—the evils which are averted by means of warfare are far greater than those arising from it, for, quite aside from everything else, it averts the deaths of all the many souls of those who convert and are yet to convert hereafter. In Letter 75 St Augustine affirms how much worse this particular evil is than the evil that arises from warfare, declaring that it is far worse

---

[275] Plutarch, *Regum et imperatorum apophthegmata* 19.1 (not to be confused with his *Apophthegmata Laconica*). Here, through yet another instance of *saut du même au même*, Trujillo's 1552 typesetter combined the Plutarch reference with the following reference to Justin, severely truncating both and omitting any mention of Justin or his Persian king. The correct reading is supplied by the Caracas manuscript (176v).

[276] Justin, *Epitome of the Philippic History of Pompeius Trogus* 19.1.10. The Persian king was Darius.

[277] Augustine, *Quaestiones S. Augustini in Heptateuchum*, Bk. 7, *Quaestiones in Iudices*, q. 49, 2–3, where Augustine insisted the story of Jephthah and his daughter does not mean that God approves of human sacrifice.

[278] Jean Gerson, *Regulae morales* 73 (abridged), in the section *De avaritia*. An edition available at the time was *Libellus canonum moralium Ioannis Gersonis* (Erfurt: Wolfgang Shenck, 1500, fol. 14v).

[279] The 1552 printing (followed by Galmés) offered the reading *por la idolatria sola, o por ella o por excusar las muertes*, where the second *o* ('or') is nonsensical. The Caracas manuscript (176v) correctly offers *y* ('and').

for a single soul to die unbaptized than for an infinite number of men to be killed, innocent though they might be.[280]

(5) And so I must reiterate that his [Las Casas's] claim that ignorance absolves them of the sin of performing human sacrifice to their gods is a doctrine which cannot be borne among Christians *if Catholic, Christian truth is to be preserved*. After all, by that same logic all the idolaters in the world would be exonerated by virtue of having all laboured under the selfsame blindness that is the conviction that their sacrifices served to worship certain beings whom they held to be gods, which is all completely inexcusable, as St Paul says in his Epistle to the Romans, Chapter 1: '*For even though they knew God, they did not honour him as God ... and they exchanged the glory of the incorruptible God for an image in the form of corruptible mankind and of birds*',[281] etc.

And if these barbarians are within their rights to defend their religion and idolatry, as would seem to be implied in the summary of his [Las Casas's] book and as the esteemed bishop went so far as to state outright in his *Confesionario*,[282] it would follow that they are within their rights to condone this practice and, consequently, that their worship of their idols is just and free from sin, although it is even more sinful to endorse the crime than to commit it. This cannot be tolerated among Catholics, for idolatry is the worst of all sins *and goes against natural reason* in the estimation of all theologians; and ignorance of natural law does not serve to exonerate anyone, as theologians and canonists alike concur.

(6) And as to his claim that deeming human sacrifice a good thing constitutes a probable opinion as it is the opinion held by the wisest members of the community, in which connection he adduces Aristotle, I would counter that the Philosopher [Aristotle] does not consider the least barbarous men among the barbarians to be wise or sensible but rather only those who live among organized, civilized peoples, as he states in the first book of his *Politics* in the context of his discussion of barbarians.[283]

And the case of Abraham in his [Las Casas's] example actually works against him, for God did not ultimately permit him to sacrifice his son. And the same goes for the sacrifice of first-born sons, whereby he ordered the first-born offspring of animals to be substituted for humans and sacrificed in their stead, as reasoned by St Augustine in the aforementioned work.[284]

---

[280] Augustine, Letter 250.2 [formerly Letter 75] (to Auxilius).

[281] Romans 1:21, 23.

[282] Las Casas, *Confesionario* (1546).

[283] Aristotle, *Politics* 1. It is unclear which passage exactly Sepúlveda had in mind, for Aristotle nowhere expresses himself in precisely these terms, but in general for Aristotle's views on these matters see 1.2 (1252a30–b9), 1.6 (1255a28–30), 3.14 (1285a16–27), and 7.7 (1327b20–31).

[284] i.e. Augustine, *Quaestiones S. Augustini in Heptateuchum*, Bk. 7, *Quaestiones in Iudices*, q. 49, 2; see further n. 277 above.

And so, to claim that they are not obliged to believe those who bring tidings of the faith of Christ and of natural law is manifestly contrary to the gospel of Mark 16—'*He who believes and is baptized will be saved; but he who does not believe will be condemned*'[285]—for God condemns no one for failing to do something they are under no obligation to do.

Twelfth objection

(1) As to his claim that what Pope Alexander [VI] meant in his bull was for the gospel first to be preached to those barbarians and then, upon their conversion to Christianity,[286] that they should become subject to the sovereigns of Castile—not insofar as control of particular things are concerned, nor with a view to enslaving them or depriving them of their realms, but rather purely at the level of overall jurisdiction by means of a reasonable degree of tribute paid towards the protection of the faith and instruction in matters of sound behaviour and good governance— and that this was spelled out in another bull,[287] issued by Pope Paul III, I would respond that Pope Alexander's intention (as is clear to see from the bull itself) was for the barbarians first to be subjugated to the sovereigns of Castile and then for the gospel to be preached to them afterwards.

For this was the approach adopted from the outset by command of the Catholic monarchs in accordance with the wishes of the pope, who himself went on to live a full nine or ten more years after issuing that bull and hence was perfectly cognizant of the manner in which the conquest was being conducted over there, just as all subsequent popes have likewise been aware of it and sanctioned it: not only by refraining from stipulating anything to the contrary but also by each in turn issuing further bulls, dispensations, and concessions for the churches with cathedral status that have been erected[288] over in that part of the world and likewise for the bishoprics and monasteries there.

For the bull of Paul III was designed only to apply to those soldiers who went marauding around, without royal authorization, enslaving the barbarians in question, committing all manner of other offences and treating the barbarians like beasts, which is what led him to specify in that bull that they were to treat them as human beings and fellow men, for they were rational animals.

---

[285] Mark 16:16.
[286] Alexander VI, *Inter caetera* (1493).
[287] Paul III, *Sublimis Deus* (1537).
[288] Reading the Caracas manuscript's *erigido* for the 1552 edition's *elegido* (177r).

(2) For to claim, as he [Las Casas] does, that they are not to be subjugated from the outset but rather only upon conversion to Christianity does not make the first bit of sense. For if it is lawful to subjugate them on one account—namely, for the protection of the faith and to prevent them from abandoning it and lapsing into heresy—why should it not follow that it is all the more lawful on two sets of grounds, namely for the aforementioned reason and, more to the point, for another, more pressing one, namely to stop them from standing in the way of preaching and of the conversion of those receptive to the faith, as well as for the purposes of getting rid of idolatry and wicked practices?

I would sooner say that, if forced to differentiate between these two stages in the process, it would stand more to reason to propose that we should have kept them in a state of subjugation until we had preached the faith to them, eradicated their idolatry, and converted them to Catholicism, thereby fulfilling the objectives of the Church, whereupon they would in turn be required to be returned to their previous state of freedom and self-governance, as opposed to *refraining* from subjugating them at the outset so as not to subject them to violence or harm—even though they deserve to be stripped of everything on account of their sins and idolatry—and then, once they had renounced their idolatry and embraced the faith, proceeding to use force against them and deprive them of their domains to prevent them from abandoning the faith again.

To do so would be to punish them for something they have not done, which goes against divine and natural law; indeed it would be akin to one who fancies himself overly clever advising a compassionate prince that a fellow who had spent a lifetime embroiled in grave sin and immense wrongdoing should be punished in word only, have all his past deeds forgiven, and be welcomed into the monarch's household like one of his own, and then, once the man in question had reformed, for the aforementioned adviser to bend the prince's ear again and counsel him to sentence the man in perpetuity to the galleys out of suspicion and concern that someone who had led such a dissolute life for so long might easily slip back into his sinful old ways. This would be one of the greater strokes of nonsense of which one can conceive: forgiving the sins of the past while meting out punishment for those which have not yet been committed.

(3) And, what is more, I would say that to grant that, upon conversion to Christianity, they and their foremost nobles are then obliged to submit to the sovereigns of Castile flies in the face of all the points he [Las Casas] has advanced in the interests of averting warfare. For if the sovereigns of Castile have, as he claims, the right to subjugate them in the manner described upon their conversion to Christianity, it surely follows that—if they refuse to pledge obedience—it is just to use force to oblige them to do so, for which war is necessary. This would in turn mean that war could justly be waged against them on far flimsier grounds than the ones I propose; and so he undoes everything he has previously said on the subject by the very terms of his own concession.

(4) As a result, this and everything else the esteemed bishop writes proves, upon closer inspection, to be designed to demonstrate that all the conquests undertaken to date—even with all directives duly observed—have been unjust and tyrannical and thus also to serve to corroborate the case made in his *Confesionario* (which could more rightly be termed defamatory libel against our sovereigns and people, as is indeed the view His Majesty's councils took of it) and to convince the emperor to refrain from undertaking any more conquests hereafter, which would constitute dereliction of duty on His Majesty's part and a failure to fulfil Christ's commandment to spread the faith—a duty he is bound by the church to discharge—and, in turn, that those wretched peoples who remain unconquered would not get the opportunity to convert to the faith.

(5) For, in the absence of the mandate to subjugate them, military personnel who at their own expense ensure the preachers' safety would cease to go as they have done to date, nor would the king foot the bill, for he has plenty of other, more pressing financial demands in his kingdom over here, and there are scarcely sufficient funds to support the preachers even here at home. And even if he did wish to bear the cost and send people over, he would be unable to find anyone willing to travel such distances even to the tune of thirty ducats a month, when nowadays they spare themselves neither danger nor expense in the interests of the gains they expect to reap from the gold and silver mines with the aid of the Indians they have subjugated. And if anyone should think to suggest that the Indians should shoulder the cost themselves, since this is all being done for their own good, it goes without saying that they would never acquiesce to this except under duress and upon defeat in war, which brings us back full circle to the first point.

And so preachers would not go, and even if they did go they would not be welcomed in but rather subjected to the same treatment as those who, at the instigation of the bishop on the selfsame grounds, were sent to Florida last year without any military accompaniment. And even if the preachers were not killed, a hundred years of preaching would still not be as effective as fifteen days' worth of it with the Indians subjugated beforehand, affording the former the freedom to preach openly and the latter the liberty to convert should they so wish, free from fear of their own priests or *caciques*. The opposite is the case in contexts where they are not first subjugated.

(6) And verily the esteemed bishop has gone to such lengths and efforts to foreclose all possible pathways by which to justify conquest and unseat all the premises on which the justice of the emperor's position is founded that he has given nonpartisan observers, particularly those who have read his *Confesionario*, no little grounds to realize and report that his primary purpose all along has been to

convince all and sundry that the dominion exercised over the Indies by the sovereigns of Castile is wholly unjust and tyrannical; however, he allows them their title on patently flimsy, baseless grounds so as to pander to His Majesty by any means possible, since he more than any other has the power to visit good and ill upon him.

(7) And so, to draw to a conclusion, I submit that it is lawful to subjugate these barbarians from the outset so as to rid them of their idolatry and wicked rites and to prevent them from standing in the way of preaching—on the contrary, they will be in a position to convert more freely and easily—and also from apostatizing after their conversion and relapsing into heresy; rather, they will be able to grow ever surer in the faith and abandon their barbarous rites and practices thanks to their interactions with Christian Spaniards. I trust that I have by means of these responses satisfied the objections and arguments of the esteemed bishop and of those who subscribe to his view. Almost all of what I have advanced here is addressed in my book [the *Democrates secundus*] and in the digest thereof [the *Apologia*]. The latter was printed at Rome after scrutiny and a positive assessment in the estimation of three immensely learned, redoubtable gentlemen—the vicar of the pope, the master of the Holy Palace, and an auditor of the Rota[289]—and unanimously praised by numerous other vastly erudite members of the Roman Court, as is evident from the very fact of being sent to press. This approval, together with the Bull of Concession of Alexander and the further endorsements issued by the other popes in the manner I have outlined, ought to suffice to dispel every last trace of doubt or misgiving harboured towards the digest, which is available in printed form, as also towards the book itself, of which multiple manuscript copies are in circulation throughout all of Spain.[290] For everything else I refer the reader directly to that material, where more detailed discussion of all this is offered.

Thanks be to God.

---

[289] Respectively, Felipe Archinto, Egidio Foscario, and Antonio Agustín.

[290] Though unprinted, copies of the *Democrates secundus* were certainly circulating in Spain in manuscript form, in particular circles at least.

Bartolomé de las Casas's 'Twelve Replies'

These are the replies offered by the bishop of Chiapa to counter the solutions to the twelve objections which Dr Sepúlveda prepared in response to the foregoing *Summary* of the bishop's *Apología*[291]

The bishop of Chiapa's prologue to the esteemed members of the assembly

Most illustrious and eminent sirs, most reverend and learned fathers: so far, in the material I have read out and submitted in written form to this august assembly, I have inveighed against the adversaries of the Indians of our Indies of the Ocean Sea as a collective, without singling out any one by name, although I could certainly point to a few who toil away and devote their every waking hour to composing treatises in the service of their principal objective, which is to say the justification and defence of the lawfulness of the wars—source of so much devastation and destruction, downfall of so many kingdoms of such magnitude, vast populations, and an infinitude of souls—which have been and could be waged upon them and of the idea that waging such wars against them in order first to subjugate them before they have so much as heard Jesus Christ's name through the preaching of the faith can be endured under Christian law.

Now it strikes me that the most reverend and distinguished Dr Sepúlveda has revealed and declared himself to be the arch-proponent and champion of these wars in the course of his response to the lines of reasoning, proof-texts, and counterarguments which I compiled in my *Apología*—part of which I read out before your excellencies and lordships—in the interests of exposing and repudiating the wickedness and tyrannical injustice of the aforementioned warfare, which also goes by the name of 'conquest'. And since he has seen fit to unmask himself and did not shrink from being deemed the aider and abettor of such abominable impieties

---

[291] At the end of the Caracas manuscript (fol. 228r), this appears as 'And these are the responses of the bishop of Chiapa against the solutions which Dr Sepúlveda gave to the objections which he noted in the summary that Master Friar Domingo de Soto drew from the said bishop's "Defence".'

which bring such disgrace upon the faith, dishonour to the name of Christianity, and spiritual and temporal ruin to the greater part of the human race, it seems to me only right to impugn him openly and oppose him outright if the poisonous cancer which he wishes to spread throughout those realms to their detriment and destruction is to be stemmed.

I therefore beg of you, illustrious lordships, mercies, and worships, to consider this momentous, perilous business not as a matter in which I have any vested interest—for my only interest here is to defend it in my capacity as a Christian—but rather as a matter bearing on God and his honour, faith and the universal church, as well as on the spiritual and temporal well-being of the sovereigns of Castile, who will be answerable for the perdition of so many souls of all those who have perished and stand to do so hereafter unless the door to the disastrous course of warmongering advocated by Dr Sepúlveda is slammed shut. And this excellent assembly must not brook the fallacious reasoning of which he avails himself so as to camouflage and gild his deleterious, vicious viewpoint as he affects to strive for, champion, or defend so-called apostolic authority and the right to dominion over those Indies on the part of the monarchs of Castile and León.

For no Christian can in good conscience lawfully champion and defend apostolic authority or the dominion of a Christian monarch by means of unjust wars, mountains and fields awash with innocent human blood, and the defamation and desecration of Christ and his faith. Rather, in accord with Dr Sepúlveda's fabricated argument, the Apostolic See is defamed and robbed of its authority, the true God is dishonoured, and the true title and sovereignty of the king is—as any right-thinking Christian will easily perceive—obliterated and wrecked. This title and sovereignty cannot be established on the basis of invading those lands and populations and robbing, killing, and terrorizing them under the pretence of preaching the faith—which is precisely how those tyrants who have laid waste to that world by killing such a vast multitude of innocent people in such a cruel and indiscriminate fashion have behaved in the course of their invasions—but rather by means of peacefully, sweetly, and lovingly preaching the gospel so as to introduce, establish, and genuinely institute the faith and kingdom of Jesus Christ in a morally upstanding fashion.

Anyone seeking to grant our sovereigns, the monarchs, the right to supreme jurisdiction over those Indies on any other basis is mightily blind, hateful to God, disloyal to his king, and an enemy of the Spanish populace, whom he is guilty of deceiving most contemptibly, since in actual fact such a person wishes to swell the ranks of hell with souls. And so as to prevent such masses from ending up in that most accursed condition, it would behove your lordships, mercies, and worships (as befits such learned Christian individuals as yourselves) to quash so deleterious and evil a stance.

CONTAINED HEREIN IS A DEBATE OR DISPUTATION   291

And though I am convinced that I have already at length in my *Apología* addressed and responded to all conceivable arguments adducible in support of that viewpoint, nonetheless, seeing as the doctor has reprised the points which he believes support his cause by extracting twelve objections from the summary of my *Apología*, it is only right that I should reply to him, demonstrating that each and every one of his solutions is trifling, ineffectual, and worthless.

First reply

(1) With regard to what the reverend Dr Sepúlveda says in response to what I said about there being many other peoples besides those of the Promised Land who were also idolatrous yet whom God did not order to be destroyed and so forth, the doctor presupposes that this is tantamount to saying that the inhabitants of the Promised Land were therefore not destroyed on account of idolatry either, etc. To this I would answer that the doctor is jumping to conclusions and putting words into my mouth, for it is not my view that they were not destroyed on account of their idolatry and the other great sins of which they were guilty, nor solely on account of the promise which God made to Abraham, since God gives both reasons as grounds for these matters (Deuteronomy 9),[292] but rather that God commanded that they alone should be destroyed and not the others who did not dwell within those bounds—although they too were idolaters and sinners—and that that commandment was reserved for the former peoples in particular for the pair of reasons offered by St Thomas in 4, distinction 39, article 1, ad 1,[293] while St Augustine in Sermon 105 of his sermons *On the Liturgical Season* offers a compelling further explanation for singling them out in this way.[294] For when the commandment is limited to a specific group, the general law stands in opposition to it.[295] The reverend doctor is therefore wrong to reason that, just because God ordered those

---

[292] Deuteronomy 9:4–5.

[293] Aquinas, *Scriptum super libros Sententiarum Magistri Petri Lombardi*, Bk. 4, dist. 39, art. 1, ad 1. This was Aquinas's commentary on Peter Lombard's *Sententiae*.

[294] The sermon to which Las Casas refers here as Sermon 105 of the *Sermones de tempore* (on the seasonal celebrations of the liturgical year) is not, in fact, to be found within Augustine's *De tempore* sermons. This is, rather, a pseudo-Augustinian work which can be found at Pseudo-Augustine, *Sermones suppositii* 34 (in the numbering of the Appendix to vol. 5 of the 1683 Maurist edition; see *PL* 39, cols. 1811–13), '*alias* de tempore 105'. The sermon is now commonly attributed to Caesarius of Arles and assigned the number 114. See the edition by Germain Morin (1937–42) and the translation by Sister Mary Madeleine Mueller in the second volume of Caesarius's sermons, vol. 47 of the *Fathers of the Church* series (Washington, DC: Catholic University of America Press, 1964), 161–66. We thank James J. O'Donnell for his help in tracking this down.

[295] 'The general law' here renders 'el derecho común', which in turn renders the Latin *ius commune*, a term from Roman law dating back to the jurist Gaius and defined by Adolf Berger as 'the general law, common to all, the law binding on all peoples or all Roman citizens' (*Encyclopedic Dictionary of Roman*

peoples to be destroyed, it follows from this that war waged to subjugate the Indians before they have had the chance to hear any preaching is lawful in that it rids them of idolatry.

(2) And another thing: what underlying rationale did the doctor perceive in the fact of God having ordered the destruction of the aforementioned seven tribes of Canaan in view of their sins and idolatry and everything else combined on account of the promise made to Abraham in the Old Testament—an era of such intransigence towards gentile populations the world over, whereas under the present era of grace and love Christ commanded that they should all without exception be preached to, entreated, invited, and brought to God by means of blandishments, thereby inducing them to give up their rites and idolatry—such that he was led to conclude that the Indians ought by means of warfare to be brought into the fold (it would be more appropriate to say 'driven away" and 'scared off') as the means of inducing them to forswear their idolatry and all other hindrances to preaching. It is obvious that the reverend doctor is availing himself of specious logic here.

(3) And for another thing: if he claims that he is not proposing that the war to be waged against the Indians is to be undertaken so as to destroy and kill them but rather with a view to subjugating them, it would be instructive to be enlightened on his views at to whether war can be waged without killing anyone or whether the soldiers will kill, rob, capture, traumatize, torment, and drive away at least some proportion of people in the course of these wars, or, alternatively, just how many of them exactly the doctor would have killed, captured, robbed, tormented, traumatized, and driven into the mountains to be fodder for tigers, and where exactly he would draw the line?

(4) And another: how does he reconcile what he says about those other peoples who dwelt outside the Promised Land, whose impieties were (in his view) not so thoroughgoing, being subjugable to the faithful Jewish people through war on account of their heathenism and idolatry, with what it says in Deuteronomy Chapter 23, namely, '*You shall not abhor an Edomite, for he is your brother, nor an Egyptian, for you were a stranger in his land*'?[296] For where was there more idolatry than in Egypt, source of all idolatrism?

(5) And another: how would the doctor account for the distinction drawn by God in the example he adduces from Deuteronomy 20,[297] in which he commanded

---

Law: Transactions of the American Philosophical Society, v. 45, pt. 2, 527, Philadelphia: 1953). In English, the Latin term is often translated 'the common law', but this can be confusing, given the separate development of the English 'common law'.

[296] Deuteronomy 23:7.
[297] Deuteronomy 20:10, 15–17.

CONTAINED HEREIN IS A DEBATE OR DISPUTATION   293

that whenever they went forth to wage war against any city from among those that were '*far away*' and distant—which is to say, those that lay outside the Promised Land—the first thing they should do was to offer peace to them, yet when it came to the inhabitants of the Promised Land they were not to offer them peace but rather put them all, young and old alike, to death by the sword? For the interpretations advanced by St Thomas, St Augustine, Nicholas [of Gorran], and El Tostado do not seem to satisfy the doctor. '*When you approach a city to fight against it*', he says, '*you shall first offer it terms of peace*',[298] and, further along: '*So you shall do to all the cities that are very far away from you and ... which do not number among the cities of which you are to take possession. But in the cities which are to be given to you, you shall not leave anything alive, but deal death to it with the blade of the sword*',[299] etc.

Therefore there must indeed have been some difference between the seven Canaanite nations and those peoples not of the Promised Land, albeit not the distinction which the doctor wishes to draw (namely that the sins of those outside the Promised Land were not inveterate, on account of which the faithful were apparently not to kill them but rather to subjugate them by means of warfare), but rather the one drawn by the venerable exegetes of the Holy Scripture, namely the commandment which the Israelites had received from God instructing them to exterminate the former [i.e. the Canaanites] and broker peace and live in harmony with all the rest, as the Master of Histories [Peter Comestor] remarks with regard to the passage in question in Chapter 11 of his history of Deuteronomy, saying: '*but with neighbouring peoples they should be as peaceful as possible and make covenants with them*'.[300] So says the Master [of Histories], from which it seems clear that the Jews were never permitted to wage war against any other people outside the Promised Land on account of idolatry and heathenism unless they had endured some additional form of harm or abuse at their hands, as Nicholas [of Lyra] also notes in that connection,[301] as do both El Tostado—in Question 1 [of his discussion of Deuteronomy 20] and in his commentary on the second book of Chronicles, Chapter 8, Question 5[302]—and Cajetan.[303]

---

[298] Deuteronomy 20:10.

[299] Deuteronomy 20:15–17.

[300] Peter Comestor, *Historia scholastica*, in ch. 11 of the chapters devoted to Deuteronomy. In the edition published in Lyon in 1543 (publisher unnamed), this passage is on fol. 79v.

[301] This passage rehearses Las Casas's refutation of Sepúlveda's views on Deuteronomy in ch. 13 of the *Apologia* (67v; Poole, 105), where he likewise cites Nicholas of Lyra, El Tostado, and Cajetan.

[302] See n. 51 above. Again, for his discussion of Deuteronomy, *Quaestio* 2 is actually of more relevance than the *Quaestio* 1 here adduced.

[303] The reference is to Tommaso de Vio (Gaetano) in his commentary on Aquinas, *ST* II-II, q. 66, art. 8, available in *Sancti Thomae Aquinatis Opera Omnia Iussu Impensaque Leonis XIII P.M. Edita*, vol. 9 (Rome: Typographia Polyglotta, 1897), 94. Las Casas refers to this passage again in ch. 41 of his *Apologia* (182v; Poole, 263), as does Sepúlveda in the conclusion to his own *Apologia* (V.2).

294   SEPÚLVEDA ON THE SPANISH INVASION OF THE AMERICAS

(6) Furthermore: why is there no mention in the entire Old Testament of the faithful Jewish people waging war against any group outside the Promised Land on account of idolatry and heathenism alone? It goes without saying that, if they had ever waged such a war on those grounds, there would be a record of it in one of the books of the Holy Scripture. As it is, of all the wars which the Jews waged against any peoples who dwelt outside the Promised Land, there is not a single instance— from the Book of Exodus all the way to the tale of the Maccabees—in which the cause was idolatry or heathenism as opposed to offences and abuses suffered at their hands. And if there were such a case, why did the doctor not allude to it?

This proves the utter falsehood of what the doctor maintains about the interlinear gloss on the words '*so you shall do to all the cities that are very far away from you*', where '*far away*' is taken to mean '*of different religion*'.[304] The reverend doctor would use this gloss to prove that the Jews were permitted to wage war against infidels on grounds of religious difference alone, and that we Christians today may do likewise. Just how contrary this is to the gospel of Christ, who said, '*Go forth and teach all the nations, baptizing them in the name of the Father, the Son and the Holy Spirit, teaching them to observe all the commandments I have given you*',[305] and to the words '*He who believes will be saved, but he who does not believe will be condemned*',[306] and how contrary to the entire doctrine and deeds of the Apostles and practice of the universal church, let any learned Christian be the judge.

(7) But for clearer evidence still of just how back-to-front the doctor has got things, let the selfsame gloss he adduces speak for itself. For at the very same point in that gloss in the words immediately preceding, which he passed over in silence as they did not serve his purposes, the whole of Deuteronomy 20 is expounded in an allegorical and moral sense. And seeing as this interpretation is not supposed to be open to debate, as Dionysius and St Augustine both state,[307] yet nonetheless the doctor adduces the gloss in his favour, he must by the same token suffer it to be used against him.

The gloss on that passage says that 'to fight against a city'[308] is a reference to 'the conclaves of the heretics or the outside world or any outsider, who opposes

---

[304] See n. 205 above.

[305] Matthew 28:19–20.

[306] Mark 16:16.

[307] Augustine and Dionysius (in reality, pseudo-Dionysius the Areopagite) seem to be adduced here in support of taking biblical teachings—here, specifically that of Deuteronomy 20—in an allegorical sense as opposed to in the more literal form which Sepúlveda champions. Augustine's discussion of the interpretation(s) of Deuteronomy 20 can be found in the *Glossa Ordinaria* (fol. 353r–353v in the 1545 Trechsel edition). Pseudo-Dionysius does not discuss Deuteronomy 20 specifically but does advocate non-literalist interpretation of the Old Testament at, for instance, *Divine Names*, ch. 4, §11; and see also his ninth letter, to *Titus the Hierarch*, discussing biblical language about God that is confusing when taken literally but needs proper mystical explanation; as well as the Pseudo-Dionysian *Celestial Hierarchy* (9.3) also cited in ch. 42 of Las Casas's *Apologia*, in which he argues against action against idolaters on the grounds that, according to Dionysius, the angels accomplish that task among the nations without violence. Perhaps, then, this is what he was thinking about here, as an alternative to violent human action to spread the gospel.

[308] Deuteronomy 20:10.

the spirit'. And on the phrase, 'you shall first offer it terms of peace',[309] the same gloss says that by proclaiming 'peace to this house' [you shall offer] 'Christ, who is our peace, who makes both sides into one'. And on the words, 'However, if it does not make a covenant with you, then you shall attack it',[310] the gloss says: 'On the authority of Scripture'. And on the words, 'You shall smite it with the blade of the sword', the gloss clarifies: 'which is the Word of God'. And then, further along, on the words, 'Thus you shall do to all the cities that are very far away from you',[311] the gloss offers the words which the doctor draws upon to his own detriment: 'of a different religion'.

For if, according to this very gloss, the cities and communities of the heretics are first to be offered Christ himself, who embodies true peace, through preaching as opposed to armed means, and, in the event that they prove unwilling to receive him by means of the faith, that we should engage them in combat in which our weapons are the authorities of the Scripture and of truth, smiting them with the sword that is the Word of God, and if God further stipulates that this is how we should deal with all cities and confederacies far away from us (which is to say: that are outside the church on account of their heathenism), then it follows that to all heretics— and most especially to those others who have never received the faith nor caused any offence to the church—we should first offer peace, proclaiming and bringing them tidings and knowledge of Christ himself, son of God, who is the truth. And the fight waged against them must be by means of the authorities of the Scripture, and wounds inflicted with the sword of the gospel by means of harmless, sweet preaching performed with meekness and humility.

(8) And that our implacability towards and fight against the infidels should be by means of the sword of the Word of God (as the gloss says) and that it is with that that we are to slay them[312] wherever they refuse to receive us is demonstrated in Isaiah 11, on the subject of the coming of Christ and of precisely this most gentle manner of preaching of the gospel: *'Then a rod will spring from the stem of Jesse'*,[313] and, shortly afterwards, *'And he will strike the earth with the rod of his mouth, and slay the wicked with the breath of his lips'*,[314] etc. This is a very different type of war and death indeed from the one envisioned by Dr Sepúlveda.

(9) And so, how does the doctor find support in this gloss—just because it says *'of different religion'*—for the notion that infidels who have never received the faith should first have war waged upon them for no other reason than their idolatry and

---

[309] Deuteronomy 20:10.

[310] Deuteronomy 20:12. The word here translated as 'covenant' is *'foedus'* in the Latin—or *fedus*, as it is spelled in the 1552 text. In the Tudela Bueso *Tratados* edition this is mistranscribed as *'sedus'* (seat).

[311] Deuteronomy 20:15.

[312] We follow the spacing of the manuscripts here (CR, 207r; MR, 233r): 'y con él los ayamos de matar' (where *él = el cuchillo de la palabra de Dios*, 'the sword of the Word of God') for the 1552 edition's 'y con ellos ayamos de matar'.

[313] Isaiah 11:1.

[314] Isaiah 11:4.

296 SEPÚLVEDA ON THE SPANISH INVASION OF THE AMERICAS

heathenism, or for the idea that the Jews could subjugate any other peoples on the same grounds? It would appear that the reverend doctor is injuring himself with his own weapons and wounding himself in the forehead. And it is astounding how, to stop himself from tumbling down, he clutches at twigs which have no strength either, like foliage or fronds. It emerges, then, that his claim that difference of religion alone constituted grounds for subjugating infidels through warfare either in the Old Testament or at any other time before or since—and least of all under the law of grace—is false indeed.

(10) To counter my point about how the examples in the Old Testament are not meant as models for imitation in the New Testament but rather sources of admiration, as is evident from many testimonies of the saints and canons from [Gratian's] *Decretum* of the church (2, q. 7, Chapter '*Nos si*'; 22, Q, 2, Chapter '*Si quis*'; and 14, q. 5, Chapter '*Dixit dominus*'),[315] the reverend doctor answered that this does not apply to the precepts of natural law, such as cases of idolatry, which was punished, etc. To this I would say that nothing he says on that subject is of the slightest consequence, for he does not offer a satisfactory response to the testimonies and arguments put to him and his followers in my *Apología*.[316]

(11) With regard to the testimony of St Cyprian in his book, *Exhortation to Martyrdom*,[317] I would respond that St Cyprian's thrust and wording are the complete opposite of Dr Sepúlveda's; for what St Cyprian means to convey there is that reversion to idolatry on the part of gentiles who had once received the faith (something which in St Cyprian's day was practically an hourly occurrence) should not be tolerated by any Christian, even if he should be put to death on that account.

And for this reason he [St Cyprian] endorses and promotes the act of martyrdom, adducing those words from Deuteronomy 13: 'If your brother ... or your son ... asks of you, "Let us go and serve other gods", ... you shall not give him

[315] *Decretum* C. 2, q. 7, c. 41 (*Nos si*) is largely devoted to Gratian's comment on a letter of Leo IV to the Frankish king Louis II in which Gratian expounds the view that popes and other spiritual leaders have the authority to correct secular leaders, through excommunication if necessary. C. 22, q. 2, can. 19 (*Si quis*) is a passage from Gregory I's *Moralia in Iob* (18.3), countering those who think swearing by the Old Testament will suffice to justify their actions and thus is in keeping with the general context of denouncing improper use of the Old Testament as a model for Christian behaviour. C. 14, q. 5, can. 12 (*Dixit Dominus*) is a passage from Augustine's question 39 on Exodus (in the *Quaestiones in Heptateuchum*, Bk. 2), discussing God's command to Moses to have the Israelites 'borrow' gold and other precious stuff from Egyptian neighbours before fleeing Egypt: the point is likewise that one cannot take this injunction in the Old Testament as a literal guide to proper Christian action.

[316] As noted at n. 30, Las Casas frequently mentions his *Apología/Apologia* in his 'Replies' and we generally take it as the Spanish *Apología*. However, Las Casas appears to have used his Latin *Apologia* as his source for his 'Replies' on at least one occasion, as noted at n. 413. In the manuscripts (CR, 207v; MR, 233v), Las Casas adds: 'folio 38, página 1a'. This is the first of several specific references to page numbers of the *Apologia* in this manuscript—all of them omitted in the printed version. These numbers do not correspond to the folio numbers of the surviving manuscript of the Latin *Apologia*.

[317] Cyprian, *Ad Fortunatum de exhortatione martyrii*, §5 (quoted in Gratian, *Decretum*, C. 23, q. 5, c. 32).

CONTAINED HEREIN IS A DEBATE OR DISPUTATION   297

your consent and your eye will not pardon him and your hand shall be upon him,[318] etc. And further along it says that if one of the Hebrews' own cities—not one of the cities of the idolatrous gentiles who had not received the law and did not number among the peoples of the Promised Land—were to be utterly polluted with idolatry, then the whole city should be devastated and destroyed, which is expressed as follows: 'If you should hear in one of your cities, which the Lord your God shall give to you to live in, anyone saying ... "Let us go and serve other gods",[319] you shall kill them', etc. This is patently a reference to the Hebrews themselves, for that the Canaanites were to be exterminated by the Israelites upon their arrival was not in doubt. Still less is it a reference to the other idolaters who dwelt outside the Promised Land, for it says: 'If you should hear [i.e. Si audieris] in one of your cities, which the Lord your God shall give to you ...',[320] etc. And this is the very 'Si audieris' which the chapter 'Si audieris' (~~22~~ 23, q. 5) in the canons from [Gratian's] Decretum adduced by Dr Sepúlveda takes as its point of departure.[321] Gratian appealed to this in support of his own point, namely to prove that killing wrongdoers does not go against the fifth commandment of the Decalogue.

St Cyprian concludes, then, in a holy and learned fashion by reasoning *a minori* as follows: if prior to the coming of Christ, *with regard to the worship of God* it was lawful and divinely mandated that apostatizing from the faith once received and reverting to idol worship should be punishable by death, then this was all the more to be observed in the wake of Christ's Advent.[322] This is what St Cyprian says and sets out to accomplish in that book, as can be seen there in Chapter 5;[323] and to underscore the point further he spends the other chapters expounding just how terrible the sin of idolatry is and how draconian the punishment which God routinely metes out for it. What emerges is thus manifestly the opposite of what the doctor alleges, and the proof offered in this reply ought to suffice for the doctor to be resoundingly repudiated by such illustrious individuals as yourselves as the most intransigent and unjust adversary of the Indians that he is, without rhyme or reason, and all of his own volition.

---

[318] Deuteronomy 13:6, 8.

[319] Deuteronomy 13:12–13. *Interficies eos* is a restatement of Deuteronomy 13:9 or a paraphrase of Deuteronomy 13:15.

[320] Deuteronomy 13:12.

[321] Gratian, *Decretum*, C. 23, q. 5, c. 32. This canon is taken from Cyprian, here quoting Deuteronomy 13:12.

[322] Cyprian, *Ad Fortunatum de exhortatione martyrii*, §5, as in n. 317 above. The words '*circa Deum colendum*' ['with regard to the worship of God'] are taken directly from Cyprian's Latin, and then the latter part of the sentence is Las Casas's translation into Spanish of the rest of Cyprian's remark on that subject.

[323] See previous note.

Second reply

(1) With regard to the second objection, which revolves around the parable '*compel them to come in*'[324] and in which connection the reverend doctor raises the matter of the two eras of the church as defined by St Augustine, everything in his answer is frivolous and false, and he does not say a single thing worth countenancing or even dignifying with an answer, and he falsely adduces the letters of St Augustine, for they all explicitly contradict his position, given that St Augustine is referring only to heretics, not to gentiles, as far as our purposes are concerned. That the church never forces or obliges anyone to do anything to which they have not made a commitment is amply demonstrated in my *Apología*.[325]

Third reply

(1) With regard to what he says in the third objection, namely that St Augustine is referring in those letters to pagans as well as to heretics, I would answer that when St Augustine includes or alludes to the case of the pagans it is not because he is equating the two, but rather because he is talking about the law which Constantine passed to outlaw idolatry among his own subjects. The law in question is the first one [in the *Codex Justinianus*]: see the chapter '*On pagans and their temples*',[326] and note also the other laws passed in turn by subsequent emperors, his successors.

That the laws in question were designed with reference to those idolaters who were imperial subjects can be clearly seen, to begin with, from the fact that Constantine directed the aforementioned first law at Taurus,[327] who was a praetorian prefect and governor or adjutor of a particular province, and the same goes for the laws passed by the other emperors, as is evident from their titles; and indeed any ruler is fully within his rights to outlaw idolatry in his own kingdom—as is true of any other public sin, only in this case even more rightly so—thereby putting a stop to all notorious villainy. Secondly, it goes without saying that nobody has the power to impose laws beyond their own territory and jurisdiction, as is plain to see in the last law of the Title *De jurisdictione omnium judicum*.[328] The third

---

[324] Luke 14:23.

[325] Las Casas deals with this in his Latin *Apologia*, ch. 42, 185r–189v; Poole, 267–73. In the manuscripts (CR, 208r; MR, 235r), this reference includes page references: 'en la hoja 7, página 2a, con las siguientes y en la hoja 31, página 1a de nuestra Apologia'.

[326] *Codex Justinianus*, Bk. 1, tit. 11: '*De paganis et templis eorum*'. The near-identical chapter ('*De paganis, sacrificiis, et templis*') in the *Codex Theodosianus* (Bk. 16, tit. 10.4) might also spring to mind, but, crucially, the law issued to the praetorian prefect Taurus is not the first item there, whereas it is first in the *Codex Justinianus*.

[327] Both Las Casas and Sepúlveda attribute this imperial law to Constantine (presumably Constantine I), but in fact it was a law issued by Constantius II in 354.

[328] *Codex Justinianus*, Bk. 3, tit. 13, law 7: '*De jurisdictione omnium judicum et de foro competenti*'. The part of this title which he does not quote, '*de foro competenti*', is in fact the part most germane to Las Casas's purposes, for it concerns the proper remit of a judge's jurisdiction.

CONTAINED HEREIN IS A DEBATE OR DISPUTATION   299

point can be gleaned from the first law in the chapter in the title *de summa trinitate*, which opens with the words: '*all the peoples over whom the rule of our clemency reigns*,'[329] etc.

Thus, he [Constantine] cannot mean for this to be imposed upon those populations not subject to him, as the doctors indeed observe in that connection; and see also the chapter *Canonum statuta* [of the title] *de constitutionibus*.[330] It follows, then, that the emperors imposed the aforementioned laws against idolatry only upon those idolaters who were their subjects and who dwelt within the bounds of the empire.

(2) As to what the doctor goes on at this point to say about force having been used in St Gregory's day against non-subject gentiles too in the course of the wars waged by Gennadius purely so as to be in a position to preach the gospel to them once they had been subjugated, I would say, with all due respect, that this is entirely false, as can be seen from the very letters of the saint himself which Sepúlveda adduces.

For in the letter which begins '*si non ex fidei*', St Gregory expresses his gratitude to Gennadius the Patrician and praises his wars because, by dint of strenuous fighting, he succeeded in triumphing over the infidel tyrants and seizing back certain communities known as Dacans, whom they had usurped from the church, and also against the heretics who were corrupting the Christians. The matter of the former can be seen from these words which appear in the letter in question: '*For it is our understanding that Your Excellency has rendered many greatly useful services for the pasturing of the sheep of the blessed Peter, prince of the Apostles, by restoring to him sizeable regions of his patrimony which had been denuded of their own cultivators by supplying—that is, by reinstating—its Datian or Dacan inhabitants*.'[331]

---

[329] *Codex Justinianus*, Bk. 1, tit. 1: '*De summa Trinitate, et Fide Catholica, et ut nemo de ea publice contendere audeat*', corresponding to the Edict of Thessalonica, issued by Gratian, Valentinian II, and Theodosius in 380.

[330] The reference is clearly to X.1.2.1, i.e. ch. 1 (the incipit is *Canonum statuta*) of title 2 (*De constitutionibus*) of Bk. 1 of the *Decretals* of Gregory IX, a chapter taken from a decree of the Council of Meaux (845). But Las Casas surely meant to refer to the modification of this chapter issued by Boniface VIII (1294–1303), in which he declared, contrary to the council's ruling, that ignorance of the law was a legitimate excuse for a wrongdoer. Boniface's ruling is in *Sextus liber Decretalium*, Bk. 1, tit. 2, c. 1.

[331] Gregory I, Letter 1.75 (= 1.73 Norberg), to Gennadius, exarch of Africa. Las Casas's version of the Latin differs somewhat from the way the text appears in editions of Gregory's letters (for example, Froben's of 1550) or in Gratian, C. 23, q. 4, c. 49. He glossed the participle in the phrase *largitis ... habitatoribus* ('with settlers having been supplied') by adding 'i.e. [= *id est*] *restitutis*' ('that is to say, restored'), to suggest that Gennadius was simply resettling people who had already been under Roman (and hence Christian) authority but had been carried off by barbarians beyond the borders of the empire. Also, while most texts of this letter offer either 'Datians' or 'Dacans', Las Casas included both: *datiorū vel dacorū*. Commenting on this passage, John R. C. Martyn maintains that '[t]hese *datitii* (or *dedititii*) were enslaved barbarian captives of the Romans, who cultivated plots of land (*datitia*) in return for taxes on produce, more profitable than the free farmers' contributions. The word only appears here in Gregory.' (*The Letters of Gregory*, Mediaeval Sources in Translation 40: Toronto: Pontifical Institute of Mediaeval Studies, 2004, vol. 1, 187n349.) It is doubtful that Las Casas had any idea who they really were, but he made a strategic guess here.

(3) It goes without saying that in the case of the infidels at issue here [i.e. the 'Indians'] St Peter does not strictly speaking have any sheep, nor rightful territory nor places divested of their original inhabitants needing to be returned to him; and nor are they enemies or foes of the church worthy of the phrase '*in wars against our enemies*', as shall emerge from what follows, for we submit that they are people who reside peacefully in their own realms and lands and have not ousted us from any of ours. This means that the wars waged by Gennadius were not with a view to subjugating them solely in order to preach the faith to them.

This second point can likewise be demonstrated courtesy of St Gregory in Letter 72—which antedates the aforementioned one likewise addressed to Gennadius—in which, referring to the heretics and infidel tyrants alike, he says: '*Just as the Lord has made Your Excellency shine with the light of victories in wars against our enemies in this life, so too should you combat the enemies of his church with every fibre of your mind and body ... both by vigorously opposing the enemies of the Catholic Church in public wars on behalf of the Christian people and also strenuously engaging in ecclesiastical battles as warriors of the Lord, for it is known that—if they are (heaven forfend) given the opportunity to inflict harm—men of heretical religion rise up violently against the Catholic faith, striving as best they can to infuse the limbs of the Christian body with the poison of their heresy, thereby polluting it. For we have learned that they, to whom the Lord is opposed, are lifting their necks up against the Catholic Church and that they wish to overturn the faith of the Christian name. But let Your Eminence quash their attempts and pin down their arrogant necks with the yoke of righteousness.*'[332]

It follows from this that, in the letters to which the doctor refers, St Gregory is speaking about infidel enemies who were guilty of usurping cities and lands belonging to the church (meaning either the Vandals or else Moorish peoples from Mauritania, who were savage heathens; Victor the Bishop makes reference to both groups in Book 2 of his *Historia ecclesiastica*,[333] as does Paul the Deacon in Book 1, Chapter 17, of his history of the Lombards)[334] and about the Manichean and Arian heretics (of whom there were a great many in Africa at that time—as can likewise be seen from Victor's *Historia* in his discussion of persecution in Africa—responsible for splintering and poisoning the church). And these are the wars of which he [St Gregory] sang the praises to Gennadius. And it is for this reason that he [Gregory] ends by beseeching God for solace, praying that, once the obstacles which made it impossible to preach to them or which kept them from converting

---

[332] Gregory I, Letter 1.74 (*PL*); 1.72 (Norberg). The letter is quoted in its entirety in Gratian, *Decretum* C. 23, q. 4, c. 48.

[333] Victor Vitensis (Victor of Vita), *Historia persecutionis africanae provinciae, temporibus Genserici et Hunirici regum Wandalorum*, Bk. 2. See the useful modern translation by John Moorhead, *History of the Vandal Persecution* (Liverpool: Liverpool University Press, 1992).

[334] Paul the Deacon [Paulus Diaconus], *Historia Langobardorum*, 1.17.

CONTAINED HEREIN IS A DEBATE OR DISPUTATION   301

had been removed by neighbouring or nearby peoples, the holy name might be spread.

(4) This means that the wars in question were not waged simply to eradicate idolatry or to subjugate peaceful heathens by means of bloodshed, as the doctor would have it, twisting the statements of the saints to suit his purposes with no grounds nor justification whatsoever, as will be obvious from everything just said. And as this has already been abundantly demonstrated in my *Apología* by means of all manner of other arguments and proof-texts, there is no need to return to this point again in what follows.

Fourth reply

(1) With regard to the fourth objection,[335] my response to the doctor's argument in the foregoing reply goes a long way to answering this next one as well. But as for his contention that it is incumbent upon the prelates and above all the pope to encourage kings to undertake lawful wars, as when Pope Adrian prevailed upon Charlemagne to wage war upon the Lombards, I would say that the doctor is forever trying to parry all possible objections which manifestly pose problems to his purpose by appealing to a single argument or authority, like a man bent on curing both the cataract in his eye and the gash at the back of his head with a single compress.

(2) As to the point at issue here I would say that it is for prelates and above all the pope to urge and command Christian monarchs to defend the holy universal church and—should it prove necessary to this end—to wage wars and wreak devastation upon all those who affront and assail it, as was the case with the Lombard tyrants and the powerful heretics and any heathens or individuals of greater and lesser status who seek to beset and bedevil it. And in this context the prophecy and second era to which St Augustine refers find fulfilment: '*all kings of the earth shall bow down before him*'[336]—a notion in which the doctor exults and which he believes serves his cause.

But the conclusion to be drawn from this is not that it is for prelates or the pope to encourage monarchs to follow in the footsteps of Mohammed, harassing and ravaging, robbing, capturing, killing, and devastating peaceful, tranquil populations (albeit heathen ones) who reside and dwell in their own lands and kingdoms, without causing trouble to us or any other nation. Jesus Christ, supreme pontifex from whom the pope and prelates derive their spiritual and hence also temporal

---

[335] After the first sentence, the first three sections of this Reply represent additions to the 1552 edition; they are missing in both manuscripts (*CR*, 290v; *MR*, 237r). See Abril-Castelló's discussion of this extensive omission: 'La bipolarización Sepúlveda–Las Casas', 244 and n. 35.

[336] Psalm 72 (71):11. Augustine cites this Psalm in Letter 173.10.

302 SEPÚLVEDA ON THE SPANISH INVASION OF THE AMERICAS

authority, entrusted these peoples to them and ordered them to bring them to his holy faith and into his church by means of peace, love, and Christian deeds, speaking to them as to meek sheep, wolves though they might be.

And so, the duty of the supreme pontiff, general vicar of Christ, and of the prelates—all of whom are likewise representatives of the Son of God himself in their respective bishoprics—is, rather, to prevent any Christian monarch who conceives a desire to undertake these kinds of unjust wars from embarking upon or engaging in them even so much as in thought, and the monarchs are obliged to obey them as they obey Jesus Christ himself, on pain of mortal sin and being guilty of committing gross sacrilege. And this can be seen from the passage in St Thomas (*Secunda secundae*, q. 40, art. † 2 ad 3)[337] which the doctor adduces (though it is hardly to his advantage to do so), in which he [St Thomas] says that the power or art or virtue of a given end should determine, direct, and prescribe the means to be employed to achieve that end.

(3) The end towards which Christ, the pope, and the prelates—and so too the sovereigns of Castile, devout Christians themselves—strive, as they are duty-bound to do, in the Indies and in relation to the Indies is the preaching of the faith for the salvation of the people there. And the means to this end are not robbing, aggrieving, capturing, and dismembering men or devastating kingdoms and causing the faith and Christian religion to reek and be reviled among peaceful heathens; this is the sort of behaviour expected of cruel tyrants, enemies of God and of his faith, as we have by now demonstrated, discussed, and addressed on many occasions in our bid to counteract the doctor's obstinacy and blindness.

(4) As to the rest of what he reports from St Thomas in his discussion of the matter of Constantine (at *Secunda secundae*, q. 10, art. 11), *namely that the rites of the infidels 'are not to be tolerated in any way'* among one's own gentile subjects:[338] we grant that this is indeed the case in instances where it can be done without uproar and the death and destruction of the peoples in question and without adversely affecting their likelihood of conversion or posing a menace to any other matter of importance, which is what St Thomas actually says there—and not by means of the sorts of verbal contortions and glosses of which Dr Sepúlveda avails himself, but rather perfectly plainly.

And these are his very words, which the doctor ought to shrink from relaying and refrain from glossing in the terms of his warped, murky interpretation: '*The rites of infidels are not to be tolerated in any way, except perhaps for the purposes of*

---

[337] Aquinas, *ST* II-II, q. 40, art. 2 (not 1, as in the 1552 printing) ad 3. Las Casas expands and paraphrases here. The standard English translation of the English Dominicans offers: 'every power, art, or virtue that regards the end, has to dispose that which is directed to the end'.

[338] Aquinas, *ST* II-II, q. 10, art. 11, co. Las Casas introduces the Aquinian citation with a paraphrasing Latin lead-in of his own, hence the italicized text without inverted commas. '*Ritus infidelium*' [the rites of infidels] occurs on many occasions in—and is the whole subject of—q. 10, art. 11, albeit not in that very sentence.

CONTAINED HEREIN IS A DEBATE OR DISPUTATION   303

averting some evil, in other words, to avoid a scandal or the devastation which might ensue from it or the obstruction to the salvation of those who, thus tolerated, would slowly be converted to the faith. For this reason the church once upon a time tolerated the rites of heretics and pagans, back when the population of infidels was extremely large.[339] These are St Thomas's words. What clearer proof could there be of the way in which the doctor falsifies and warps the pronouncements of the saints, just as he does with the Holy Scripture? And St Thomas's words there likewise reveal the sheer irrelevance of the gloss which the doctor supplies at that point, namely *'which is to say, before there were Christian princes who could exercise coercion'*, for which the burden of proof remains with him.

(5) What could be more grievous than inspiring the heathens with hatred, abhorrence, and loathing for the faith before they have even heard its doctrine? What greater form of destruction than butchering countless people in the course of warfare? What greater barrier to the salvation of the heathens than casting vast numbers of souls down into hell and prompting those who escape with their lives never to convert; or if, out of fear, they do go through the motions of converting, for their faith never to be true, but merely feigned? And where has the church ever had within its reach a greater multitude of heathens more amenable, more lacking in impediments to embracing the faith and more readily receptive to conversion (so long as tyrants do not annihilate them before they have had the chance to be exposed to preaching) than the Indians in our Indies?

The teachings of St Thomas, which Dr Sepúlveda himself adduces in support of his own cause, are thus at variance with the misguided notions which the doctor wickedly propounds.[340] And so the poisoned arrows in which he trades and which he burns to launch contrary to all that is good and to the detriment of the law of the gospel, turn against him and become lodged in his own breast.

(6) And as for the passage he adduces from St Thomas in the eighth article there [i.e. in q. 10] in which,[341] in the course of enumerating the grounds for warfare against heathens who obstruct the faith, he identifies three modes of obstructionism—namely through profane behaviour, by persuading others to abandon it or not to embrace it in the first place, or by means of public persecution—I would firstly say that he is arraigning St Thomas on false charges here in claiming that his discussion there is of the grounds for the wars waged by Gennadius and the imposition of the gospel under duress, for St Thomas says no

---

[339] Aquinas, *ST* II-II, q. 10, art. 11, co.

[340] The word here translated as 'wickedly propounds' is *'dogmatiza'* (from *dogmatizar*): note that the lexicographer Sebastián de Covarrubias in his early seventeenth-century dictionary, the *Tesoro de la lengua castellana o española*, notes of the cognate adjective *'dogmatizante'* (under *'dogma'*, 3) that 'we always take it in the pejorative sense to refer to someone who teaches errors contrary to the faith; the Holy Inquisition punishes those people severely, rightly, and justly'. If taken in the full sense of the word, this would indeed be a strong charge levelled at Sepúlveda.

[341] Aquinas, *ST* II-II, q. 10, art. 8, co.

304 SEPÚLVEDA ON THE SPANISH INVASION OF THE AMERICAS

such thing.[342] Secondly I would say that none of the three aforementioned grounds for war militates against the Indians, for obvious reasons.

(7) And as to what he next proceeds to adduce from St Thomas, q. 94, art. 3, ad 2,[343] in support of the idea that idolatry entails immense blasphemy, we have already demonstrated in our *Apología* that anyone runs the risk of going astray here, whether from ignorance or from malice. This is because, in the first passage just cited (q. 10, art. 8),[344] St Thomas is not referring to the sort of blasphemy that arises from accidental idolatry, which is the sort whereby idolaters mean no offence to God; on the contrary, they believe that, in so doing, they are worshipping and serving him [God], though in reality it is blasphemy arising from idolatry, *but of the accidental variety, which is to say, unintentionally on the idolaters' part.* And this is the variety to which St Thomas is referring in the aforementioned q. 94,[345] and is, when it comes to infidels who have not previously received the faith, for no mere mortal judge to punish. This can be demonstrated by the fact that, in performing the rites and ceremonies prescribed by their laws, the Jews and the Moors are blatantly committing blasphemy due to the blasphemy which those practices entail, just as all that they do in the course of their rites and ceremonies contravenes, jeopardizes, and damages our holy faith, and thus counts as an instance of the accidental variety, as per the testimony of St Jude Thaddaeus the Apostle in his canonical pronouncement: '*But these people blaspheme all the things that they do not understand.*'[346] All the same, the church does not punish them for it, for it tolerates these practices in them, although they are their subjects and it would be easy and straightforward for it to do something about it.

(8) But the sort of blasphemy which the church penalizes and punishes is the type in which the Moorish and Turkish infidels engage on purpose by disparaging, undermining, or profaning our faith so as to prevent those who would otherwise embrace it from doing so, for instance by casting aspersions on Our Saviour Jesus Christ or on his saints or his church. This is the type of blasphemy to which St Thomas is referring in the aforementioned q. 10, art. 8,[347] as noted in that connection by Cajetan and by the most learned *maestro* Vitoria in their respective interpretations of that eighth article.[348]

---

[342] Las Casas's first point here ('I would firstly say ...') is a late edition to the 1552 edition, for it is missing in the manuscripts (*CR*, 210r; *MR*, 238r).

[343] Aquinas, *ST* II-II, q. 94, art. 3, ad 2.

[344] Aquinas, *ST* II-II, q. 10, art. 8, co.

[345] Aquinas, *ST* II-II, q. 94, art. 3, ad 2.

[346] Jude 1:10.

[347] Aquinas, *ST* II-II, q. 10, art. 8, co.

[348] Cajetan's commentary on Aquinas's *ST II-II*, q. 10, art. 8, may now be consulted, for instance, in *Angelici Doctoris Sancti Thomae Aquinatis Summa Theologica in Quinque Tomos Distributa, cum Commentariis Thomae de Vio Cardinalis Cajetani ...* (Padua, 1698), 78; the commentary on the article in question is headed '*Num bene fieret, si infideles cogerentur ad fidem*'. On Vitoria's comments—offered in the course of his lectures—on this article, see *Vitoria, Comentarios a la Secunda secundae de Santo Tomás,* 6 vols., ed. by Vicente Beltrán de Heredia (Salamanca: Biblioteca de Teólogos Españoles, 1932).

CONTAINED HEREIN IS A DEBATE OR DISPUTATION   305

(9) In other words, St Thomas does not mean that war may be waged against infidels on account of blasphemy of every kind. Dr Sepúlveda is mistaken, then, as is demonstrated at greater length in our *Apología*. Everything else which the reverend doctor adduces or rather mangles from the letters and pronouncements of St Augustine is improperly and wrongly adduced and entirely baseless, for his procedure is to scour the statements and doctrine of the saints solely with a view to finding things with which he can mask, excuse, or festoon his own poisonous doctrine.[349]

Fifth reply

(1) As to the way he addresses the fifth objection, submitting his own interpretation and elucidation of the meaning of the Apostle St Paul's words in 1 Corinthians 5— '*For what business of mine is it to judge those who are outside?*'[350]—I would say that, just as the doctor readily offers that interpretation off the top of his head, so too can it be just as readily dismissed, for he offers no proof; and what the jurists have to say about such behaviour is that, '*We blush to speak with no legal basis*' (in the chapter *de collationibus* from the law which opens '*illam*', etc.).[351]

This is especially true given that what he says runs counter to the meaning ascribed to those words by all the Greek and Latin doctors. And in my *Apologia* I have already proven by means of ten utterly watertight arguments and numerous irrefutable authorities that it is not for the church to punish idolatry or any other sin committed by heathens who never received the faith there in their remote regions within their own self-contained territory. For it does not have the right of contentious jurisdiction over them other than in the six exceptions which I listed there.[352] When he says that '*the power to which a given end pertains should dictate the means to that end*',[353] it is the truth—insofar, at least, as '*the means are proportioned to the end*'[354] and lead to the accomplishment of that end or are of use. But as

---

[349] This concluding dig at Sepúlveda's methods ('for his procedure is ... ') was a flourish added to the 1552 printing, as was 'or rather mangles' ('o arreboruja') earlier in the sentence; these are missing in the manuscripts (*CR*, 210r; *MR*, 238v).

[350] 1 Corinthians 5:12.

[351] Though Las Casas attributes this saying to 'the jurists', it was coined by the great medieval civil lawyer, Bartolus de Saxoferrato (Bartolo da Sassoferrato, 1313–1357). The source given in the text is Book 6 of the *Codex Justinianus*, Title 20 (*De collationibus*), Lex 19 (*Illam*), on which Bartolo's comment took the form '*Erubescimus aliquid dicere sine lege*'. Despite his citation of commentary on the *Codex*, however, Las Casas's citation of it here ('*Erubescimus cum sine lege loquimur*') corresponds to the way it appears in Bartolo's comment on a similar law in *Novels* (*Novellae constitutiones*), 18.5. We are grateful to Benjamin Straumann for helping clarify this.

[352] 'Contentious jurisdiction' is a legal term.

[353] Aquinas, *ST* II-II, q. 40, art. 2, ad 3.

[354] Aquinas, *ST* I-I, q. 47, art. 1, arg. 3.

306 SEPÚLVEDA ON THE SPANISH INVASION OF THE AMERICAS

for the things that serve to hinder or even to forestall that end, or most especially those things which are destructive to that end, these should be cast out far from themselves as things which are harmful and inimical to that end.[355]

(2) Everything which the doctor asserts is so clearly utterly deleterious to the goal which God, the church, and the sovereigns of Castile share as their common objective and which the latter are obliged to attain by means of conventional, Christian means befitting of the cause, namely the honour and glory of the Holy Name, the establishment of the faith, and the salvation of all those souls by preaching the gospel sweetly, lovingly, and peacefully.

For to have wars precede the gospel—which, as the doctor notes, was and is the route espoused by Mohammed to spread his sect—is (as all right-thinking Catholic men know only too well) a source of affront to the honour of God, causes the infidels to loathe and detest the name of Christianity and Christ himself, constitutes a surefire way to decimate and devastate the peoples with whom the Indies are so densely populated, and, lastly, condemns an infinitude of souls to perish and burn in hell for all eternity, meaning that God and the church and the sovereigns of Castile are thwarted in their aforementioned objective, giving rise to so many abominable evils. This is what Dr Sepúlveda has embraced and established as his principal purpose, as I have abundantly and unequivocally demonstrated in any number of my Spanish and Latin writings, including my aforementioned *Apología*, in my bid to disprove him and his followers.

Sixth reply

(1) As to what he claims that I said about Christ not having granted power over the whole world to St Peter, for he did not possess such power *in actu* but only *in potentia*, I deny what he says, for no statement to that effect is to be found anywhere in my whole *Apologia*. What I said there[356] and will say again now is that heathens who have never received the faith are not properly speaking part of the forum of the church, not least—among the various other pieces of evidence or proof which I adduced—because they are not current subjects of Christ, for the fact of the matter is that infidels and sinners are rebels who are not subject to Christ owing to their lack of faith and recalcitrant spirit, as can be seen in Romans 10—'*Not all obey*

---

[355] The italicized words outside inverted commas here are not from Aquinas, but appear to be Las Casas's own Latin extrapolation. Venancio Carro cites precisely this phrase (along with the preceding Aquinian dictum) as representing the thought of Las Casas (*La teología y los teólogos-juristas españoles ante la conquista de América,* 2nd ed. (Salamanca: Biblioteca de Teólogos Españoles, 1951), 637).

[356] In Las Casas's Latin *Apologia,* this is in ch. 6 ([fol.] xxx; Poole, 56). In the manuscripts he again supplies a specific page number (not corresponding to the surviving manuscript of the *Apologia*): 'Lo que dixe allí en la hoja 34, página 1a y en las siguientes ...' (*CR*, 211r; *MR*, 239v).

CONTAINED HEREIN IS A DEBATE OR DISPUTATION   307

the gospel[357]—and Exodus 10, where, with Moses as his mouthpiece, God said to Pharaoh: '*How long will you refuse to humble yourself before me?*'[358]

(2) It follows, then, that the people at issue here are subjects not *in actu* but *in potentia*, since all humans and creatures of this world belong to Christ, even *qua* man, as regards the *actual* power and authority granted to him by his eternal Father (Matthew, final chapter).[359] I concluded from this that, when it comes to heathens and bad Christians, Christ is invested with one type of might or power *in actu* and another *in potentia*. The first sort is ascribed to Christ insofar as he can exercise his power and jurisdiction over them if he so chooses, but he abstains from doing so, and so in this regard can be said to possess it *in habitu*, which is to say *in actu primo*, like someone who possesses some kind of knowledge and omits to use it or take it into account. Christ shall commute it into *actu secundo* once the heathens and sinners convert, or when each reaches the end of their days, or on Judgment Day, when he will dispose of all as he sees fit. In Book 2 of his *De anima*, the Philosopher discusses these two types of *actus*—the first denoting the stage at which it is *in habitu,* and the second being when *potentia*, operating through the agency of *habitus*, produces some form of action.[360]

The second form of power which I stated that Christ wielded *in potentia* is in relation or with respect to heathens and sinners, who, even in their unconverted state, are self-evidently Christ's subjects or *in potentia* primed to become so; and this will then become the case *in actu* and *cum effectu* ['with effect'] if and when they come to the faith through baptism and to grace by means of penitence and charity. I illustrated the difference between these two powers or modalities of power by means of three passages from St Paul—Hebrews 2, 1 Corinthians 15, and Philippians 3—and also with reference to St Thomas's discussion of the passages in question in his commentaries.[361] I also offered plenty of other arguments to substantiate this, although really it is more than sufficient simply to adduce those proof-texts, as they are quite unequivocal. From this it followed that the heathens in question do not fall within the forum or jurisdiction of Christ *cum effectu* and *in actu* as outlined above.

---

[357] Romans 10:16. The Vulgate has '*non omnes **obedierunt** evangelio*' and most translations likewise render a past tense; however, Las Casas here has '*non omnes **obediunt***' and so, to reflect this, we here offer a translation in the present tense.

[358] Exodus 10:3.

[359] Matthew 28:18. The manuscripts read 'Mathei ultimo' (*CR*, 211r; *MR*, 240r), which the 1552 edition shortened to 'Matth. vl.' Tudela misread this as the Roman numeral VI and printed 'Mateo cap. 6', which Galmés oddly expanded to '*Math*. VI.6', in which he has been followed by Denisova.

[360] Aristotle, *Metaphysics* 9, which is concerned with potentiality and actuality, would seem a more obvious reference here; however, Las Casas expressly cites Aristotle's *De anima* 2, presumably because Sepúlveda, following (if perhaps somewhat misconstruing) Aquinas in *ST* II-II, q. 4, art. 3, ad 1, had done so: see further n. 253 above.

[361] The passages (with the commentary of Aquinas) are: Hebrews 2:8 (Aquinas, C. 1, Lectio 2, §§116–20); 1 Corinthians 15:24–25 (Aquinas, Caput 15, Lectio 3, §§936–44); Philippians 3:21 (Aquinas, Caput 3, Lectio 3, §145).

(3) As a result, I demonstrated that heathens are not properly subject to the 'forum' or jurisdiction of the church but rather are *in potentia* so. I mean this with reference to contentious jurisdiction, and, among other lines of reasoning, I advanced the following logical sequence by these means: if we grant that the church possesses and is bound to have or possess subjects insofar as they are the subjects of Christ in his capacity as prince of the Christian republic—for the infidels in question are Christ's subjects *in potentia* in the manner described—then it follows that they are also subjects *in potentia* of his republic, the church. That this syllogism is sound is evident from the fact that the church cannot wield greater or more effective power or jurisdiction over the heathens than Christ himself possessed when he was bodily present on earth, or than he possesses up in heaven today; nor can the authority of the church exceed that which we find written and proclaimed in Holy Scripture.

I also demonstrated this by means of an explicit pronouncement to this effect from St Thomas in III, q. 8, art. 3, ad 1, which reads: '*For those who are infidels, even though they are not actually members of the church, are nonetheless potential members of the church. This potentiality is based on two principles: firstly and above all on the power of Christ, which is sufficient for the salvation of the entire human race, and secondly on free will.*'[362] *These are his words.* St Thomas is nothing if not clear and adroit here in his discussion of Christ's 'habitual' power, which is sufficient for the salvation of the entire human race, yet there is no sign of him saving all of humanity *cum effectu*; it must, then, be that he possesses that power *in habitu* while the subjection of the infidels to Christ and his church is *in potentia*, for they may convert to God of their own free will if they so wish. And so it emerges that I do not deny that Christ possesses power and jurisdiction *in actu* over all the humans of the world, faithful and unfaithful alike, as the doctor takes me to mean.

(4) What I do dispute is the notion that, notwithstanding the fact that in his capacity as a man he is invested with all the divine power which his Father granted to him to see to it that natural law is upheld and the gospel preached, he then failed to refrain from bringing it fully to bear upon those infidels who had not received the faith until such time as they converted or until the end of their days or of the world: for my contention is that he *did* refrain from exerting it. And this is what it means to possess power *in habitu* or *in actu primo*; but it does not follow from this, as the doctor is at pains to argue, that Christ granted St Peter and to his own church the power or jurisdiction to punish the heathens who never received the faith and who dwell in their own lands and distant realms without causing any offence to the faith. The reverend Dr Sepúlveda will never succeed in proving this claim for as long as he lives. All this goes to show that the syllogism in which he so exults does not hold true: '*They do not have it* in actu, *therefore they do not have it at all.*' For the

---

[362] Aquinas, *ST* III, q. 8, art. 3, ad 1.

antecedent can be taken with reference to cases actu secundo, *but not* actu primo [*i.e.* in habitu]. *Hence if they have something* in habitu, *then it does rightly follow that they thus simply have it. That is not so, etc., which is the line of argument our distinguished doctor espouses.*[363]

(5) Everything else which the reverend doctor goes on to say in the course of answering this Sixth Objection likewise works against him, as any right-thinking reader will easily be able to discern, especially his claim that the emperors turned a blind eye to idolaters—even the ones who were their own subjects—so as to avoid the strife and damages which would inevitably arise from any attempt to rid them of their idolatry. And this makes up no small part of the refutation of his view which I offer throughout my *Apología* at various points; but if it were possible to vanquish idolatry among both subject and non-subject peoples without tumult, danger, damages, and difficulties, who but an idolater could deny or doubt that quashing it would be a just course of action? And so the doctor would do better to concede this point to me than to deny what I say.

Seventh reply

(1) As to the use to which he puts the esteemed canonists' comments on the chapter *Quod super his*, in *De voto*,[364] claiming that they state there that heathens can be vanquished and punished on account of their sins against nature and idolatry alone, and that it is preposterous of me to suggest that this only applies to cases in which they are profaning the name of the Creator in territories which formerly belonged to Christians, I would reply that Dr Sepúlveda is as mistaken here as he is about everything else. The reasons I provide on this count in my *Apologia* are more than enough to elucidate what the canonists mean by what they say there. They would do it themselves if they were still alive, so that their doctrine, interpreted as the doctor interprets it, might cease to be used in support of such intolerable great absurdities, the obliteration of peoples and realms, slander and abomination of the faith, and all manner of other things unbecoming to such learned men as they.

(2) This is most especially true seeing as the canonist doctors do not hold that peaceable heathens who are not guilty of active heathenism—but rather only of

---

[363] The first statement here (in inverted commas) is taken from what Sepúlveda says in the Sixth Reply, where he attributes this axiom to Aristotle in *Metaphysics* 9. The rest of the text (which I have not put in inverted commas) is then presumably Las Casas's own extrapolation of it, continuing in Latin for the sake of style and logical flavour.

[364] This is a reference to X.3.34.8, i.e. the *Decretales* of Gregory IX, Bk. 3, tit. 34 (*De voto*), cap. 8 (*Quod super his*). This was a rescript written by Innocent III to Hubert Walter, Archbishop of Canterbury, and the canonists commenting on it are Innocent IV, Hostiensis, Joannes Andreas, and Panormitanus. See further n. 263 above and *Apologia* III.2.xii.

310   SEPÚLVEDA ON THE SPANISH INVASION OF THE AMERICAS

heathenism of the sort which theologians term *of the purely negative variety*[365]—deserve to be ravaged and put to the sword simply because they are idolaters and have other abominable vices. For if preaching and the doctrine of the faith, imparted in the manner prescribed by Christ, serve to remove and drive out idolatry and all these vices, as our own experience attests is the case among the Indians each and every day—experience of which Dr Sepúlveda himself is in notably short supply—how could such redoubtable doctors say or believe that they should be vanquished in war prior to preaching? It seems overwhelmingly likely that if the canonists had had the opportunity to encounter and make contact with infidels such as these Indians—so utterly different from the Turks and Moors who were around and known to the canonists in their own day—they would most certainly never have said or opined the things that the doctor goes about claiming. And so the reverend doctor arraigns the esteemed canonists on false charges indeed.

Eighth reply

(1) As to the way the doctor parrots ideas about barbarians which he would have done better not to parrot, for he does not even understand what St Thomas means and attempts to distract from that fact by appealing to Aristotle's doctrine in the *Politics*,[366] I would say that—of the four types of barbarian which I scrupulously delineated in my *Apología*—the Indians are barbarians of the second category.[367]

These, then, are barbarians of the sort discussed by the Philosopher in the third book of his *Politics*[368]—not those from *Politics* 1—which is to say the same sort as many highly civilized and intelligent nations were and remain still today, and as was true of the Three Wise Men according to St Chrysostom,[369] and indeed of our own Spanish forebears, as noted by Pompeius Trogus at the end of Book 44—which is the last book of his whole history—where he says: '*Nor would the Spaniards submit to the yoke, even after their country was overrun, until Caesar Augustus, having subdued the rest of the world, turned his victorious arms against them. He reduced this*

---

[365] i.e. of the non-active sort, in that they have never before heard tell of Christianity (in contradistinction to the 'active' category of heathen who knows of Christianity but repudiates it anyway).

[366] Aquinas, *Sententia libri politicorum* (*Commentary on Aristotle's* Politics), Bk. 1, lect. 1, c. 23. The reference to Aristotle is probably to *Politics* 1.2 (1252a30–b9) and 1.6 (1253a28–30).

[367] Las Casas's second category of 'barbarians' covers those who speak a language unfamiliar to the person applying the term. This corresponds, then, to the original Greek sense of *barbaros*. Las Casas discusses this idea further in his Latin *Apologia* in ch. 2 (14v–16r; Poole, 30–31).

[368] Aristotle, *Politics* 3.14 (1285a16–27). Las Casas cites this discussion of barbarian kingships at some length in ch. 2 of his *Apologia* (15v–16r; Poole, 31–32).

[369] As is evident from ch. 2 of the *Apologia* (15r; Poole, 31), Las Casas is thinking of two passages from St John Chrysostom's 7th Homily on Matthew, on the Magi as especially wise barbarians (in the sense of non-Greeks), not the sometimes cited Homily 6 (though that too refers to the Magi as barbarians). The Latin version quoted by Las Casas in the *Apologia* may be found on pp. 48–49 of the *Secundus Tomus Operum Divi Ioannis Chrysostomi* published by Johann Herwagen in Basel in 1539. For the Greek texts (and a somewhat different Latin translation), see *PG* 57, cols. 75 and 77.

barbarous and savage people into the form of a province, and brought them by the influence of laws to a more civilized way of life.[370] *Those are his words.*

(2) And so given that the Spanish people were themselves once a barbarous, savage lot, one might inquire of the reverend doctor whether it would strike him as an equally appropriate and advisable course of action for the Romans to have subjected them to a similar *repartimiento*, granting each tyrant his share in the manner employed in the Indies and causing all our forefathers, in the course of mining the silver and gold which Spain used to boast, to perish in body and soul, in accordance with the procedure advocated by the doctor by means of his odious, counterfeit fabrications. Or whether he would like St James to have put this into practice in Córdoba any more than I should like to have seen it done in Seville.[371]

(3) The Indians are so intelligent and quick-witted, so capable and receptive to any moral science or speculative doctrine, and for the most part thoroughly well organized, prudent, and reasonable in their governance, boasting many eminently just laws; moreover, they have derived such great benefit from matters of the faith and Christian religion and in developing good habits and reforming their vices whenever they have received instruction from missionaries and other upstanding individuals, and with every passing day they continue to make progress as much as any people of the world discovered after the Apostles ascended to heaven or yet to be discovered today. I need not rehearse the remarkable progress they have made in the mechanical and liberal arts, such as in reading and writing, in singing and with all musical instruments, in grammar and logic, and in all other areas in which they have been instructed and to which they have been exposed.

(4) And since God has withheld details of all this from Dr Sepúlveda (which will likely prove a source of no little damage to his conscience), it would have been far more becoming of a man so learned in other matters and held in such high esteem if—to avoid plunging into this great labyrinth of error—he had, prior to weighing in on a subject in which he was unversed, first thought to consult those servants of God who had spent countless days and nights toiling to preach to and convert those people, instead of getting ahead of himself by rashly lending credence to the ungodly, tyrannical men who prevailed upon him to compose his treatise to justify the plundering, robbery, and killings they have perpetrated and the usurped states of which they have seized possession by means of vast bloodshed and the death and perdition of untold numbers of innocents.

(5) And what most blights the reverend doctor in the eyes of all right-minded, god-fearing people with first-hand experience of the Indies is the fact that he

---

[370] Justin, *Epitome of the Philippic History of Pompeius Trogus*, translated by J. C. Yardley with introduction and explanatory notes by R. Develin (Atlanta: Scholars Press, 1994), 44.5.

[371] Las Casas's sardonic quip invites Sepúlveda to imagine St James, bellicose evangelist of Spain in popular legend, subjecting the ancient inhabitants of Sepúlveda's Córdoba—and of Las Casas's own native Seville—to the sort of violent conversion that Sepúlveda advocated for the Amerindians. This corresponds to a rhetorical set-piece in ch. 4 of Las Casas's Latin *Apologia* (23v; Poole, 43–44).

312 SEPÚLVEDA ON THE SPANISH INVASION OF THE AMERICAS

invokes and appeals to Oviedo in his utterly false, despicable *History* which he dubbed 'general', presenting him as an unimpeachable source of authority when really Oviedo numbered among the ranks of plundering tyrants and exterminators of Indians—as he himself admits in the prologue to Part I, column 6, and in Book 6, Chapter 8—and, in short, one of their capital foes.[372] Let right-thinking people decide for themselves whether this person is an appropriate witness to be used against the Indians. And yet our doctor calls this man an earnest, industrious chronicler, for he found him to be just to his taste in providing fodder for the dearth of truths in which he trades, for that *Historia* contains almost as many lies as pages. I have amply demonstrated as much in other works of mine and in my *Apología*.

Ninth reply

(1) Turning now to the way he counters the ninth objection, namely my assertion that war is more an impediment to the conversion of the Indians than an aid, for the harm it causes them fills them with hatred for the Christians, not to mention the behaviour and lifestyle of the soldiers being such that their manifold wickednesses preclude any possibility of the religion they profess being deemed a good one, to which his mercy, our most reverend doctor, responds that the delirious patient also takes against the physician that cures him and the mischievous boy against the teacher who punishes him, but that this is no reason to refrain from either activity, as St Augustine says in the relevant letter[373] (etc.): to all this I would retort that, although this will go without saying in the eyes of any Christian with even half their wits about them, while my position is crystal-clear, the answer and solution of the very reverend doctor is so tenebrous[374] that it is unbecoming to Christian eyes or ears, as I have demonstrated at great length in my *Apología*.

(2) However, seeing as the doctor feigns ignorance of my rebuttal of this false assertion of his, I shall state by way of response that he is most grievously mistaken in drawing this analogy, for the Indians do not belong to the class of delirious

---

[372] Gonzalo Fernández de Oviedo, *Historia general de las Indias* (Seville: Juan Cromberger, 1535). Sepúlveda had cited Pt. 1, 3.6 in his Eighth Objection. In col. 6 of the prologue (+iiir) Oviedo mentioned serving as official assayer (Veedor de las Fundaciones de Oro); and in Bk. 6, ch. 8 (fol. lxviir–v) he mentioned impressive gold nuggets he'd inspected and weighed in his official capacity.

[373] Augustine, Letter 185.2.7 (to Boniface). The manuscripts have 'en la Epístola 50' (CR, 231v; MR, 244v). See also Letter 93 (to Vincentius), at 1.2 and 2.4.

[374] Our translation follows the reading of the manuscripts (CR, 213v; MR, 244v), which offer: 'es mi posición clara: y la respuesta y solución del muy reverendo Doctor tan escura'. The 1552 edition offers: 'es imposición clara la respuesta del reverendo doctor: y solución tan obscura', which one could render: 'the doctor's answer is manifestly an invention of his own devising and a solution so tenebrous …'. Not only does the reading of the manuscripts make more sense, with a pointed contrast between Las Casa's 'clear' position and Sepúlveda's 'obscure' answer, but it is clear that the typesetter made a very natural error in misreading 'mi posición' as 'imposición', which led to a desperate attempt to alter the following words to fit this misconstrual.

CONTAINED HEREIN IS A DEBATE OR DISPUTATION   313

individual to whom St Augustine refers, for St Augustine is talking about inveterate, unrepentant heretics, as can be seen as plainly as the sun is bright (if I may
be forgiven the turn of phrase) in Letters 48 and 50 on which the doctor draws in
order to dissemble his audacity.[375]

In the latter of these letters St Augustine is writing to Count Boniface, a devout
Christian, explaining to him the difference between Donatist and Arian heresies
and accounting for why the heretics were up in arms about the laws the emperors
had passed against them at the behest of the church: for, although at first they
found these rules difficult to endure, just as it is hard for the deranged to endure
the lash, later on—once they had come to their senses, recognized the error of their
ways and proceeded to convert—they derived great joy from them. St Augustine
comments: *'For the same thing happens to the Donatists as to the accusers of the
holy Daniel, for just as the lions were turned against the latter, so the laws are against
the former.'*[376] And a little further along there: *'These laws, which appear to be inimical to them, are in fact very much for their sake, since many people have been reformed thanks to them and continue to be reformed every day, and they give thanks
for having been reformed and for having been delivered from that deranged wickedness.'* And somewhat further along still: *'For the physician is a source of vexation to
the delirious individual and the father to his unruly son'*, etc.

Small good, then, does it do the doctor to seek to avail himself of St Augustine's
point about the heretics with reference to the Indians, for heretics can be obliged by
force to return to the faith to which they pledged through baptism, since they are
already subjects of the church; but the same is not true of the Indians, for they are
not subjects, in that they were never baptized, and therefore they are not deranged,
which is to say obstinate and unrepentant.

By the same token, neither are they unruly children or youths of the sort whom
the church is duty-bound to force along to school with the lash, for they would
first of all need to become children of the church through baptism; but for as long
as they are not its children, the church is neither required nor permitted to bring
them into the fold by means of lashes and violence, in accordance with that passage from 1 Corinthians 5: *'For what business is it of mine to judge those who are
outside?'*,[377] but rather by means of blandishments and sweet, meek, mild, peaceful,
loving, Christian conversation, approaching them like sheep among wolves—not
as wolves and plundering brigands among the most meek and guileless sheep—in
accordance with the instruction issued to the church by its Prince, Teacher, and

---

[375] Augustine, Letter 93 [formerly Letter 48] (to Vincentius); Letter 185 [formerly Letter 50] (to
Boniface). These letters are devoted in their entirety to the question of the proper way to deal with
heretics.

[376] Augustine, Letter 185.2.7, discussing Daniel 6:24. The following pair of passages is likewise from
185.2.7. Galmés (p. 167) inadvertently omitted the second passage, apparently through haplography.

[377] 1 Corinthians 5:12.

Redeemer (Matthew 10; Luke 10)[378] and as the Apostles did and as the whole universal church has always done.

And this is why in their discussion of the passage in question (*'What business of mine are those who are outside?'*),[379] St Augustine in his discussion of it in his sermon *'On the centurion's slave-boy'*[380] and elsewhere, together with the *Glossa Ordinaria Interlinearis* and every single one of the holy doctors writing in Greek and Latin alike, all concur that *'this is to say that blandishments—not anger—are to be employed with these infidels so that they can come to reap the benefits of Christ through love and sweetness'.*[381]

And St Gregory imparts the same lesson in Book 11, Letter 15, and it is also to be found in the *Decretum* [of Gratian], dist. 45, chapter *'qui sincera'*: *'Those who are sincere about wishing to attract those who are strangers to the faith must strive to do so with blandishments, not harshness, so that the unpleasantness does not drive away the minds of those whom the restoration of reason could easily call back',* etc.[382] And in Book 1, Letter 34—lest anyone think that he said it inadvertently—he reiterates the point: *'It is necessary to bring those at variance with the Christian religion to the unity of the faith by means of meekness and kindness, advising and persuading them, so that those whom the sweetness of preaching and the prospect of fear of future judgment could induce to believe are not driven away by means of threats and terrors. So they ought to gather together in a friendly way to listen to the Word of God from you, rather than be terrified by a harshness that is extended beyond proper bounds.'*[383] These are St Gregory's words. What clearer testimony against the false allegations of the reverend doctor could there be than this?

(3) Furthermore, towards the end of his letter to the monk Demophilus, St Dionysius says: *'Indeed, it is proper to teach the ignorant, not harm them with punishments, just as we also do not torture the blind, but lead them by the hand.'*[384] And a little further on: *'It is therefore a source of great horror when someone whom Christ, in his immense goodness, sought in the mountains when they had

---

[378] Matthew 10:16; Luke 10:3.

[379] 1 Corinthians 5:12.

[380] Augustine, [*Sermones ad populum*,] Sermon 62, 7.11. (Las Casas would have known this sermon as Sermon 6 in the category *Sermones de Verbis Domini*: see n. 120 above, and ch. 7 in his *Apologia*.)

[381] What Las Casas has in mind here is in fact the *Glossa Interlinearis* (not, as he says, the *Glossa Ordinaria*), which uses Augustine's Sermon 62.7.11 (see previous note) to gloss 1 Corinthians 5:12. The text Las Casas offers here is a blend of Augustine's words there—especially *'Blandiendum est illis, ut audiant veritatem'*—with his own loose paraphrase of what he asserts is the learned scholarly consensus on the matter.

[382] This letter from Gregory I to Paschasius, bishop of Naples, is now numbered 13.12 (as in *PL* 77, cols. 1267–68) or Norberg 13.13. This letter is, as Las Casas notes here, quoted in its entirety in Gratian, *Decretum*, D. 45, c. 3. (Like Las Casas, Gratian knew this letter as Book 11, Letter 15.) Composed in 602, this letter from Gregory to Paschasius concerns the proper treatment of the Jews in the bishop's city.

[383] Gregory I, 1.35 (*PL* 77, col. 489) = Norberg 1.34. Like the later letter to Paschasius, this letter of 591 to Peter, bishop of Terracina, concerns the proper treatment of Jews within a bishop's city.

[384] Pseudo-Dionysius the Areopagite, Letter 8.5 ('To Demophilus the Monk'); see *PG* 3, cols. 1095–96. Las Casas quotes this passage (and the next) in ch. 3 of the *Apologia* (21v).

CONTAINED HEREIN IS A DEBATE OR DISPUTATION   315

gone astray, called back as they fled and, upon finding them, carried back upon his holy shoulders ends up being tormented, rejected, and driven away by you.' Does the figure of Christ scouring the mountains for a lost sheep fleeing in fear—which is precisely what the simple, meek heathens are like—and then lifting it onto his shoulders, having gone to such lengths to locate it at great effort and with difficulty, seem to indicate that Christ would be glad to see his Christians go after those who had never received the faith nor done anything to offend us with blows of the lance and sword as the means to convert them to the faith, as Dr Sepúlveda would have it?

In a letter penned to the Philippians (Chap. 10), St Polycarp the Martyr, disciple of St John the Evangelist, likewise says: 'Be you all subject to one another, taking care to be irreproachable in your conduct among the gentiles, so that you may both receive praise for your good deeds and also so that the Lord may not be blasphemed through you. But woe betide him who causes the name of the Lord to be blasphemed! Therefore you should all teach sobriety and also be sober in your own conduct',[385] etc. Does putting the infidels to the sword and hacking them to pieces on account of and in the course of warfare prior to preaching the faith to them count as irreproachable interaction and commendable ministrations to the infidels of the sort which will prompt them to give thanks to the Christians and refrain from blaspheming Christ? Do butchering and slaughtering constitute examples of the restraint and sobriety by means of which we, in our capacity as Christians, are to interact and teach? And will we ourselves escape that 'woe betide', with its threat of eternal damnation, on the day of our own judgment if we pursue that course of action as our means of preaching of the faith? And will anyone who endorses and advocates that course evade that same 'woe betide'?

The degree to which the doctor is right to base his argument about the lawfulness of getting the Indians to convert by waging war on them before preaching the faith to them solely on the analogy of the madman and the mischievous boy will be only too clear. Killing, robbing, traumatizing, terrorizing, aggrieving, and capturing the Indians, raping and disgracing their wives and daughters, and filling them with hatred for the faith and the Christian religion, all of which number among the soldiers' actions: what manner of paving the way is this that the doctor has devised? It would seem, rather, to be a way of paving and securing the path of whatever robbery, kidnap, and violent appropriation they have perpetrated; for that is the sole objective of the tyrants. And once such actions have been perpetrated, how could upstanding clergymen and friars possibly effect anything positive, as he says the Apostles did? And does the selfsame arrow of the claim that this is 'as the Apostles

---

[385] The original Greek text for ch. 10 of Polycarp's *Epistle to the Philippians* is lost: the text offered by Las Casas here is taken from the Latin version published in 1498 in Paris by Jacobus Faber Stapulensis (Jacques Lefèvre d'Étaples); it can also be consulted at *PG* 5, col. 1014, where it is included along with the Greek text which is available for chs. 1–9.

316 SEPÚLVEDA ON THE SPANISH INVASION OF THE AMERICAS

did' not come back to strike the reverend doctor? Were the Apostles in the habit of sending plunderers, robbers, killers, reprobates, and abominable tyrants ahead of them, as the doctor would see sent?

(4) Furthermore, the doctor then goes on to adduce something else, namely the words of St Augustine in Letter 48: 'If the infidels had fear instilled in them but were not offered any teaching, this might look all too akin to dreadful tyranny. Then again, if they were to be given instruction but not instilled with fear, having become hardened by the ingrained nature of their customary ways … ',[386] etc. To which my question would be: why does the doctor pull an extra word—'infidels'—from out of his own sleeve and insert it here? For St Augustine says no such thing: he simply says 'if they had fear instilled in them but were not offered any teaching' in the course of making his case with regard to the Donatist heretics, as will be obvious from the title of the letter itself and throughout the whole thing; for that title is: 'Letter from the Blessed Augustine to the Vincentius the Donatist and Rogatist, rejoicing at seeing many heretics rectified in their way of thinking', etc. St Augustine is not, then, lumping all heathens together indiscriminately in his discussion. It is consequently imperative, when reading what the esteemed doctor adduces, to keep a close eye on his hands as he composes and, similarly, on his tongue as he speaks. I do not wish to say any more on this subject, for it would be to go on at undue length. Let the reverend doctor read my *Apología*, in which he will find all his false allegations refuted in minute detail.

Tenth reply

(1) As to what he says in answer to the tenth objection, namely that the pope has the power and mandate to preach the gospel both himself and through the ministry of others throughout the whole world, we grant that this is indeed the case; but the corollary which the reverend doctor extrapolates from this—namely that heathens can be forced to listen to preaching—is not at all self-evident, and a considerably more fine-grained inquiry into the truth of the matter than the one the doctor performs would need to be undertaken in order for this to become adducible as evidence. For we see that when Christ, Son of God, sent the Apostles out to preach, he did not command them to use force against those who did not wish to listen to them, but rather to withdraw peacefully from that place or city and shake off the dust from their feet upon it, reserving punishment for its inhabitants for their final judgment, as can be seen in St Matthew 10.[387]

(2) Furthermore, when the Samaritans did not wish to welcome his very own royal and divine self into the city of Samaria, and the Apostles sought permission to

---

[386] Augustine, Letter 93.1.3 [formerly Letter 48] (to Vincentius).
[387] Matthew 10:14–15.

CONTAINED HEREIN IS A DEBATE OR DISPUTATION   317

smite them with fire from the sky (which would certainly be a more effective course of action than the wars the doctor proposes!), he roundly rebuked them for this suggestion, for he had not (he said) come to cause the perdition of souls which the doctor is only too happy to see cast down into hell, but rather for their salvation, as can be seen in the Gospel of St Luke, Chapter 9.[388]

(3) This pair of testimonies offers two overwhelmingly compelling and powerful arguments from the Holy Scriptures, from which we must take our lead and doctrine in directing and organizing our lives and shaping our behaviour. One of them is *ab exemplis* ['by example'], and the other is *ab auctoritate negative* ['by negative precedent'].[389] The latter admittedly has little traction in contentious civil disputes, yet looms large indeed in the Holy Scripture. Our Saviour availed himself of both types when he saw that they were useful for our instruction, and the church, the councils and the holy doctors make use of them too. In the former case, the argument proceeds *affirmative* ['positively'] as follows: virtuous, wise, sensible men— to say nothing of the saints themselves—performed particular actions in such and such a manner in which they may be emulated; therefore we should also perform these actions and imitate them in so doing. In the latter case, the argument runs as follows: with regard to a particular matter with a bearing on our edification in life—especially where leading a Christian life is concerned—and the preservation of a good conscience in observing the law of God, virtuous, sensible men *refrained from* doing a particular action (which under more appropriate circumstances they would not have shrunk from doing), thereby avoiding certain sorts of unfavourable consequences; therefore we too should refrain from the thing in question and shrink from those and other equally troublesome outcomes.

(4) Our Saviour availed himself of the first variety, *ab exemplis affirmative*,[390] as reported in Matthew 12, where he defended his disciples against aspersions cast by the Jews, saying: 'Have you not read what David did when he became hungry, how he entered the temple and ate the consecrated bread, which was not lawful for anyone else to eat?'[391] By this example he demonstrated that it was lawful for the disciples to help themselves to the ears of corn in order to eat, even on the Sabbath. He availed himself of the latter sort in John 8, where it says: '*This Abraham did not do.*'[392]

And the church too has recourse to this sort: neither Christ nor his Apostles ever granted forgiveness to those who did not repent and reform; therefore we should not grant it either, which is to say, we should not absolve those who are in a state

---

[388] Luke 9:54–55.

[389] The opposition being set up is between *ab exemplis affirmative* ('by example in the positive sense', i.e. by positive example) (as below), here rendered simply as *ab exemplis* ('by example'), and *ab auctoritate negative* ('by negative precedent', i.e. by express prohibition).

[390] See previous note.

[391] Matthew 12:3–4. This quotation is not italicized as Las Casas cites it in Spanish-language form.

[392] John 8:40.

of mortal sin (24, q. 1, chapter '*legatur*', and 1, q. 2, chapter '*quam pio*').[393] And see also the Council of Elvira, Canon 6 60: if anyone should smash the idolaters' idols by force and against their will and were to be killed there on that account, we see fit and decree that this person should not be included in the ranks of the martyrs, for there is no record or mention in the Gospel of the Apostles ever having done such a thing at any point.[394] And St Thomas, in *Secunda secundae*, q. 10, art. 12, likewise reasons there *in that passage by negative precedent*, as follows: the practice of the universal church is a source of great authority—more so than the sayings of any one saint, such as St Jerome or St Augustine; and since the church was not in the habit of baptizing children born to infidels against their parents' will, it follows that we should not do so either.[395]

(5) And so this is all to say that whatever actions prudent, wise, virtuous men did or did not perform—and this goes even more so for the actions which the saints undertook or refrained from undertaking or avoided, and most of all for those of our God and Saviour and his Apostles—we too should do or not do, undertake or avoid, and it is on this basis, imitating and doing what they did and not doing what they did not, that we must conduct our lives and mend our ways. For if this were not the case, St Paul would not have said in Ephesians 5, '*Therefore be imitators of God, as beloved children*',[396] and in Philippians 3: '*Brethren, join in following my example, and observe those who walk according to the pattern you have in us*',[397] etc. And as St Gregory Thomas says: '*Every action of Christ is an instruction to us*.[398]

And the grounds for following the examples of virtuous, good men in acting or abstaining from action is because those who are virtuous and good are well versed in the nature of things which are doable and points of good practice, for they are more guided by, and closer to, reason, which is the surest guide in all we do. This is why the Philosopher in Book 2 of his *Ethics* says that the mean of virtue is whatever is determined in accordance with the view of the wise.[399] And those who count as wise in this regard are not those who consider matters in the abstract but rather

---

[393] Gratian, *Decretum*, C. 24, q. 1, c. 2 (*Legatur*), a letter on the subject of the pope's inability to absolve the sins of a dead person; and Gratian, *Decretum*, C. 1, q. 2, c. 2 (*Quam pio*), a papal letter asserting that no money should change hands between those who agree to convert and those inducing them to do so.

[394] The Libertine Council or Concilium Eliberritanum, also known as the Synod of Elvira (at Granada), issued sixty canons (though many are not regarded as original); here canon 60 itself is meant. (The same error is in the manuscripts: *CR*, 216r; *MR*, 248r.)

[395] Aquinas, *ST* II-II, q. 10, art. 12, co.

[396] Ephesians 5:1.

[397] Philippians 3:17.

[398] Aquinas, *ST* III, q. 40, art. 1, ad 3. On these words of Aquinas's, see for instance Richard Schenk, O.P., '*Omnis Christi actio nostra est instructio*: The Deeds and Sayings of Jesus as Revelation in the View of Thomas Aquinas', in *La doctrine de la révélation divine de saint Thomas d'Aquin*, edited by Léon Elders (Rome: Libreria Editrice Vaticana, 1990), 104–31. For *Christi* (present both in the 1552 edition and the manuscripts: *CR*, 216r; *MR*, 248r), Tudela Bueso (in the *Tratados*) and Galmés incorrectly read *christiani*.

[399] Aristotle, *Nicomachean Ethics* 2.6.15 (1106b7–1107a2). Here, the word 'mean' ('the mean of virtue') is used to render the Greek 'μεσότης', the proper moral midpoint between two extremes.

CONTAINED HEREIN IS A DEBATE OR DISPUTATION   319

in practical terms, with an eye to what can be done in practice. And in the sixth book of that same work he [Aristotle] shows that, in matters of virtue, we should accept and acquiesce to the resolutions and determinations of the wise without any further evidence or testimony, just as we accept proofs in the mathematical sciences.[400]

(6) For since the saints and servants of God (especially the Apostles) were and are incomparably wise in matters of virtue—and infinitely more so Christ himself, invested with the wisdom of the Father himself—it is self-evident that we must emulate the deeds of Christ and his followers in terms of what they did or refrained from doing and use those principles to inform and govern our own lives and set the compass of our behaviour. For when Christ dispatched the Apostles to preach, he set out how they were to behave in the event of coming upon people who did not wish to listen to them or welcome them in,[401] and this was to shake off the dust from their shoes as a sign of their sin but not to force them to listen, which, had he deemed the latter an appropriate practice, he would not have hesitated to teach, prescribe, and state; but he showed that it was a bad course of action in rebuking St John and St James on that account,[402] in view of which it would be outrageous, presumptuous, and sinful indeed of us to act to the contrary.

(7) And so it turns out that my position on this is neither false nor new-fangled, as the doctor slanderously alleges, but rather a point of Catholic, Christian doctrine. And the learned men who accept my view as true are not opposed to this; for it is one thing for the church to hold the power to remove the obstacles which have been maliciously put in the path of preaching, and quite another to force the heathens to harken to preaching against their will. For the former can be lawfully done, whereas the latter cannot. And so it is not the opinion of these men that diverges from what I affirm, but rather only that of the reverend doctor, straying from the path of true reason.

(8) Lastly, whatever comes of this article, either way this objection is in no way to the Indians' detriment, for they do not put up any resistance to listening to the evangelical doctrine so long as it is preached to them without murder, robbery, and tyranny, as commanded by Jesus Christ and as required by the purest, truest, meekest Christian religion; it is a different story altogether[403] if preaching is undertaken in the manner so perversely prescribed by the doctor. For, under those circumstances, they are quite right to refuse to hear it and in persecuting and massacring those who would foist it upon them and in deeming it an evil thing at variance with all reason.

---

[400] Aristotle, *Nicomachean Ethics* 6.11.6 (1143b12–14) appears to correspond most closely to this idea.

[401] Matthew 10:14.

[402] Luke 9:54–55.

[403] Here begins an addition ('otra cosa es ... ') that Las Casas made to the 1552 printing; it is not present in the manuscripts (*CR*, 216v; *MR*, 245v).

Eleventh reply

(1) As to the way he counters the eleventh objection, in which I state that if it were necessary to resort to warfare to free the innocents from persecution, even more innocents would die, and of any two given evils or ills it is necessary to choose the lesser, the doctor says that I have got my sums wrong, for more than twenty thousand people were sacrificed in New Spain each year, meaning that in the thirty years that have elapsed since New Spain was conquered six hundred thousand have been spared: the first thing I would say by way of response is that the doctor and I should compare our calculations.

(2) The second thing to point out is that it is not true to say that twenty thousand people were sacrificed each year in New Spain—nor one hundred, nor even fifty—for if that had been the case then we would not find such abundant numbers of people there as we do indeed find. That is just the tyrants talking, seeking to justify and vindicate their tyrannical acts of violence in oppressing, persecuting, and tyrannizing those Indians whom they spared from the awful harvest they reaped and kept as slaves. And those who seek to champion their cause, such as the doctor and his followers, support this outcome.

(3) The third thing to say is that the doctor has got his own arithmetic all wrong, for it would be truer and far more fitting to say that the Spanish have upon arrival in each province sacrificed more people to that most beloved and adored goddess of theirs, Greed, in any given year of those spent in the Indies than the Indians to their gods in a hundred years across all the Indies put together. The sky, the earth, the elements, and the stones all testify to this and cry out in lament, and even the very tyrants responsible for it do not deny it; just observe how all those realms were brimming with inhabitants when we invaded each in turn, and compare the situation to which we have reduced them today, for they are devastated and annihilated. Immense shame and flagellating turmoil ought to assail us, since godfearingness seems to be in such short supply, for seeking to excuse or exonerate such wicked, unspeakable crimes, when, faced with more land in length and breadth than all of Europe and much of Asia combined stretching before our very eyes,[404] we have with utmost cruelty, injustice, and tyranny depopulated, depleted, and devastated it all through plundering and appropriation in a matter of forty-five or forty-eight years and all for the sake of goods and riches—lands which we once saw full to bursting and densely populated with the most civilized of people.

And if the most reverend Dr Sepúlveda were to reflect upon this in a more kind and charitable frame of mind, he would realize that my arithmetic is better than his. And he would do well to clarify, seeing as he weeps for the death of the unbaptized

---

[404] The phrase is the 1552 edition's expansion of the manuscripts' 'tres mil leguas de tierra' (CR, 217r; MR, 250v). Similarly, in the previous sentence the 1552 edition added 'extirpados' ('rooted out', 'annihilated') to the manuscript's simple 'destruidos'.

CONTAINED HEREIN IS A DEBATE OR DISPUTATION   321

when it comes to Indians sacrificed, who will have amounted in number to ten or a hundred (and even if it were a thousand or ten thousand, which it is not), how it is that his soul is not stricken, his innards rent asunder, and his heart broken at the twenty million souls that have perished in the intervening period without having received the faith or the sacraments? They could all have been saved, for God has made them so eminently receptive to the faith, and instead they have been condemned because the Spanish have deprived them of the opportunity and occasion to convert and repent by butchering them contrary to all reason and justice and all in the interests of robbing and capturing them.

(4) Fourthly, I would say that the esteemed doctor is putting words into my mouth when he claims that I sought to come up with arguments to exonerate the practice of human sacrifice, when even those gentiles of the so-called civilized, unbarbaric sort considered the practice an abomination, as Pliny, Book 30, Chapter 1 reports.[405] My stance on this is not about excusing them in the eyes of God, for I do not know what God makes of them, for his judgment is inscrutable; rather, I wish to demonstrate by means of manifest arguments that they suffer from ignorance and labour under a pall of probable error which means that they will not credit it the first time, or even the first several times, that Christians inform them that human sacrifice goes against natural law and is a sin, and consequently they cannot be justly punished on this account by humans or indeed any mortal judgment. And I would even go so far as to say that they will never be obliged to believe any preacher of our holy faith who keeps company with the tyrants, warmongers, plunderers, and killers that the doctor would like to dispatch. And to maintain what he does is much further removed from Christianity than what I propose, which is the opposite, as any right-minded Christian will recognize and concede.

And I would go further and say that it is no straightforward matter to prove to them that it is against natural law to perform human sacrifices to the true (or false, if deemed and held to be true) God; rather, there are sound, probable, and practically inarguable grounds on which the opposite case can be made. I discussed these at length in my *Apología* and read them out in the presence of many theologians and learned individuals,[406] and, availing themselves of many of these same arguments, a particular group of barbarians even succeeded in convincing the Romans of this when the latter tried to ban them from performing human sacrifice, as recounted by Plutarch in his *Problems*, p. 465.[407] And the Romans themselves, finding themselves overpowered and greatly beleaguered by Hannibal, sacrificed a Gaulish man and woman and a Greek man and woman in the Forum Boarium in order to placate the gods, who they believed must be angry at them, as Plutarch reports in the

---

[405] Pliny the Elder, *Naturalis historia*, 30.3.12.

[406] This last phrase ('y se leyeron en presencia de muchos teólogos y letrados') was added in the 1552 printing: it is not present in the manuscripts (CR, 217r; MR, 251v).

[407] Plutarch, *Roman Questions* 83, which Soto noted that Las Casas had mentioned in Valladolid (and which features in ch. 34 of his *Apologia* at 153v; Poole, 223).

322 SEPÚLVEDA ON THE SPANISH INVASION OF THE AMERICAS

same place,[408] as does Livy in Decade III, Book II.[409] And in Italy, the dire straits endured on account of famine and other misfortunes persuaded people to offer the first fruits of humans killed in sacrifice, although they had some misgivings, as reported by Dionysius of Halicarnassus in Book 1 of his history of the Romans.[410]

And the Gauls frequently performed this sort of sacrifice, particularly in times of terrible disease or under other life-threatening circumstances, such as war. And their rationale for this was that they felt, where curing or saving human lives was concerned, that the immortal gods would not be appeased unless human life was offered up in turn. Julius Caesar attests to this in Book 6 of his *Commentaries on the Gallic War*, where he says the following: '*All Gaulish people are extremely devoted to religious rites and for this reason those who are afflicted with serious illness or en-gaged in dangerous combat either sacrifice humans as victims or pledge to perform such sacrifices, for they believe that unless the life of a human is offered in exchange for human life, the might of the immortal gods cannot be placated. They have estab-lished sacrifices of this same kind in the public sphere.*'[411] That is what he says.

And there were no people in the world—or just a few shy of all—who were not in the habit of performing human sacrifice to the gods (including in Spain itself, as evidenced by Strabo in Book 3 of his geographical work *De situ orbis*),[412] induced to do so by natural reason: for this and so much more is owed to God by all mortals, and even if the doctor were to devote several more days to duly studying the matter than he has hitherto devoted, he will not be able to prove beyond all doubt that sacrificing humans to the true (or false, but deemed to be true) God goes against natural law, *even setting aside any explicit divine or human law*.[413]

(5) As to what the reverend doctor goes on to say about killing innocent people in the course of just warfare being an accidental occurrence, or that they will not qualify as sins so long as the prince is of sound intention in his soul, etc., I would answer that it is the killing of innocent people in a sinless fashion in the course of just warfare which may be termed accidental. And it only counts as *per accidens*

---

[408] Plutarch, *Roman Questions* 83. This is also quoted at length in ch. 34 of the *Apologia*, as in the previous note.

[409] Livy, *Ab urbe condita* 22.57.

[410] Dionysius of Halicarnassus, *Antiquitates Romanae* 1.24. This is quoted at length in ch. 36 of the *Apologia* (161r; Poole, 235).

[411] Julius Caesar, *De bello gallico* 6.16.

[412] Strabo, *Geography* 3.3.6. Note that the name actually given for Strabo's work in the main body of the text here is '*De situ orbis*' ['On the layout of the world']. This was indeed an alternative title under which Strabo's work was sometimes published: for instance, the Greek-to-Latin translation of Strabo's work by Guarino of Verona (1374–1464)—which Las Casas was clearly using here, as is clear from his quotation of this same passage in ch. 34 of the *Apologia* (154r)—went by that name. However, the title '*De situ orbis*' may also lead to confusion, as this is also the title of a work by fellow geographer Pomponius Mela. In the facsimile of the 1552 edition of this Reply published by Hanke ed. (p. 400), in fact, Strabo's name has been crossed out—but then rewritten in the margin.

[413] The italicized words translate a Latin phrase in the original, reflecting what appears to be the source of most of this passage: the beginning of ch. 36 of Las Casas's Latin *Apologia*. As noted at n. 30, this indicates that Las Casas was already at work on this Latin manuscript while penning these 'Replies' in late 1550 or early 1551. (Galmés's edition prints an intrusive comma and *a* between *seclusa* and *omni*.)

CONTAINED HEREIN IS A DEBATE OR DISPUTATION   323

and hence excusable in those cases where there is no other way for the just war in question to be brought to an end or victory attained except by means of the action which will result in the death or killing of the innocents along with the wicked or guilty: for instance, when it proves necessary to attack and overthrow a fortress as a result of which some children who happen to be in there too will die. But if it is not necessary to storm the fortress in order to secure victory, especially in cases where there is good reason to believe that there are definitely or almost certainly innocents present within, then it no longer counts as *per accidens* but *per se*, with the killing of whatever innocents met their end there constituting a primary aim in itself. And therefore the king—if it was he that issued the order—and all those who carried it out would be guilty of mortal sin and would be, and are, obliged to make reparations for all the harm caused,[414] nor shall there be any salvation for them unless they sincerely repent.

And the reason for this is that, seeing as warfare and all the actions perforce performed in the course thereof (such as killings, robberies, and all the rest) are deeds which are evil *per se*, war should never, ever be waged unless as a last possible resort and out of purest necessity. St Augustine says as much in 23, q. 1, C. '*Noli*': '*It is a matter of will for there to be peace, whereas war is born of necessity*.'[415] And Pope Nicholas [I], in a chapter of q. 8 of the aforementioned *Causa*, says: '*Unless necessity compels it, battles should be abstained from not only during Lent but at all times*,'[416] etc. And necessity is the sole mitigating factor preventing these actions which are *per se* evil or otherwise somehow execrable from being mortal sins. For if, for instance, in the example given, the storming of the fortress is not a matter of necessity, then obviously blame accrues for the deaths and injuries sustained not only by the innocent but also by the guilty. For this kind of war is unjust from the outset, as veraciously asserted by the most reliable theologians.

(6) And so it is in the case of the Indies, where there is no need whatsoever to engage in warfare. For if the aim is to get rid of and extirpate the vices whereby the Indians kill people for the purposes of human sacrifice, which only occurred in a few places (though this point would still stand even if the practice had indeed been widespread), this can be most readily accomplished by means of preaching the gospel alone, not through cruel warfare. And so, given the moral certainty that there are infinite innocents among them in the form of countless children, women, and adults who neither engage in nor approve of these depravities, it is impossible to wage war on the grounds suggested by the doctor without being guilty of the

---

[414] This key reference to the necessity of reparations was oddly omitted by Galmés (p. 175), though it is present in both the 1552 edition and in both manuscripts (CR., 217v; MR., 252v).

[415] Augustine, Letter 189.6. Sections 4–6 of this letter (to Boniface) are quoted in Gratian, *Decretum*, C. 23, q. 1, c. 3 (*Noli existimare*), which, as Las Casas's mode of referencing here makes clear, has certainly been his source for the Augustinian text.

[416] The text in question is the *Ad consulta Bulgarorum* of Pope Nicholas I, but consulted, as the mode of referencing again makes clear, through Gratian, *Decretum*, C. 23, q. 8, c. 15. *Ad consulta Bulgarorum* is a document produced in the context of the Photian Schism.

324   SEPÚLVEDA ON THE SPANISH INVASION OF THE AMERICAS

most terrible mortal sin and being obliged to make restitution for all the damages caused.

The passage he adduces from Gerson is thoroughly at odds with his cause and, if he reconsiders it with dispassionate eyes, in fact works considerably more in favour of my own case against him, for Gerson says: '*Only the best interests of the republic or the need to avoid a public catastrophe considerably worse than any private ill arising from warfare exonerates mortal sin.*'[417] It is obvious that the defamation of the faith and abhorrence of the Christian religion arising from the most execrable warfare—impediment to the salvation of so many—which the doctor would have precede the gospel, the damnation to which those whom the tyrants immediately butcher and kill are in turn immediately doomed, and the deaths of countless innocents who are not to blame for the sins in question (even in those lands in which they *are* practised)—such as children, women, labourers, those who do not perpetrate such acts, and many others again who would not do so were it not for the fact that their princes and priests had established and decreed these practices—is by far the greater and more damaging ill.

(7) The same goes for the impulse, zeal, and predilection for robbing, capturing, and persecuting those people and wishing to wage war on them of which the tyrants seem to have boundless reserves with not a care spared for the sinfulness of their behaviour, as a result of which they exist and live in a perpetual state of mortal sin. No doubt, as I have demonstrated beyond all doubt in my *Apología*, this is all very much to the public good—far preferable to having a handful of innocents die as victims of human sacrifice![418] And this is something that happens to the reverend doctor time and again: the proof-texts which he adduces in support of his position, twisting them against the grain of their rightful interpretation, come hurtling straight back at him along the true course, measure for measure, landing squarely in opposition to his outrageous design.

(8) As to what the eminent doctor next proceeds to contest, namely the notion that, if those idolaters or barbarians are right to defend their own religion and idolatry—as I am purported to claim and as I do indeed openly affirm in my *Confesionario*—then it follows that they are also within their rights and free from sin in worshipping their idols, etc., my response is to reiterate that, on the understanding that they are labouring under the fallacy or false conviction of believing those gods of theirs to be the true God (or in worshipping and revering the one they hold to be the true god by means of idol worship), not only do they have just—or one might rather say 'probable'—grounds for defending their religion, but are also themselves obliged to do so by natural law that if they do not duly mount their

---

[417] Jean Gerson, *Regulae Morales*, 73 (in the section '*De avaritia*'). See n. 278 above.

[418] The sarcastic comment about a 'grande bien público', as well as the preceding insistence that the Spanish oppressors are in a state of mortal sin, are flourishes added to the 1552 edition. The dig at Sepúlveda's method in the next sentence also contains late amplifications. In preparing the printed edition, Las Casas clearly enjoyed ratcheting up his personal attacks on Sepúlveda.

CONTAINED HEREIN IS A DEBATE OR DISPUTATION 325

defence of it—even to the point of losing their lives in defending their religion and their idols or gods if need be—then they are guilty of mortal sin and will go to hell for that sin alone.

The reason for this—without going into any of the many others offered in my *Apología*—is that, as humans, we are all by nature obliged to love and serve God more than our very own selves, and therefore to defend his honour and divine worship to the death if necessary, *when the situation and occasion require it*, as can be seen in Romans 10, '*confession is made with the mouth, resulting in salvation*,'[419] as the doctors and St Thomas, (*Secunda secundae*, q. 3, art. 2)[420] note in that connection. And the deaths of all the martyrs point to the same conclusion. And there is no difference whatsoever in terms of the obligation incumbent upon those who know the true God—as is the case for Christians such as ourselves—as opposed to those who do not know him, so long as they deem and consider some god to be the true one, just as there is no difference between a man who refrains from knowing another's wife so as not to commit the sin of adultery in violation of the Sixth Commandment and a man who believed and was convinced that he was obliged to know such a woman and that he would be breaking the divine command in *refraining* from doing so. It is clear that if he did not then go ahead and know her, he would be guilty of mortal sin, misguided though this conviction is. The reason for this is that a misguided belief binds and obliges just as much as a correct one, *albeit not in the same way*. '*Because true conscience binds simply and* per se, *whereas erring conscience binds* per accidens *and only under certain circumstances, namely insofar as something bad is perceived to be good, from which it follows that if action is taken sin is not avoided, but if action is not taken sin is nonetheless incurred*', according to St Thomas, in *Summa theologica*, *Prima secundae*, q. 19, arts. 5 and 6,[421] and in the second book of his commentary on the *Sentences* [of Peter Lombard], in dist. 39, q. 3, art. 3 *passim*,[422] and also in other places.

For since idolaters believe and are taught that those idols are the true God or that the true God is served and worshipped or ought to be served and worshipped by means of them—for in truth the universal notion of God does not point or lead to anything but the true God (according to St John Damascene, Gregory of Nazianzus, St Augustine, Boethius, St Thomas, and all the saints who address themselves to this subject)[423]—and are through natural reason also aware of the first principle

---

[419] Romans 10:10.

[420] Aquinas, *ST* II-II, q. 3, art. 2, s.c.

[421] Aquinas, *ST* I-II, q. 19, art. 5, ad 2, and art. 6.

[422] Aquinas, *Scriptum super libros Sententiarum Magistri Petri Lombardi*, Bk. 2, dist. 39, q. 3, art. 3.

[423] Here Las Casas is rapidly citing several authorities to whom he makes fuller reference in ch. 35 of his *Apología*, at 155r–v and 157r–v. For John Damascene, he has in mind *De orthodoxa fide*, ch. 1; for Gregory of Nazianzus, he means the work translated by Petrus Mosellanus Protegensis (Peter Schade) as *De theologia* and published in Basel by Johann Froben in 1523 under the title *Divi Gregorii Episcopi Nazanzeni De theologia libri quinque* (in the *Apología* he refers to 'column 11', which is on p. B6r of that edition and seems appropriate); for Augustine, *De civitate Dei* 10.4, among other possible occasions on which Augustine voices this sentiment; for Boethius, *De consolatione philosophiae*, Bk. 3, Prosa 10, ll. 23–27; and for Aquinas, *Summa contra Gentiles*, Bk. 3, ch. 119.

326 SEPÚLVEDA ON THE SPANISH INVASION OF THE AMERICAS

agendorum ['of things to be done'], namely that God must be obeyed, worshipped, and served, which is one of the elements of synderesis and is upheld fully among the infidels, it follows—given their fallacious understanding and aforementioned error and the binding nature of conviction—that they are obliged to defend their god (or the gods whom they believe to be the true god) and their religion, just as we Christians are obliged to defend our own true God and the Christian religion, and if they fail to do so then they are guilty of mortal sin, just as we would be guilty of sin for failing to do so wherever the need arose.

(9) But this is where the parallel ends: for we, in so doing, prove ourselves worthy, whereas they, in so doing, are doomed to eternal damnation; indeed, for them, both action and inaction alike entail flouting the divine commandment. And on the understanding that all men are obliged by natural law to defend their god or the gods whom they deem the true god, Cicero in his eleventh speech, delivered in defence of Marcus ~~Fontero~~ Fonteius, excoriates the Gauls for being degenerate and departing from the practice of all other nations in not going to war in defence of their gods, saying: '*Do you suppose that those sorts of people are swayed by the sanctity of a sworn oath and the fear of the immortal gods when giving evidence? The Gaulish people are so very different from the custom and nature of the other peoples of the world in that, while other nations wage battles in defence of their own religion, the Gauls wage wars against the religion of everyone else*',[424] etc. These are Cicero's words. The doctor tries to claim that acceptance of the fact that they are within their rights or labouring under a probable impression in defending their gods or being obliged to do so must mean also accepting that they are equally right and free from sin in honouring and serving their idols and practising idolatry: but this does not follow. And since his mercy failed to notice the type of misapprehension under which the idolaters labour and the nature of an erring conscience, he proceeded along logically flawed lines in his argument.

(10) As for the rest of what he asserts about probable opinions, etc., I say that, among any populace one might care to mention, an opinion is deemed probable not in line with the rules of reason *in the absolute sense*, but because this is how it appears to the experts in any given business or art and they make use and approve of it accordingly, even if it happens to be in error.

(11) The same goes for those considered wisest and most sensible in any given community who govern and rule over the young and the masses, even though in truth they are mistaken and not at all wise or sensible when it comes to true reason, especially in matters of the faith and divine law. For there can be true virtue only where there is true knowledge of God, as St Augustine says.[425] In this same vein jurists say that '*the commonly held opinion leads to probable error*' as noted

---

[424] Cicero, *Pro M. Fonteio*, 13.30. Note that the 1552 text, and subsequent editors following it, all print 'Fontero' here. The manuscripts, however, correctly read *Marco Fonteio* (CR, 219r; MR, 254v).

[425] Augustine, *De civitate Dei* 8.8.

CONTAINED HEREIN IS A DEBATE OR DISPUTATION   327

in Book 6 [of the *Decretals*] in a gloss offered in connection with *De postulatione prelatorum* (which has but a single chapter), and also in *lex* 2 ff. *De juris et facti ignorantia*.[426]

I should like to inquire of the reverend doctor whether or not he deems the Romans to have been an organized, civilized people, with sensible individuals, philosophers, and wisemen represented among the population? Therefore whatever they endorsed, did, and upheld could be termed probable, even if it was in fact woefully misguided. For in matters of gods and idolatry, the opinion which the Romans so punctiliously observed and endorsed is the one that could, therefore, be said to be the 'probable' one for them and their nation; for lesser, lowerranking folk are not to go asking the intellectuals of other nations whether or not what their superiors are doing or instigating is probable from the point of view of true reason. Therefore it is not known as the 'probable opinion' with regard to the rules of reason *in the absolute sense*, but rather because it is what is considered best and practised and endorsed by those deemed the wisest and most sensible in any given nation. Therefore everything the reverend doctor adduces at all points in his discussion of this matter is devoid of substance and worth alike.

(12) With regard to his ensuing assertion that my point about God having commanded Abraham to sacrifice his son to him works more against me than against him, I would say that he makes his case very poorly by appealing to the fact that God did not then permit Abraham to perform the sacrifice. I ask of him: why was it that God commanded him to perform this sacrifice? Clearly, besides the great mystery he wished to represent and the test of obedience to which he wished to subject his servant, it was also in order to convey that everything is owed to him and that if he did not ultimately allow the boy to be sacrificed to him, it was by the grace of his infinite goodness and the mercy he had on Isaac.

This point can be proven by means of the vow of Jephthah, who sacrificed his own daughter in fulfilment of his pledge. He did this, misguided though it was, because he saw that God had instructed Abraham to do this, as El Tostado notes in

---

[426] This dictum derives from a gloss of Panormitanus (Nicolò de' Tudeschi) offered in connection with the one and only chapter ('*Capitulum unicum*') of tit. 5 '*De postulatione praelatorum*' in Book 1 of the Sixth Book of the *Decretales* (i.e. *Liber Sextus Decretalium*, Boniface VIII's appendix to Gregory IX's *Decretales*), as Las Casas's first reference indicates. Panormitanus was using it more specifically in the context of the consensus of university professors ('*communis opinio **doctorum** inducit probabilem errorem*'); see further Alexander Russell, *Conciliarism and Heresy in 15th-Century England* (Cambridge: Cambridge University Press, 2017), 174n93. The second reference given is to the *Digest*, Bk. 22, tit. 6: '*De juris et facti ignorantia*'; see especially the second extract, from the jurist Neratius Priscus. Las Casas's immediate source for both the dictum and this pair of references, however, would appear to have been the entry '*De opinione*' in the so-called *Summa Sylvestrina* of Silvestro Mazzolini da Prierio *alias* Prierias (1456/7–1527), a compendious theological reference work where this information is presented in near-identical form to Las Casas's citation practice here. In his *Apologia* (ch. 31, 140v; Poole, 206), Las Casas cited the *Summa Sylvestrina*'s entry '*De bello*', so he certainly knew the work. Frequently reprinted after its *editio princeps* of 1515, it was properly known as *Summa summarum quae Sylvestrina dicitur*.

that connection (Judges 11, q. 48 and q. 52).[427] And the Holy Scripture itself would appear to show God's approval of Jephthah's vow and its fulfilment, as can be seen in St Paul's Epistle to the Hebrews, Chapter 11, where the Apostle lists Jephthah among the saints.[428] And this can also be seen from what it says of Jephthah in Judges 11, namely that the Spirit of the Lord descended upon Jephthah just before he made his vow, to say nothing of the fact that God did after all then go on to grant him victory over his enemies, which is what he had hoped to obtain when he made his pledge in the first place.[429] In light of all this it would appear that God accepted the terms of this vow and, in turn, that human sacrifice must have been gratifying to him. In view of these arguments and scriptural passages, St Augustine cannot bring himself to condemn Jephthah outright, as can be seen in his Questions on the Book of Judges, q. 49,[430] which is the very one the doctor adduces in support of his own argument. And so, seeing as Jephthah believed he was gratifying God in making that vow and since God himself, it would appear, did not condemn it—at least once the vow had already been made—for the trio of reasons just outlined, it is hardly unconscionable for the infidels likewise to have believed that offering human sacrifices to God (or to those whom they considered God) is something owed to God and which gratifies him. And if he did not ultimately allow Abraham to sacrifice his son, it was not because this was not owed to him, but rather out of his infinite goodness and the mercy he had on Isaac, and indeed because he had resolved to derive his own flesh from him. The same goes in part for what I note about the first-born sons whom he ordered to be sacrificed to him but then wished to be replaced by a lamb or shekels, or by doves or turtledoves (Exodus 13 and 34; Leviticus 27; Numbers 8; Luke 2).[431]

(13) And with regard to the final point of this objection I would say that from now until Judgment Day no heathens shall ever be obliged, in the eyes neither of God nor of men, to embrace the faith of Jesus Christ for as long as those bearing its tidings continue to be warmongers, killers, robbers, and tyrants, as Dr Sepúlveda would wish it and as he yearns to dispatch. And until such time as its proclaimers and preachers are virtuous men who lead truly Christian lives and do not keep company with tyrants, those words from the gospel—'*but he who does not believe will be damned*'[432]—shall never apply to the infidels, and least of all to the Indians and those of their ilk, despite the fact that they can and will still go to hell for other sins which cannot be absolved without faith.

---

[427] El Tostado (Alonso de Madrigal), *Commentaria in Judices et Ruth*, ch. 11, qs. 48 and 52. From here on, the discussion of Jephthah is an addition to the 1552 printing, not present in the manuscripts (*CR*, 219v; *MR*, 256r).

[428] Hebrews 11:32–34.

[429] Judges 11:29–32.

[430] Augustine, *Quaestiones in Heptateuchum*, Bk. 7, *Quaestiones in Iudices*, q. 49, 2–3.

[431] Exodus 13:13 and 34:20; Leviticus 27:3–7 and 27:26; Numbers 8:16–18; Luke 2:23–24.

[432] Mark 16:16.

Twelfth reply

(1) Coming now to the final objection: the errors and egregious propositions which Dr Sepúlveda amasses there, shrouded and glossed with the feigned zeal of serving royal interests, are so enormous, at such variance with all evangelical truth and Christianity as a whole, and worthy of such singular punishment and censure of the severest sort that no right-minded Christian should be surprised by our desire to indict him not only in a lengthy written tract but as a capital enemy of the Christian republic, abettor of cruel tyrants, scourge of the human race, and sower of the most mortal blindness throughout these Spanish realms. But proceeding with as much restraint as possible, as the law of God requires of us, offering just a brief response to each element in turn, the enormity of the error of his views will be laid bare.

(2) His opening claim about it having been Pope Alexander's intention for the Indians first to be subjugated by means of warfare—or, as the doctor (with all due respect) always calls it in his writings in both Spanish and Latin, 'conquest'—is a patent falsehood. This can be seen from the terms of the Bull of Concession, wherein the exposition of the basis on which the supreme pontiff founds his entire objective—namely the conversion and salvation of the souls there—runs as follows: '*They (that is to say, your envoys) have discovered certain islands and mainlands inhabited by a very large number of people dwelling in a peaceful fashion.*'[433] And further on: '*We exhort you most earnestly by the Lord and by the holy baptism which you have received which renders you beholden to apostolic commands and by the innards of Our Lord Jesus Christ we fervently entreat you that, since you propose to launch and undertake this expedition of this sort with eager zeal for the true faith, you should likewise conceive both a desire and a sense of duty to induce the peoples living on those islands and lands to embrace the Christian faith.*' And later on: '*And, furthermore, we command you by the virtue of your holy obedience (in accordance with your promise, and as your utmost devotion and royal magnanimity leave us in no doubt that you will indeed do) that you must dispatch upstanding, god-fearing, learned, skilled, experienced men to the aforementioned mainlands and islands to instruct the aforementioned inhabitants and residents in the Catholic faith and school them in good conduct, adhering to these principles with every due diligence.*' This is what it says there. For if Pope Alexander was aware, thanks to the reports of the monarchs themselves, that the discoverers they had sent to uncover that world had found that its inhabitants dwelt in peace, why would the pope have endorsed so-called 'conquest' and directed the monarchs first to subjugate them by means of

---

[433] Alexander VI, *Inter caetera* (1493). The first extract rearranges and abridges the wording. In the second extract, *misericordiae* is missing after *viscera* ('bowels'), both in the 1552 edition and in the manuscripts (CR, 220r; MR, 257r).

warfare and only afterwards to preach the gospel to them, as the reverend doctor asserts in his writings?

(3) Furthermore: if the pope, in issuing them with instructions to bring about the conversion of these peoples to the Christian religion, beseeches the monarchs by virtue of the holy baptism they received and by the innards of Jesus Christ, where does the reverend doctor get the idea that the pope's intention was to prevail upon the monarchs to go about sooner subjugating them in warfare rather than first preaching the gospel to them?

(4) Furthermore: if the Supreme Pontiff avails himself of another formal directive (where it reads: '*And, furthermore, we command you by virtue of your holy obedience*', etc.)[434] to require the Catholic monarchs to send upstanding, God-fearing, learned, skilled, expert men to the Indies to instruct its peaceful inhabitants, how can the doctor take the bull of the aforementioned concession to mean that Pope Alexander was in favour of bloodthirsty conquest and that he prioritized robbery, violence, death, extermination of populations, and the perdition of peoples over the preaching of the gentle law of the gospel? Why did the doctor not include and point to the words or clauses of the bull in which the pope signalled his approval of this abominable course of action worthy of Mohammed himself? It is plain to see that the doctor is woefully mistaken.

(5) And so that his error and misapprehension are put beyond all doubt, let consideration and attention be paid to what the doctor then goes on to add at that point, levelling a major allegation at the Catholic monarchs that cannot be borne by His Majesty and yet affecting to be thereby rendering him a service, namely his claim that, in accordance with the intention of the Supreme Pontiff (back in the days when Pope Alexander himself was still alive), the monarchs supposedly stipulated by their royal authority that the Indians were to be subjugated through warfare from the outset.

That these are terrible charges wrongly levelled at the sovereigns by the esteemed doctor can be demonstrated, for one thing, from the very first instruction which, in their capacity as Catholics, they ordered to be issued to the First Admiral [Christopher Columbus] when they first sent him back to the Indies after his initial discovery of it, dispatching him together with farmers and unwarlike people charged not with conquest, robbery, and murder but with settling, building upon, and cultivating the land and drawing those tame, humble, mild, peaceful people to them by means of meekness, sweet edifying conversation, and acts of charity and love.

In this connection the sovereigns state the following in the first article of the aforementioned first instruction: 'First and foremost, since our Lord God saw fit

---

[434] Alexander VI, *Inter caetera*, in Davenport, *European Treaties Bearing on the History of the United States*, 74.

CONTAINED HEREIN IS A DEBATE OR DISPUTATION   331

in his holy mercy to unveil these islands and mainland to the king and queen, our lords, by dint of the efforts of the aforementioned sir Christopher Columbus, their admiral, viceroy, and governor of the lands in question, who has reported to Their Highnesses that he perceived the people he found living there to be very well suited to conversion to our holy Catholic faith, for they have neither law nor creed, this has proved most gratifying to Their Highnesses and continues to gratify them, for it is meet in all things to seek above all else to be of service to God, Our Lord, and to the glory of our holy Catholic faith. Therefore, wishing our holy Catholic faith to be expanded and amplified, Their Highnesses order and enjoin the afore-mentioned admiral, viceroy, and governor to seek and strive by every means and manner possible to induce the inhabitants of the islands and mainland in question to convert to our holy Catholic faith. And to assist with this, Their Highnesses are dispatching the faithful friar Father Buyl, along with a number of other men of the cloth, whom the admiral is to take with him. These clergymen, with the aid and efforts of the Indians who were brought here, who will have a good under-standing and command of much of our language by now, should endeavour to give them a thorough grounding in the particulars of our holy faith, striving to in-struct them in it as best they can. And so that this may be most effectively accom-plished, the aforementioned admiral must, once the fleet has safely arrived there, endeavour and see to it that all those who have made the crossing in the fleet, and all those who do so hereafter, treat the Indians most kindly and lovingly and re-frain from aggrieving them in any way, seeking to establish dialogue and good relations between the two sides and behaving as impeccably as possible. And the admiral should likewise give freely from the gifts of the wares sent along by Their Highnesses for the purposes of bartering and treat the Indians with the utmost respect. And in the event of one or more individuals treating them poorly in any way whatsoever, the aforementioned admiral, in his capacity as Their Highnesses' viceroy and governor, should punish them most severely by the powers vested in him for this purpose by Their Highnesses',[435] etc. This is the official edict of Their Highnesses.

It is for your lordships, mercies, and worships now to judge if there is any basis to Dr Sepúlveda's position and whether or not there are grounds to credit what he claims and what response he might deserve and indeed what manner of recom-pense from the monarchs. If the monarchs, having been informed that the inhab-itants of the Indies were peaceful and well suited to conversion, instructed the first admiral at the first opportunity from the outset in the very first directive they is-sued to seek to convert them to the faith by any means and manner possible and, so

---

[435] For the text of this directive, see Las Casas, *Historia de las Indias* 1.81. See also Martín Fernández de Navarrete, *Colección de los viajes y descubrimientos que hicieron por mar los españoles desde fines del siglo XV,* vol. 2 (Madrid: Imprensa Real, 1825), 66–72.

as to inspire them all the more to do so, to offer and give freely of the wares which they had provided from their own royal estate for the purposes of bargaining or to exchange for gold, silver, and pearls, and to show the utmost respect to the Indians, and for all Spaniards to treat them very well and lovingly, and for anyone who failed to do so to be roundly punished, perhaps the doctor might enlighten us as to how he came to accuse the Catholic monarchs of ordering the despicable acts of tyranny, which he advocates contrary to God and his law, to be committed in the name of 'conquest' from the outset?

Ordering utmost care to be taken over all possible ways and means of converting them, treating them with utmost respect and generously offering them gifts from the bartering reserves and merchandise in order to inspire them to embrace the faith, commanding the Spanish to deal lovingly with them and for anyone who failed to do so to be roundly punished: are these statements from which one can conclude that the monarchs ordered wars to be waged and the Indians conquered prior to preaching the gospel to them?

Or was the idea rather that, having first inspired in them an eminently understandable hatred for the faith and for those responsible for bringing it to them, they were then to convert them and bring them into the fold of the Christian religion? The sovereigns clearly grasped the pope's intention considerably better than the doctor, who would seek to construe it by distorting it, as he is wont to do with all his sources.

(6) His mistakenness and misapprehension in this regard can, secondly, be proven by means of a clause in the will of Her most serene Majesty, the esteemed Queen Isabel herself, who, unassailed by throes of high emotion, seemed to grasp the pope's intention a mite better than our doctor here. It reads as follows: 'Furthermore, with regard to the time when the islands and mainland of the Ocean Sea, both discovered and yet to be discovered, were granted to us by the Holy Apostolic See, our chief objective—for which we sought permission from Pope Alexander, honoured be his memory, who had granted us the concession—was to seek to prevail upon and draw in the inhabitants of those lands and convert them to our holy Catholic faith and to send prelates, men in holy orders, clergy, and other learned, God-fearing individuals to the aforementioned islands and mainland to instruct the denizens and inhabitants there in the Catholic faith, teach and instil good habits in them, and to do all the above with due dedication, as outlined at greater length in the terms of the aforementioned concession; and so I most dearly beseech the king, my lord, and entreat and command the princess, my daughter, and her husband, the prince, to maintain and uphold this, and for this to remain their principal objective, in which they should exercise all due diligence. And they should neither allow nor suffer the Indian inhabitants and residents of the aforementioned Indies and mainland, both conquered and remaining to be conquered, to sustain any injury either to their persons or to their property, but rather order them to be properly and justly treated. And if any such injury is sustained, they should make amends and see to it in a manner wholly compliant with that which

CONTAINED HEREIN IS A DEBATE OR DISPUTATION   333

has been enjoined and entrusted to us by the terms of the concession.'[436] *These are her words.*

Does it not strike your lordships, mercies, and worships that, in so ardently prescribing peace, meekness, and love as the means by which to entice and attract the Indians to the faith, the most serene queen is rather more in accord with the intention of the pope and of God than our doctor with his violence, tyranny, and warmongering? The doctor, then, is most sorely mistaken and seeks to mislead this venerable council, and, in his toadyism, promises to prove the downfall of future monarchs as well as of the current one, His Majesty.

The archives of the Royal Council of the Indies teem with numerous other edicts, directives, royal missives, dispensations, and laws issued at different points in time both by the previous monarchs and by His Majesty with a view to preventing and averting warfare and stipulating that the Indians are not to be subjected to war or to any other form of abuse but rather to be cured, by peaceful, loving means, of the terror with which they are struck—humble and meek as they are—at the sight of the Spanish who cut such fearsome figures and in the wake of the cruelty endured at their hands and instead to be rendered amenable to lending their ears to the preaching of the gospel undisturbed, freely, and of their own volition and so become devoted to our Christian faith. For there is nothing preventing them from embracing our holy faith but the fear which the Spaniards inspire in them and the abuses they commit.

This in turn sheds light on another facet of Dr Sepúlveda's mistakenness and blindness, for he should know that the harm, robberies, killings, and depredation wrought upon more than three thousand leagues of the most blissful, densely populated land were all without exception performed and perpetrated by the tyrants in the Indies without authorization from the sovereigns of Castile; on the contrary, everything has been carried out against their express orders and injunctions, as demonstrated in my *Thirty Propositions*[437]—which I penned by way of elucidation and defence of my *Confesionario*—and in various other writings of mine. And so the reverend doctor's skulduggery is left without a truthful leg to stand on, rendered null and void. In our *Apología* we have responded at great length to instances where the very learned doctor's quibbles about the clauses of Pope Alexander's bull could seem to have some specious plausibility.[438]

(7) It also follows from all this that what the doctor then goes on to say—namely that in granting bulls, dispensations, and indulgences for the establishment of

---

[436] Codicil XI to the Testament of Isabel. See *Testamentaria de Isabel la Católica*, edited by Antonio de la Torre y del Cerro (Barcelona: Vda. Fidel Rodríguez Ferrán, 1974), 97.

[437] The *Thirty Propositions* ('*Aquí se contienen treinta proposiciones muy jurídicas*') formed another of the tracts that Las Casas published with Sebastián Trujillo in Seville in 1552. See Las Casas, *Obras completas*, vol. 10, 197–214, for an edition with introduction by Ramón Hernández, O.P.

[438] Las Casas offers this refutation of Sepúlveda's interpretation of *Inter caetera* in ch. 59–62 of his Latin *Apologia*. In the manuscripts (*CR*, 221v; *MR*, 261r), he again offers page numbers: 'desde la hoja 163 haste el fin de a primera parte'.

334 SEPÚLVEDA ON THE SPANISH INVASION OF THE AMERICAS

churches, cathedrals, bishoprics, monasteries, and other spiritual things the pope was signalling his approval of this war and tyrannical conquest—is not only wicked but absurd and utterly preposterous. The extent to which Christ makes deals with the Devil, and the bearing which this has on the case at hand, is for your lordships, mercies, and worships to judge.

(8) What the doctor then proceeds to reason is a fine effort to force a correspondence or equivalence, treating two different phases, or rather two different sets of circumstances, as if they were one and the same: namely, subjugating the Indians before they have received the faith as opposed to doing so only once they have already embraced it of their own free will.[439] In this connection he contends and posits that it is equally if not more pressing to remove the obstacles put in the path of preaching the faith (which the Indians themselves have never put there nor will ever do of their own accord, which is tantamount to saying unless they are provoked with good reason or grounds to do so) as it is to get them to keep the faith once they have received it, which is the second phase or circumstance. In so doing, he is conflating our right or mandate to preach the faith to those who have never received it with the need to preserve it in those who already have. His mistakenness in all this is plain to see, for he fails to allow for the vast gulf separating the two aforementioned phases or situations and the consequent discrepancy in terms

[439] From this point until the end of §10, the published text of this part of Las Casas's Twelfth Reply as offered in his 1552 printing—and, consequently, as followed in the main body text of the translation we offer here—represented a marked departure from the version to be found in the manuscripts. (See further the preface to this translation.) In a significant revision of that earlier view, the 1552 version moved to affirm the right of Amerindian communities to reject Spanish rule even after conversion: the 'ideological and tactical revolution' (246) which occupied Vidal Abril-Castelló in his seminal 1984 article, 'La bipolarización Sepúlveda–Las Casas'. The original—far shorter—version of the same passage as contained in the manuscripts (CR, 222r; MR, 261v–262r) is as follows:

'What the doctor then takes this to mean is a fine effort to force a correspondence or equivalence, treating two distinct phases as if they were one and the same: on the one hand, the subjugation of the Indians prior to receiving the faith; on the other, proceeding to do so after they have embraced it of their own free will (in view of the fact that they are recent converts to it or to stop them from corrupting it with sins and heresies or indeed to prevent them from abandoning it altogether by means of apostasy). The most reverend doctor has thus failed properly to appreciate the true nature of the distinction here in terms of the rights and particularity peculiar to each of the two phases, for, when it comes to the former,* we only have the right to preach to them and to avail ourselves of all the means proportionate to and necessary for this end, among which warmongering, robbing, capturing, and killing do not number. When it comes to the latter of the two phases, by contrast, our right to action is far stronger and more robust, for it is incumbent upon us to reinforce, uphold, preserve, and defend the holy faith and Christian religion, and it was with an eye to this phase and out of the most befitting necessity and by means of this most just of titles that the Apostolic See had the foresight to grant and donate supreme jurisdiction and dominion over that world (albeit without depriving the local rulers of their own) to a Catholic monarch. And so, once he has properly grasped the nature of the difference at issue here, he will find that my position on this does not represent the undoing of all that I said on that subject before, as the illustrious doctor alleges. And seeing as I have already expanded on the matter at length by composing a dedicated treatise devoted to demonstrating the true, juridical title which the sovereigns of Castile and León have to supreme, universal dominion over that world of the Indies, I shall say no more about it here.'

* Here we read 'en cuanto' ('with regard to') for what the Caracas edition (mis)prints as 'no cuanto'.

of right or mandate which obliges us to adopt two different courses of action in pursuing these two distinct ends.

(9) For, when it comes to the former, we only have the right or mandate to preach to them and to avail ourselves of all possible means required for and appropriate to preaching and to gospel law, none of which includes or extends to warfare, robbery, enslavement, or murder. But when it comes to preserving, upholding, and defending the faith of those who have already received it, we have stronger, more robust rights and a more binding mandate. The rationale behind this is that, once people have received the faith, it perforce falls to us to maintain, uphold, preserve, and defend it, particularly where recent converts are concerned, seeing as they are much more easily corrupted by means of sin, heresy, or apostasy. But we are not under so stringent an obligation when it comes to preaching the faith, since we do not know whether the infidels in question will wish to receive it, for that is at their discretion and we cannot force them to embrace it.

As regards the second case, right, or mandate (which, as already mentioned, is of a more stringent and binding nature), the grounds were far more noble and necessary than in the first, on account of which the Apostolic See was justly and prudently able to proceed to concede and grant universal supreme dominion and sovereignty over that world—yet at the same time without depriving the native rulers or inhabitants of their own sovereignty—to a Catholic monarch who would uphold and preserve them in the faith; but the grounds for action are not so compelling in the case of the right to preaching alone. The main and most inarguable reason for the difference between the two—not counting the one already mentioned above—is because the church cannot force people to embrace the faith but it *can* compel them to keep it.

(10) Furthermore: prior to being baptized the infidels are not subjects of the church, as discussed above and as demonstrated at great length in my *Apología*.[440] And so, to speak *without restrictions*, they cannot have a ruler deposed or indeed imposed by the church (nor would they owe obedience to any such imposed ruler), other than very much *on an ad hoc basis* and under highly specific circumstances, for instance if the ruler in question were single-handedly responsible for obstructing the preaching of the faith. After they have converted, however, the church has far more solid grounds on which to exercise its temporal jurisdiction over them by virtue of their subject status, as will be self-evident. And this principle is universal: namely, if the church were to perceive something to be necessary or highly expedient for the preservation and defence of the faith and Christian religion and as a safeguard against future eventualities and dangers, it is entirely right and just for it to enact the measure in question by the power vested in it by its apostolic duty and role as Christ's representative on Earth. This is even more the case in

---

[440] Las Casas's lengthy refutation of the claim that infidels are subject to the authority of the church takes up chs. 6–29 of his Latin *Apologia*.

instances where so little detriment and so many benefits accrue to the native rulers themselves and all the peoples there, as is the case with imposing a supreme, universal monarch upon that whole world, or at least to serve as an imperial overlord to command, direct, and govern them and establish universal Christian laws to enable them to be bettered in their temporal state and maintained and upheld in their spiritual condition as Christians.

And in the event that, upon conversion to Christianity, they should not wish to accept and obey that supreme ruler (though this will hardly be the case among the Indians, especially among the larger, settled communities, as they are by nature so thoroughly meek, humble, and obedient), it still does not follow from this that war can be waged on them on that account (as Dr Sepúlveda claims) so long as they continue to keep the faith and observe due justice. This is because attention should always be paid to the ultimate aim and purpose on account of which this supreme, universal ruler is to be imposed upon them, namely for the Indians' own good and benefit, and always with an eye to ensuring that this supreme rulership does not turn into a source of harm, ruin, and destruction for them. For in that eventuality there is no room for doubt: in fact, from that moment onwards one could even go so far as to call that rulership unjust, tyrannical, and wicked insofar as it served the ruler's own good and interests over the well-being and common benefit of the subjects. And this is abhorred and abhorrent from the standpoint both of natural reason and of all human and divine laws. And it is in this sense, and this sense only, that I mean the nineteenth of my *Thirty Propositions*[441]—the one in which I say that kings, lords, and other groups of that nature in the Indies[442] are obliged to recognize the sovereigns of Castile as their rulers, monarchs, and emperors—to be taken and understood.

The reason for this is that, even though refusal to accept them is a sin, nonetheless—in the interests of averting the strife and irreparable damages which warfare would invariably entail and if the stated goal, namely the spiritual and temporal well-being of all those peoples, is to be honoured—they cannot be forced to submit by means of warfare without this too constituting the gravest mortal sin. Therefore the sensible, Christian avenue or way of implementing, establishing, and perpetuating the aforementioned reign and sovereign rule over those realms, which our illustrious monarchs are duty-bound and obliged to exercise and implement, is the peaceful, kindly, loving, Christian way, namely winning over the spirits and minds of those people—rulers and subjects alike—by means of love and good, well-intentioned actions. Without hesitation or delay, the Indians will come with

---

[441] For this nineteenth of the *Thirty Propositions*, see vol. 10 of the *Obras completas*, 209.

[442] For the phrasing here ('los reyes e señores e comunidades de aquel orden de las Indias'), cf. the beginning of the nineteenth of Las Casas's *Thirty Propositions*: 'Todos los reyes y señores naturales, ciudades, comunidades y pueblos de aquellas Indias son obligados a reconocer a los reyes de Castilla por universales y soberanos señores y emperadores ...'.

CONTAINED HEREIN IS A DEBATE OR DISPUTATION   337

open arms, dancing and frolicking, to offer themselves in submission and to serve them swiftly and gladly, as my own extensive experience and findings reliably show.

I have addressed myself to this subject at length in many writings of mine composed in Latin and Castilian alike, in particular the one I penned with a view to establishing the true legal title of the monarchs of Castile and León to universal, sovereign dominion over the Indies.[443] And seeing as the doctor fails to recognize all the aforementioned points which obtain *de facto* and *de jure*, nor the distinction between the circumstances or phases outlined above, nor the purpose of this rule, the manner in which it is to be brought about, the form of governance and all the other things which are and ought to be ordered concerning or directly involving the Indians in order to achieve that end (that end being, as already mentioned, exclusively their own good, benefit, profit, and development), the doctor consequently believes that my own statement on this subject represents (in his opinion), by the very terms of my own concession, the undoing of everything I had previously said.[444] And the reason for this is none other than that he is distorting it (as is his wont), pretending that something is amiss anytime he has the opportunity to do so in order to justify or burnish his own purpose and most duplicitous zeal.

(11)[445] And, in light of the above, what the doctor then in turn proceeds to posit—namely that the Indians deserve to be stripped of their liberty and sovereignty on account of their idolatrous sins—proves to be specious. Presumably he means to imply that they are not the lords of their own domains, realms, or estates, or that they can be stripped thereof *ipso jure*: if this is indeed what he means to suggest, then it must be that the reverend doctor does not realize that this assumption leads, by virtue of sound logical reasoning, to a major heresy now long since condemned, namely claiming or contending that temporal civil sovereignty has its basis in faith or grace. This heretical mistake originated in the primitive church, as noted by St Jerome in his commentary on the Epistle to Titus.[446] It was subsequently reprised by several others, since also condemned for it, and in our own times it has again been expanded upon by Luther.[447] By contrast, the Holy Scripture still refers on multiple occasions to heathen, idolatrous, sinful kings— such as Sennacherib, Nebuchadnezzar, Achan, and many others—as kings. And

---

[443] As his wording here indicates, this is a reference to another of the treatises Las Casas published in Seville around this time, the *Tratado comprobatorio del imperio soberano y principado universal que los reyes de Castilla y León tienen sobre Las Indas*. (While the title page gives the date 1552, the colophon dates the publication to 8 January 1553.) This work was an expansion of the 17th and 18th of the *Thirty Propositions*. See Las Casas, *Obras completas*, vol. 10, 391–543, where it is edited and introduced by Ramón Hernández, O.P.

[444] Cf. Sepúlveda's Twelfth Objection, end of §3 (where, as here also, 'por su/mi confesión' is somewhat obscure).

[445] At this point, the 1552 edition returns to following the manuscripts, with some variants noted below.

[446] Jerome, *Commentarius in Epistolam ad Titum*, 3:1–2.

[447] In referring to the revival of this 'heretical' notion, Las Casas has in mind figures such as Hostiensis; he discusses the matter further in chs. 15 and 41 of his *Apologia*.

Solomon was not stripped of his kingdom, despite being an abominable idolater. Or if what he means is that *they ought to be dispossessed by a righteous man* on the basis of the sins they commit in their heathenism alone, this is false, as I demonstrate in my *Apología* by means of incontrovertible authorities and arguments, for the right to do so is reserved for God alone, who has the power to annihilate them if he so chooses, though, in his boundless mercy, he refrains from doing so.

(12) As for his assertion that, upon closer inspection, everything I say and write is done with a view to proving that all conquests undertaken to date (even those in which all directives have been observed) have been unjust and tyrannical and to corroborating what I wrote in my *Confesionario*, etc: to the first point I would answer that his mercy is quite right, and I hereby reiterate once again that all the conquests and wars which have been waged against the Indians from the discovery of the Indies until our own times were and always have been singularly unjust, tyrannical, and infernal and have been more terrible and a greater source of monstrosities and offences against God than those perpetrated by the Turks and the Moors against Christendom. And all those who have participated in these wars have been most dastardly plunderers, assaulters, and cruel tyrants responsible for committing the most heinous, reprehensible sins in the course of waging them, and everything of which they came into possession and acquired in the process was and is by violent means, through robbery, assault, and tyranny.

On account of this—not to mention all the other damages that defy enumeration or calculation and which cannot be made good, for they are irremediable—all concerned are obliged to make restitution in full. And there will be no hope of salvation for them unless they offer them reparation insofar as their means allow and make it up to them and weep every single day of their wretched lives for their sins the extent, magnitude, and quantity of which have never before been seen or heard. And I would even go so far as to say that the illustrious doctor and any other person minded to justify or make excuses for them is guilty of the most terrible mortal sin and likewise obliged to make restitution on grounds of being the impediment to the salvation of those tyrants who might otherwise repent, as well as to the compensation which those victims of tyranny still alive or else their heirs might stand to receive were it not for him and his new-fangled, pernicious doctrine preventing them from doing so.

(13) In response to the second point I would say, as I asserted in my *Thirty Propositions* and as can be seen from what I explained just above, that neither the late sovereigns of Castile nor our current majesty ever issued a directive, edict, or dispensation stipulating that war or conquest should be waged for its own sake—and least of all against the Indians—nor did they ever countenance any such thing.[448] And if any directive or dispensation of theirs did seem to admit

---

[448] This is in *Proposición 25* of his *Treinta Proposiciones*, in vol. 10 of the *Obras completas*, 210–11.

CONTAINED HEREIN IS A DEBATE OR DISPUTATION   339

the possibility of waging war, it will have been *accidentally*, which is to say, on the basis of a thousand deceptions and false pretences both *de jure* and *de facto* represented to the monarchs by the tyrants themselves and likewise by those who had a stake in their tyrannical undertakings and so sought to defend or exonerate them. And when such a case was brought to the monarchs' attention, they would swiftly revoke and rectify it with further stipulations to the opposite effect.[449] And thus every single act of robbery, violence, destruction, death, and perdition in both body and soul of the more than twenty million people whom the aforementioned tyrants have hacked to pieces, and the three thousand leagues of land which they have destroyed and denuded of inhabitants,[450] has been carried out and perpetrated not with the authority of the monarchs of Castile but, on the contrary, flying in the face of their many explicit prohibitions issued to the opposite effect, as demonstrated above.

And I would go further still: on the off-chance that the sovereigns were, as the doctor claims, to have issued directives and dispensations to that effect (which is not to be entertained even so much as hypothetically as something that could actually befall the consciences and royal minds of the Catholic monarchs or of His Majesty or of his most scrupulous Christian Council of the Indies in existence today) authorizing the aforementioned wars and conquests to be waged and to continue to be waged today as a primary objective and end in itself purely on the pretext falsely devised by Dr Sepúlveda in the absence of any further just new motive, even in this hypothetical scenario still none of the wars waged to date would be justified nor would those waged today be justifiable or excusable and the late Catholic monarchs would be guilty of mortal sin and His Majesty today would not escape the same fate either, and they would all have been and remain obliged to offer the aforementioned restitution and recompense *in solidum*.

And this is the nature of the so-called service which the most reverend doctor renders to His Majesty and to the esteemed members of His Majesty's Royal Council of the Indies, blinding them by toadying up to them so despicably.[451] If only God would see fit to make the doctor recognize the terrible offences which his impudence causes him by means of the harm it does to the propagation of his holy faith, the temporal losses sustained by the monarchs of Castile and the damages inflicted upon all of Spain and upon the well-being and temporal and spiritual salvation of all those countless souls.

The reason for this is that, no matter how many offences his words commit, they will come to naught, for even if a piece of Scripture or doctrine of the saints expressly endorsing his misguided, accursed opinion were to exist (a tall order

---

[449] In *Proposición 26* of his *Treinta Proposiciones*, vol. 10 of the *Obras completas*, 211.

[450] This phrase, present both in the manuscripts (*CR*, 222v; *MR*, 263v) and the 1552 edition, was inadvertently omitted by Galmés (p. 188).

[451] The end of this sentence ('tan pestilentemente lisonjeándolos y cegándolos') is yet another late sharpening of the knife against Sepúlveda; it was not present in the manuscripts (*CR*, 223r; *MR*, 263v).

340   SEPÚLVEDA ON THE SPANISH INVASION OF THE AMERICAS

indeed seeing as they all go against him), it would still have proved necessary to silence and suppress it on account of the enormous scandal to which it gives rise and the incentive it provides or offers to those who are forever thirsting after and primed for robbery, murder, and capturing those defenceless people. This can be seen, quite aside from all the many other scriptural and saintly proof-texts available, from a memorable statement made by St Basil in his *Morals*, to wit: '*For even when a matter or a particular word is sanctioned by Scripture, it should nonetheless be disregarded whenever, as a result of a similar situation, other people become either more ready to sin or more sluggish for proper actions*.'[452] That is what he says.

(14) Likewise, in another of his pronouncements, St Basil goes on: 'It is a clear indication that someone does not have the charity of Christ towards his neighbour if he does something which harms his property or mind and hinders his faith, even though it might be something allowed, under special circumstances, by Scripture.'[453] These are Basil's words. All the more reason for the doctor to stop pursuing and persisting in something so despised and condemned by the whole Holy Scripture, the doctrine of all the saints, natural reason as a whole, the virtuous good sense of right-thinking men and the entirety of Christian practice of the universal church.

But since the doctor refuses to recognize the lethal, far-reaching damages and evils which he occasions and the need that thus arose for my *Confesionario* (endorsed by four supremely learned Masters of Theology—*maestros* Galindo, Miranda, Cano, and Mancio[454]—along with two fellow theologians of the rank just below,[455] Fr. Pedro de Sotomayor and Fr. Francisco de San Pablo,[456] directors of the College of St Gregory in Valladolid and now both Masters of Theology themselves) to serve as an impediment and antidote to those evils, he sees fit to refer to it as defamatory libel; and yet his own book is one which the Universities of Salamanca and Alcalá have condemned as pernicious, unsound doctrine and for which the Royal Councils have withheld printing permission on the four or five occasions on which he sought it and in which he traduces the faith of Jesus Christ and the whole Christian religion by toiling and striving for Christianity to be spread by means of war, robbery, and slaughters, as under the law of Mohammed, giving free rein to the whole of Spain to be of the view, without further thought, care, or consideration, that robbing, killing, and casting vast masses down into hell is not a sin.

---

[452] Basil the Great, *Moralia, Regula* 33, c. 2 (*PG* 31, 751–52).

[453] Basil the Great, *Moralia, Regula* 5, c. 2 (*PG* 31, 709–10).

[454] All Dominican friars and teachers: Domingo de Galindo (Salamanca), Bartolomé Carranza de Miranda (San Gregorio, Valladolid), Melchor Cano (Salamanca), and Mancio de Corpus Christi (Alcalá).

[455] The Spanish term here rendered as 'theologians of the rank just below' is '*presentado*', denoting a rank between *maestro* and *licenciado* (see Covarrubias, *Tesoro, s.v. presente*, 7).

[456] Two more Dominican friars, both at San Gregorio in Valladolid (the chapel of which was where the junta met).

CONTAINED HEREIN IS A DEBATE OR DISPUTATION   341

(15) Furthermore, in seeking to persuade them to endorse and authorize it, he is responsible for defaming His Majesty and all future monarchs in the eyes of their fellow kings and neighbouring kingdoms by causing them to be thought of and known as unjust, deficient Christians.

(16) Furthermore, Dr Sepúlveda thinks that this book of his (or rather pamphlet of libel, as I would call it)—which ruins the reputation and regard in which the Amerindians are held in the eyes of all the world and slanders these boundless populations as beasts lacking in human reason that can be hunted or ridden like brutish animals, impervious to teachings and brimming with unspeakable sins, thereby casting false aspersions on countless individuals—has nothing of the slanderous about it, despite the enormity of all the aforementioned awful characteristics, and that it should remain available and be studied as the Holy Scripture is.

I need hardly reiterate the immense audacity he exhibited in sending it to be printed at Rome (where, in the absence of most of the facts of the matter),[457] they do not grasp the venomous poison with which it brims, disguised as it is with false rhetorical flourishes), thereby flouting the condemnation of it issued by the two Universities and the rejection on the part of the aforementioned Royal Councils. If the pope's deputy and the master of the Holy Palace and all the others whom he prides himself on having had approve the book were to have been made aware of just how much falsehood and depravity it contained, the extent to which it harms and hinders the gospel, and the degree to which it is incongruent with the innate goodness, reasonableness, docility, simplicity, and natural meekness of the inhabitants of the Indies, it is scarcely to be believed that such illustrious personages as these gentlemen all no doubt are can have been so indifferent and inimical towards both themselves and the truth as to permit such heinous, lethal doctrine to be made available in published form.

(17) He also alleges something else no less absurd, unworthy of being heard by prudent, pious ears—on the contrary, it should be repudiated and despised for being so full of worldliness and secularity, *like a man who doesn't know the things of God*[458]—namely that, if the practice of conquering and subjugating the Indians through warfare were discontinued, soldiers would (he claims) cease to go at their own expense as has been the case up until now, nor could they go at the king's expense, for everything in his possession is required for his kingdoms over here; and even if the latter *did* wish to bear the cost of sending people,[459] he would be unable to find anyone willing to go for thirty ducats a month, 'when nowadays they spare themselves neither danger nor expense in the interests of the gains they expect to

---

[457] Here the parenthesis is closed prematurely and ungrammatically in the 1552 printing.

[458] The phrase set off by dashes translates yet another intensification of animus against Sepúlveda added to the 1552 printing.

[459] The 1552 edition has 'y aunque quisiese a su costa gente'. The manuscripts supply the necessary infinitive 'embiar' ('enviar') before 'gente' (*CR*, 223v; *MR*, 265v).

reap from the gold and silver mines with the aid of the Indians they have subjugated', etc. These are all Dr Sepúlveda's own words.

Could it be any more glaringly obvious just how little the doctor understands of the facts of this matter into which he has been so desperate to plunge so blindly? Or the degree to which he shows himself to be flying in the face of human and divine law and natural reason in his myopic way? He even goes so far as to assert that nobody embarks on the crossing to the Indies with a view to anything other than subjugating and capturing the people there and exploiting them most tyrannically. He says as much in Spanish, albeit cryptically phrased. This, then, is the course of action the doctor seeks to promote, as will be apparent.

That the doctor has no understanding of this whole business is evident from the fact that he ought, before weighing in on it all, to have known that one of the most decisive factors that have led to the robbery, depopulation, and destruction of this vast mass of realms in the Indies and the reason for the failure to respect and obey their natural king [i.e. the king of Spain] has been the fact that tyrants volunteering to raise fleets and undertake conquests at their own expense have been allowed to do so. The funds for this did not, however, come from their estates over here but rather from the riches acquired through robbery, plundering, and depredation committed in certain regions with a view to rising to the rank of frontier commanders, proceeding to plunder and destroy other regions. His Majesty and his Royal Council of the Indies have ample experience of this by now, having seen it occur time and again, and they condemn it as wicked and evil.

(18) Furthermore: the doctor's mistakenness in this regard is greater still, for there are so many people keen to travel to the Indies for free that one of the main burdens borne by the *Casa de Contratación* in Seville since at least the year 1500, and in more recent years here at the Council as well, has been to endure the endless badgering of those seeking permission to make the crossing to the Indies.[460]

(19) Furthermore: the most reverend doctor ought to know that the lands across that whole hemisphere are so fertile and productive that they will make a rich man out of anyone minded to take advantage of them without needing to resort to exploiting the Indians. And hardworking, industrious people—not good-for-nothing sorts like soldiers—are already over there and their presence suffices to ensure that the Indians who still have not been pacified after the tyrannies they have endured at Spanish hands do not come to visit harm upon the clergymen: so much so, in fact, that they never approach at all, or only very rarely, unless they are stirred up and sought out.

---

[460] The Casa de la Contratación ('House of Trade'), established in Seville in 1503, had broad powers regarding overseas trade and travel. In addition to settling legal disputes, drafting maps, training pilots, and probating wills of Spaniards who died overseas, it also, as Las Casas notes, regulated emigration to the Indies.

CONTAINED HEREIN IS A DEBATE OR DISPUTATION   343

(20) Furthermore: the doctor should also be aware that the Indians have never done any harm to Christians unless first provoked by the litany of abuses and incomparable ravages suffered at their hands. Even in such instances, they never visited any harm upon friars once they had been apprised of the difference between clergymen and laypeople and between the nature of the different objectives motivating the former and latter respectively. For they are by their nature overwhelmingly peaceful, harmless, and utterly meek.

(21) Furthermore: the most reverend doctor ought to realize that it is preposterous and out of all reasonable proportion to seek to subdue the Indians and pave the way for preaching to them by sending tyrants with cruel, unruly armed forces to people who are already profoundly distressed, aggrieved, and dumbfounded by the evils and ravages they have been made to suffer; rather, it should be first essayed from the lands or provinces with Spanish settlements nearest at hand, broached by clergy with the aid of peaceful Indians with whom there is already shared acquaintance, familiarity, and trust, which is precisely what my fellow Dominican friars and I did when, approaching from Guatemala, we availed ourselves of this strategy and engaged in peaceful negotiations, thereby succeeding in converting those provinces which the king consequently ordered to be named the provinces of Verapaz, which is to say 'true peace', where these days, to the glory of God, the most marvellous Christianity now reigns—a fact of which the most reverend doctor is unaware.

The provinces in question were, quite rightly and with good reason, in a state of frenzy and turmoil on account of the unlawful wars which the Spanish had waged on them, and the first person to enter and bring peace to the area was the Blessed Friar Luis,[461] who would go on to be killed in Florida, a fact which the reverend Dr Sepúlveda attempts to exploit to his advantage. But little good does it do him: for even if they had massacred all the Dominican friars and St Paul himself along with them, this would still not increase the legitimacy of action against the Indians a single jot more than there was before—which, as it was, was already zero. This is because the port at which Friar Luis was put ashore by those wicked sailors, who were supposed to be steering clear of that area as per their instructions,[462] had been the site of the arrival and disembarkation of four fleets of cruel tyrants guilty of perpetrating unconscionable cruelties against the Indians of those parts, affronting, aggrieving, and corrupting the land for a thousand leagues all around.

As a result they [the Indians] have all the right in the world to be at war with the Spanish—and indeed with all Christians—from now until Judgment Day.[463]

---

[461] i.e. Fr. Luis de Cáncer, a Spanish Dominican friar who had known Las Casas through involvement in the Dominican missionary project in Verapaz and was later killed in Tampa Bay, Florida, in 1549.

[462] For this relative clause in the 1552 edition, the manuscripts (CR, 224v; MR, 267r) offered a gratuitous slur on sailors generally: 'que no suelen hazer sino por maravilla cosa buena' ('who are not in the habit of performing any good action, absent a miracle').

[463] This sentence was added to the 1552 edition; it is not in the manuscripts (CR, 224v; MR, 267r). But see the next note.

And having never seen or come into contact with clergy before, they had no way of knowing that these were missionaries, especially as the latter kept company with the very men who have brought them such evil and ruin, to whom they were, moreover, similar in mien, clothing, beard, and language and whom they would see eating, drinking, and making merry all together like firm friends. And if the sailors had taken the aforementioned Father Fr. Luis to the place which had been indicated and decided upon by those of us over here and on which the blessed man had set his sights, he would not have been killed, for it appears that the other friars, his companions, asked the pilot to put them ashore elsewhere up or down the coast, in other provinces, but he, on the pretext of wanting first to go to the island of Cuba to replenish their water supplies, deposited them there in New Spain, and there was nothing they could do about it.

And even if they had been killed in another province (although this was not in fact the case) this would not detract from my argument, for the infidels have killed other men better than they and better than any alive in the world today on the same account. And it is a most noble holy tenet for some of God's servants to lay down their lives for the gospel. For they are of more use in the conversion of the heathens after their precious death than they could ever be toiling and sweating away down here. And so we place our hope in God that Fr. Luis Cáncer, who was such a devoted servant of his, can and will continue to be of service in the conversion and salvation of those who put him to death. For since they know not what they do, and as far as they are concerned they are killing not friars or servants of God but mortal enemies at whose hands they have suffered so much,[464] our Lord God shall look upon them with merciful eyes in keeping with the merits of the very blessed Fr. Luis.

And this is the right road, divine and royal, and the pattern[465] instituted and endorsed by God himself for preaching the gospel and converting souls—not the diametrically opposed one advocated by the doctor, which every divine, rational, and human law condemns. And if the divinely sanctioned method does not lead to the conversion of the faithful of the Indies this year, God—who died for them—will convert them next year, or ten years from now. And the reverend doctor should not presume to be more zealous than God himself, nor in a greater hurry to convert souls than he; rather, the esteemed doctor should restrict himself to modelling himself after God, for God is the teacher and he the student. And therefore his mercy should be content with advocating the mode and procedure established by

---

[464] Here the manuscripts offered: 'against whom they are waging a very just and rational war—against the Spaniards, I mean—and not just today but from here on to the Day of Judgment; meanwhile, no recompense is being made to them for the harms and disasters and slaughters they have received' (CR, 224v; MR, 267v).

[465] This translation follows the reading of the manuscripts (CR, 224v; MR, 267v): 'Y esta es la recta vía divina y real y forma de predicar ... '. The 1552 printing offers: 'Y ésta es la recta vía divina e forma real de predicar ...'.

CONTAINED HEREIN IS A DEBATE OR DISPUTATION   345

Christ, our God, and not devise another course of action contrived by the Devil himself and espoused by his emulator and apostle Mohammed by means of such great villainy and human bloodshed. And so the most reverend Dr Sepúlveda proves to have his facts of the matter quite wrong.

(22) That he is similarly mistaken on the legal front will be no less evident. Quite aside from all the many other grounds for this which emerge perfectly plainly from his dialogue and summaries in both Spanish and Latin too, this can be demonstrated by, firstly, the way the doctor locates and predicates the entire legal title of the sovereigns of Castile and León to supreme dominion over that world of the Indies on military prowess and on our superiority in terms of physical might. This approach has always characterized, and continues to characterize, places over which tyrants ruled and rule.

His second mistake on the legal front is that he appears to imply that he does not believe that the sovereigns of Castile and León are, by virtue of their commitment to the objective of preaching the gospel and the conversion and good governance of the realms and republics of those Indies, obliged to bear all the costs associated with achieving that objective. To suggest otherwise is to do the monarchs an offence and disservice, setting them on the road to ruin by misleading them and toadying up to them to such dangerous effect. And, in the absence of other suitable sources of funding, they should be prepared to meet these expenses from their income and tributes from their own realms here, for the simple reason that, as mentioned, they have undertaken to discharge this duty. This obligation only increases in light of the vast quantity of treasure which they have obtained and continue to receive from those Indies every single day.

The third sign that the doctor is mistaken on the legal front is that he can be seen to invert and disrupt the natural order of things, making the means into an end and a main object out of the ancillary. The aim of this whole matter, which in God's eyes constitutes the main objective, is the preaching of the faith—the expansion of his church—not throughout the wastelands and fields of those lands but rather among its native inhabitants, converting them and saving their souls. Of secondary and lesser importance is the matter of the temporal benefits which the Spaniards who go there stand to be able to reap, to which in his writings the reverend doctor frequently makes reference as if it were the principal objective. Anyone unaware of this is mightily ignorant indeed, while anyone who denies it is no more a Christian than Mohammed himself, but Christian in name only.[466] He says that it is the prospect of the gold and silver mines and the labour of the Indians which lures them there; and I can well and truly believe it, for they have certainly always shown it to be the case by their actions, for what motivates them is not the honour of God nor

---

[466] A final intensified jab at Sepúlveda added to the 1552 edition; not found in the manuscripts (CR, 225r; MR, 268v).

zeal for his faith nor to succour and aid in the salvation of their fellow humans and nor is it to serve their king, as they forever boastfully claim to be the case, but rather exclusively their greed and ambition to tyrannize and rule over those Indians, whom they wish to be shared out, as if they were beasts,[467] in an eternal, tyrannical, hellish *repartimiento*, which, bluntly put, is nothing more than dispossessing and ousting or expelling the sovereigns of Castile from that whole world and arrogating it to themselves, usurping their supreme royal jurisdiction from them and setting themselves up as tyrants in finest fashion. And this is what the most reverend Dr Sepúlveda advocates with all his might, although at heart I do not believe that he can be truly cognizant of the damage he is doing.

(23) In order to counteract this blindness and plague and put a halt to all these other countless evils, prevent the sovereigns of Castile from losing the Indies, and avert the utter perdition of so many people and the extermination of such boundless lands, as will otherwise shortly come to pass, and so as to stay the scourges which God rains down upon the whole of Spain on this account and which he will soon unleash more cruelly still, as my fifty years' experience of this business indicates, I have spent the past thirty-five years toiling at this court.

And it is towards this end that I direct my every effort, and not at all with the aim of undermining the Castilian sovereigns' title to supreme dominion there, nor with a view to shutting the doors of its justification, as the doctor makes me out to be doing: rather, I close the doors to false titles, which are all hollow and of no substance, and open them up to the most lawful, robust, compelling, impeccable Catholic ones, as befits true Christians. And, in my quest to identify, establish, substantiate, and proclaim them, I should like to think that I have devoted a touch more time and effort than the doctor has. What you will find written in this connection in my dedicated treatise on the matter will clearly attest to this.[468] It was with a view to achieving this aim or aims, expelling such heedless or unheeded sins from those lands over there and these realms here, that I composed my *Confesionario*.

Thanks be to God.

To the praise and glory of our Lord Jesus Christ and of the most holy virgin St Mary, his mother. The present work was published in the most noble and loyal city of Seville at the press of Sebastián Trujillo (book printer), opposite the Church of Our Lady of Grace. Completed on the tenth day of the month of September in the year 1552.

---

[467] 'Como si fuesen bestias': added to the printed edition; not in the manuscripts (CR, 224r; MR, 269r).

[468] Most likely a reference to the *Tratado comprobatorio*, an expansion of the 17th and 18th of the *Treinta proposiciones*. See above, n. 443.

Appendix: Final points of argument presented to the congregation by Sepúlveda (12 April 1551)

Most distinguished, illustrious and reverend Sirs:[469]

I, Dr Sepúlveda, declare that it has come to my attention that some of the esteemed members of this congregation would prefer the principal question under discussion here—namely the subjugation of the barbarians—to be sooner pronounced upon by theologians, to whom consideration of such matters more properly falls, than to jurists; and since this could be readily accomplished by having theologians debate the matter in their presence, I beseech your lordships and mercies to grant me an audience with the congregation so that I might offer three or four arguments in support of my position and invite the responses of those most reverend fathers who hold the opposite view;[470] and if their answer is deemed satisfactory in the estimation of the other members of the congregation, then I shall acknowledge that I have been mistaken and tear up everything I have committed to paper on the subject. But if their responses prove so flimsy and fallacious as to be inadmissible, then it will be clear to all who is the defender of the truth which nowhere emerges more plainly than by means of a debate and disputation in which both sides address each particular in turn.

To counter those who discredit or contest the bull and decree of Pope Alexander VI in which he grants authority to the Catholic monarchs of Spain and their successors and exhorts them to carry out the conquest of the Indies by first subjugating those barbarians (over whom he grants them rule and jurisdiction) and thereafter bringing about their conversion to the Christian religion, the following arguments may be adduced:

First of all, the chapter '*Per venerabilem*' from *Qui filii sint legitimi*,[471] which stipulates on the basis of the divine law enshrined in Deuteronomy 17 that when the adjudication of the Apostolic See is sought on points of uncertainty, as indeed occurred right at the start of this conquest of the Indies, the verdict of the pope

---

[469] The phrase, 'Final points of argument presented to the congregation by Sepúlveda (12 April 1551)', which we are adopting as our title, appears at the very end (p. 31) of Bonet de Sotillo's transcription of the manuscript of this text (pp. 29–31 of Giménez Fernández's ed.). The fuller reference as given on p. 31 in fact specifies that it was on 'Wednesday 12 April' ('Miércoles XII de abril 1551'); however, as the footnote there points out (31n1), 12 April 1551 was not a Wednesday. A possible correction to Wednesday 22 April is proposed; conversely, Abril-Castelló, 'La bipolarización Sepúlveda–Las Casas (p. 241), accepts 12 April as certain. Though certainly the junta reconvened at Valladolid in April 1551 for the second session, the precise shape of events there is murky on this and other points: see further next note.

[470] Sepúlveda reports in his *Proposiciones temerarias* (§5) that he was granted this audience. It is unclear how this written statement of his position may or may not correspond to any speech indeed delivered. He reports that he discussed with the theologians his interpretation of the bulls of Alexander VI and Paul III. Abril-Castelló's 'La bipolarización Sepúlveda–Las Casas' remains the best account of the second session.

[471] X 4.17.13. Sepúlveda cites this same chapter of Book 4 of Gregory IX's *Decretals* repeatedly in his *Apologia*: see III.2.xiii; III.4.xxxii; III.4.xxxv; V.20. The rendering of Title 17, '*Qui filii sint legitimi*', has gone somewhat awry in Bonet de Sotillo's transcription (p. 29).

348 SEPÚLVEDA ON THE SPANISH INVASION OF THE AMERICAS

must be heeded and anyone who defies it must die on that account[472] (which is to say, be excommunicated).

Likewise, the chapter '*Nulli*', 25, q. 1, in which it says: *No one is permitted, on pain of losing his position, to violate either holy conciliar resolutions or decrees of the Holy See.*[473]

Likewise, St Thomas, in the final article of his *Quodlibetal Questions* 9,[474] says that the pope may prove mistaken in individual matters and circumstances because such cases are conducted on an uncertain basis, namely by means of the testimonies of men as to the matters at issue; but when it comes to matters pertaining to the universal state of the church, as where the faith or customs are concerned,[475] while it would be possible for him to be mistaken in a personal capacity inasfar as he is human, he cannot go wrong by the grace of the Holy Spirit who governs the church, in which connection see John 14: *the spirit will come and teach you all truth*;[476] and, so, to claim that the pope *may err in such matters is*, in the opinion of certain doctors,[477] *heretical, as noted by Sylvester* [Silvestro Mazzolini da Prierio *alias* Prierias] *in his entry on 'canonization'.*[478] But even if a scenario were somehow to arise in which the pope appeared mistaken in the context of a decree pertaining to *the faith or customs*, this would have to be determined by another

---

[472] Deuteronomy 17:8–12.

[473] Gratian, *Decretum,* C. 25, q. 1, c. 4—a decretal of Pope Hilarius. (Note that this is not the same chapter as the one also entitled '*Nulli*' to which Sepúlveda refers in the *Proposiciones temerarias* in §15, which is a decretal of Gregory IV: *Decretum,* D. 19, c. 5.) Bonet de Sotillo (p. 29) mistranscribes '... *sine status sui periculo* ...' as '... *sive* ...' (and '*constitutiones*' as '*constituitiones*'), which creates a sense problem.

[474] Thomas Aquinas, *Quaestiones Quodlibetales* 9, or, in short form, *Quodlibet* 9—which Bonet de Sotillo misconstrues and transcribes as 'Onolibeto 9°' (p. 29). The passage in which Aquinas discusses this is indeed to be found at *Quodlibet* 9, q. 8, co. (or, by an earlier referencing system, *Quodlibet* 9, q. 7, art. 16); but in fact Sepúlveda is here drawing not on Aquinas directly but rather on the paraphrase of this portion of *Quodlibet* 9 offered in the *Summa Sylvestrina* of Silvestro Mazzolini da Prierio *alias* Prierias, in his entry on canonization (*Canonizatio sanctorum*): see further n. 478 below.

[475] Here there is a problem with the manuscript reading: Bonet de Sotillo (who gives 'que tocan al estado a la fee o a las costumbres', p. 30) catches it partially, noting (p. 30, n. 1) that the words 'universal de la iglesia' (from the fuller original phrase 'al estado universal de la iglesia') have been crossed out; but in fact 'al estado' should also be deleted, for the whole phrase at this point is an accidental reduplication of 'al universal estado de la iglesia' from the previous clause: the replication has then been caught and duly suppressed, but with 'al estado' inadvertently surviving. That this is the case is clear from the fact that this all represents Sepúlveda's rendering of the original phrasing of his source, the *Summa Sylvestrina*: '*Quaedam vero pertinent* **ad statum universalem** *totius ecclesiae,* **vel quantum ad fidem,** *ut determinationes circa ea quae sunt fidei,* **vel quantum ad mores,** ...' (fol. LVIv, col. 1).

[476] This is a version of John 14:26, drawing also on John 14:17 (and John 14 more broadly).

[477] What Sepúlveda has here generalized to 'certain doctors' in the plural was originally a more specific reference—in the singular—to the view of John of Naples: the passage of the *Summa Sylvestrina* which Sepúlveda is following here has '*quod in talibus possit errare* **secundum D**[octorem] **Io**[annem] *est hereticum*' (fol. LVIv, col. 1).

[478] As noted in n. 474 above, Sepúlveda's discussion of Aquinas in *Quodlibet* 9 here is in fact taken from the paraphrase of it included under the entry on 'canonization' in the *Summa Sylvestrina*—as Sepúlveda hereby reveals. For Prierias's formulation, see e.g. *Summa Sylvestrina* (Strasbourg, 1518), fol. LVIv, col. 1, referring to St Thomas '*in 9. quo*[d]*l*[ibeto] *q*[uaestione] *ultima*', which Sepúlveda more or less reproduces for his reference here (and which, in turn, also explains Bonet de Sotillo's garbling of it: see n. 474 above, and next note).

CONTAINED HEREIN IS A DEBATE OR DISPUTATION   349

pope or council: it is not for private citizens, learned though they might be, to pronounce on the matter of whether the pope is mistaken or not (it behoves them, rather, simply to obey), for to do so would constitute an almighty outrage and colossal aberration for the Christian republic and governance of the church, especially in a case such as this concerning Alexander's decree as to how to go about converting a new world to the faith. For, as St Thomas says there in the aforementioned *Quodlibetal Questions* 9, art. ~~15~~ 16: '*More faith ought to be deposited in the personage of the pope alone when he is deciding or adjudicating a matter in the church than in a whole crowd of wise men.*'[479]

Moreover, in his book on [*Precept and*] *Dispensation*,[480] St Bernard [of Clairvaux] remarks the following: '*From whom, finally, would divine counsel be sought other than from the man to whom the dispensation of the mysteries of God has been entrusted? Therefore, we ought to listen to the man whom we consider to occupy the place of God as though he were in fact God—at least in those matters which are not manifestly contrary to God.*' This is most especially so in the case of an edict such as the one under discussion here [i.e. Alexander VI's bull], which is consistent in every regard with what it says in the *Decretal* of Pope St Gregory in the chapter '*Si non*', 23, q. 4,[481] and with the opinions and proclamations of St Augustine and St Ambrose and with the ancient practice of the church under the faithful emperors and is praised by all Christians and accords with Holy Scripture in the Old and New Testaments alike, as established and corroborated by the subsequent graces and dispensations issued by every pope to succeed Alexander, and is predicated on the authority and mandate to preach the gospel throughout all the world which Christ bestowed upon his vicar [i.e. the pope]; and for the latter to be accomplished most expediently it is necessary to subjugate the heathens to the Christians, to which end he was rightly granted the authority by the combined authority of the relevant chapters[482]—'*Praeterea*', '*Prudentiam*', and '*Suspicionis*'—from the title *De officio delegati*,[483] in which it is stipulated that anyone charged with accomplishing a primary task is by that same token rightfully entrusted with all that which is ancillary

---

[479] Bonet de Sotillo (p. 30) gives this as 'Quod, liberto [*sic*] 9': again, it is a reference to Aquinas, *Quodlibet* 9—or, rather, to Pierias's paraphrase of *Quodlibet* 9 in his *Summa Sylvestrina*. It would appear that the passage meant is, again, actually based on *Quodlibet* 9, q. 7, art. 16 (or, by modern referencing convention, *Quodlibet* 9, q. 8, co: see n. 6 above), not art. 15. Pierias in fact offers no article reference here at all, and efforts to recall it seem to have led to this misquoting (or perhaps, simply, subsequent transcription error).

[480] Bernard of Clairvaux, *De praecepto et dispensatione* (*PL* 182); the passage in question is at *PL* 182, col. 873. Note that Bonet de Sotillo (p. 30) gives '*De Dispensas*', and the Latin offered for the citation there is also somewhat garbled. We have translated directly from *PL* 182.

[481] Gratian, *Decretum*, C. 23, q. 4, c. 49, i.e. Gregory I's letter to Gennadius, 1.75 Norberg (1.73 *PL*).

[482] In her transcription of this sentence, Bonet de Sotillo (p. 30) gives '*juntamente*' ('all together') for what we would take to be '*justamente*' ('justly', 'rightly')—though our translation serves to capture both. The same is true in the next clause, where we likewise take Bonet de Sotillo's '*juntamente*' to be '*justamente*', though we have again translated so as to allow for both.

[483] X.1.29.5, 21, 39. Bonet de Sotillo (pp. 30–31) gives '*de off icii*, | *delege*' (and '*prudentia*' for '*prudentiam*'); see further n. 243 on the name of this Gregorian title.

to and necessary for that end. St Thomas's asseveration in the *Secunda secundae*, q. 40, [art.] 2, ad [3] likewise attests to this: '*The power*', he says, '*to which a given end pertains should dictate the means to that end*.'[484] He vouchsafes this view in the course of discussion of a case bearing a great similarity to the matter under consideration here, which is to say the just wars which the popes exhort the Catholic monarchs to undertake for the sake of the divine and spiritual end that is the conversion of the heathens.

---

[484] Aquinas, *ST* II-II, q. 40, art. 2, ad 3. Bonet de Sotillo (p. 31) prints: '22 [i.e. *II-II*] *questión*, 40 *artículo*, 2 *adizión* [sic]'.

Outrageous, Scandalous, Heretical Notions

(*Proposiciones temerarias, escandalosas, y de mala doctrina*)

Preface to the translations of *Proposiciones temerarias* and *Declaración*

The *Proposiciones temerarias* is the last, the latest, and—together with the *Declaración* which accompanies it—no doubt also one of the least well known of the Sepúlvedan works included in this volume. Its full title is (some variant of): *Proposiciones temerarias y de mala doctrina que notó el doctor Sepúlveda en el libro de la conquista de Indias que hizo imprimir el Obsipo de Chiapa* (*Outrageous, heretical notions which Dr Sepúlveda identified in the book on the conquest of the Indies published by the bishop of Chiapa*).[1] In it, Sepúlveda returns to the fray and reprises the subject of the Valladolid disputations for a final time, despite by now wishing—or at least affecting to wish—to put the whole business behind him once and for all.[2] More specifically, he sets out in the *Proposiciones temerarias* (*PT*) to take issue with the *Aquí se contiene una disputa o controversia* account of the matter which Las Casas had had printed in Seville in September 1552—without Sepúlveda's knowledge, much less permission.[3] In so doing, Las Casas had, moreover, clearly sought to afford himself the last word on the subject by rounding off the volume with his set of torrential responses to Sepúlveda's (answers to Las Casas's earlier) *Objections*. The *PT* can thus in turn be understood as Sepúlveda's own reply to Las Casas's *Replies*.[4]

---

[1] In truth, 'title' is something of a misnomer: the 'titles' offered here and in what follows are, rather, descriptions of the content of the *PT* as given in the various manuscripts in which it is contained. This is the descriptive 'title' as offered in MS. *S* (there, as a short-form variant on fol. 10*v*) and in MS. *C*—the pair of *PT* manuscripts that has recently come back to light. It is not quite the version of the title with which the reader may already be familiar from Fabié(–Denisova) and those who follow him: that form is owed to MS. *M*, on which more below. For present purposes, the orthography of these and other early modern elements cited in what follows has been mostly modernized.

[2] Note Sepúlveda's opening gambit at *PT*, §1.

[3] See Letter 113, from Sepúlveda to Antoine Perrenot de Granvelle, in Sepúlveda, *Obras completas*, vol. 9.2: *Epistolario*, §3, p. 325. Sepúlveda repeatedly insists, both here in his letter to Granvelle and in the *PT* itself (§1), on the fact that Las Casas had printed that work 'without licence', which he presents as a grave misdemeanour and in which regard he has been enthusiastically followed by modern scholars; though see further our discussion of this matter in the Introduction, p. 53.

[4] Sepúlveda himself refers to his *PT* as a '*respuesta*' ('response') to Las Casas's *Aquí se contiene* (Letter 113, §2, p. 324: '*Ahora con esta carta envío a V. S.* [*una*] **respuesta** *que ... escribí contra los errores y desatinos de*[*l*] [*de*] *fray Bartolomé de las Casas*' ('Enclosed herein I am sending you [i.e. Granvelle]

Sepúlveda on the Spanish Invasion of the Americas. Luke Glanville, David Lupher and Maya Feile Tomes, Oxford University Press. © Luke Glanville, David Lupher, and Maya Feile Tomes 2023.
DOI: 10.1093/oso/9780198863823.003.0006

352   SEPÚLVEDA ON THE SPANISH INVASION OF THE AMERICAS

On this occasion, however, Sepúlveda's mode of 'response' to Las Casas's unilateral publishing action took a rather radical form of its own: for this time his rejoinder was not directed at Las Casas himself but instead prepared with a view to denouncing him and his volume before the Inquisition.[5] The *PT*, then, is—as its title suggests—devoted to outlining the doctrinally dubious elements which Sepúlveda wished to bring to the Inquisition's attention and see the *Aquí se contiene* formally indicted as heresy. Indeed, the *PT* seemingly formed part of some kind of dossier or at least pair of denunciation documents, for it is accompanied by a shorter companion piece—known to us from just one manuscript—entitled *Declaración de cómo las excusas de los errores del libro del Obispo de Chiapa no son bastantes ni relievan nada* (*Itemization of the grounds on which the pretexts offered for the falsehoods in the bishop of Chiapa's book neither suffice nor serve to exonerate anything*). In it, Sepúlveda enumerates five key doctrinal problems dissected at greater length in the *PT*. As such, the *Declaración* can be seen as a form of précis of, or heuristic index to, the more expansive exposition of the *PT*, to which it stands in relation. Indeed, from the reader's perspective, the *Declaración*—which was clearly written after the *PT*—presupposes familiarity with the content of the *PT* throughout. We present them here too as a pair.

Like the texts contained in *Aquí se contiene* itself, the *PT* and *Declaración* are both in Castilian Spanish (albeit with a substantial admixture of Latin in both, especially in the *PT*). Indeed, Sepúlveda—who by preference wrote in Latin—expressly comments on the question of language use in the *PT*, presenting the choice of Castilian as a conscious decision taken to enable those who had been keeping abreast of the preceding vernacular instalments of this most textual of 'debates' to read this latest contribution to it, too.[6] His anticipation of a reasonably large readership thereby

---

a reply which I composed to refute the falsehoods and mistakes contained in Fray Bartolomé de las Casas's book' [i.e. *Aquí se contiene*]). See also Ángel Losada, *Juan Ginés de Sepúlveda: a través de su 'Epistolario' y nuevos documentos* (1949; reprinted in Madrid: Consejo Superior de Investigaciones Científicas, 1973), 208–09, referring to the *PT* as Sepúlveda's '*contrarréplica*' ('counterreply') to *Aquí se contiene*. Eduardo Briancesco et al., *Caminando hacia el tercer milenio: evangelización y liberación* (Buenos Aires: Ediciones Paulinas, 1986), 87, adopt the same formulation; and see further Henry Raup Wagner, with the collaboration of Helen Rand Parish, *The Life and Writings of Bartolomé de las Casas* (Albuquerque: University of New Mexico Press, 1967), 189. It is curious that Losada should refer in his remarks there (208) to the *PT* as a '*célebre opúsculo*' ('renowned little work'), given that its reception history has been patchy to say the least—and to which Losada himself inadvertently contributed: see further below.

[5] Wagner and Parish, *The Life and Writings*, 189, speculating over whether or not Sepúlveda was the notorious individual who reported Las Casas to the Inquisition: 'Was Sepúlveda the accuser? I infer so from a curious writing … : [the *PT*]'; indeed, in view of style and mode, the *PT* (and its companion piece, the *Declaración*) 'may well be an actual denunciation'. See also Vidal Abril-Castelló, 'La bipolarización Sepúlveda-Las Casas y sus consecuencias: La revolución de la duodécima replica', in *La ética en la conquista de América*, edited by Demetrio Ramos et al., 229–88 (Madrid: Consejo Superior de Investigaciones Científicas, 1984), 249.

[6] Letter 113, §6, p. 326: 'The treatise [i.e. the *PT*] is presented in the vernacular tongue, like the printed book itself [i.e. *Aquí se contiene*], so that anyone who understands the former may also be in a position to understand the latter' (our translation). He has earlier (in §3, p. 324) referred explicitly to the

also emerges: after all, he could easily have plumped for Latin if his target audience had been the rarefied circle of the Inquisition alone. The *PT* and *Declaración* differ crucially from the texts of the *Aquí se contiene* volume, however, in that they never saw publication in their own day and remained in manuscript until long after Sepúlveda's death. Any contemporaries who engaged with the *PT* both during and after Sepúlveda's lifetime—there is evidence of both—will have accessed the text by means of handwritten copies, not through printed editions. In fact, the *PT*—and *Declaración*—remained in manuscript for over three centuries after their production sometime in the mid-1550s.

Three manuscripts of the *PT* are known to exist today, one of which also contains the *Declaración*. Of these, two date from the sixteenth century itself and will have been produced during Sepúlveda's own lifetime; and one of these, prepared very shortly after the time of the *PT*'s apparent composition, may even have been known to Sepúlveda himself. Neither, however, is a Sepúlvedan autograph. Sepúlveda refers to the production of at least two copies of the work: in a letter of 15 March 1554 to Antoine Perrenot de Granvelle (bishop of Arras), he discusses the composition of the *PT* and mentions that he has already had one copy sent to the Inquisition (where it may, in turn, have been copied out any number of times for the adjudicators' purposes) prior to dispatching this letter; and in that same missive he enclosed a second copy of the *PT* for Granvelle's own perusal in the hope that he would recommend to Charles V that Inquisitorial proceedings be mandated. He also instructed Granvelle to make further copies still if he wished to show it around more widely.[7] Moreover, if Sepúlveda wrote the *PT* in Castilian Spanish in order to allow interested parties to engage with it, then it was clearly produced in anticipation of an active readership, which is to say in the expectation of many copies. The three *PT* manuscript witnesses known to us today will therefore by no means represent the sum total of copies of the *PT* that once existed[8]—though whether any of the others has survived remains to be seen. Further copies of the *Declaración*, for which we currently have just one manuscript witness, may also yet await discovery. Libraries in Spain, France, Italy, and beyond would reward scouring to that effect.

The fact that the *PT* is a work known from the early modern period only through manuscripts as opposed to printed editions means not only that it circulated differently at the time but inevitably that it has had a markedly different reception history from the texts of *Aquí se contiene*, or indeed from many of Sepúlveda's

---

fact that *Aquí se contiene* is itself in Spanish ('en romance'). Of course, the substantial recourse to Latin throughout the *PT* ultimately still presupposes a certain type of reader.

[7] Letter 113, §§3, 4, and 6, pp. 325–26. He claims (§6)—albeit most likely by way of *captatio benevolentiae*—that the copy enclosed for Granvelle was produced under dissatisfactory circumstances and leaves much to be desired in terms of presentation.

[8] Not least because *M*, which is not a copy of either *S* or *C* and corresponds to a different part of the stemma, must itself have been copied from a copy which is now lost or unknown.

354 SEPÚLVEDA ON THE SPANISH INVASION OF THE AMERICAS

other works. It was not included, for instance, in the definitive sixteen-volume Pozoblanco series of editions of Sepúlveda's *Obras completas* produced around the turn of the twenty-first century.[9] At times it has even been disputed that it was by Sepúlveda at all.[10] Moreover, the *PT* features an initially curious alternation of grammatical person—at times the author of the text writes as Sepúlveda in the first person, at others in the third—which might also appear to suggest that the work is not really Sepúlvedan, or at least not wholly. However, the evidence that can now be marshalled—notably the much overlooked letter to Granvelle in which Sepúlveda discusses the *PT*'s composition, along with the comparative evidence now available from our trio of recently reunited manuscripts (to say nothing of the text's highly characteristic Sepúlvedan style, complete with favoured idioms)—serves to indicate that it certainly was.[11]

The likely date for the *PT*'s composition has also thus become much more secure. Where previously exponents of the view that this opuscule was not Sepúlveda's own also held that it was likely composed after his death (in 1573),[12] it now appears clear that it was composed—by Sepúlveda himself—between late 1552 and early 1554, most likely in the latter portion of 1553. The *terminus post quem* is certainly 10 September 1552, which is when Las Casas's *Aquí se contiene*—the work which the

---

[9] It was, however, certainly known to the Pozoblanco editors, for reference to it is included in volume IX.2 of 2007 (edited by Ignacio J. García Pinilla and Julián Solana Pujalte) in the form of Sepúlveda's own letter about it to Granvelle, pp. 324–27 (Letter 113); and note the editors' remarks in the footnotes there: p. 325n570, and p. 326n573. However, neither the matter nor the omission is further discussed.

[10] In 1981, Anthony Pagden asserted that the *PT* 'has some claim to derive from a writing or writings by Sepúlveda although it was evidently composed after his death'. See Anthony Pagden, 'The "School of Salamanca" and the "Affair of the Indies"', *History of Universities* 1 (1981): 71–112, at 107–108n157. This view may perhaps have been influenced by the fact that Antonio María Fabié's edition (*Vida y escritos de don Fray Bartolomé de las Casas, Obispo de Chiapa*, vol. 2 (Madrid: Miguel Ginesta, 1879), 543–69), on which Pagden was certainly relying, runs together adjacent sections of MS. *M*—which indeed contains one piece of writing clearly *not* by Sepúlveda, on which more below—as well as by the fact that Sepúlveda refers to himself in the third person when offering part of his own account in the *PT* (§§2–5, on which also more below). Losada (*Juan Ginés de Sepúlveda*, 198) is somewhat non-committal, observing at one point that the *PT* is merely 'attributed' to Sepúlveda, although in general it is clear that he more than accepts the attribution: see especially pp. 208–10. Fabié is also thoroughly convinced: see next note. Others again have changed their mind, going from agnostic to vigorously in favour: see, to pick an example entirely at random, David A. Lupher, *Romans in a New World: Classical Models in Sixteenth-Century Spanish America* (Ann Arbor: University of Michigan Press, 2003), 355n38 and 112.

[11] Even without reference to Sepúlveda's letter to Granvelle or to manuscripts *S* and *C*, Fabié upon first printing the *PT* in 1879 came out strongly in favour of it as a genuine Sepúlvedan text (vol. 2, 543n1). More recently, Natalia K. Denisova, in her *Proposiciones temerarias* (Madrid: Fundación Universitaria Española, 2019), also accepts the *PT* as certainly Sepúlvedan. As for stylistic evidence, see for instance n. 15 below for a turn of phrase which evidently formed part of Sepúlveda's idiolect; also n. 40 on his repeated use of '*anotaciones*' to refer to the *PT*. Stylistic evidence is not conclusive, of course, for style can be imitated—but it contributes to the overall balance of probabilities.

[12] See, for instance, Pagden, 'The "School of Salamanca"', 107–108n157. See also Antonio Sierra Corella, *La censura de libros y papeles en España y los índices y catálogos españoles de los prohibidos y expurgados* (Madrid: Imp. Góngora / C. F. D. Archiveros, Bibliotecarios y Arqueólogos, 1947), 186. The idea that the *PT* was composed after Sepúlveda's death relies on ignoring the date of 1571 included in MS. *M*—or, alternatively, on the tradition which takes this 1571 to be 1591, on which n. 34 below. The latter in turn relies on ignorance of Sepúlveda's letter to Granvelle in which he personally discusses the *PT*.

OUTRAGEOUS, SCANDALOUS, HERETICAL NOTIONS   355

PT is devoted to filleting and denouncing—was published. The *terminus ante quem* is 15 March 1554,[13] date of the aforementioned letter from Sepúlveda to Granvelle, complete with enclosed copy—by which time he had allegedly also already dispatched a copy to the Inquisition, suggesting that the true date of completion is earlier still. In that same letter Sepúlveda himself offers some comment on the matter of the time frame, all couched in the language of extreme recency. Indeed, in his March 1554 remarks to Granvelle he refers to *Aquí se contiene* as having 'only just' come to his attention (*'no vino a mí noticia hasta agora'*).[14] This might reasonably be taken to imply that he must have composed the *PT* perhaps at some point in early 1554 itself. However, the 'recency' of his encounter with Las Casas's volume must certainly be taken more expansively than that, for by the time he writes to Granvelle in March 1554 he had not only encountered the *Aquí* but scrutinized it, penned his denunciation of it, and even begun making and distributing copies.

Further encouragement towards a more elastic interpretation of his use of the language of 'recency' is the fact that he refers to *Aquí se contiene* itself as having been published during *'los días pasados'*—which might initially seem a surprising thing to say from the vantage point of 1554 (after all, *Aquí se contiene* had been printed back in September 1552) but is actually just an example of an early modern pattern of idiomatic usage in which 'days' can be taken to mean an extended period of time, stretching readily to many months or more.[15] Las Casas's publication of *Aquí se contiene* is thus to be understood as having taken place in recent times only in the broadest sense—and the 'recency' of Sepúlveda's own encounter with it (and, hence, of his composition of the *PT*) may by the same token stretch back across any number of months preceding. This in turn serves to point us more likely back into 1553 than to early 1554. Indeed, one of our surviving *PT* manuscripts (*M*) contains an invaluable intrusion whereby the copyist, battling to construe an enigmatic abbreviated element, solves the problem in a manner which inadvertently provides invaluable temporal information: although what must in fact have been offered at this point will have been some kind of abbreviation (such as '*añs*') for the Latin word '*antecedens*',[16] the copyist has mistaken this as a reference to a

[13] MS. *S* is itself catalogued in the Archivo General de Indias (AGI) as dating from 1554, which, if correct, would further serve to confirm this as the *terminus ante quem*.

[14] Letter 113, §5, p. 325. He also claims only to have come across it at all courtesy of a friendly monk who loaned him a copy (§3, p. 325).

[15] Sepúlveda's reference to the publication of *Aquí se contiene* as having occurred during '*los días pasados*' ('in recent/bygone days') is in his letter to Granvelle (Letter 113) at §2, p. 324. In the *PT* itself (§4) there is an instance of a similar form of usage, where Sepúlveda refers to the Valladolid assembly being reconvened '*después de algunos días, que fueron seis o siete meses*': there, what might at first be taken as a rather snide remark ('in a few days' time, which ended up being six or seven *months*') is in fact simply another instance of this same early modern idiomatic usage whereby '*día*' can be used to denote an extended period of time. On this usage, see on *día²* in Sebastián de Covarrubias Orozco's 1611 *Tesoro de la lengua castellana o española*, edited by Felipe C.R. Maldonado and Manuel Camarero (Madrid: Editorial Castalia, 1995).

[16] MSS. *S* and *C* both have '*añs*', an abbreviation for Latin '*antecedens*' ('antecedent', 'premise'), which gives a sense of what the manuscript from which *M* was copied will likely also have had at this point, and how this could readily have been construed as a reference to a year.

356 SEPÚLVEDA ON THE SPANISH INVASION OF THE AMERICAS

year (Latin *annus*; Castilian *año*), of which they in turn seek to make sense by duly supplying one: '*anno dmî 53*', i.e. '*anno domini 53*'—'in the year of Our Lord [15]53' (*M*, fol. 8*v*). Though this constitutes a dissatisfactory reading in other senses, the (mis)construal of it as a reference to the moment of enunciation at Sepúlveda's time of composition of the *PT* is quite invaluable for our purposes, constituting our only internal piece of dating information contained in any of the manuscripts. The copyist must, moreover, have known a thing or two about the context, for 1553 certainly accords with, and so seems to serve to confirm, what we too would—based on the *termini post* and *ante quem*—propose as the most likely date of the *PT*'s composition. It would seem, then, that the *PT* was composed after 1552, before March 1554, and almost certainly in 1553—perhaps sometime towards the latter part, such that it was still exercising Sepúlveda as a matter of import when he came to write to Granvelle in March the following year.

At the same time, the '*días pasados*' do still bespeak a comparatively swift turn-around overall: whatever the precise date of composition, a total of no more than eighteen months can have elapsed between the publication of *Aquí se contiene* and Sepúlveda's composition of the *PT*. By contrast, the *PT* did not then re-emerge onto scholarly horizons until the last quarter of the nineteenth century, when a transcription of it was published in the second volume of Antonio María Fabié's *Vida y escritos de don Fray Bartolomé de las Casas, Obispo de Chiapa*, vol. 2 (Madrid: Miguel Ginesta, 1879), 543–59, where it is included as '*Apéndice XXV*' ('Appendix 25'). There it is entitled *Proposiciones temerarias, escandalosas y heréticas que notó el Doctor Sepúlveda en el libro de la Conquista de Indias que Fray Bartolomé de las Casas, Obispo que fue de Chiapa, hizo imprimir <u>sin licencia</u> en Sevilla, año de 1552, cuyo título comienza 'Aquí se contiene una disputa o controversia ...*' (*Outrageous, scandalous, heretical notions which Dr Sepúlveda identified in the book on the Conquest of the Indies published by Friar Bartolomé de las Casas, former bishop of Chiapa, <u>without</u> <u>licence</u> in Seville in 1552, of which the title begins: 'Contained herein is a debate or disputation ...*'), in line with the manuscript (*M*) which Fabié consulted, on which more below. (The underscored emphasis on the work's unlicensed state—on which more in the Introduction (p. 53)—is also taken from that manuscript.) Following this, there was certainly some awareness and renewed interest in the *PT* in the twentieth century, notably among eminent Sepúlvedan–Lascasian scholars such as Ángel Losada and Henry Raup Wagner.[17] More recently, the text was reprinted in full in 2019 by Natalia Denisova, who reproduces the text of Fabié's 1879 transcription verbatim.[18]

It is regrettable, then, that the version offered by Fabié in 1879 contains a substantial number of difficulties arising from misreadings and/or mistranscriptions

---

[17] Losada, *Juan Ginés de Sepúlveda*, 653–54, 663; see also 198, 206, esp. 208–210, 331; Wagner and Parish, *Life and Writings*, 189.

[18] Denisova, *Proposiciones temerarias*, 193–213.

of the *PT* text—especially, though by no means exclusively, of its Latinate portions. Moreover, as mentioned, Fabié's transcription is based on consultation of just a single manuscript (*M*), which—now that it can be compared with two more—is notable for its high incidence of unconvincing variant forms (one of which—however revealing for our purposes—we have just noted): the other two manuscripts which have since come to light offer preferable readings on practically all occasions. We have termed this trio of currently known manuscripts *S*, *C*, and *M*—for reasons on which more in the next section. *S*, which has only just come back to light, is the oldest. *C*, which is the youngest, is a copy of *S*. By contrast, *M* (the manuscript known to Fabié) was produced not long after *S* but offers a somewhat divergent text and also differs from the *S~C* tradition in a number of other key regards—most notably the fact that, for all its problems, it is the only manuscript witness for the *Declaración*. We are fortunate to have had the opportunity to consult this trio and generate a systematic collation to inform our own translation.[19] This is the first treatment of the *PT*, then, to take into account three different manuscripts. It is also the first translation of the *PT*—and *Declaración*—into English, or indeed any language.

The manuscripts

Manuscript *S*

This manuscript, which is the oldest, is held in the Archivo General de Indias (AGI) in Seville; call number: PATRONATO, 252, R.16.[20] It was previously held in the Archivo General de Simancas and it is in that context that it first enters the written record, hence *S*—though, felicitiously, this designation does double duty for both the locations at which it is known to have been held. Manuscript *S* is entitled: *Proposiciones temerarias, scandalosas y de mala doctrina que notó el doctor Sepúlveda en el libro de la conquista de Indias que fray Bartolomé de las Casas, obispo que fue de Chiapa, hizo imprimir en Sevilla sin licencia anno* [*sic*] *1552, cuyo título comienza así: Aquí se contiene una disputa o controversia &c.* (*Outrageous, scandalous, heretical notions which Dr Sepúlveda identified in the book on the conquest of the Indies published by Friar Bartolomé de las Casas, former bishop of Chiapa, without licence in Seville in 1552, of which the title begins: 'Contained herein is a debate or disputation, etc ...'*). Later in the manuscript (fol. 10*v*) the title appears again in the abbreviated form which we have adopted as our main designation: *Proposiciones temerarias y de mala doctrina que notó el doctor Sepúlveda en el*

---

[19] For reasons of space this collation is not offered in our volume: however, we signal moments of particular interest or difficulty in the footnotes, and we take this opportunity to express our hope that a proper critical edition of the *PT* text in Spanish and Latin, based on a careful collation of the manuscripts, will someday appear.

[20] It can be consulted online at: http://pares.mcu.es/ParesBusquedas20/catalogo/show/126843

358   SEPÚLVEDA ON THE SPANISH INVASION OF THE AMERICAS

libro de la conquista de Indias que hizo imprimir el Obsipo de Chiapa (*Outrageous, heretical notions which Dr Sepúlveda identified in the book on the conquest of the Indies published by the bishop of Chiapa*).

Manucript *S* was held at the great state repository of Simancas (just outside Valladolid) until 1785, when all papers pertaining to the Americas were transferred by royal decree from locations across Spain to the AGI in Seville. Although it contains no internal evidence for its date of publication, in the AGI catalogue it is listed as dating from 1554—a year, or at least a place in relative chronology, assigned on the basis of evidence drawn from the other papers contained in the wider Lascasian manuscript sheaf (PATRONATO, 252) to which it belongs.[21] If this date is correct, then it means that manuscript *S* will have been produced very shortly after Sepúlveda had penned the original in late 1553(?), and may even have been a copy of which he was aware. It is not itself a Sepúlvedan autograph, for *S* is certainly not in Sepúlveda's hand, which is substantially attested—and entirely different. It is possible, however, that it was copied directly from the (or an) autograph; there is even evidence to suggest that this task was discharged by one of Sepúlveda's celebrated, if anonymous, scribes: the handwriting in *S* bears a decided similarity to that of the sixteenth-century scribe who produced, for instance, one of the foremost contemporary manuscripts—the so-called 'Regio' or 'R' codex—of Sepúlveda's *De rebus gestis Caroli Quinti historia*, now held in the Real Academia de la Historia.[22] There, that scribal hand is used for the main text while interlinear corrections are offered by Sepúlveda himself,[23] which in turn means that if the same scribe was indeed involved in the production of our MS. *S*, Sepúlveda will have known the individual in question and most likely, therefore, also this very copy of the *PT*, to which he may even have given his express seal of approval. Moreover, although it would not pay to be led any further into undue speculation at this point, this possibility is rendered at least *a priori* reasonably probable by the fact that prolific writers such as Sepúlveda tended to work with the same pool of trusty regular scribes time and again. Pending further graphological analysis, suffice it for now to say that MS. *S* is certainly very early and, moreover, that the fact the copyist even had access to it at this stage suggests that it will likely have been produced in or near Sepúlveda's own circle, or else perhaps in the Inquisitorial sphere to which Sepúlveda had submitted a copy by March 1554—or might MS. *S* be, conceivably, that very copy?

Although he had not had access to *S* himself, Fabié—who consulted only *M*—did have second-hand knowledge of its existence: he refers in 1879 to a catalogue entry in an 'old inventory' ('*un inventario viejo*') left behind at Simancas after the

---

[21] This tranche of AGI documents grouped together as 'PATRONATO, 252' can be consulted in its entirety here: http://pares.mcu.es/ParesBusquedas20/catalogo/contiene/126827

[22] On the 'Regio' codex, see José Antonio Bellido Díaz, '*Indefessae labor limae Sepulvedanae* en los libros 19 y 20 de la *De rebus gestis Caroli Quinti historia*', *Exemplaria classica* 12 (2008): 195–248, described at 199, with samples of this 'R' scribal hand reproduced at 200–06. Samples of Sepúlveda's own hand can also conveniently be consulted in some of the interlinear annotations reproduced in this same article.

[23] See Bellido Díaz, '*Indefessae labor limae Sepulvedanae*', 204–06.

OUTRAGEOUS, SCANDALOUS, HERETICAL NOTIONS   359

relocation of all its 'Indies'-related documents to Seville in 1785: in it, a work entitled '*Proposiciones temerarias y de mala doctrina que notó el Doctor Sepúlveda en el libro de la Conquista de Indias, que hizo imprimir el Obispo de Chiapa*' is listed.[24] However, while this serves to attest to his apparent awareness that the manuscript in question had by then been transferred to Seville, it is not clear that he or anyone else ever sought it there, and *S* thus does not appear to have been examined by any scholar of the *PT* prior to now. Colleagues from Simancas helped us to locate it in the AGI in June 2022.

Manuscript *C*

This manuscript is to be found in the Biblioteca General Histórica of the University of Salamanca; call number: MS 2058.[25] It was originally held elsewhere in Salamanca, at the Colegio Mayor de Cuenca, hence *C*. This manuscript is a high-quality copy of *S* and bears the short-form version of the title: '*Proposiciones temerarias y de mala doctrina que notó el Doctor Sepúlveda en el libro de la conquista de Indias que hizo imprimir el Obispo de Chiapa*'. Unlike *S*, however, it is not a stand-alone item but rather occupies part (fols. 145r–157v) of a more substantial manuscript containing several items all said to be copied '*... de las bullas, breves y otros papeles originales que están en los Archivos Reales de la villa de Simancas*' ('*...* from the bulls, briefs, and other original documents held at the Royal Archives in the town of Simancas').[26] That version *C* of the *PT* was transcribed from a copy of the manuscript originally held at Simancas—which has now just resurfaced at the AGI in Seville, as above—is thus advertised squarely on *C*'s title page.

Sure enough, *C* is a close and careful copy of the *S* text with only very minor deviations or transcription errors. Descriptions of *C* suggest that it can be dated to sometime in the seventeenth or possibly eighteenth century,[27] in turn attesting to interest in the matter after Sepúlveda's own lifetime. One wrinkle in this regard is that, while the type of handwriting would appear to point to the earlier date, it could also be an archaizing mode adopted as a form of affected stylization, so could

---

[24] See Fabié, vol. 2, 158–59. Losada was also in some sense aware of *S*, since the manuscript we have now termed *C* alludes in its own frontmatter, which Losada dutifully reproduces on p. 654 of his *Juan Ginés de Sepúlveda*, to having been copied out from a manuscript held at Simancas.

[25] See Óscar Lilao Franca and Carmen Castrillo González (eds), *Catálogo de manuscritos de la Biblioteca Universitaria de Salamanca. Vol. II: Manuscritos 1680–2777* (Salamanca: Ediciones de la Universidad, 2002), 402–03.

[26] The full title of MS 2058 is: '*Patronazgo Real de las Indias, en que estan las concessiones de los Summos Pontifices de las Conquistas, Demarcaciones, Patronazgo y Erecciones de Yglesias con otras cosas tocantes a ellas, que por mandado del rey don Philippe III deste nombre se copio de las bullas, breves y otros papeles originales que estan en los Archivos Reales de la villa de Simancas*'. See Lilao Franca and Castrillo González, *Catálogo de manuscritos*, 403. The first item contained therein is in turn described as an '*Inventario de las bullas, breves y lo demas contenido en este libro ...*': note the similarity of this formulation to that of the aforementioned 'old inventory' mentioned by Fabié, as above.

[27] Lilao Franca and Castrillo González (*Catálogo de manuscritos*, 402) list it as seventeenth-century. Losada (*Juan Ginés de Sepúlveda*, 654), describes the handwriting as eighteenth-century. See also Ángel Sanz Tapia, 'Juan Ginés de Sepúlveda: *Propossiçiones Temerarias, Escandalosas ...*', in *AA. VV., Cisneros y el Siglo de Oro de la Universidad de Alcalá* (Universidad de Alcalá: Centro Internacional de Estudios Históricos 'Cisneros' / Fundación General de la Universidad de Alcalá, 1999), 250.

360 SEPÚLVEDA ON THE SPANISH INVASION OF THE AMERICAS

potentially also be consistent with the later, eighteenth-century dating. We can at least say for sure that the *terminus ante quem* is 1798: the year in which the Colegio Mayor de Cuenca was dissolved as an institution by royal decree, whereupon its valuable manuscript collection—including our *C*—was transferred in 1802 to the Real Biblioteca in Madrid. It was while held at the Real Biblioteca—where it was catalogued as MSS. 271[28]—that it was encountered by Losada and, consequently, it is by this call number that it has been known to all scholars until now.[29] References to this Madrid-listed copy of the *PT* appeared in the first (1949) edition of Losada's *Juan Ginés de Sepúlveda: a través de su 'Epistolario' y nuevos documentos* and are repeated verbatim in the reissued second edition of 1973. However, between the two but unbeknownst to Losada, this copy of the *PT* had in fact—like all erstwhile Cuencan manuscripts—been moved back to Salamanca by governmental decree in 1954 on the occasion of the 800th anniversary of Salamanca University's foundation.[30] The still widely reproduced bibliographical details from Losada 1973 were therefore already outdated at the time of its publication: in truth, this manuscript has been back at Salamanca, where we located it in September 2021 in the University's Biblioteca General Histórica, hiding in plain sight for the past seventy years. This leaves just one *PT* manuscript currently still known to be held in Madrid: Manuscript *M*.

Manuscript *M*

This manuscript is held in the Biblioteca Nacional de España (BNE) in Madrid (hence *M*); its call number is MSS./17508.[31] It appears to date from 1571 and certainly—as corroborated by the style of handwriting—from some time towards the later sixteenth century.[32] It is thus significantly earlier than *C* and second in age only to *S*; however, it is discussed in third and final position here, for it represents a separate branch of the stemma (whereas *C* is a copy of *S*). It is also the manuscript which contains the only hitherto known copy of the *Declaración*. In fact, *M* contains three pieces: not only copies of the *PT* and *Declaración* but

[28] Or, more fully, Pal. VII-E-4, 2-D-2, 271.
[29] Losada 1949/1973, 653–54 and 663: these bibliographical details have been widely followed and reproduced. Its former call number for the Real Biblioteca is sometimes also given as MS. 2813 (Losada 1949/1973, 382; Denisova, 193n1) or 2.813 (Sanz Tapia, 'Juan Ginés de Sepúlveda', 249). It is unclear to what this refers and could, conceivably, simply be an *erratum*: after all, it occurs only once, at Losada 1949/1973, p. 382—not in his main descriptions of the manuscripts at pp. 653–54 and p. 663. Might it simply be the RB call number (271) inadvertently rendered as '281', to which an extraneous '3' somehow then became attached? (In this regard it may be worth noting that the footnotes on p. 382 of Losada 1949/1973 are all in the '30s' (i.e. all begin '3-') and are printed in font indistinguishable from that of any number in the main text.
[30] By Franquist decree of 5 May 1954, all manuscripts originally from Salamanca were ordered to be returned from the RB in Madrid to their city of origin and rehoused at Salamanca University.
[31] It is available to consult online: http://bdh-rd.bne.es/viewer.vm?id=0000134053&page=1
[32] The style of handwriting is dated as follows—Fabié (vol. 1), 298n1: late sixteenth century; Fabié (vol. 2), 543n1: late sixteenth or early seventeenth century; Losada 1949/1973, 382: sixteenth century; Losada 1949/1973, 654: seventeenth century; Denisova, 193n1: late sixteenth century. In the current version of the BNE catalogue, MS 17508 is merely described as dating from 'entre 1501 y 1600?', but, in view of the commentary, it certainly has a date—or a *terminus post quem*—of 1571.

OUTRAGEOUS, SCANDALOUS, HERETICAL NOTIONS 361

also—located between the two—a discursive commentary on the *PT* composed by an anonymous third party. The commentary, which for reasons of space we are regrettably unable to include here, offers a series of approving observations about the *PT* and adduces further pieces of evidence—mainly proof-texts—in favour of Sepúlveda's position.[33] Thus, whereas *S* (in stand-alone form) and *C* (as part of a wider compilation) present their transcriptions of the *PT* unaccompanied by any other document associated with it, MS. *M* is a veritable mini dossier of documents devoted to the *PT*, as follows:

a) Fols. 1*r*–23*v*: Sepúlveda's *PT* itself. This item, which occupies the lion's share of *M*, thus corresponds (manuscript variants—and copying errors—notwithstanding) to the content of *C* and *S*. It is entitled *Proposiciones temerarias, escandalosas y heréticas que notó el Doctor Sepúlveda en el libro de la Conquista de Indias que Fray Bartolomé de las Casas, Obispo que fue de Chiapa, hizo imprimir sin licencia en Sevilla, año de 1552, cuyo título comienza 'Aquí se contiene una disputa o controversia ...'* (Outrageous, scandalous, and heretical notions which Dr Sepúlveda identified in the book on the conquest of the Indies published by Friar Bartolomé de las Casas, bishop of Chiapa, without licence in Seville in 1552, of which the title begins: 'Contained herein is a debate or disputation ...'). It is copied in a distinctive hand.

b) Fols. 24*r*–31*v*: the anonymous third-party commentary on the *PT*. It has no title, but is listed in the BNE catalogue information as '*Observaciones sobre el escrito anterior*' ('Observations on the foregoing document', i.e. the *PT*). This piece is dated 8 October 1571,[34] thus furnishing us with the date, or at least the *terminus post quem*, for the production of the manuscript from this point onwards (if not indeed for the manuscript in its entirety). The piece is said to have been composed at the monastery of San Francisco in Granada. Its anonymous author speaks freely in the first person and identifies himself (fol. 31*v*)—in all but name—as working at the behest of Dr Francisco de Valdecañas y Arellano, *oídor* of Granada. Importantly, the handwriting in this section of the manuscript differs somewhat from that in the other two—though whether that is because a different individual indeed penned the commentary or whether the same individual as copied the Sepúlvedan material was at this point simply writing in a different mode is unclear. Transcription and spontaneous composition famously constitute different

---

[33] Though, as Wagner and Parish (*The Life and Writings*, 189n14) summarize, this commentary ultimately also 'exonerates Casas but says that Sepúlveda's doctrine was more popular'.

[34] Different editors have read this date (on *M*, fol. 31*v*) in different ways. For '8 October', see Fabié (vol. 2), 566 (and, following this, Denisova, 222); also Losada 1949/1973, 663. However, Fabié (vol. 1), 298n1, offers '18 October': this could simply be a typo; though it is true that the numeral in question leaves room for interpretation as both '8' and '18' (or even, conceivably, '28'). More significantly, some have read '1571' here as '1591': see e.g. Sierra Corella, *La censura de libros*, 186; Sanz Tapia, 'Juan Ginés de Sepúlveda', 249. We read '8 [or 18] October 1571' and take MS. *M* to date from within Sepúlveda's lifetime.

362   SEPÚLVEDA ON THE SPANISH INVASION OF THE AMERICAS

writing practices, so the unevenness in hand need not—necessarily—pose a problem for the idea that the whole manuscript could be the work of a single individual. Further graphological analysis would be required to be able to pronounce on this with greater certainty.

c) Fols. 37r–40r (NB. Fols. 32r–36v are uninscribed): the *Declaración* or, to give it its full title again, *Declaración de cómo las excusas de los errores del libro del Obispo de Chiapas no son bastantes ni relievan nada*. This is copied out in the same hand as the *PT* (and so also differs in the same manner and degree from that in which the commentary is written). In the *Declaración*, Sepúlveda itemizes—and swiftly refutes—the salient points of heterodoxy identified in Las Casas's 1552 *Réplicas*. As such, it represents a summary of those lines of argument on which he elaborated at greater length in the *PT*, and, based on internal evidence, it is clear that the *Declaración* was composed after *PT* itself.

Prior to its arrival at the BNE, MS. *M* was held in the private collection of renowned nineteenth-century Sevillian-born scholar and bibliophile Pascual de Gayangos y Arce (1809–1897), who lived in Madrid, London, and beyond. It was still in his possession at the time of Fabié's writing in the 1870s: Fabié thanks him for granting him access to it.[35] Upon Gayangos's death, his collection of books and manuscripts—including the one we are now calling *M*—was acquired by the BNE in 1899.[36] How Gayangos himself first came into possession of the manuscript is currently unknown, as are its previous locations in the seventeenth and eighteenth centuries—although, as the 1571 commentary reveals, the original context of production of the manuscript is apparently *granadino*. This manuscript copy of Andalusian-born Sepúlveda's *PT* thus has its own Andalusian connection and, three centuries later, came to the attention of fellow Andalusian-born Gayangos. It also bears considering whether there was particular contemporary interest in the *PT* at Granada in 1571 because Sepúlveda himself had by then withdrawn to his birthplace at nearby Pozoblanco, where he was to die in 1573. If *M*'s date of 1571 is correct, then the production of this copy of the *PT* will—like *S*—have occurred during Sepúlveda's own lifetime, and not so very far away from him.

* * *

M thus offers several advantages. It is a veritable mini dossier devoted in its entirety to Sepúlveda's 1554 denunciation of Las Casas, featuring not only the *PT* itself but the only currently known copy of its companion piece, the *Declaración*, as

---

[35] See Fabié, vol. 1, 298n1, together with vol. 1, xi–xii; and see further vol. 2, 543n1. Like Gayangos, Fabié was originally from Seville and the two were colleagues in the Academia de la Historia.

[36] See Pedro Roca, *Catálogo de los manuscritos que pertenecieron a D. Pascual de Gayangos existentes hoy en la Biblioteca Nacional* (Madrid: Tipografía de la Revista de Archivos, Bibliotecas y Museos, 1904). For the dating of the transfer of Gayangos's collection to the BNE, see p. 5. For the *PT*, see p. 316, where it is listed as Nº 996.

OUTRAGEOUS, SCANDALOUS, HERETICAL NOTIONS   363

well as a near-contemporary sixteenth-century commentary also unattested else-where. Unlike with *S* or *C*, we also know when and where (at least a part of) this manuscript appears to have been produced. Moreover, whoever produced it (sin-gular or plural) clearly had a vested interest in, and good knowledge of, the subject matter: *M* is, after all, the manuscript which offers the gloss of the year of the *PT*'s composition as 1553, which—though the presence of a temporal gloss at this point in the text betrays a shaky grasp in other regards—at least suggests an informed understanding of the circumstances of the *PT*'s original production. (Alternatively, it is of course possible that the manuscript from which MS. *M* was copied already contained the intrusive—if illuminating—temporal gloss, which is here simply re-produced.) Moreover, the anonymous author of the commentary—who may or may not have been the same person as the scribe—discusses the *PT* authoritatively and appears to have been expressly commissioned by Valdecañas to provide this written statement of opinion, suggesting that he was intimately acquainted with the text—or at least that, in the process of discharging his assigned duty, he will cer-tainly have become so. A high degree of familiarity with the matter is also indicated by the fact that the compiler(s) of *M* evidently had sight of Sepúlvedan material to which access is not necessarily to be taken for granted: not only the *PT*, of which copies were in wider circulation and of which at least three have survived, but also the *Declaración*, which—if indeed it was prepared as part of a denunciation in-tended for the Inquisition itself—will not have been so readily accessible and for which *M* is indeed currently our only witness. This too suggests some degree of privileged or at least particular decree of acquaintance with the matter—and, just possibly, even with Sepúlveda himself?

At the same time, *M* also poses a number of problems. As a document it is by far the most untidy of our three manuscripts, featuring unpolished handwriting(s) and an unsystematic—and decidedly uneconomical—pattern of folio usage. (This in turn, at least, on balance speaks *against* the idea that the whole manuscript might, rather, be a work of later compilation by someone who transcribed the pair of Sepúlvedan texts alongside the anonymous *PT* commentary: this would not pro-vide a good explanation for the blank folios left between items, nor for the change in hand from one to the other and back again.) Unlike the relatively clean-copy *S* and highly elegant *C*, then, *M* was clearly more of a working document. More to the point, the version of the *PT* text offered in *M* diverges markedly from that offered in *S~C*: the *M* text has a large number of variant readings—whether introduced by the *M* scribe or already present in the source from which *M* was copied—to which the readings of *S~C* are in almost all instances preferable. *M* also has a number of reasonably substantial omissions vis-à-vis the text contained in *S~C*. Moreover, as *M* was the only manuscript consulted by Fabié in the nineteenth century, these problems have all been faithfully reproduced (and some new ones introduced)[37]

---

[37] See, for instance, n. 42 of the *PT* below.

364 SEPÚLVEDA ON THE SPANISH INVASION OF THE AMERICAS

in Fabié 1879, and, in turn, in Denisova 2019. Moreover, Fabié and Denisova do not distinguish clearly—or in some cases at all—between *M*'s pair of Sepúlvedan texts (our *a* and *c*) as opposed to the third-party commentary (*b*): Fabié runs together *a* and *b*[38]—even though there is a marked change of subject position from *a*'s Sepúlvedan focalization to *b*'s own first-person stance—and offers an obvious demarcation only of the *Declaración* (our *c*). Denisova simply runs together all three,[39] thereby creating a confusing impression for the reader attempting to make sense of the shifting voices and focalization in evidence across the apparently monolithic text, which is in fact three separate texts.

This translation

In what follows, we offer translations into English of the *PT* as contained in *S~C* (and of which the *M* variant can be consulted at *M*, fols. 1–23*v*) and of the *Declaración*, which is only attested in *M*. In practical terms we have, for the former, worked primarily from *C*, as it is the most readily legible—though with an eye always to any meaningful points of divergence from its source, *S*, at which point we generally follow *S*. We do not follow *M* (to which *S~C* are not related) for the *PT*, though a couple of key points of interest are signalled in the footnotes. Major difficulties with Fabié's transcription of the *PT* from *M* (followed by Denisova) are also noted; however, we have not sought to signal all such points systematically. We have introduced section numbers to divide up the *PT*.

The broader procedure and stylistic approaches adopted correspond to those already discussed for the translation of *Aquí se contiene*, as outlined above at pp. 234-35. Just a couple of features of note bear highlighting here. The first is Sepúlveda's use of Latin in the *PT*, which is extensive—far more so than in the *Objections*. Moreover, his use of Latin here (and, to a lesser degree, in the *Declaración*) is not restricted mostly or even primarily to points of citation: rather, it is the vehicle for several extended meditations of his own in which he uses Latin to develop a particular line of thought in full. These switches might seem the absent-minded slips of one who wrote by preference in Latin but in fact, upon closer inspection, almost invariably prove to serve to impart a philosophical air at key junctures in the argumentation, or when being especially barbed in deriding Las Casas's own use of logical reasoning. As before, these Latin portions have been rendered in italics to give the Anglophone reader a textured sense of the alternation between Castilian-language (in non-italicized formatting) and Latin-language (italicized) passages in the original.

The second feature of note is that, though he opens and concludes in the first person, Sepúlveda on occasion refers to himself in the *PT* in the third person. This has likely contributed to some of the above-mentioned confusion around the

---

[38] See Fabié, vol. 2, 559–60.
[39] Denisova, *Proposiciones temerarias*, 193–213.

authorship of the *PT*—especially when reading Fabié–Denisova's undifferentiated transcriptions of *M* (which, until now, was the only form in which the *PT* was available), which give an odd impression of a patterning from first person (*PT*, §1) to third (§§2–5) and back to first (*PT*, §§6–17), in turn bleeding seamlessly into the remarks of the anonymous commentator, who also speaks in the first person and refers to Sepúlveda in the third. Then, in the *Declaración*, the use of the first person corresponds to the Sepúlvedan subject position again. In reality, however, this to-and-fro in the *PT* should not be taken as evidence to suggest that it was not a Sepúlvedan work. For one thing, Sepúlveda has form: there are other occasions on which he refers to himself in the third person.[40] In this instance, moreover, the mid-*PT* switch to the third person is a marked usage which occurs for the purposes of a discrete section (§§2–5): the brief history offered by way of summary of the course of events thus far and the pretty pass to which everything has now come. This grammatical patterning can thus be best understood in terms of the function of the *PT*, which Sepúlveda composed with the express view of sending it to the Inquisition—but also in anticipation of a broader readership. Crucially, then, this third-person survey section would appear to be designed to constitute a sort of set-piece 'authorized account' of the vicissitudes of his dispute with Las Casas: one which he presumably hoped would go down in history as the definitive version, *contra* Las Casas's earlier 1552 account, thereby allowing a version of the narrative with a strongly Sepúlvedan bias to prevail, despite the third-person pretence to objectivity. In writing of himself in the third person he was thus anticipating, even modelling, the hoped-for mode of contemporary commentators and perhaps especially future historians in their discussion of his role in events. Writing in the third person also made this portion more readily excerptable and copiable, primed for transplantation into the annals of history.

In reality, as bibliographical fate would have it, the reception trajectory of the *PT* has been fraught and—far from constituting any kind of definitive account— the text has instead been long forgotten and decidedly underserved in modern scholarship: distorted in Fabié–Denisova, omitted altogether from the Pozoblanco *Obras completas*. Though our efforts are (as ever) naturally by no means to be taken as any kind of endorsement of this 'authorized' Sepúlvedan version of events, we hope that our inclusion of a translation of the *PT* here—produced from an enhanced version of the text generated from comparative inspection of the three surviving manuscripts and accompanied by the *Declaración*—will at least constitute a useful corrective.

---

[40] Sepúlveda does something similar for instance in his letter to Granvelle (Letter 113, §4, p. 325) when describing how he would like to see the king respond to the *PT* by '... mandando que lo hagan examinar por las anotaciones que contra él hizo el doctor Sepúlveda' ('... ordering it [Las Casas's *Aquí se contiene*] to be examined in light of the criticisms of it which Dr Sepúlveda had penned'), referring to himself in the third person here as if inhabiting and ventriloquizing the subject position of the king, almost as if thereby willing the desired outcome into reality.

366 SEPÚLVEDA ON THE SPANISH INVASION OF THE AMERICAS

Outrageous, scandalous, heretical notions which Dr Sepúlveda identified in the book on the conquest of the Indies published by Friar Bartolomé de las Casas, former bishop of Chiapa, without licence in Seville in 1552, of which the title begins: 'Contained herein is a debate or disputation, etc...'

(1) By exercising forbearance and holding my tongue, I thought that I would succeed in getting the esteemed bishop of Chiapa to let me live in peace and turn my attention to other scholarly matters, untroubled by old quarrels, since I had already settled to my own satisfaction the dispute and debate regarding the justice of the conquest of the Indies into which, on his account, I entered with him and a series of other learned theologians.[41] For this reason I had refrained from responding to the replies he composed to the answer I presented at the assembly of the councils to his twelve objections or *to the barking with which he hounded me and strove to damage my reputation* by claiming that the things I write are scandalous notions that fly in the face of all gospel truth and go against all Christianity, and calling me an abettor of tyrants, scourge of the human race, and sower of the most mortal blindness, all because I defend the truth against the falsehood which he himself sowed, from which grave ills have arisen both here and over in the New World. But I see now that a man *for whom it did not suffice to pour out the venom of his bitterness among a select crowd of redoubtable individuals on whose patience he has trespassed, but has also seen fit, by the printing of a little book, to oblige even men of immense accomplishment to bear witness and pay heed*,[42] can know no peace nor is capable of affording others any respite either; and so he leaves me no choice but to respond for the sake of my honour, *lest anyone interpret my silence as the pricks of conscience.*

---

[41] Our translated title corresponds to the full form of the title of the *Proposiciones temerarias* as given in the oldest of the three manuscripts at our disposal, *S*. More broadly its short-form version of this title, *Proposiciones temerarias y de mala doctrina que notó el Dr Sepúlveda en el libro de la conquista de Indias que hizo imprimir el Obispo de Chiapa*, which appears on fol. 16 of manuscript *S* and is in turn adopted as the main title in manuscript *C*. Note that what we are here translating as 'heretical' is, in its Spanish original in *S*, 'de mala doctrina' (*Proposiciones temerarias, escandalosas y de mala doctrina*): 'of unsound doctrine'; in other words, 'unorthodox' or 'heretical'. The latter solution has the advantage of also coinciding more closely with the variant form of the title offered in manuscript *M*, with which readers may already be familiar from Fabié's 1879 edition of the text (and Denisova's of 2019), which itself employs the word 'heretical' (*Proposiciones temerarias, escandalosas y heréticas*) as opposed to the periphrasis 'de mala doctrina'.

[42] In this Latin passage, as so often, manuscript *M* (and hence Fabié's printed text) is full of errors that could have been corrected had manuscripts *S* and *C* been consulted. Here, notably, one should read *effudisse* ('pour out') for *offendisse*, and *impresso libello* ('a little book having been printed') for *in presenti bello*. Sepúlveda's phrase *virus acerbitatis suae* ('the venom of his bitterness') is taken from Cicero, *De amicitia* 23.87. For the phrase *praeclari facinoris* ('immense accomplishment'), with its unusual positive sense of *facinus*, see Cornelius Nepos, *Vitae* 20 (Timoleon), 1.5.

OUTRAGEOUS, SCANDALOUS, HERETICAL NOTIONS   367

For my own part I would be prepared to go on enduring and secretly nursing the injury that has been done to me were it not for the fact that it is inextricably mixed up with the common interest and with the affront and contempt which he inflicts upon God by disseminating such impious views and upon our sovereigns and people in charging them with tyranny and manifest villainy by means of a public announcement in the guise of a document printed without licence, and so I shall respond only to those elements which especially deal with this. But first and foremost, since Las Casas goes around blithely recounting his own version of all manner of things pertaining to this matter both orally and in writing, it strikes me as necessary to start by offering a brief, faithful, and true account of what is going on, going back to the very beginning.[43]

(2) In the wake of the arrival of a certain group of clergymen who had been dispatched from the Indies by the Spaniards over there to come and seek an audience with our lord the emperor and king in connection with various edicts he had issued,[44] the subject of the justice of the conquest of the Indies became a major topic of discussion at court. As a result the Most Reverend Cardinal the Archbishop of Seville, President of the Council of the Indies,[45] who had heard Dr Sepúlveda declare that he considered the conquest to be just, holy, and conducted precisely as it ought in the manner that is standard for just wars and that he could prove as much beyond any shadow of a doubt, entreated him to do right by God and his king by committing something to paper on that subject; and so in a matter of just a few days Dr Sepúlveda composed just such a book, which, seeing as it had been inspected and approved by all those at court who read it, he in turn presented to the Royal Council of Castile, requesting a licence to have it printed.

It was submitted for examination first to Dr Guevara, of the aforementioned council, then to Fr. Diego de Vitoria, and thirdly to Dr Moscoso, in accordance with Dr Sepúlveda's wishes for it to be scrutinized by a number of people so as to confer greater gravitas upon it; and the book, having met with approval from each of them, the licence was just on the cusp of being issued when certain figures of authority staged an intervention,[46] saying that, excellent though the book might be, it was not a suitable moment for it to be printed. Faced with this obstacle,

---

[43] At this point Sepúlveda switches to referring to himself in the third person and continues in this vein until the point marked by an asterisk on p. 370. See the preface to this translation on this pattern of usage.

[44] The New Laws of 1542.

[45] García de Loaysa.

[46] Here the scribe of *M*, which has a variant reading at this point, has attempted to introduce a key point of clarification by specifying that these 'figures of authority' hailed from the Council of the Indies.

Dr Sepúlveda wrote to the emperor to report what was going on, and His Majesty responded very graciously and supplied him with a special dispensation to present before the Royal Council, instructing them to examine the book carefully and, provided that they did not find in it anything of substance that counselled against it, to grant a licence for it to be printed; and so it was submitted yet again to the *licenciado* Francisco de Montalvo, and he gave it his approval, too.

(3) At this juncture the bishop of Chiapa arrived from the Indies and, having been apprised of all this through the assistance of other individuals who were aggrieved at the prospect of the book's publication, he contrived for it to have to undergo examination all over again, seeking to accomplish through machinations and dealings what he did indeed then manage to do. The book was submitted to Salamanca and to Alcalá, where the bishop succeeded in getting what he wanted by means of machinations, fabrications, and favour-mongering. As a result, those from Alcalá answered that they believed the book ought not to be printed, for which they offered no rationale, even though the letter from the Royal Council had instructed them to justify their verdict. Those from Salamanca gave the same response, providing reasons which the Royal Council deemed frivolous and insubstantial. Dr Sepúlveda objected to this affront and beseeched the Royal Council and our lord the prince to summon the most erudite, well-versed theologians from both Salamanca and Alcalá to come and debate the matter with him before the Royal Council in the presence of a number of other learned theologians who would sit in judgment on the matter.

(4) Thereupon the emperor, having presumably been consulted, ordered the Council of the Indies to join forces with a series of key individuals from the various other councils in addition to four theologians, who all duly presented themselves at the stipulated time, as in the wake of this pronouncement they had been appointed right away by the Council of the Indies. Of the four theologians, three were Dominican friars, highly learned individuals in their own right but all with such a clear conflict of interest in the matter, having themselves argued that the conquest of the Indies was unjust in their writings and sermons, that the *fiscal* of the Royal Council spoke out in opposition and lodged appeals, declaring that the emperor had been misled in naming those priests and requesting that other theologians come in their stead, or, at least, should join their ranks, and he floated a few names, including Dr Moscoso and Dr Sepúlveda; but in the end it was decided that the configuration decreed by His Majesty should not be altered in any way, except for the fact that Dr Sepúlveda should also appear in the assembly, not in the capacity of judge but in order to give his opinion on the matter which His Majesty had commanded the assembly to consider and to provide his reasons for his view in the presence of the aforementioned gentlemen, which is what he duly did in the first session, in a speech before those gentlemen lasting two or three hours. The bishop of Chiapa then turned up at the second session with a book of ninety sheets and asked them to listen to him while he read it out, and he read from his book for five

OUTRAGEOUS, SCANDALOUS, HERETICAL NOTIONS   369

or six days, until, tired of hearing him speak, they ordered him to stop reading and for a summary of that book to be prepared instead.

Friar Domingo de Soto—one of the four theologians—duly produced a summary that ran to nine [double-sided] pages, of which copies were given to all the gentlemen in question and likewise to Dr Sepúlveda, who penned a three-page response, and a copy of this response in turn was ordered to be distributed to the aforementioned gentlemen and so it was done, and they were commanded to submit their verdicts a certain while hence[47] (which ended up being a period of six or seven months), whereupon the priests all dispersed to their respective monasteries while Dr Sepúlveda went back to Córdoba.

When he returned at the appointed time as instructed, it was only to discover that the bishop of Chiapa—either on his own or in collaboration with others—had produced a twenty-one-page reply to his answer, to which Dr Sepúlveda did not respond at that point for there was no need, since he had already answered everything and, moreover, because he found that the gentlemen in question had paid such little notice to Las Casas's replies that few if any of them had even read them, although they had all been supplied with a copy.

(5) But Dr Sepúlveda did attend another session of the assembly, where he engaged in a lengthy debate and quarrel with those reverend fathers regarding the arguments he [Sepúlveda] had advanced and the bulls of Pope Alexander and of Pope Paul to which he appealed in that connection; and, in the end, although back at the first congress opinion had been divided,[48] subsequently the esteemed jurists of the councils all ultimately resolved to follow the opinion of the canonist doctors in the chapter *Quod super his* of *De voto*, in which the latter conclude in favour of the justice of the wars waged by Christians against infidels on account of their idolatry or for failing to observe natural law in some other way—as was the case with the Indians—with the aim of subjugating them and forcing them to observe it, which is one of the four arguments advanced by Dr Sepúlveda in his book.[49] Any one of those arguments alone would suffice to justify the conquest (though few and far between were those who did not subscribe to them all anyway), as they

---

[47] This is the other example of Sepúlveda using the term 'días' in the early modern idiomatic sense that denotes an extended period of time on which we remarked above in connection with the likely timeframe of the *PT*'s composition: see discussion at p. 355. Note that in MS. *M* (and so, as ever, also in Fabié–Denisova), this idiomatic usage has been ironed out—be it simply as a transcription error (perhaps in the form of a sort of reverse haplography which led the copyist's eye straight to 'meses': 'months') or perhaps an attempt at clarification—and consequently what in *S~C* reads 'después de algunos **días**, que fueron seis o siete **meses**' (*S*, fol. 2v; *C*, fol. 147r) in turn there simply reads 'después de algunos meses, que fueron seis o siete' (*M*, fol. 4v).

[48] i.e. a reference to the first phase of 1550.

[49] The *doctores canonistas* alluded to here are the ones Sepúlveda had mentioned in his Seventh Objection: Innocent IV, Hostiensis, Joannes Andreas, and Panormitanus. See also his *Apologia*, III.2.xii. in our numbering (§6 in Moreno Hernández's edition). These canonists were commenting on Innocent III's decretal *Quod super his*, which became ch. 8 of title 34 (*De voto*) of Bk. 3 of the *Decretales* of Gregory IX.

370 SEPÚLVEDA ON THE SPANISH INVASION OF THE AMERICAS

all acknowledged publicly, declaring that they held the conquest to be just for that reason alone even in the absence of any of the others and that not a single one of them was in any doubt on that point.

Of the four theologians,[50] one went to the Council [sc. of Trent] and another did not wish to give his view—presumably to avoid betraying his own convictions or so as not to offend his friends—while Fr. Bernardino de Arévalo, a man noted for his learning and holiness, duly tendered a written statement of his opinion in which he showed himself to be in agreement with Dr Sepúlveda's view on all four counts, and he furthermore also submitted a book devoted to justifying the conquest which he had composed in most learned and earnest fashion in support of the aforementioned opinion, and it was decided that all were to be required to submit their verdict in writing so that it could be sent to the emperor as they had been instructed. All the esteemed members of the assembly and the whole court are witnesses to the truth of everything declared in the foregoing section, which, in any case, is all a well-known matter of public record.

* * *

(6) I offer this truthful account by way of response to the false reports included at the start and indeed dotted throughout the whole of the bishop of Chiapa's book on the matter, and, as regards the question of the legality of the conquest, all I can say is that the arguments he managed to marshal at Alcalá and Salamanca, as well as everything that all those who have wished to defend his view have said, have all already been more than thoroughly answered in that book of mine [i.e. *Democrates secundus*] which can be found in circulation across all of Spain thanks to the many copies which were ordered to be made at court, at Salamanca, and at Alcalá, as well as in the summary thereof which was printed at Rome,[51] in view of which it is not necessary to go around repeating the same point a thousand times as he does, *imagining that he is making himself heard through his verbosity—or, to be rather more precise, that in the presence of an uninformed crowd it is possible to overwhelm the brightness of truth with murkiness in the manner of seditious tribunes stirring up the masses.*

So, leaving aside everything else, I shall respond only with a view to settling matters with a bearing on the honour of God and of our sovereigns and nation—as is my duty—and on my own honour. This will all be undertaken simultaneously,[52] accounting for why I said what I did in some of my responses to those error-ridden objections of his—for it seemed to me that some of the ideas he advances cannot be

---

[50] Melchor Cano was the theologian who went to Trent; the one chary of submitting an opinion was Bartolomé de Carranza. Soto voted against Sepúlveda. See Sepúlveda's letter of 1 October 1550 to Martín Olivano (*Obras completas* IX.2, 270, letter 95, §8).

[51] i.e. *Apologia pro libro de justis belli causis* (Rome, 1550).

[52] Reading *juntamente* with *S* and *C* for *M*'s *justamente*.

OUTRAGEOUS, SCANDALOUS, HERETICAL NOTIONS   371

maintained by Christian folk *without detriment to the Catholic faith*—which ideas he seeks to defend tooth and nail.

(7) Getting down to business, then, and deferring in every particular to the opinion of those better versed in such matters—and most especially to that of the Catholic Church—I would say, with regard to the third point in Friar Domingo de Soto's summary of the bishop of Chiapa's book in which he says that, although all of humanity is subject to Christ *qua* man *in potentia*, this is not the case *in actu*, that *this proposition is heretical for it is manifestly against that passage in the Gospel, in Matthew 28, which reads: 'All power is given unto me in heaven and on earth'.*[53] For these words clearly state that Christ *qua* man was granted power and jurisdiction over the whole world and that he really does possess it; conversely, to say that he does not possess it *in actu* is tantamount to saying that he does not possess it at all, for the following logical sequence holds, as all philosophers agree: *if something is not possessed* in actu *then it is not possessed*, as Aristotle states in the ninth book of his *Metaphysics*.[54]

And as for his denial (in the Sixth Reply) of ever having said any such thing, it can be found right there in the printed book in question at the aforementioned point in the summary where it is plainly stated, and even the very words to which he has recourse in that Reply—namely that infidels are not current subjects of Christ—attests to it, and the pretext he offers for this—that he took 'subjects' to mean those made subject through faith and grace—is baseless, irrelevant, and indicative of a man who has managed to realize that he does not know what to say; for the issue under discussion is the power and jurisdiction which Christ *qua* man possessed—and granted via St Peter to the church—over faithful and unfaithful alike, and he seeks to plead the case for his wrongful view by claiming that he was talking about subjugation *through faith which has been shaped by grace* and that this type of subjection pertains to Christ *qua* God more than *qua* man.

(8) Furthermore, in the Eleventh Reply the bishop of Chiapa says that there are sound, probable, and nigh-incontestable grounds on which it may be reasoned that offering human sacrificial victims to the true God or to a false one does not go against natural law; and, a little further on, he substantiates this by claiming that there were very few peoples who were not in the habit of performing human sacrifice to their gods, having been induced by natural reason to do so. As can be seen from these words and from what is contained in the summary (folio 16.6), he is clearly stating that sacrificing innocent humans to false gods does not go against natural law.

---

[53] Matthew 28:18.
[54] Aristotle, *Metaphysics*, Bk. 9, esp. chs. 6–9, where (using the language of the standard Latin translation), Aristotle stresses the primacy of *actus* over *potentia*. See Sepúlveda's references to the *Metaphysics* in his 6th Objection in *Aquí se contiene una disputa*.

372 SEPÚLVEDA ON THE SPANISH INVASION OF THE AMERICAS

The impiety and heresy of such a notion can be proven as follows: This assertion manifestly condones the worship of idols and contradicts Sacred Scripture;
therefore it is impious and beyond heretical. The logical consequence is proved by
the premise: If it is not against the law of nature to sacrifice human victims to false
gods, then the pagans who once used to do this did not sin by acting against the law
of nature, for they were not subject to any divine law except natural law, according
to the consensus of theologians, on which see Aquinas I-II, q. 98, art. 5.[55] I examine
the minor premise: to sacrifice human victims to false gods is condemned as a very
serious sin in the Sacred Scriptures of the Old and New Testaments. Therefore, it
conflicts with Divine Scripture to say that it is not a sin. The antecedent[56]—that is
to say, that it is condemned as a very serious sin—I prove thus: idolatry and murder
are everywhere condemned in Sacred Scripture as very serious sins, which is clearer
than would need to be proved. See canon 'Quod omnibus', with gloss, [C.] 32, q. 7.[57]
Moreover, to sacrifice human victims—that is, innocent human victims—to false
gods is most especially idolatry and murder; therefore the conclusion holds. And
so the Holy Scripture terms these sacrifices 'impieties' (Deuteronomy 9), or, in like
vein, 'abominations' (Deuteronomy 12): 'Every abomination', it says, 'which the
Lord hates they have performed for their gods, offering their sons and daughters
and burning them with fire'. And it was on account of these sins, it says, that they
were destroyed (Deuteronomy 9 and 18).[58]

Likewise, if sacrificing the spoils of pillage is an abomination in the eyes of God,
then sacrifice that takes the form of murder will be all the more so still, and in
fact, in another passage (Ecclesiasticus 34[:24]), the former is even equated to the
latter: '*Akin to one who kills a son before his father's eyes*', it says, '*is the person who*

---

[55] Aquinas, *ST* I–II, q. 98, art. 5, co.

[56] We follow here the reading of *S* and *C*: *añs.s.*, i.e. *antecedens scilicet*, taking *antecedens* as direct
object of *probo*, with *scilicet* ('that is to say', 'i.e.') introducing the clarification *quod damnetur ut
gravissimum peccatum*. But the generally inferior manuscript *M* (followed by Fabié and Denisova) offers
the tempting alternative reading *anno dmî 53*, which would conclude the previous words *Ergo pugnat
cum scriptura divina dicere non est peccatum*, yielding the sense: 'Therefore it conflicts with Divine
Scripture to say that it is not a sin in the Year of Our Lord [15]53'. This would provide a plausible date for
the composition of this document. While highly attractive, this reading seems to us more likely to result
from confusion over the reading and construction of *añs.s.*

[57] *M* offers 'c. Cum omnibus', but *S* reads 'c. quod omnibus', neither of which is a chapter *incipit* in
Gratian's *Decretum*, C. 32, q. 7. But Sepúlveda was evidently thinking of c. 13 ('Flagitia') of q. 7, a passage from Augustine's *Confessions* (3.8.15) that asserts that even the hypothetical universality of a practice contrary to nature would be no excuse for those who indulge in it—a forceful contradiction of the
view of Las Casas cited in the Spanish words just before this Latin passage. The key sentence in the
Confessions begins, 'quae si omnes gentes facerent … ', and it seems likely that by including the gloss's
lemma on this ('Que si omnes') Sepúlveda's autograph manuscript gave rise to the later manuscript variants. This gloss (by Johannes Teutonicus) spells out Augustine's point even more fully: 'It is argued that
one is not excused from blame on the excuse of either joining with many others or following custom
(*ratione multitudinis vel consuetudinis*)'. Sepúlveda may have found this passage through the entry
natura in the *Margarita Decreti* of Martinus Polonus, a handy index to Gratian often printed with early
editions of the *Decretum*, including Amerbach's 1512 Basel edition, where the passage from Augustine
in Gratian appears on fol. 541. We thank Anders Winroth of the University of Oslo for casting light on
this obscure reference.

[58] Deuteronomy 9:27; 12:31; 9:4–5; 18:12.

offers a sacrifice from the property of the poor'. Moreover, if the pagans, guided by natural reason, were within their rights to worship their idols with acts of murder and were not guilty of sin or injustice in so doing—a claim which is impious and wicked— then I prove the following logical sequence: he who is led by natural reason follows eternal law, for indeed its proper image is natural law. This is equivalent to saying that they acted in accordance with what it says in Psalm 4[:5–6]: *'Offer the sacrifices of righteousness; put your trust in the Lord. Many say, "Who will show us any good?" The light of your countenance has been signed upon us, Lord'. That the 'light' in question is natural reason is the unanimous interpretation of the holy doctors, for which see Aquinas I-II, q. 19, art. 4 at the end.*[59]

Therefore, to claim that sacrificing humans to false gods, which entails both idolatry and murder, does not violate natural law is an impious error characteristic of a brazen man either little versed in theology or else who holds the Catholic faith in little regard and to whose attention it has not come that the commandments of the Decalogue are all natural laws and that anyone who flouts any of them is flouting natural law, as all theologians agree, on which see St Thomas I-II, q. 100, art. 1 and 8 and art. 11;[60] in [Gratian's] *Decretum*, ch. *'Non est'*; § *'his itaque'*; dist. 6;[61] Scotus and other theologians 3. sen. dist. 37;[62] for sacrificing innocent humans to false gods is self-evidently against the First Commandment, *on worshipping only one God*, and against the one on murder.[63]

(9) And to his point that many people engaged in this practice, I counter that they were all barbarians, and if a civilized, right-thinking populace did on occasion ever do so, then in that regard they were not civilized at all but barbarous, just as virtuous men are from time to time led into sin in the throes of high passion and in this regard they are not virtuous at all and are not to be imitated, such as when St Peter denied Christ out of fear or when David *overcome by lust, contrived the death of Uriah*, and in fact there are a great many occasions on which wise men are not immune to the blindness of the masses. So to claim that they were motivated by natural reason in acting as they did is an even greater error and blasphemy than the previous point, for it is tantamount to saying *that, in so doing, they were behaving rightly and wisely since they were following the light of natural reason, which is the*

---

[59] Aquinas, *ST* I-II, q. 19, art. 4, co.

[60] Aquinas, *ST* I-II, q. 100, arts 1, 8, and 11.

[61] Gratian, *Decretum*, D. 6, c. 3. The body of this chapter is an extract from Isidore of Seville's *Sententiae*, Bk. 3 (*Sententia de summo bono, c. 6*); its incipit is 'Non est [peccatum …]'. 'His itaque' is the incipit of Gratian's own comment on this extract, in the same chapter of Distinctio 6.

[62] The reference is to Duns Scotus's commentary on the third of the four books of Peter Lombard's *Sententiae*. As Sepúlveda indicates, Distinctio 37 addresses Lombard's discussion of the question of whether the sins condemned by the Decalogue are necessarily violations of natural law. (Lombard had offered the objection that if they were, there would have been no need to have them in writing. Also, there were divinely-ordered violations of the Decalogue, as when the Israelites fleeing Egypt were commanded to steal from their Egyptian neighbours.) In the edition of Scotus's commentary published in Paris by Jean Granion in 1513, Distinctio 37 is on fols. LXVII–LXVIIIv.

[63] i.e. the Sixth Commandment.

374   SEPÚLVEDA ON THE SPANISH INVASION OF THE AMERICAS

sole perfect type of reason (as St Thomas says in Prima secundae, *q. 68, art. 2) and the guide of human will (q. 71, art, 6).*[64] *Therefore, Las Casas claims that the practices in which the idolaters were wont to engage in the perverse state of mind which their sins had engendered in them (as Paul notes in Romans 1[:28]) is something which they did on account of natural reason, which is a stupid, impious, and exceptionally heretical thing to say.*

(10) In the aforementioned Eleventh Reply, he [Las Casas] goes on to say that idolaters are so duty-bound by natural law to honour the false gods whom they hold to be true ones that if they fail to do so, even to the point of laying down their lives in defence of their religion[65] and their idols if necessary, then they are guilty of mortal sin. *This assertion is likewise impious and heretical and is of a piece with the previous one, since it defends idolatry as something in which it is right to engage.* For, although the erring conscience of which he speaks forces them to idolatry and, even worse, to defend idolatry, it forces them in such a way that they are not exempt from committing a sin.[66] But to say that they are obliged to do so by natural law is to argue *that they are behaving rightly, justly, and wisely, for any person who observes natural law observes divine law, from which natural law is derived, on which see St Thomas, I-II, q. 91, art. 2;*[67] *which in turn would mean that such a person is acting rightly, justly, and wisely in engaging in idol worship, and in so doing proves pleasing to God and has been blessed with the approval of their fellow men, according to the teaching of Paul in Romans 14.*[68] *All which is impious and wicked to claim.*

The argument he offers in support of the idea that the majority of peoples were prompted by natural reason to perform human sacrifices to their gods is that this much and more is owed to God, which is essentially saying *that it is implanted*[69] *in natural reason for men to worship God by means of the sacrifice of their most precious things—which we ourselves gladly admit. But to conclude from this that it is likewise inherent in natural reason that whatever one supposes to be God must be worshipped in the same manner is the mark of a man hallucinating in broad daylight and doing his utmost to undermine the very foundations of natural morality. For in the same manner it would be possible to deduce that, if it is instilled by natural*

---

[64]   Aquinas, *ST* I-II, q. 68, art. 2 co (paraphrased); *ST* I-II, q. 71, art. 6, co, where Aquinas refers to the '*regula voluntatis humanae*' ('the rule/guide of human will') as *duplex*: one aspect is 'human reason'; the other, primary, aspect is 'eternal law, which is, so to speak, God's reason' (*lex aeterna, quae est quasi ratio Dei*).

[65]   Following *S* and *C* ('*de su religion*'), omitted by *M*.

[66]   Sepúlveda clearly has in mind here Aquinas's discussion of the supposed binding force of an erring conscience (*conscientia errans*; Sepúlveda's '*la consciencia errante*'): *ST* I-II, q. 19, a. 5 co. Our translation 'even worse ... etc.' follows *S* and *C*: 'que aun es peor, obligales de manera que haziendolo ...' (for which *M*, followed by Fabié, has 'que aunque es peor obligalles que haziendola').

[67]   Aquinas, *ST* I-II, q. 91, art. 2 co.

[68]   Romans 14:18.

[69]   All manuscripts correctly read *insitum* here, but Fabié read *iusitum* here and in two other instances of the word in these lines, both of which were correct in all three manuscripts. This is an indication that Fabié's Latinity was even shakier than that of the scribe of *M*.

OUTRAGEOUS, SCANDALOUS, HERETICAL NOTIONS   375

reason in all men that they should follow everything that is good, then it is likewise instilled by natural reason that whatever any particular individual supposes to be good must immediately be followed—a doctrine that would lead to the collapse of all moral teaching. For this would give rise to a situation in which the most intemperate men, cast down into the depths of evils, who, relying on natural reason,[70] suppose the good to be bad and the bad good, would pursue the basest pleasures, which they consider to be things that are good and engender happiness, choosing the bad in place of the good through corrupted reason. This error in choosing[71] is the source and origin of every sort of wickedness, as the Philosopher [Aristotle] declares in the third book of the [Nicomachean] Ethics.[72] For although the will by nature seeks the true good, it then seeks perversely and unnaturally what it supposes to be good, as the aforementioned Philosopher testifies in the second book of the Eudemian Ethics.[73]

Therefore, in order for the wickedness and misguidedness of this shameful, nefarious claim to be clearly exposed,[74] one must understand what Aristotle teaches in the book On the Movement of Animals: *that in whatever action a man undertakes with due thought, he avails himself of a certain syllogism, the conclusion of which is the action itself.[75] Therefore a pious and upright man, in order to worship God correctly, has recourse to a syllogism along the following lines: Whatever is god ought to be worshipped by the sacrifice of the best things: So this thing is God, and these are the best things: Then, in accord with this conclusion, this thing ought to be worshipped by the sacrifice of these things. He worships the true God with the best things—that is, with virtues and piety. And since he does not take any kind of falsehood as his minor premise, through a good process of reasoning he acts rightly and piously.[76]*

The worshipper of idols, however, may indeed be availing himself of the same syllogism, but with a false minor premise that declares a created being to be God. This error drives him into the impiety of worshipping created beings in place of God. Therefore he is led not by natural reason, which is the guide of the will, but rather is swept away by error and a deficient understanding. This error is doubled in those who

---

[70] Reading *ratione naturali nitentes*, following *S* (but correcting its dative *rationi*). *M*, followed by Fabié, has the correct ablative *ratione naturali*, but reads *in res* for *nitentes*. *C* has *intentes* for *nitentes*.

[71] Reading *in eligendo* with *S* and *C* for *M*'s *intelligendi*.

[72] Aristotle, *Nicomachean Ethics* 3.1.4 (1110b28–30).

[73] Probably a reference to *Eudemian Ethics* 2.10 (1227a18–30). Fabié misread *M*'s somewhat unclear numeral as referring to Bk. 5 (which is identical to Bk. 5 of the *Nicomachean Ethics*). Manuscripts *S* and *C* clearly cite Bk. 2.

[74] Following *S*'s *et ignorantia* [our 'misguidedness'] *patefiat*. *M* (followed by Fabié) omitted *ignorantia* and mangled *patefiat* to *puto fiat*. Apparently, the verb *patefacio* lay beyond the erudition of the scribe (and of the modern editors).

[75] Aristotle, *De motu animalium*, §7 (701a8–b1). 'Undertakes' renders the *obit* of *S* and *C*; *M* has *edit*. 'Of whose' renders the *cuius* of *S* and *C*; *M* has *eius*. Fabié's punctuation reveals that he failed to understand this passage.

[76] Reading *per bonam consequentiam recte pieque facit S* and *C*. *M* has the absurd *probo nam recte pie quod consequentiam facit*, duly followed by Fabié and Denisova. (Again, we are mentioning in these notes only the most egregious errors of the only printed texts that so far exist. We hope it is clear that a proper edition of this work is long overdue.)

offer up human sacrifices: they imagine the created being to be God, and they consider an impious and wicked sacrifice, condemned by natural and divine law, to be pious, when in fact no animal is by nature less suited to be sacrificed than man—see the Philosopher [Aristotle], Politics Bk. 7, ch. 2,[77] and likewise according to the testimony of the Sacred Scripture, which declares sacrifices of this sort to be abominations which God opposes (Deuteronomy 18).[78]

For just as, if one wishes to receive a true prince with preparations fit for a king, one ought to set out an elegant and sumptuous feast with the most precious things, but things from the sorts of food proper for dining-tables, not with horsemeat just because one happens to have to hand a horse more valuable than any foodstuffs, by the same token it would be ritually proper to sacrifice to God the best among animals, but on the proviso they are of the kind[79] suitable for sacrifice and not the kind God would reject in sacrifices. And yet, if we are looking for the truth, we are commanded by the law of nature to sacrifice no animal at all, even to the true God. For otherwise the practice of animal sacrifice would not have been suspended through gospel law and Christian custom—to say nothing of sacrificing a human being, which the old law similarly deplores.

(11) It stands even more to reason, then, that those idolaters who worshipped multiple[80] gods did not have the universal conception of God as properly befits him, namely *best, greatest, and almightiest, creator of all good things*, which can only betoken one single God, for any entity that does not boast these characteristics is not God, and only one [God] alone can exhibit all these features, meaning that those idolaters who worshipped birds, beasts, and snakes as gods on account of some quality with which they imagined these entities to be invested—as noted by St Paul in Romans 1[81]—were manifestly mistaken in so doing, not only in believing those animals to be gods, but also for failing to grasp what it means to be God.

One example will suffice for all. While it is true that all men by the law of nature seek happiness, nonetheless it does not follow from this that the Epicureans, who believe that the enjoyment of bodily pleasures[82] is happiness, are permitted to consort with prostitutes. And in that practical syllogism which the aforementioned employ—all things productive of pleasure are to be adopted;[83] visiting prostitutes is productive of pleasure; therefore I am permitted to visit prostitutes—the major premise also is false, as in the case of the view espoused by these people who

---

[77] Aristotle, *Politics* 7.2 (1324b40–42). *M* has 'Polit. 2, cap. 2', printed by Fabié and Denisova. *S* and *C* correctly offer 'pol. 7, c. 2'.

[78] Deuteronomy 18:12. *M* has 'Deut. 19', printed by Fabié and Denisova. *S* and *C* correctly offer 'Deut. 18'.

[79] Reading *ex eo genere* with all three manuscripts; Fabié has *excogenere*.

[80] Reading *muchos* with all manuscripts; Fabié read *nuestros*.

[81] Romans 1:22–23.

[82] Reading *frui voluptatibus corporeis* (*S*, *C*) for *M*'s *in voluptatibus corporeis*.

[83] Reading *adsciscenda* (*S*, *C*) for *M*'s *admittenda*.

OUTRAGEOUS, SCANDALOUS, HERETICAL NOTIONS 377

only understand happiness in what St Thomas calls a purely verbal and equivocal sense.[84]

The same thing happens in the case of idol-worshippers, who have a false understanding about God. By worshipping idols they do not understand God except in a purely verbal and equivocal sense; rather, they apprehend created beings that have some power or excellence—as, for example, if someone were to imagine that the sun were a god because of its excellent light and warmth salutary for plants and animals and were to worship it in the form of a statue with human victims, that person would not understand God, for indeed he would be worshipping him neither in himself nor contingently; rather he would be worshipping the statue contingently, but the sun (that is, an exceptional created being) in itself. For if someone among the pagans used to piously worship the true God as author of all good things and the first cause of all things (as the Philosopher [Aristotle] understood), but did so in the form of a gold or silver statue and by the name of Jupiter, that man was not a worshipper of idols.[85] For it is not the name or the image that constitutes idolatry. For God is called upon throughout the nations by very many[86] names, and we Christians ourselves make use of images.

(12) Furthermore, it is incorrect to say that an erring conscience is binding, for that is the proper task of just law. Thus, such a conscience offers no excuse for sinning. The sin lies not in failing to do what it [the erring conscience] says or orders, but in the disdain we believe one shows for right reason in not abiding by that which one actually believes to be the case: i.e. that it is a greater sin to perform that action—especially with regard to matters prohibited by natural law, as is the case about which we are now speaking.[87] Thus the armature which the proponent of this notion [i.e. Las Casas] constructed upon the flimsy straws of erring conscience so as to defend his impious error comes tumbling down in sundry ways.

(13) And to say what he says *simply,*[88] *unconditionally, and without support* around the beginning of his Eleventh Reply—that he doesn't know what judgment God passes on idolaters who sacrifice innocent human beings to false gods— makes this impious error of his even worse and casts even more doubt upon its

---

[84] Sepúlveda implies that the phrase *nisi nomine tenus et equivoce* is taken from Aquinas, but we have not located these precise words. Aquinas's main discussion of the Epicureans' views on pleasure is at *ST* I-II, q. 34, art. 2 co.

[85] Fabié prints *idolare* where all three manuscripts correctly offer *idolorum.*

[86] Reading *plurimis* (*S, C*) for *M*'s *pluribus.*

[87] Sepúlveda is indebted here to Aquinas's discussion of the supposed binding and excusing power of *conscientia errans* in *ST* I-II, q. 19, art. 5 co and art. 6 co. *M* follows this passage with a Latin version of the same idea (missing in *S* and *C*): '*Therefore, he who acts against his erring conscience or false reasoning sins not because he is failing to act in accord with its guidance, but because he is doing as much violence as he can to divine law and holds right reason in contempt, in that he considers the things he is doing to be forbidden*'.

[88] Reading *pure* (*S, C*) for *M*'s *quiere. Pure* is part of the Latin phrase that continues with *et sine conditione sive suppositione.* Also, our translation here ignores the incorrect paragraph break that *M* (followed by Fabié) introduced between *conditione* and *dize.* This error is not found in *S* and *C*.

author. For to harbour doubts about God's judgment in a matter as clear as this is to run counter to the Catholic faith and the precepts of the Decalogue, and is an indication that one is not a Christian, or that one lacks understanding or the common sense of prudent men. For when someone who knows perfectly well that God condemns idolaters and murderers (which is what those who sacrifice innocent humans to false gods are) goes on to say that he doesn't know what judgment God passes on them, he is in effect saying that he harbours doubts about gospel law and even natural law, since knowledge in this matter is taken for certainty on faith, in accord with the common understanding of learned men—in which sense are to be taken those words in the chapter *Ex litteris* [in the title] *De sponsalibus*[89]—as opposed to knowledge by means of *post hoc* demonstration (in case he would like to get off the hook with that sort of childish flimflam).

(14) In the Eleventh Reply he also says the following words: 'I would even go so far as to say that they (which is to say the infidels) will never be obliged to believe any preacher of our holy faith who keeps company with tyrants, warmongers, plunderers, and killers'.

This claim about the infidels not being obliged to believe the preachers of Christ's faith is impious and heretical, for it goes expressly against that passage from the Gospel of St Mark 16—*Go into all the world, and preach the gospel to every creature. He that believes and is baptized shall be saved; but he that does not believe shall be damned*[90]—for God does not condemn anyone for not doing what they are under no obligation to do, in view of which the point about keeping company with soldiers and wicked men who are more interested in robbing than anything else does not change anything, for a war which is just in and of itself does not cease to be so simply because its soldiers are ill-intentioned, and if they go along more with a view to plundering than of enacting justice then they are guilty of sin, as St Augustine says,[91] but even so they are not obliged to make restitution of what they have pillaged, as attested by St Thomas (II-II, q. 66, art. 8);[92] and so preaching does not forfeit any of its holiness due to the presence of soldiers who are not there to preach but to subjugate the barbarians and ensure that the preachers come to no harm, and for this they do not need to be saints. After all, if this were the case then heretics would not be obliged to believe the preachers during Inquisitorial proceedings either owing to the presence of the soldiers and those administering

---

[89] This refers to one of two possible chapters (7 and 10) beginning *Ex litteris* in title 1 (*De sponsalibus*) of Bk. 4 of the *Decretales* of Gregory IX. Both chapters are letters of Pope Alexander III, and both deal with the pope's authority to intervene in disputes over the validity of marriage vows. The point for Sepúlveda here would be the impossibility of going against papal authority.

[90] Mark 16:15–16.

[91] Pseudo-Augustine, Sermon 82 of the *Sermones supposititii* (*PL* 39, col. 1904), but in Sepúlveda's day it was known as Sermon 19 of the category *De verbis Domini*. But Sepúlveda clearly derived this reference from the passage in Aquinas that he proceeds to cite. The words of Pseudo-Augustine are '*propter praedam militare peccatum est*'.

[92] Aquinas, *ST* II-II, q. 66, art. 8 ad 1.

OUTRAGEOUS, SCANDALOUS, HERETICAL NOTIONS   379

secular justice who are there to lead them to the stake upon the conclusion of the preaching should they refuse to convert or in cases where they have relapsed.

And even if the preachers themselves harboured such wicked intentions as the ill-intentioned soldiers, the infidels would still be obliged to believe them and the preaching itself would not cease to be just and holy in its own right, just as Mass, baptism, and the other sacraments do not lose their validity and holiness just because those who administer them are evil sinners, nor should the kind of preaching in question be a source of concern to good Christians, for St Paul takes delight in it: '*Some indeed*', he says, '*preach Christ even of envy and rivalry; and some also of good will*';[93] and shortly afterwards:[94] '*What does it matter? Just this, that Christ is proclaimed in every way, whether out of false motives or true, and in that I rejoice*';[95] and that good doctrine must be embraced when imparted by bad and good alike *Christ himself teaches in the Gospel of St Matthew by means of these words: The scribes and the Pharisees sit in Moses' seat. So obey them and do everything they tell you to do; but do not do what they do, for they do not practice what they preach.*[96]

(15) In the Twelfth Reply he says that all conquests of the Indies undertaken to date, even in cases where all the directives have been properly observed, have been unjust, tyrannical, and infernal.

This claim is erroneous, scandalous, and based on an outrageous piece of heresy, for it hinges on arguing that the decree or special grace which Pope Alexander VI established and granted to the Catholic monarchs for the purposes of subjugating the Indians to their dominion and thereafter having the gospel preached to them— and so too the bull,[97] and the rescript thereto,[98] which functions in the same manner as the other *Extravagantes*—is ineffectual and not to be obeyed because it was not within the pope's power to mandate this. To suggest such a thing is condemned by the church as heresy: chapter '*Nulli*', dist. 19; chapters '*Violatores*' and '*Generali*', 25, q. 1, with the corresponding glosses;[99] and that this claim hinges on this intolerable notion can be proven by the fact that its proponent [i.e. Las Casas] knows full well, for it is a point of common knowledge, that all the conquests have

---

[93] Philippians 1:15.

[94] Fabié amusingly printed the *et paulo post* of the manuscripts as *et Paulo post*, presumably influenced by *San Pablo* a few words earlier.

[95] Philippians 1:18.

[96] Matthew 23:2–3.

[97] *Inter caetera*, 1493.

[98] This is a reference to '*Dudum siquidem*' (26 September 1493), which was a response to a query of the Catholic monarchs and which has often been called an 'extension of the donation'.

[99] Gratian, *Decretum*, D. 19, c. 5 (a decretal of Gregory IV, beginning '*Nulli fas est …*' 'No one is allowed to wish or be able to transgress the precepts of the Apostolic See'); C. 25, q. 1, c. 5 (a decretal of Pope Damasus, beginning '*Violatores canonum …* ' 'Those who willingly violate the canons are severely judged by the holy fathers'); C. 25, q. 1, c. 11 (a decretal of Pope Adrian, beginning '*Generali decreto …*' 'By a general decree we have determined that that person be cursed by anathema and be eternally charged by God as a denier of the Catholic faith who in any way believes that a judgment of kings, bishops, or Roman pontiffs should be violated—or who allows it to be violated'). *M* has *Generalis* here, but *S* and *C* correctly give *generali*.

380   SEPÚLVEDA ON THE SPANISH INVASION OF THE AMERICAS

from the very outset had that bull and decree as their basis, and if that bull has any force and authority then it goes without saying that the conquest is just, which our proponent denies; for he plainly reveals his conviction that the pope did not have the power to issue that decree and grace through his dogged insistence that the church has no jurisdiction over infidels.[100]

This is the primary basis for his false claim regarding the injustice of the conquest, as can be seen in his Fifth and Sixth Replies and also from what he says in the Twelfth Reply, namely that, prior to baptism, infidels are not subjects of the church, nor is the church in a position to depose or impose rulers upon them, nor are they obliged to show obedience, all of which diametrically contradicts the bull and concession; and the camouflage of which he avails himself in order to mask this outrageous assertion is to contend that the bull confers neither authority nor endorsement for the procedure of first subjugating those pagans and exposing them to teachings only afterwards, denying that it says anything to that effect.

It is a great travesty and intolerable impudence to set out to dim people's understanding of patently obvious matters by means of spurious arguments; for the pope plainly praises the Catholic monarchs' objective as holy and commendable in view of the fact that '*they wish, by divine grace, to subjugate those people to themselves and so subject them to the Catholic faith*'[101] and greatly encourages them in their proposed venture, enjoining upon them that, since they are moved by religious zeal to wish to undertake this expedition (which is to say conquest and war, as everyone who understands Latin knows), they should strive to make them [sc. the infidels] convert to the Catholic faith, for that is the ultimate and chief objective; and so as to induce them to embark upon this more gladly and eagerly still, he makes a grant to them and their successors of all those islands and mainlands, complete with their realms, cities, towns, and other localities, along with their rights, jurisdictions, and dependencies. And even though the bull states all this perfectly openly, our proponent insists that this is not what it says, as though he were addressing children or slow-witted men who lack all knowledge of Latin.

---

[100] Of course, this is not exactly what Las Casas was arguing: rather, he sought to draw a distinction between 'active' infidels (those who knew of the faith and still chose to reject it) versus those who had never come into contact with it at all and so never embraced it in the first place. It is the latter over whom, he says, the church has no direct jurisdiction. Sepúlveda's formulation here, then, is a somewhat coarse representation of Las Casas's position, resulting in an (inadvertent?) extension of his claim to all categories of infidel. Offering a point of clarification in this regard, manuscript *M* (17*v*) here has '*infieles negativos*' ('negative infidels', i.e. *not* those of the active sort) where *S* (7*v*) and *C* (154*r*) both just have '*infieles*'. This *M* clarification restates Las Casas's position more accurately, and it is certainly a key detail, for it is around this that Sepúlveda is here basing his whole discussion of Las Casas's principal point of alleged heresy. Moreover, from what Sepúlveda goes on to say, it is clear that he is in fact taking Las Casas to task specifically over what he argues about '*negative*' infidels, as astutely glossed by *M*.

[101] This corresponds reasonably closely to what the *Inter caetera* indeed says on this point, namely: '... *illarumque* [*sc. insulae*] *incolas et habitatores vobis divina favente clementia subiicere et ad fidem catholicam reducere proposuistis*' ('and you have proposed, with the support of divine clemency, to subject the dwellers and inhabitants of those [islands] to you and to subject them to the Catholic faith').

OUTRAGEOUS, SCANDALOUS, HERETICAL NOTIONS   381

Thus to claim that the bull does not say what it so patently does say is all just another way of clearly insinuating[102] that the whole thing is a farce and that the pope was not within his rights to do this, although he [Las Casas] does not quite dare to come straight out and say it in so many words, and it is against such an outrageous assertion that the above adduced decrees can be rightly brought to bear, for, even though it might theoretically be permissible to say that the pope can err *beyond the bounds of faith and in moral decrees if abandoned by the Holy Spirit by whose guidance he governs the church*, it is not likely that he should actually go astray, nor should one even think so, and to claim that he does err is grave impudence on the part of private individuals and anyone who espouses any such idea comes under grave suspicion of seeking to undermine the power of the church, which is why such a person is condemned as a heretic in the above cited chapters. Only another pope, who embodies the personage of the whole church, or a general council, which fulfils the same function, can give the say-so to have something amended and establish what is just and true, but it is not for judges and private individuals to pass judgment on laws and decrees which have already been issued, but rather to make their judgments in accordance with them (Chapter '*In istis*', dist. 4),[103] and this goes all the more for a decree of such importance pertaining to the universal administration of the church and the procedure to be followed in converting a new world to the Catholic faith; and to suppose that the Holy Spirit would permit the pope to err in this regard is to cast aspersions on the faith, and in particular, by means of the selfsame set of outrageous fabricated allegations, is directly at odds with the pronouncement of Pope St Gregory (Chapter '*si non*', 23, q. 4) in which he unequivocally states that wars waged upon gentiles by Christians specifically with a view to expanding the church and the faith, in the interests of preaching the gospel and the name of Christ to them once they have been subjugated, are just and holy.[104] This was the approach adopted by Gennadius, exarch of Africa, towards the populaces most immediately adjacent to the Roman empire in inland Africa, for to suggest that he was motivated by other factors is an intolerable piece of effrontery, for St Gregory himself says that Gennadius proceeded as he did purely with a view to subjugating them so that the name of Christ could be preached to them more expediently.

(16) As to what he says about his *Confesionario* and, in the same breath, about my own book: returning to what I said there in the preface, which is the truth of the matter, I reiterate that the Royal Council did not ever issue any kind of ruling

---

[102] Reading 'es querer dezir por rodeo' (*S, C*), for *M*'s 'es dezir por todo'.

[103] Gratian, *Decretum*, D. 4, c. 3, a short passage from c. 31 of Augustine, *De vera religione*, with a longer comment by Gratian. The Augustine passage declares judges powerless to change laws: '*non licebit iudici de ipsis iudicare, sed sucundum ipsas*' ('A judge may not pass judgment *on* them, but *in accord with* them'). *M* garbles this reference as 'Cap. 1 In istis, dist. 4' (in fact, it is c. 3), but *S* and *C* give the proper reading.

[104] Gratian, *Decretum*, C. 23, q. 4, c. 49. This is the letter from Gregory to Gennadius that frequently surfaced in *Aquí se contiene*: 1.75 (*PL* 77, cols 529–30); Norberg 1.73.

382   SEPÚLVEDA ON THE SPANISH INVASION OF THE AMERICAS

against my book other than to prorogue its licence to be printed, and once it had been published in Rome, where it was examined and endorsed by the deputy of the pope, the master of the Holy Palace, and an auditor of the Rota[105] and unanimously lauded by Rome's intellectuals, the Royal Council did not take exception to this, although there were mutterings in other quarters on the grounds that, since it had been printed *pending the litigation* with regard to the matter of its publication, its existence in printed form ought not to be tolerated; but no action was ever taken against it except at Salamanca courtesy of the meddling of the bishop of Chiapa and his overzealous friends, nor did this prevent numerous copies of it from continuing to do the rounds publicly at court without anybody else raising objections or saying a word about it to me, although I was in possession of copies thereof and openly gave them out to anyone who wished to have a read, and so they circulated among and were read by those gentlemen of the Royal Council and of the assembly and all learned men at court.

By contrast, when that *Confesionario* of his came to the attention and into the hands of the Royal Council, they ordered it to be examined and scrutinized and it was deemed and adjudged false, scandalous, and outrageous, and Las Casas was hauled up before the Royal Council on that account and rebuked most roundly by the esteemed president in the presence of the other members, and the order went out that the *Confesionario* was to be rounded up and confiscated from monasteries across all of Castile, as was indeed then done, and the same instruction was issued with respect to the Indies; and it is also known and widely acknowledged that my book, which has been circulating throughout all of Christendom in the form of copies and summaries, has exposed the error of the ways of those who had advanced the opposite view in writings prior to my own, and it has since also prompted eight men from the ranks of the most learned theologians and canonists of our nation to write in favour of the conquest of the Indies, pursuing a variety of lines of reasoning with immense learning and prowess, all of which boil down to and fall under one of the four lines of argument I outlined right from the very start of my book, any one of which suffices to justify the conquest. The eight men in question are: Fr. Alonso de Castro, Fr. Luis de Carvajal, and Fr. Bernardino de Arévalo (Franciscans), as well as Dr Honcala (canon of the cathedral of Ávila), all of whom are excellent theologians; along with the esteemed bishop of Michoacán,[106] who had spent many years in the Indies, *licenciado* Gregorio López from the Council

---

[105]   Felipe Archinto, Gil Foscarario, and Antonio Agustín.

[106]   Vasco de Quiroga, bishop of Michoacán from 1536 until his death in 1565. He was in Spain from 1547 to 1554, during which time he was often called upon to advise the Council of the Indies. Though still celebrated by the indigenous inhabitants around Lake Pátzcuaro, and frequently cited for his utopian projects inspired by his reading of More's *Utopia*, his 1535 *Información en derecho* took a dim view of the cultural level of the Amerindians, emphasizing their cruelty and barbarism, claiming that they lived 'sin ley y sin rey'.

of the Indies, the Archdeacon of Mallorca, and another Mallorcan doctor, all great canonists.

As to his claim that four *maestros* and two theologians of the rank just below them (whom he names)[107] numbering among the most learned, authoritative members of his Order countersigned his *Confesionario*, which contains all the same reprehensible ideas,[108] I would say that it is scarcely to be believed that such learned, redoubtable men would put their names to such heretical great nonsense, or perhaps they perused the book only cursorily and signed it under the pressure of pestering and machinations, which are certainly not qualities alien to its author; and conceivably once one of them had signed the book under such circumstances, the others followed suit so as to get out of having to read the whole book, which is substantial and tedious, little suspecting the perversity of the doctrine it contained and paying attention only to the main gist, as was demonstrated by one of the most eminent members of their number, who, when questioned by another highly learned, redoubtable clergyman (who had read the notes I penned and was abreast of the whole business) as to how he could have had put his name to a book full of such specious stuff,[109] expressed his amazement at the account the latter gave of its content and said he had never seen any such thing or at least he had not paid heed to it.

And when Fr. Domingo de Soto penned his summary of the book [Las Casas's *Apología*], noticing and shrinking from its unsound doctrine, he set about camouflaging and rectifying those passages, *but it was wasted effort; for in the case of an incurable disease the diligence of doctors is of little use, especially when the blind temerity of the sick man, revelling in his disease, spurns the principles of the art of medicine.* This is what happened to him [Las Casas] in the Replies after I had exposed the wounds all the more, *for even amid the compresses which—though the ailment was incurable—had nonetheless been carefully and scrupulously applied, the ailment kept on bursting forth afresh with the same frenzy as before.* Thus, though he cunningly contrives to find ways of turning his personal quarrels, of which he is never in short supply, into matters of public interest, *just as seditious people are accustomed to do, he would be taken aback if perchance some reasonably sane*[110] *man should wish to sully his own good cause by recklessly mixing it up with his bad cause and his rashness.*

* * *

[107] See Las Casas's Twelfth Reply, §14.

[108] Reading 'donde tambien se contienen estos errors' (*S, C*); *M* has 'dando tambien estos errores'.

[109] This translation renders several words carelessly omitted from *M* (and hence absent from the printed editions): 'y sabia todo lo que pasava, come avia firmado libro que contenia tales errores...'.

[110] *Modo sanus*, in all three manuscripts. Fabíe printed *modus sanus*.

384   SEPÚLVEDA ON THE SPANISH INVASION OF THE AMERICAS

(17) Thus far I have responded for the sake of the honour of God and of our sovereigns and people; I now wish to double back to salvage my own, which will be just a matter of a few words for it will suffice to expose the contrivance and machinations which the bishop of Chiapa has always employed against me. The fact of the matter is that, realizing that all the arguments he adduces to refute the truth which I champion are futile and utterly flimsy, he resolved to plunge everything into disarray by means of false allegations and fabrications quite beside the point. For what I [in actual fact] assert and have set out in writing is, briefly put, that the conquest of the Indies performed with a view to subjugating those barbarians, ridding them of their idolatry, and forcing them to observe natural law against their will if necessary—and then, having subjugated them, to preach the gospel to them with all due meekness without recourse to any force whatsoever—is just and holy, and that, once they have been subjugated, they should be neither killed nor enslaved nor stripped of their estates but rather turned into vassals of the king of Castile and made to pay an appropriate amount of tribute as appointed and required by our sovereigns and as stipulated in the instructions issued to the captains-general whom they have dispatched, and that anything done in breach of this is wrongfully done and a grave sin for which it will be arduous indeed to account before God, and anything taken by force—above and beyond that which can be lawfully seized in war—is robbery and must be restored, and the bone of our contention is to establish whether or not all the above—as set out in my writings—is true; and the bishop of Chiapa, who has read my views on this a thousand times in my writings, instead of refuting it expends his whole life on recounting the cruelties and robberies which the soldiers have perpetrated and even those they have not perpetrated, falsely alleging that I support them and condone these evils, even though he and everyone else who has read my book, which has been disseminated throughout all of Christendom, knows that I said the opposite and that these evils strike me as even more awful than they strike him and in my book I condemn them as severely as can be, although I do not devote as much time to it as he does, for he speaks and thinks of nothing but exaggerating them by any convoluted means possible, although it is all completely beside the point which is at issue here, for the cruelties, robberies, damages, and sins which soldiers commit in practically all wars do not detract from the justice of the war in any way if the warfare itself is just per se, and anything rightfully seized in accordance with the law of warfare is not robbery nor is there any requirement to make restitution, as St Thomas says (II-II, q. 66, art. 8).[111] And so everything Las Casas imputes to me is false, as everyone who has read my book knows—and he better than anyone else.

---

[111] Aquinas, *Summa Theologica* II-II, q. 66, art. 8.

Appendix: Itemization (*Declaración*) of the grounds on which the pretexts offered for the falsehoods in the bishop of Chiapa's book neither suffice nor serve to exonerate anything

The first falsehood is the claim that the infidels are not subject to Christ *in actu*, which goes against what it says in the Gospel: *All power is given unto me in heaven and in earth* (Matthew, final chapter).[112] The pretext offered for this interpretation is that he [Las Casas] took this to mean that they were not rendered subject *in terms of faith and grace*, which is an irrelevant point, for the bone of our contention concerns the jurisdiction and forum of the church and of Christ, and indeed it is precisely in that connection that the bishop offers the remark in question (as can be seen from fol. 36*v* and fol. 38*v*),[113] meaning that this pretext is utterly fallacious and nothing but nonsense.

The second doctrinal problem is to say that the heathens were acting under the influence of natural reason and natural law in sacrificing humans to their false gods whom they believed to be true ones: the issue to note here is the fact that the bishop himself claims that he does not mean to suggest that the infidels should be absolved

---

[112] Matthew 28:18. This Itemization (*Declaración*) is a digest of, or reader's guide to, the *Proposiciones temerarias* (*PT*). The unnamed Lascasian 'book' here alluded to is thus the same as the work to which the *PT* is more explicitly devoted to filleting: Las Casas's *Aquí se contiene* volume of 1552, containing Sepúlveda's own (responses to Las Casas's) *Objections* and Las Casas's subsequent *Replies*, with which the *PT*—and, hence, also this *Declaración*—in turn engages. The word here rendered as 'falsehood' (or, below, as 'doctrinal problem' *et sim.*) all correspond to Sepúlveda's original term, '*error*': by this he clearly in fact means out-and-out 'heresy', but, as that is a verdict at which he was hoping the Inquisition itself would officially arrive, he generally refrains from putting it directly into their mouths; and, so, nor have we into Sepúlveda's.

[113] The folio page references offered here and throughout the *Declaración* correspond to the pagination of Las Casas's printed 1552 *Aquí se contiene* volume. Readers wishing to follow up these references can do so courtesy of Galmés's 1992 *Aquí se contiene* edition, which conveniently tracks the original folio pagination in the margins. (Denisova 2019, pp. 75–192, also includes it, albeit text-internally as opposed to marginally.) Sepúlveda employs a system of referencing whereby *a* and *b* correspond to what by modern referencing conventions would be *r*[*ecto*] and *v*[*erso*]. To ease the consultation process, *a* and *b* have therefore been converted throughout this document to *r* and *v* (although note that Galmés and Denisova both simply use bald numerals for *recto* pages): thus, for instance, Sepúlveda's original 38*b* has here become 38*v* (while e.g. 46*a* would become 46*r*, i.e. Galmés–Denisova's 46: see next note). To complicate matters further, however, many of the folio references offered in *M* (our only witness for the *Declaración*) are wrongly recorded: we have therefore first converted everything to *r* and *v*, then in turn employed the usual strikethroughs to supply further corrections. Some of these errors appear to be simple counting mistakes, quite possibly on Sepúlveda's own part: easy enough to do, for the original 1552 *Aquí se contiene* does not print the folio pagination—it merely offers the occasional quire number—so it is easy to miscount, or to factor in the frontmatter differently at different times. Sepúlveda may also have been working from hastily taken notes, or even from memory: in his letter to Granvelle (Letter 113, §3, p. 325) he refers to having only had access to *Aquí se contiene* thanks to a copy loaned by a friend. Other errors again, meanwhile, are garden-variety copying errors, likely introduced later: in the first of the two references to which this footnote attaches, for instance, *M* gives '86*b*' (written in a manner which looks like '86 6', which indeed is what Fabié, p. 567, and Denisova, p. 223, both print)—but *Aquí se contiene* runs to just 61 folio pages. It seems clear that '36*b*' [our 36*v*] must be meant: the context corresponds to the subject-matter discussed by Las Casas there (and '3' is easy to mistake for '8'). The ascending numerical order from 36 to 38 which results from this amendment also makes better logical sense. The same is true of several of the other corrections we offer, where the amendment results plausibly in references located on adjacent folios.

of their sins in this regard, which is untrue, for he plainly strives to exonerate them by saying, firstly (on fol. 47v 46r),[114] that he does not know what judgment God reserves for them in this instance, and to be in any doubt over this is un-Christian. He next says that they are labouring under a probable error and proceeds to assert that there are sound, probable, and nigh-incontrovertible grounds that can be adduced in favour of the idea that performing human sacrifice to idols believed to be true gods is consistent with natural law, for if the reasons are sound and probable then they lead to sound conclusions; and then, on fol. 48r 46v, he goes on to assert that most populaces were in the habit of performing human sacrifices to their gods under the influence of natural reason, all of which is a bid to exculpate them and endorse these practices, for he claims that the sins they perpetrated *in a wrongful manner and in ignorance of the law of nature by which we are commanded to worship the one true God* were in fact undertaken *under the influence of natural law, which is an impious and wicked assertion*. For to argue that, when already in a state of mortal sin, it follows *by virtue of natural law* that a further mortal sin in turn be committed *is utterly false*, for *every mortal sin goes against natural law, as all theologians concur*, and to claim that something can be a mortal sin and yet still be done *by the lights of natural law* is to be guilty of contradiction; *thus to invoke natural law in a wrongful fashion constitutes an impious obstinacy*, which is something that cannot be tolerated among learned, Catholic men.

The third falsehood is fundamentally akin to the second, and the pretext advanced for it likewise pure fraudulence, as I have demonstrated at length in my commentary.[115]

The fourth problem is to maintain that the infidels are not obliged to believe those who preach the gospel if they come in the company of soldiers, robbers, and murderers: this is at variance with that passage of the Gospel which says that *he who believes and is baptized will be saved; but he who does not believe will be condemned*.[116] The justification ventured in this instance, namely the idea that the infidels are not obliged to believe the first utterance or tidings to pass the preachers' lips, hardly serves to further the bishop's cause: for what he actually says (on fol. 46v 46r)[117] is that they are not obliged to believe them the first time round or indeed on any other occasion either, and on fol. 50v 50r[118] he asserts that from now until

---

[114] The Lascasian remark in question occurs in *Aquí se contiene* at fol. 46r (i.e. Galmés/Denisova's 46), not 47v. This reference and the next, where we have in turn had occasion to correct 48r to 46v, would then fall on adjacent pages, which further confirms the plausibility of the correction. See previous note.

[115] This is a reference to the *PT*, where this point is discussed at §§10–12. The phrase used to denote the *PT* here is '*en las anotaciones*' ['in my notes' or 'commentary']. Sepúlveda also refers to the *PT* as his '*anotaciones*' in his Letter to Granvelle (Letter 113, §4, p. 325).

[116] Mark 16:16.

[117] The remarks in question are in Las Casas's Eleventh Reply (§4). Sepúlveda's fuller discussion of this point is in the *PT*, §14.

[118] The reference in *M* (fol. 38v) here is to 50b, i.e. our 50v—though in fact 50r (i.e. Galmés's 50) must be meant. Note that Fabié and Denisova both print a bald '50' here, albeit not because they had adopted the same numbering system as Galmés, but because Fabié missed the 'b' in the manuscript (which is indeed somewhat confusingly given on that occasion as an upper-case 'B'—though note the same pattern

OUTRAGEOUS, SCANDALOUS, HERETICAL NOTIONS   387

Judgment Day they will never be obliged in the eyes either of God or of men to believe the preachers for as long as those who come to bear tidings and preach remain unvirtuous types who fail to exemplify the truly Christian way of life and continue to keep company with soldiers (whom he terms tyrants), and he even goes so far as to suggest that, unless the preachers who come are themselves virtuous, exemplary Christians, the heathens will not be obliged to believe them even in the *absence* of soldiers[119]—all of which I have proven to be both impious and false. As to the rest of what it says in that justification with regard to the mode to be employed in preaching the gospel: nobody would deny that that is the right way to proceed, and it is indeed the very method espoused by the preachers who travel over to that part of the world, and the bishop does not make any move to contest this, nor is it of relevance for our purposes. The example I adduced with regard to the form of preaching that occurs in Inquisitorial proceedings concerns those who, even when not relapsed heretics, persist stubbornly in the error of their ways, of which the preacher strives to disabuse them.[120]

The fifth falsehood is the assertion that all conquests of the Indies undertaken to date, even in cases where all relevant directives were duly observed, have been unjust and tyrannical, which is outrageous and, moreover, predicated on a preposterous notion which has been condemned as heretical[121] (in the chapter 'Nulli', dist. 19, in the chapter 'Generali', and in the chapter 'Violatores', 25, q. 1),[122] for it entails arguing that the pope did not have the authority to issue the decree and

of usage in the reference immediately preceding, also at *M*, fol. 38*v*—after an uncharacteristically large space and thus does not belong quite so obviously to the folio page reference). More importantly for our purposes, the rendering of the latter portion of this sentence has gone haywire in Fabié's transcription (followed verbatim by Denisova) and has a fairly substantial omission: see next note.

[119] This passage continues to draw on what Las Casas says in the Eleventh Reply (§13). Note that there is a significant copying error in Fabié's transcription from *M* of the preceding four clauses of this sentence: he appears to have fallen prey to a classic scribal error known as *saut du même au même*, whereby the eye jumps from one identical word to another (in this case, the abbreviation 'Xpianos': 'Christians') repeated later in the same passage, thereby causing the intervening portion of text to be omitted (here in bold: '... *en la vida verdaderamente Xpianos y sin compañia de soldados que el llama tiranos de manera que si no son virtuosos y muy buenos Xpianos los predicatores aunque vayan sin soldados ...* ', *M*, fol. 38*v*). This results in a truncated sentence which he has attempted to render less grammatically curious through adjusted punctuation. Denisova has in turn followed Fabié's transcription exactly and so omits the same portion. By contrast, the translation we offer here renders the full sentence as found on fol. 38*v* of *M*. For more on the phenomenon of *saut du même au même* (an extended form of haplography), see, e.g., L. D. Reynolds and N. G. Wilson, *Scribes and Scholars: A Guide to the Transmission of Greek and Latin Literature*, 4th ed. (Oxford: Oxford University Press, 2013), 227.

[120] The example to which Sepúlveda here refers is offered in the *PT* at §14—the only other occasion on which he draws this particular comparison in any of his Valladolid texts. This in turn constitutes key evidence that the *Declaración* was prepared after, or at least in conjunction with, the main body of the *PT*, to which it stands in inextricable relation. From the reader's perspective, the *Declaración* thus continually presupposes familiarity with, and access to, the *PT* itself.

[121] Here Sepúlveda *does* avail himself of the term 'heresy' ('*heregía*' [*sic*]), which, for the reasons outlined above in n. 113, makes this moment all the more emphatic, for he is now drawing attention to something which really has been formally condemned—a technicality on which he hopes to see Las Casas hoisted.

[122] Gratian, *Decretum*, D. 19, c. 5; C. 25, q. 1, c. 5; C. 25, q. 1, c. 11.

388 SEPÚLVEDA ON THE SPANISH INVASION OF THE AMERICAS

concession which he granted to the Catholic monarchs by means of his bull. The justification for this is that, in the course of his discussion elsewhere,[123] the bishop argues that the pope is quite within his rights to render the Indians subject to the king of Castile so long as those *caciques* who pose no obstacle to preaching or conversion are not deprived of their dominions and, by the same token, that war was not to be waged against them to that end either, and that this is how the bull is to be understood. My answer to this is that, in the printed book at issue here,[124] he [Las Casas] states outright that the church does not have jurisdiction over the infidels and is not to depose or impose rulers upon them and that the latter in turn do not owe obedience, all of which is diametrically at odds with the bull, as I have demonstrated, and his recourse to this proviso stipulating these further conditions is spurious, baseless, and against the terms of the bull, which grants the authority to subjugate those barbarians by warfare if necessary—not so as to punish them for any wrong committed against us but rather because it is the most effective way of getting them to convert, which is the ultimate goal, as exemplified under analogous circumstances by Gennadius, exarch of Africa, whom St Gregory praises so fulsomely (chapter '*Si non*', 23, q. 4).[125] These fallacies, then, are indefensible in the eyes of learned, righteous men, and to resort to special pleading in the bid to justify them *is a sophistical abuse of that aphorism which runs, 'Though Plato is our friend, it nevertheless remains right and proper for our dearer friend to be the truth'.*[126]

---

[123] Las Casas indeed makes this argument not in *Aquí se contiene* but in another of his published treatments of the subject: the *Treinta proposiciones muy jurídicas*—specifically in Propositions 17 and 18, to which Sepúlveda is here alluding. He may also conceivably have had Las Casas's *Tratado comprobatorio* in mind.

[124] Sepúlveda is referring to Las Casas's discussion of this point in the Twelfth Reply (§10) of the much mentioned *Aquí se contiene*. The reason he here respecifies that this is the work meant is because the reference immediately preceding has just pointed the reader to a different Lascasian work—the *Treinta proposiciones*.

[125] Gratian, *Decretum*, C. 23, q. 4, c. 49—Gregory I's letter to Gennadius (1.75 Norberg; 1.73 *PL*).

[126] Sepúlveda is here drawing on a famous maxim, '*Amicus Plato, sed magis amica veritas*' ('Plato is our friend, but an even better friend is the truth'), with roots in Aristotle's *Nicomachean Ethics* (1096a 16–18) and above all in Plato's *Phaedo* (91B). Here, the implication is that Las Casas was effectively availing himself of the sentiment encapsulated in this proverb in claiming that, much though the combined weight of the church fathers and other authorities might point towards one conclusion, it is nonetheless essential to cleave to truth itself and therefore be prepared to dispute textual authority ('Plato') where necessary. Baulking at what he takes to be yet another instance of Lascasian irreverence vis-à-vis the church fathers, Sepúlveda here thus accuses Las Casas of proceeding by the supposed logic of the aphorism in an intolerably sophistical manner. For more on the proverb itself, see Leonardo Tarán, '*Amicus Plato, sed magis amica veritas*: From Plato and Aristotle to Cervantes', *Antike und Abendland* 30/4 (1984): 93–124 (repr. in his Collected Papers, 1962–1999, Leiden: Brill, 2001, 1–46), with particular attention to patterns of usage in the early modern Hispanic context. In general, see also Henry Guerlac, '*Amicus Plato* and Other Friends', *Journal of the History of Ideas* 39/4 (1978): 627–33.

Postscript

From Valladolid to the 'Black Legend'

An avid reading public greeted the appearance of the account of the 1550–51 Valladolid debate that Sebastián Trujillo printed for Las Casas on 10 September 1552, for it appears that an anonymous printer had 'pirated' it before the year was out.[1] But nearly a century passed before *Aquí se contiene* was published again in its entirety—two editions appearing in quick succession. In 1645, the Venetian printer Marco Ginammi issued his Italian translation under the title *Conquista dell'Indie Occidentali*—including the original Spanish in parallel columns (with the Latin passages untranslated and breaking the columnar format). The Republic of Venice's relations with both Spain and the papacy were very strained in this period, and Ginammi was manifestly cashing in on anti-Spanish sentiment among his customers. The following year saw the republication of *Aquí se contiene* in the Iberian Peninsula itself, but under highly fraught circumstances. It appeared with four of the other 1552 Lascasian treatises (with the *Brevísima relación de la destrucción de las Indias* inevitably taking first place) in Barcelona from the printer Antonio Lacavallería, who gave the collection the title *Las obras del Obsipo D. Fray Bartolomé de las Casas, o Casaus*. The year of publication, 1646, was in the midst of the Catalan Revolt against Philip IV (also called *La Guerra de los Segadores,* 1640–52), a secession movement allying Catalonia with France against Castile. As Roger Chartier has noted, 'This 1646 publication of five Las Casas treatises is part of this context of war, and it unites Catalans and Indians as previous or as potential victims of Castilian tyranny.'[2]

---

[1] Anthony Pagden, 'The "School of Salamanca" and the "Affair of the Indies"', *History of Universities* 1 (1981), 71–112, at 94, and at 112n205 he reports that 'the pirated edition has a different border and initials and different lines at the end of the title'. He cites Clive Griffin for this information, but Griffin's own reference to this pirated edition in *The Crombergers of Seville* (105 and n21) cites only Pagden's article! Pagden also referred to this elusive reprint in *The Fall of Natural Man*, 234n5. Web searches readily yield what appear to be multiple copies of both printings, each with colophons claiming that they were printed by Trujillo. Isacio Pérez Fernández, O.P., industriously listed locations of copies of the two printings in his magisterial *Inventario documentado de los escritos de Fray Bartolomé de Las Casas*, revised by Helen Rand Parish (Bayamón: CEDOC, 1981), 593 and 596–601. Pérez referred cautiously to 'otra edición de 1552 distinta de la presente', without either characterizing one as 'pirated' or taking a stand on which of the two (which he labelled 'A' and 'B') came first (and was hence presumably 'official').

[2] Roger Chartier, *Won in Translation: Textual Mobility in Early Modern Europe* (Philadelphia: University of Pennsylvania Press, 2022), 18. On the same page, Chartier discusses the 1645 Venetian edition. Anthony Pagden claimed that *Aquí se contiene* was 'reprinted in Paris in 1646 as part of the French propaganda campaign against Spain' (*The Fall of Natural Man*, 234n5). In 'The "School of Salamanca"', 112n205, cited in support of this is E. Vacas Galindo's 1908 *Fray Bartolomé de*

390 SEPÚLVEDA ON THE SPANISH INVASION OF THE AMERICAS

Thus, both the Venice and Barcelona editions appealed to anti-Castilian fervour in their target audiences and implicitly invited readers to imagine the fate of distant Amerindians as awful premonitions of what might befall Venetians and Catalans in their European homelands. But in pursuing this entrepreneurial publishing strategy, these seventeenth-century editions of the sixteenth-century account of the Valladolid debate were anticipated by a slew of translated extracts that, starting in 1578, appeared in Flemish/Dutch, French, English, German, and Latin. All were implicitly polemical publications, some explicitly marketing themselves as warnings to nervous readers facing possible Spanish aggression and—to use a word common in the titles of these works—'tyranny'. All of these extracts from *Aquí se contiene* were included as supplements to translations of Las Casas's incendiary and harrowing *Brevísima relación*. Thus, these accounts of the debate between Sepúlveda and Las Casas played a supporting role in the *Brevísima relación*'s star performance in the dramatic and lurid 'Black Legend' of Spanish imperialism in early modern Europe.[3]

These translated extracts from our treatise, in editions too numerous to list here in full,[4] can be classified in two groups:

1) The Low Countries tradition

This Flemish/Dutch tradition[5] appended short extracts from two of Las Casas's 'Replies', followed by more extensive extracts from another of Las Casas's 1552 tracts, *Entre los remedios*.[6] This vigorous tradition began with the publication of

---

Lascasas: Disputa o controversia con Ginés de Sepúlveda, but the only reference to a 1646 edition there seems to be on p. ix, where the editor, the Marqués de Olivart, refers to Lacavallería's Barcelona edition.

[3] For the history of the 'Leyenda negra', see the study that named the phenomenon: Julián Juderías, *La leyenda negra y la verdad histórica* (Madrid: 1914); see also William S. Maltby, *The Black Legend in England: The Development of Anti-Spanish Sentiment, 1558–1660* (Durham, NC: Duke University Press, 1971) and Jeremy Lawrance, *Spanish Conquest, Protestant Prejudice: Las Casas and the Black Legend* (Nottingham: Critical, Cultural and Communications Press, 2009).

[4] A useful, though now dated, survey of many of these translations of the *Brevísima relación* is Joseph Sabin, *A Dictionary of Books Relating to America,* vol. 3 (New York: Sabin, 1870), 392–98. The scholarly literature on early modern translations of the *Brevísima relación,* to which extracts from our treatise were appended, is vast. Among the best recent studies are: Lawrance, *Spanish Conquest, Protestant Prejudice*; Rolena Adorno, 'The Not-So-Brief Story of the *Brevísima relación de la destrucción de las Indias*', in *Bartolomé de las Casas, O.P: History, Philosophy, and Theology in the Age of European Expansion,* edited by David Orique, O.P. and Rady Roldán-Figueroa, 29–57 (Leiden and Boston: Brill, 2019); Chartier, *Won in Translation,* ch. 1, 'Publishing: The Seven Lives of the *Brevísima relación de la destrucción de las Indias*', 1–27.

[5] For an extensive survey of early Flemish/Dutch translations of the *Brevísima relación,* see Pieter Anton Tiele, *Mémoire bibliographique sur les journaux des navigateurs néerlandais* (Amsterdam: Frederik Muller, 1867), 319–32.

[6] The extracts from Las Casas's 'Replies' are from the 11th, §2 and beginning of §3 (more Amerindians died as a result of offerings to the Spaniards' 'beloved goddess Greed' than to their own gods) and the 12th, §24 (the Spaniards were not motivated by God or king but by a desire to become tyrants at the expense of royal authority).

POSTSCRIPT: FROM VALLADOLID TO THE 'BLACK LEGEND' 391

Seer cort Verhael vande destructie van d'Indien ... (Antwerp or Brussels, 1578), followed the next year by a reissue under the title *Spieghel der Spaenscher Tirannije* ... , some variation of which title remained standard, beginning with the new edition published by De Jonge in Amsterdam in 1596 and frequently reprinted in subsequent years. In 1620 Jan Cloppenburg in Amsterdam issued not only an edition in Dutch (still using the 1578 translation), but also one in French (*Le miroir de la Tyrannie Espagnole* ...)—both embellished by prints taken from the Frankfurt edition of De Bry (see below). Significantly, these twin Cloppenburg editions of 1620 were divided into two parts: the second was an account of Spanish atrocities in the Low Countries, illustrated 'by a blood-curdling new set of engravings showing tortures and murders of Dutch Protestants'.[7]

2) The Miggrode tradition

We derive this name from Jacques de Miggrode, the Flemish translator responsible for the first translation of Las Casas's *Brevísima relación* into French, published first in Antwerp or Brussels in 1579 and then in Paris in 1582 (reprinted by G. Cartier in Geneva that same year).[8] Miggrode offered in his appendix a much more generous selection of the other 1552 tracts than the 1578 Flemish translation had offered: the 'portion of a letter' to Prince Philip ('Un pedazo de una carta y relación'); the extracts from the *Entre los remedios* included in the 1578 Flemish translation; the prologue to the *Tratado comprobatorio*; and, finally, generous selections from *Aquí se contiene*: Las Casas's 'Argumento', Sepúlveda's preface to his 'Objections', Las Casas's preface to his 'Replies', and the short extracts from the Eleventh and Twelfth Replies included in the Flemish edition of 1578. Miggrode prefaced his translation of the *Brevísima relación* with an eloquent preface offering Las Casas's account as a dire warning for the translator's readers in the Low Countries, suggesting that any weakening of resolve in the face of Spanish imperialism could lead to scenes as harrowing as those Las Casas had evoked of America. Indeed, the edition published in Antwerp (or Brussels) in 1579 makes the point clear as early as the title-page: 'Pour servir d'example & advertissement aux xvii Provinces du pais bas' ('to serve as an example and warning to the 17 Provinces of the Low Countries').

In 1583, a translator still known only as M. M. S. published in London a vigorous English translation of Miggrode's French translation and its appendices, reproducing on the first page of text the words from the Flemish edition of the French translation: 'to serve as a President [precedent] and warning, to the xii [*sic*] Provinces of the lowe Countries'.[9] Though the English translator duly included Miggrode's

---

[7] Lawrance, *Spanish Conquest, Protestant Prejudice*, 31, with sample plates on p. 51.

[8] *Tyrannie et Cruautez des Espagnols, perpetree es Indes Occidentales, qu'on dit Le Nouveau Monde* ... (Antwerp: François de Raveleghien, 1579).

[9] *The Spanish Colonie, or Briefe Chronicle of the Acts and gestes of the Spaniardes in the West Indies* ... (London: William Brome, 1583). Miggrode's name here is mangled as 'James Aliggrodo'.

392 SEPÚLVEDA ON THE SPANISH INVASION OF THE AMERICAS

preface warning of Spanish 'tyranny' in the Low Countries, English subjects of Queen Elizabeth would have had no trouble applying the lesson to themselves in a time of increasing tension with Spain—just five years before the sailing of the Spanish Armada. In 1625, Samuel Purchas included an abridged version of 1583 translation of the *Brevísima relación* in *Purchas his Pilgrimes,* including the extracts from *Aquí se contiene* appended to that translation.[10]

Miggrode's French translation of the *Brevísima relación*—including his selections from *Aquí se contiene*—also formed the basis for the impressive editions that the celebrated printer and engraver Theodor de Bry published in German and Latin in Frankfurt in 1597 (repr. 1599) and 1598 (repr. 1614), vividly illustrated with his engravings of Spain's atrocities in the Americas (illustrations soon adopted, as noted above, in the 'Low Countries tradition').[11] On the title-page of the German edition, De Bry followed Miggrode in offering this material as 'Warnung' and insists that it is being issued in German for the very same purpose as that of the Flemish translator ('ins Hochteutsche umb ebenmässiger Ursachen willen übergesetzt').

Thus, substantial portions of *Aquí se contiene* played a strong supporting role in the development of the so-called 'Black Legend' (*Leyenda negra*) of Spanish tyranny and atrocities in the New World—and the Low Countries—by way of translations of extracts in Flemish/Dutch, French, English, German, and Latin. Also, as noted above, the two complete seventeenth-century translations of the treatise played their own role, in Venice and Catalonia, in the passionate tradition of anti-Castilian propaganda in early modern Europe—indicating that the 'Black Legend' was by no means confined to Protestants.

An echo of this European career of *Aquí se contiene* can be detected, we suspect, in a pronouncement delivered 'with great emotion' by Samuel Johnson to his supper-mate James Boswell in London's Turk's Head coffee-house on 28 July 1763: 'I love the University of Salamancha; for when the Spaniards were in doubt as to the lawfulness of their conquering America, the University of Salamancha gave it as their opinion that it was not lawful.'[12] While Johnson is unlikely to have

---

[10] Samuel Purchas, *Purchas his Pilgrimes* (London: William Stansby, 1625), The Fourth Part, Bk. 8 ch. 4, 1567–603. The extracts from *Aquí se contiene* are on pp. 1601–03. For a helpful discussion of Purchas's use of these Lascasian texts, see Jonathan Hart, *Representing the New World: The English and French Uses of the Example of Spain* (New York and Basingstoke: Palgrave, 2000), 218–22. For Purchas's use of José de Acosta, see pp. 79–84 of Andrew Fitzmaurice, 'The Salamanca School in England', ch. 2 of *Sovereignty, Property and Empire, 1500–2000* (Cambridge: Cambridge University Press, 2014), a perceptive study that transcends the usual focus on the 'Black Legend'.

[11] *Wahrhaftige Anzeigung der Hispanier grewlichen, abschewlichen und unmenschlichen Tyranney, von ihnen in den indianischen Länder ... begangen* (Frankfurt: De Bry, 1597); *Narratio Regionum Indicarum per Hispanos quosdam devastatarum verissima* (Frankfurt: De Bry, 1598).

[12] James Boswell, *Boswell's Life of Johnson,* edited by George Birkbeck Hill, revised and enlarged by L. F. Powell (Oxford: Clarendon Press, 1934), vol. 1, 455. In a note in Appendix G on p. 550, Powell pointed out that the University of Salamanca's decision was limited to Sepúlveda's book, and he cited Fabié on Las Casas, Bell on Sepúlveda, and Menéndez Pelayo's edition of the *Democrates secundus,* none of which, of course, was available to Johnson. Powell ventures no guess as to the source of Johnson's awareness of the 'Affair of the Indies'.

POSTSCRIPT: FROM VALLADOLID TO THE 'BLACK LEGEND'   393

come across a copy of the 1583 *Spanish Colonie*, and the subsequent two English translations of the *Brevísima relación* of 1656 and 1689 did not include the supplemental material, Johnson had surely dipped into the enticing pages of *Purchas his Pilgrimes*—which later famously served as the inspiration for Coleridge's 'Kubla Khan'.[13] There, on p. 1602 of The Fourth Part, he would have read this version of Las Casas's words from the 'Argumento' of *Aquí*: 'The Lords of the Royall Counsaile of Castile, as wise and just Judges, determined therefore to send the said Booke to the Universities of Salamanca and Alcala, the matter being for the most part therein Theologically handled, with commandement to examine it, and if it might be printed, to signe it: which Universities after many exact and diligent disputations, concluded, that it might not be printed, as contayning corrupt doctrine'. This, it seems to us, is the most likely source of Doctor Johnson's memorable outburst. Thus, what has become surely the most famous pronouncement in English on the 'Affair of the Indies' is revealed as a belated response to the still controversial and endlessly troubling intervention of Juan Ginés de Sepúlveda in the question of the justice of the Spanish invasion of the Americas.

---

[13] The first post-1583 English translator of the *Brevísma relación* was John Milton's nephew John Phillips, who dedicated it to Lord Protector Cromwell in support of his Caribbean ambitions: *The Tears of the Indians* (London: Nathaniel Brook, 1656). A year after the Glorious Revolution, an anonymous translation appeared under the stirring title, *Popery Truly Display'd in Its Bloody Colours* (London: R. Hewson, 1689). Perhaps it shouldn't be surprising that in 1898, amidst the propaganda war against Spain preceding and during the Spanish–American War, Phillips's translation was reissued, abridged, and illustrated with illustrations from De Bry by the New York publisher J. Boller, under the title, *An Historical and True Account of the Cruel Massacre and Slaughter of 20,000,000 People in the West Indies by the Spaniards* (adapted from the subtitle of *Tears of the Indians*), but sporting on its front cover a more timely alternate title, over a De Bry illustration: *Horrible Atrocities of Spaniards in Cuba*.

Bibliography of Post-1492 Works

Abril-Castelló, Vidal, 'La bipolarización Sepúlveda–Las Casas y sus consecuencias: La revolución de la duodécima replica', in *La ética en la conquista de América*, edited by Demetrio Ramos et al., 229–88 (Madrid: Consejo Superior de Investigaciones Científicas, 1984).

Adorno, Rolena, *The Polemics of Possession in Spanish American Narrative* (New Haven: Yale University Press, 2007).

Adorno, Rolena, 'The Not-So-Brief Story of the *Brevísima relación de la destrucción de las Indias*', in *Bartolomé de las Casas, O.P.: History, Philosophy, and Theology in the Age of European Expansion*, edited by David Orique, O.P. and Rady Roldán-Figueroa, 29–57 (Leiden and Boston: Brill, 2019).

Allemann, Daniel, 'Empire and the Right to Preach the Gospel in the School of Salamanca, 1535–1560', *The Historical Journal* 62/1 (2019): 35–55.

Andrés Marcos, Teodoro, *Los imperialismos de Juan Ginés de Sepúlveda en su Democrates Alter* (Madrid: Instituto de Estudios Políticos, 1947).

Anghie, Antony, *Imperialism, Sovereignty and the Making of International Law* (Cambridge: Cambridge University Press, 2005).

Baccelli, Luca, 'Nihil humanum a me alienum puto: Sepúlveda e l'umanità degli Indios', in *Guerra giusta e schiavitù naturale: Juan Ginés de Sepúlveda e il dibattito sulla Conquista*, edited by Marco Geuna, 89–116 (Milan: Edizioni Biblioteca Francescana, 2014).

Bartelson, Jens, *War in International Thought* (Cambridge: Cambridge University Press, 2018).

Bell, Aubrey F. G., *Juan Ginés de Sepúlveda* (Oxford: Oxford University Press, 1925).

Bellido Díaz, José Antonio, '*Indefessae labor limae Sepulvedanae* en los libros 19 y 20 de la *De rebus gestis Caroli Quinti historia*', *Exemplaria classica* 12 (2008): 195–248.

Benjamin, Katie Marie, *A Semipelagian in King Charles's Court: Juan Ginés de Sepúlveda on Nature, Grace, and the Conquest of the Americas* (Th.D. diss., Duke University Divinity School, 2017).

Benton, Lauren, Adam Clulow, and Bain Attwood (eds), *Protection and Empire: A Global History* (Cambridge: Cambridge University Press, 2018).

Berger, Adolf, *Encyclopedic Dictionary of Roman Law: Transactions of the American Philosophical Society*, vol. 45, pt. 2 (Philadelphia: 1953).

Blaise, Albert, *Lexicon Latinitatis Medii Aevi (Corpus Christianorum)* (Turnhout: Brepols, 1975).

Boswell, James, *The Life of Samuel Johnson*, edited by *George Birkbeck Hill*, revised and enlarged by L. F. Powell, vol. 1 (Oxford: Clarendon Press, 1934).

Bradbury, Scott, 'Constantine and the Problem of Anti-Pagan Legislation in the Fourth Century', *Classical Philology* 89/2 (1994): 120–39.

396 BIBLIOGRAPHY

Briancesco, Eduardo, et al., *Caminando hacia el tercer milenio: evangelización y liberación* (Buenos Aires: Ediciones Paulinas, 1986)

Brown, P. R. L., 'St. Augustine's Attitude to Religious Coercion', *Journal of Roman Studies* 54/1-2 (1964): 107-16.

Brunstetter, Daniel R., and Dana Zartner, 'Just War against Barbarians: Revisiting the Valladolid Debates between Sepúlveda and Las Casas', *Political Studies* 59/3 (2011): 733-52.

Cajetan (Tommaso de Vio Gaetano), 'Commentary on Aquinas's Summa Theologica', in *Sancti Thomae Aquinatis ... Opera Omnia Iussu Impensaque Leonis XIII P.M. Edita*, vol. 8 and 9 (Rome: Typographia Polyglotta, 1895 and 1897).

Campos, Edmund Valentine, 'West of Eden: American Gold, Spanish Greed, and the Discourse of English Imperialism', in *Rereading the Black Legend: The Discourses of Religious and Racial Difference in the Renaissance Empires*, edited by Margaret R. Greer, Walter D. Mignolo, and Maureen Quilligan, 247-69 (Chicago: University of Chicago Press, 2017).

Cañizares-Esguerra, Jorge. 'The "Iberian" Justifications of Territorial Possession by Pilgrims and Puritans in the Colonization of America', in *Entangled Empires: The Anglo-Iberian Atlantic, 1500-1830*, edited by Jorge Cañizares-Esguerra, 161-77 (Philadelphia: University of Pennsylvania Press, 2018).

Cano, Melchor, 'De dominio Indorum', in *Corpus Hispanorum de Pace*, vol. 9, edited by Luciano Pereña, 555-81 (Madrid: Consejo Superior de Investigaciones Científicas, 1982).

Carman, Glen, 'Human Sacrifice and Natural Law in Las Casas's *Apologia*', *Colonial Latin American Review* 25/3 (2016): 278-99.

Carranza, Bartolomé de, 'Ratione fidei potest Caesar debellare et tenere Indos novi orbis?', in *Misión de España en América: 1540-1560*, edited by Luciano Pereña Vicente, 38-57 (Madrid: Consejo Superior de Investigaciones Científicas, 1956).

Carro, Venancio Diego, *La teología y los teólogos-juristas españoles ante la conquista de América*, 2nd ed. (Salamanca: Biblioteca de Teólogos Españoles, 1951).

'Carta del Consejo de Indias a Su Majestad el Rey sobre la Prohibición de las Conquistas en la Junta de Valladolid [1554]', in *Corpus Hispanorum de Pace*, vol. 8, edited and translated by Luciano Pereña et al., 320-24 (Madrid: Consejo Superior de Investigaciones Científicas, 1984).

Cassi, Aldo Andrea, *Ultramar: L'invenzione europea del nuovo mondo* (Rome-Bari: 2007).

Castilla Urbano, Francisco, 'La consideración del indio en los escritos sepulvedianos posteriores a la Junta de Valladolid', *Cuadernos Americanos* 142 (2012/14): 55-81.

Castilla Urbano, Francisco, *El pensamiento de Juan Ginés de Sepúlveda: Vida activa, humanismo y guerra en el Renacimiento* (Madrid: Centro de Estudios Políticos y Constitucionales, 2013).

Castilla Urbano, Francisco, 'The Debate of Valladolid (1550-1551): Background, Discussions, and Results of the Debate between Juan Ginés de Sepúlveda and Bartolomé de las Casas', in *A Companion to Early Modern Spanish Imperial Political and Social Thought*, edited by Jörg Alejandro Tellkamp, 222-51 (Leiden: Brill, 2020).

Castro, Alfonso de, *De iusta haereticorum punitione* (Antwerp: 1568).

Cerdá y Rico, Francisco, et al., 'De vita et scriptis Joannis Genesiae Sepulvedae', in *Juan Ginés de Sepúlveda, Opera, cum edita, tum inedita, accurante Regia historiae academia*, vol. 1, i-cxliii (Madrid: Academia de la Historia, 1780).

Chartier, Roger, *Won in Translation: Textual Mobility in Early Modern Europe*, translated by John H. Pollack (Philadelphia: University of Pennsylvania Press, Material Texts Series, 2022).

Clayton, Lawrence A., *Bartolomé de las Casas: A Biography* (Cambridge: Cambridge University Press, 2012).

Clayton, Lawrence A., and David M. Lantigua (eds), *Bartolomé de las Casas and the Defense of Amerindian Rights: A Brief History with Documents* (Tuscaloosa: University of Alabama Press, 2020).

Coroleu Lletget, Alejandro, 'The *Fortuna* of Juan Ginés de Sepúlveda's Translations of Aristotle and of Alexander of Aphrodisias', *Journal of the Warburg and Courtauld Institutes* 59 (1996): 325–32.

Coroleu Lletget, Alejandro, 'Introducción filológica', in Juan Ginés de Sepúlveda, *Obras completas, vol. 3: Demócrates Segundo*, edited by Alejandro Coroleu Lletget, clviii–clxxx (Pozoblanco: Ayuntamiento de Pozoblanco, 1997).

Coroleu Lletget, Alejandro, and Julián Solana Pujalte, 'Un nuevo manuscrito del *Democrates secundus sive de iustis belli causis* de Juan Ginés de Sepúlveda', *Analecta Malacitana* 20/1 (1997): 127–31.

Covarrubias, Diego de, 'De iustitia belli adversus indos', in *Corpus Hispanorum de Pace*, vol. 6, edited and translated by Luciano Pereña et al., 343–63 (Madrid: Consejo Superior de Investigaciones Científicas, 1981).

Covarrubias Orozco, Sebastián de, *Tesoro de la lengua castellana o española*, edited by Felipe C. R. Maldonado and Manuel Camarero (Madrid: Editorial Castalia, 1995).

Davenport, Frances Gardiner, *European Treaties Bearing on the History of the United States and Its Dependencies to 1648* (Washington, D.C: Carnegie Institute of Washington, 1917).

De la Torre y del Cerro, Antonio (ed.), *Testamentaria de Isabel la Católica* (Barcelona: Vda. Fidel Rodríguez Ferrán, 1974)

Denisova, Natalia K., *Proposiciones temerarias: Recopilación de textos de Juan Ginés de Sepúlveda, Bartolomé de Las Casas y Domingo de Soto que tratan del debate del Nuevo Mundo* (Madrid: Fundación Universitaria Española, 2019).

Encinas, Diego de, *Libro Primero de Provisiones, Cédulas, Capítulos, y Cartas ... tocantes al buen govierno de las Indias* (Madrid: Imprenta Real, 1596).

Erasmus, Desiderius, *Collected Works of Erasmus: Volume 84: Controversies with Albert Pio*, edited by Nelson H. Minnich (Toronto: University of Toronto Press, 2005).

Evans, Robert F., *Four Letters of Pelagius* (London: Black, 1968).

Fabié, A. M., *Vida y escritos de Fray Bartolomé de las Casas, Obispo de Chiapas*, vols. 1 and 2 (Madrid: Miguel Ginesta, 1879).

Fernández-Santamaría, J. A., *The State, War, and Peace: Spanish Political Thought in the Renaissance 1516–1559* (Cambridge: Cambridge University Press, 1977).

Fitzmaurice, Andrew, *Humanism and America: An Intellectual History of English Colonization, 1500–1625* (Cambridge: Cambridge University Press, 2003).

Fitzmaurice, Andrew, *Sovereignty, Property and Empire, 1500–2000* (Cambridge: Cambridge University Press, 2014).

Gentili, Alberico, *De jure belli libri tres*, vol. 2, translated by John C. Rolfe (Oxford: Clarendon Press, 1933).

Geuna, Marco (ed.), *Guerra giusta e schiavitù naturale: Juan Ginés de Sepúlveda e il dibattito sulla Conquista* (Milan: Edizioni Biblioteca Francescana, 2014).

398 BIBLIOGRAPHY

Geuna, Marco, 'Ripensare Sepúlveda e la tradizione della guerra giusta', in *Guerra giusta e schiavitù naturale: Juan Ginés de Sepúlveda e il dibattito sulla Conquista*, edited by Marco Geuna, v–xviii (Milan: Edizioni Biblioteca Francescana, 2014).

Glanville, Luke, *Sovereignty and the Responsibility to Protect: A New History* (Chicago: University of Chicago Press, 2014).

Glanville, Luke, *Sharing Responsibility: The History and Future of Protection from Atrocities* (Princeton: Princeton University Press, 2021).

Gong, Gerrit W., *The Standard of 'Civilization' in International Society* (Oxford: Clarendon Press, 1984).

Gould, Eliga H., 'Entangled Histories, Entangled Worlds: The English-Speaking Atlantic as a Spanish Periphery', *American Historical Review* 112/3 (2007): 764–86.

Griffin, Clive, *The Crombergers of Seville: The History of a Printing and Merchant Dynasty* (Oxford: Clarendon Press, 1988).

Grotius, Hugo, *De jure belli ac pacis libris tres*, vol. 2, edited by Francis W. Kelsey (Oxford: Clarendon Press, 1925).

Guerlac, Henry, '*Amicus Plato* and Other Friends', *Journal of the History of Ideas* 39/4 (1978): 627–33.

Gutiérrez, Gustavo, *Las Casas: In Search of the Poor of Jesus Christ* (Maryknoll, NY: Orbis, 1993).

Hanke, Lewis, *The Spanish Struggle for Justice in the Conquest of America* (American Historical Association, 1949).

Hanke, Lewis, *Aristotle and the American Indians: A Study in Race Prejudice in the Modern World* (Chicago: Henry Regnery, 1959).

Hart, Jonathan, *Representing the New World: The English and French Uses of the Example of Spain* (New York and Basingstoke: Palgrave, 2000).

Hernández, Ramón, O.P., 'Los tratados impresos por Bartolomé de las Casas', in Bartolomé de las Casas, *Obras completas, vol. 10: Tratados de 1552*, edited by Ramón Hernández O.P. and Lorenzo Galmés O.P., 1–21 (Madrid: Alianza, 1992).

Herzog, Tamar, 'How Did Early-Modern Slaves in Spain Disappear? The Antecedents', *Republic of Letters* 3/1 (2012): 1–7.

Humphries, Mark, 'Rufinus' Eusebius: Translation, Continuation, and Edition in the Latin Ecclesiastical History', *Journal of Early Christian Studies* 16/2 (2008): 143–64.

Jones, Ellen, *Literature in Motion: Translating Multilingualism across the Americas* (New York: Columbia University Press, 2022).

Juderías, Julián, *La leyenda negra y la verdad histórica* (Madrid: Tipografía de la Rev. de Arch., Bibl. y Museos, 1914).

Kinsella, Helen, *The Image before the Weapon: A Critical History of the Distinction between Combatant and Civilian* (Ithaca, NY: Cornell University Press, 2011).

Kolb, Robert, 'Origin of the Twin Terms *jus ad bellum/jus in bello*', *International Review of the Red Cross* 37/320 (1997): 553–62.

Kristeller, Paul Oskar, *Renaissance Thought: The Classic, Scholastic, and Humanist Strains* (New York: Harper Torchbooks, 1961).

Kristeller, Paul Oskar, *Eight Philosophers of the Italian Renaissance* (Stanford: Stanford University Press, 1964).

BIBLIOGRAPHY 399

Kristeller, Paul Oskar, *Iter Italicum: A Finding List of Uncatalogued or Incompletely Catalogued Humanistic Manuscripts of the Renaissance in Italian and other Libraries, Vol. 2: Italy: Orvieto to Volterra [and] Vatican City* (Leiden: Brill, 1967).

Lantigua, David M., 'The Freedom of the Gospel: Aquinas, Subversive Natural Law, and the Spanish War of Religion', *Modern Theology* 31/2 (2015): 312–37.

Lantigua, David, 'Religion within the Limits of Natural Reason: The Case of Human Sacrifice', in *Bartolomé de las Casas, O.P: History, Philosophy, and Theology in the Age of European Expansion*, edited by David Thomas Orique, O.P. and Rady Roldán-Figueroa, 280–309 (Leiden: Brill, 2018).

Lantigua, David M., *Infidels and Empires in a New World Order: Early Modern Spanish Contributions to International Legal Thought* (Cambridge: Cambridge University Press, 2020).

Las Casas, Bartolomé de, *Conquista dell' Indie Occidentali di Monsignor Fra Bartolomeo dalle Case* (Venice: Marco Ginammi, 1645).

Las Casas, Bartolomé de, *Aquí se contiene una disputa o controversia....* (Barcelona: Antonio Lacavallería, 1646).

Las Casas, Bartolomé de, *Obras escogidas de Fray Bartolomé de las Casas: Opúsculos, cartas, memoriales*, vol. 5, edited by Juan Pérez de Tudela Bueso (Madrid: Ediciones Atlas, 1958).

Las Casas, Bartolomé de, *Tratados de Fray Bartolomé de las Casas*, vol. 1, transcribed by Juan Pérez de Tudela Bueso with prologues by Lewis Hanke and Manuel Giménez Fernández (Mexico City: Fondo de Cultura Económica, 1965, repr. 1974 & 1997).

Las Casas, Bartolomé de, *History of the Indies*, translated and abridged by Andrée M. Collard (New York: Harper & Row, 1971).

Las Casas, Bartolomé de, 'Carta a los Dominicos de Chiapa y Guatemala acerca de las ventas de las encomiendas del Perú [1563]', in *Corpus Hispanorum de Pace*, vol. 8, edited and translated by Luciano Pereña et al., 235–50 (Madrid: Consejo Superior de Investigaciones Científicas, 1984).

Las Casas, Bartolomé de, *A Short Account of the Destruction of the Indies*, edited and translated by Nigel Griffin with an introduction by Anthony Pagden (London: Penguin, 1992).

Las Casas, Bartolomé de, Aquí se contienen treinta proposiciones muy jurídicas, edited by Ramón Hernández O.P., in *Bartolomé de las Casas: Obras completas*, vol. 10: Tratados de 1552, edited by Ramón Hernández O.P. and Lorenzo Galmés O.P., 197–214 (Madrid: Alianza, 1992).

Las Casas, Bartolomé de, *Aquí se contienen unos avisos y reglas para los confesores*, edited by Lorenzo Galmés, in *Bartolomé de las Casas, Obras completas, vol. 10: Tratados de 1552*, edited by Ramón Hernández O.P. and Lorenzo Galmés O.P., 367–88 (Madrid: Alianza, 1992).

Las Casas, Bartolomé de, *Tratado comprobatorio del imperio soberano*, edited by Ramón Hernández O.P., in *Bartolomé de las Casas, Obras completas, vol. 10: Tratados de 1552*, edited by Ramón Hernández O.P. and Lorenzo Galmés O.P., 391–543 (Madrid: Alianza, 1992).

Las Casas, Bartolomé de, *In Defense of the Indians*, edited and translated by Stafford Poole (DeKalb, IL: Northern Illinois University Press, 1992).

400 BIBLIOGRAPHY

Las Casas, Bartolomé de, *The Only Way*, edited by Helen Rand Parish, translated by Francis Patrick Sullivan, S.J. (New York: Paulist Press, 1992).

Las Casas, Bartolomé de, 'Historia de las Indias', in *Obras Completas*, vols. 3–5, edited by Miguel Ángel Medina, with introductory material by Jesús Angel Barreda and Isacio Pérez Fernández (Madrid: Alianza, 1994).

Lawrance, Jeremy, *Spanish Conquest, Protestant Prejudice: Las Casas and the Black Legend* (Nottingham: Critical, Cultural and Communications Press, 2009).

Lilao Franca, Óscar, and Carmen Castrillo González (eds), *Catálogo de manuscritos de la Biblioteca Universitaria de Salamanca. Vol. II: Manuscritos 1680–2777* (Salamanca: Ediciones de la Universidad, 2002).

Liso, Saverio di, *Bartolomé de Las Casas, Juan Ginés de Sepúlveda: La controversia sugli indios* (Bari: Edizioni di Pagina, 2016).

Llorente, Juan Antonio, *Histoire critique de l'Inquisition d'Espagne,* vol. 2 (Paris: 1817).

Locke, John, *Two Treatises of Government*, edited by Peter Laslett (Cambridge: Cambridge University Press, 1960).

Losada, Ángel, *Juan Ginés de Sepúlveda: a través de su 'Epistolario' y nuevos documentos* (Madrid: Consejo Superior de Investigaciones Científicas, 1949; repr. 1973).

Losada, Ángel, 'Introducción', in *Juan Ginés de Sepúlveda: Democrates Segundo, o de las justas causas de la guerra contra los Indios*, edited by Ángel Losada, vii–xxxii (Madrid: CSIC, Instituto Francisco de Vitoria, 1951; repr. 1984).

Lupher, David A., *Romans in a New World: Classical Models in Sixteenth-Century Spanish America* (Ann Arbor: University of Michigan Press, 2003).

Mair, John, *In secundum Sententiarum* (Paris: Jodocus Badius (Ascensius) and Jean Petit, 1510).

Maltby, William S., *The Black Legend in England: The Development of Anti-Spanish Sentiment, 1558–1660* (Durham, NC: Duke University Press, 1971).

Mansi, Gian Domenico, *Sacrorum conciliorum nova et amplissima collection*, vol. 23 (Venice: Antonio Zatta, 1779).

Mazzolini, Silvestro, *Summa summarum quae Sylvestrina dicitur* (Bologna, 1515).

Mégret, Frédéric, 'From "Savages" to "Unlawful Combatants": A Postcolonial Look at International Humanitarian Law's "Other"', in *International Law and Its Others*, edited by Anne Orford, 265–317 (Cambridge: Cambridge University Press, 2006).

Menéndez y Pelayo, Marcelino, 'Advertencia preliminar', *Boletín de la Real Academia de la Historia* 21/4 (1892): 257–59.

Moorhead, John, *History of the Vandal Persecution* (Liverpool: Liverpool University Press, 1992)

Moreno Hernández, Antonio, 'Introducción' to the edition of the Apologia, in Juan Ginés de Sepúlveda, *Obras completas*, vol. 3, cxxviii–clxxxvi (Pozoblanco: Ayuntamiento de Pozoblanco, 1997).

Morison, Samuel Eliot (ed.), *Journals and Other Documents on the Life and Voyages of Christopher Columbus* (New York: Heritage Press, 1963).

Moyn, Samuel, *Humane: How the United States Abandoned Peace and Reinvented War* (New York: Farrar, Straus and Giroux, 2021).

Muldoon, James, *Popes, Lawyers, and Infidels* (Philadelphia: University of Pennsylvania Press, 1979).

BIBLIOGRAPHY 401

Muñoz Machado, Santiago, *Sepúlveda, Cronista del Emperador* (Barcelona: Edhasa, 2012).

Mylius, Arnold, 'De vita scriptisque … Sepulvedae', in Juan Ginés de Sepúlveda, *Ioannis Genesii Sepulvedae Cordubensis … Opera quae reperiri potuerunt Omnia*, unpaginated (Köln: Arnold Mylius in Officina Birckmannica, 1602).

Nájera, Luna, 'Masculinity, War, and Pursuit of Glory in Sepúlveda's *Gonzalo*', *Hispanic Review* 80/3 (2012): 391–412.

Navarrete, Martín Fernández de, *Colección de los viajes y descubrimientos que hicieron por mar los españoles desde fines del siglo XV*, vol. 2 (Madrid: Imprensa Real ,1825).

O'Driscoll, Cian, 'Re-negotiating the Just War: The Invasion of Iraq and Punitive War', *Cambridge Review of International Affairs* 19/3 (2006): 405–20.

O'Gorman, Edmundo, 'Estudio preliminar', in *Bartolomé de las Casas: Apologética historia sumaria*, vol. 1, edited by Edmundo O'Gorman, xxi–xxxvi (Mexico City: Universidad Nacional Autónoma de México, Instituto de Investigaciones Históricas, 1967).

Orford, Anne, 'Jurisdiction without Territory: From the Holy Roman Empire to the Responsibility to Protect', *Michigan Journal of International Law* 30/3 (2009): 981–1015.

Orique, David Thomas, O.P., *To Heaven or To Hell: Bartolomé de las Casas's Confesionario* (University Park, PA: Pennsylvania State University Press, 2018).

de Osma, Pedro, and Fernando de Roa, *Comentario a la Política de Aristóteles*, vol. 1, edited by José Labajos Alonso (Salamanca: Universidad Pontífica de Salamanca, 2007).

Oviedo, Gonzalo Fernández de, *La historia general de las Indias* (Seville: 1535; repr. Salamanca, 1547).

Pagden, Anthony, 'The "School of Salamanca" and the "Affair of the Indies" ', *History of Universities* 1 (1981): 71–112.

Pagden, Anthony, *The Fall of Natural Man: The American Indian and the Origins of Comparative Ethnology* (Cambridge: Cambridge University Press, 1982; rev. 1986).

Pagden, Anthony, *The Burdens of Empire: 1539 to the Present* (Cambridge: Cambridge University Press, 2015).

Pagden, Anthony, and Jeremy Lawrance, 'Introduction', in *Vitoria, Political Writings*, edited and translated by Anthony Pagden and Jeremy Lawrance, xiii–xxviii (Cambridge: Cambridge University Press, 1991).

Pagden, Anthony, and Jeremy Lawrance, 'Glossary', in *Vitoria, Political Writings*, edited and translated by Anthony Pagden and Jeremy Lawrance, 369–82 (Cambridge: Cambridge University Press, 1991).

Parry, J. H., and Robert G. Keith (eds), *New Iberian World: A Documentary History of the Discovery and Settlement of Latin America to the Early Seventeenth Century, vol. 1, The Conquerors and the Conquered* (New York: New York Times Books, 1984).

Pérez Fernández, Isacio, O.P., *Inventario documentado de los escritos de Fray Bartolomé de las Casas*, revised by Helen Rand Parish (Bayamón, P. R.: Centro de Estudios de los Dominicos del Caribe, 1981).

Pérez Martín, Antonio, *Proles Aegidiana*, vol. 2 (Bologna: Publicaciones del Real Colegio de España, 1979).

Pietropaoli, Stefano, 'Las Casas e Sepúlveda: due modelli del diritto internazionale moderno', in Marco Geuna (ed.), *Guerra giusta e schiavitù naturale: Juan Ginés de Sepúlveda e il dibattito sulla Conquista*, 157–68 (Milan: Edizioni Biblioteca Francescana, 2014).

402 BIBLIOGRAPHY

Pietschmann, Horst, 'Aristotelischer Humanismus und Inhumanität? Sepúlveda und die amerikanische Ureinwohner', in *Humanismus und Neue Welt*, edited by Wolfgang Reinhard, 143–66 (Weinheim: VCH, 1987).

Pike, Frederick B. (ed.), *Latin American History: Select Problems* (New York: Harcourt, Brace, and World, 1969).

Pomponazzi, Pietro, 'On the Immortality of the Soul', translated by William Henry Hay II, revised by John Herman Randall Jr, with an introduction by John Herman Randall Jr and annotations by Paul Oskar Kristeller, in *The Renaissance Philosophy of Man*, edited by Ernst Cassirer, Paul Oskar Kristeller, and John Herman Randall Jr, 257–381 (Chicago: University of Chicago Press, 1948).

Poole, Stafford, 'Preface', in *Bartolomé de las Casas: In Defense of the Indians*, edited and translated by Stafford Poole, xix–xxvi (DeKalb, IL: Northern Illinois University Press, 1992).

Pufendorf, Samuel, *Of the Law of Nature and Nations*, translated by Basil Kennett (London: 1729).

Purchas, Samuel, *Purchas his Pilgrimes: The Fourth Part* (London: William Stansby, 1625).

Quirk, Robert E., 'Some Notes on a Controversial Controversy: Juan Ginés de Sepúlveda and Natural Servitude', *Hispanic American Historical Review* 34/3 (1954): 357–64.

Real Academia de la Historia, *Catálogo de la colección de D. Juan Bautista Muñoz*, vol. 1 (Madrid: Real Academia de la Historia, 1954).

Reynolds, L. D., and N. G. Wilson, *Scribes and Scholars: A Guide to the Transmission of Greek and Latin Literature*, 4th ed. (Oxford: Oxford University Press, 2013).

Rivera, Luis N., *A Violent Evangelism: The Political and Religious Conquest of the Americas* (Louisville, KY: Westminster/John Knox, 1992).

Roca, Pedro, *Catálogo de los manuscritos que pertenecieron a D. Pascual de Gayangos existentes hoy en la Biblioteca Nacional* (Madrid: Tipografía de la Revista de Archivos, Bibliotecas y Museos, 1904).

Roland, G., *Quartus tomus operum Divi Ioannis Chrysotomi* ... (Paris: 1546).

Russell, Alexander, *Conciliarism and Heresy in 15th-Century England* (Cambridge: Cambridge University Press, 2017).

Sabin, Joseph, *A Dictionary of Books Relating to America*, vol. 3 (New York: Sabin, 1870).

Salter, Mark B., *Barbarians and Civilization in International Relations* (London: Pluto Press, 2002).

Sánchez Gásquez, Joaquín J., 'La *Pro Alberto Pio Carpensi, Antapologia in Erasmum Roterodamum* de Juan Ginés de Sepúlveda: Testimonio de una singular asímilación cultural y retrato de un humanista', *Humanistica Lovaniensia* 47 (1998): 75–99.

Sanderlin, George, *Bartolomé de las Casas: A Selection of His Writings* (New York: Knopf, 1971).

Sanz Tapia, Ángel, 'Juan Ginés de Sepúlveda: *Propossiçiones Temerarias, Escandalosas* ...' , in *AA. VV., Cisneros y el Siglo de Oro de la Universidad de Alcalá*, 249–51 (Universidad de Alcalá: Centro Internacional de Estudios Históricos 'Cisneros' / Fundación General de la Universidad de Alcalá, 1999).

Schäfer, Christian, 'La *Política* de Aristóteles y el Aristotelismo político de la conquista', *Ideas y valores* 119 (2002): 109–35.

Schäfer, Christian, 'Einleitung', in *Juan Ginés de Sepúlveda, Democrates secundus / Zweiter Demokrates*, edited, translated, and introduced by Christian Schäfer, xiii–lxxiv (Stuttgart-Bad Cannstatt: Frommann-Holzboog, 2018).

BIBLIOGRAPHY   403

Schäfer, Christian, 'Conquista and the Just War', in *A Companion to Early Modern Spanish Imperial Political and Social Thought*, edited by Jörg Alejandro Tellkamp, 199–221 (Leiden: Brill, 2020).

Schenk, Richard, O.P., '*Omnis Christi actio nostra est instructio*: The Deeds and Sayings of Jesus as Revelation in the View of Thomas Aquinas', in *La doctrine de la révélation divine de saint Thomas d'Aquin*, edited by Léon Elders, 104–31 (Rome: Pontificia Accademia di San Tommaso d'Aquino / Libreria Editrice Vaticana, 1990).

Schwartz, Daniel, 'The Principle of the Defence of the Innocent and the Conquest of America: "Save Those Dragged Towards Death"', *Journal of the History of International Law* 9/2 (2007): 263–91.

Sepúlveda, Juan Ginés de, *Ioannis Genesii Sepulvedae Cordubensis … Opera quae reperiri potuerunt Omnia* (Köln: Arnold Mylius in Officina Birckmannica, 1602).

Sepúlveda, Juan Ginés de, *Opera, cum edita, tum inedita, accurante Regia historiae academia* (Madrid: Imprenta Real de la Gaceta, 1780).

Sepúlveda, Juan Ginés de, *Democrates Alter, sive de justis belli causis apud Indos*, edited by Marcelino Menéndez y Pelayo, *Boletín de la Real Academía de Historia* 21/4 (1892): 257–369.

Sepúlveda, Juan Ginés de, *Tratado sobre las justas causas de la guerra contra los indios* (México: FCE, 1941, repr. 1979 and 1996).

Sepúlveda, Juan Ginés de, *Democrates Segundo, o de las justas causas de la guerra contra los Indios*, edited by Ángel Losada (Madrid: CSIC, Instituto Francisco de Vitoria, 1951; repr. 1984).

Sepúlveda, Juan Ginés de, 'Postreros apuntamientos que dio Sepúlveda en la congregación', in *Bartolomé de las Casas, Tratado de Indias y el doctor Sepúlveda*, edited by Manuel Giménez Fernández, 29–31 (Caracas: Fuentes para la Historia Colonial de Venezuela, 1962, repr. 1988).

Sepúlveda, Juan Ginés de, 'Dialog über die gerechten Kriegsgründe', translated by Dietmar Schmitz, in *Der Griff nach der neuen Welt*, edited by Christoph Strosetzki, 210–69 (Frankfurt: Fischer, 1991).

Sepúlveda, Juan Ginés de, *Obras completas, vol. 9.1: Epistolario*, edited by Ignacio J. García Pinilla and Julián Solana Pujalte (Pozoblanco: Ayuntamiento de Pozoblanco, 1997).

Sepúlveda, Juan Ginés de, *Obras completas, vol. 9.2: Epistolario*, edited by Ignacio J. García Pinilla and Julián Solana Pujalte (Pozoblanco: Ayuntamiento de Pozoblanco, 1997).

Sepúlveda, Juan Ginés de, *Democrate secondo, o della giusta causa della guerra contro gli Indos*, translated by Giuseppe Patisso (Galatina: Congedo, 2008).

Sepúlveda, Juan Ginés de, *Democrate secondo, ovvero sulle giuste cause di guerra / Democrates secundus sive de iustis belli causis,* edited and translated by Domenico Taranto (Macerata: Quodlibet, 2009).

Sepúlveda, Juan Ginés de, *Democrates secundus / Zweiter Demokrates*, edited, translated, and introduced by Christian Schäfer, Politische Philosophie und Rechtstheorie des Mittelalters und der Neuzeit, Reihe I: Texte, Bd. 11 (Stuttgart-Bad Cannstatt: Frommann-Holzboog, 2018).

Sepúlveda, Juan Ginés de, *Proposiciones temerarias : recopilación de textos de Juan Ginés de Sepúlveda, Bartolomé de Las Casas y Domingo de Soto que tratan del debate del Nuevo Mundo*, edited by Natalia K. Denisova (Madrid : Fundación Universitaria Española, 2019).

404 BIBLIOGRAPHY

Sepúlveda, Juan Ginés de, and Bartolomé de las Casas, *Apologia*, edited and translated by Ángel Losada (Madrid: Editora Nacional, 1975).

Shaw, Brent D., *Sacred Violence: African Christians and Sectarian Hatred in the Age of Augustine* (Cambridge: Cambridge University Press, 2011).

Sierra Corella, Antonio, *La censura de libros y papeles en España y los índices y catálogos españoles de los prohibidos y expurgados* (Madrid: Cuerpo Facultativo de Achiveros, Bibliotecarios y Arqueólogos, 1947).

Simms, Brendan, and D. J. B. Trim (eds), *Humanitarian Intervention: A History* (Cambridge: Cambridge University Press, 2011).

Simpson, Gerry, *Great Powers and Outlaw States: Unequal Sovereigns in the International Legal Order* (Cambridge: Cambridge University Press, 2004).

Soto, Domingo de, *In quartum Sententiarum* (Salamanca: Juan María de Terranova, 1561–62).

Soto, Domingo de, *Relección 'De dominio'*, edited by Jaime Brufau Prats (Granada: Universidad de Granada, 1964).

Soto, Domingo de, 'Sumario', in *Relecciones y Opusculos*, vol, 1, edited by Jaime Brufau Prats, 68–194 (Salamanca: Editorial San Esteban, 1995).

Tarán, Leonardo, '*Amicus Plato, sed magis amica veritas*: From Plato and Aristotle to Cervantes', *Antike und Abendland* 30/4 (1984): 93–124 (repr. in his Collected Papers, 1962–1999, Leiden: Brill, 2001, 1–46).

Taranto, Domenico, 'La "Bolla Alessandrina" e la guerra giusta: Note sul rapporto tra l'ecclesiastico, il politico e il religioso in Sepúlveda', in *Guerra giusta e schiavitù naturale: Juan Ginés de Sepúlveda e il dibattito sulla Conquista*, edited by Marco Geuna, 31–52 (Milan: Edizioni Biblioteca Francescana, 2014).

Tiele, Pieter Anton, *Mémoire bibliographique sur les journaux des navigateurs néerlandais* (Amsterdam: Frederik Muller, 1867).

Toste, Marco, 'Invincible Ignorance and the Americas: Why and How the Salamancan Theologians Made Use of a Medieval Notion', *Rechtsgeschichte—Legal History* 26 (2018): 284–97.

Truyol y Serra, Antonio, 'In Memoriam Ángel Losada García', in Juan Ginés de Sepúlveda, *Obras completas*, vol. 3, VII–X (Pozoblanco: Aynuntamiento de Pozoblanco, 1977).

Tubau, Xavier, 'Canon Law in Juan Ginés de Sepúlveda's *Democrates secundus*', *Bibliothèque d'Humanisme et Renaissance* 73/2 (2011): 265–77.

Tuck, Richard, *The Rights of War and Peace: Political Thought and the International Order from Grotius to Kant* (Oxford: Oxford University Press, 1999).

Vacas Galindo, Fray Enrique, O.P., *Fray Bartolomé de Lascasas: Disputa o controversia con Ginés de Sepúlveda* (Madrid: Revista de Derecho Internacional y Política Exterior, 1908).

Vattel, Emer de, *The Law of Nations*, edited by Béla Kapossy and Richard Whatmore (Indianapolis: Liberty Fund, 2008).

Vitoria, Francisco de, *Comentarios a la Secunda secundae de Santo Tomás*, 6 vols., edited by Vicente Beltrán de Heredia (Salamanca: Biblioteca de Teólogos Españoles, 1932).

Vitoria, Francisco de, 'On Dietary Laws, or Self-Restraint', in *Vitoria, Political Writings*, edited and translated by Anthony Pagden and Jeremy Lawrance, 205–30 (Cambridge: Cambridge University Press, 1991).

Vitoria, Francisco de, 'On the American Indians', in *Vitoria, Political Writings*, edited and translated by Anthony Pagden and Jeremy Lawrance, 231–92 (Cambridge: Cambridge University Press, 1991).

Vitoria, Francisco de, 'On the Evangelization of Unbelievers', in *Vitoria, Political Writings*, edited and translated by Anthony Pagden and Jeremy Lawrance, 339–52 (Cambridge: Cambridge University Press, 1991).

Vitoria, Francisco de, *De legibus* (Salamanca: Ediciones Universidad Salamanca, 2010).

Vollet, Matthias, 'Sepúlveda: Traductor y comentarista de Aristóteles, *Política I*', *Ideas y Valores* 119 (2002): 137–43.

Wagner, Henry Raup, with the collaboration of Helen Rand Parish, *The Life and Writings of Bartolomé de las Casas* (Albuquerque: University of New Mexico Press, 1967).

Wolff, Christian, *Jus gentium methodo scientifica pertractatum*, vol. 2, edited by Joseph H. Drake (Oxford: Clarendon Press, 1934).

Index of Authors and Works Cited in the Translated Texts

For the benefit of digital users, indexed terms that span two pages (e.g., 52–53) may, on occasion, appear on only one of those pages.

Actus Silvestri, 248–49
Ambrose, 105–6, 116–17, 153, 208, 210, 212, 217, 221–22, 279, 349–50
  De Abraham, 159
  De Cain et Abel, 105–6, 116–17, 184–85, 188–89, 203–4
  De officiis ministrorum, 109, 122, 123, 128, 132, 158, 180
  De Paradiso, 166n.346
  De Tobia, 159
  Expositio Evangelii secundum Lucam, 260, 263
  Letter 6, 138
  Letter 17, 209–10, 279
  Letter 18, 209–10, 279
Pseudo-Ambrose
  De vocatu gentium, 126–27
Andreas, Joannes
  Commentary on *Quod super his*, 119n.158, 205, 280n.263, 309n.364, 369n.49
Anselm of Laon
  Glossa interlinearis, 242n.38, 270n.205
Aquinas
  In Epistolam ad Romanos, Caput Primum, 186–87
  Quaestiones disputatae. De veritate, 245–46
  Quaestiones Quodlibetales, 348–49
  Scriptum super libros Sententiarum Magistri Petri Lombardi, 243–44, 291–92, 325
  Sententia libri Ethicorum, 163
  Sententia libri Politicorum, 202–3, 267n.192, 280, 310
  Summa contra Gentiles, 325–26
  Summa theologica
    I-I, q. 47, 305n.354
    I-II, q. 19, 168–69, 325, 372–73, 374n.66, 377n.87
    I-II, q. 34, 376–77
    I-II, q. 49, 277–78
    I-II, q. 68, 373–74
    I-II, q. 71, 373–74
    I-II, q. 91, 374
    I-II, q. 94, 266n.189

I-II, q. 98, 124, 372
I-II, q. 100, 266n.189, 373
II-II, q. 1, 125
II-II, q. 2, 125
II-II, q. 3, 325
II-II, q. 4, 307n.360
II-II, q. 10, 119–20, 204, 210, 211, 246, 254–55, 257, 272–73, 274, 279, 302–4, 317–18
II-II, q. 12, 252, 254–55
II-II, q. 24, 169
II-II, q. 33, 215, 220n.103
II-II, q. 39, 146–47
II-II, q. 40, 134–35, 273, 276, 281, 302, 305n.353, 349–50
II-II, q. 65, 155
II-II, q. 66, 108n.121, 153, 159, 378–79, 384
II-II, q. 91, 93n.76
II-II, q. 94, 204, 274, 280, 304
II-II, q. 108, 103
II-II, q. 188, 131n.226
III, q. 8, 251–52, 308
III, q. 40, 318
III, q. 44, 245–46
III, q. 59, 245–46
Pseudo-Aquinas (Ptolemy of Lucca)
  De regimine principum, 108–9, 135, 175n.360, 202–3, 205, 211–12, 213–14, 276
Aristotle, 94, 120, 123–24, 149, 190, 377
  De anima, 277–78, 307
  De motu animalium, 121–22, 375
  De partibus animalium, 97n.93
  Eudemian Ethics
  Magna Moralia, 97, 122
  Metaphysics, 122, 217, 276, 277–78, 307, 309n.363, 371
  Meteorologica, 122
  Nicomachean Ethics
    Bk 2, 95n.87, 218, 318–19
    Bk 3, 163n.338, 169n.350, 374–75
    Bk 5, 93n.75, 96n.89, 103n.109, 143–44, 145–46, 169, 219
    Bk 6, 318–19

408 INDEX OF AUTHORS AND WORKS CITED IN THE TRANSLATED TEXTS

Aristotle (*cont.*)
  Bk 7, 96n.88, 113n.133, 145
  Bk 10, 88n.60, 92n.73, 109, 110n.127, 122,
    123, 140–41, 212
  Politics
  Bk 1, 88, 97, 99n.100, 100n.101, 101,
    152n.298, 155, 156n.311, 161n.331,
    178n.369, 202–3, 221–22, 267, 284, 310
  Bk 2, 104n.112, 111n.130, 175, 177
  Bk 3, 102n.106, 121–22, 128, 145–46, 157n.313,
    175n.361, 176, 206, 219, 266–67, 310–11
  Bk 7, 88n.60, 375–76
  Rhetoric, 264–65
  Topics, 264–65
Pseudo-Aristotle
  De mundo, 121, 122
Pseudo-Athanasius of Alexandria
  On 1 Corinthians, 252
Augustine, 86, 94, 116–17, 132, 134, 146, 149–50,
    166, 168, 171, 184–85, 205, 210, 212, 221–
    22, 248–49, 292–93, 294, 298, 301, 305,
    313, 317–18, 349–50
  Confessions, 372
  Contra Faustum, 91, 93, 95, 96, 105, 108, 122,
    124, 128, 152, 165, 180, 187–88, 206
  Contra litteras Petililani, 130–31, 151–53,
    201, 208
  De civitate Dei, 108–9, 121, 157, 178, 202–
    3, 325–27
  De consensu Evangelistarum, 91
  De doctrina christiana, 94, 130
  De natura et gratia contra Pelagium, 124, 126
  De sermone Domini in monte, 91, 156
  De spiritu et littera, 124
  De vera religion, 381n.103
  Enchiridion de Fide, Spe, et Caritate, 129, 137
  *Epistola ad Catholicos contra
    Donatistas*, 130–31
  In Evangelium Ioannis tractatus, 91, 245–46,
    273n.221
  Letter 16 (Maximus to Augustine), 121
  Letter 76, 246
  Letter 93, 101–2, 118–19, 137, 138, 140, 141–
    42, 152, 184–85, 209–10, 211–12, 215,
    216–17, 271–72, 273, 275–76, 279, 281,
    312–13, 316
  Letter 105, 246
  Letter 127, 245–46
  Letter 138, 91, 101–2, 109–10, 118–19, 133,
    275–76, 279
  Letter 173, 137, 138, 208, 246, 271–72, 275, 279
  Letter 185, 152, 204–5, 217, 246, 247, 271–72,
    275, 278, 281, 312–13
  Letter 189, 88–89, 201, 323

Letter 250, 144–45, 282, 283–84
  Quaestiones in Heptateuchum, 131, 136, 200–1,
    206, 282–83, 284, 296n.315, 327–28
  Sermones ad populum, Sermon 62, 252–54,
    278, 314
  Sermones ad populum, Sermon 88, 103
Pseudo-Augustine
  De vita christiana, 258
  Quaestiones veteris et novi testamenti, 164
  Sermon 82, De verbis Evangelii Lucae, 95–96,
    105–6, 378–79
  Sermones supposititii, 291–92
Augustinus Hibernus
  De mirabilibus sacrae scripturae, 129n.216

Basil the Great
  Moralia, Regula, 339–40
Bede
  Historia ecclesiastica gentis Anglorum, 216–17,
    249–50, 266–67, 279n.262
  Homiliae 23 (on birthday of John the
    Baptist), 143
  In Lucae evangelium exposition, 263
Bernard of Clairvaux
  De praecepto et dispensatione, 146–47,
    212, 349–50
Pseudo-Berosus
  *Berosi sacerdotis Chaldaici Antiquitatum...libri
    quinque*, 182–83
Boethius
  De consolatione philosophiae, 325–26
Bonaevallis, Arnaldus (Arnaud de Bonneval)
  De cardinalibus operibus Christi, 93–94
Boniface VIII
  Decretales, Bk. 6 (*Sextus Liber Decretalium*)
    1.2.1, 299
    1.5, 326–27

Caesar, Julius
  De bello gallico, 157–58, 322
Cajetan, 186–87
  Commentary on Aquinas, Summa theologica,
    117n.152, 205, 220–21, 293, 304
Cassiodorus and Epiphanius Scholasticus
  Tripartite History, 249n.93
Castro, Alfonso de
  De iusta haereticorum punitione, 221–22
Chrysostom, John
  Homilies on (the Epistle to) Titus, 258
  Homily 72 on the Gospel of John, 249
  Opus Perfectum, 249, 259, 310–11
Pseudo-John Chrysostom
  Opus Imperfectum in Matthaeum, 131, 245–46,
    249, 257–58

INDEX OF AUTHORS AND WORKS CITED IN THE TRANSLATED TEXTS 409

Cicero, 123–24
  De amicitia, 366n.42
  De officiis, 157, 172
  Pro M. Fonteio, 326
  Tusculan Disputations, 109
Pseudo-Clement
  Recognitiones, 265
Codex Justinianus, 209n.66, 298, 298n.328,
  305n.351
Comestor, Peter
  Historia scholastica, 293
Curtius, Quintus
  Historiae Alexandri Magni, 282–83
Cyprian, 93–94, 149–50
  Ad Fortunatum de exhortatione martyrii,
    116–17, 182–83, 184–85, 203–4, 270–
    71, 296–97

Damascene, John
  De orthodoxa fide, 325–26
Digest, 92, 95n.83, 108, 173n.356, 327n.426
Dionysius of Halicarnassus
  Antiquitates Romanae, 321–22
Pseudo-Dionysius the Areopagite
  De caelesti hierarchia, 125–26, 245–46, 294
  Divine Names, 95, 169n.348
  Letter 8, 314–15

El Tostado (Alonso de Madrigal), 292–93
  Commentaria in Deuteronomium, 243–44, 293
  Commentaria in Judices et Ruth, 327–28
  Commentaria in librum secundum
    Paralipomenon, 243–44
  Paradoxa, 124
Eusebius
  De praeparatione evangelica, 265
  Ecclesiastical History, 209–10, 248n.90
  De vita beatissimi imperatoris Constantini,
    209–10, 256n.141

Gerson, Jean
  Regulae morales, 143, 218, 283–84, 324
Glossa interlinearis, 241–42, 244n.53, 270, 314
Glossa ordinaria, 295
Gratian
  Decretum (Part 1)
    D. 4, c. 3, 381
    D. 6, c. 3, 373–74
    D. 9, c. 11, 92–93
    D. 13, cc. 1-2, 143, 218
    D. 19, c. 5, 379–80, 387–88
    D. 37, c. 15, 164n.340
    D. 38, c. 10, 162n.337
    D. 45, c. 3, 201, 247, 272–73, 314

    D. 45, c. 5, 201, 272–73
    D. 56, c. 10, 249–50
    D. 74, c. 7, 152n.296
    D. 83, c. 3, 106n.116
    D. 86, c. 3, 178n.371
  Decretum (Part 2)
    C. 1, q. 2, c. 2, 248–49, 317–18
    C. 2, q. 7, c. 41, 244–45, 296
    C. 11, q. 3, c. 60, 152n.297
    C. 11, q. 3, c. 92, 166n.346
    C. 11, q. 3, c. 101, 166n.345
    C. 14, q. 5, c. 10, 180n.374
    C. 14, q. 5, c. 12, 244–45, 296
    C. 22, q. 2, c. 19, 245, 296
    C. 22, q. 4, c. 6, 143n.277
    C. 23, q. 1, c. 2, 317–18
    C. 23, q. 1, c. 3, 201, 323
    C. 23, q. 1, c. 4, 180n.373
    C. 23, q. 2, c. 2, 200-1
    C. 23, q. 4, c. 1, 103n.110
    C. 23, q. 4, c. 38, 208, 246, 271–72, 275
    C. 23, q. 4, c. 41, 209–10, 216–17, 271–72, 275
    C. 23, q. 4, c. 42, 271–72, 275, 279
    C. 23, q. 4, c. 48, 300n.332
    C. 23, q. 4, c. 49, 185n.390, 210–11, 212,
      250–51, 272, 349–50, 381, 387–88
    C. 23, q. 4, c. 50, 117n.150, 184n.386
    C. 23, q. 5, c. 32, 203–4, 270–71, 296–97
    C. 23, q. 5, c. 33, 201, 208
    C. 23, q. 5, c. 39, 132n.233, 203–4
    C. 23, q. 5, c. 49, 106n.115, 117n.149,
      153n.302, 184n.383, 189n.397
    C. 23, q. 6, c. 3, 209, 211–12
    C. 23, q. 8, c. 10, 135
    C. 23, q. 8, c. 15, 136n.253, 323
    C. 25, q. 1, c. 4, 348
    C. 25, q. 1, c. 5, 379–80, 387–88
    C. 25, q. 1, c. 11, 379–80, 387–88
    C. 32, q. 7, c. 13, 372n.57
Gregory I, 273n.221
  Ad Edilbertum anglorum regem, 279
  Letters
    Book 1, 138, 184–85, 210–11, 217, 274–75,
      299, 300
    Book 3, 117n.150, 184n.386, 260
    Book 11, 201, 209–10, 216–17, 249–50, 279
  Moralia in Iob, 91–92, 127, 143, 154, 218, 244–
    45, 266–67, 296
  Regula pastoralis, 162
Gregory IX
  Decretals
    1.2.1, 299
    1.7.2, 214–15
    1.29.5, 134n.243, 276, 349–50

410 INDEX OF AUTHORS AND WORKS CITED IN THE TRANSLATED TEXTS

Gregory IX (*cont.*)
    1.29.21, 135n.244, 349–50
    1.29.39, 281, 349–50
    3.34.8, 205, 255–56, 280, 310, 369–70
    3.42.3, 201, 208, 247–48, 256
    4.1.7 or 10, 377–78
    4.17.13, 206, 213–14, 224, 347–48
    5.6.14, 255–56
Gregory of Nazianzus
    De Theologia, 325–26

Haymo of Halberstadt
    In epistolam ad Romanos, 132n.233
Homer
    Iliad, 88, 175
Hostiensis
    Commentary on *Quod super his*, 119n.158,
        205, 280n.263, 309n.364, 369n.49

Innocent IV
    Comments on a letter ("*Maiores*") by Innocent
        III to the Archbishop of Arles, 247–
        48, 255–56
    Commentary on *Quod super his*, 119n.158,
        185n.391, 205, 255n.140, 280n.263,
        309n.364, 369n.49
Institutes, 173n.356
Isidore of Seville, 99, 110, 166
    Etymologiae, 95, 156–57
    Sententiae, 373n.61

Jerome, 86, 166, 317–18
    Chronicon, 209–10
    Commentaria in Evangelium Matthaei, 260
    Commentarius in Epistolam ad Titum,
        337–38
    Commentarii in Ezechielem, 132
    Letter 60, 249n.93
Pseudo-Jerome
    Regula monachorum, 94
Justin
    *Epitome of the Philippic History of Pompeius
        Trogus*, 282–83, 311n.370

Lactantius
    Divinarum institutionum, 265
Las Casas
    Apología/Apologia, 238–39, 240, 268, 269, 284,
        289–90, 291, 296, 298, 301, 304, 305–7,
        309, 310, 311–12, 316, 321–22, 324,
        325, 333, 335–36, 337–38, 368–69, 370,
        371, 383
    Aquí se contiene una disputa o controversia,
        366, 387–88

*Aquí se contienen treinta proposiciones muy
    jurídicas*, 333, 336, 338–39, 346n.468,
    388n.123
Confesionario, 284, 287–88, 324–25, 333, 338,
    340, 346, 381–83
*Tratado comprobatorio del imperio soberano
    y principado universal que los reyes de
    Castilla y León tienen sobre Las Indas*,
    337n.443, 346n.468, 388n.123
Livy
    Ab urbe condita, 321–22

Mair, John
    In primum et secundum Sententiarum,
        212, 221–22
Mazzolini, Silvestro [Sylvius]
    Summa Sylvestrina, 213–14, 327n.426, 348–49

Nicholas I, Pope
    Ad consulta Bulgarorum, 323n.416
Nicholas of Gorran, 292–93
    *Postilla elucidativa et magistralis super
        Epistolas Pauli*, 243–44
Nicholas of Lyra
    Postillae perpetuae in universam S. Scripturam,
        204–5, 221–22, 244–45, 274, 293

Orosius
    Historiae adversus paganos, 248–49
Oviedo, Gonzalo Fernández de
    Historia general de las Indias, 110n.129, 202,
        280, 311–12

Panormitanus (Nicoló de' Tudeschi)
    Commentary on *Quod super his*, 119n.158,
        205, 280n.263, 309n.364, 369n.49
Paul the Deacon
    Historia Langobardorum, 249–50, 300–1
Plato, 94, 120, 123–24
    Phaedo, 388n.126
Pliny the Elder
    Naturalis historia, 144, 282–83, 321
Plutarch
    Quaestiones Romanae, 265, 321–22
    Regum et imperatorum apophthegmata, 282–83
Polycarp
    Epistle to the Philippians, 315

Ramírez, Don Antonio
    On War against the Barbarians, 198–99
Richard of Middleto(w)n [Ricardus de
        Mediavilla]
    *Super quattuor libros sententiarum Petri
        Lombardi quaestiones subtilissimae…*, 252

INDEX OF AUTHORS AND WORKS CITED IN THE TRANSLATED TEXTS   411

Roa, Fernando de
  Comentario a la Política de Aristóteles,
    221–22

Saxoferrato, Bartolus de (Bartolo da
    Sassoferrato), 305n.351
Scotus, John Duns, 127
  Quaestiones in quattuor libros Sententiarum,
    212, 221–22, 373
Sepúlveda
  Apologia, 238, 288, 341, 381–83
  Democrates primus, 87
  Democrates secundus, 198–200, 220, 221–23,
    237–38, 241–42, 288, 340, 341, 367–68,
    369–70, 381–83, 384
Strabo
  Geography, 322

Terence
  Heautontimoroumenos, 130
Theophylact
  Enarratio in evangelium S. Lucae, 246

Vincent of Beauvais (Vincentius Bellovacensis)
  Speculum historiale, 260–61
Vitensis, Victor (Victor of Vita)
  Historia persecutionis africanae provinciae,
    temporibus Genserici et Hunirici regum
    Wandalorum, 300–1
Vitoria, Francisco de, 128
  Comentarios a la Secunda secundae de Santo
    Tomás, 304
  De legibus, 266n.189, 304
Voragine, Jacopo de
  Golden Legend, 254n.135

Index of Biblical Passages Cited in the Translated Texts

For the benefit of digital users, indexed terms that span two pages (e.g., 52–53) may, on occasion, appear on only one of those pages.

Old Testament, 270–71, 294, 295–96

Genesis
6:12, 182n.375
14:8–16, 98n.95, 131n.227
14:21, 158
15:13–20, 270n.206
15:16, 207n.58, 242–43
18-19 182–83
19:24-25 242n.41

Exodus
10:3, 306–7
13:13, 266n.190, 327–28
22:28, 120–21
23:4, 133n.239
23:7, 264
32, 203–4
32:29, 116n.143, 184–85
34:20, 327–28

Leviticus
12:6, 266
18:1–5, 203–4
18:3, 270
18:21, 270
18:24–30, 270
18:27–28, 115n.141, 184n.384
18:29, 115n.142, 185n.388
19, 270
20:2–5, 203–4
20:2–6, 270
20:4–5, 115n.138, 183n.378
20:23, 270
26:6, 88n.58
26:27–33, 244–45
26:30–31, 241–42
27:3–7, 327–28
27:26, 327–28

Numbers
8:16–18, 327–28

Deuteronomy
2:4–5, 164n.341
2:9, 164n.341
2:18–19, 164n.341
6:16 136n.251
7:1, 253
7:1–2, 242–43
7:1–6, 243–44
7:5, 253
9:1–5, 243–44, 270
9:4, 115n.139, 203, 241–42
9:4–5, 291–92, 372
9:5, 242–43
9:27, 372
12:2, 204
12:2–3, 241–42, 243–44, 270
12:29–31, 270
12:31, 115, 203, 372
13:6 & 8, 296–97
13:9, 296–97
13:12, 296–97
13:12–13, 296–97
13:12–15, 182–83
13:15, 296–97
16:20, 106n.117
17:2–3, 212–13, 224
17:8–12, 347–48
18:9–12, 115, 203
18:12, 182–83, 372, 375–76
20, 294
20:1, 243–44
20:10, 241–42, 292–93, 294n.308, 295n.309
20:10–11, 218
20:10–12, 139, 207
20:10–14, 174n.357
20:11, 107n.118, 241–42
20:12, 295n.310
20:12–14, 241–42
20:14, 158
20:15, 139, 207, 241–42, 243–44, 270, 295n.311
20:15–17, 174n.358, 292–93
23:7, 242–43, 292

414 INDEX OF BIBLICAL PASSAGES CITED IN THE TRANSLATED TEXTS

Deuteronomy (*cont.*)
25:2, 155
32:35, 98

Judges
11:29–32, 327–28
20, 98n.96

2 Samuel
12:26–31, 158

2 Kings
16:3, 116
17:1–8, 116
17:1–23, 164–65
18:3–4, 204–5
23:4–20, 204–5
24:1-25:21, 164–65

2 Chronicles
8, 243–44

Psalms
2:8, 277–78
4:5–6, 372–73
4:6, 93, 130n.220
34:14, 88n.58
72:11, 137n.259, 208n.60, 246n.81, 271–72,
   301n.336
72:12–13, 132n.231
76:11, 246
79:6, 117
82:1 & 6, 120–21
106:35–41, 116, 203–4
106:49, 203–4

Proverbs
12:29, 101
13:22, 152
21:1, 146
24:11, 132
29:19, 140

Isaiah
11:1, 295
11:4, 295

Jeremiah
23:29, 245–46

Daniel
2:37–38, 148
3:29–30, 205n.44
4:34–37, 205n.44

6:24, 313
14:21, 278
14:22, 204–5

Joel
2:32, 126

Jonah
3:6–10, 204–5

New Testament, 349–50, 372

Matthew
3:2, 261n.171
5:8–9, 93n.74
5:16, 249n.97, 257–58
7:12, 92n.69, 134n.241
8:5–13, 252n.120
9:9–13, 245–46
10:7–8, 259n.158
10:10, 136n.250
10:12, 263
10:13, 260–61n.168
10:14, 319n.401
10:14–15, 263, 316
10:16, 250n.100, 259n.159, 313–14
11:29, 258n.154
12:3–4, 317
13:28–30, 264n.181
18:15–17, 214n.86
19:16–21, 92n.68
19:17–19, 206n.52
21:5, 262n.175
21:9, 124n.193
22:38, 206n.52
23:2–3, 379
28, 135
28:18, 205, 277, 307, 371, 385
28:18–20, 119n.159, 206
28:19–20, 276, 294n.305

Mark
1:4, 261n.171
16:9, 246n.72
16:15, 262, 276, 277
16:15–16, 378–79
16:16, 285, 294n.306, 328n.432, 386n.116
16:20, 215n.91

Luke
2:14, 88n.57
2:23–24, 327–28
3:3, 261n.171
6:27–29, 89n.62

INDEX OF BIBLICAL PASSAGES CITED IN THE TRANSLATED TEXTS   415

6:29, 91n.63
7:1–10, 252n.120
8:2, 246n.72
9:3, 260
9:54–55, 316–17, 319n.402
10:3, 313–14
10:5, 88n.58, 263
10:6, 260–61n.168
10:7, 177n.365
10:10–12, 263
10:30–37, 132n.228
12:13–14, 243n.50
12:14, 252
14:15–24, 207–8, 208n.60, 247n.87
14:21, 101n.104
14:21–23, 138n.260
14:23, 245, 271, 274n.232, 298n.324
24:46–47, 261–62

John
1:12, 120–21
3:17, 262n.174
8:40, 317
10:11, 277
10:14, 277
10:16, 277
14:12, 245–46
14:17, 348–49
14:23, 92n.71
14:26, 348–49
15:13, 266n.191
18:23, 91n.66
21:17, 277

Acts of the Apostles
4:12, 124n.192
9:1–19, 246n.72
9:3–8, 137n.258
10:34–35, 126n.201
17:23, 255
17:34, 254
23:3, 91n.65

Romans
1:14, 261n.173
1:19–20, 120
1:20, 186n.392
1:21, 123n.187
1:21–23, 284
1:22–23, 376
1:28, 373–74
2:12–15, 124
2:14, 118n.154
2:14–15, 93n.78

2:21–23, 260n.164
2:24, 257–58
3:8, 142n.276, 202
8:18, 124n.195
10:10, 325
10:12, 126n.202, 142n.275, 261–62
10:15, 136n.249
10:16, 306–7
13:1, 148
13:4, 98n.99, 132n.234
13:8–9, 92
14:18, 374
15:3 & 7, 201
15:27, 177n.365

1 Corinthians
1:24, 186–87
5:11, 254n.132
5:12, 118n.153, 129n.217, 202, 220n.102,
    254n.130, 254n.133, 305, 313–14, 314n.379,
    314n.381
5:12–13, 243n.50, 251–52, 275
6:12, 157n.314
9:10, 214–15
13:12, 125n.196
14:38, 162n.336
15:24–25, 307
15:27, 251–52
15:28, 251–52

2 Corinthians
3:6, 113n.132
10:5, 247, 255n.138, 257n.146
10:6, 247

Galatians
3:26, 121n.168
3:28, 261–62
4, 133n.236

Ephesians
4:11–13, 135n.248
5:1, 318
5:5, 127n.210
6:5 & 9, 159n.328

Philippians
1:15, 379n.93
1:18, 379n.95
2:15, 258–59
3:17, 318
3:19, 114n.135
3:21, 307
4:5, 259n.156

416 INDEX OF BIBLICAL PASSAGES CITED IN THE TRANSLATED TEXTS

Colossians
3:22, 159
4:1, 159, 178n.367

1 Thessalonians
5:22 171n.354

1 Timothy
1:13, 162n.334
2:4, 129n.218, 133n.240, 142n.275
5:8, 178n.370
6:16, 186–87

2 Timothy
4:2, 245–46

Titus
2:7, 258n.153
2:15, 245–46

Hebrews
2:8, 251–52, 277–78, 307
11:6, 125, 186–87
11:32–34, 327–28

James
2:19, 123
2:26, 123

1 Peter
2:12, 258–59
2:18, 103, 159

Jude
1:10, 304

Apocrypha

Wisdom
10:19, 152
12, 203–4
12:3–6, 116

Ecclesiasticus
10:28, 151
15:14, 136
17:12, 130, 132, 210n.69,
    256n.144
34:24, 372–73

1 Maccabees
2:23, 182–83
9:36–40, 98n.97

2 Maccabees
6:11, 164–65
14:35, 266n.189

General Index

For the benefit of digital users, indexed terms that span two pages (e.g., 52–53) may, on occasion, appear on only one of those pages.

Abraham
  descendants of, 127
  and God's command to sacrifice Isaac, 266,
    284, 327–28
  and God's promise of land, 39, 242–43, 270,
    291–92
  retribution for injuries to Lot, 97–98, 131–32,
    158
  and Sodom, 164–65
  and the Sabbath, 317
Abril-Castelló, Vidal, 230–31, 233–34, 269n.202,
  334n.439, 347n.469
Adorno, Rolena, 82–83n.48
Adrian, Pope, 273, 301, 379n.99
adultery, 95–96, 162–63, 169
  prohibition of, 91–92, 260, 325
  as a sin against nature, 128–29, 254–55
Afghanistan, 2001 invasion of, 59–60
Agustín, Antonio, 7, 193, 194, 198, 224, 288n.289,
  382n.105
Alcalá de Henares, University of, 3–4, 23, 24
  rejection of *Democrates secundus*, 22–23, 25,
    28, 199–200, 238, 340, 368, 370, 392–93
Alexander of Aphrodisias, 6, 8–9
Alexander the Great, 25–26, 267
Alexander III, Pope, 134–35, 378n.89
Alexander VI, Pope
  donation of, 14, 18–19, 20, 26–27, 46, 47, 50–
    51, 146, 147, 194, 212–13, 226–27, 268,
    269, 285, 329–30, 347–50, 379–80. *See*
    also papal bulls: *Inter caetera*
Ambrose, 16–17, 19, 25, 31–32, 72. *See also* Index
  of Authors and Works Cited in the
  Translated Texts
Amerindians
  as apes, 13, 75–76, 82, 110n.128, 113
  as barbarians, 13–15, 29, 37–39, 111–17, 202,
    241, 257, 266–67, 280, 310–12
  as beasts, 13, 48–49, 76–77, 82, 113–14, 202,
    280, 341, 345–46
  benefits of subjugation, 2, 6–7, 13, 105, 114,
    142–46, 149, 219

cases where subjugation unnecessary, 219
  as civilized, 113, 267, 311
  governance of (by Spaniards), 21, 28–29, 84–
    85, 175–79, 384
  as *homunculi* ('lesser humans'), 13, 74–75,
    111–12, 181–82, 187–88
  humanity and rationality, 6–7, 10, 113
  inferiority of, 13, 38, 111–13
  as natural slaves (*see* slavery: natural slavery)
  See also dominium: Amerindian; human sacrifice:
    Amerindian; slavery: enslavement
    of Amerindians and its prohibition;
    tyranny: of Amerindian rulers
Andreas, Joannes, 17n.63
Andrés Marcos, Teodoro, 77–78, 206n.53
Anghie, Anthony, 61
Antonio, Nicolás, 192, 193
Apostles, the, 316–18
  authority of, 119, 202, 275–76
  method of evangelism, 18–19, 31, 43, 88,
    135–36, 137, 201, 207–8, 209–10,
    215–16, 217, 254, 259, 281, 313–14,
    315–16
  See also Bible: New Testament: Great
    Commission; and Index of Biblical
    Passages Cited in the Translated Texts:
    Matthew 28 & Mark 16
Aquinas, Thomas, 6, 25, 28, 29
  Commentary on Aristotle's Politics, 38
  Summa theologica, 32, 40
  See also Index of Authors and Works Cited in
    the Translated Texts
Archinto, Felipe, 198, 224, 288n.289, 382n.105
Arcos, Miguel de, 223
Arévalo, Bernardino de, 33, 50–51, 370, 382–83
Argote, Francisco de, 28–29
Arianism, Arian heretics, 248–49, 300–1, 313
Aristotle, 20–21, 29, 36, 44
  Italian Aristotelianism (= Paduan Averroism),
    5–6
  on natural slavery (*see* slavery: natural
    slavery)

418 GENERAL INDEX

Aristotle (*cont.*)
  works
    Metaphysics, 6
    Politics, 12–15, 37–39
  See also Index of Authors and Works Cited in
    the Translated Texts
Augustine, archbishop of Canterbury,
  249–50
Augustine, bishop of Hippo, 15, 16–17, 25,
  28, 29
  on evangelism and the Donatists, 18–20, 39–
    40, 41–42, 74
  on just war, 16
  on punishment, 16, 31–32, 39–40, 72–73
  See also Index of Authors and Works Cited in
    the Translated Texts

barbarians, categories of, 37–38, 266–67,
  310–12. *See also* Amerindians: as
  barbarians
Benjamin, Katie Marie, 4–5
Bible
  Old Testament, 39
    Deuteronomy 20, 19
    Proverbs, 16–17
    Psalms, 16–17
  New Testament, 39
    Do unto others (Matthew 7:12), 18
    Great Commission (Matthew 28:18-20),
      15, 42
    judging outsiders (1 Corinthians 5:12),
      16, 39
    Parable of the banquet (Luke 14:15-24), 19,
      31–32, 39–40
    Parable of the good Samaritan (Luke 10:
      25-37), 16–17
    Vulgate, 85
  See also Index of Biblical Passages Cited in the
    Translated Texts
biblical precedents, 2–3, 39, 71, 72–73, 74, 80,
  117, 131–32, 182–83, 244–45, 254,
  255–56, 266, 270–71, 281, 296, 317,
  318. *See also* Christ: as model for
  Christian behaviour
'Black Legend' (La leyenda negra), 56, 389–93
blasphemy, 23–24, 40, 142, 162, 200, 257–58,
  304–5, 315, 373–74. *See also* war: as
  punishment for blasphemy
Bologna, 3–4, 9–10
  Colegio de San Clemente, 3–5, 7–9, 10n.27,
    198n.18
Boswell, James, 392–93
Brufau Prats, Jaime, 78, 228–29, 257n.145
Bry, Theodor de, 390–91, 392

Caesar, Julius, 84. *See also* Index of Authors and
  Works Cited in the Translated Texts
Cajetan (Gaetano), Tommaso de Vío, 8–9, 17–18,
  25, 72–73, 80, 186–87
  Commentary on Aquinas's *Summa theologica*,
    18–20, 30
Cáncer, Luis, 48, 343n.461, 344
cannibalism, 6–7, 13, 43–44, 58–59, 61–62, 111–
  12, 113, 149
Cano, Melchor
  approval of the *Confesionario*, 26–27, 340
  correspondence with Sepúlveda, 23–26, 29–
    30, 31–32
  on papal jurisdiction, 46n.195
  on Spain's wars and evangelism, 34, 42,
    43n.184, 50
  and the Valladolid Junta, 33, 51, 52, 370n.50
canon law, canonists, 2–3, 4–5, 18n.67, 28, 29–30,
  41, 45, 51, 63–64, 81, 255–57, 280,
  284, 309–10, 369–70, 382–83. *See also*
  Gratian's Decretum and Gregory IX's
  Decretals in Index of Authors and
  Works Cited in the Translated Texts
Capdevila, María Teresa Bermejo de, 229
Caracas
  Biblioteca Nacional de la Historia, 231
Carpi, 7–8
Carranza, Bartolomé de
  approval of the *Confesionario*, 26–27,
    46, 340
  on papal jurisdiction, 46n.195
  on Spain's wars and evangelism, 34, 42,
    43n.184
  and the Valladolid Junta, 33, 51, 370n.50
Carvajal, Luis de, 223, 382–83
Cassi, Andrea, 75–76
Castilla Urbano, Francisco, 10n.27, 76–77,
  80n.47, 192n.3
Castro, Alonso de, 382–83
Catalonia, Catalans, 389–90, 392
Celestine III, Pope, 134–35
Charlemagne, 135, 273, 301
Charles V (Holy Roman Emperor = Charles I
  of Spain), 9–10, 22, 52, 55, 65–66, 86,
  87, 90, 110–11, 114, 133, 237–38, 333,
  338–39, 353, 367–68
  calling the Valladolid debate, 33, 239,
    368–69
  See also New Laws
Chartier, Roger, 389
Christ
  his temporal power, 135, 213–14
    in actu, 39, 251–52, 277–78, 306–9,
      371, 385

GENERAL INDEX   419

in habitu, 39, 251–52, 277–78, 306–9
in potentia, 39, 251–52, 277–78,
    306–9, 371
as model for Christian behaviour, 25, 31, 201,
    205, 217, 318, 344–45
See also Bible: New Testament; and relevant
    passages in Index of Biblical Passages
    Cited in the Translated Texts
Church, Catholic. *See* canon law; ecclesiastical
    jurisdiction
Ciceronian dialogues, 8, 81
Circumcellions, 253, 278
civilization, levels of (*civilitas, humanitas*),
    13, 21–22, 37–39, 59–61, 82, 84–85,
    101, 105, 113, 157, 176, 267. *See also*
    Amerindians: as barbarians; and
    barbarians: categories of
Clement VII, Pope (Giulio de' Medici), 8–10,
    23, 111
Cloppenburg, Jan, 390–91
Coleridge, Samuel Taylor, 392–93
Columbus, Christopher, 330–31
conscience. *See* ignorance, invincible or
    otherwise; probable error
consent, Amerindian, to Spanish rule, 50, 54–55,
    233–34
Constantine, 211–12, 217, 248–49, 273, 278,
    279, 302
    supposed edict against pagans, 19, 31–32,
    72–73, 138, 142, 149–50, 184–85,
    209–10, 255–56, 274, 275, 298–99
Constantius II, 138n.261, 209–10
Córdoba, 3–4, 65–66, 198–99, 223, 311, 369
Coroleu Lletget, Alejandro, 7, 65, 66–68, 69, 70,
    73n.21, 74, 78
Cortés, Hernan de, 90, 112
Council of the Indies (*Consejo de Indias*), 1, 12,
    26–27, 34, 192n.3, 202, 333, 339
    deliberating *Democrates secundus*, 22,
    237–38
    and the Valladolid debate, 33, 50n.211,
    51n.215, 52, 239, 368–69
Council of Castile, Royal, 22–23, 25, 32–33, 34,
    237–38, 367
Councils, Church
    Eighth Council of Toledo, 154, 167, 218
    Elvira, 317–18
    Fifth Lateran, 5–6
    First Council of Lyon, 95
    Fourth Council of Toledo, 201, 208, 246,
    273n.221
    Seventh Council of Toledo, 143
    Trent, 22n.87, 51, 370
Covarrubias, Diego de, 23n.93

Crombergers (Sevillan publishing family),
    52n.222
Cromwell, Oliver, 393n.13
Cuba, 11, 343–44
Cyprian of Alexandria, 72

Dacans, 299
Damasus, Pope, 178–79, 379n.99
Datians, 299
David, king of Israel, 158, 317, 373–74
Decalogue, the, 92, 119, 296–97, 377–78
    and natural law, 15, 46, 91–92, 206, 276, 373
Democrates, 12
Denisova, Natalia K., 228, 353–54, 356, 363–64
Díaz de Rivas, Pedro, 65–66
dispossession (and confiscation) of goods
    of barbarians, 150–53
    imposed with moderation, 155–61
    of those defeated in a just war, 71, 84, 154–55,
    188–90, 204
    of unbelievers, idolaters, and heretics, 8–9,
    116, 130–31, 152–53, 162, 184–85,
    209–10, 273, 279, 337–38
Dominicans, 46n.195, 50, 51, 59–60, 73,
    247–48
    in the Americas, 8–9, 10, 32–33, 139, 343
    opposing Sepúlveda, 3, 15, 69–70
    supporting Las Casas, 340n.454
    supporting Sepúlveda, 22, 69, 221–23
    at Valladolid, 33–34, 368–69
dominium
    Amerindian, 14, 24, 28–29, 47, 84, 200, 233–
    34, 335, 337–38
    infidel, 8–9, 17–18, 73, 78n.41, 117–18, 205
    natural slaves, 13–14
    Spanish in the Americas, 26–27, 34–35,
    237, 268, 287–88, 290, 335, 345,
    379–80
Donatism, Donatists, 16, 18–20, 31–32, 41–42,
    74, 137, 141, 208, 211–12, 246–47,
    313, 316. *See also* relevant letters of
    Augustine in Index of Authors and
    Works Cited in the Translated Texts
Dorico, Valerio and Luigi, 194, 224
Duns Scotus, John, 25. *See also* Index of Authors
    and Works Cited in the Translated
    Texts

ecclesiastical jurisdiction, 1–2, 16, 31–32,
    39–40, 41, 43, 49, 117–20, 202,
    251–54, 255, 275–79, 305–9, 335–36,
    371, 379–80, 385, 387–88. *See also*
    Christ: his temporal power; and papal
    jurisdiction

420 GENERAL INDEX

Egypt, Egyptians, 93, 94, 242–43, 292, 296n.315, 373n.62
Elizabeth I, queen of England, 59, 391–92
Elvira, Council of. *See* Councils, Church
encomienda, encomenderos, 11, 33, 51, 52, 84, 237
  and Las Casas, 11, 26–27, 54, 57
  and Sepúlveda, 21–22, 55–56, 85
Epicureans, 376–77
Epstein, Lewis, 195
Erasmus, Desiderius, 7–8, 10, 23, 252n.116
  Ciceronianus, 8
  Erasmian pacifism, 8
Española, 8–9
evangelization
  coercive, 18–20, 31–32, 133–42, 207–16, 312–16
  forcing infidels to listen to preaching, 19–20, 42–43, 46, 59-60, 140, 213–14, 216–17, 262–63, 267–68, 281, 316–19
  impediments and obstacles to conversion, 28–29, 136, 270–71, 300–1, 319, 334–35, 387–88
  obstruction of faith, 32, 39–40, 47–48, 211, 250–51, 262, 274, 280, 300–1, 302–4
  obstruction of preaching, 41, 42, 47–48, 256, 262, 300–1, 319, 334–36
  peaceful but following subjugation, 6–7, 18–20, 31–32, 133–37, 207–16, 282–85
  peaceful and without subjugation, 26–27, 49, 257–62, 312–16, 330–32, 333, 334–35, 336–37, 343
  peaceful method of, 10, 18–19, 43, 48–49, 290, 306, 313–14, 343–45
  usefulness of fear in, 19–20, 31–32, 40, 41–42, 48–49, 139–42, 145–46, 149–50, 156–57, 207–9, 211–12, 215–17, 247, 261, 281, 287, 303, 312–16, 333
  See also Donatism, Donatists; war: to facilitate evangelization
evils, choosing the lesser of two, 43–44, 56, 102–5, 142–46, 154, 167, 218, 256, 263–64, 282–84, 320

Fabié, Antonio María, 192–93, 354n.11, 356–57, 358–59, 362, 363–65
fear. *See* evangelization, usefulness of fear in
Ferdinand II, king of Aragon, 53, 114, 212–13
Florida, 48–49, 140, 287, 343
Foscarario, Gil, 198, 224, 288n.289, 382n.105

Gaeta, 9, 73, 186–87
Galindo, Domingo de, 340

Galmés, Lorenzo, O.P., 228
García de Loaysa, Francisco, Archbishop of Seville, 12, 367
García-Pelayo, Manuel, 55–56, 65, 67, 77
Gaul, Gauls, 84, 157–58, 321–22, 326
Gayangos y Arce, Pascual de, 362
Gennadius, exarch of Africa, 19, 31–32, 72–73, 138, 184–85, 210–11, 217, 250–51, 272, 273–75, 299–301, 303–4, 381, 387–88
Genoa, 9–10
Gentili, Alberico, 58–60
Giménez Fernández, Manuel, 229
Ginammi, Marco, 389
Ginés de Sepúlveda, Juan. *See* Sepúlveda
Goths, 248–49, 267
Granvelle, Antoine Perrenot (Bishop of Arras), 34, 53–54, 56, 192n.3, 351n.3, 353–56
Gratian, 63. *See also* canon law, canonists, and Index of Authors and Works Cited in the Translated Texts
Great Commission. *See* Bible: New Testament; and *also* Index of Biblical Passages Cited in the Translated Texts
greed, Spanish, 44, 57, 90, 150–51, 320, 345–46
Gregorio, *licenciado*, 12–13, 382–83
Gregory I, Pope, 19, 25, 31–32, 72–73. *See also* Index of Authors and Works Cited in the Translated Texts
Gregory IV, Pope, 244n.59, 348n.473, 379n.99
Gregory IX, Pope, 63. *See also* Index of Authors and Works Cited in the Translated Texts
Griffin, Clive, 53, 389n.1
Grotius, Hugo, 58–60
Guatemala, 51, 343
Guevara, Francisco, 221–22, 367–68

Hanke, Lewis, 2, 9n.23, 15, 33, 75–76, 79, 195
Hannibal, 321–22
Haro, Antonio Ramírez de, bishop of Segovia, 198–99, 238
Henry VIII vs. Catharine of Aragon, 4–5
heresy, 5n.9, 25, 30–31, 87–88, 215–16, 286, 288, 300, 313, 335
  Las Casas accusing Sepúlveda, 47, 337–38
  Lutheran, 7–8, 14, 65–66, 110–11, 337–38
  Sepúlveda accusing Las Casas, 1, 46, 47, 53–54, 348–49, 352, 366, 371, 372, 373–74, 378–80, 381, 383, 385n.112, 387–88
heretics (vs. infidels), 31–32, 39–40, 130–31, 140, 141–42, 151–52, 153, 209–12, 217, 221–22, 246–48, 272–75, 295, 298–305,

312–13, 316. *See also* Donatism, Donatists

Hernández, Ramón, O.P., 53

Holy Land, the, 41, 116, 151–52, 255

homunculi. See Amerindians: as *homunculi*

Hostiensis, Cardinal (Henry of Segusio), 14, 17–18, 29–30, 71, 72–73, 337n.447, *See also* Index of Authors and Works Cited in the Translated Texts

humanism, humanists, 4–6, 5n.11, 7, 8, 9–10, 15, 23, 28, 55–56

human sacrifice

Amerindian, 6–7, 13, 15, 16–17, 18, 29–31, 113–17, 131–32, 149, 174, 181–82, 203, 206, 207, 241

ancient, 44–45, 114, 115–16, 118, 164, 170, 203–4, 270, 282–83, 321–22

Las Casas's defence of Amerindian, 43–46, 51, 61–62, 263–66, 320–28

Sepúlveda's rebuttal, 282–85, 371–76, 377–78, 385–86

idol-worship (passim)

Amerindian's reasonable defence of, 45, 324–27

early Christian suppression of, 31–32, 39–40, 142, 149–50, 209–10, 279, 298–99

early Christian toleration of, 40, 279, 309

punishment (or suppression) of, 1–2, 24, 30–31, 32, 40, 113–17, 151–53, 174, 200, 251–54, 278, 304–5, 337–38, 372–78

See also blasphemy; human sacrifice; Israelites: God's punishment of; Israelites: wars against Canaanites etc; Israelites: and peoples outside the Promised Land; war: to punish idolatry and other violations of natural law; war: unbelief as just reason for war

ignorance, excusable or otherwise, 44–45, 161–71, 203, 264–66, 282–83, 284, 320–28, 385–86. *See also* probable error

imperium. See rule, nature of Spanish (in America)

infidels. *See* ecclesiastical jurisdiction; heretics (vs. infidels); Muslims (Mohammedans, Moors, Saracens); papal jurisdiction; and war: unbelief as just reason for war

Innocent III, Pope, 64, 106, 201n.21, 206n.53, 208n.61, 213n.79, 213n.81, 214n.88, 224n.112, 256n.142

Innocent IV (Sinibaldo de Fiesco), canon lawyer and pope, 17–18, 29–30, 40n.171, 41, 58n.248, 71. *See also* Index of Authors and Works Cited in the Translated Texts

Inquisition, Council of the, 53–55, 226, 352–53, 362–63, 364–65, 378–79, 386–87

Iraq, 2003 invasion of, 58–60

Isabel I, queen of Castile, 53, 212–13, 332–33

Israelites

enemies of Assyrians and Babylonians, 15, 114–16, 164–65

fleeing Egypt, 348n22

God's punishment of, 15, 114, 151–52, 203–4, 245

and peoples outside the Promised Land, 19, 39, 173–74, 243–44, 270–71, 292–97

refraining from enslaving defeated enemies, 84

sacrifices, 127

wars against Canaanites, Amorites, and others of the Promised Land, 15, 39, 71, 72, 80, 114–17, 151–52, 161–62, 164–65, 182–83, 184–85, 188–89, 241–44, 270–71, 278

Jephthah and his daughter, 283n.277, 327–28

Jerome, 16–17. *See also* Index of Authors and Works Cited in the Translated Texts

Jews, post-Old Testament, 152–53, 210, 246, 247–48, 304. *See also* Israelites

John the Baptist, 261–62

Johnson, Samuel, 392–93

Judgement Day, 43, 251–52, 255, 263, 264, 307, 315, 344

Julian the Apostate, 278

jurists (specialists in Roman law), 30–31, 43, 59, 84, 99–100

at Valladolid, 33, 50–51, 239, 347, 369–70

Kristeller, Paul Oskar, 5, 66–67

Lacavallería, Antonio, 389

Ladrada, Rodrigo de, 11–12

Lantigua, David, 45n.191

Las Casas, Bartolomé de

background, 11–12

role in opposing publication of *Democrates secundus*, 22–28, 237–38, 368

at Valladolid junta and aftermath, 33–56, 239, 368–69

works

Apologética historia sumaria, 52, 226n.1, 238–39n.30

422 GENERAL INDEX

Las Casas, Bartolomé de (*cont.*)
  Apologia (Latin), 37–38, 38n.166, 52, 55,
      226n.1, *See also* Index of Authors and
      Works Cited in the Translated Texts
  Apología (Spanish), 34–35, 52, 234. *See also*
      Index of Authors and Works Cited in
      the Translated Texts
  Aquí se contiene una disputa, 34–37, 52–55
    differences between 1551 and 1552
        versions, 49, 233–34, 301n.335,
        334n.439
    editions, 227–29, 389–93
    manuscripts, 230–34, 389
    See also Index of Authors and Works
        Cited in the Translated Texts
  *Brevísima relación de la destruición de las
      Indias*, 52, 56, 389, 390, 391–93
  Confesionario, 26–27, 32–33, 45, 46, 48,
      52, 57. *See also* Index of Authors and
      Works Cited in the Translated Texts
  Doce dudas, 49, 50
  Entre los remedios, 390–91
  Erudita et elegans explicatio, 54–55
  De thesauris, 50
  Tratado comprobatorio, 52, 391. *See also*
      Index of Authors and Works Cited in
      the Translated Texts
  Treinta proposiciones muy jurídicas, 26–27,
      49, 52. *See also* Index of Authors and
      Works Cited in the Translated Texts
  De unico vocationis modo, 41
  See also human sacrifice: Las Casas's defence of
      Amerindian
law
  canon. *See* canon law, canonists
  human, 89, 152, 210, 322, 344–45
  international, 57–58, 61
  of nations (*ius gentium*), 26, 57–58, 71, 84–85,
      98, 99–100, 147–48, 154, 156–60, 162,
      172, 173, 188–90, 267
  natural (*passim*)
    authority of, 12, 90–93, 296, 371–73, 377,
        385–86
    congruence of natural and divine law, 6–7,
        90–91, 114, 115, 116, 322, 374
    known to all men, 93–94, 162, 270–71, 284, 296
    salvific when followed, 123–27
    See also war: to punish idolatry and other
        violations of natural law
  positive, 8–9
  Roman, 84, 160, 161, 172

Leopoldus, 12
Libya, 2011 intervention in, 59
licence to print
  denied for *Democrates secundus*, 22–28,
      34–35, 37, 55–56, 80, 237–38, 367–68,
      381–82
  not acquired for *Aquí se contiene una disputa*,
      36–37, 52–54, 356, 367
Liso, Saverio di, 228–29
Llorente, Juan Antonio, 54–55
Locke, John, 58–59
Lombard, Peter, 12–13
Lombards, the, 135, 273, 301
López, Gregorio, 50n.211, 382–83
Losada, Ángel, 4n.7, 8n.22, 10n.27
  and *Democrates secundus*, 65–66, 68–69,
      76–80, 150n.290
  and Las Casas's *Apologia*, 238–39n.30
  and *Proposiciones temerarias*, 351–52n.4,
      354n.10, 356, 359–60, 359n.24
  and Sepúlveda's *Apologia*, 193n.6,
      194–95, 196
Low Countries, 59, 390–92
Luther, Martin; Lutherans, 4–5, 7–8, 9, 10, 12, 14,
      65–66, 87, 110–11, 337–38
Lyon, First Council of. *See* Councils, Church:
      First Council of Lyon
Lyra, Nicholas of, 25. *See also* Index of Authors
      and Works Cited in the Translated
      Texts

Madrid
  Biblioteca Real del Palacio, 65–67, 192–93,
      359–61
  Real Academia de la Historia, 194,
      230–31, 358
Mair, John, 12–13, 18–19. *See also* Index of
      Authors and Works Cited in the
      Translated Texts
Mancio de Corpus Christi, 340
Manichean heretics, 300–1
Melanchthon, Philip, 7
Mendoza, Luis de, Count of Tendilla and
      Marqués of Mondéjar, 68–69, 86
Menéndez y Pelayo, Marcelino, 55–56, 65, 67,
      77, 79–80
Mexico. *See* New Spain
Mexico City / Tenochtitlan, 11–12, 16–17,
      55n.236, 112
Miggrode, Jacques de, 391–92
Milton, John, 393n.13

Mirandola, Pico della, 7–8
Mohammed, 260–61, 301–2, 306, 330, 340, 344–46. *See also* Muslims
Montalvo, Francisco de, 22, 221–22, 367–68
Montesinos, Antonio de, 8–9
Montezuma, 112
Moreno Hernández, Antonio, 191–93, 194, 195, 196
Moscoso, Álvaro, 34, 69, 221–22, 367–69
Moses, 115–16, 124, 127, 184–85, 296n.315, 306–7
Moxó y Francolí, Benito María, 231
Mühlberg, 1547 battle of, 65–66, 79–80
Muslims (Mohammedans, Moors, Saracens), 41, 42, 104, 211, 255–56, 262, 304, 309–10, 338. *See also* Mohammed
Mylius, Arnold, 69–70, 191–92, 194

Nájera, Luna, 195n.16
natural law. *See* law: natural
Nebuchadnezzar, 148, 164–65, 204–5, 337–38
New Laws (*Leyes nuevas*, 1542), 1, 11–12, 26, 32–33, 55, 237n.27, 367
New Spain, 11–12, 16–17, 33, 34, 44, 77, 106–7, 113, 131–32, 191–92, 207, 223, 282, 320, 343–44
Nuñez Vela, Blasco, 11–12

Oliván, Martín, 50–51
Oviedo y Valdés, Gonzalo Fernández de, 38–39. *See also* Index of Authors and Works Cited in the Translated Texts

Pagden, Anthony, 2, 13–14n.44, 69n.18, 76–77, 82, 354n.10, 389n.1, 389–90n.2
Pagliai, Bruno, 227–28
Panormitanus (Nicolò de' Tudeschi), 17n.63
papal bulls
    Apostolici regiminis, 5–6
    Inter caetera, 14, 18–19, 20, 26–27, 46, 47, 50–51, 146, 147, 194, 212–13, 226–27, 268, 269, 285, 329–30, 347–50, 379–80
    Sublimis Deus, 10–11, 46, 47, 50–51, 226–27, 268, 285, 347n.470
papal jurisdiction, 2–3, 20, 24, 46n.195, 47, 129, 184–85, 187–88, 202, 205–6, 233–34, 252, 275–79, 301–5, 335–36, 347–50, 379–80. *See also* Christ: his temporal power; and ecclesiastical jurisdiction
papal authority and infallibility, 347–50, 380, 387–88

parables. *See* Bible: New Testament; and relevant passages in Index of Biblical Passages Cited in the Translated Texts
Paris 391
    University of, 12–13
Patisso, Giuseppe, 67, 77, 79–80
Paul, St
    submission of serfs to lords, 54
    response to being struck, 23
    on judging those outside the Church, 16, 39, 72–73
    Romans 2:14, 17n.65
    See also Index of Biblical Passages Cited in the Translated Texts
Paul III, Pope, 10–11, 46, 47, 50–51, 226–27, 268, 285, 347n.470, *See also* papal bulls
Pelagius, British heretic, 258n.152
Pereda, Julián, 67, 77
Pérez Fernández, Isacio, O.P., 229, 389n.1
Peru, 11–12, 33, 34, 51, 52, 191–92
Peter, St, 126, 260
    and Cornelius, 125–26
    denial of Christ, 373–74
    submission of serfs to lords, 54
    vicar of Christ, 134–36, 205, 247–48, 277, 299–300, 306–7, 308–9, 371
    See also Index of Biblical Passages Cited in the Translated Texts
Phelan, John Leddy, 79
Philip, Prince (later Philip II), 27, 27n.114, 36n.156, 52, 74, 90, 150n.290, 391
Philip IV, 389
Phillips, John, 393n.13
philosophers, pagan, monotheism of, 17n.65, 29, 68–69, 73, 74, 80, 93, 94, 120–27, 186–87
Pio, Alberto, Prince of Carpi, 7–9, 23n.95
Pizarro, Gonzalo, 11–12
Plato, Platonic dialogues, 8, 81. *See also* Index of Authors and Works Cited in the Translated Texts
Pomponazzi, Pietro, 5–6, 7–8, 9
    De immortalitate animae, 5–6
Poole, Stafford, 52n.223, 195, 238–39n.30
Powell, L. F., 392n.12
Pozoblanco, 3–4, 362
preaching. *See* evangelisation
precipice (metaphor), 18, 133–34, 146
probable error, probable opinion, 44, 264–65, 284, 321–27, 371–77, 385–86. *See also* ignorance, excusable or otherwise

424 GENERAL INDEX

Promised Land. *See* Israelites: wars against
    Canaanites, Amorites, and others of
    the Promised Land
protection of innocents. *See* war: to protect
    innocents
Protestantism, Protestants, 56, 57–58n.244,
    58–60, 390–91, 392. *See also* 'Black
    Legend'; Luther, Martin; Lutherans
Pufendorf, Samuel, 58–59
punishment. *See* war: as punishment for blasphemy;
    and war: as punishment for idolatry and
    other violations of natural law
Purchas, Samuel, 391–92
    Purchas His Pilgrimes, 391–93

Quirk, Robert E., 83
Quiroga, Vasco de, 382n.106

Ramírez, Antonio, Bishop of Seville, 198–99,
    220–21, 238
reparation. *See* restitution
Repartimientos, 237, 311, 345–46
'Responsibility to Protect', 59, 61–62. *See also*
    war: to protect innocents
restitution, 108
    whether owed by individual Spaniards,
        26, 47, 48, 57, 322–24, 338,
        378–79, 384
    whether owed by the Spanish Crown, 47, 49,
        339
robbery. *See* theft
Rome, Romans, Roman empire (ancient).
        See also law: Roman
    as examplars of virtue, 123–24
    Romans and human sacrifice
        as practitioners of, 44–45, 321–22
        as suppressors of, 265, 282–83
    Roman idol-worship, 209–10, 327
    Roman rule
        civilizing mission, 187–88
        justice of, 108–9, 118, 150, 202–3
        limited extent of, 117–18
        moderate nature of, 177
    Romans in Spain, 38–39, 110–11
    wars of the Romans
        moderation in warfare, 84, 157
        Roman rules of war, 108
        waged to impose rule on inferior peoples,
            109–10

Rome (modern), 8–9, 10, 87, 111, 224, 238, 288,
    381–82
    Biblioteca Vallicelliana, 66–67, 78

Salamanca
    University of, 13–14, 23, 31–32, 34, 65–66,
        193, 359–60, 392–93
    University theologians' approval of
        Confesionario, 26–27, 340
    University theologians' judgment against
        Democrates secundus, 22–24, 25, 28,
        199–200, 238, 340, 368, 370, 381–82,
        392–93
Samaritans, 260, 263, 316–17
Sánchez Gásquez, Joaquín J., 7
San Pablo, Francisco de, 340
Santander
    Biblioteca Marcelino Menéndez Pelayo, 67
Sarmatians, 248–49
Saverio de Zelada, Francisco, 66–67
Schäfer, Christian, 31n.131, 65, 67–69, 74, 75–77,
    78, 79, 80, 84n.51
Schmitz, Dietmar, 67, 77, 79–80
Scythians, 112, 248–49
Sepúlveda, Juan Ginés de
    as Aristotelian philosopher and translator, 1,
        3–4, 5–7
        shifting views on Aristotelian 'natural
            slavery', 2, 6–7, 15, 29, 37
    background, 3–10
    as humanist, 1, 5–8, 28
    as theologian, 1, 3–5, 7–8
    works
        Antapologia pro Alberto Pio, 7–8
        Apologia 1–2, 4–5, 17n.63, 27–33, 37, 47, 55,
            191–224
            circumstances of composition, 27–29,
                194–95
            confiscation of, 34
            editions, 194–95
            main arguments, 29–33
            manuscripts, 191–93
            translations, 195 (*see also* Index of
                Authors and Works Cited in the
                Translated Texts)
        *Cohortatio ad Carolum ut Bellum Suscipiat
            in Turcas*, 9–10
        Declaración, 351–53, 360–64
        De fato et libero abritrio, 4–5, 8–9

GENERAL INDEX 425

Democrates primus, 9–10, 12, 15, 81 (*see also* Index of Authors and Works Cited in the Translated Texts)

Democrates secundus (*Democrates alter*), 1, 3, 4–5, 6, 8, 10–22
  circumstances of composition, 1, 12, 367
  editions and translations, 77–78
  main arguments, 10–22
  manuscripts, 65–77 (*see also* Index of Authors and Works Cited in the Translated Texts)

De orbe novo, 55–56, 65–66

De rebus gestis Caroli Quinti historia, 65–66, 358

De regno et regis officio, 55–56

De ritu nuptiarum et dispensatione, 4–5

Gonsalus (*Dialogus de appetenda gloria*), 8, 15, 81

'Postreros apuntamientos' ('Final points of argument'), 50–51, 226–27, 229, 231

Proposiciones temerarias, 36–37, 46, 47, 50–51, 53–55, 56, 226–27, 351–65
  date and circumstances of composition, 354–56
  editions, 356, 360–65
  manuscripts, 353, 356–65

translations
  Alexander of Aphrodisias, Commentary on Aristotle's *Metaphysics*, 6, 8–9
  Aristotle, *De ortu et interitu*, 3–4
  Aristotle, *Politics*, 14, 83

serfs, serfdom, 20–21n.78, 54, 83–84, 175–76n.362

Serrano, Pedro, 55

Seville, 12, 311, 342
  Archivo General de Indias (AGI), 357–59
  and the printing of Las Casas's treatises, 34–35, 52–53, 54–55, 225, 226, 227–28, 351

Sigüenza, University of, 3–5

Simancas
  Archivo General de Simancas, 357–59

Sisebut (Visigothic king), 210

slavery
  of defeated in war, 20–21, 150–61, 171–74, 188–90

enslavement of Amerindians and its prohibition, 2, 6, 10–11, 20–21, 26–27, 28–29, 47, 55–57, 175–79, 200, 268, 335, 384 (see also *encomienda*)

natural slavery (Aristotle and after), 2, 6, 12–15, 20–21, 25–26, 29, 36, 37–39, 60–61, 83–85, 150–53 (*see also* war: to subjugate barbarians to civilized rule)

terminology, 20–21n.78, 83–85, 99–100, 175–76, 189

Socratic/Platonic dialogues, 8, 81, 91–92

Sodom (and Gomorrah), 97–98, 129, 158, 164–65, 182–83, 184–85, 241–42, 244–45, 255–56, 263

sodomy, 111n.130

Solomon, 337–38

Sotillo, Dolores Bonet de, 229, 231

Soto, Domingo de, 3–4, 50, 239, 370n.50, 383
  De dominio, 34, 42, 46n.195
  In quartum Sententiarum, 42–43n.183
  member of Valladolid junta, 33, 51, 370n.50
  Sumario (summary of presentations of Las Casas and Sepúlveda at Valladolid), 35–37, 42–43, 45–46, 47, 53, 225–26, 228–29, 230–31, 233–34, 239, 240–69, 369

Sotomayor, Pedro de, 340

sovereignty. See *dominium*

Spaniards
  superiority of (acc. to Sepúlveda), 13, 110–11
  governance of Amerindians. *See* Amerindians: governance of

Spanish Armada (1588), 391–92

Spanish-American War (1898), 393n.13

Spartans, 98, 104, 157, 177

Sylvester I, Pope, 248–49, 257–58, 273

Taranto, Domenico, 65, 74, 78, 79, 80

theft, 38–39, 56–57, 92, 128–29, 134–35, 137, 140, 247, 254–55, 260, 323, 328, 330, 333, 335, 338–40, 342, 384, 386–87

Tierra Firme (Panama and environs), 34, 191–92, 280

Toledo
  Archivo y Biblioteca Capitular, 66–67
  See also Councils, Church

426 GENERAL INDEX

tribute
   Amerindian, 20–21, 46, 55, 56–57, 181–82,
      268, 285, 345, 384
   in Deuteronomy, 19, 107, 139, 173–74, 207,
      218, 241–42
   and the *encomienda*, 11
   exacted from those defeated in just war, 173,
      178
   parallels today, 59–60
Trujillo (Trugillo), Sebastián, 52n.222, 53, 225,
      227–28, 230, 346, 389
Tudela Bueso, Juan Pérez de, 228
Turks, 9–10, 41, 263, 304, 309–10, 338
tyranny
   of Amerindian rulers, 71–72, 80
   defense of innocents from (*see* war: to protect
      innocents)
   of Spanish invaders, 26, 32–33, 38–39, 44,
      48–49, 56, 57–58, 59–60, 220, 287–88,
      289–90, 297, 302, 311–12, 315–16,
      320–21, 324, 328–29, 331–32,
      333–34, 336, 338–39, 342–43, 345–46,
      366–67, 379, 386–88. *See also* 'Black
      Legend'

unbelief. *See* war: unbelief as just reason
      for war

Valdecañas y Arellano, Francisco de (*oídor* of
      Granada), 361–63
Valladolid, 11, 12, 74
   Colegio de San Gregorio, 35
   junta (conference) of 1550–1551
      course of, 33–50, 225–27, 239, 368–69
      origins, 1, 8–9, 239, 367–69
      second session, 50–51, 369–70 (*see
        also* Sepúlveda: *works*: 'Postreros
        apuntamientos')
Vandals, 211, 300–1
Vattel, Emer de, 58–59
Velasco y Ceballos, Fernando José de,
      66–67
Venice, Venetians, 112, 389–90, 392
Verapaz, 48–49, 343, 343n.461
Vitoria, Diego de, 22, 32–33, 69, 221–22,
      367–68
Vitoria, Francisco de, 25, 50n.211, 78n.41
   on consent of the governed, 50
   death of, 23
   on evangelism and subjugation, 18–19, 42
   and Melchor Cano, 24

   on natural slavery and subjugation of
      barbarians, 13–14, 14n.46, 14n.47,
      20–21
   on papal jurisdiction, 46n.195
   on punishment of violations of natural law, 16,
      29–31, 43, 58n.248
   on war to protect innocents, 24, 30–31, 43
Vives, Juan Luis, 7, 8

Wagner, Henry Raup (and Helen Rand Parish),
      54–55, 352n.5, 356, 361n.33
war
   Christians permitted to wage, 9–10
   civil, 102–5, 160
   defensive, 97 (*see also* war: justifications and
      consequences of resistance)
   dispossession of those defeated (*see
      dispossession (and confiscation): of
      those defeated in a just war)
   to facilitate evangelization, 18–20, 31–32,
      41–43, 133–48, 149–50, 187–88,
      207–16, 245–51, 257–63, 281, 312–19,
      330–32, 347, 349–50, 379–81, 384,
      387–88
   holy, 7–8, 131
   justifications and consequences of resistance,
      16–17, 20–21, 45, 47–48, 99, 107–8,
      146, 174, 200, 216, 233–34
   just war
      consequences for defeated, 154–61
      impossibility of justice on both sides,
        161–71
      just conduct in war, 57–58, 107–10, 292,
        322–23, 377–78, 384
      just reasons for war, 94–99
      possibility of, 87–90
      traditional requirements (or rules), 94–99,
        107–10, 180
   vs. pacifism (*see* Erasmus)
   to protect innocents, 16–17, 30–31, 43–46,
      131–32, 149, 207, 263–66, 282–85,
      320–28
   to punish blasphemy, 39–40, 41, 204–5, 206,
      244–45, 274, 280, 304–5
   to punish idolatry and other violations of
      natural law, 15–16, 29–30, 39–41,
      113–20, 127–34, 149, 203–7, 241–57,
      270–71, 272–75, 280, 291–97, 298–305,
      309–10, 337–38, 369–70
   to subjugate barbarians (or natural slaves)
      to civilized rule, 12–15, 29, 37–39,

114, 142–46, 149, 187–88, 202–3, 257, 266–68, 280, 310–12
to subjugate unwilling Amerindians upon conversion, 47–48, 49–50, 286, 334–37
unbelief as just reason for war, 17–18, 118–20, 132, 205, 241–42, 254–55
unjust wars, guilt in waging and ignorance as excuse, 161–65

wars of dubious justification
rulers sinful in waging, 170–71
soldiers sinless in waging, but justly liable to suffering, 165–70, 171–74
Wolff, Christian, 58–59

Zeno of Elea, 190
Zumárraga, Juan de, 16n.60

The manufacturer's authorised representative in the EU for product safety is
Oxford University Press España S.A. of el Parque Empresarial San Fernando de
Henares, Avenida de Castilla, 2 – 28830 Madrid (www.oup.es/en or product.
safety@oup.com). OUP España S.A. also acts as importer into Spain of products
made by the manufacturer.

www.ingramcontent.com/pod-product-compliance
Lightning Source LLC
Chambersburg PA
CBHW071244060725
29174CB00014B/88